IMAGES
of America

KINGS MOUNTAIN

ON THE COVER: Several yokes of oxen drag a train of logs down a denuded Purisima Canyon skid road on the way to the Borden-Hatch mill (1854–1870). The man with the bucket, the "grease monkey," poured water or tallow, rendered from oxen slaughtered because of illness, onto the trail to grease the skids and make moving the load easier. Sometimes a system of cables, run from huge spools and looped around trees, was used to help the oxen by pulling the logs. The man and the boy to the left are sitting on a "barber chair" stump, so nicknamed for the shape that resulted when a section of a tree trunk, while the tree was being felled, split off. (Courtesy Ken Fisher.)

IMAGES
of America

KINGS MOUNTAIN

Stacy Trevenon

ARCADIA
PUBLISHING

ISBN 978-0-7385-5829-5

Published by Arcadia Publishing
Charleston, South Carolina

Printed in the United States of America

Library of Congress Control Number: 2007943431

For all general information, please contact Arcadia Publishing:
Telephone 843-853-2070
Fax 843-853-0044
E-mail sales@arcadiapublishing.com
For customer service and orders:
Toll-Free 1-888-313-2665

Visit us on the Internet at www.arcadiapublishing.com

This book is dedicated to the Kings Mountain community,
gracious pioneers who love art and the living canvas around them.

Contents

Acknowledgments		6
Introduction		7
1.	Early Days: The Roots of a Mountain Enclave	9
2.	Toppling Giants: Logging Techniques and Tools	13
3.	A Sturdy Breed: Lumbermen and Lumber Mills	29
4.	Dairying: A Gentler Life	45
5.	Mountain Life: Peaks, Gulches, and Crossroads	55
6.	Years of Unrest: Development and Subdivisions	65
7.	A Community United: The Kings Mountain Art Fair	79
8.	Treetop Talent: Mountain Folk Artists	101
9.	Full Circle: Kings Mountain Today	115
Bibliography		127

ACKNOWLEDGMENTS

It is not easy, in this demanding age, to make time to help another. It is rare to find an entire township stepping up to do the same. But very quickly, while compiling this book, I found that willingness and generosity are common denominators up on Kings Mountain. As if they share genetic traits, people on the mountain—and previous residents who once lived there—have been uniformly kind, helpful, and generous with time and resources.

First and foremost, my deepest appreciation goes to the mountain's undisputed historian, Ken Fisher, who despite his highly demanding schedule and business commitments was an unfailing fount of information and outstandingly generous with his knowledge and photographs.

I also offer warmest thanks to mountain residents Ardyth Woodruff, David Wendt, Zanette Cornman, and Bill Goebner for their time, ready assistance, information, and warm common sense.

I want to gratefully thank the mountain residents who also gave of their time and experience: Terry Fotre; Dan and Katy Katzenberger; Sybil and Dennis Plank; Deb, Joe, and Logan Rockmore; Rebecca Holland; and Steve Michelson. Thanks also to those who welcomed me into their homes and memories: Phil and Barb Kreiss, Don Roesch, and Sally and Gil Richards.

I offer heartfelt thanks to the following: Carol Peterson, archivist of the San Mateo County Historical Association, for her thorough and capable aid; Mitch Postel, president of the San Mateo County Historical Association, for his kind support; Dick Tagg and Jeanne Thivierge of the Woodside Community Museum for generously opening their files and not watching the clock; Mary "Molly" Spore-Alhadef, librarian, local history collection of the Redwood City Library, for her gracious and knowledgeable assistance; John Poultney, editor, Arcadia Publishing, for his professionalism and support; and Clay Lambert, my editor at *Half Moon Bay Review* newspaper for okaying all the vacation days that went into this book.

My love and thanks go to my family for encouragement, and last but by no means least, to my husband, Doug, for optimism, technical savvy, and tireless support on the home front.

INTRODUCTION

Definitions vary as to the exact location of Kings Mountain. Technically it lies within unincorporated San Mateo County and uses the Woodside zip code, 94062. A close look at maps reveals Woodside's high northwestern reaches, and that, colloquially and informally, is Kings Mountain. It is an enclave defined by homes either along Skyline Boulevard, which bisects the region, or tucked along nearby winding, narrow mountain roads. There are also a couple of fine restaurants rich in their own histories, a palette of personalities from everyday folk to millionaires, and a unique community ethic.

Kings Mountain lies in an area dubbed Sierra Morena, or "Brown Mountain," by early Spanish explorers. Resident and local historian Kenneth L. Fisher defines Kings Mountain proper as that area bordered by Highway 92 to the north and Bear Gulch West to the south, 800 feet in elevation or higher. The Kings Mountain Volunteer Fire Brigade defines the region in terms of their response area: from the intersection of Skyline Boulevard and Highway 92 south eight or nine miles to Skeggs Point and including all the mountain roads branching off Skyline that are otherwise inaccessible to traffic, no matter how far they meander into the hills. Longtime resident and fine-art painter Rebecca Holland puts it on still another level: "Kings Mountain is a state of mind."

That state of mind evolved through several distinct phases of its history, as the mountain's population and economics waxed and waned, its people learned to make the best of natural and man-made resources, and aesthetic beauty became its economic and psychic backbone.

Its earliest roots lie with Native American hunters and gatherers. The Spanish and Mexicans who came next found the mountain inhospitable since its steep wooded terrain and cool climate discouraged farming. But upon the Gold Rush, redwood trees, an ideal medium for building a new country, became the "gold in them thar hills." With "environmentalism" a century away, logging meant economic survival, so tenacious lumbermen knuckled down to tackle literally towering odds. They wound up denuding the mountain but set a lasting precedent of perseverance and resourcefulness.

"Kings Mountain" was named almost casually after the King family and their hotel, saloon, and other amenities set up in 1868 in the heart of the mills. Communities came and went through the 1870s: early Woodside around dentist Robert O. Tripp's landmark store, Summit Springs, Greersburg, Portola Valley, West Union, and thriving, showy Searsville with its school and resort waters—later submerged under a man-made lake. And there was Whiskey Hill, with an oak tree that once bore a sign declaring that underneath it lay the body of a horse thief hanged there.

The world of the lumber mills had a Wild West glamour with an edge, but another, more refined element came with the advent of dairying in the 1850s. Then came the first half of the 20th century, when the prewar and war years brought change. The mills and dairies disappeared. Large land grants and mill parcels were subdivided to foster a new kind of building boom. Tavern patrons and vacation-home owners dodged Prohibition.

Contemporary times brought a patina of modernity. The mountain's award-winning elementary school opened in 1953. Maintained roads made life easier. The area became home for employees of the San Francisco Airport and Peninsula businesses. Homeowners leveraged stunning views into equity: in a flip-flop of history, in an area once famous for logging, sleek homes sprang up, many built on the property of the rustic cabins of mountain pioneers. Mountain history was reshaped: potential logging, by a contemporary mountain mill and for business dealings with overseas interests, drew protests in the 1960s.

Challenges were, of course, synonymous with mountain life. Those who lived there had to be hardy and patient. Today, while there are no more grizzlies or runaway logs, new obstacles defy the convenience-minded. Mountain life can be relatively isolated. Year-round, cell phone coverage is spotty at best. In the winter, storms knock out power, rain-slicked roads become deadly, and thick veils of tule fog drop visibility to just a few feet.

But with a resilience worthy of their forebears, contemporary mountain folks meet the challenges. Living far from clogged cities and fast-paced urban life on the mountain—with its wooded beauty, crisp air, and a close-knit camaraderie vanishing in modern times—is a choice they willingly embrace.

The only time the mountain overflows with visitors is every Labor Day weekend with the annual Kings Mountain Art Fair, celebrating its 45th year in 2008. This mountain institution grew over four decades from a little crafts show into a nationally recognized and respected event that hinges on highest-end art to handmade fine crafts. Over those years, the strictly noncommercial fair brought and sustains fire protection in a vulnerable area, built an attractive community center that is a mountain focal point, supports a remarkable elementary school and a number of other local groups, and, run solely by volunteer effort, coalesces the mountain community across all economic and social lines.

Today the clear-aired mountain, fringed with second-growth redwoods, is home to some 350 households occupied by a modern generation of personalities as distinctive as their ancestors. It boasts two fine restaurants with their own histories and sees a regular influx of summertime hikers, bicyclists, and motorcyclists besides the stalwart folk who brave the elements year-round. Its annual art fair unites residents in common goals. Linking the residents through communication is the Kings Mountain Association and the mountain's newsletter, the *Echo*. Modern iconoclasts like birth control pill inventor Carl Djerassi, football's Joe Montana, and rock legend Neil Young have lived on its outskirts. And rapidly growing second-growth trees have restored the forest canopy, reaching for the towering stature of their predecessors, oddly mirroring the perseverance of the loggers who once leveled them.

The mountain and its art fair are historical and cultural tapestries, and this small book can do little more than scratch the surface of their many stories. Every attempt has been made to represent historical material accurately, though multiple printed and human resources sometimes conflict. This volume attempts only to present an overview and convey a unique sense of time, place, and community that characterizes the mountain, yesterday and today. As longtime art fair volunteer Joe "Rocky" Rockmore puts it, speaking as much of the mountain as the fair, "We all enjoy it because we see our neighbors, everyone works hard and has fun. I don't see a compelling need to change anything."

One

Early Days
The Roots of a Mountain Enclave

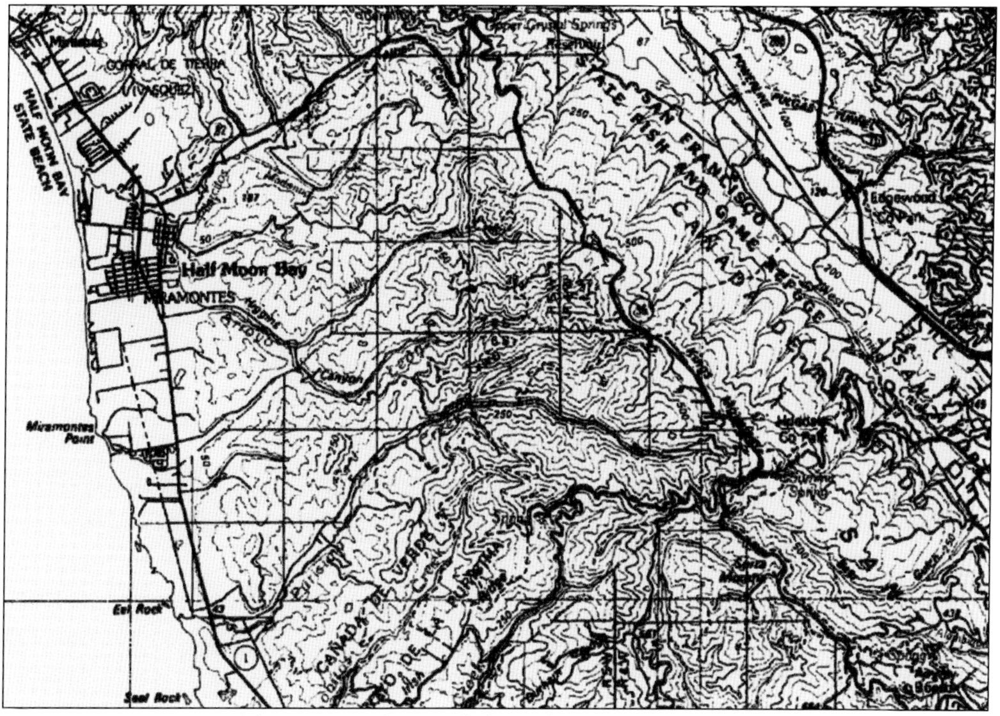

Kings Mountain rises like a 2,000-foot wall from the western edge of Crystal Springs Lake, bisecting the San Francisco Peninsula and separating populated cities and coastline. Stretching approximately 12 miles, fluctuating 4 to 5 miles in width, this unincorporated San Mateo County community spans roughly 60 square miles. It is crisscrossed by a network of creeks—Tunitas ("little sea apples"), Lobitos ("little wolves"), Bear Gulch, Arroyo Leon, Alambique, San Francisquito—which watered the redwoods that fed the mountain's booming 19th-century logging industry. It is pocked by steep ravines, including Soda, Tripp, and Apple Tree, gulches that stymied early loggers but defined the area's beautiful but exacting character. Through it, paved or dirt roads branching off the modern Skyline Boulevard, with names taken from early residents like Froment, Harkins, or Comstock, keep alive a whiff of the past. (Courtesy U.S. Geological Survey.)

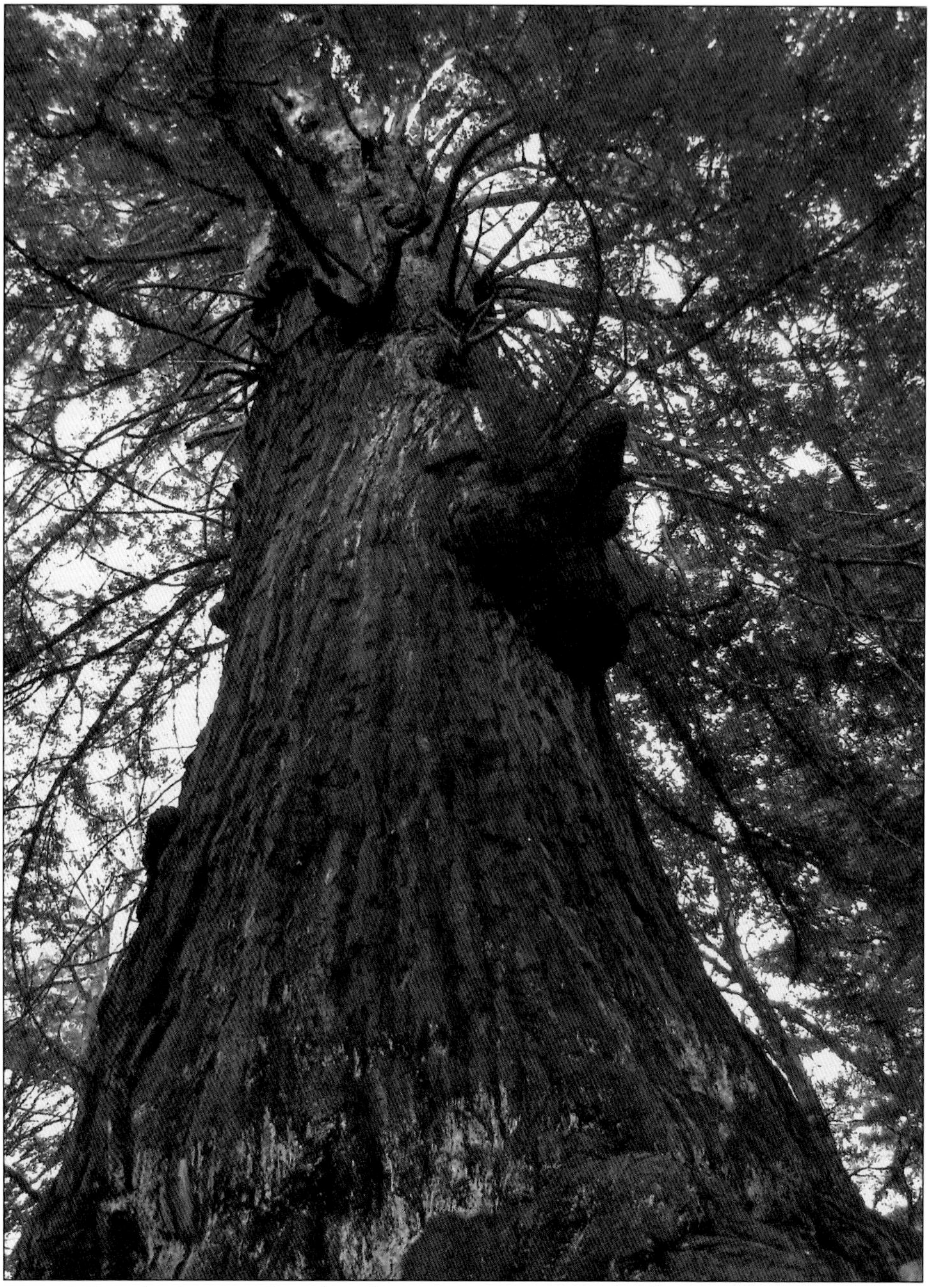

Along with Douglas fir, tan oak, and madrone, *Sequoia sempervirens*, long-lived California redwoods (some live 2,000 years or more), bristled up and down the slopes and ravines of Kings Mountain. Conifers (which produce cones carrying seeds), they were described in 1840 by the Reverend Walter Colton as spreading "emerald sails to the wind, compact as the royals of a ship." One such old-growth colossus, nicknamed "Methuselah," stands just off Skyline Boulevard. Another, discovered in 1870, measured 75 feet in circumference. Yet another giant, when hollowed, housed six or seven wood-choppers and their bunks. Weather-resistant and plentiful, redwood lured Spanish priests building missions along the coast and early settlers building houses and towns. (Courtesy the author.)

The Native Americans who passed through Kings Mountain en route inland or to the ocean, depicted in this sketch by Ludovik Choris, official botanist with an 1816 Russian expedition, were dubbed "Costanoans" by the Spanish explorers. They were described as hostile, friendly or simple, dark-skinned, with a peaceful, nomadic hunting-gathering lifestyle; they were skilled in weaving baskets for gathering and preparing food, chiefly acorns, crustaceans, and shore birds. (Courtesy Gilbert Richards.)

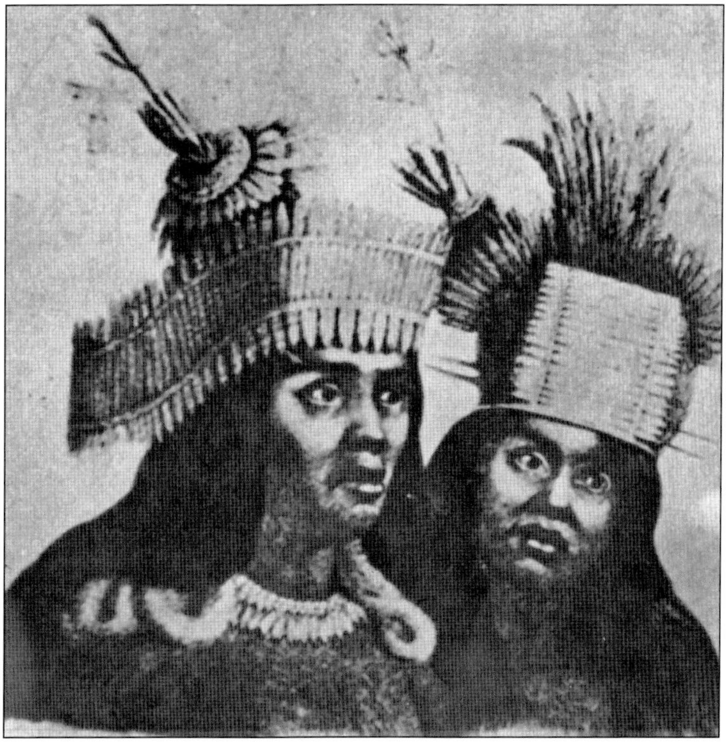

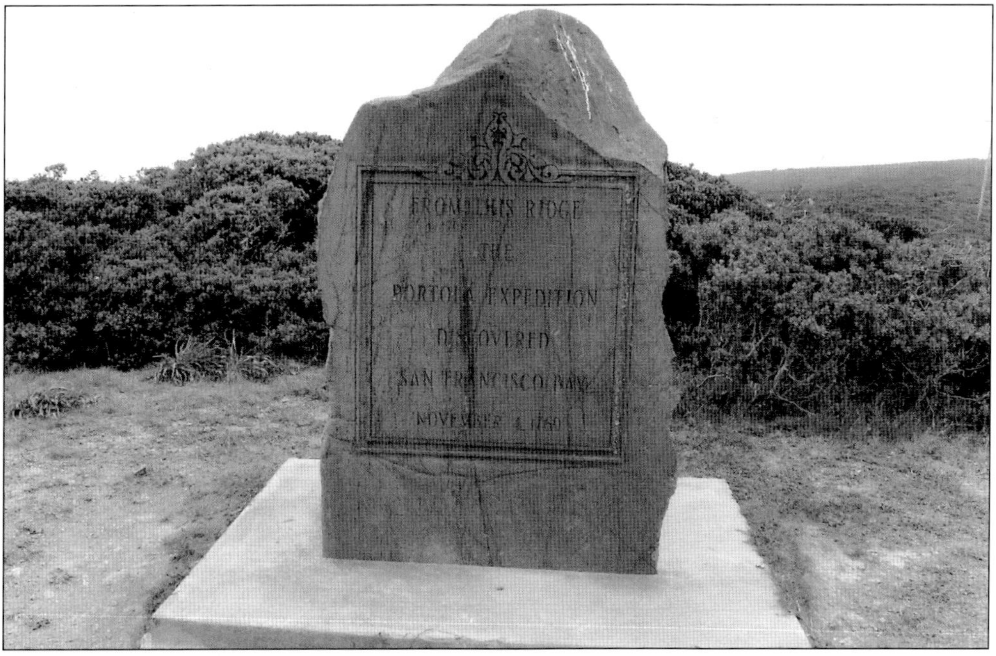

The Woodside region into which Kings Mountain is tucked, and its environs, entered history on November 4, 1769, when Capt. Gaspar de Portola, governor of the Californias (1767–1770), led more than 60 footsore and ailing men into the fog-shrouded foothills slightly north of Kings Mountain in search of a land route to Monterey Bay. What they found that day—though they missed its significance—was the San Francisco Bay. (Courtesy the author.)

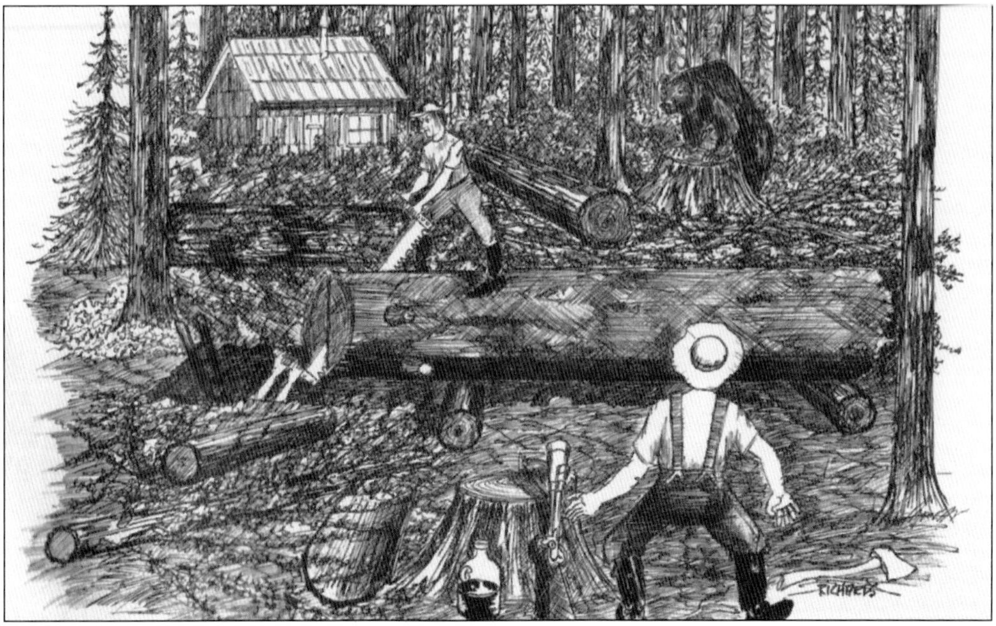

Grizzly bears were ubiquitous mountain residents. Encounters between early mountain residents and bears were not uncommon, as dramatically depicted in this sketch by Gilbert Richards, artist, avid historian, and author of *Crossroads: People and Events of the Redwoods of San Mateo County.* A harrowing battle between man and bear gave landmark Bear Gulch, and later the road, its name. (Courtesy Gilbert Richards.)

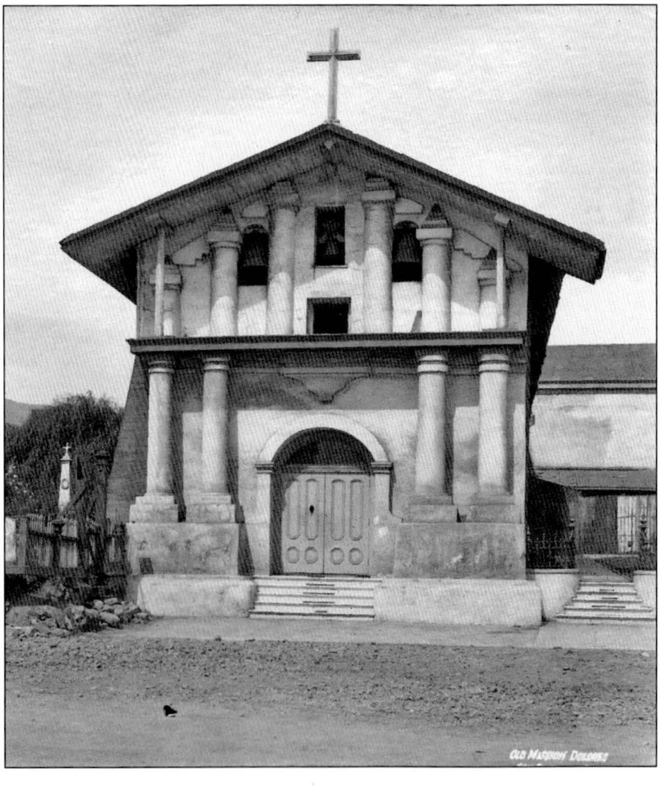

Spanish padres seeking to colonize and baptize picked lumber-rich locations to build missions. Soldiers and Native Americans braved grizzlies—sometimes with fatal results—to fell trees for wood used in doors and trim for Mission Santa Clara (1777) and Mission Dolores in San Francisco (1776). The city's oldest building and survivor of the 1906 earthquake, Mission Dolores is shown here in the late 1800s. It was only a matter of time before lumbering and milling boomed on Kings Mountain. (Courtesy Mission Dolores.)

Two

Toppling Giants
Logging Techniques and Tools

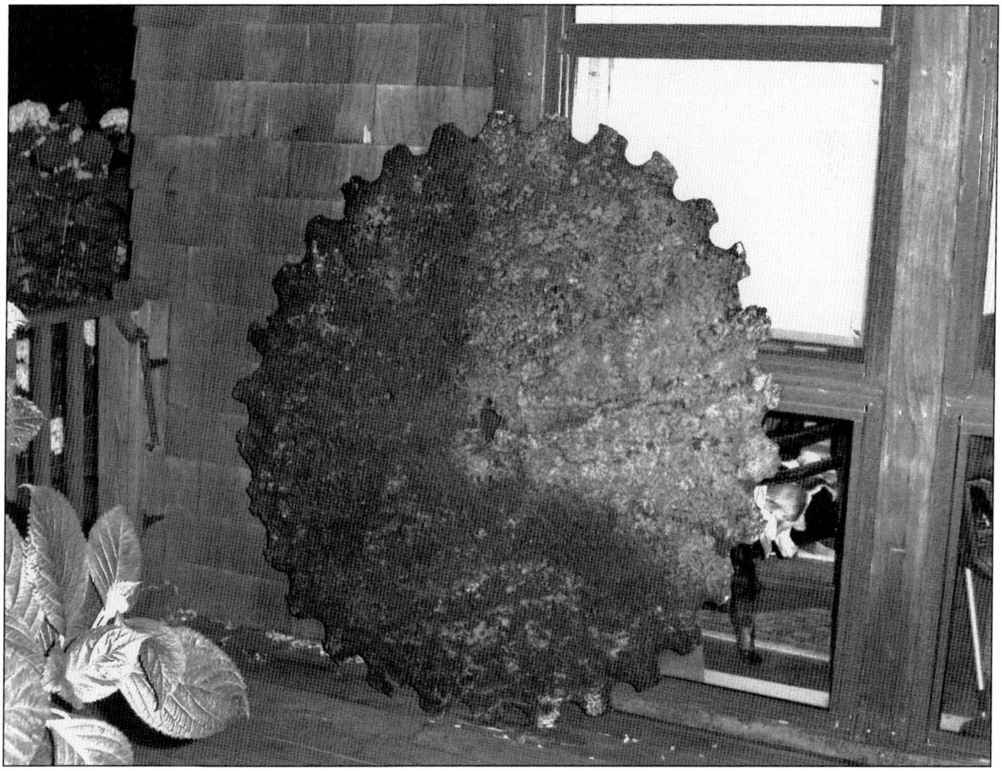

Redwood trees excited little attention among Kings Mountain's early Spanish and Mexican residents in the late 1700s and early 1800s. Wood was not the material of choice for the Spanish, and the Mexicans were adobe-minded. That changed as newcomers saw the trees as raw material for growing cities. Environmentalism as we know it was nonexistent: indeed, the giant trees were nuisances given Pres. James Polk's "Manifest Destiny" of taming the new country into farmland. The discovery of gold at Sutter's Mill in 1849 unleashed a building rush, and on Kings Mountain, as wood was recognized as a viable resource, the first trickle of loggers became a stream. They attacked the forests with simple tools, such as this 60-inch saw blade dating from the period 1900–1906, which could only cut a log through half its own diameter. In time, the loggers developed technology, pooled their muscle, brought in oxen and mule teams, harnessed steam power, and finally introduced the donkey engine. Felling the giants became an industry. (Courtesy the author, from Ken Fisher's collection.)

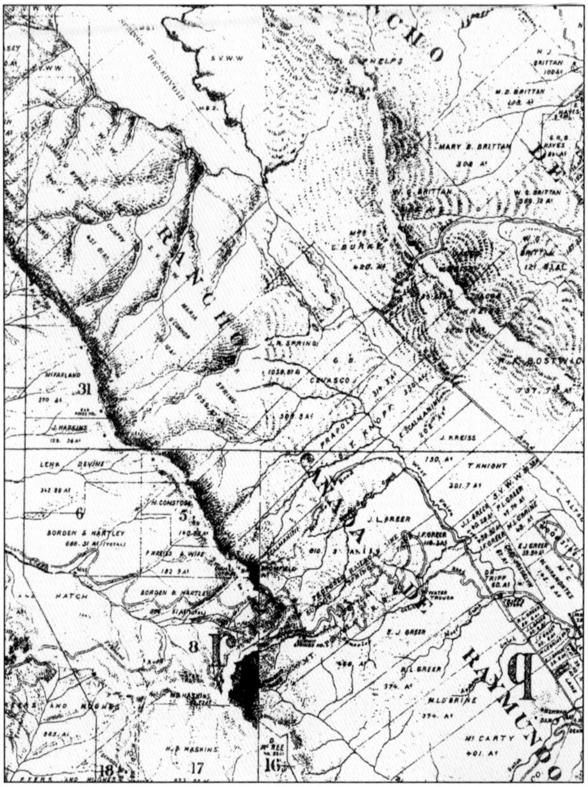

Much mountain land, where the mills sprang up and the Kings Mountain community grew, was initially contained in Mexican land grants Rancho Canada de Raymundo (12,545 acres issued August 3, 1840, to John Copinger) and Rancho Canada Verde y Arroyo de la Purisima (8,905 acres issued in 1835 to Jose Antonio Alviso). This map was drawn in 1894 by surveyor, engineer, and artist Davenport Bromfield. Born July 2, 1862, in Australia, Bromfield came to love the mountain as county engineer from 1891 to 1893. He was also gentle and humble, and respected nobility of character. He married Mary Ware, 10 years his senior, after whom he later named the mountain's Ware Road. Into his 80s, he still surveyed land and drew up maps. He died August 22, 1954. (Above, courtesy San Mateo County Historical Association; below, courtesy Ken Fisher.)

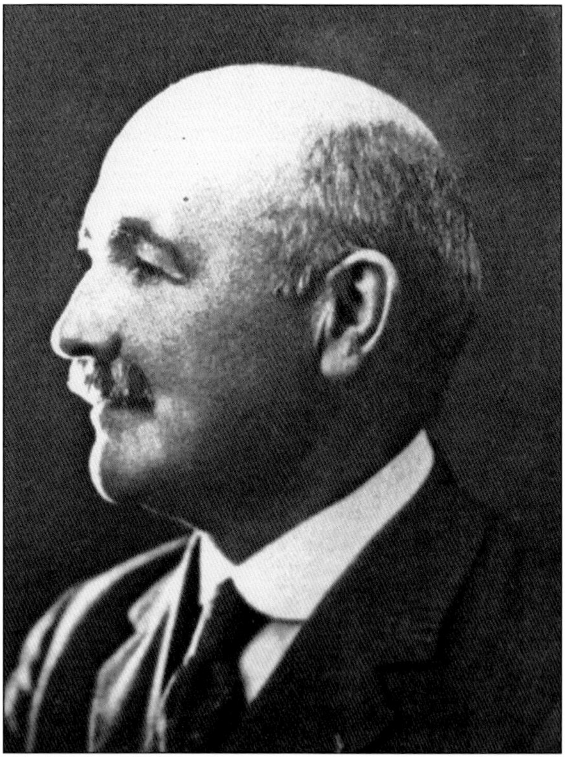

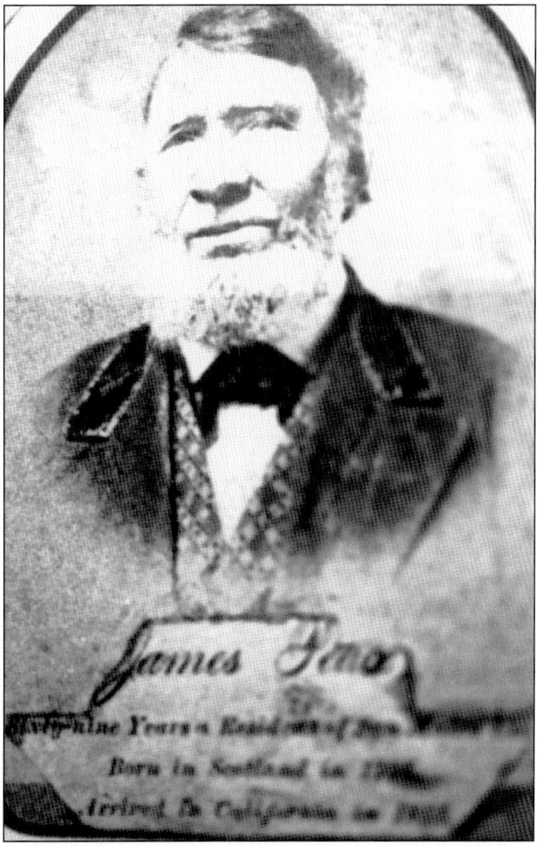

Arguably the first recorded Kings Mountain resident, James Pease was born in 1795 on one of Scotland's Orkney Islands. He came to California with the Hudson's Bay Company in the mid-1830s and deserted his vessel at Monterey in June 1838, supposedly sheltered by a lady sympathetic to deserters, Juana Briones. He drifted to the redwoods with William "Bill-the-Sawyer" Smith, also known as Guillermo Bill, who came here at 19 to build a mill. Pease applied his carpentry skills to work for Smith and then John Copinger, and he built a cabin high on the mountain's north end. The map points Pise Hill and Pise Lookout are thought to be misinterpretations of Pease's Scottish-accented pronunciation of his own name. He died October 12, 1890, by drowning and is buried in Union Cemetery in Redwood City. (Both courtesy Ken Fisher.)

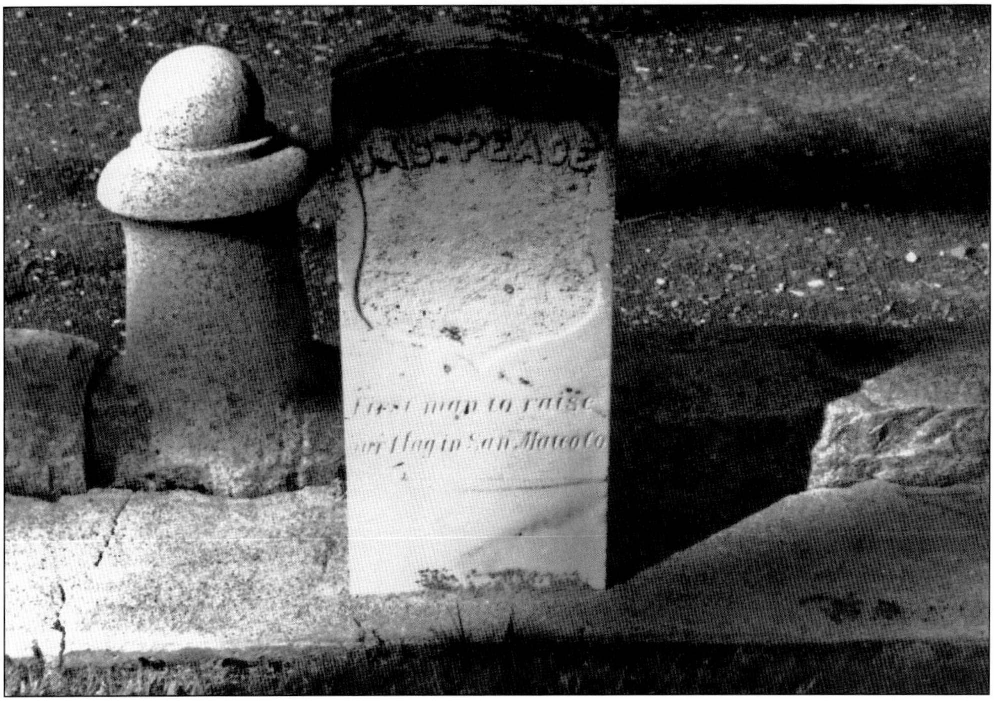

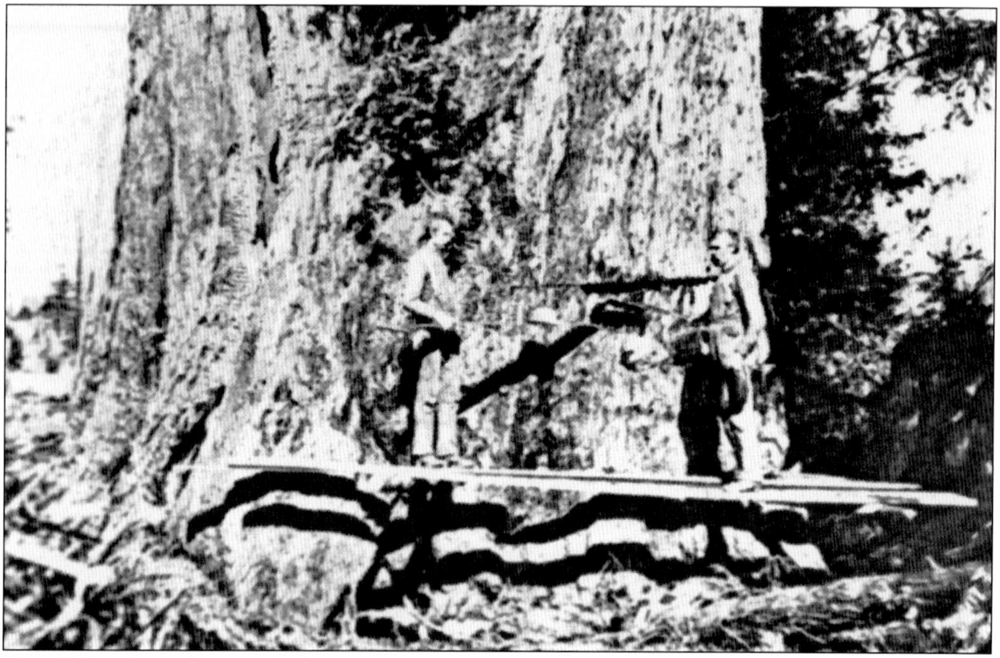

Two "fallers" stand on a platform resting on supporting springboards driven into the tree. The highly skilled fallers planned the cut so the giant would topple just the way they wanted: on level ground so it would not shatter and angled uphill so gravity would help in hauling it away. (Courtesy Ken Fisher.)

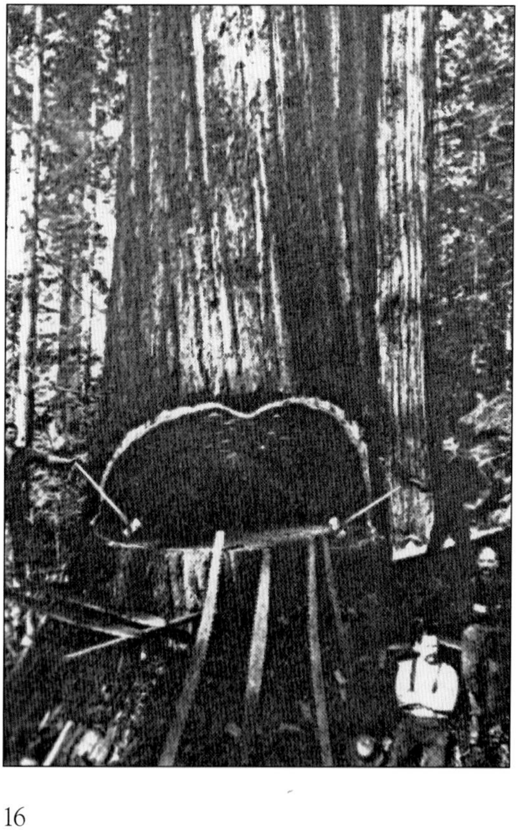

The fallers first leveled the earth behind the tree, then used saw and axe to make an undercut facing the direction it was to fall. Partway through the trunk, they placed a straight stick into the cut to adjust the angle. Then they switched to a two-man saw on the other side. A loud crack meant it was time to yell "Tim-BER!" (Courtesy Ken Fisher.)

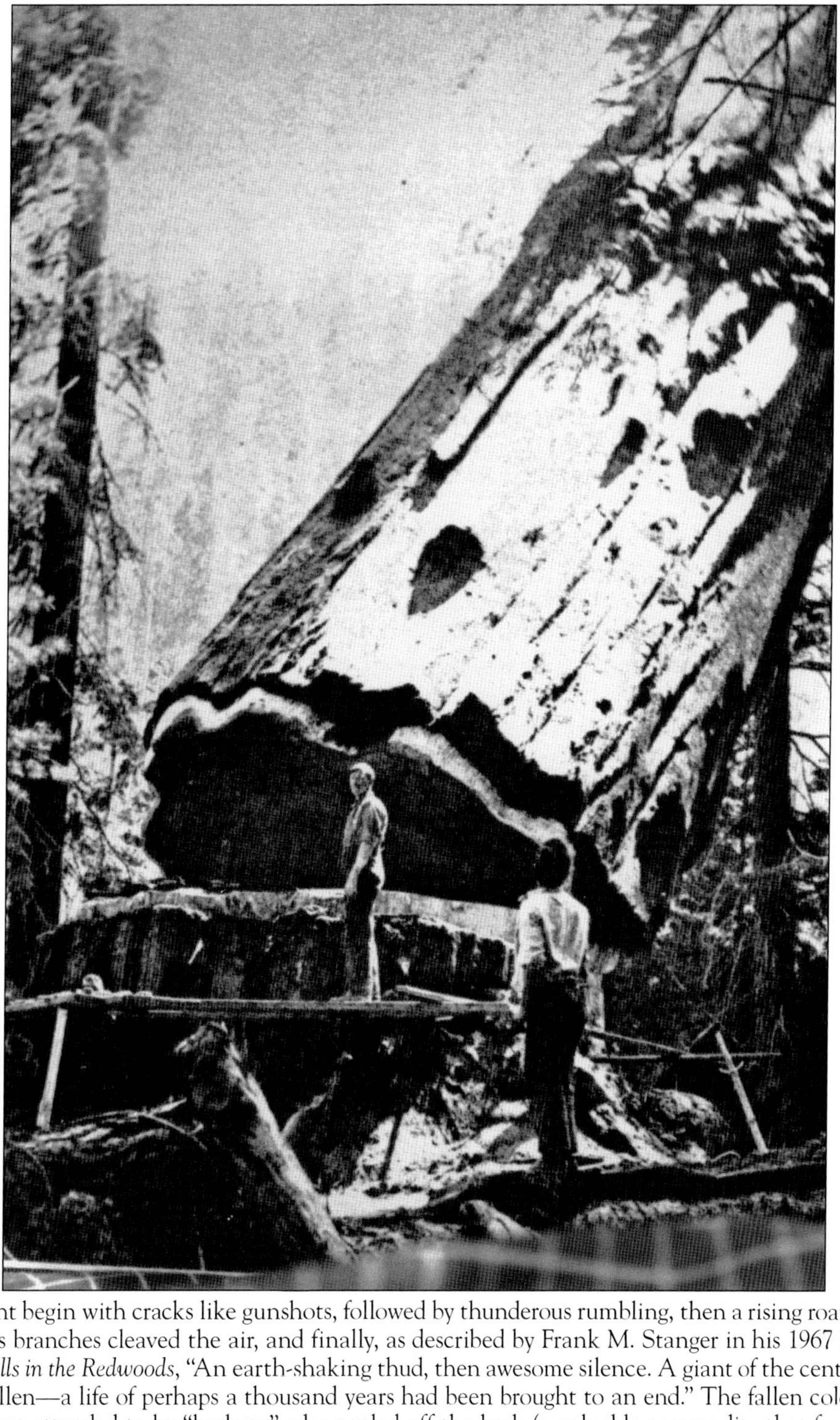

It might begin with cracks like gunshots, followed by thunderous rumbling, then a rising roar and rush as branches cleaved the air, and finally, as described by Frank M. Stanger in his 1967 book *Sawmills in the Redwoods*, "An earth-shaking thud, then awesome silence. A giant of the centuries had fallen—a life of perhaps a thousand years had been brought to an end." The fallen colossus was then attended to by "barkers," who peeled off the bark (a valuable commodity that found a ready market in peninsula tanneries). Then they trimmed off branches and cut the trunk into manageable segments of 16 to 18 feet. The process took a week or more. (Courtesy Ken Fisher.)

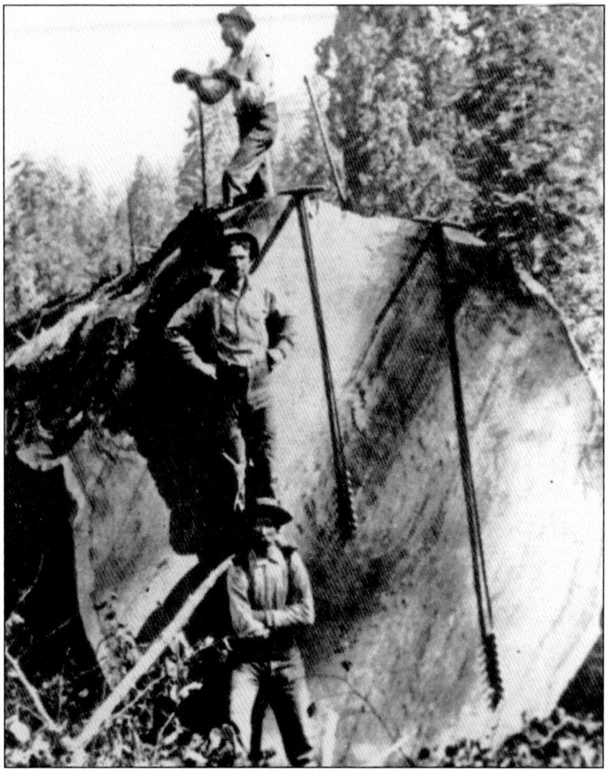

Larger trees of 10 to 12 feet or more in diameter were simply too big to be milled with early saw blades. So lumbermen drilled holes into the downed trunks with augers, packed dynamite into the holes, and blasted the logs into pieces small enough to work. The process was effective but wasteful. (Courtesy Ken Fisher.)

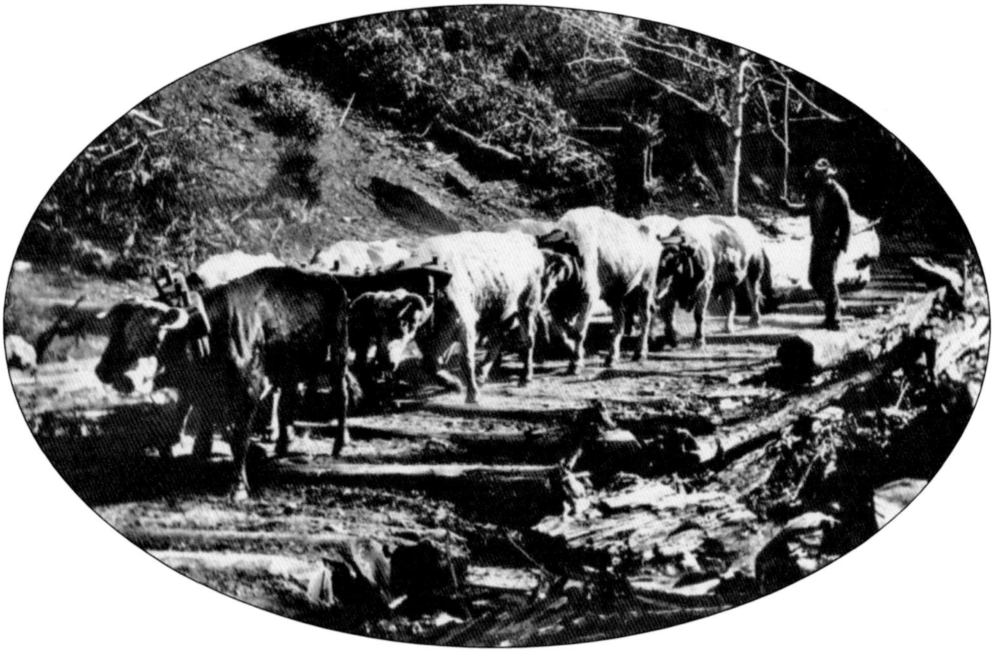

The segments of logs, "dogged" one behind the other like cars of a train, were hauled to the mills by four to eight teams of oxen. Skid roads like this one, over which the teams hauled the logs, were built downhill, with short segments of logs tamped into the dirt to bear the weight and define the road. (Courtesy Redwood City Library.)

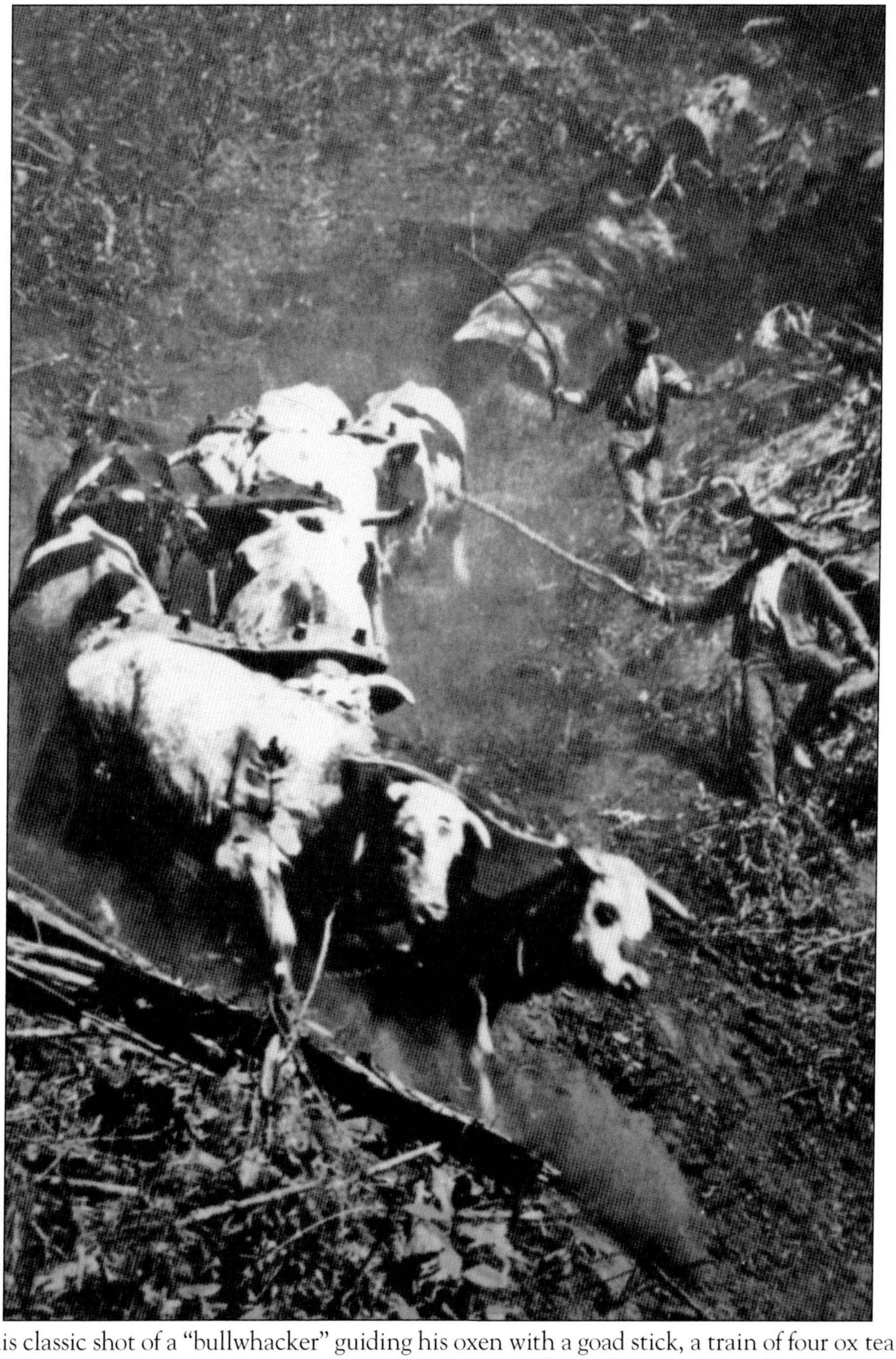

In this classic shot of a "bullwhacker" guiding his oxen with a goad stick, a train of four ox teams drags logs down a steep mountain trail in the late 1880s. This bullwhacker later fought in World War I and survived to live a long life until his death in an auto accident at age 95. The dust kicked up by the heavy-hoofed oxen indicates it was probably summertime; trees were felled in winter but "yarding," or hauling them to the mill, shut down when rain-soaked roads posed hazards to men and beasts dragging heavy loads. It might be April or even May before sodden trails dried out enough to permit loggers and teams to resume work. (Courtesy Ken Fisher.)

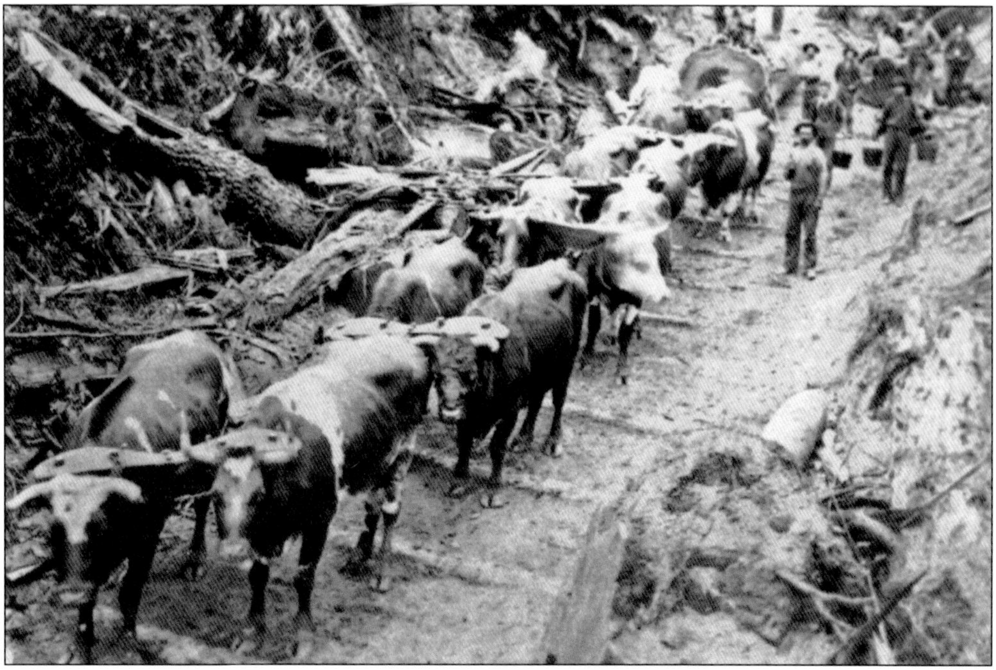

A rare 12-ox team in the Tunitas, linked by short chains, hauls a load. On the log is the head bullwhacker, who commanded a dusty dignity and a respected salary. He directed his beasts (by name) with jerk lines on the left or "near" side and the right or "off" side, spoken word, and his goad. At his command, first the rear team, then the ones in front successively, strained forward until the load creaked into motion. (Courtesy Ken Fisher.)

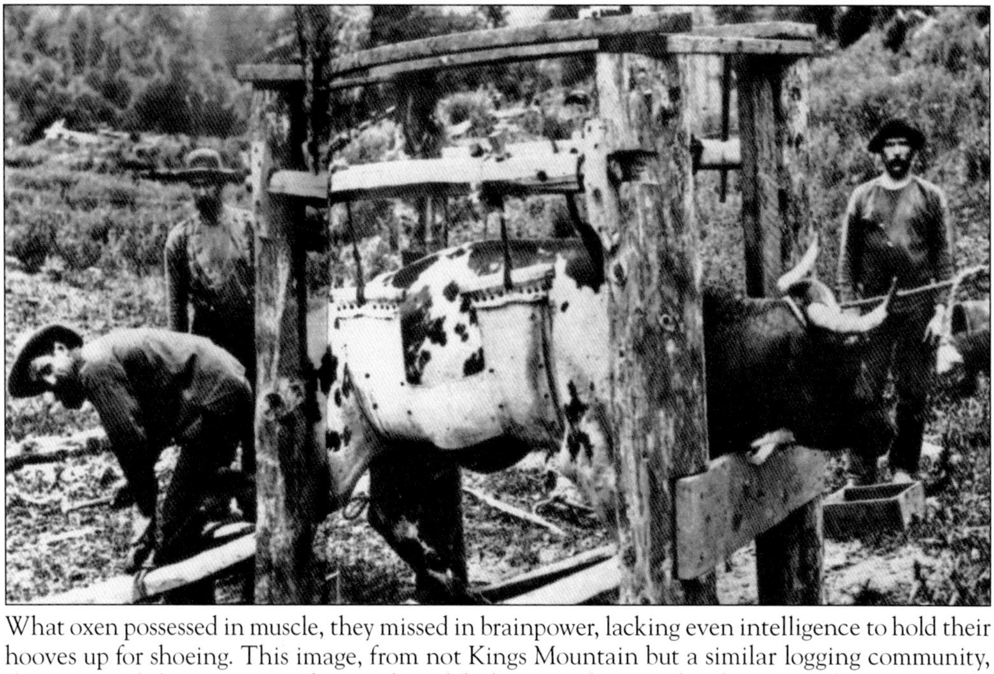

What oxen possessed in muscle, they missed in brainpower, lacking even intelligence to hold their hooves up for shoeing. This image, from not Kings Mountain but a similar logging community, shows typical slings oxen tenders made to lift the ox and suspend it, hooves within easy reach, while being shod. (Courtesy Ken Fisher.)

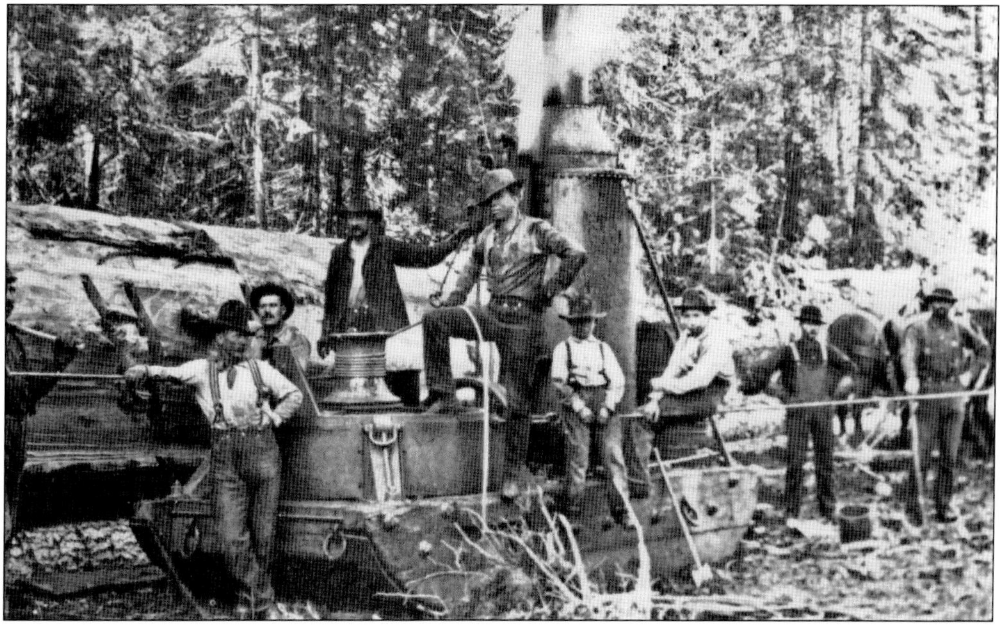

This photograph, though not from Kings Mountain, shows a technological leap forward: the steam donkey engine, invented in 1881. Averaging about 60 horsepower, it changed logging—and peace and quiet—on the mountain forever. According to an 1876 Bingham-Willamette Company advertisement, it was "a machine so infernal that when fired up the darn thing would drive every critter within ten miles a hi-tailin' it for the brush!" (Courtesy Ken Fisher.)

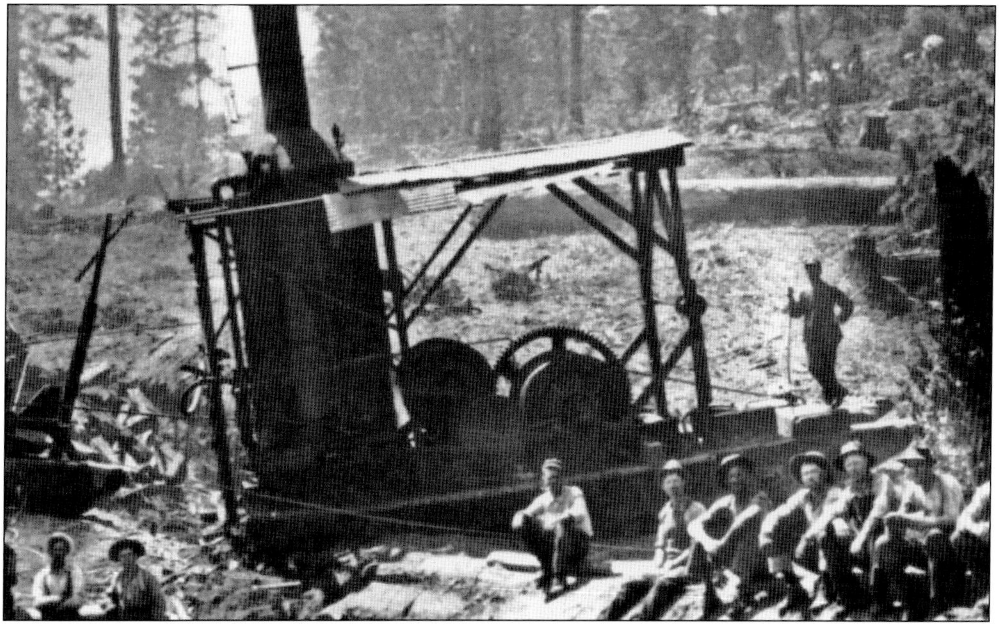

Unlike earlier donkey engines with vertical capstan configurations, later models, like this c. 1910 one, had horizontal spool configurations. The Bingham-Willamette Company built thousands, which worked mills as far as India. Weighing up to 9,000 pounds, powered by boilers, gears, levers, and drums, they burned 1,600 board feet of lumber daily. Their day ended with the Depression and the advent of Caterpillar tractors. (Courtesy Ken Fisher.)

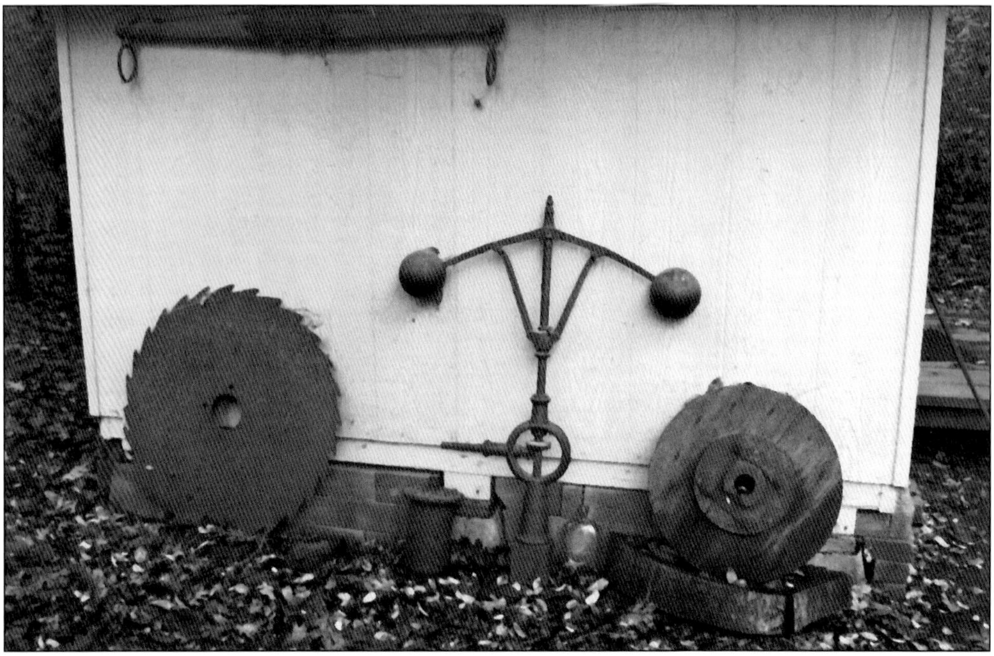

Mounted on a donkey engine, the T-shaped "governor," from around 1860, regulated the speed of the engine with heavy balls. The shingle saw blades were used at the turn of the 20th century. The single tree hanging overhead was part of the harness that linked horse and wagon. The little round object is a *c.* 1875 cable drum. (Courtesy the author, from Phil Kreiss's collection.)

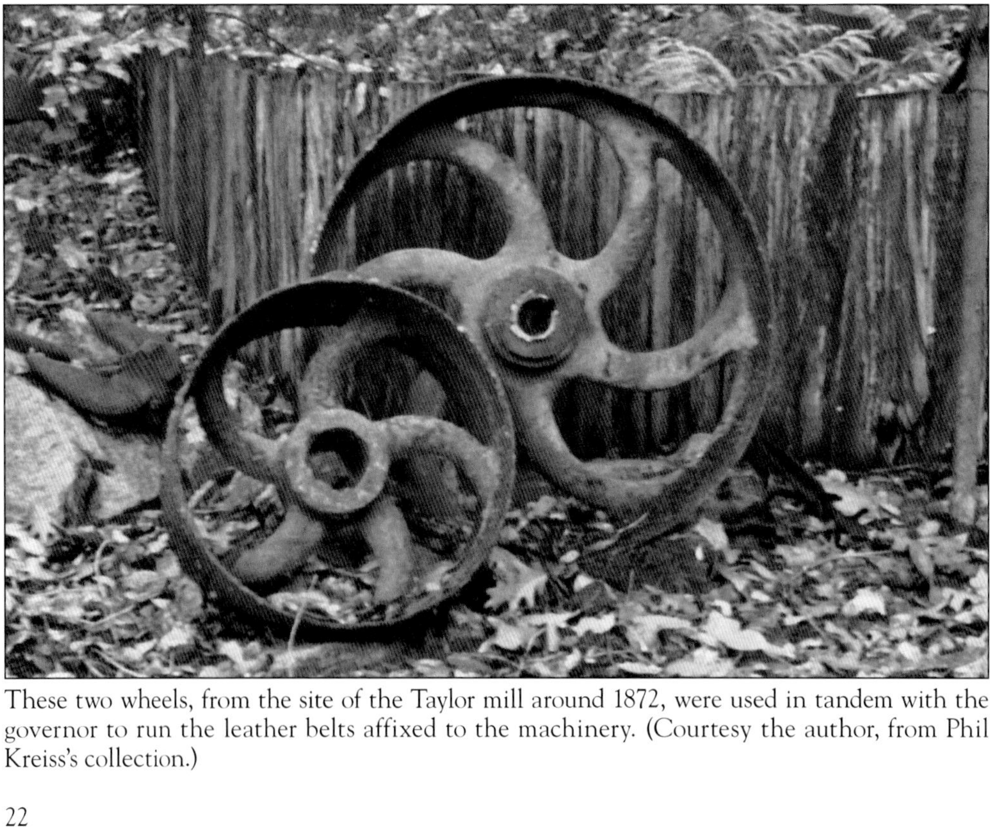

These two wheels, from the site of the Taylor mill around 1872, were used in tandem with the governor to run the leather belts affixed to the machinery. (Courtesy the author, from Phil Kreiss's collection.)

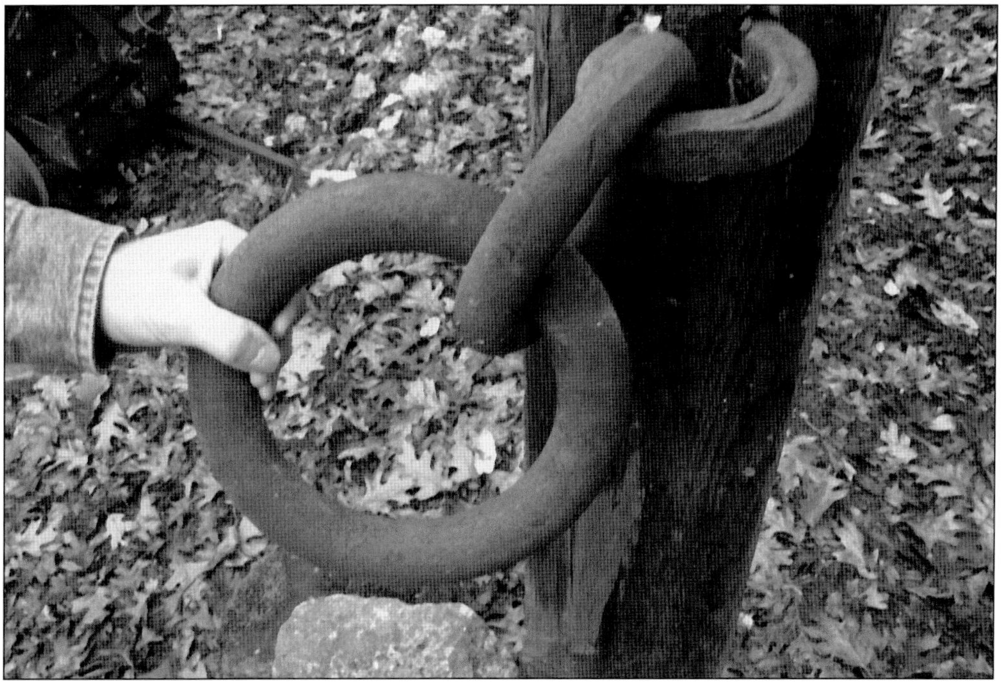

It took a heavy iron ring like this, held by an adult to show perspective, to secure multiple oxen for shoeing or otherwise tending. This ring was taken from the abandoned Virginia mill site (1900–1906) with permission by Phil Kreiss. (Courtesy the author, from Phil Kreiss's collection.)

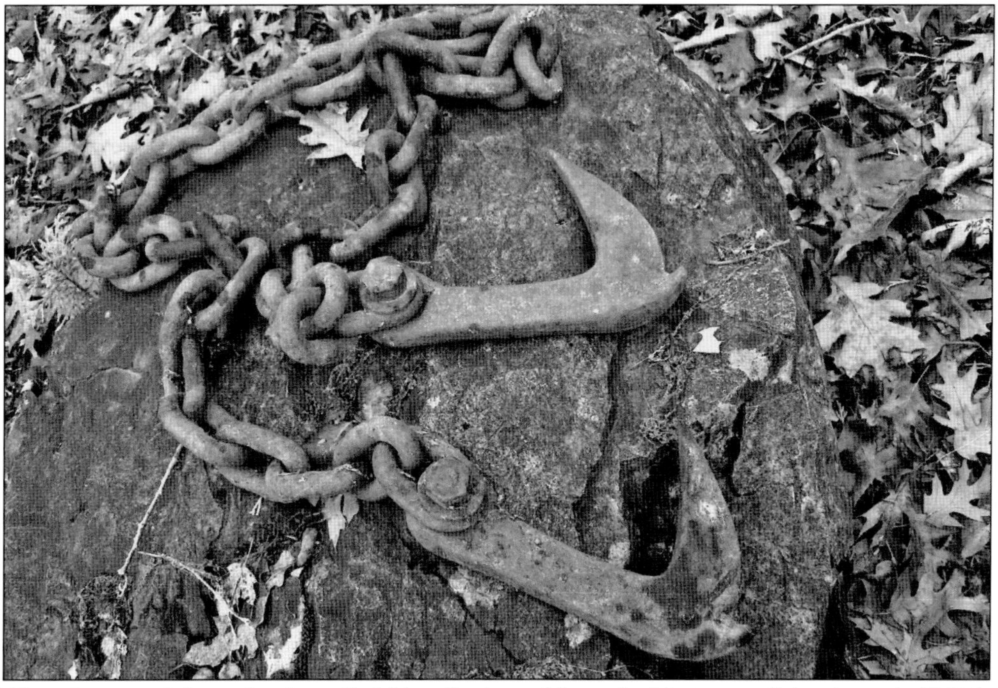

These heavy, solid-iron hooks, called "dogs," salvaged from the Virginia mill (in the early 1900s), were used to drag logs downhill to the mill. The hooks, perhaps 14 inches high and linked by chain, were used in tandem. (Courtesy the author, from Phil Kreiss's collection.)

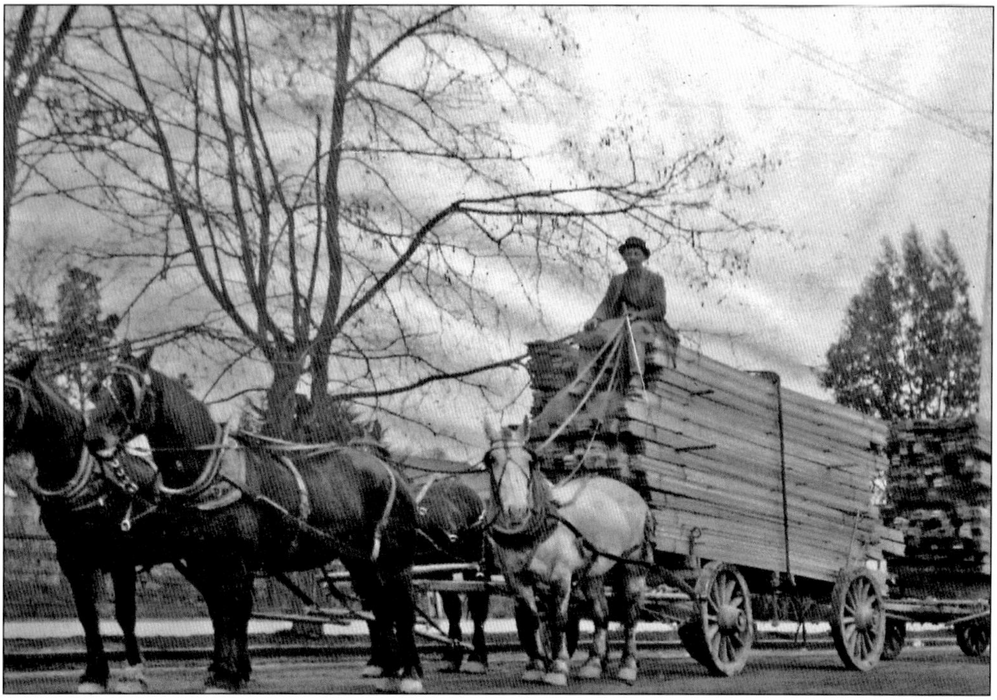

"Teaming" by horse or mule teams, above, was one way to transport worked logs from the mountain down to the Redwood City ports. Redwood, hewn into lengths, was stacked on wagons or carts for transportation. But slabs or logs were not the only things that made up the loads. The wagon assembly below, loaded with tan bark, is shown after making a stop on its way down the mountain to port in Redwood City. (Above, courtesy Redwood City Library; below, courtesy Woodside History Archives.)

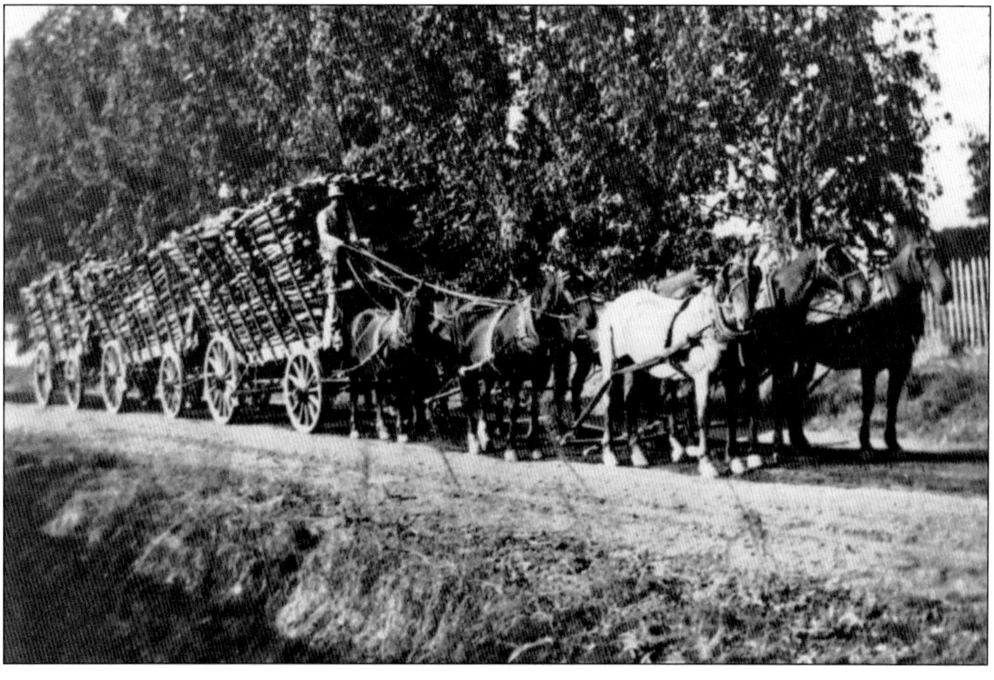

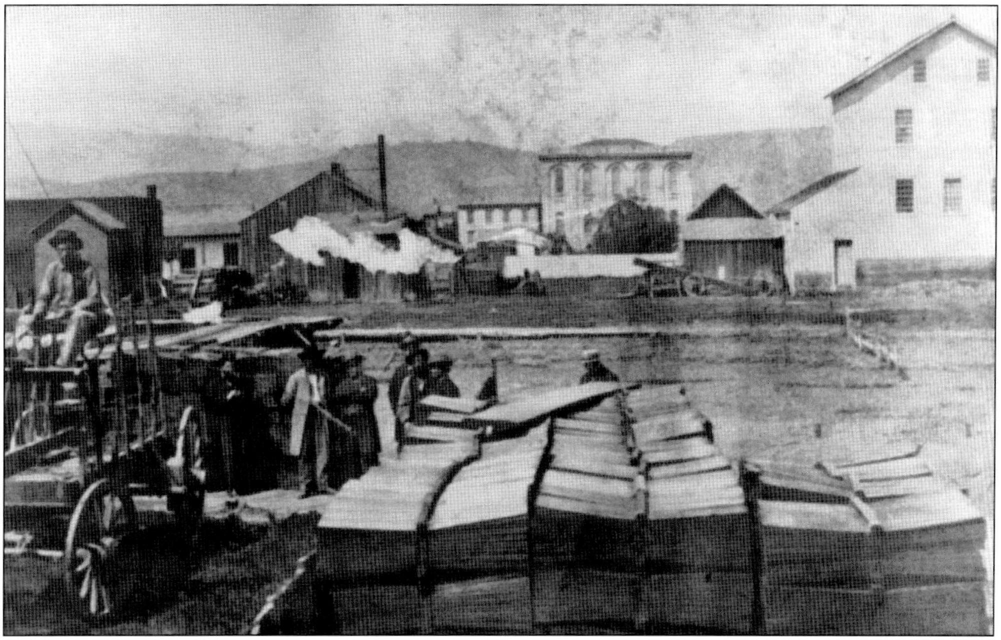

Ox or mule teams, above, were not the only means of transporting lumber. In 1850, Dr. Robert O. Tripp sent a shipment of lumber from the woods to San Francisco by raft. This gave G. M. Burnham the idea of a shallow-draft sailing boat he named *Redwood*, the first such vessel to be used in the lumber trade. The Redwood City port soon took shape, with docks like this one in front of the original county courthouse (1850–1880) from which shingles are being loaded. A familiar figure there was Charles Hanson, born in Denmark, whose four-partner company Hanson-Ackerson monopolized the Redwood City lumber trade. In its inaugural year, 1865, it shipped out $758,906 in lumber. Hanson bought several mills on the mountain and in nearby La Honda like the one below. Then he tapped the rich northwest timber lands in Tacoma, Washington, and set up the Tacoma Mill Company in Redwood City. (Both courtesy Redwood City Library.)

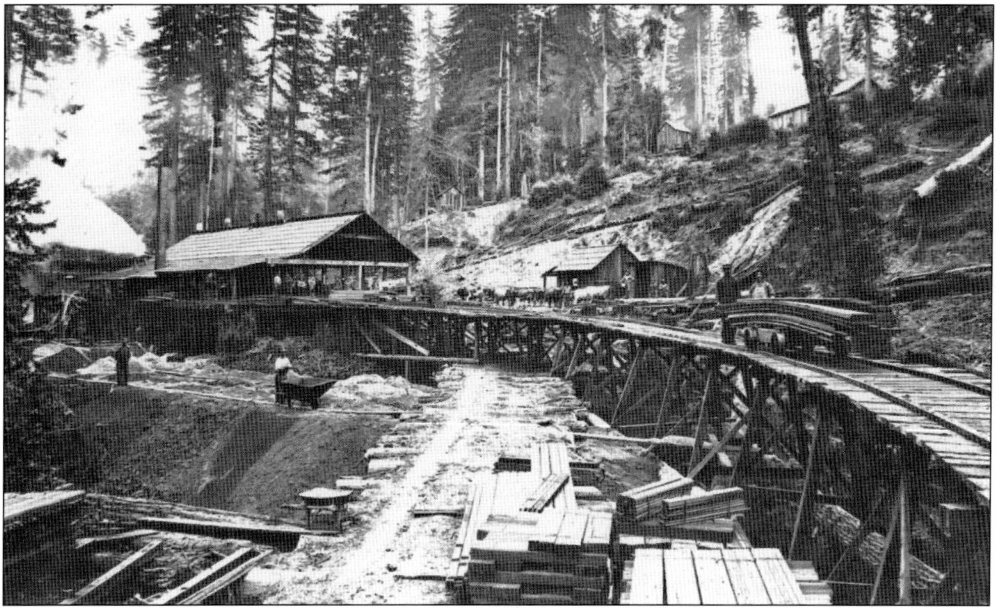

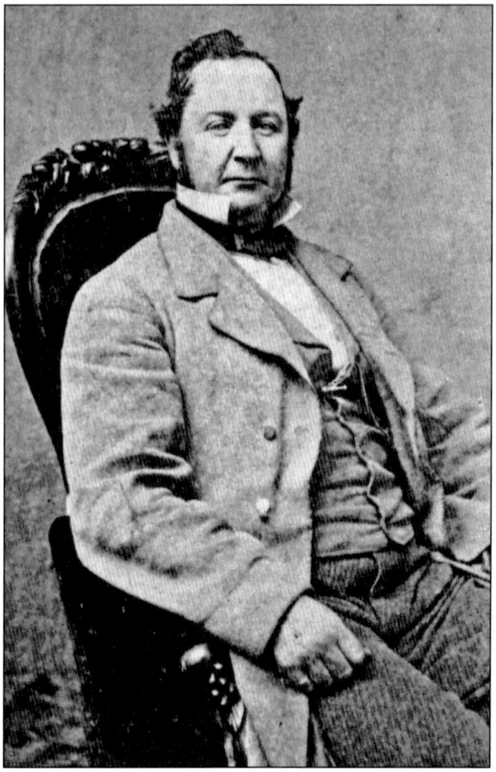

Smooth-talking Charles Brown, left, supposedly built one of the peninsula's first sawmills, along with fellow seminal mill owner Dennis Martin. Born in New York in 1814, Brown came to San Francisco on a whaling ship he left behind with aid from deserters' sweetheart Juana Briones. He married in 1837 and in 1846 bought 2,880 acres between Alambique and Bear Gulch Creeks, paying for it with lumber, which he called Mountain Home Ranch. Often controversial, Brown allowed a distillery to be built on the creek; authorities ignored it, and it closed after lending its name to Alambique (Spanish for "distillery") Creek. He did build a small, water-powered mill and this adobe, below, in 1849. Widowed in 1850, he remarried and relocated to Lake Merced in 1853, where he died poor. His adobe, now a private residence, survives. (Both courtesy Woodside History Archives.)

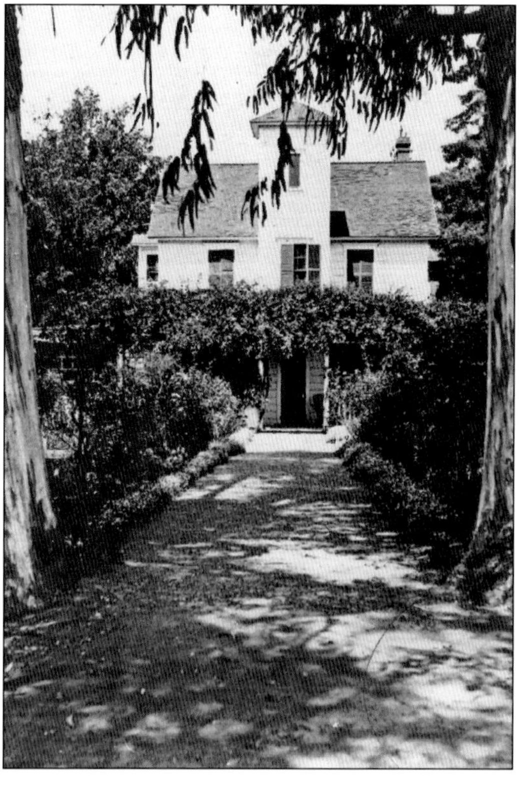

John Greer (above), captain of the brig *Wild Duck*, was the second Irish husband of Maria Louisa Soto, who secured the title to Rancho Canada de Raymundo upon the death of her first husband, John Copinger. Copinger, born in 1811 in Dublin, Ireland, was a disgraced naval officer who obtained 12,540 mountain acres in 1839. He married pioneer's daughter Soto, and they had two children, but he died eight years to the day after their wedding as a prisoner in the Mexican War. In 1850, Maria married Greer, born in 1808, who left sailing to "see the elephant" in the gold fields and became a justice of the peace and school board trustee before dying on February 13, 1885. This Copinger-Greer adobe, below, was built in 1840. Legend prevails that in order for Greer, a Protestant, to be buried in his wife's family's Catholic cemetery, his grave had to be dug 3 feet deeper than usual—safely out of consecrated ground. In fact, he is buried in Union Cemetery. (Right, courtesy Ken Fisher; below, courtesy Woodside History Archives.)

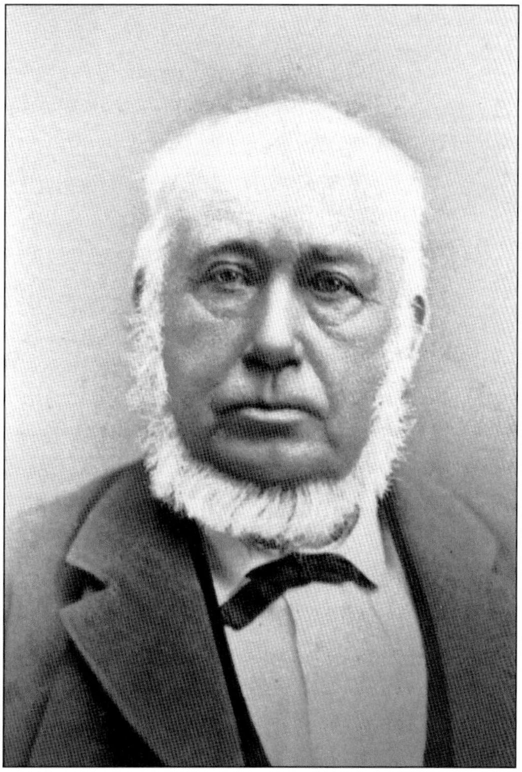

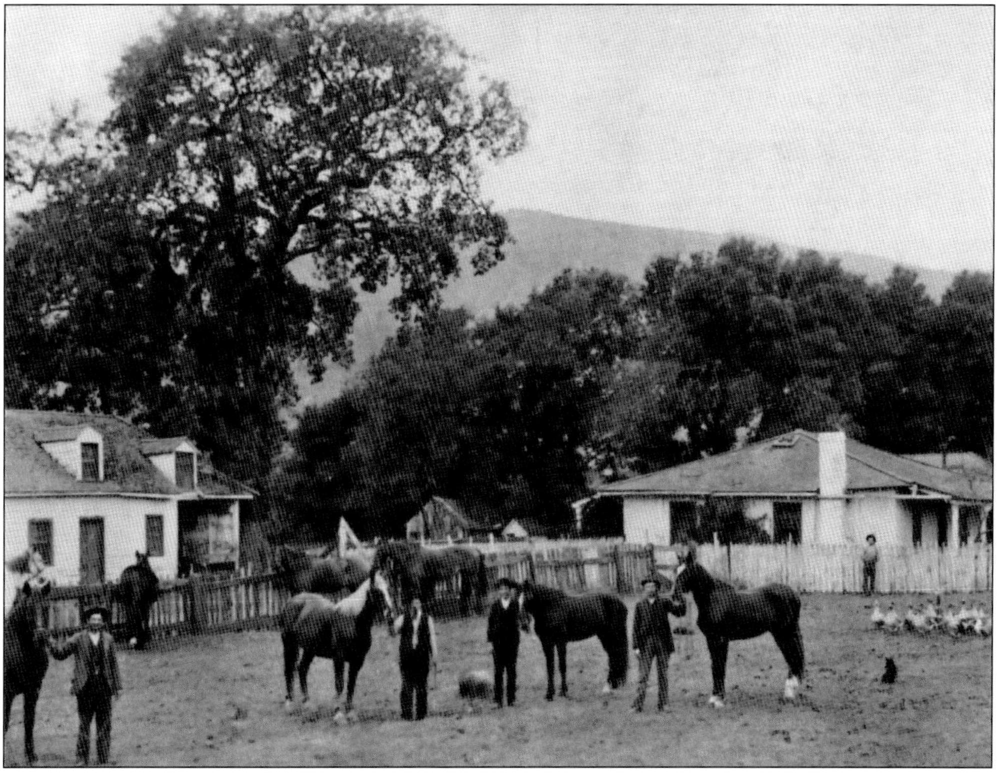

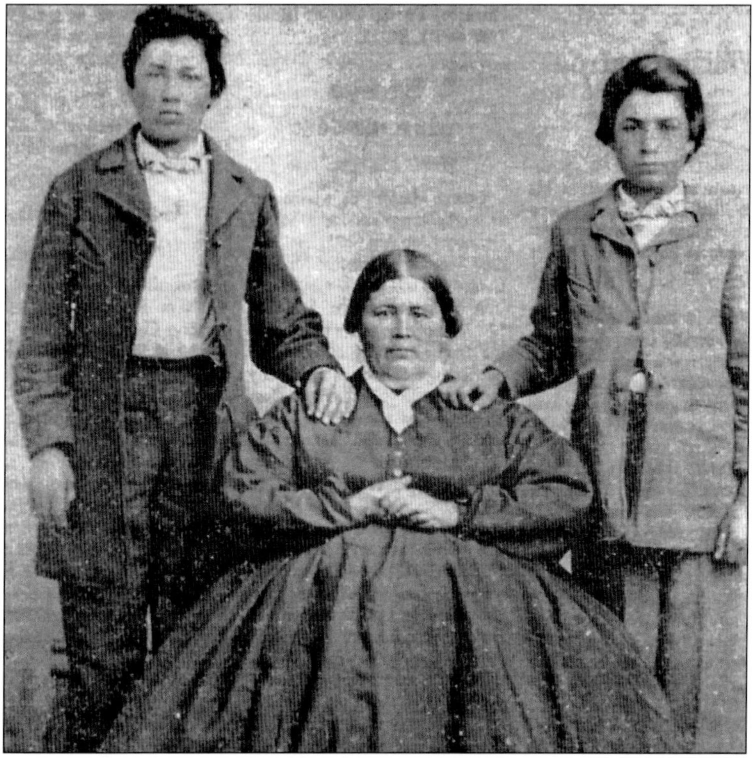

Capt. John Greer's stepdaughter, Manuela Copinger, became a strong-willed adult who married vaquero Antonio Miramontes of Portola Valley and shared with him a penchant for living beyond their means. At left, Maria Louisa Soto Copinger Greer poses around 1864 with her sons Robert (1851–1901), left, and Lucas (1852–1945). She died unexpectedly on May 7, 1883. (Courtesy Woodside History Archives.)

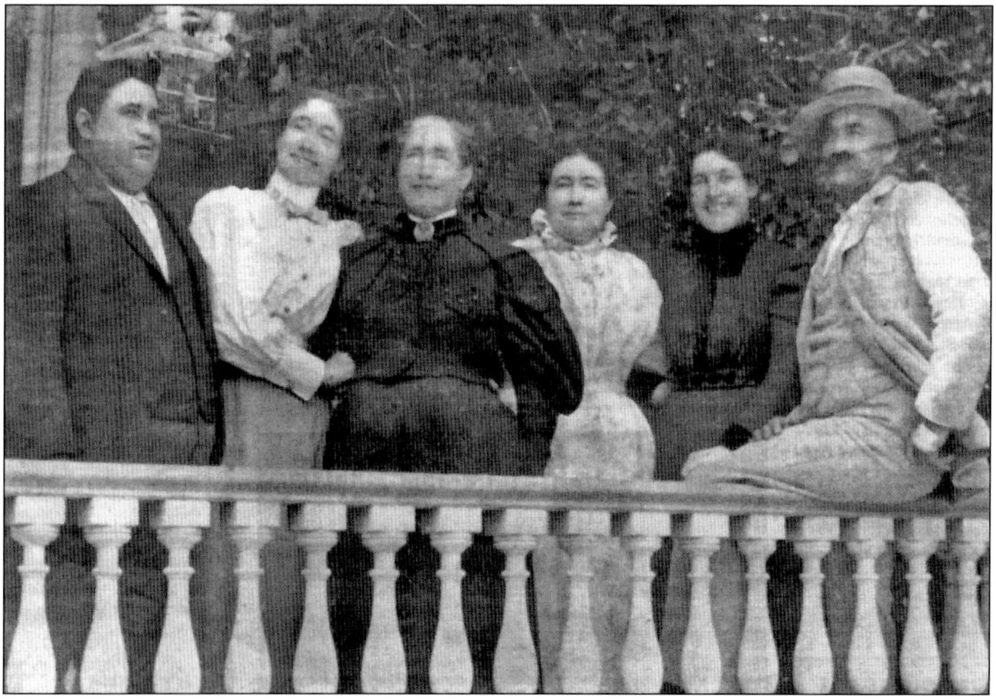

The Greer family, now adults, is shown at a family reunion. The men are Robert Greer, far left, and Lucas Greer, far right. Manuela Copinger is the second woman from the left. (Courtesy Woodside History Archives.)

Three

A Sturdy Breed
Lumbermen and Lumber Mills

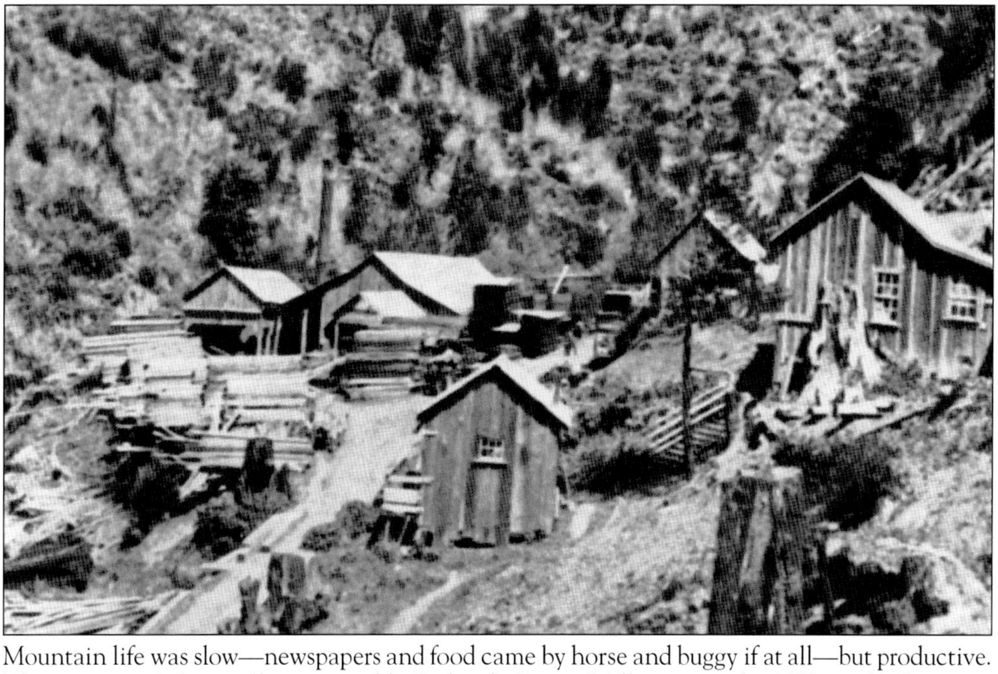

Mountain life was slow—newspapers and food came by horse and buggy if at all—but productive. The mountain's first mill was arguably Richard's Steam Mill, running by 1852 on the Purisima Canyon rim. By 1853, fifteen mills were operating on Kings Mountain, yielding 20 to 25 million feet of lumber annually. Those included the Borden and Hatch mill seen here, built in 1871 in Purisima Canyon. Mills came and went: when an area was "gulched out," they were moved to untouched forest. Still, sparing only trees that were too small, twisty, or inaccessible, loggers clear-cut the area so that by 1875, only six to eight mills still functioned. The millmen were rough-and-tumble laws unto themselves. When in 1856 a widow and her pretty daughter formed a temperance league, the men listened avidly to the daughter's pleas—until she got married, whereupon she found no one to heed her. Then there was Edna "Rickety Ann" Van Winkle, who worked at the mills until marrying prominent San Francisco lawyer Francis Henie; the couple dined often with Pres. Theodore Roosevelt. The mountain saw even more colorful individuals, a phenomenon which never faded. (Courtesy Ken Fisher.)

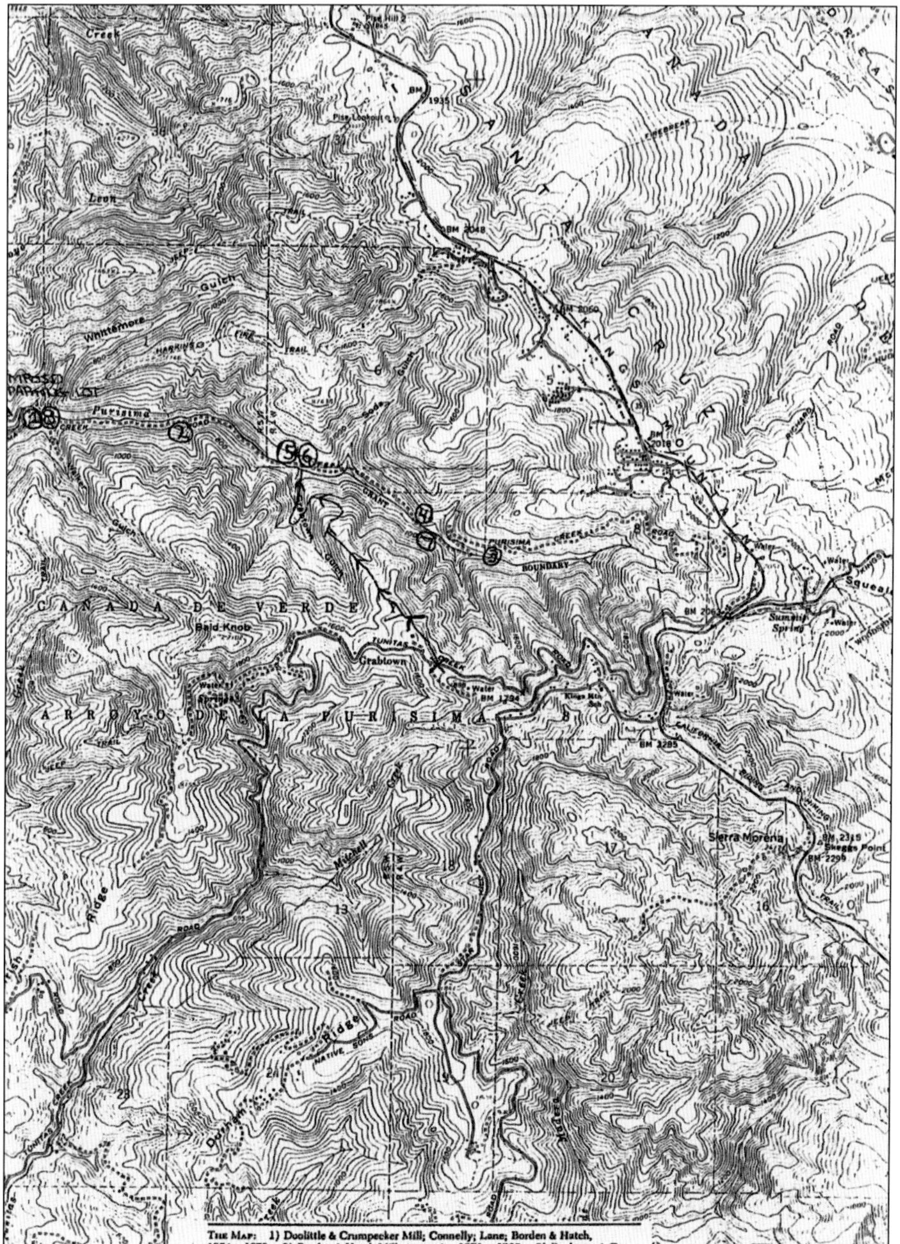

This topographical map has been adapted to show some—but by no means all—of the mills on Kings Mountain during the height of the 19th-century milling rush. This section looks at Purisima Canyon and Purisima Creek, sprung from headwaters high in the Sierra Morena and meandering through three miles of richly wooded land. The map also includes places drawn from mountain lore, like 2,102-foot-high, aptly named Bald Knob to the middle left. Or Squealer Gulch to the right, named for mill worker Bob Gibson. He lived at Summit Springs, hauled shingles, had a hook where his left hand once was, and got the nickname of "Squealer Bob" for his high-pitched voice. He would light into anyone who used that name within his hearing, though. (Courtesy U.S. Geological Survey.)

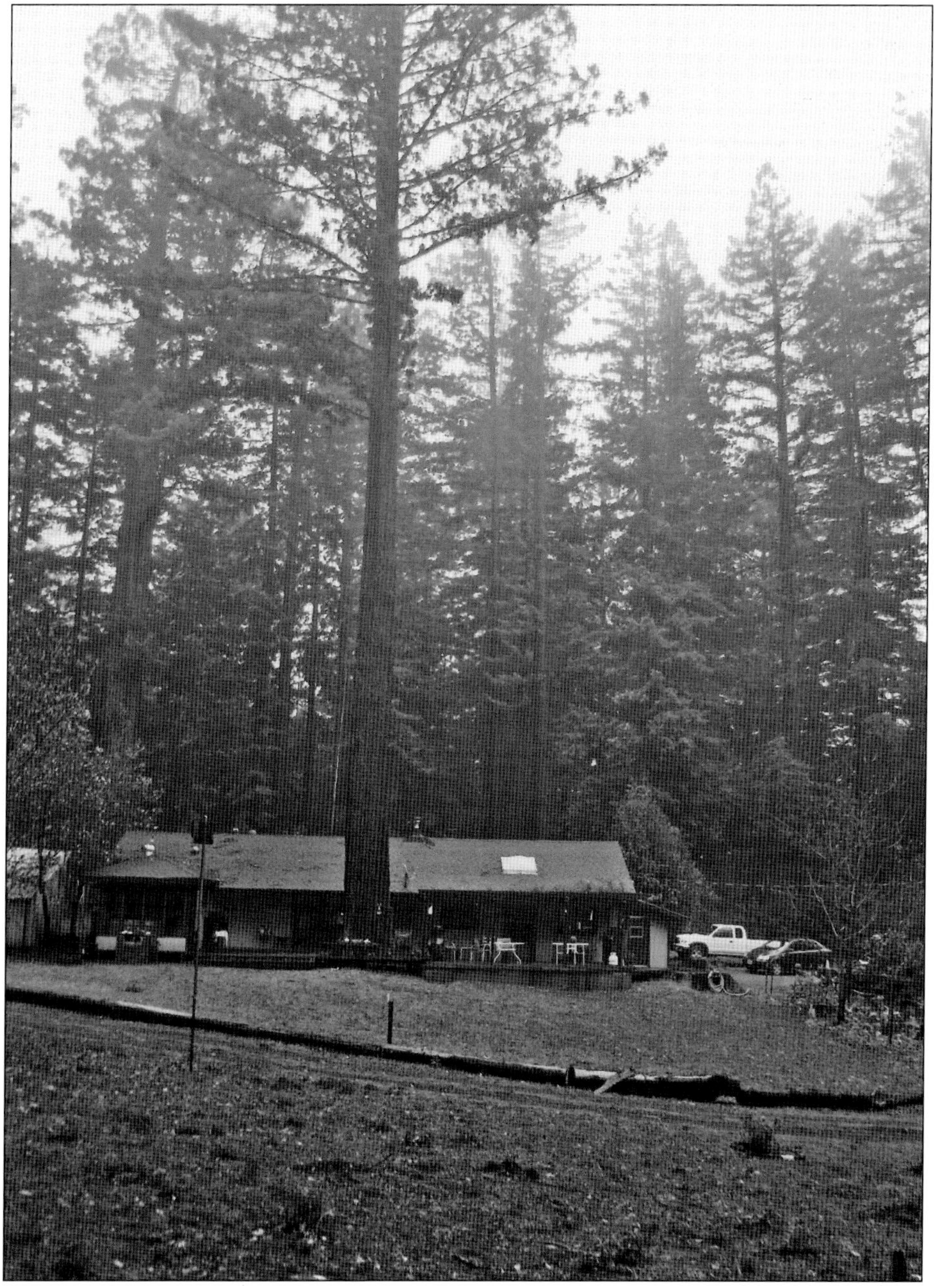

This private home stands at the epicenter of "Grabtown," still present on U.S. Geological Survey maps, but an obscure precursor to Kings Mountain. It began when French lumberman Eugene Froment opened a mill in Tunitas Canyon in 1868. That failed, but an odd settlement sprang up around it. Settlers simply helped themselves to land and put up a shack. If they left the area, someone else grabbed land and shack. One morning, Sarah Church Arnold found a barn foundation in her vegetable garden. Her neighbor suggested calling the town Grabannapolis, but her waggish nine-year-old brother Andrew said, "Why not Grabtown?" and it stuck. At one time, Grabtown housed 200 to 300 people. Fourteen families lived there in 1882. By 1900, that number had dwindled to three. Around 1890, what was left of the town burned. (Courtesy the author.)

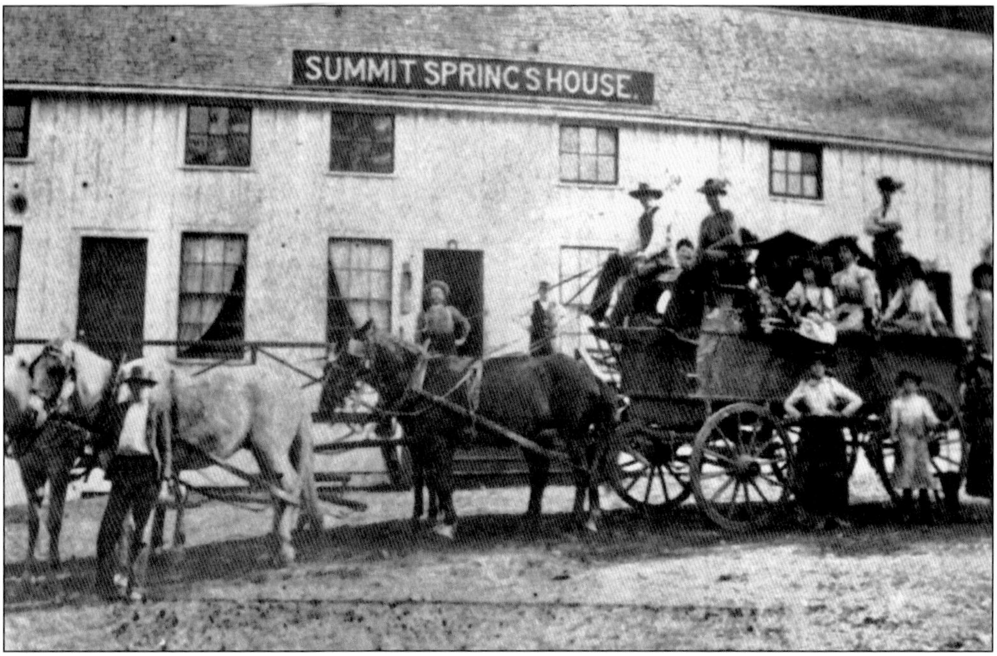

Before Eugene Froment's Tunitas Canyon mill folded in 1879, it spawned Summit Springs, near where today's Highway 35 meets Kings Mountain Road. It grew into a small but fashionable social hub on the mountain's "brow," hence the name "Brow House." There was a hotel, school, store, livery, and saloon. In 1868, Froment built the Summit Springs House, shown here, a large but no-frills hotel for teamsters making the two-day trip hauling timber along Summit Springs (toll) Road, shown in 1870. Teamsters made wages of around $50 a month plus food. (The home of mountain man Henry Bottger peeks through the trees to the left.) Year-round springs watered Summit Springs. In time, it faded into obscurity, but its name is still found on U.S. Geological Survey maps. (Above, courtesy Ken Fisher; below, courtesy Woodside History Archives.)

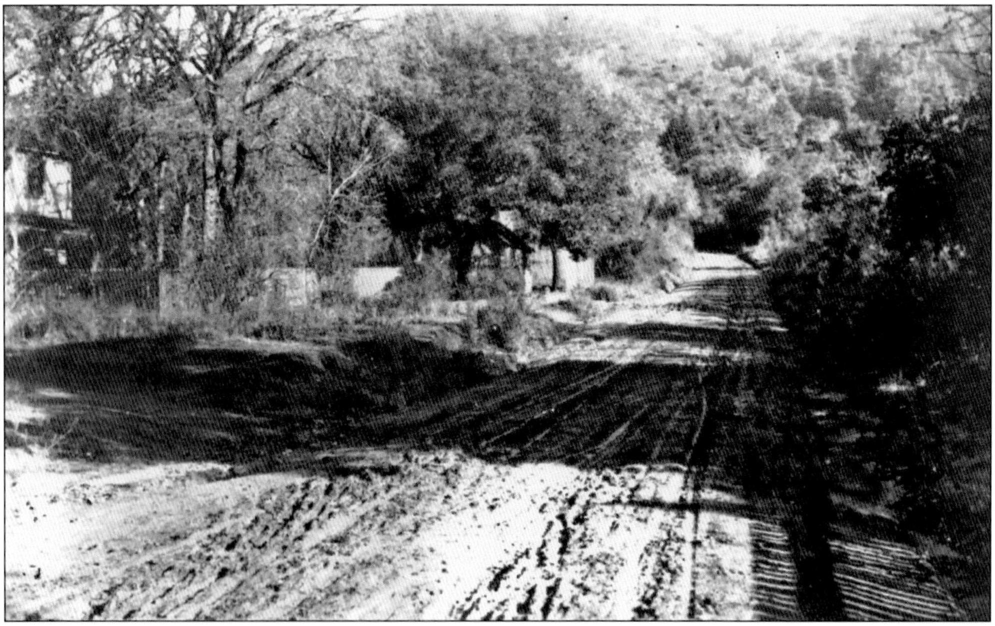

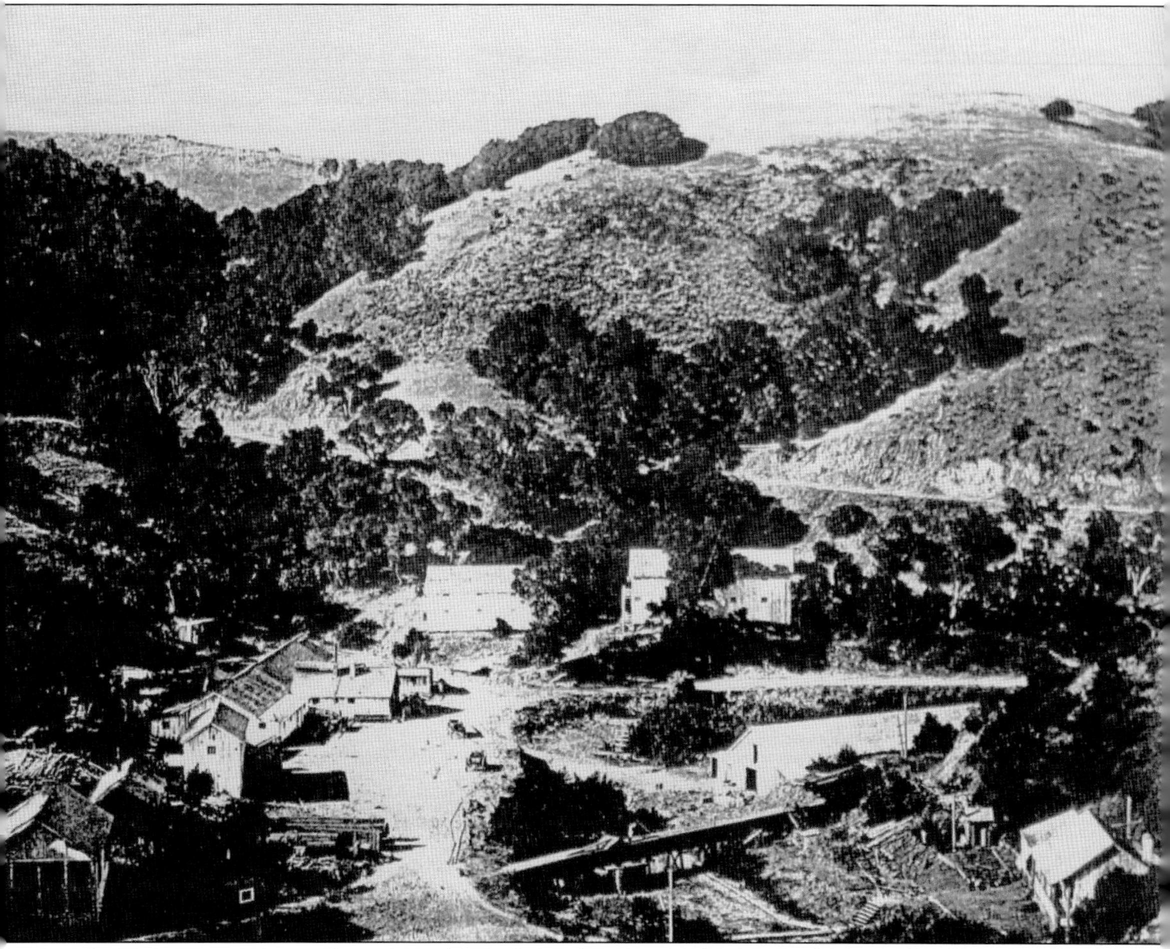

Communities came and went in the 1860s and 1870s: early Woodside around Dr. Robert O. Tripp's landmark store, Summit Springs, Greersburg and Searsville (shown here) to the south and east, Portola Valley, and Whiskey Hill, sometimes called "Last Chance," site of the infamous Hanging and Kissing Tree. It figured in the long trip from redwoods to Redwood City: The first day was spent making the summit with an overnight stay in Grabtown. The next day meant inching down the grade dragging a log that acted as a brake. Next came a stop at Whiskey Hill, less a community than a spot where bullwhackers took liquid reinforcement before plunging down Redwood Gulch to the port. Guesswork, not evidence, suggests there might have been a saloon there. In both the 1880s and Prohibition, fruitless efforts were made to substitute new names. (Courtesy Redwood City Library.)

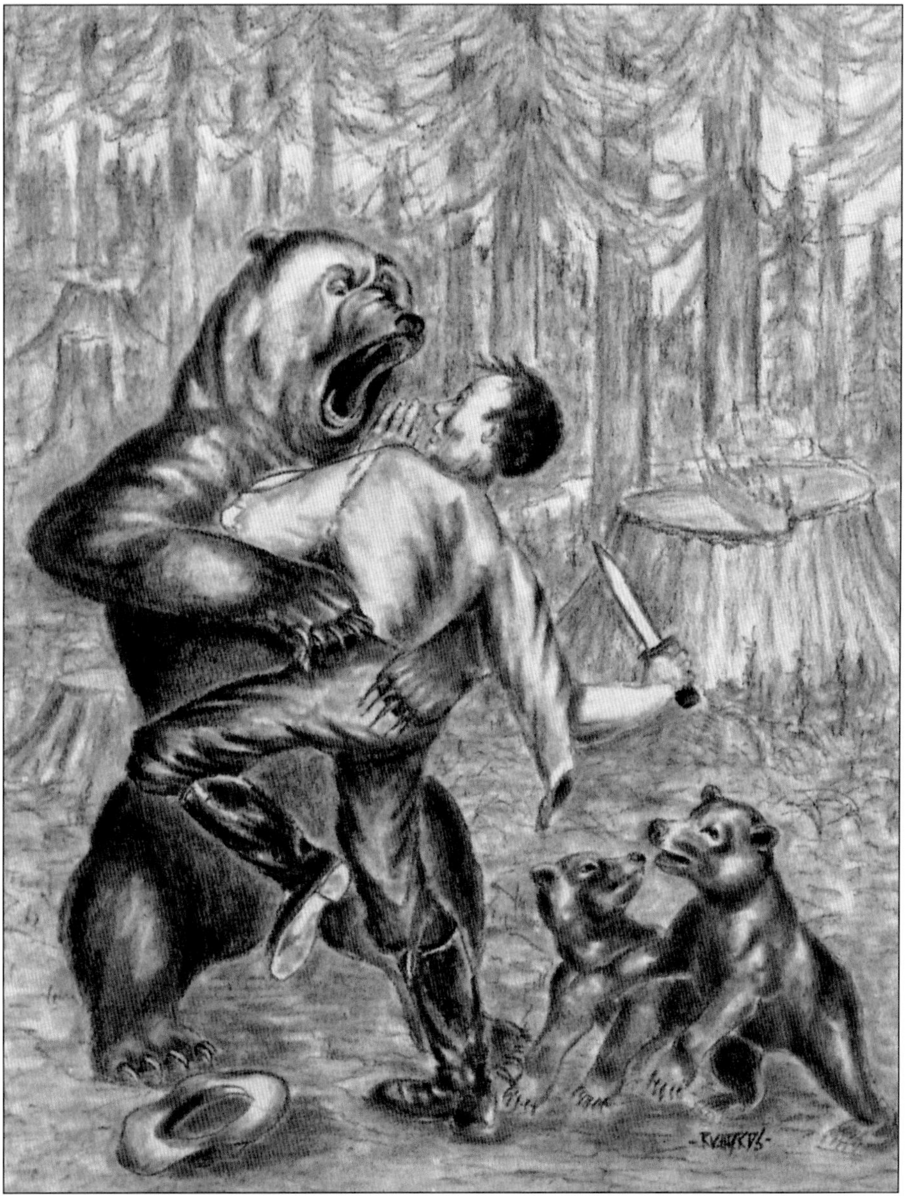

The Charles Brown Adobe figures in how Bear Gulch got named after "Grizzly" Ryder in an incident dramatically sketched by Gilbert Richards. Searching for lost calves, Ryder stopped there to chat with an old sailor and a Native American woman. Resuming his search in the brush, he stumbled on a mother grizzly with two cubs. The bear grabbed him; he struck back with his knife. She loosened her grip, and he wrenched away, rolled downhill, and played dead. The bear approached him, gave one last swipe, and ambled off. He blacked out and awakened at the adobe, where the woman tended him and the sailor stitched his gashes with sail string. They summoned a doctor who wanted to amputate, but Brown refused, declaring he would not live or die without the arms and legs God gave him. He did live many more years, until 1917, immortalized by a gulch. Grizzlies roamed Kings Mountain until 1870, when the last one in San Mateo County was poisoned by John Harkins, father of legendary hermit George, on high Whittemore Gulch. (Courtesy Gilbert Richards.)

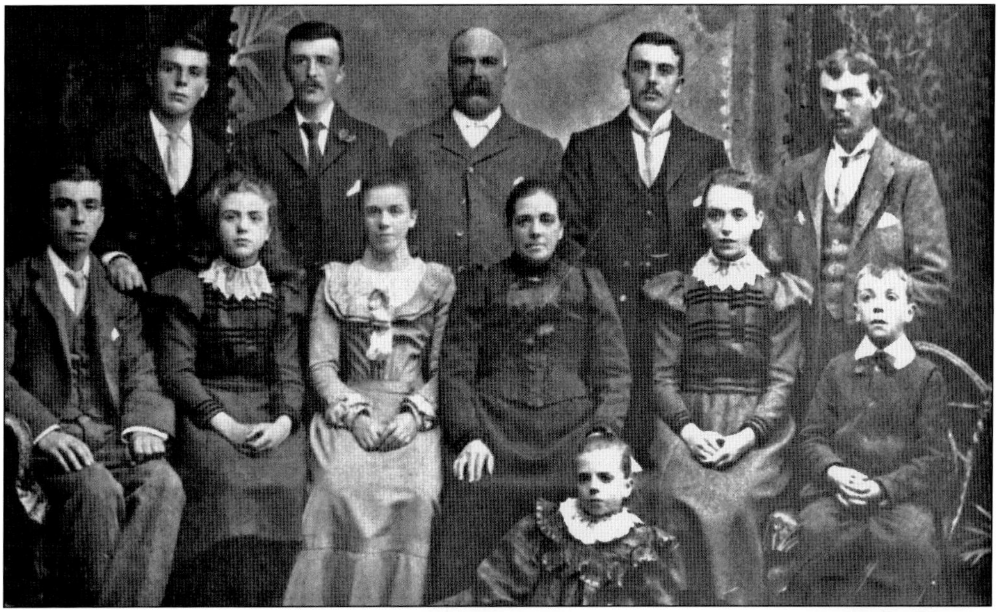

They began as squatters: Frank and Honora (pronounced Hon-oh-RAY) King built a home in 1868 on unclaimed land, started a saloon, boardinghouse, and barbershop, and raised six children. He was a stout German barber often prosecuted but never convicted of serving liquor without a license; she cooked for the mill men and was honored for her chicken dinners and huckleberry pies. Among their guests were Leland and Jane Stanford. Legend has it that when students headed up the mountain, professors would remark, "I suppose you are going up to Kings' mountain," and the name stuck. In 1888, a dispute arose over the land; Judge George Buck, shown here, decreed that while the squatters were in the wrong, they had been there so long he gave them land anyway. Frank died in 1896, and Honora stayed on the mountain, nursing hermit "Uncle" Nathan Comstock in his final days, until her death in 1924. (Above, courtesy Ken Fisher; right, courtesy Redwood City Library.)

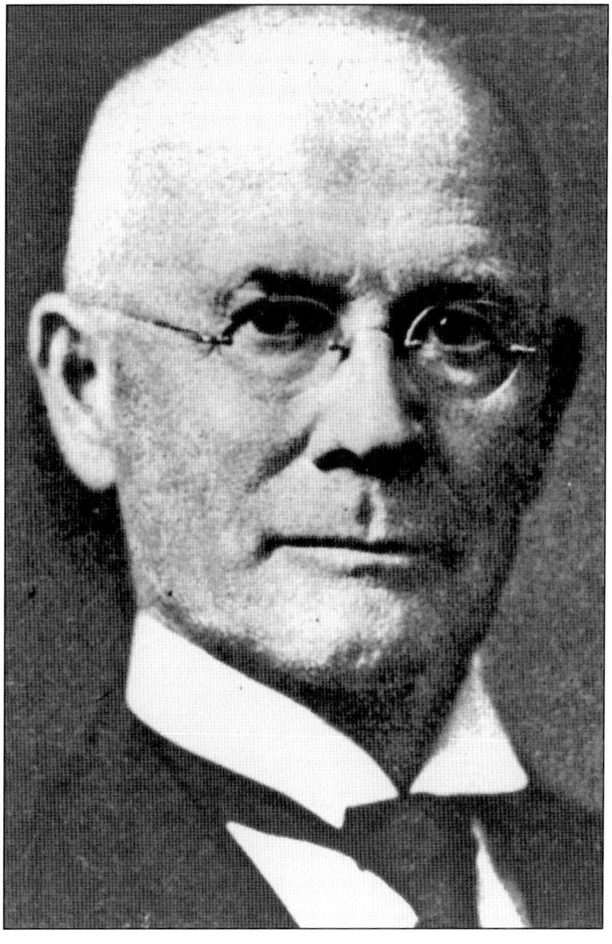

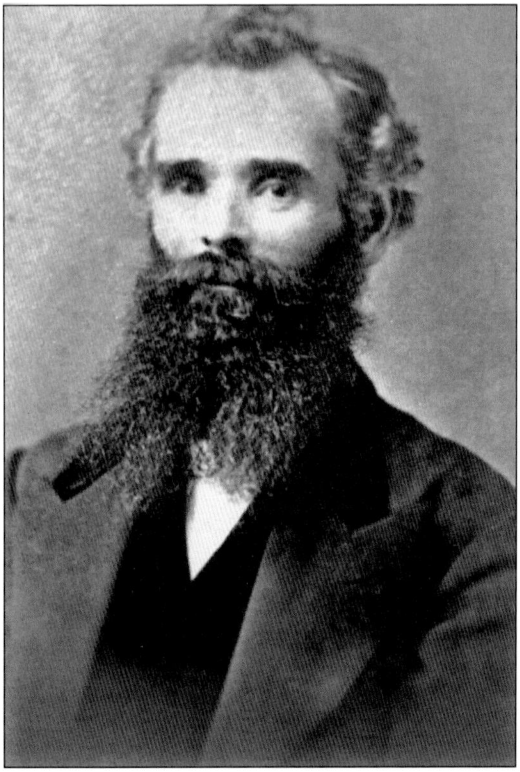

Over 70 years, Purisima Canyon, or "The Purisima," saw milling develop on the mountain. The first mill, small and water-powered, was built in 1854 by Doolittle and Crumpecker and turned out 3,000 feet of lumber per day. It was purchased in 1865 by Rufus Hatch, shown here in his logging prime, and George Borden. It peaked in 1871 with an order for the Spring Valley Water Company. (Courtesy Ken Fisher.)

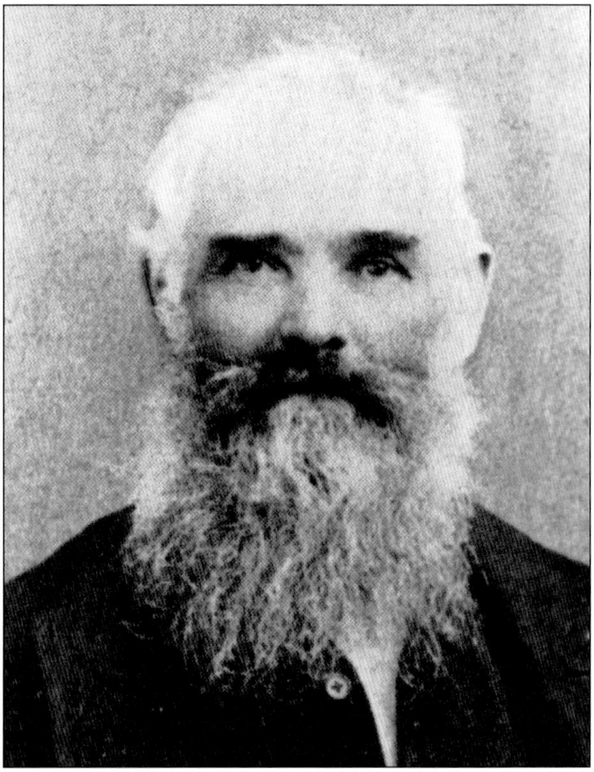

The mature Rufus Hatch was the father of county supervisor Alvin S. Hatch. In the 1890s, Rufus Hatch and partner George Borden bought Clarence Hayward's shingle mill on the upper Tunitas Canyon and added its machinery to their mill. They sought only the best timber for the water company order and now levied the new equipment on trees they had previously ignored. (Courtesy Ken Fisher.)

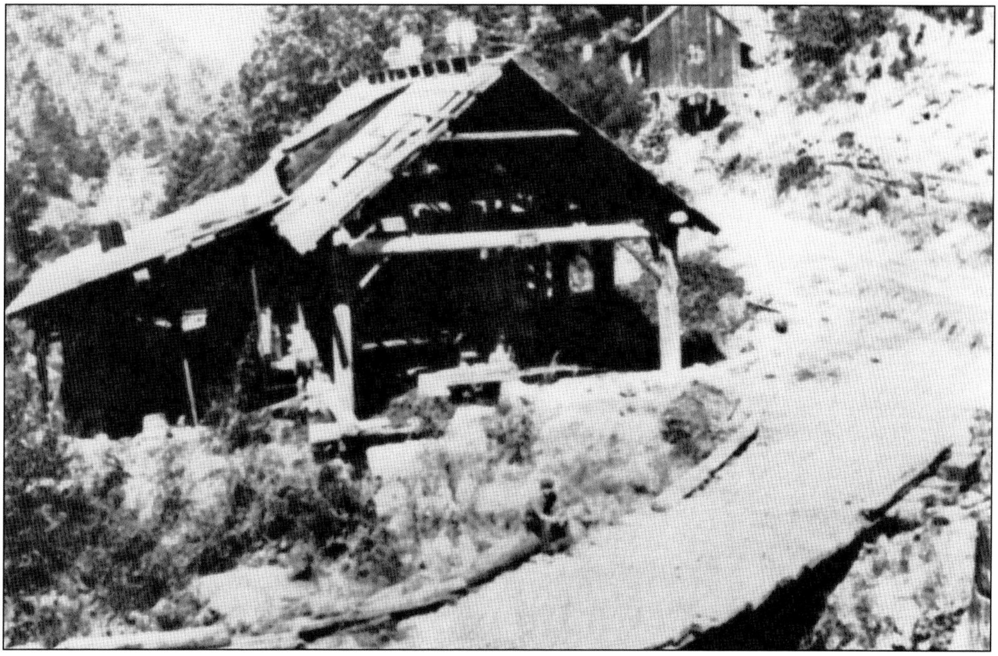

A 30-year logging partnership between the Borden and Hatch families dissolved when George Borden died in 1899 and his son Charles took over his affairs. The Hatch family took the eastern portion of the land and Charles Borden the western portion, which included this sawmill, operating from 1900 to 1906. (Courtesy Ken Fisher.)

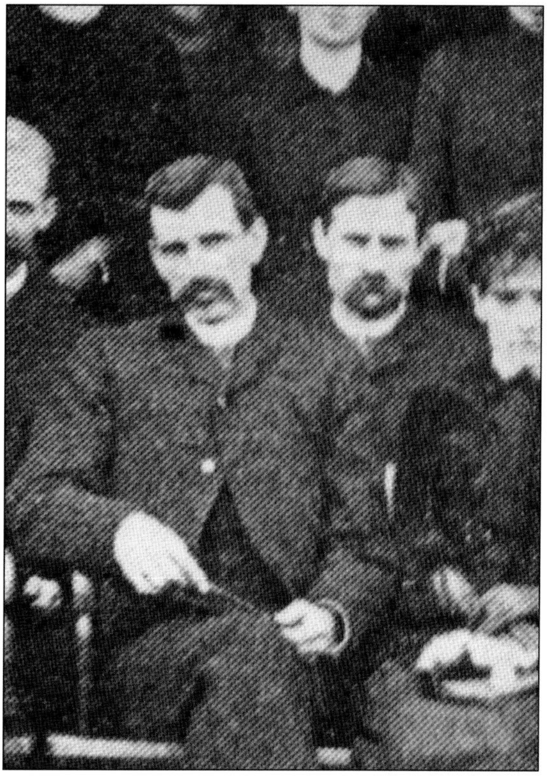

Charles Borden formed a partnership with George P. Hartley, shown here, a former county superintendent of schools whose land bordered the Purisima Creek to the north. They set up a shingle mill in 1906, which timbered out both sides of the canyon. (Courtesy Ken Fisher.)

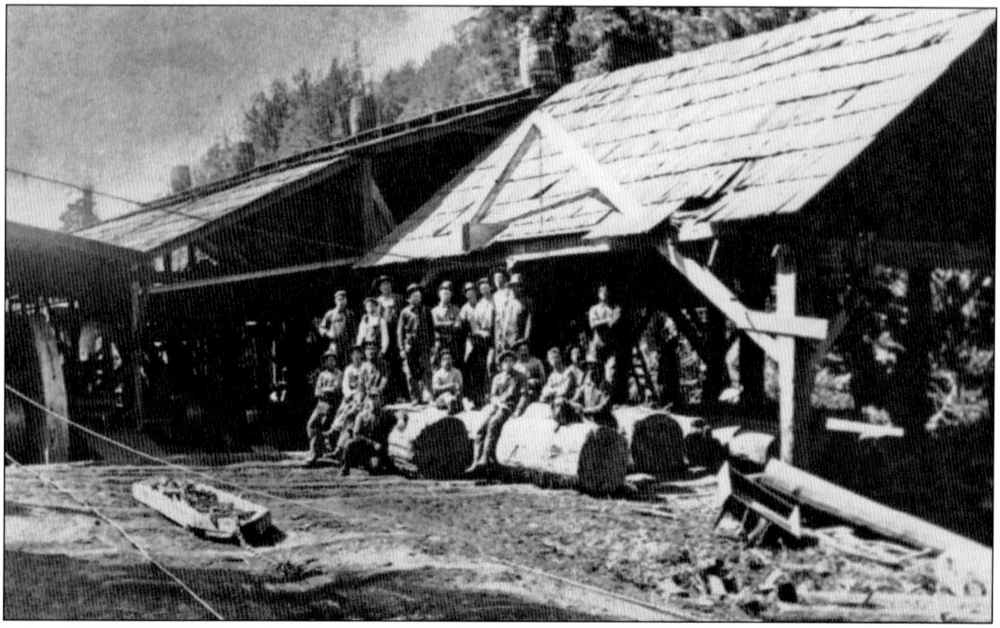

Like Charles Borden, Alvin Hatch took over his father's affairs. In 1906, he bought the Virginia Mill, shown here, and moved it to the Purisima. It was started in 1900 by three owners of the Virginia Timber and Lumber Company with an innovation called a hoist, which raised lumber on Corte Madera Creek via a half-mile, steel-rail tramway that worked well for all but the heaviest logs. (Courtesy Ken Fisher.)

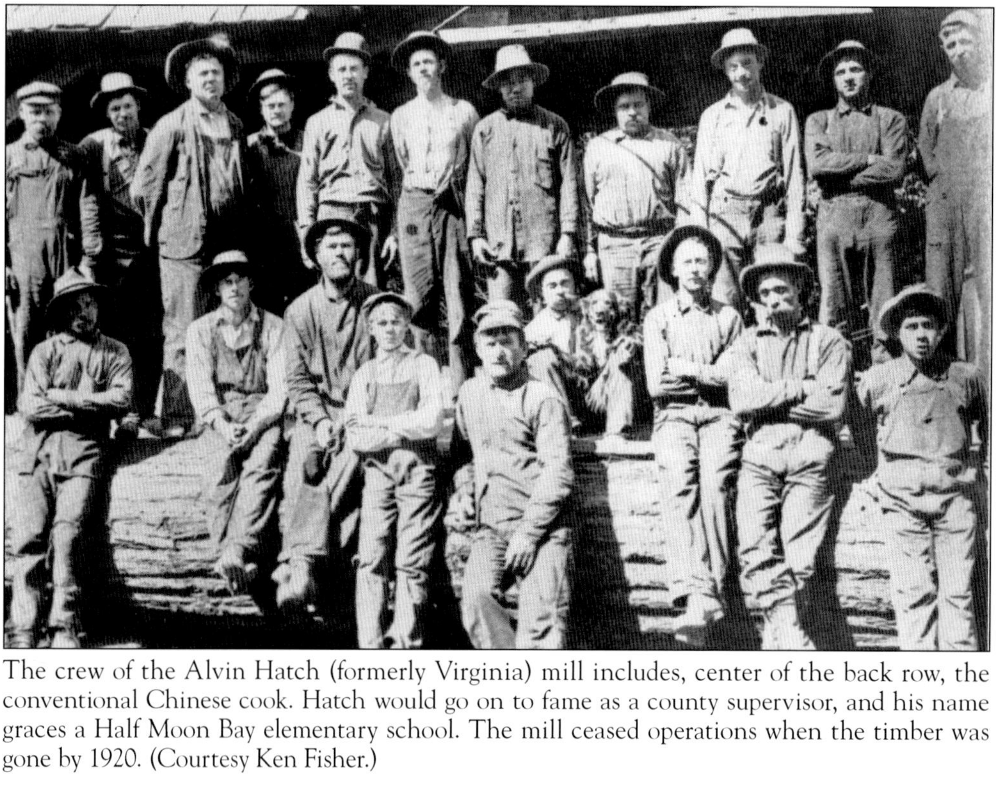

The crew of the Alvin Hatch (formerly Virginia) mill includes, center of the back row, the conventional Chinese cook. Hatch would go on to fame as a county supervisor, and his name graces a Half Moon Bay elementary school. The mill ceased operations when the timber was gone by 1920. (Courtesy Ken Fisher.)

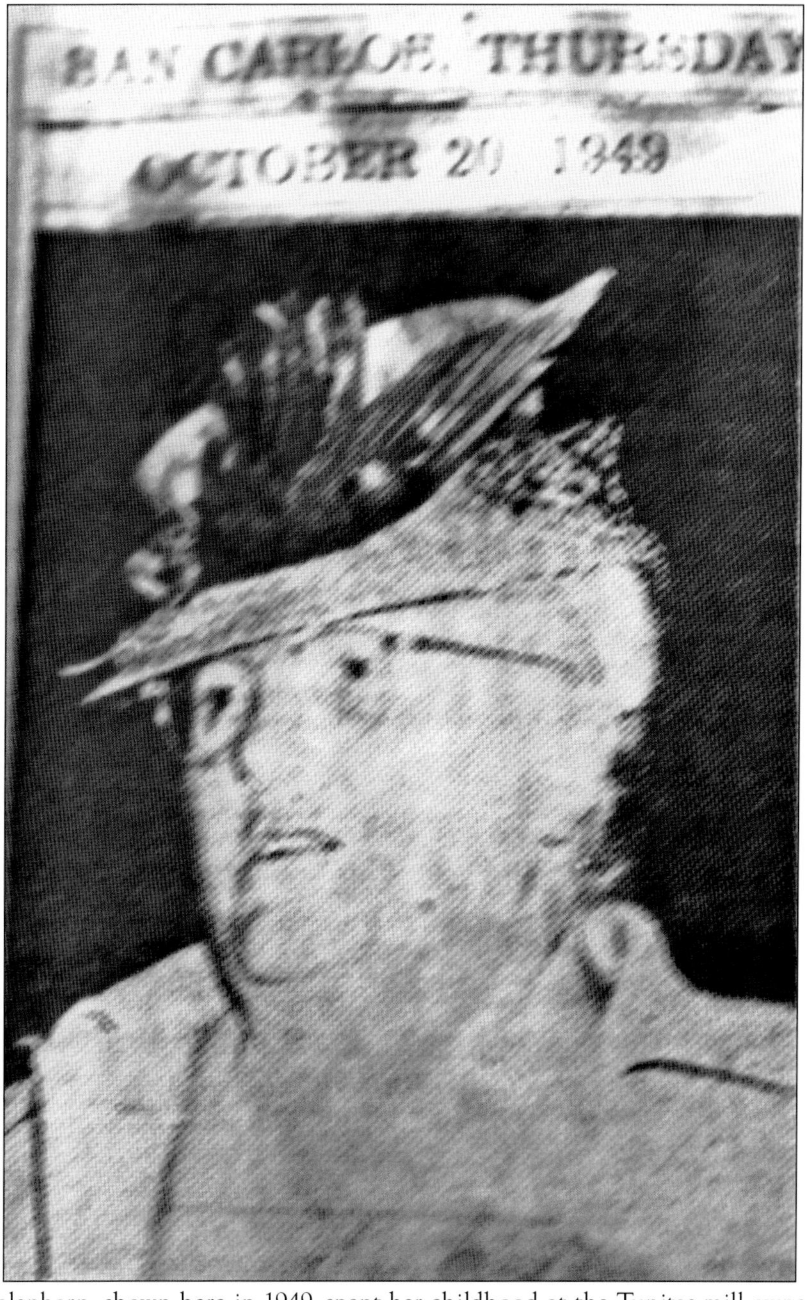

Emma Kalenborn, shown here in 1949, spent her childhood at the Tunitas mill owned by her father, Clarence Hayward. In a memoir she presented in 1944 to the San Mateo County Historical Association, she noted, "One of the most exciting days was when my father would take me part way up the skid road [and] put me on a stump beside the skid road where I could watch the oxen bring down those logs. I wish I could make you see them with the heavy yokes on their necks, the driver goading them on with his own particular vernacular and calling each one by name." She recalled another icon: "One I remember particularly, as I was fascinated by the hook he wore where his left hand was missing. He handled the heavy loads with the greatest of ease. He had a very high-pitched voice and was known as Squealer Bob." (Courtesy Ken Fisher.)

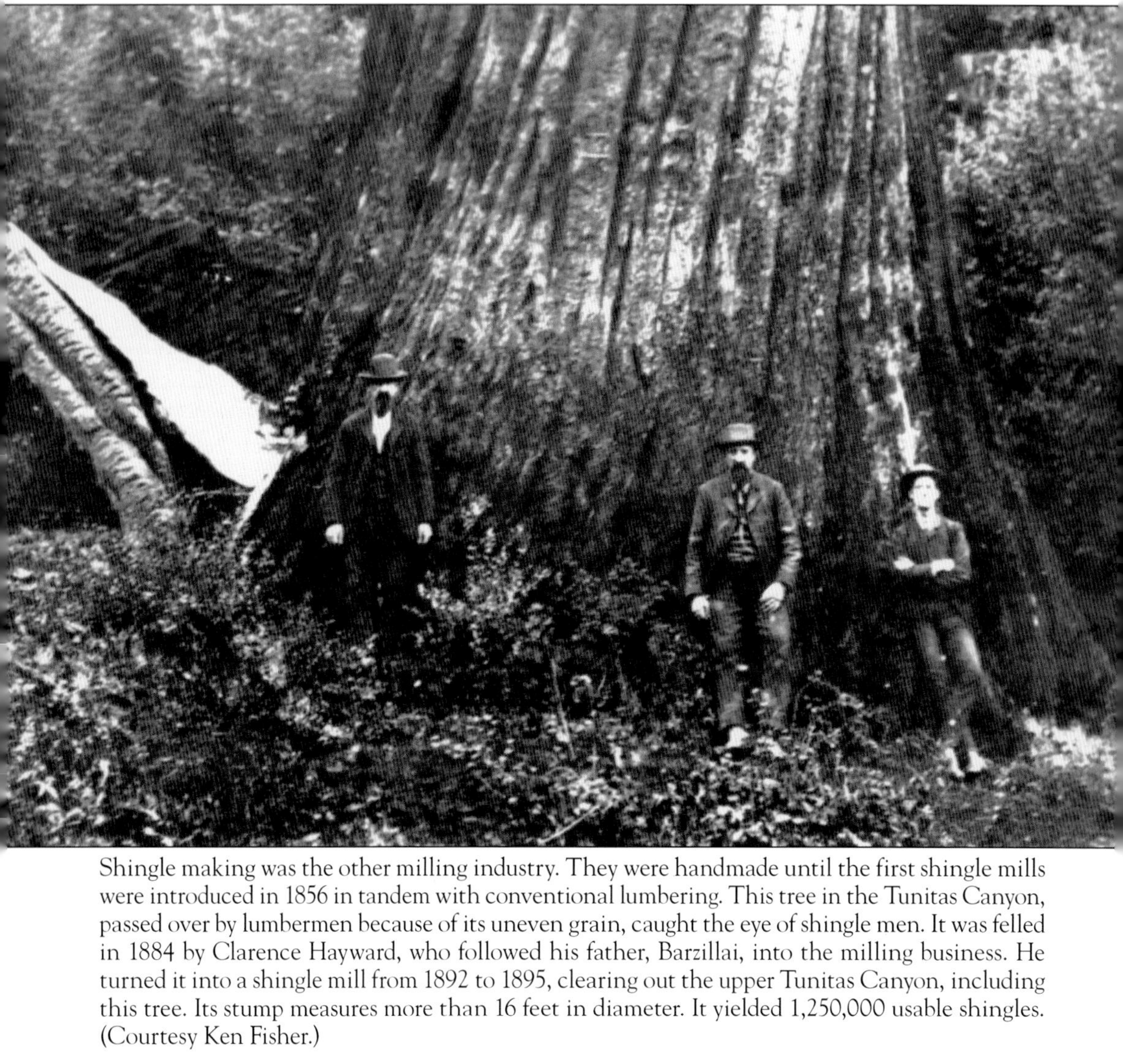

Shingle making was the other milling industry. They were handmade until the first shingle mills were introduced in 1856 in tandem with conventional lumbering. This tree in the Tunitas Canyon, passed over by lumbermen because of its uneven grain, caught the eye of shingle men. It was felled in 1884 by Clarence Hayward, who followed his father, Barzillai, into the milling business. He turned it into a shingle mill from 1892 to 1895, clearing out the upper Tunitas Canyon, including this tree. Its stump measures more than 16 feet in diameter. It yielded 1,250,000 usable shingles. (Courtesy Ken Fisher.)

Sheldon "Purdy" Pharis, the "Shingle King," born in 1828, came to the mountain in 1853 with hand tools and a work ethic, and his shingle mills led the industry. Though a bachelor and loner, he financed the mountain's one-room Pharis School District. But with position came paranoia: He died March 1, 1884, at 55, of a gunshot wound to his head. The verdict was suicide, but doubts prevailed. (Courtesy Redwood City Library.)

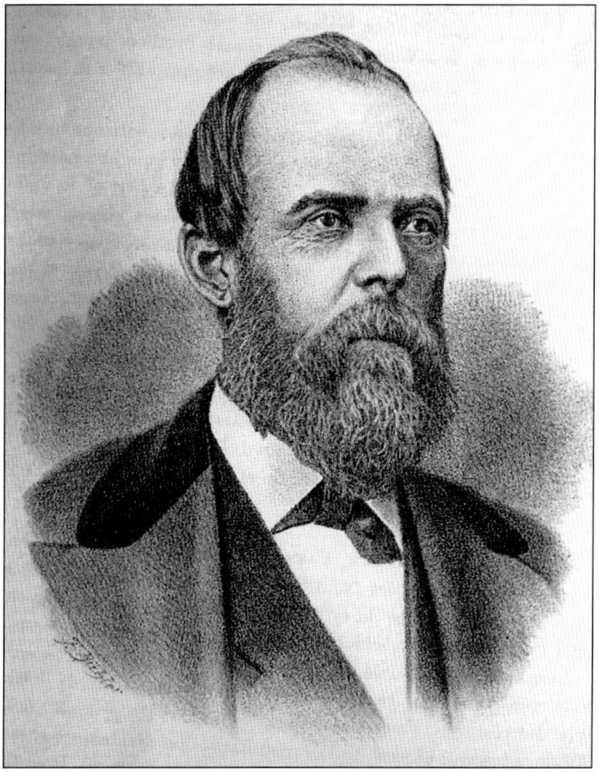

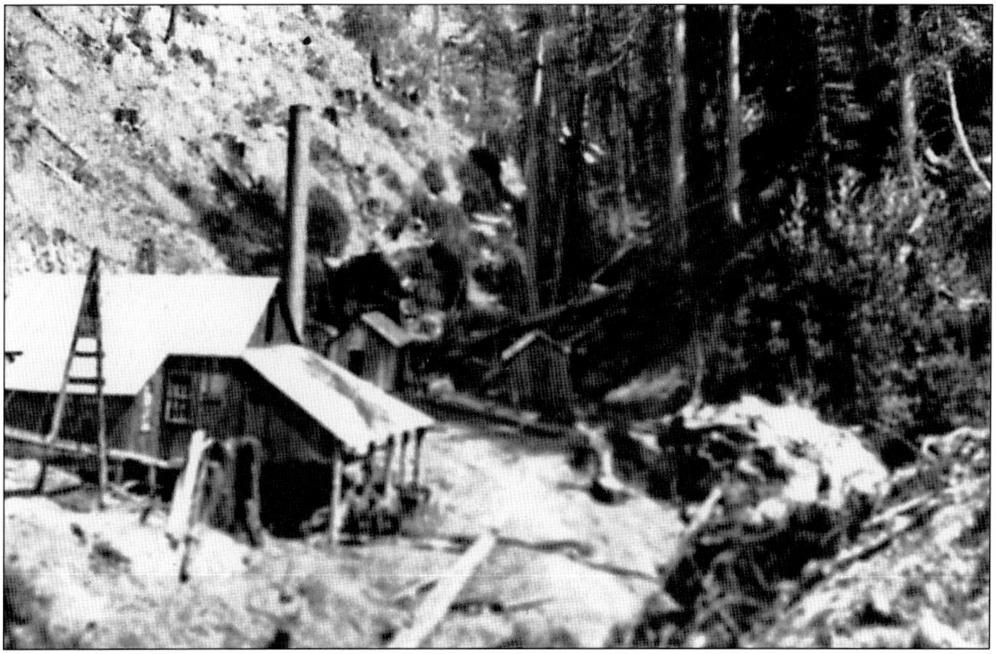

The Pharis Purisima Canyon mill, built in 1870, could turn out 100,000 shingles in a day. One of seven owned by "Shingle King" Pharis, it helped grant him respect. He produced more than 300 million shingles and became the county's largest individual landholder with more than 6,500 acres. This mill thrived until his death. (Courtesy Ken Fisher.)

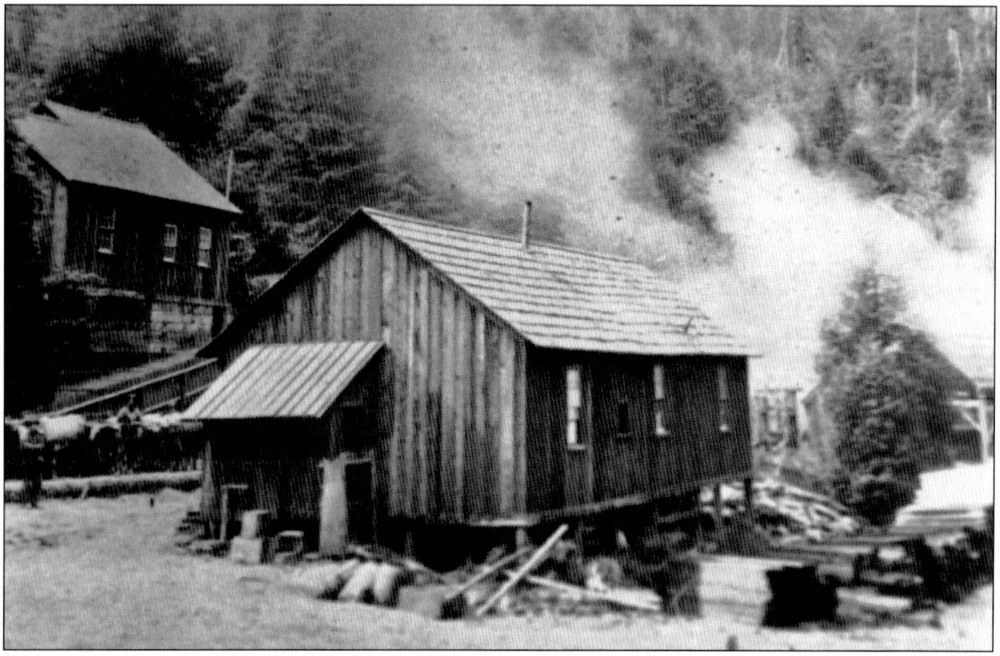

In this image of one of the Saunders mills in Tunitas Canyon is Joshua Saunders's home to the left. The oxen are walking on today's Tunitas Canyon Road. The cookhouse is at the center and the mill to the right. It and lumber piles straddle the creek. (Courtesy Ken Fisher.)

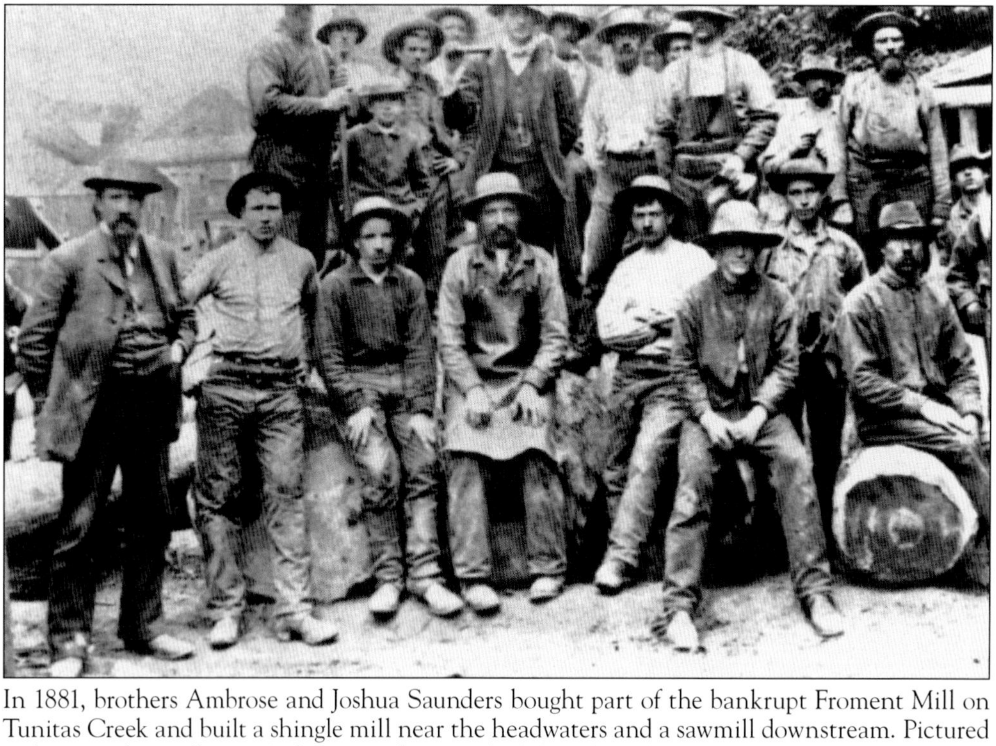

In 1881, brothers Ambrose and Joshua Saunders bought part of the bankrupt Froment Mill on Tunitas Creek and built a shingle mill near the headwaters and a sawmill downstream. Pictured is the Saunders mill crew; Joshua Saunders is at far left. After a few years of success, both brothers died in January 1886. (Courtesy Ken Fisher.)

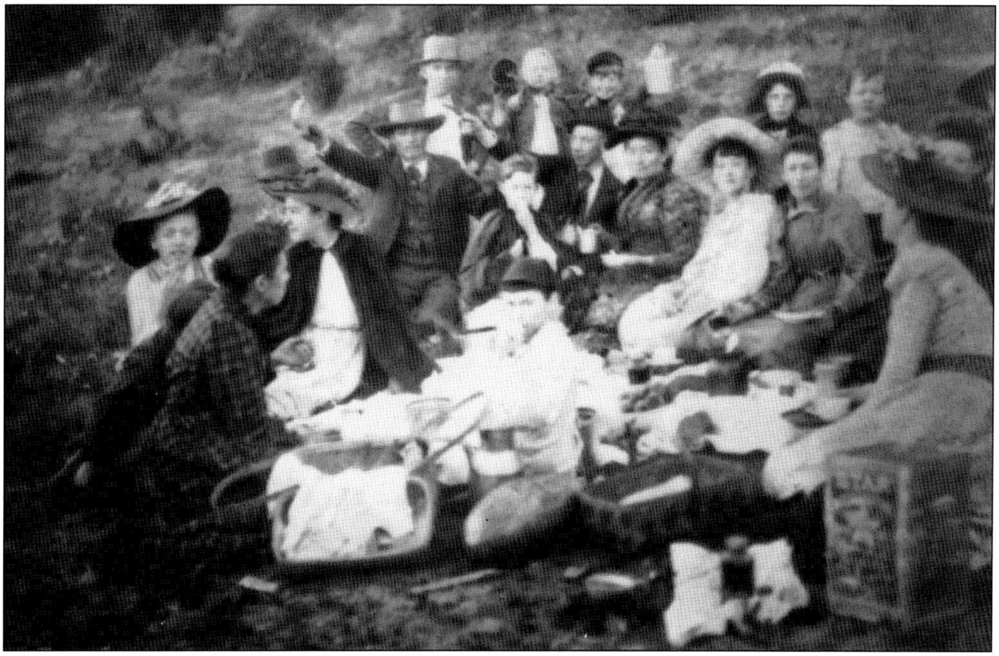

No photograph exists of beloved hermit "Uncle" Nathan Comstock, born in Rhode Island between 1808 and 1820. Allegedly an unhappy love affair drove him to the mountain, where he milled, farmed, hunted, rented his land for huckleberry parties like this one above, and built a small cabin, shown below. Six feet tall with grayish hair and flowing beard, he is described as a gentle, harmless image of Rip Van Winkle. In 1892, four years before Comstock's death, Steve Perkins found him pinned under a fallen tree and freed him. Comstock promised to remember Perkins in his will. Perkins shrugged that off until a yellowed letter with a new stamp reached him on Christmas Eve 1912, directing him to a place to dig. There he found a rusty can filled with $500 in gold coin and a note: "Let this help you in your old age as you helped me." (Both courtesy Ken Fisher.)

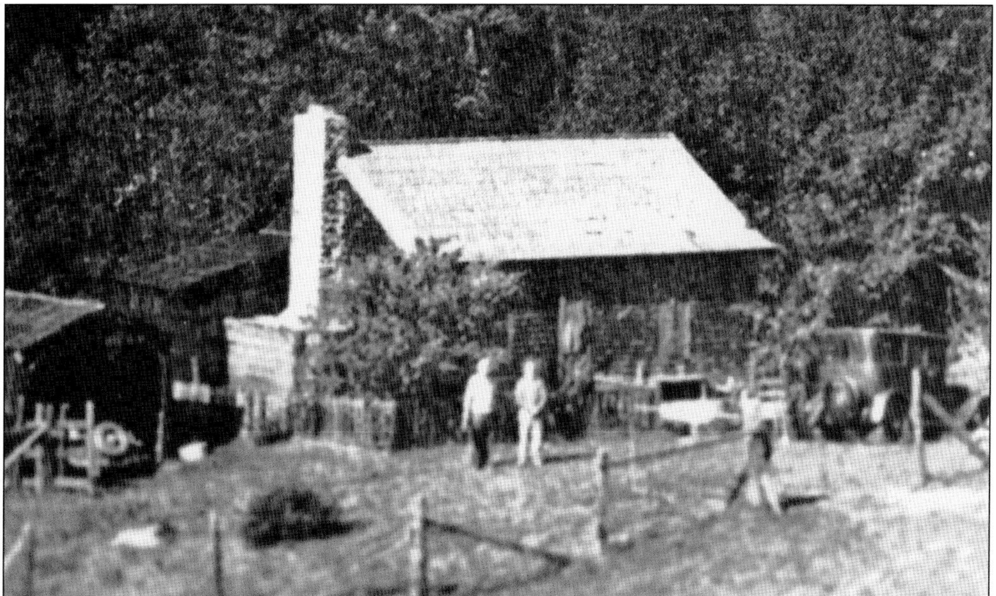

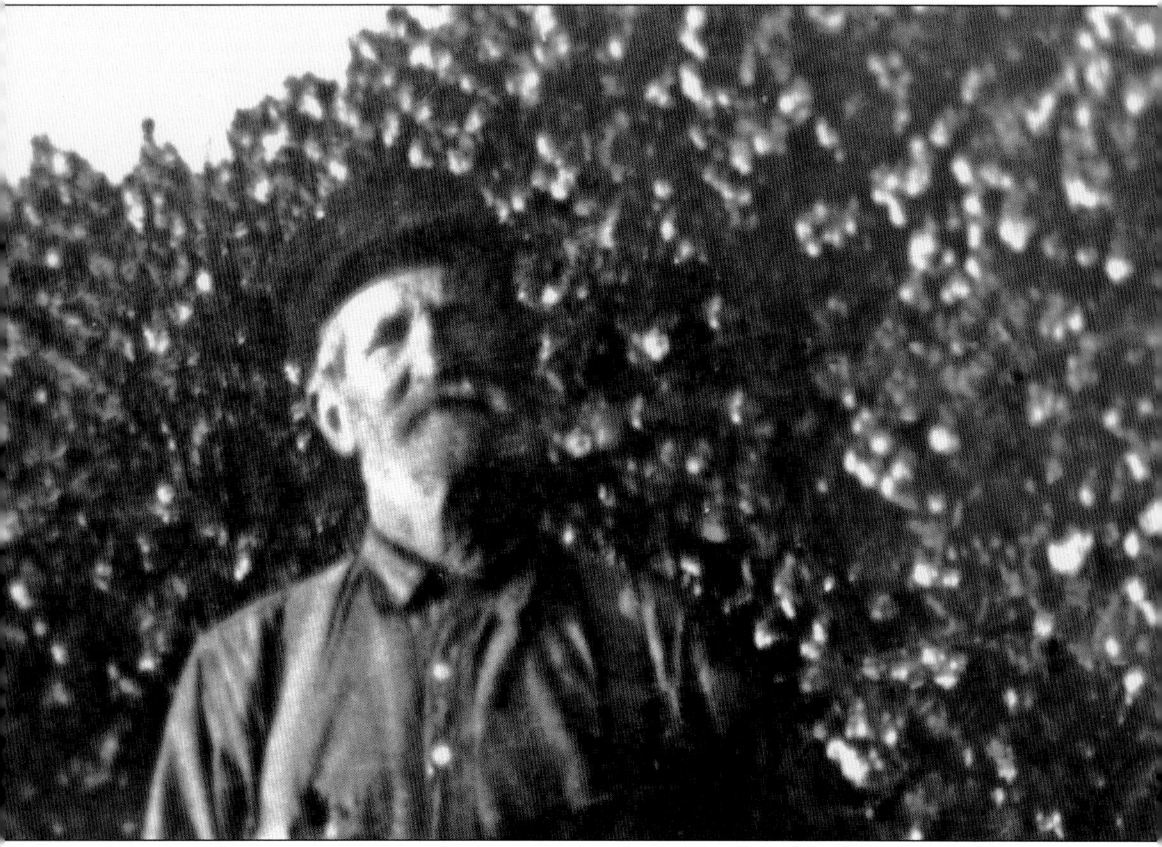

George Harkins, born in 1866, walked daily to the Pharis school as a boy. As a man, he became its next-to-last trustee. It was fitting for the solitary, bachelor hermit, a last vestige of the mountain's pioneer era. Growing up among sawmills, he went from laborer to logger, supervising the logs' dangerous downhill slide. Described as fearless, simple, outdoorsy, kindly, and honest, he kept a few cows and apple trees and hunted on his own land just west of Skyline. Little fazed him: He was known to methodically track down ne'er-do-wells who fired upon him. In 1934, he died from a small beetle boring from his ear into his brain. Of him, Davenport Bromfield wrote: "Those who met him casually, called him worthless, others who thought they knew him called him miserly, but those who knew him best appreciated him. He was just different. We are all different, but not with his difference. That made him an interesting character to all who knew him well." (Courtesy Ken Fisher.)

Four

Dairying
A Gentler Life

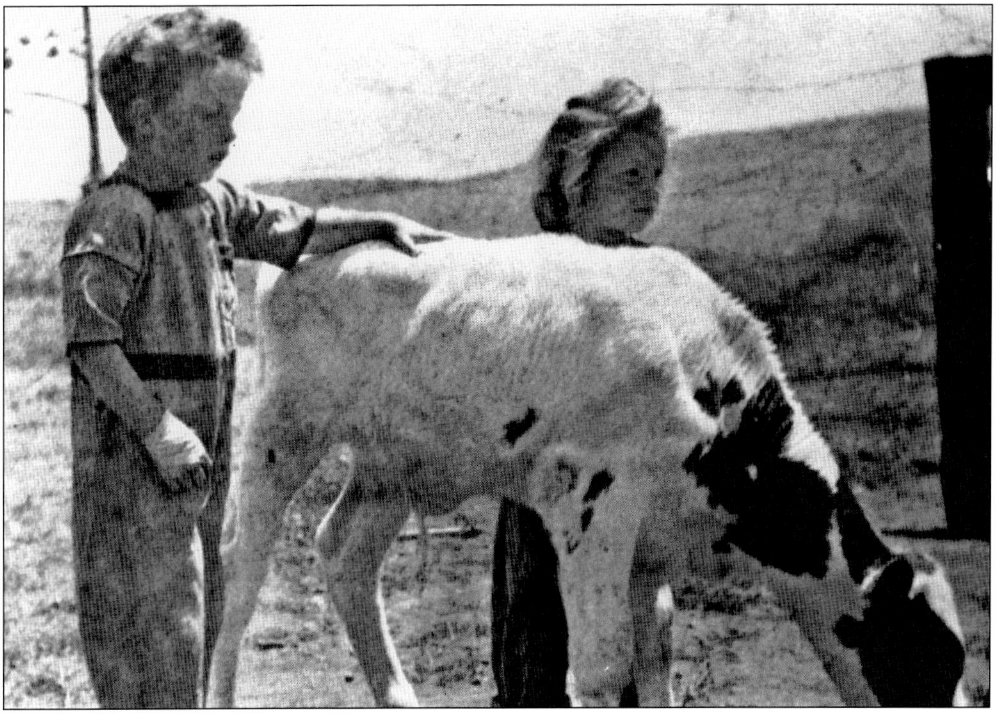

If lumbermen braved grizzlies, injury, cold, and booze, the dairymen who came in the 1850s led more genteel lives. Land on the mountain's southwest edge and treeless north face was ready-made for them by nature and history: Spanish cattle, brought in for beef and tallow, trampled out the sage and transformed the country to grassland, and the forty-niners brought in the first cattle for small home dairies. Families, like these young grandchildren of premiere cattleman Peter Van Winkle, flourished here, as did schools and churches. Perhaps the best-known dairy was Steybrae Farm, belonging to E. B. McFarland. Scottish Ayrshires were the cattle of choice for innovative mountain dairymen like J. N. Gilman. Around World War II, advanced technology, increased machinery costs, lack of interest from returning soldiers, and labor shortage as a result of a rise in postwar building phased the little dairies out. The grassland was retaken by the timeless sage. (Courtesy Ken Fisher.)

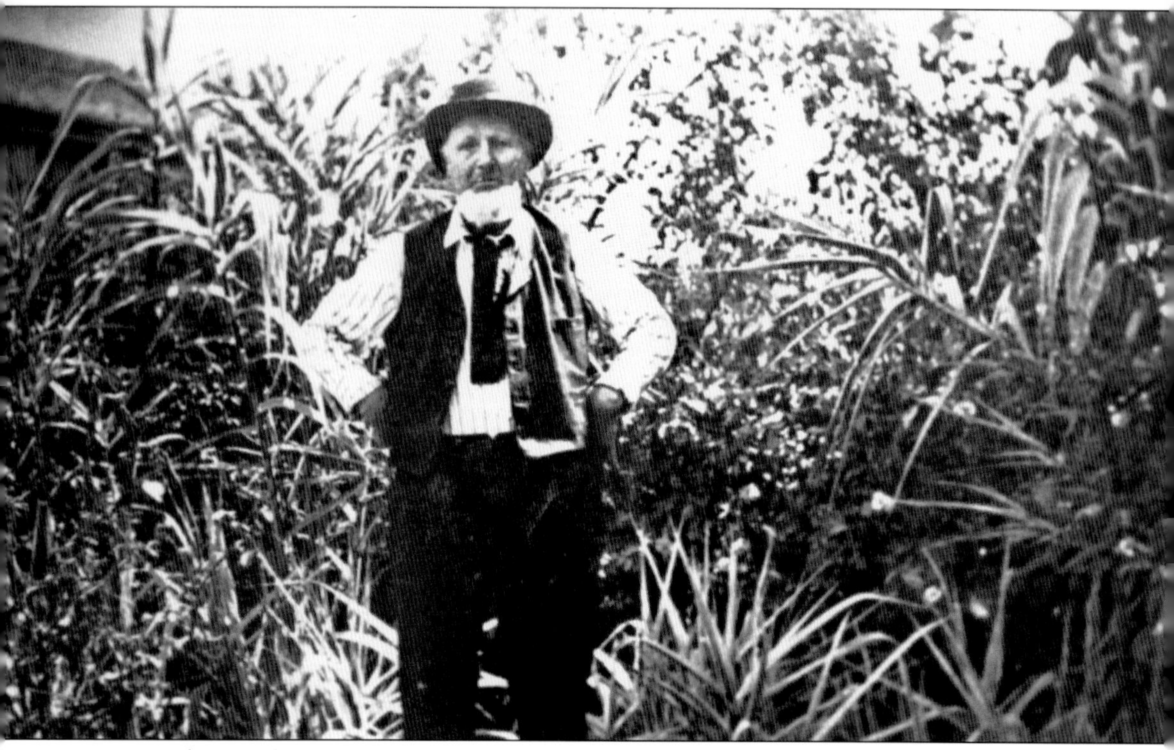

Peter Schoonmaker Van Winkle (1827–1907) came from Jersey City and painted carriages until coming west in 1849, painting a ship to pay his way through the Panama Canal. After trying the gold fields, he bought 203 acres on Kings Mountain. Enterprising and earnest, he farmed there for 30 years—beginning by casting his eye on his neighbor Thomas Moylan's young daughter, Magadelena. (Courtesy Ken Fisher.)

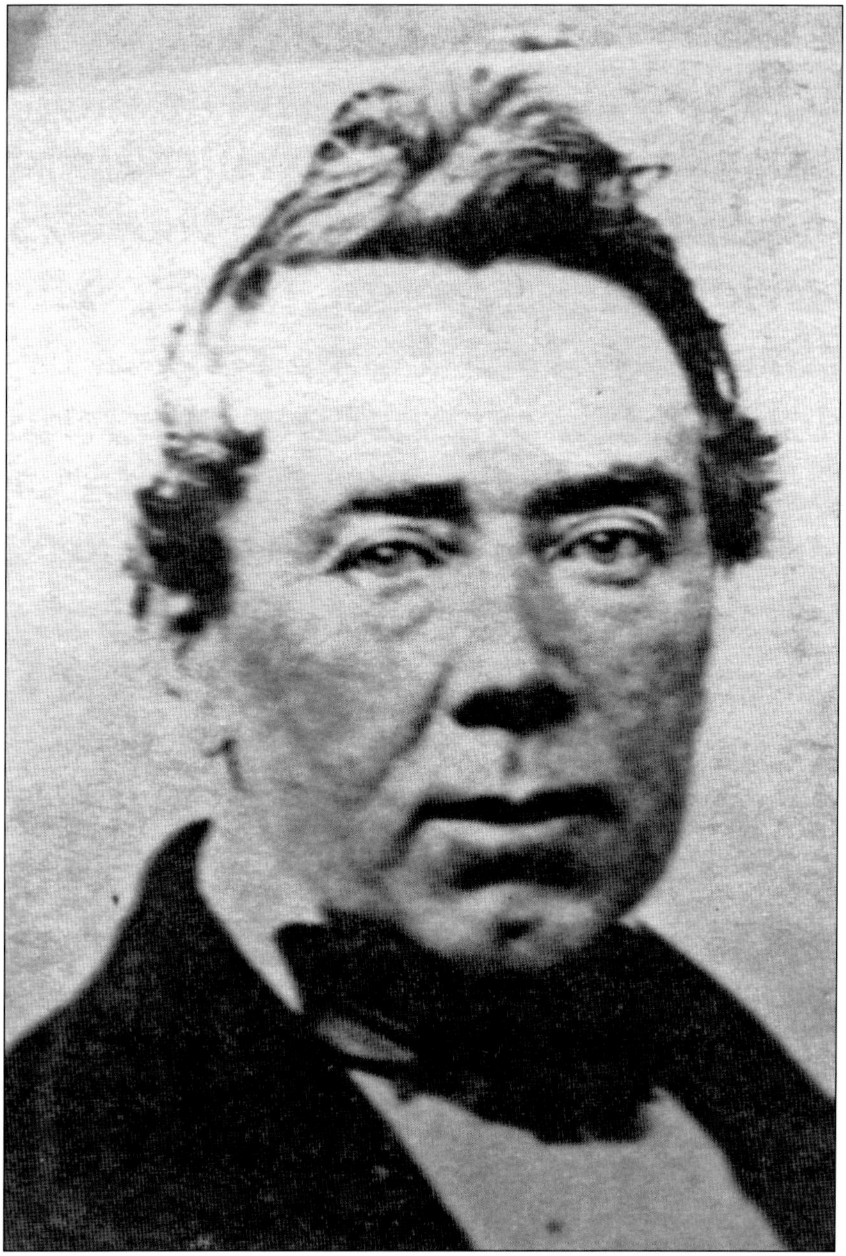

Thomas Moylan (1818–1861), a Catholic from Dublin, took his Episcopalian bride, Jane Burke, a descendant of Irish nobility, to America, where he sold coal in San Francisco. He was also a butcher and allegedly the first to bring meat in a barge to San Rafael and to graze cattle in Golden Gate Park. Upon developing symptoms of black lung disease, he moved to the purer air of Kings Mountain and welcomed the attentions of his neighbor, Peter Van Winkle, on his only surviving daughter, Magadelena. She was one day shy of her 16th birthday when she married Van Winkle, a man more than twice her age, on August 7, 1860, in San Francisco. Though she had seen tragedy (her sister and father died within a year of her wedding), she had grit: She bore 11 children (one died) and raised three sons and seven daughters, keeping the girls clear of the rough millmen. (Courtesy Ken Fisher.)

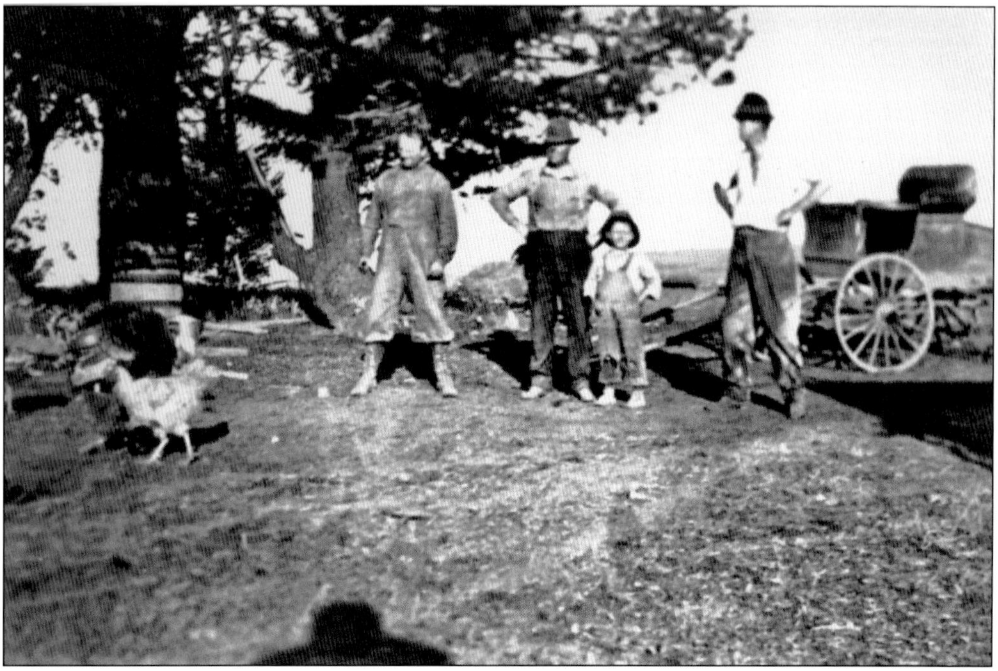

The surviving Van Winkle children included Jane Van Winkle, Matilda Levy, Elizabeth Badarous, Tom Van Winkle, Sarah Carroll, Isabel Thomson, Aimee Lee, Pierre Van Winkle, Helen Waterhouse, and John S. Van Winkle. The *c.* 1920 photograph above shows Pierre to the left. Helen Van Winkle recalled seeing the "Tower of Jewels," the lights of the 1915 Panama Pacific International Exhibition, from the ranch. The photograph below shows young Van Winkle grandchildren Peter and Harriett playing in 1917 at the family tank house. (Both courtesy Ken Fisher.)

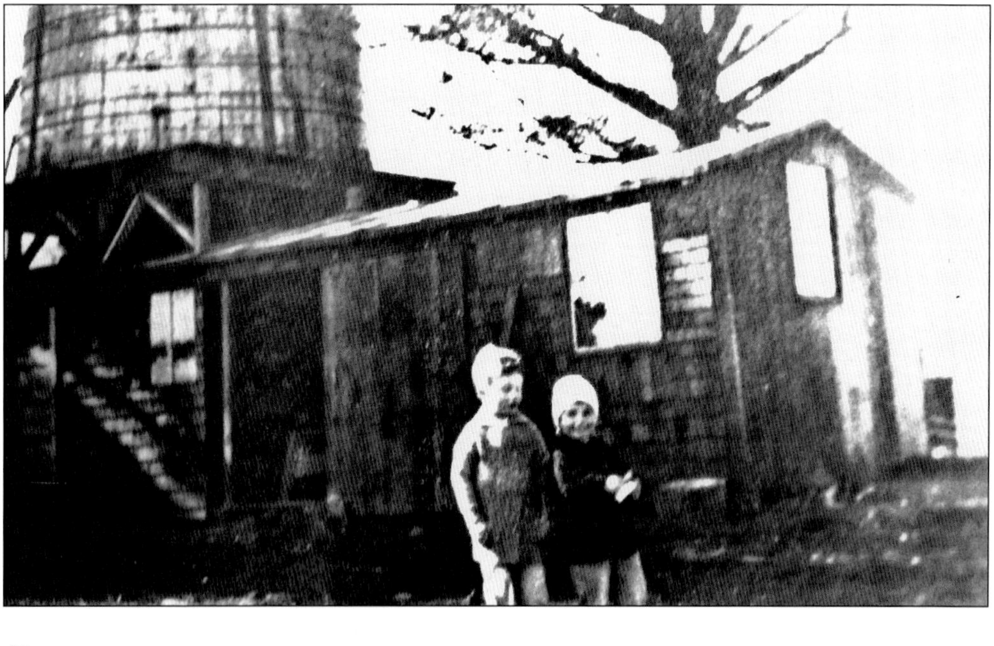

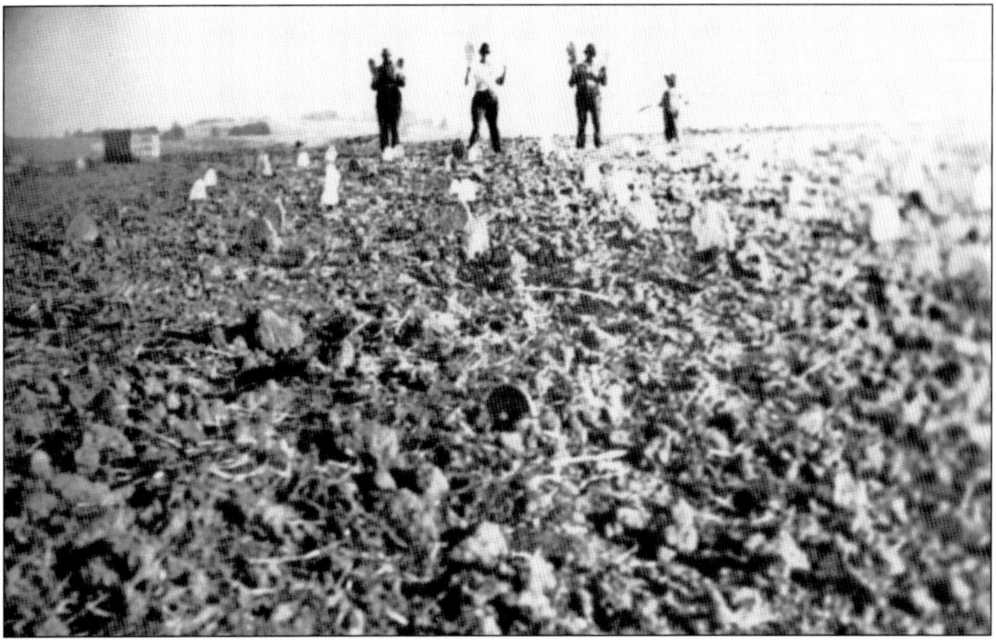

Only John Van Winkle showed serious interest in sharing his father's farming lifestyle, illustrated in these photographs of planting a field and tending stock on the Van Winkle land. The others drifted into less rigorous lives off the mountain, though they visited in the summers, and even John eventually moved into the coffee business in San Mateo. Their mother, Magadelena Moylan Van Winkle, coaxed their father into San Francisco, though he continued to work the farm as a hobby until his death in 1907. The house fell into disrepair and, shortly after the dawn of the 20th century, was dismantled for lumber. The milk house became a summer cabin. (Both courtesy Ken Fisher.)

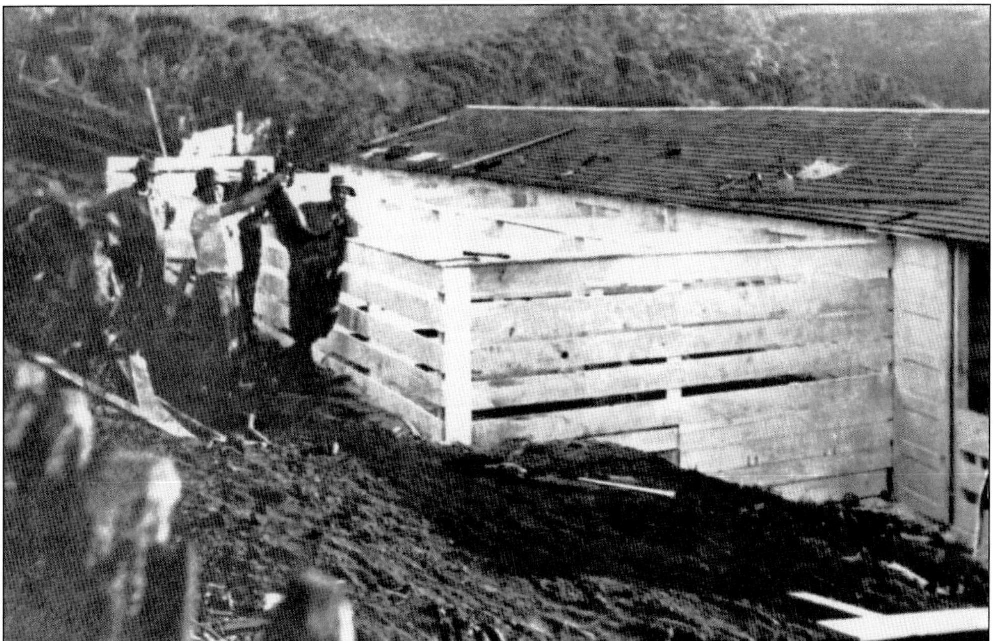

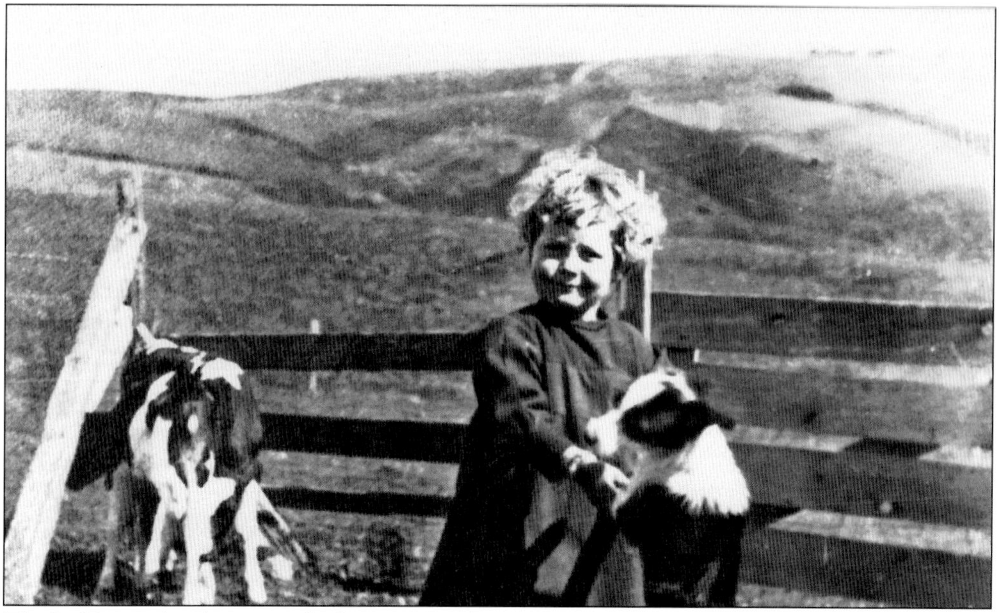

The Peddesaro family, originally from Portugal, rented space on the Van Winkle ranch beginning around 1915. Their little girl, Mary Ednah, was born there. Here she frolics with her dog and a calf in 1921. (Courtesy Ken Fisher.)

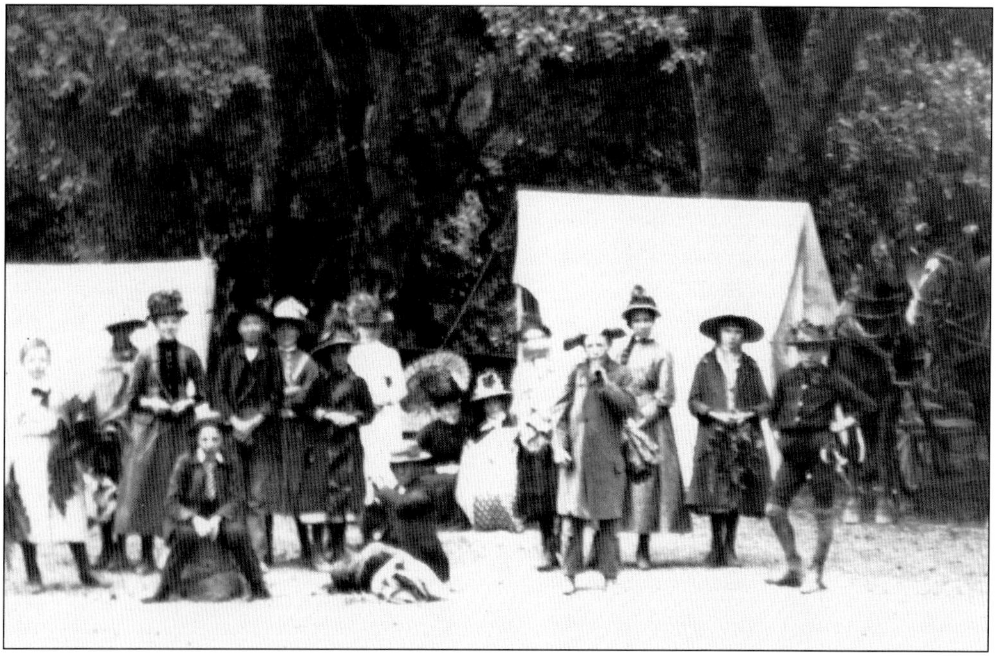

In a few places in the mountain woods, huckleberries flourished, and groups and families armed with buckets would attack the bushes on summer afternoons with visions of succulent pies. Here the Heiner family enjoys one such outing in the 1880s along Skyline, above Woodside. (Courtesy Ken Fisher.)

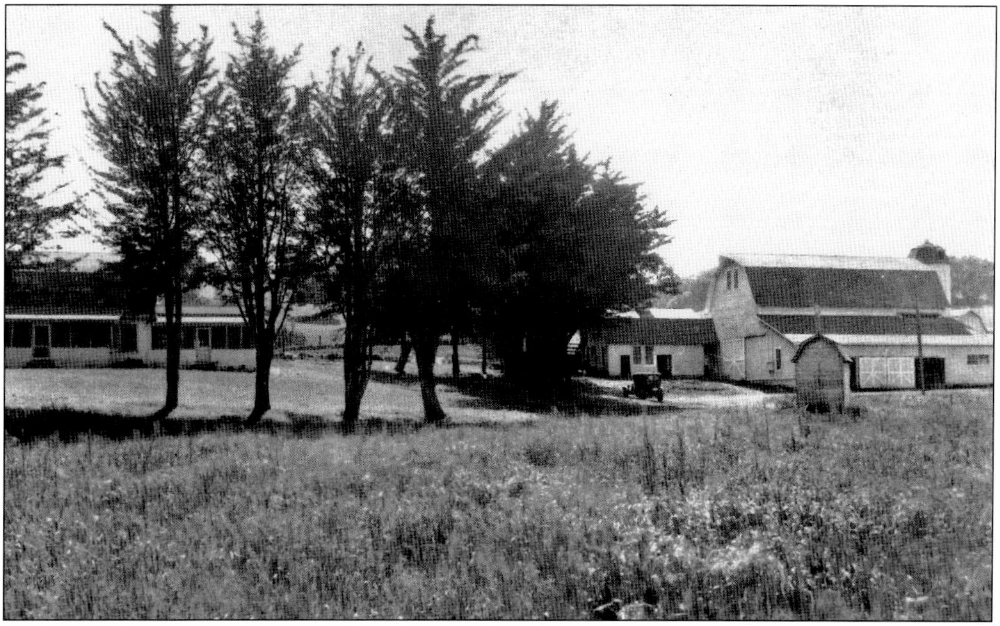

In 1921, J. N. Gilman bought nearly 63 acres, for $10 down and a takeover of a $5,000 mortgage, on today's Canada Road. As vice president and general manager of the De Laval Dairy Supply Company, he wanted a place to test De Laval equipment before marketing it. He also wanted this quiet country home and a good-looking, productive breed, so he installed a herd of Ayrshires in 1921. Equestrians dominate the land now. (Courtesy Woodside History Archives.)

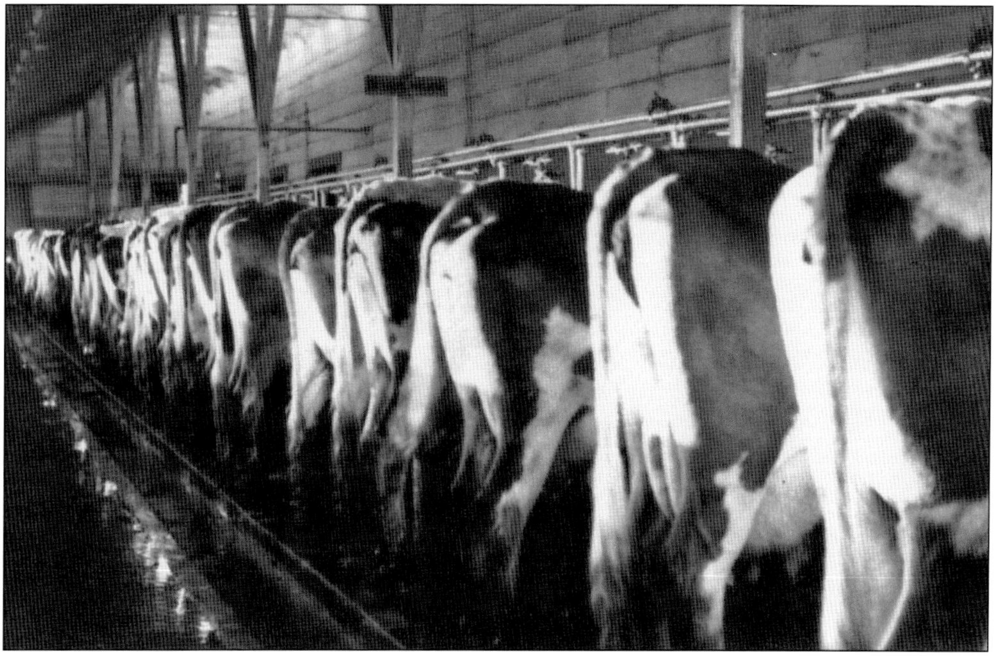

Gilman put into practice his ideas for a modern dairy in his durable Dutch barn, creating one of the first mechanized milking dairies. He put in modern cork brick floors, individual mangers and drinking bowls, individual steel stanchions like these, calf and maternity pens, and a clean transport system for feed. (Courtesy Woodside History Archives.)

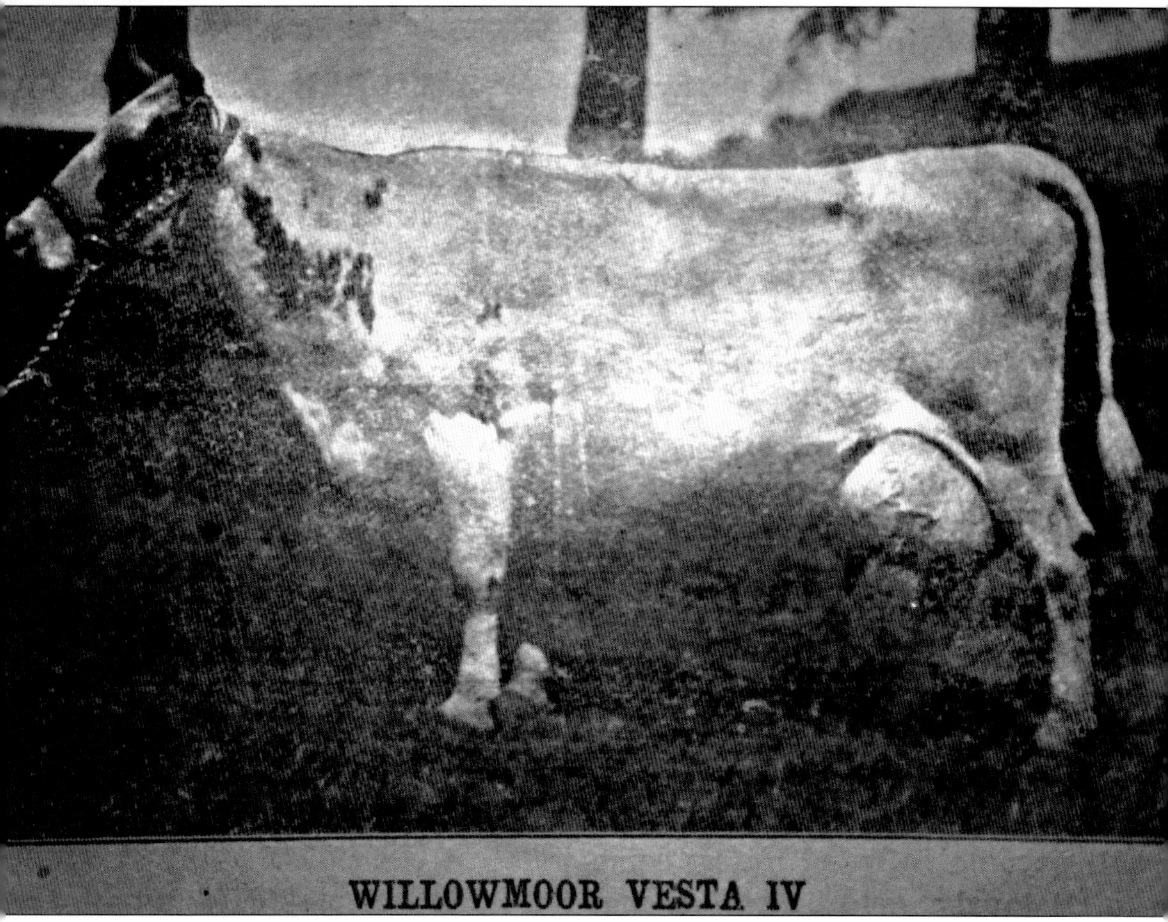

Little is known about dairyman E. B. McFarland of Steybrae Farm just west of Skyline, but much is known about his prize Ayrshire, Willowmoor Vesta IV. She was born March 26, 1912, in Washington State. At two years old, she took first prize in the Panama Pacific Exposition in San Francisco. At four, she set a world record, producing 17,755 pounds of milk that tested 4.23 percent butterfat. At nine, in 1921, she won a grand championship at the California Livestock Show in San Francisco. She is pictured at age 11. In March 1922, she was purchased by J. N. Gilman in his bid to improve his herd with carefully selected cows and herd bull Elkhorn Aggressor. Gilman was one of several mountain dairyman to boast of owning Willowmoor's offspring. He also brought home California National Livestock Show ribbons throughout the 1920s. His cows were carefully groomed: Their horns were polished and their tails braided before going before the judges to be tested for appearance and the butterfat content of their milk. (Courtesy Ken Fisher.)

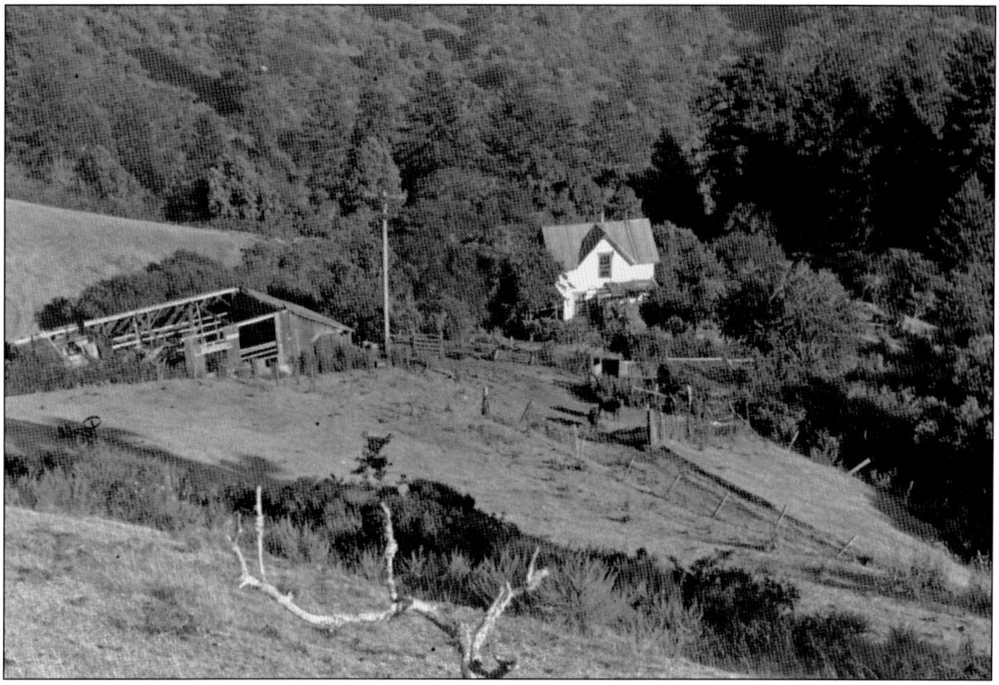

The mountain's dairying families were closely linked and not just by geography. Such was the case with the Beebes. In Tunitas Canyon, brothers Thomas G. and William W. Durham owned a square mile of land and cut what is said to be the first road on the mountain. Just south, another dairying family of Jacob Downing had an additional mile of land. In between, Thomas Beebe developed a ranch, shown here, and built a house. He did not live there alone: he married the Durhams' sister, Flora. (Both courtesy Ken Fisher.)

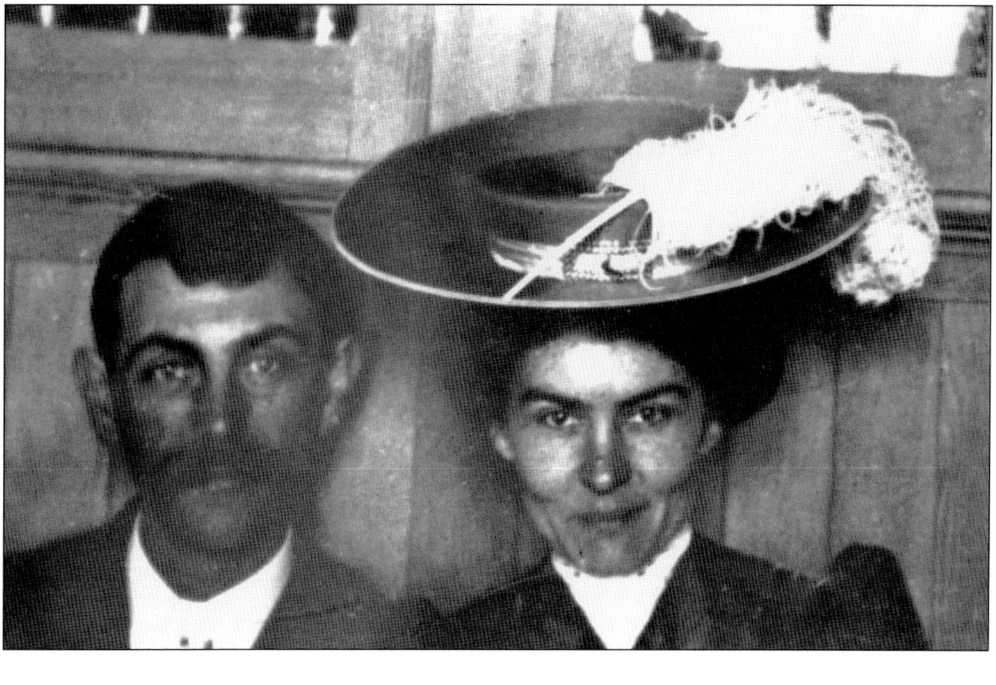

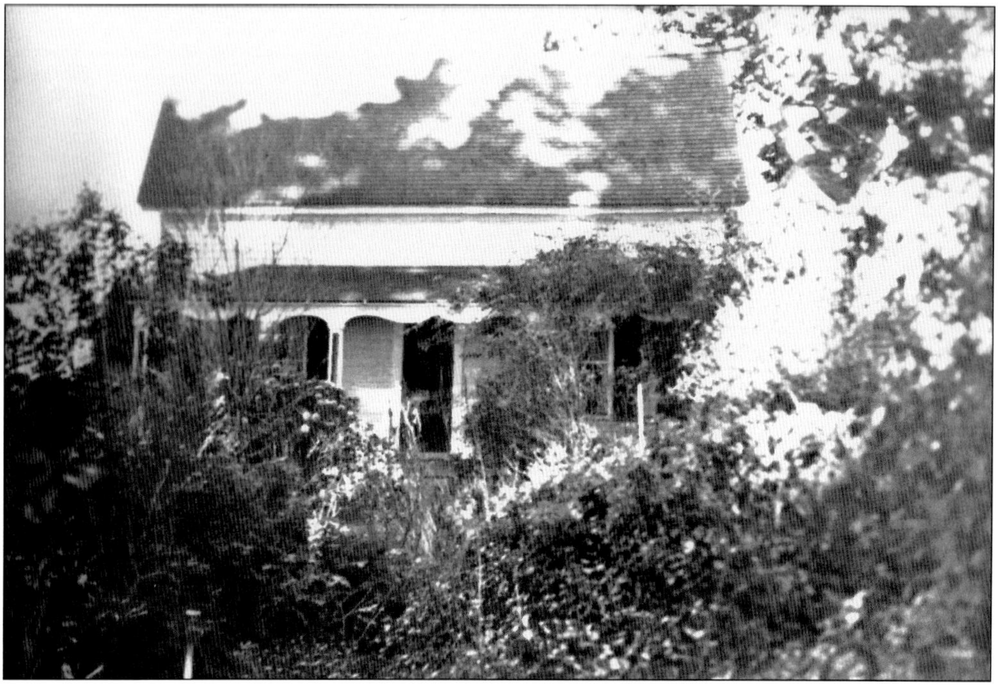

The road cut in 1857 by the Durham brothers, farmers on Kings Mountain, became today's Star Hill Road. The photographs show the stately home of W. W. Durham, in both its early days and after some remodeling. The brothers also had a dairy on Star Hill Road. W. W. Durham was a pillar of the mountain community: he married a local schoolteacher and was one of seven neighbors of Sheldon "Purdy" Pharis who served on the coroner's jury that returned the official verdict of Pharis's suicide. (Both courtesy Ken Fisher.)

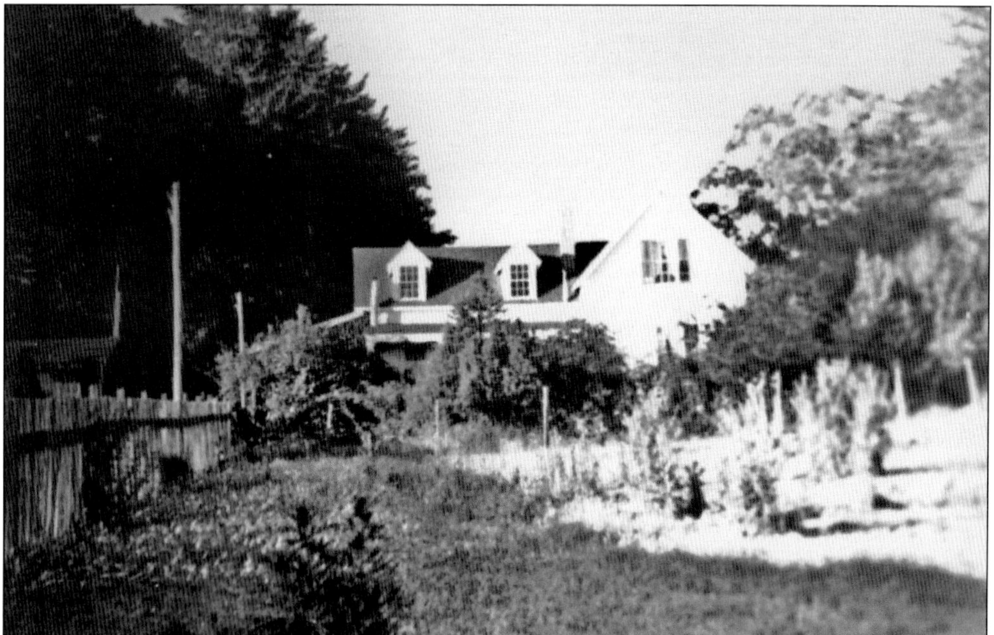

Five

Mountain Life
Peaks, Gulches, and Crossroads

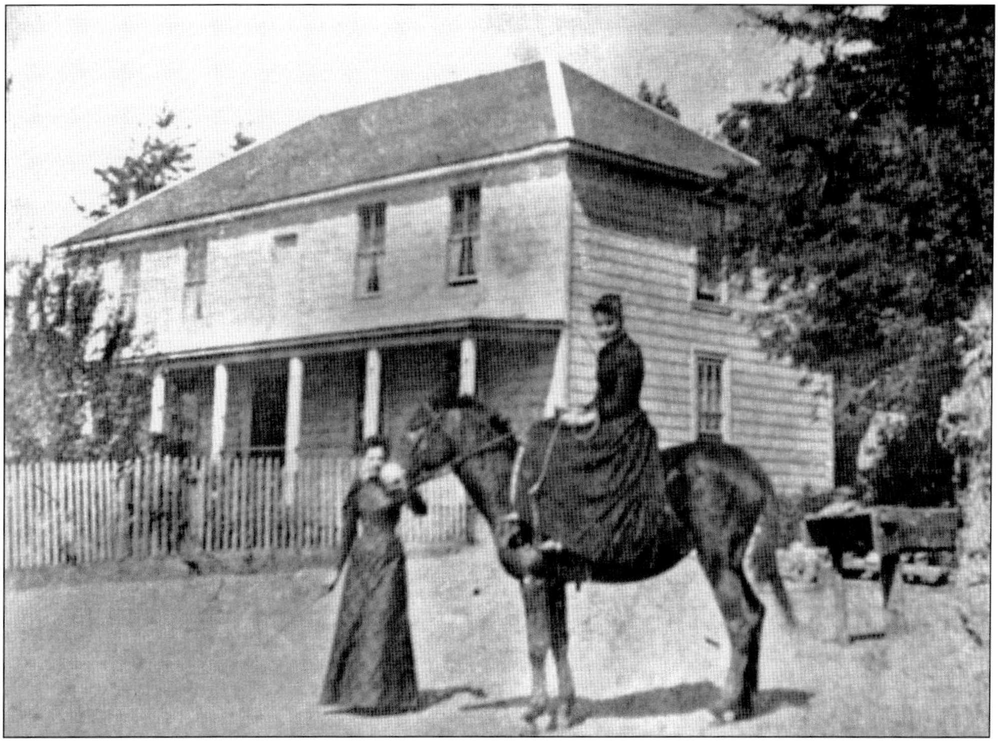

Like a giant sequoia, the essence of Kings Mountain, anchored in its people, took root and flowered to define life on the mountain: close to the natural world, sometimes yielding, other times driven. As loggers carved out paths to haul their lumber to Redwood City, little stops appeared where men and teams snatched liquid reinforcement before tackling the next stage. Honora King leveraged her cooking skills into a family hotel, shown here. Watering holes became mini-townships. Primitive networks of stage routes developed. As dairying with its civilizing influences took hold, schools sprang up, one-room institutions that hung on until a drought of students closed them. When the outside world intruded, mountain folk faced it, like the Wyman family, who sent their seven sons to fight in World War I. They survived, and the family received a presidential commendation for sending all their boys to war. Like the long-lived redwoods, Kings Mountain persevered. (Courtesy Ken Fisher.)

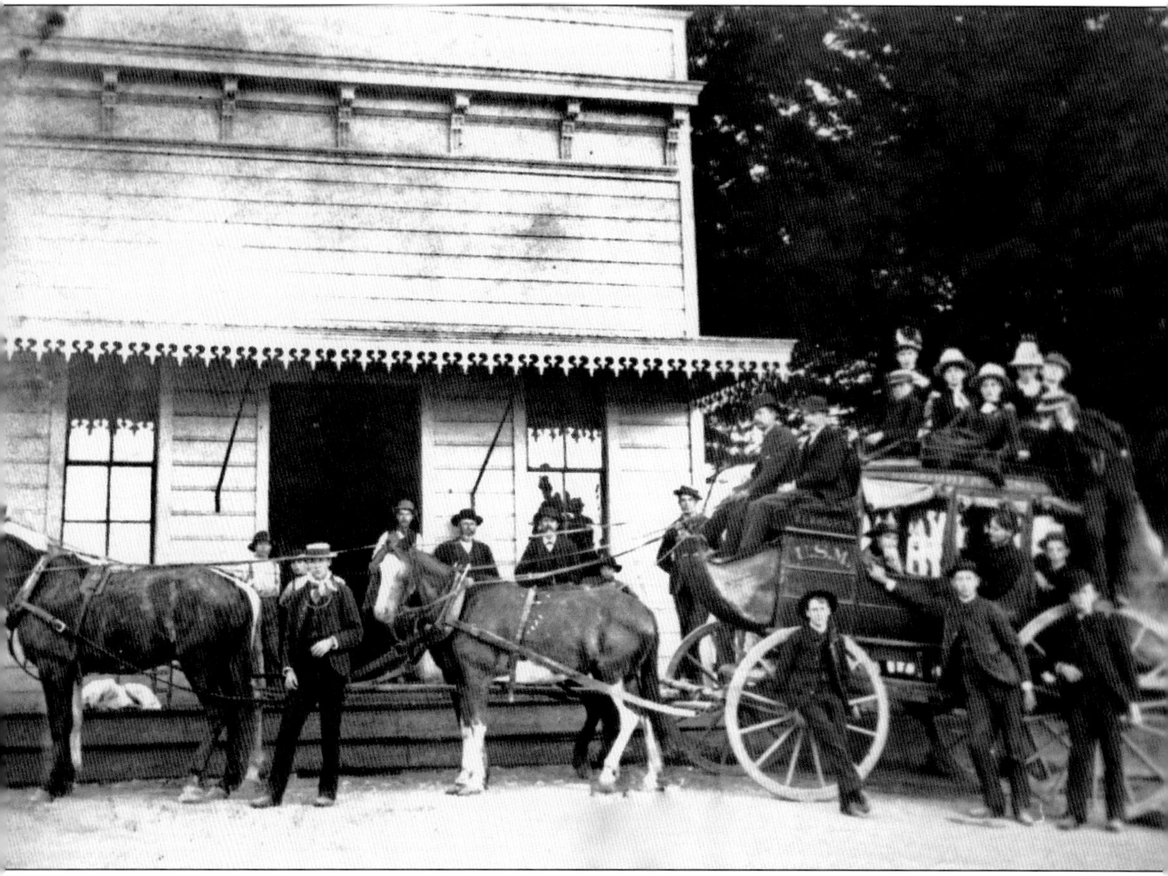

The earliest wagon route to the coast ran through Summit Springs. Here Roy Cloud and his family started the next phase in a trip from Redwood City to Woodside after visiting Byrnes Station, a mountain stage stop that became a restaurant in the next century. In the mid-1850s, stage lines were set up between San Francisco and Woodside with a stop in Searsville; the fare was just over $2. Round-trip mail delivery took one day. Early stages included the French Omnibus and Concord stages from New Hampshire, designed for speed and comfort at from $1,250 to $1,500 per stage. By the late 1860s, when a stage line was set up between coastal Pescadero and San Mateo, the westbound fare was 45¢ to Byrnes Station and $1 to the summit, but $2 eastbound, probably because of the grade. By 1907, the Ocean Shore Railroad put the brakes on stage lines. (Courtesy Ken Fisher.)

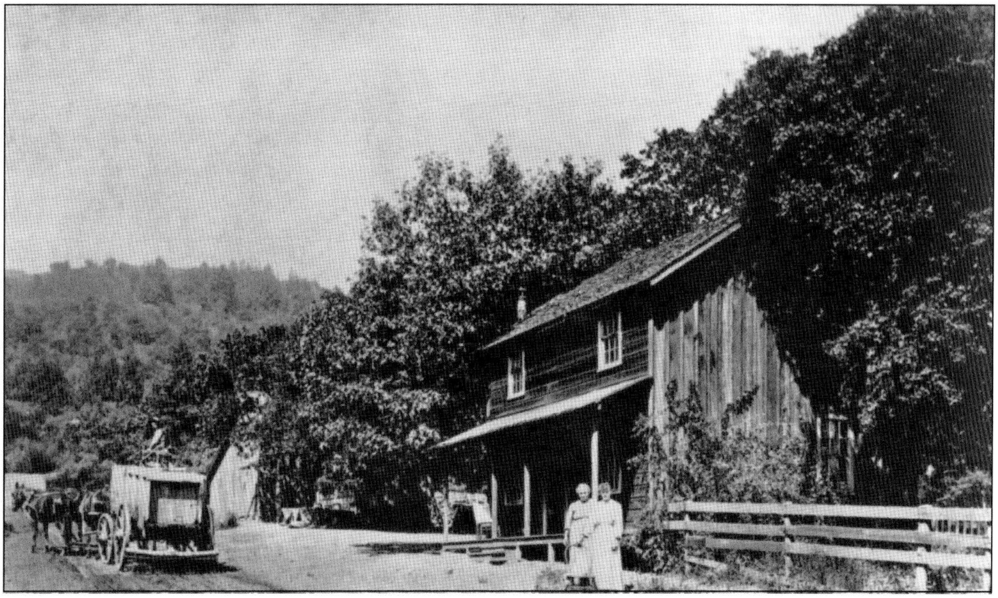

This c. 1868 Summit Springs Road tollhouse, known as the "tole" house, was where drivers paid a 25¢ toll for a horse and buggy and 10¢ for a loose cow or horse. Standing outside it is Mrs. Henry Bottger and her daughter Lucy. (Courtesy Woodside History Archives.)

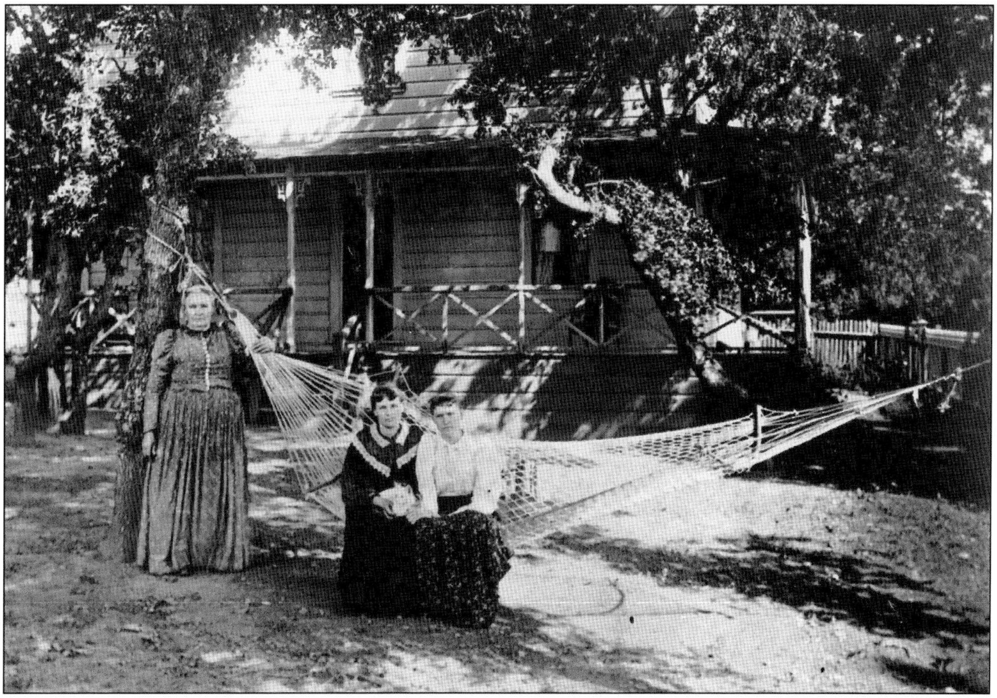

The Bottger two-story frame home was built in the late 1880s behind the tollhouse. Mrs. Bottger is shown here with daughters Lucy (left) and Edith (right). (Courtesy Woodside History Archives.)

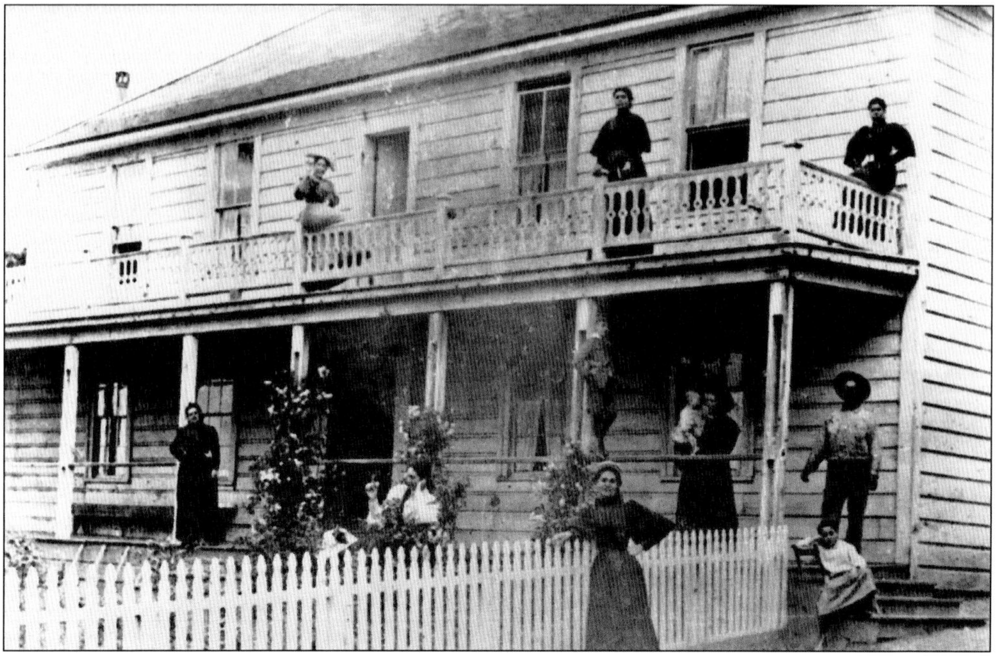

The Kings Mountain Brow House, named for its location at the mountain crest, was run by King matriarch Honora. It was a destination for lumbermen, travelers, and Stanford University students. It ceased operations in the 1890s, but King stayed until her death in 1924. The building was demolished in the 1930s. (Courtesy Ken Fisher.)

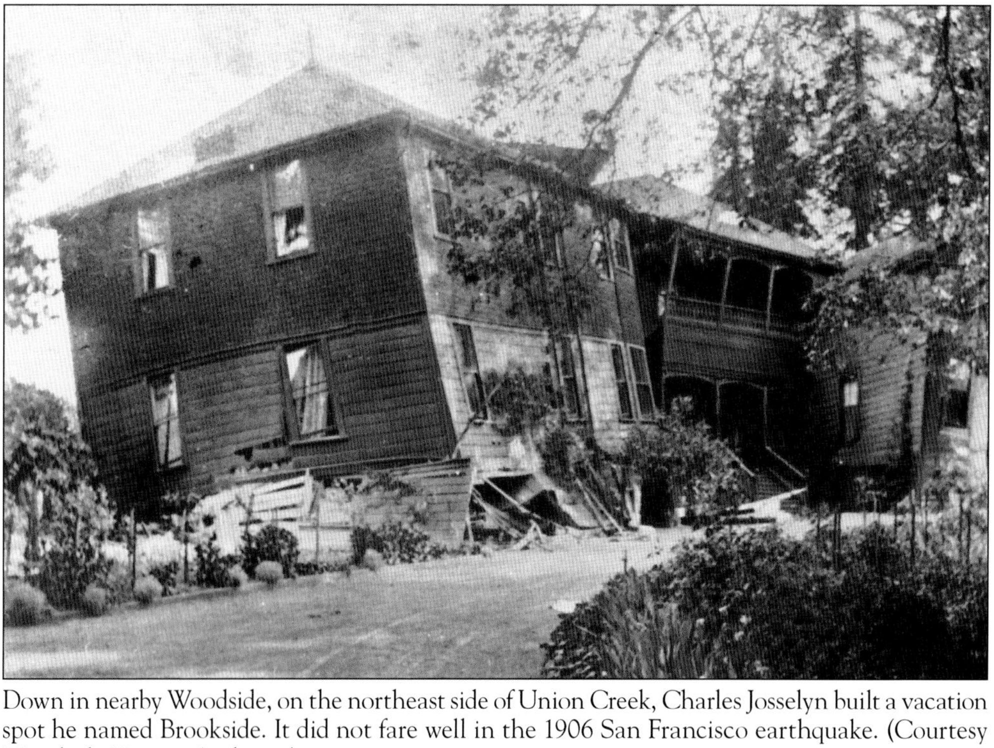

Down in nearby Woodside, on the northeast side of Union Creek, Charles Josselyn built a vacation spot he named Brookside. It did not fare well in the 1906 San Francisco earthquake. (Courtesy Woodside History Archives.)

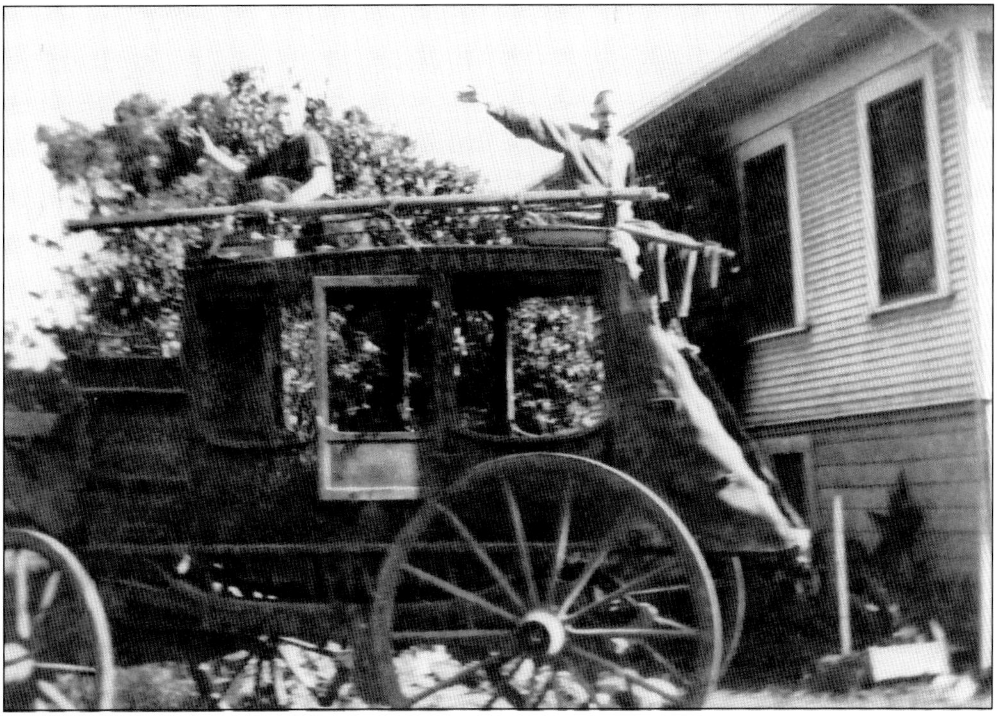

The Knights Stage started as a mail line in 1865 and in 1872 began service to San Gregorio through Summit Springs. Taking the stage meant bumps, dust, and risk of injury, so refreshment at Summit Springs was welcome. It offered stops on the mountain with spectacular ocean views, part of the allure for flatland stage riders. After 45 years, Knights ceased service in 1910. (Both courtesy Woodside History Archives.)

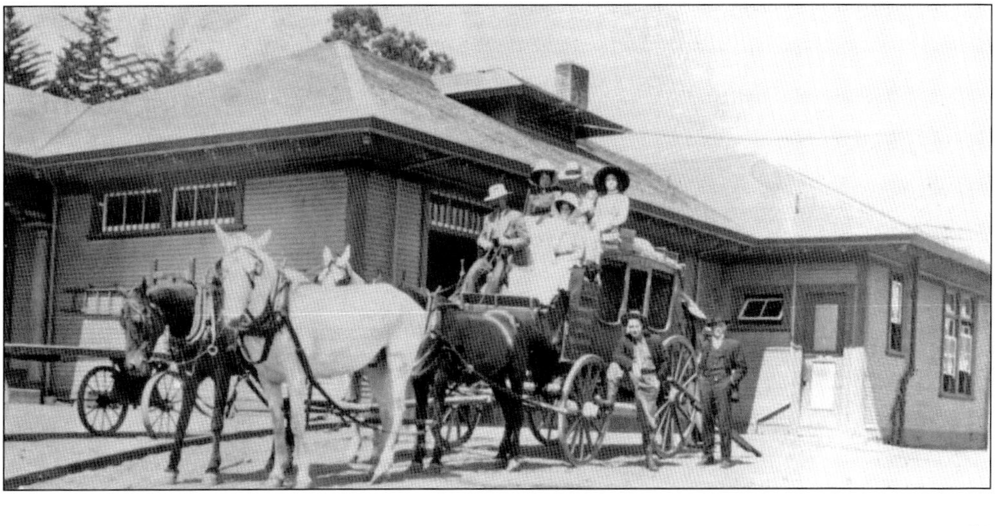

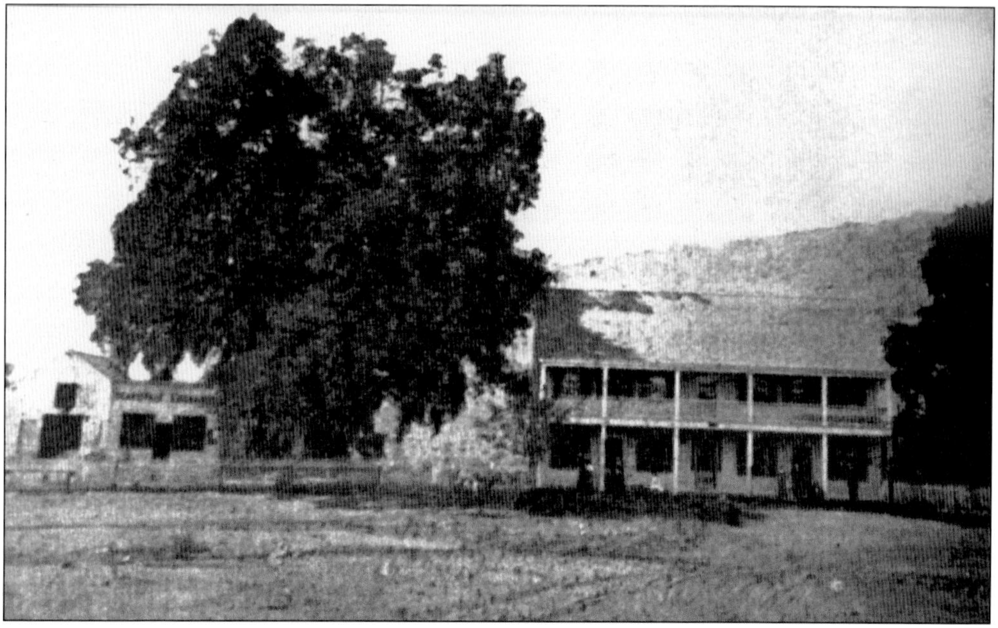

South of Kings Mountain on Skyline, Albert Eikerenkotter opened this establishment, but he also opened a summit saloon in the 1890s for the lumbermen. It was a quintessential Wild West scene: gambling, horse races, wrestling matches, shoot-outs. Once a man was caught cheating at cards; when he reached for the pot, someone jabbed a knife right through his hand. (Courtesy Woodside History Archives.)

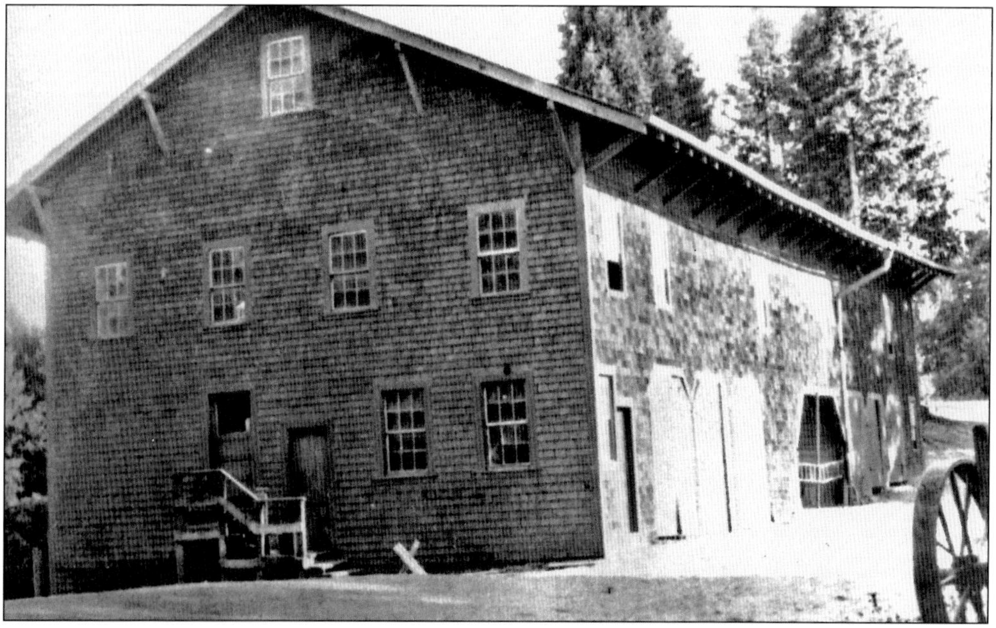

Hiram Haskins's large barn was reportedly used to change horses for the Redwood City–San Gregorio stage line—appropriate for former stage driver Haskins. A habitually gruff man who wore a six-shooter, he was one reason the Pharis suicide verdict was doubted—he had spent the night of Pharis's death at his house. The barn became boarding stables and burned in the 1970s. (Courtesy Ken Fisher.)

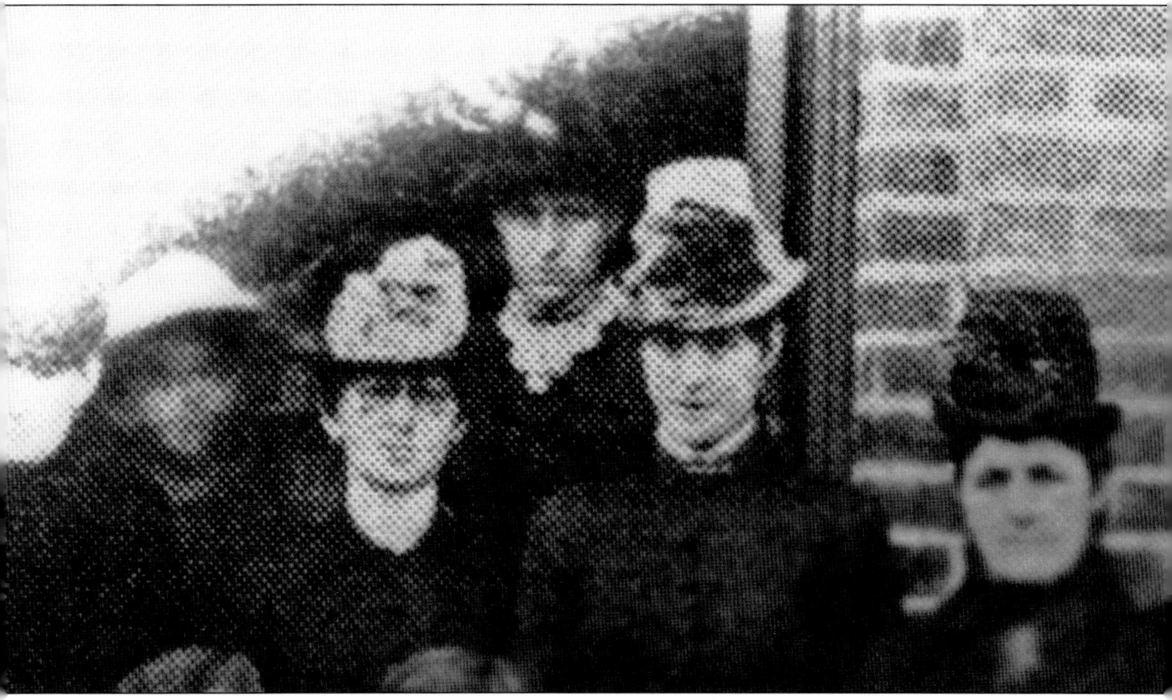

Fresh-faced Eva Greene, rear, was one of several schoolmarms who taught at the Pharis school but was unable to stand rigorous mountain life for long. In 1862, growing families on the mountain's north side necessitated formation of the Laguna School District. Eight years later, another school was formed at the mountain's crest; it burned, but Purdy Pharis financed a new school district that survived until 1912. In both schools' heyday, attendance reached 40 students, but as families drifted away, that dwindled to six in 1905. The teachers' names quaintly reflected their era: Minnie Mullen, Sadie Savage, Electra Rumsey, Lily Rose, Blanche Bean, Delia Monroe. They had primitive buildings and sporadic attendance when pupils missed school to help on the farm, but textbooks were respected and handed down with care. At their peak, the schools' budget per student was $12.64. (Courtesy Ken Fisher.)

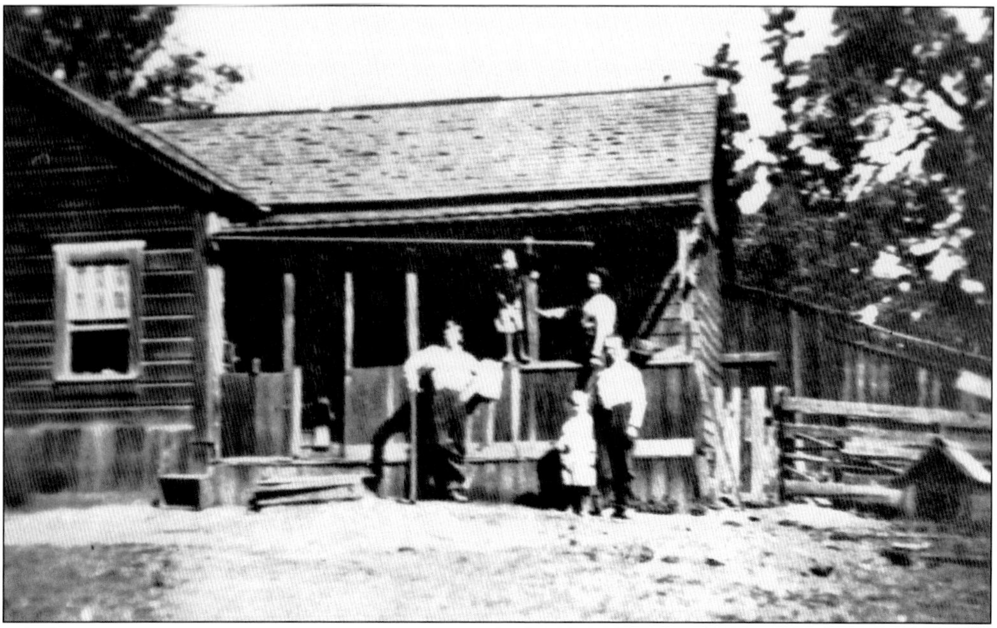

A tragic figure was Frank Furgher, who lived on the east side of Bald Knob and worked the Alvin Hatch mill. Once vandals ransacked his cabin, beat him, and left him for dead. His wife, Sophie, died young. To attend her funeral, he left their two young children at a friend's home in Redwood City. During the service, the house burned and the children died. Furgher lived out his days alone, still working at the mill. (Courtesy Ken Fisher.)

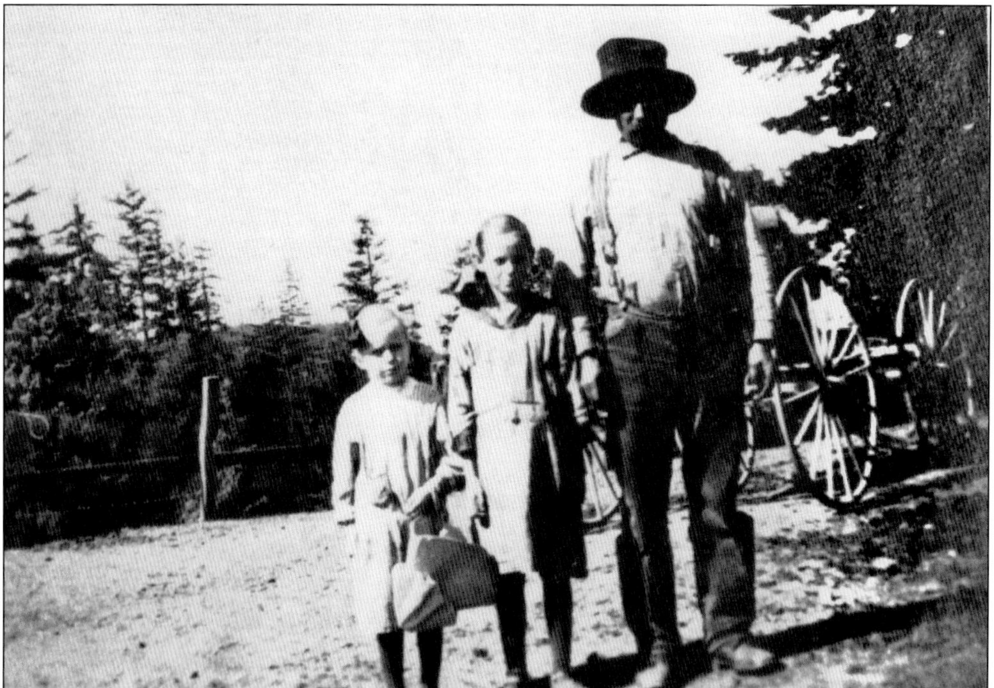

Frank Furgher, a man to whom life was not kind, stands outside his cabin on his Bald Knob property in 1914, with nieces Madeline and Kate Johansen. (Courtesy Ken Fisher.)

From 400 to 800 acres near Star Hill Road was owned by the Swett family, after whom the road where Kings Mountain Elementary School now stands is named. Frank H. Swett (right) was in law, but his son Wilbur Maurice (below) was an eye, ear, nose, and throat doctor. An active and involved man, Wilbur Swett developed a ranch, built roads and a picnic area from which visitors could see the ocean, and maintained homes around the Bay Area. His grandson, John Swett, recalls that Wilbur died in 1937 in a single-car crash on Skyline, on his way back from seeing patients in his San Francisco office. The house that was once a Swett family country home is a private residence today. (Both courtesy Dan Katzenberger.)

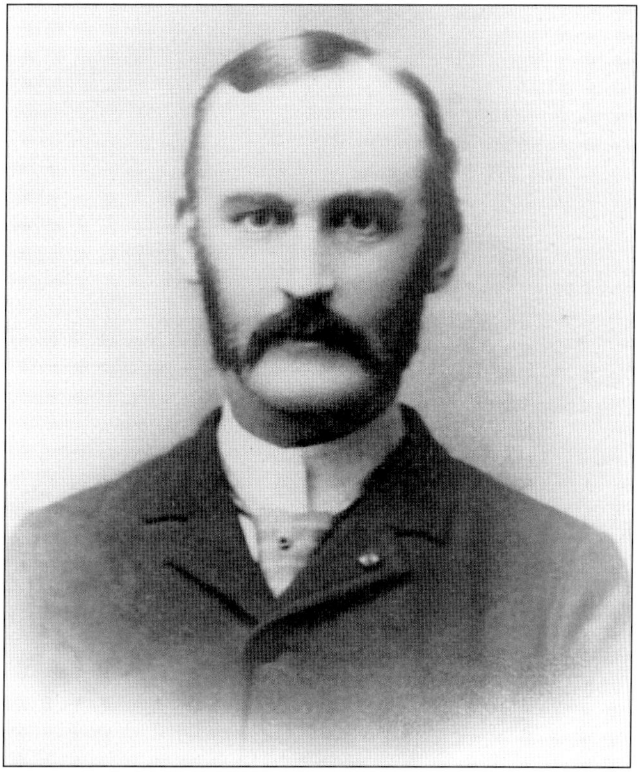

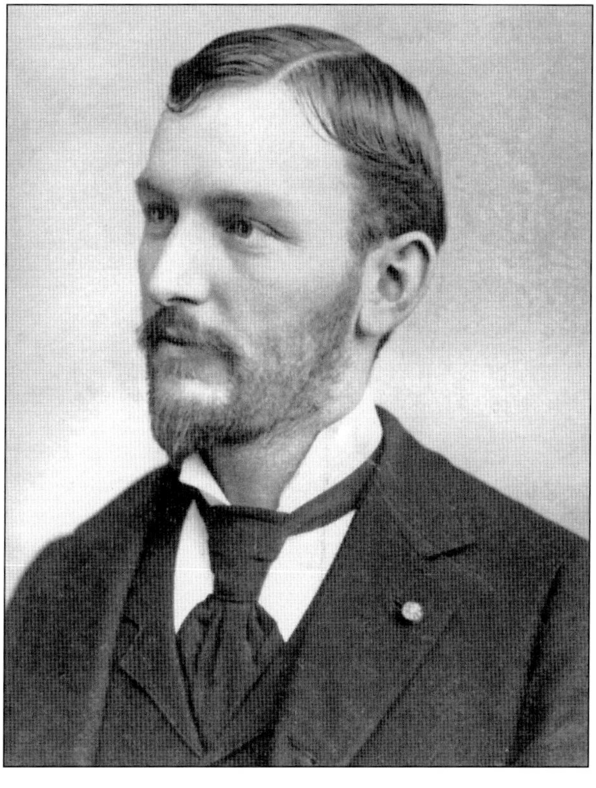

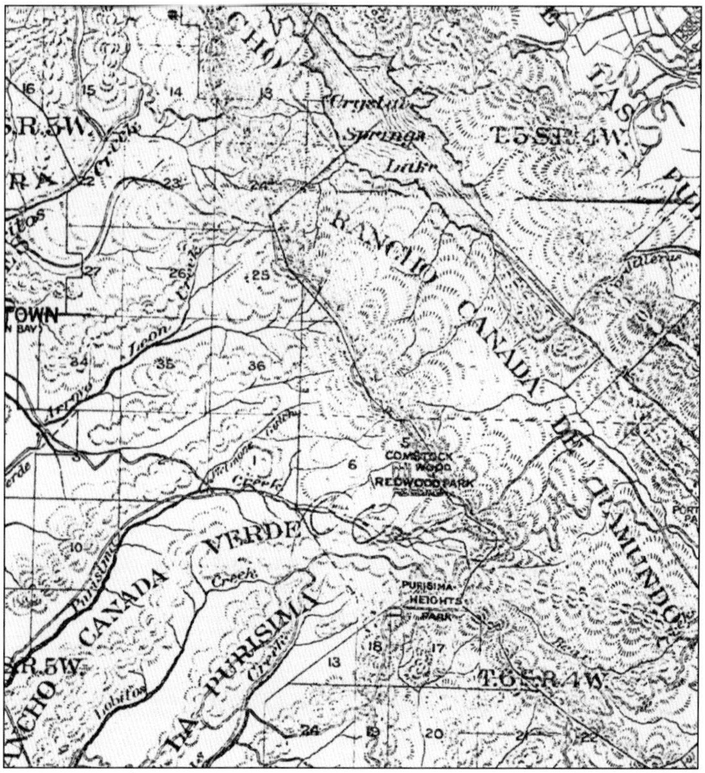

This c. 1913 "Denny's Pocket Map" of San Mateo shows the early subdivisions: Redwood and Purisima Heights Parks and Comstock Wood. Redwood Park was an early subdivision, formed in 1908; former mill owner Alvin Hatch subdivided part of his land to form Purisima Heights. (Courtesy Ardyth Woodruff.)

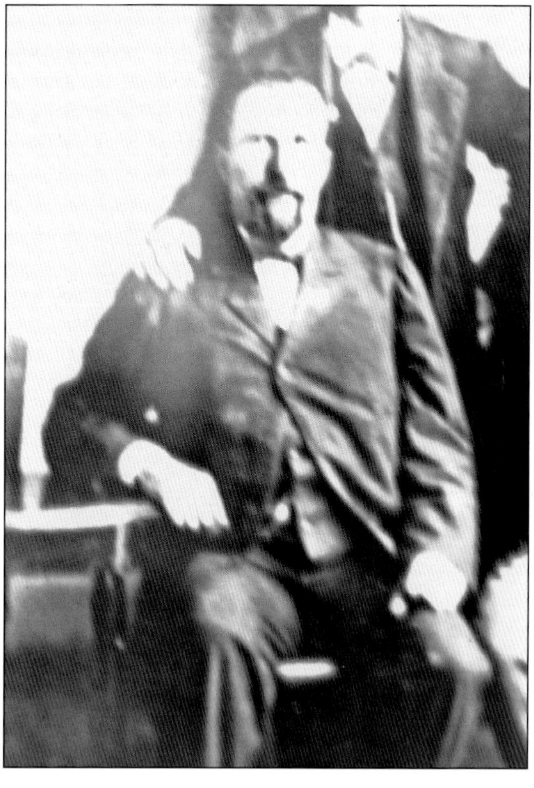

Phil Kreiss—no relation to the son of Don Kreiss, "dean" of mountain bottle collectors—and his wife, Maggie, were close friends of surveyor Davenport Bromfield, who stayed with them while visiting the mountain. Phil Kreiss originally owned the parcel that became the Redwood Park subdivision. (Courtesy Ken Fisher.)

Six

Years of Unrest
Development and Subdivisions

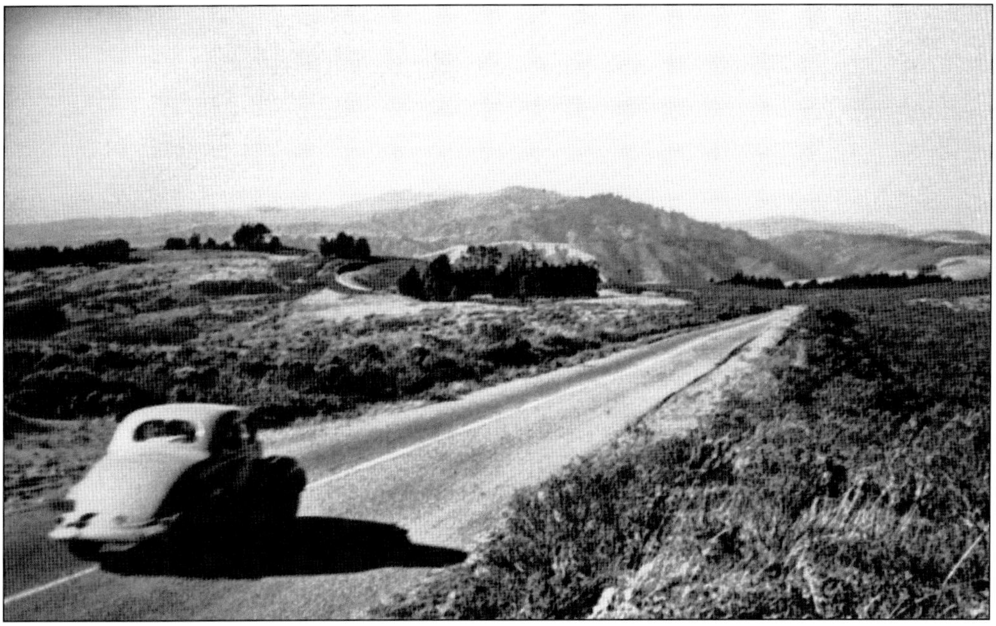

Rough-and-ready logging times downshifted in the early 20th century. School enrollment had shrunk, lack of trees and cheap Pacific Northwest lumber phased out the mills, and technology did likewise for the dairies. Perhaps the biggest harbinger of change was Skyline Boulevard (shown in 1948), built in 1923–1924, in time for the automobile craze. Mountain landowners, expecting a flood of vacationers, hurried to subdivide their land. A seminal but extreme example was Redwood Park (1908), in which a single 140-acre parcel was pulverized into tiny 25-by-100-foot lots. Alvin Hatch subdivided part of his land as Purisima Heights Park, renamed Kings Mountain Park in 1928. Surveyor Davenport Bromfield built the mountain's first summer cabin, created the Sierra Morena Woods subdivisions (1922 and 1924), sold parcels to the Sons of Norway, divvied Skyline Boulevard among his children, and named Harkins, Comstock, and Ware Roads for pioneers and his wife, Mary Ware. Bootleggers parried with Prohibition. Restaurants, complete with tourist cabins for inebriated patrons, sprang up. Vestiges of these colorful times survive among the redwoods today. (Courtesy Ken Fisher.)

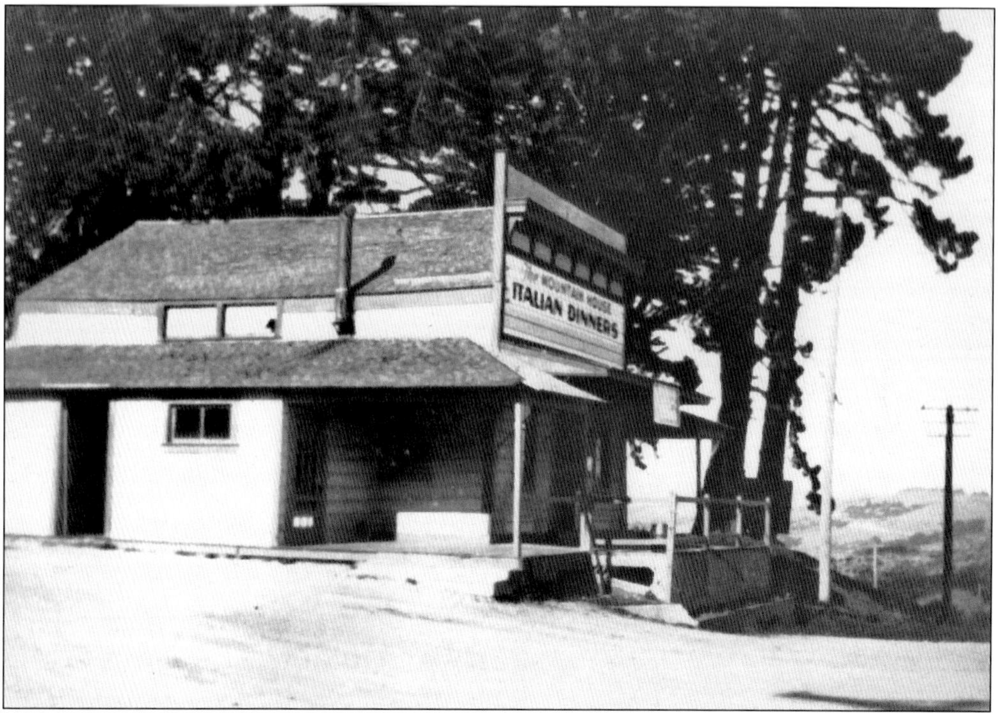

Byrnes Station, shown here in the 1930s below Highway 92 on the mountain's north face, evolved from a 19th-century stage stop. The first local restaurant to be named "Mountain House" (in 1930), it was known for its Italian dinners, as the sign proclaims. (Both courtesy Ken Fisher.)

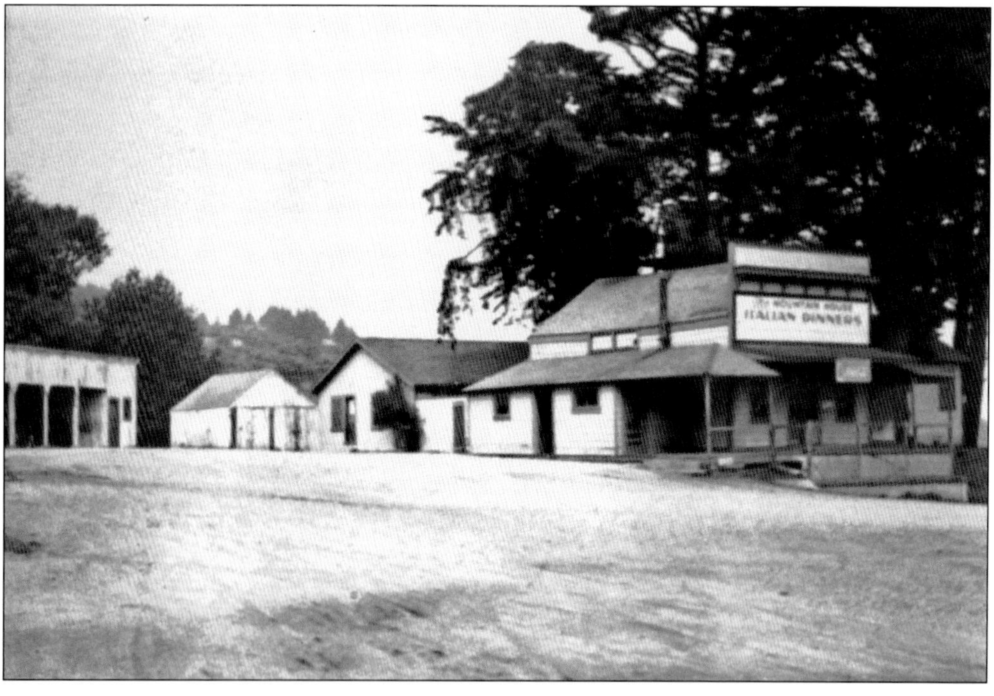

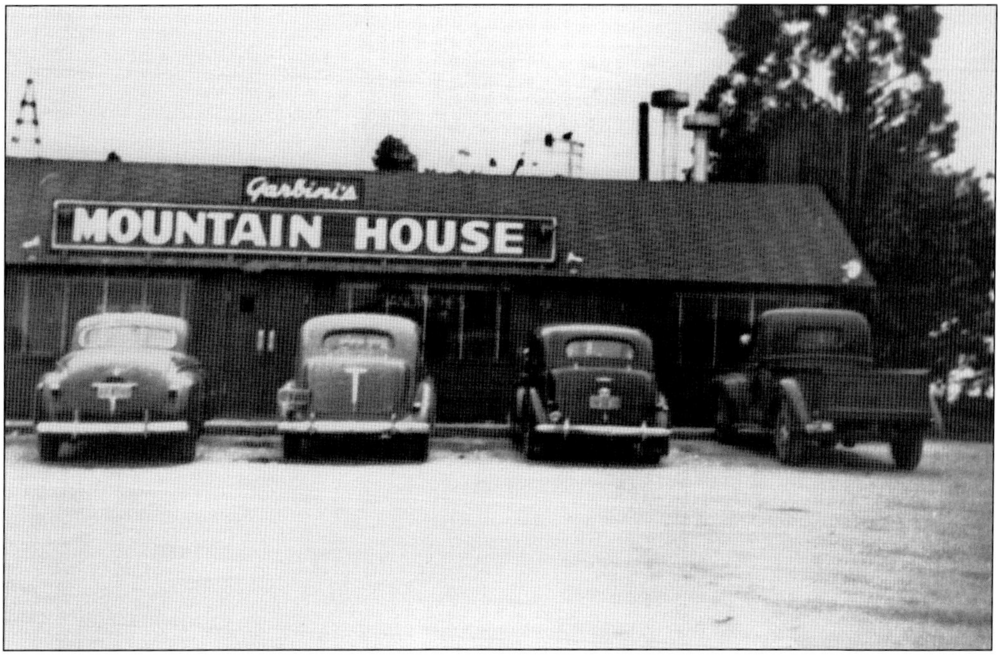

Garbini's, shown in the 1940s, was the second restaurant to be named "Mountain House." A long, low building, Garbini's gained fame as the site of the last crank phone in San Mateo County, drawing the curious to stop by to make a phone call. The restaurant built a second story with decorative blue glass. (Courtesy Ken Fisher.)

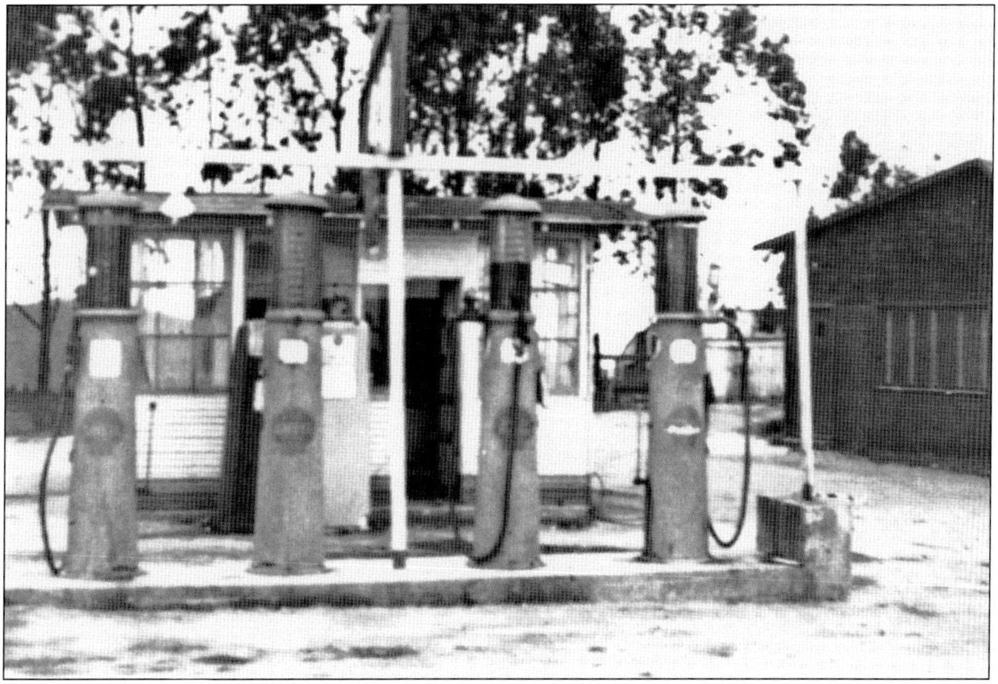

Garbini's Mountain House included one of four operating gas stations along Skyline Boulevard in the 1930s–1940s. Its gas facilities were taken down before the restaurant was torn down in the 1960s. (Courtesy Ken Fisher.)

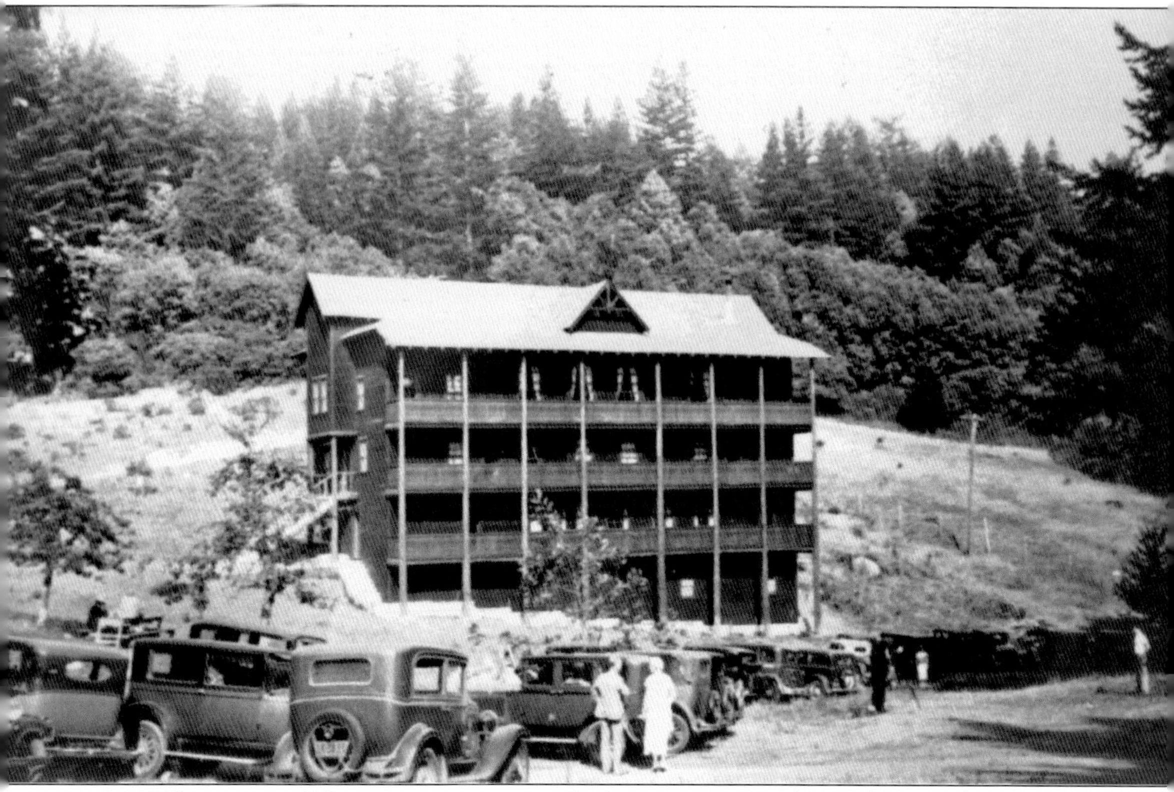

In 1908, a group of Norwegian immigrants, looking to preserve their culture in America and help the ailing among themselves, founded a lodge in San Francisco. In 1923, two members on a hunting trip discovered the beauty of Kings Mountain and, eager for a place reminiscent of Norway, bought 23 acres from Mary Bromfield and built a lodge. The building, shown here in 1930, followed Norway's "sveitserstil" architectural style, reminiscent of romantic Swiss chalets in the fjord country, and took a year for volunteers to build. A café was added in 1934 and an Olympic-sized pool in the 1950s. Though it was originally planned for the top of the hill, some members of the enclave slipped down one night and changed the marking stakes to a more aesthetic spot. The enclave, dubbed Henrik Ibsen Park after the Norwegian playwright, now provides a recreational gathering place for the 400-member Sons of Norway lodge based in San Francisco. Membership is open to those who are Norwegian-born or have a sincere interest in Norwegian culture and traditions. (Courtesy Ken Fisher.)

Glamorous soprano Berthe Andre (1892–1950) had a 20-year career singing in churches, community centers, and for the San Francisco Opera. In 1934, she bought a one-room cabin in Redwood Park for $400 and made it her occasional hideaway. Her final performance, given while she was battling terminal cancer, was Schubert's "Ave Maria" in a Yule concert at City Hall Square in Oakland on December 22, 1950. (Courtesy Zanette Cornman.)

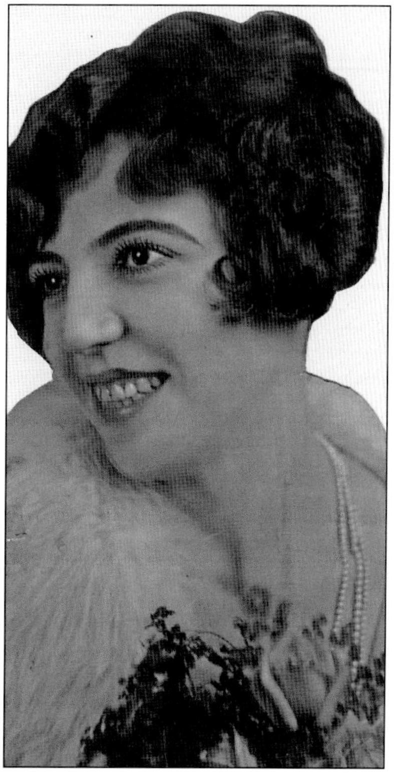

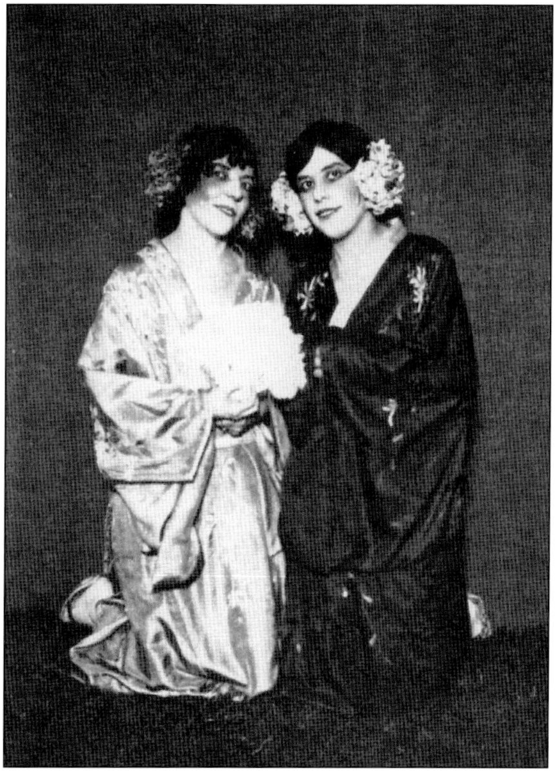

A voice teacher as well as performer, Berthe Andre often presented student recitals. Here in one such recital in 1928, she is joined by her teenage daughter Zanette (right) for a duet from the opera *Madama Butterfly*. Her daughter, now Zanette Cornman, followed her mother to the mountain, becoming a permanent resident in the mid-1950s. (Courtesy Zanette Cornman.)

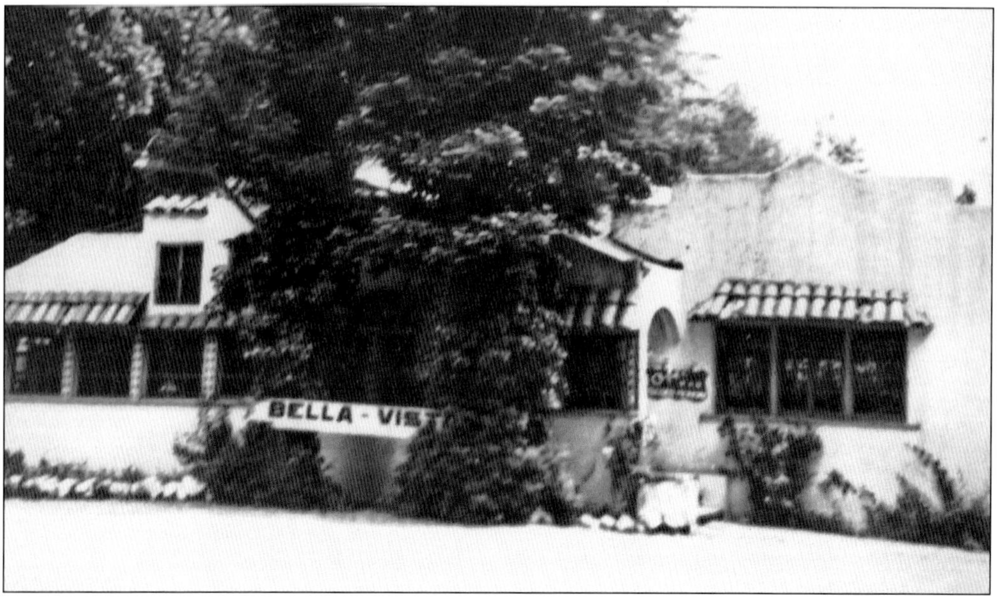

From a 1920s country inn to a roadhouse, a speakeasy, a casino, a brothel, and a hangout for Stanford University students, the Bella Vista fed its clientele while times changed around and within it. The original cocktail lounge is now the third dining room in what current co-owner John Ward (with his mother, Joan) calls "a true destination restaurant." Little has changed since this 1940s shot (above) when two tourist cabins were attached to it (below). The cabins are now gone, but the restaurant thrives as a classy, "white tablecloth" establishment with fine fare. (Both courtesy Ken Fisher.)

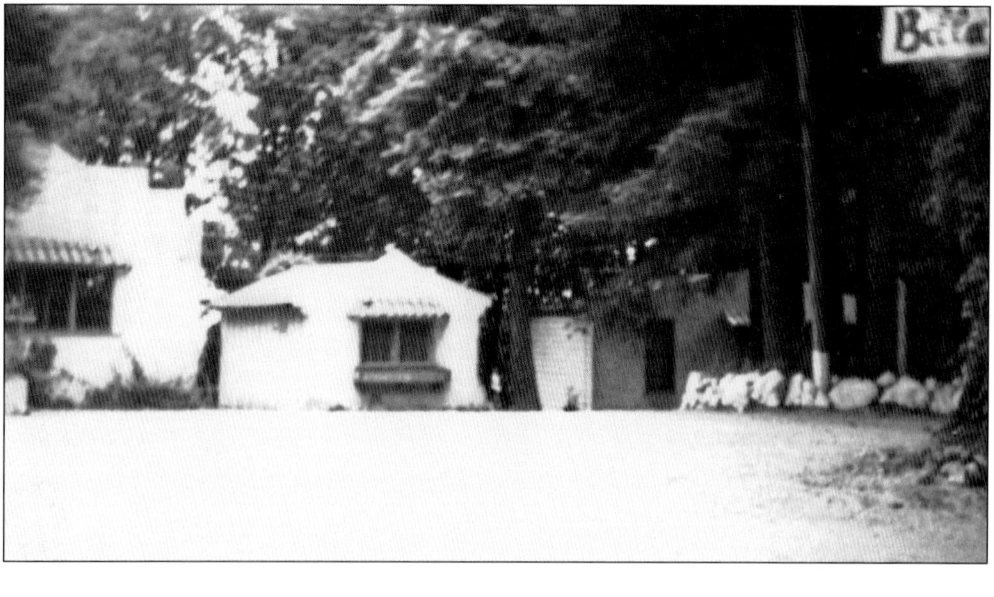

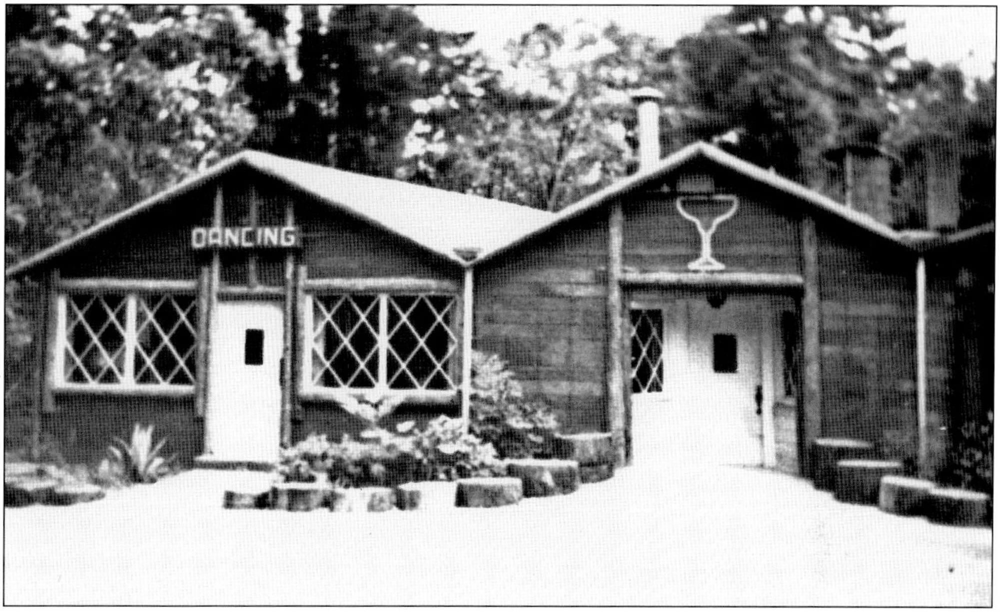

Sierra Morena, shown in the 1940s but established in the 1930s with a dining room, bar, dance floor, and three tourist cabins, was named after the Spanish name for "brown" or "dark mountain." Later it became Kelly's Place, where the bar was tended by Mr. Kelly and meals were prepared by Mrs. Kelly. No one used or even knew their first names. Eventually it became Uncle John's. It burned in 1968. (Courtesy Ken Fisher.)

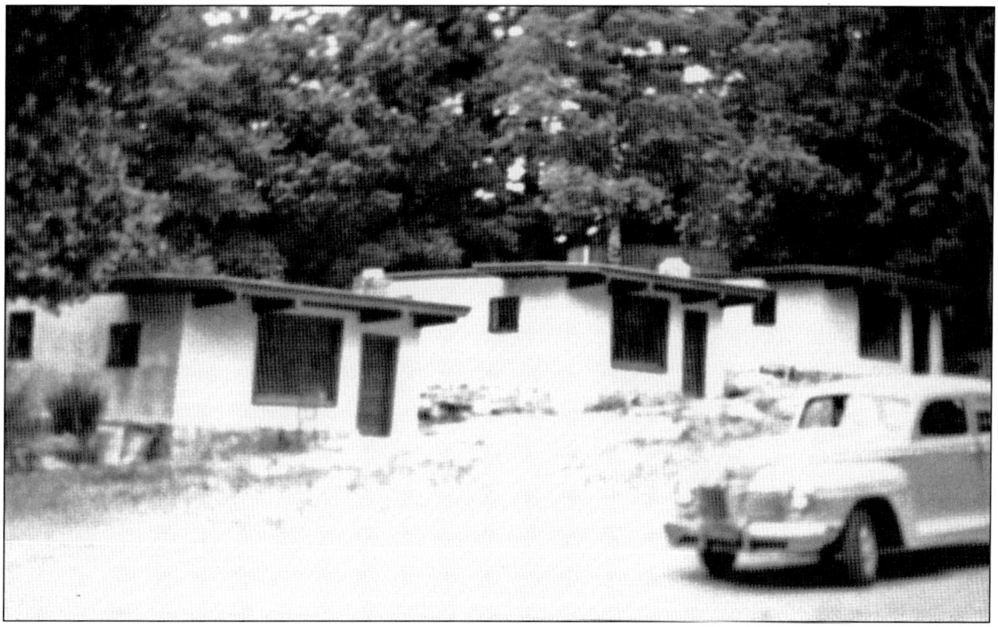

Three small tourist cabins, built in the 1930s without landscaping, adjoined the Sierra Morena Tavern. They were remodeled into an apartment unit, huddled under a steeply pitched roof, and extensively landscaped. The spaces between units were used for carports. Allegedly the unit boasted a fire pit, which lent a sentimental touch to the tavern. (Courtesy Ken Fisher.)

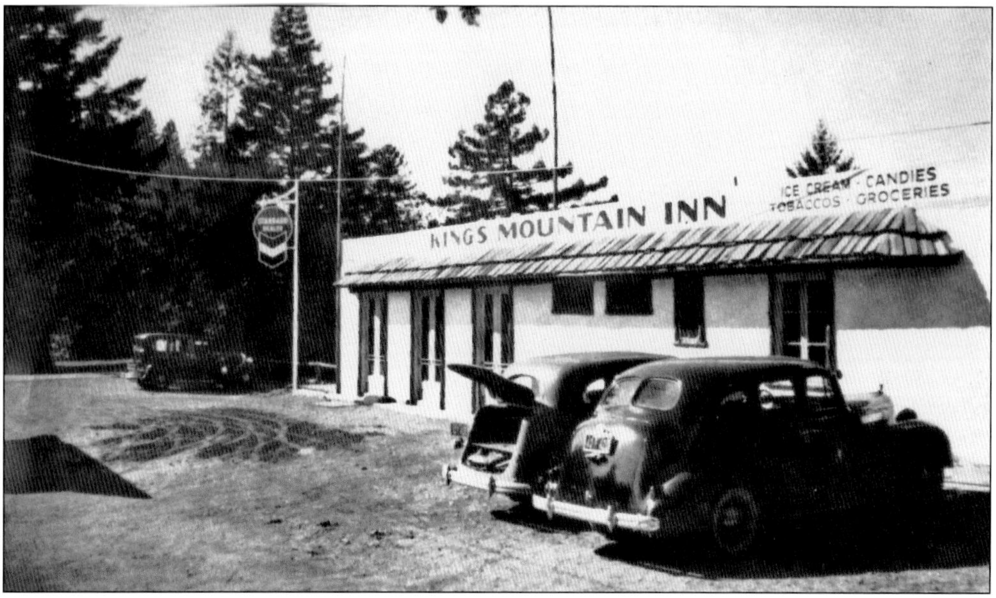

Eddie Castleman tore down the Mountain Brow House in 1938 and put up the Kings Mountain Inn in 1939 as a bar, diner, and gas station. In 1948, it was purchased by Vic and Alberta Brock. This photograph looks south from where the Kings Hotel once stood. Honora's son Walter "Doc" King liked to visit in the 1940s. To the center left is the beginning of Tunitas Creek Road and then Skyline Boulevard. (Courtesy Ken Fisher.)

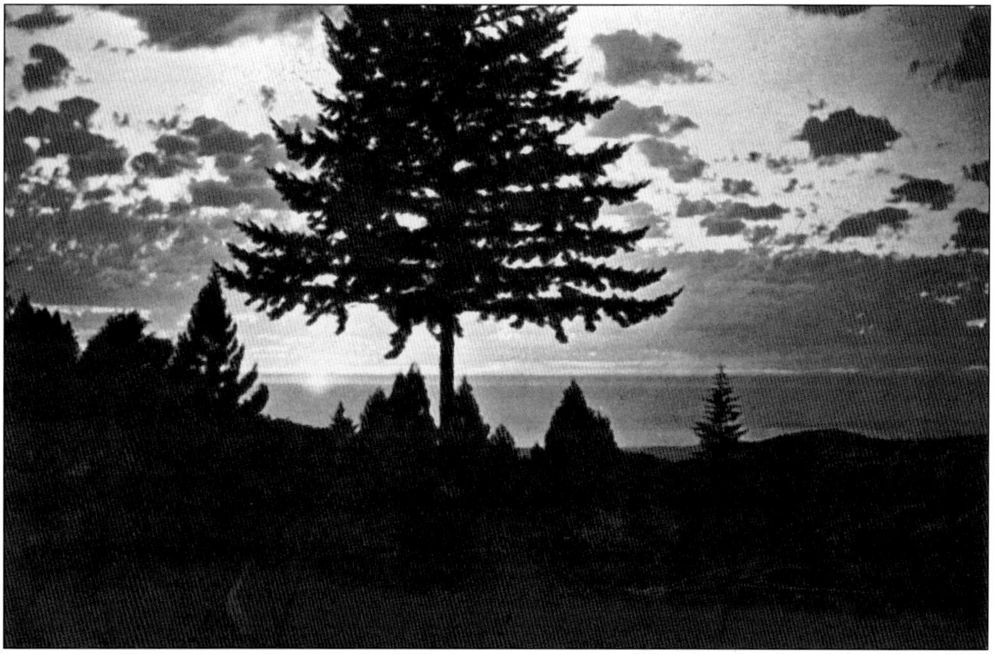

A 1950s–1960s postcard shows the sunset view from the dining room of the Brocks' Kings Mountain Inn. A paragraph on the back describes an establishment 2,070 feet above sea level, where guests can look out over 60 miles of Pacific Ocean from Half Moon Bay to the Farallone Islands and enjoy "food and cocktails at their best." (Courtesy Ken Fisher.)

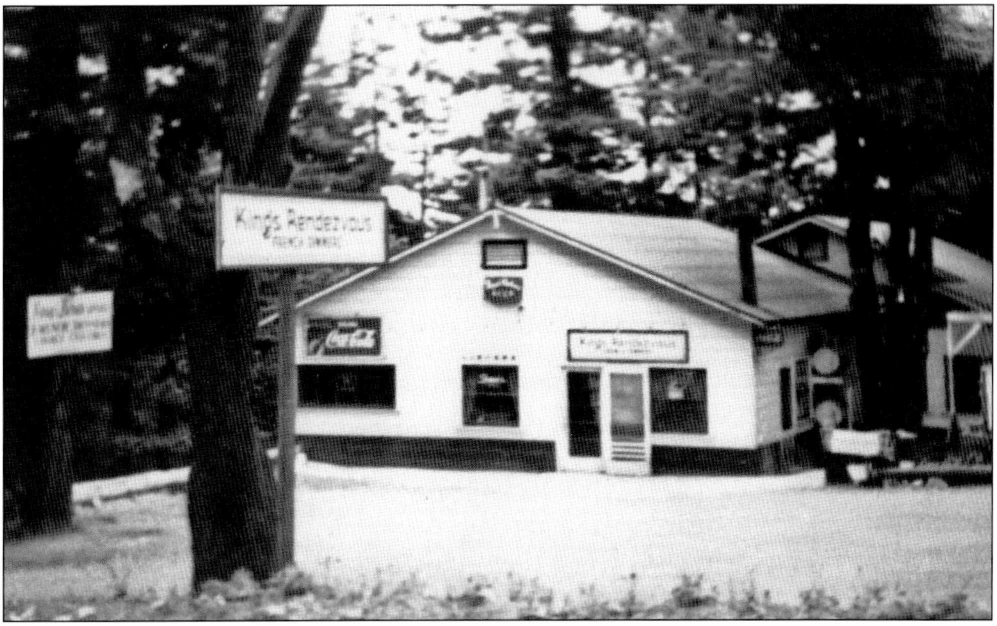

Kings Rendezvous, shown in the 1940s, was run by a formidable woman who would throw drunken customers off the deck. It was renamed the Red Pump in 1962 and shortly afterward became one of the spots where mountain men gathered informally, ostensibly to form a local fire brigade but more often to play poker. Eventually it became Alex's and finally today's Mountain House. (Courtesy Ken Fisher.)

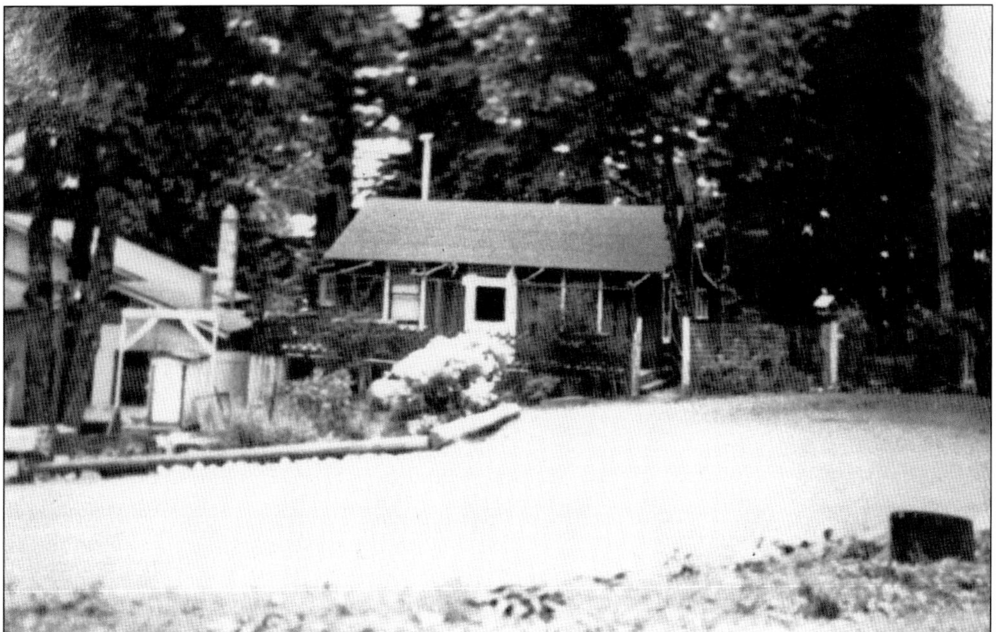

This tourist cabin adjoined Kings Rendezvous until it was torn down in 1965. Among its inhabitants were a family and, toward the end, John ?, a self-proclaimed warlock of whom colorful tales still survive. Some of them revolved around his favorite expressions: "Outta sight!" and "Far out!" (Courtesy Ken Fisher.)

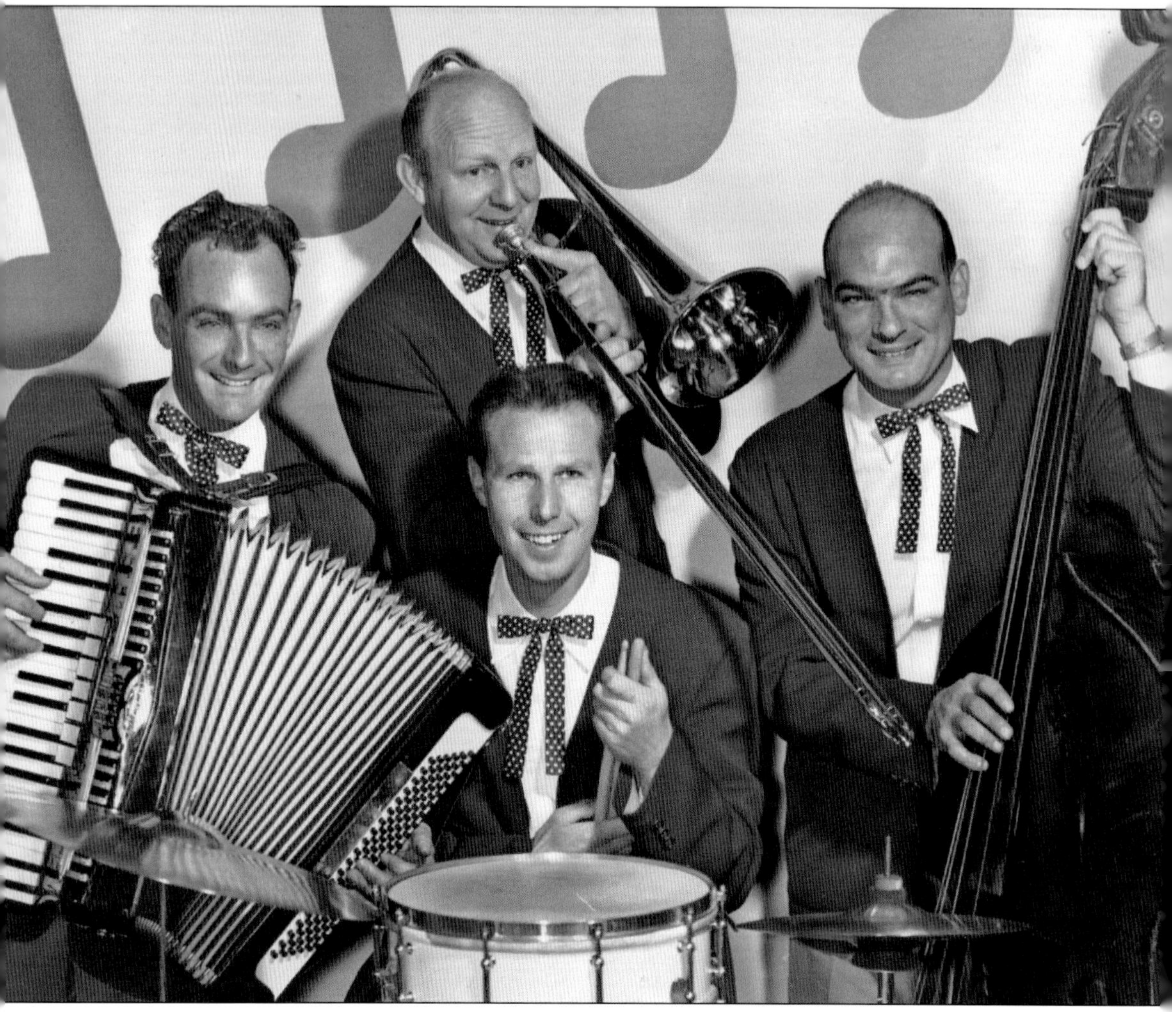

The Four Notes played swing and big band music on the peninsula from 1955 to 1965 but had ties to Kings Mountain. Johnny Barsochini (right) played the bass; his brother Leo (left) played the accordion; and Gerd Keene (center) kept the beat as the drummer. Trombonist Don Kreiss (top center) forged a unique link to the mountain as the "dean of bottle collectors." Along with his son Phil in the 1960s, he combed old mill sites to collect glass bottles, long discarded by loggers, that once held whiskey, medicines, or pickles. He unearthed hundreds of unbroken ones he called "snapshots of history," which he proudly displayed at his home and to which he added by visiting bottle shows. He also helped Dr. Frank M. Stanger, who published the definitive book *Sawmills in the Redwoods*, by leading him on research hikes to old mill sites. Don Kreiss died in 1999. (Courtesy Phil Kreiss.)

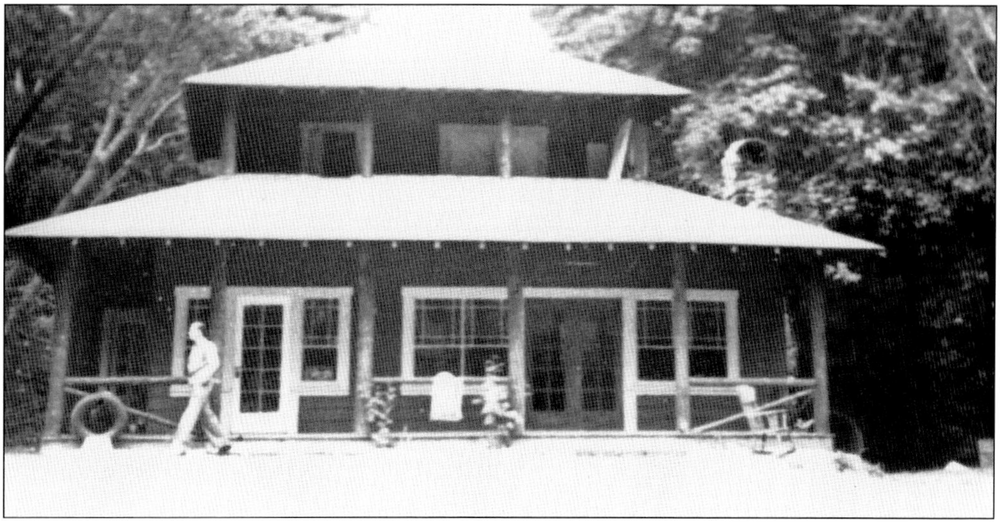

Knudson's was a small general store with one of the area's four operating gas stations in the 1940s when shown here. In the early 1960s, the owners, living upstairs, were brothers Conrad "Connie" and Ted Knudson. Connie drove a school bus, and Ted ran the store and maintained the gas pumps. Connie had married but was estranged from his wife, Al, when he died. Ted stayed on at the establishment and was eventually joined there by Al, who ran a snack bar and candy and ice cream store there until her death. In time, the gas pumps and station were removed, and the store building became a residence. (Both courtesy Ken Fisher.)

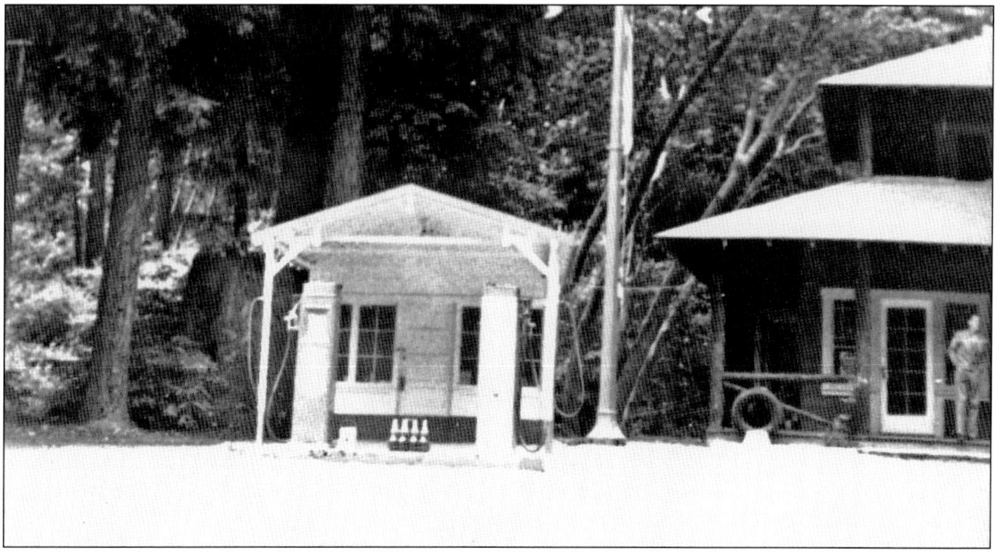

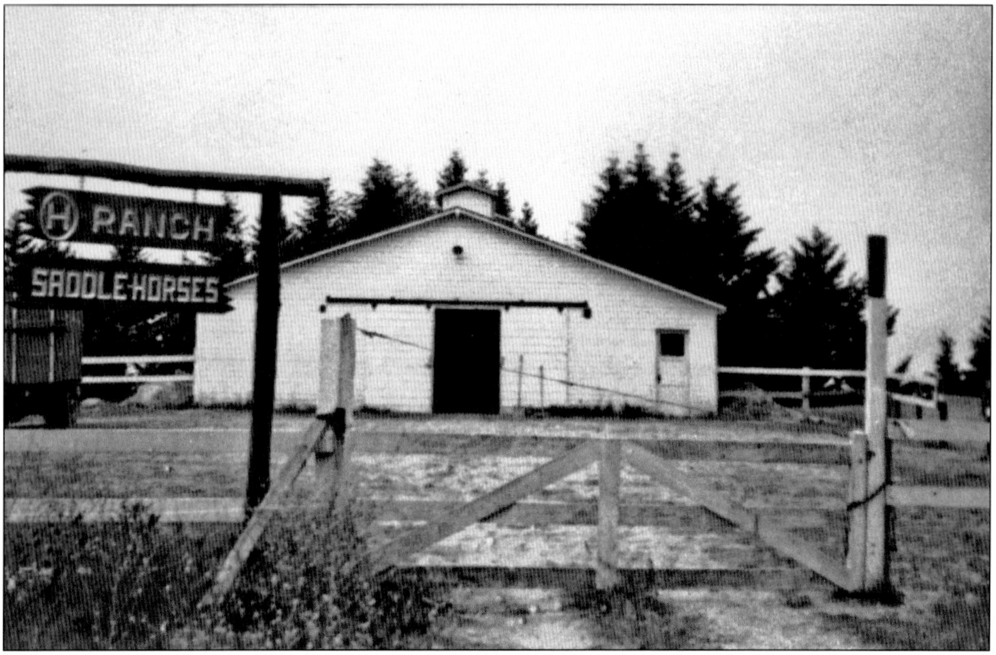

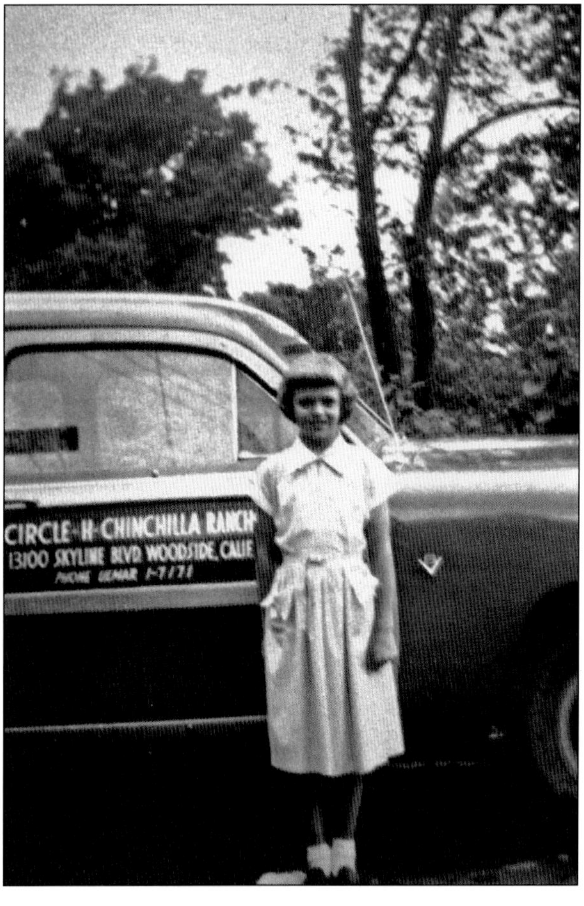

The Circle H was built in the 1940s and saw several incarnations. It became Higgins Circle H, the Vista Del Mar, the Honeywind, the Benchmark, and finally the Alpen Rose. It supposedly had an organ on which guests played polkas and also was a country store. Locals recall the night the Benchmark cook was whipping up dinner on the deep fryer and the oil ignited. He called local firefighters and asked them to stop by next time they were in the area. Concerned, they hurried out at once and found flames shooting 30 feet in the air. The Benchmark was one of the first mountain buildings to be saved from fire. A chinchilla ranch occupied a long bunker on the ranch. Later it was used as a conference facility and a country store, and is now closed to the public. (Both courtesy Ken Fisher.)

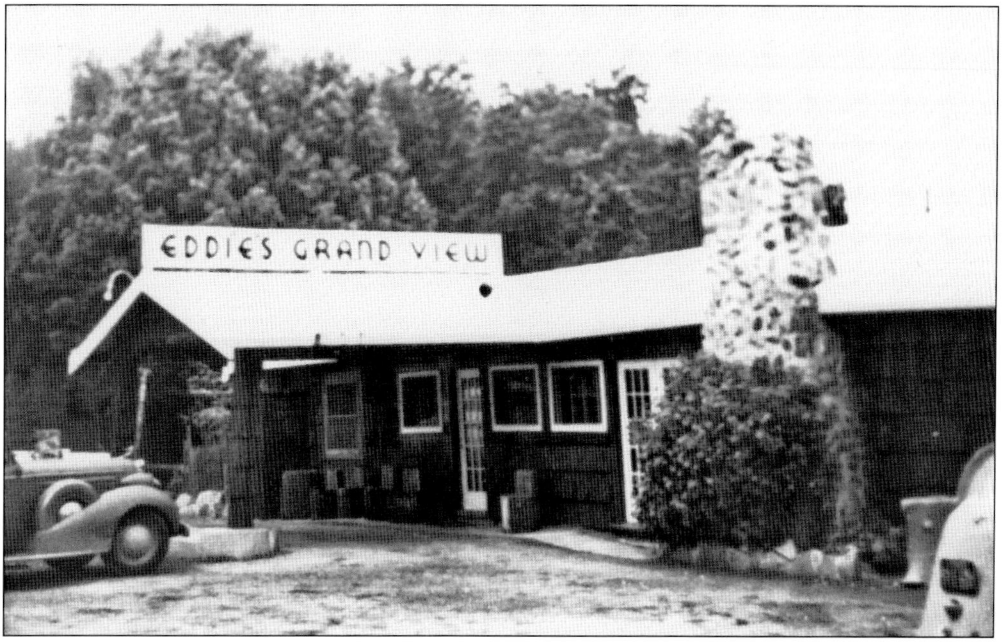

Eddie and Flo Castleman bought the restaurant they called Eddie's Grand View in 1948. Eddie allegedly gave friends free drinks and did not always pay taxes. Rumors flew that he was a bootlegger. He explained the adjacent cabins: "They stack up the drunks like cordwood and give them keys to their cars in the morning along with their bill." (Courtesy Ken Fisher.)

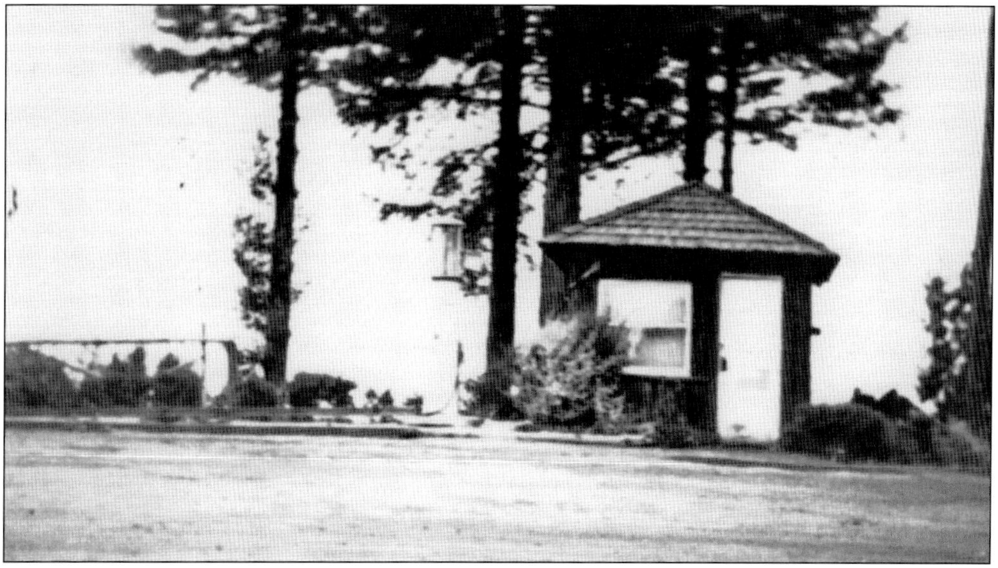

Eddie's Grand View was one of many mountain establishments with adjacent tourist cabins like this one. Eddie's cabin was torn down when the main building was remodeled into a brothel with three concrete "cribs," small areas that each held a bed and a sink. (Courtesy Ken Fisher.)

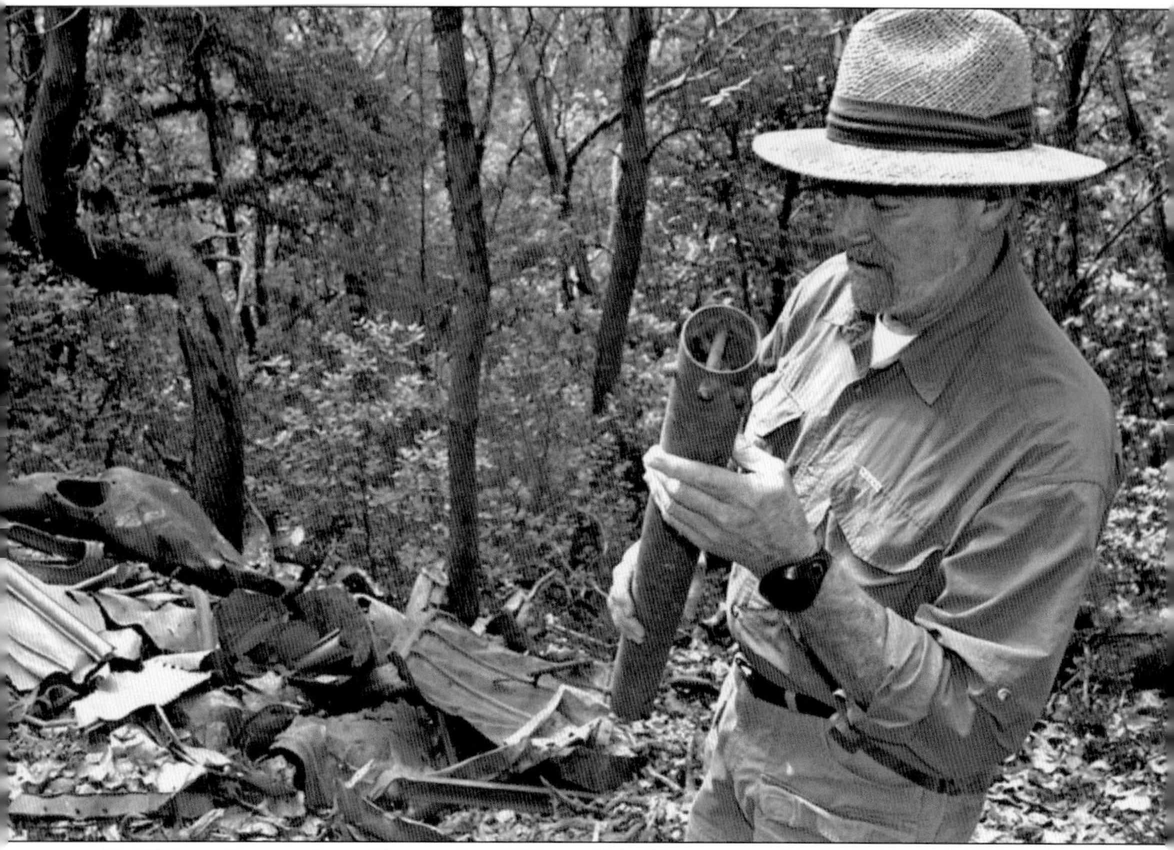

Half Moon Bay resident Christopher O'Donnell holds a piece of wreckage on the site where, on October 29, 1953, mountain tranquility was shattered by San Mateo County's worst air disaster when the *Resolution*, a British Commonwealth Pacific Airlines DC-6, slammed into the southeast side in heavy fog. This jumbo jet of its day was approaching San Francisco, one stop on its Australia–to–New York flight, with 11 passengers and 8 crew members, all lost in the disaster. Red Cross volunteers and emergency personnel, including what became the county's first forensic investigation team, recovered bodies and wreckage and doused three forest fires started by the crash. The area, now part of the El Corte de Madera Open Space Preserve, still contains evidence of the accident enshrouded in ravines. On October 29, 2006, exactly 53 years after the crash, O'Donnell had a memorial plaque in black granite with names of the victims dedicated at the Hiller Aviation Museum. Days earlier, he had carried a piece of the wreckage onto a San Francisco International Airport runway—symbolically fulfilling the ill-fated flight. (Courtesy *Half Moon Bay Review*.)

Seven

A Community United
The Kings Mountain Art Fair

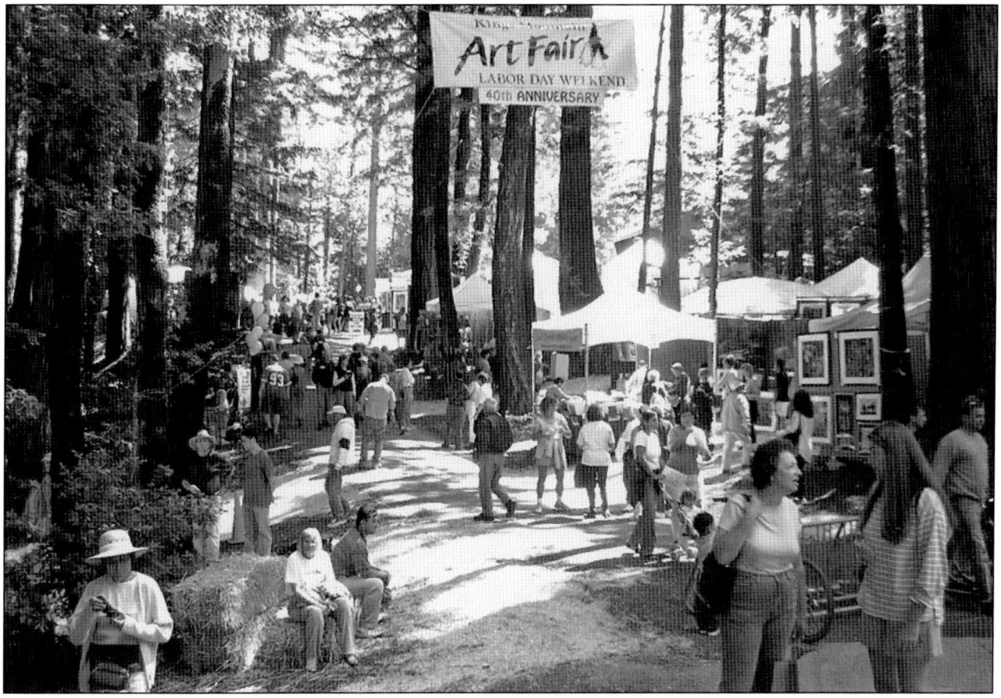

Fire is an ever-present threat on the forested mountain, and protection had been in the hands of California Department of Forestry firefighters in Belmont or San Mateo—too far away in an emergency. In 1962, the mountain's men met at the Red Pump to play poker but also to form a volunteer fire brigade with first chief Chuck Carter (no relation to later firefighter Bob Carter). Then came the disastrous Wickett's Mill fire of 1964, which "looked like the whole mountain was on fire," said resident Ardyth Woodruff, and which neighbors battled with 12 Pulaski firefighting tools and garden hoses. Serendipitously, a year earlier, a group of mountain women had held a craft show, and in an epiphany, the community realized that show could be the means to protect itself from fire. Four decades later, the Kings Mountain Art Fair has grown into a unique phenomenon: operated solely through volunteer effort, staunchly eschewing commercialism, it is a remarkable crux around which an already close community rallies every year. It revolves around art: highest quality yet affordable work by artists of the Western states and beyond as well as a small separate section for mountain artists. It is rated in the Top 10 fairs in the northwestern United States on the prestigious Harris List and among the country's top 200 art events by *Sunset Magazine*. "It's pretty unique in today's world, that so many in the community come together for a particular thing," said current executive director Dawn Neisser. "All your neighbors are there." (Courtesy Bill Goebner.)

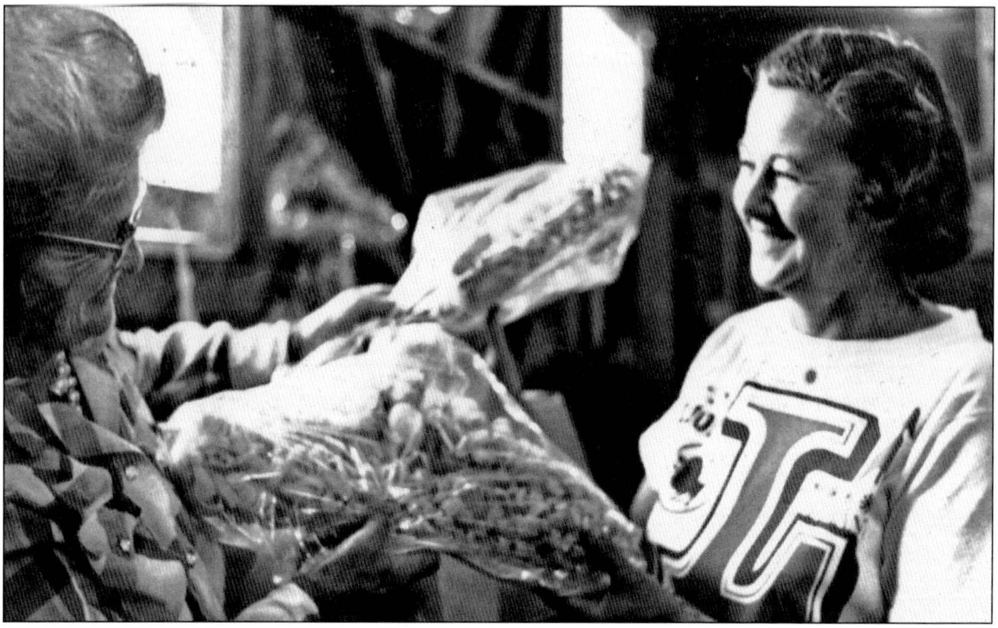

The art fair started in 1963 when the Pine Needles mountain needlework club, inspired by members Verna Littlechild, Wylda Mason, Ruth Harder, and Alberta Brock, held a crafts show. Above, Wylda (left) and fellow Pine Needle Marge Farwell plan the show. There were knitted and crocheted quilts, holiday ornaments, baby clothes, and whimsical thistle-like "teazles" with candles and Styrofoam. Ironically, one caught fire that year. (Courtesy Ardyth Woodruff.)

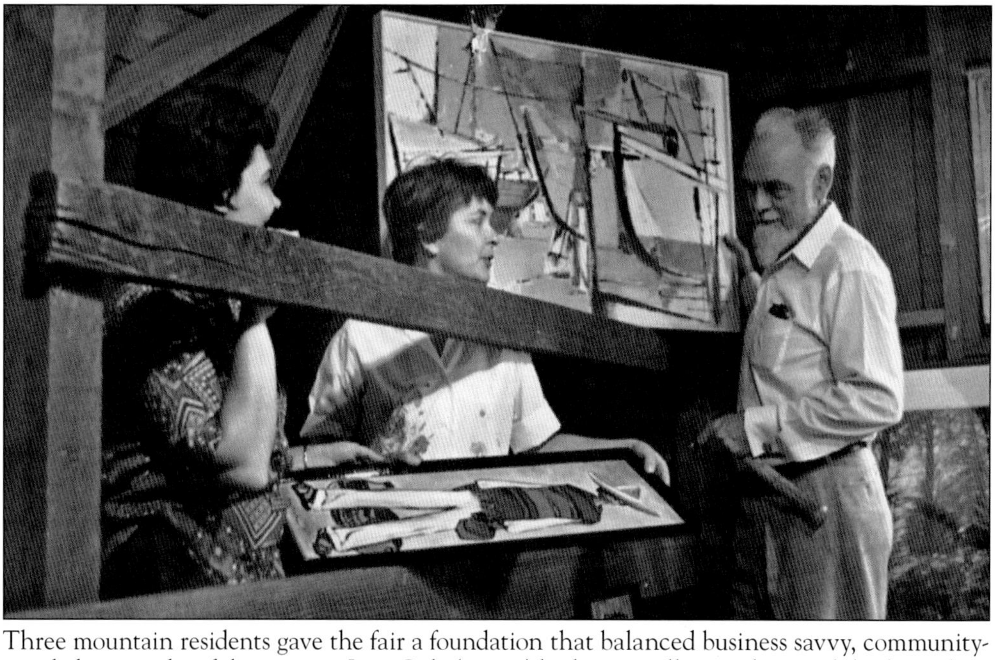

Three mountain residents gave the fair a foundation that balanced business savvy, community-mindedness, and artful creativity. Jean Cole (center) had run a gallery and wanted the fair to be a high-end juried show; she chaired it with no-nonsense benevolence for 20 years. Ardyth Woodruff (left) championed participation by local artists and children. Painter/sculptor Ken Washburn had taught art at Cornell University for 20 years. (Courtesy Ardyth Woodruff.)

Volunteers including Ken Washburn (center), Jean Cole (to his right), and Ardyth Woodruff (to his left) break ground for the first fair, June 22 and 23, 1963, in a barn belonging to John Wickett, near but not part of his mill. Then-residents Elmo and Kathy Allen used it to store and repair cars, and oil and grease were everywhere. The artists covered the floor with hay; visitors thought that looked folksy. (Courtesy Ardyth Woodruff.)

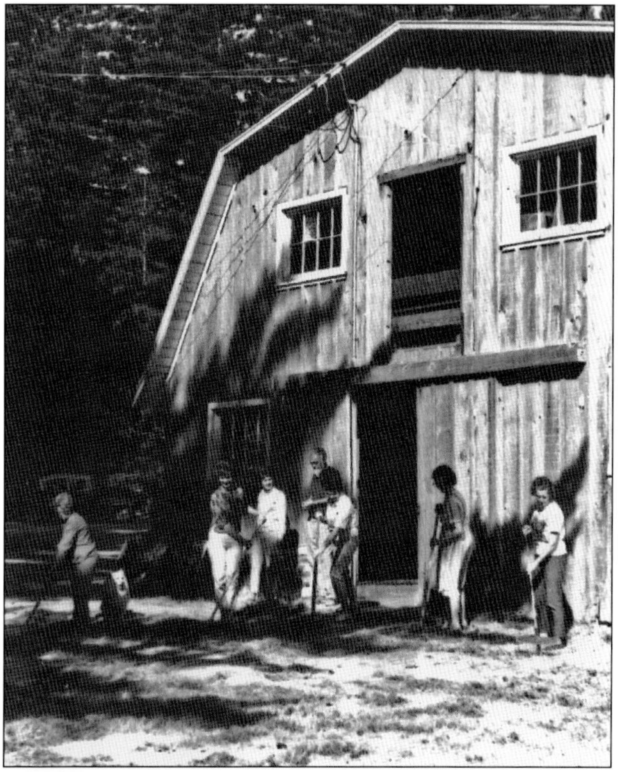

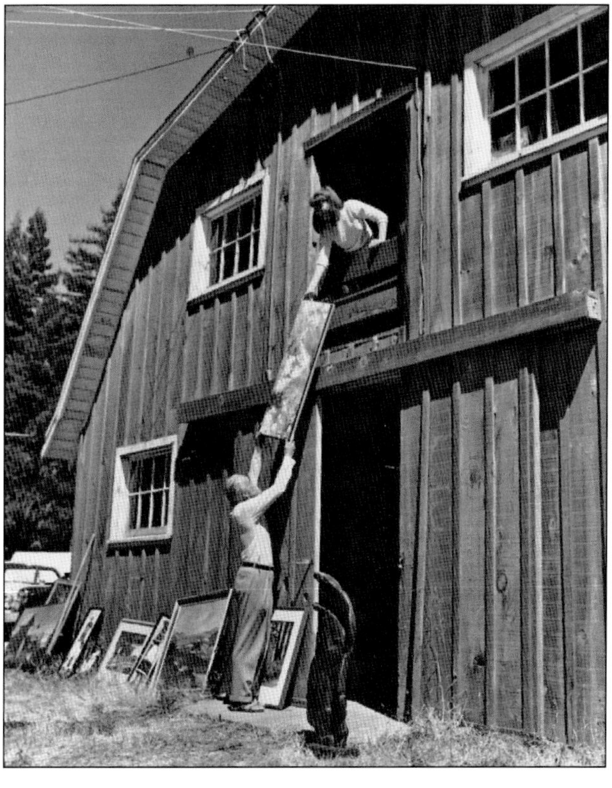

Ken Washburn hands up a painting to Michele Woodruff as they set up for the first fair. The art consisted of Pine Needles crafts on the barn's first floor and paintings and sculpture by local artists on the second. Jean Cole demanded quality: when someone submitted a painting of a farmer drowning cats, she nixed it, declaring that even if the fair was not juried, "we do have standards." The fair raised $50 but netted about $35 after expenses. (Courtesy Ardyth Woodruff.)

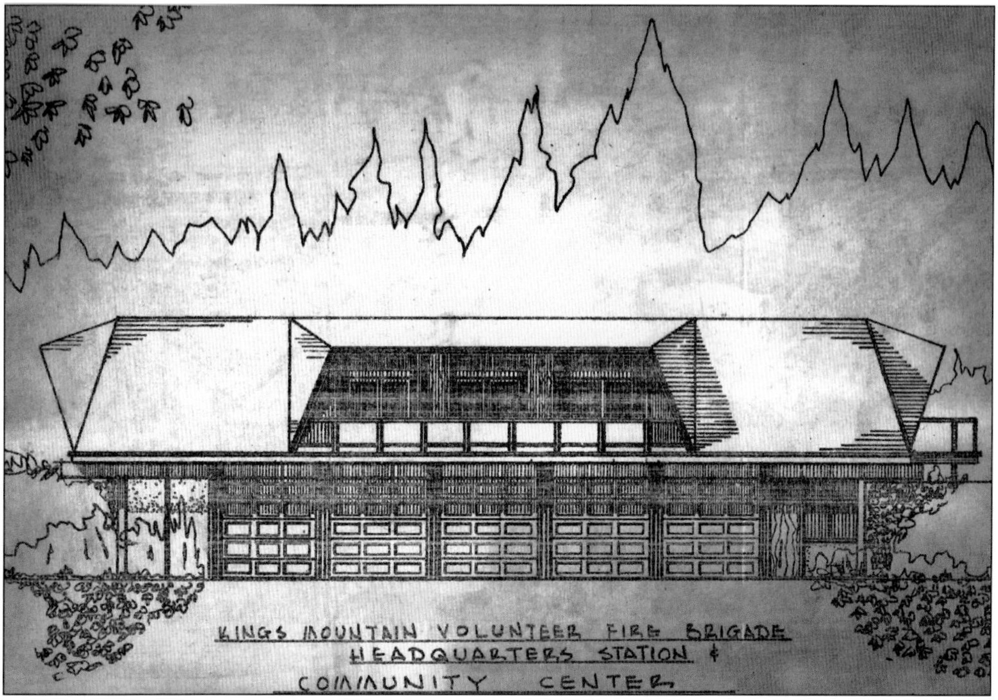

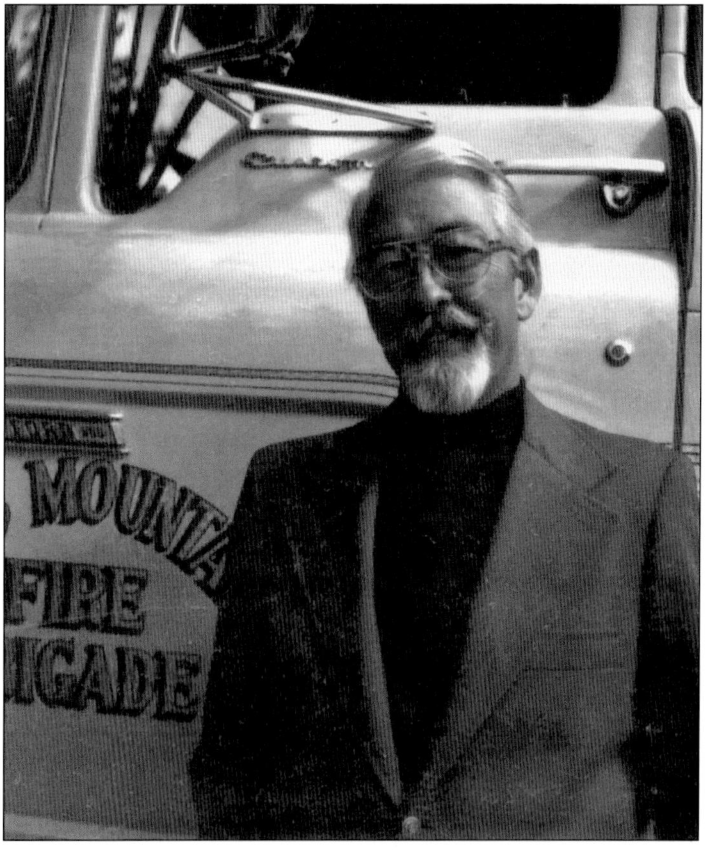

Architect John Cole, Jean's husband, designed the 5,200-square-foot building for the fledgling fire department. The firefighters wanted a one-story metal building to store equipment, but John felt it was possible to have an aesthetic building large enough to house community activities and argued that a mansard roof would help it blend into the forest. At the Red Pump one night, he drew his idea on a table napkin, and the firemen were convinced. Throughout five years of construction, he was there every weekend until it was completed. John Cole died in 1989; a commemorative plaque honoring him hangs in the center. (Both courtesy Bill Goebner.)

The phenomenon of everyone pitching in to support the community took root in 1966, when the mountain's men set to work transforming John Cole's sketches into reality. They used their own tools; plumbers or electricians donated skills and Pine Needles and other women cooked for the workers. The center was built exclusively by volunteer labor with donated materials, no tax money went into it. The resourceful builders scrounged materials, like the bright-red tiles from the bone pile of a San Jose commercial tile company, which decorate the center's restroom. The community supported the fledgling fire brigade with fund-raisers like this one below on July 15, 1967; the man in the white hat is the Mr. Kelly of Kelly's bar. His wife, known to all as simply "Mrs. Kelly," cooked for that event. (Right, courtesy Ardyth Woodruff; below, courtesy Bill Goebner.)

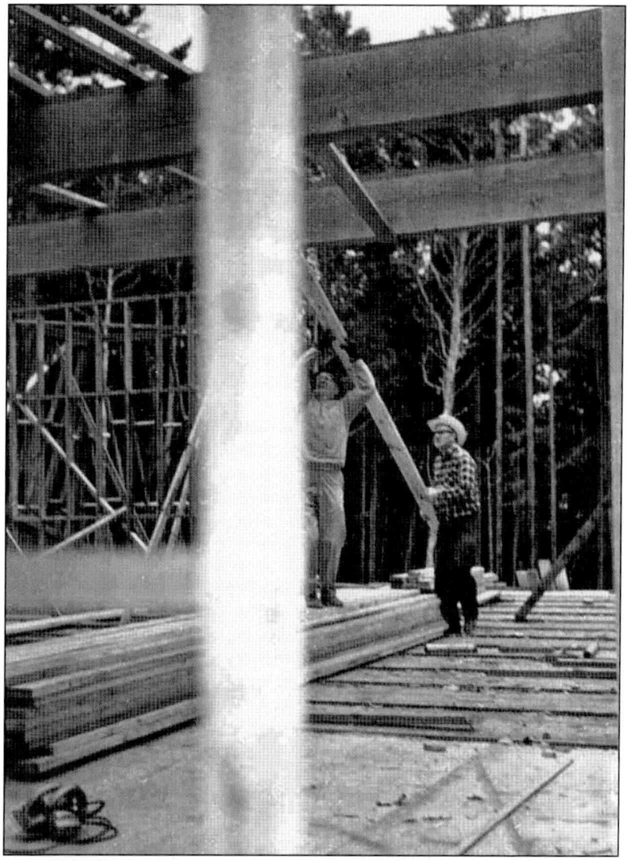

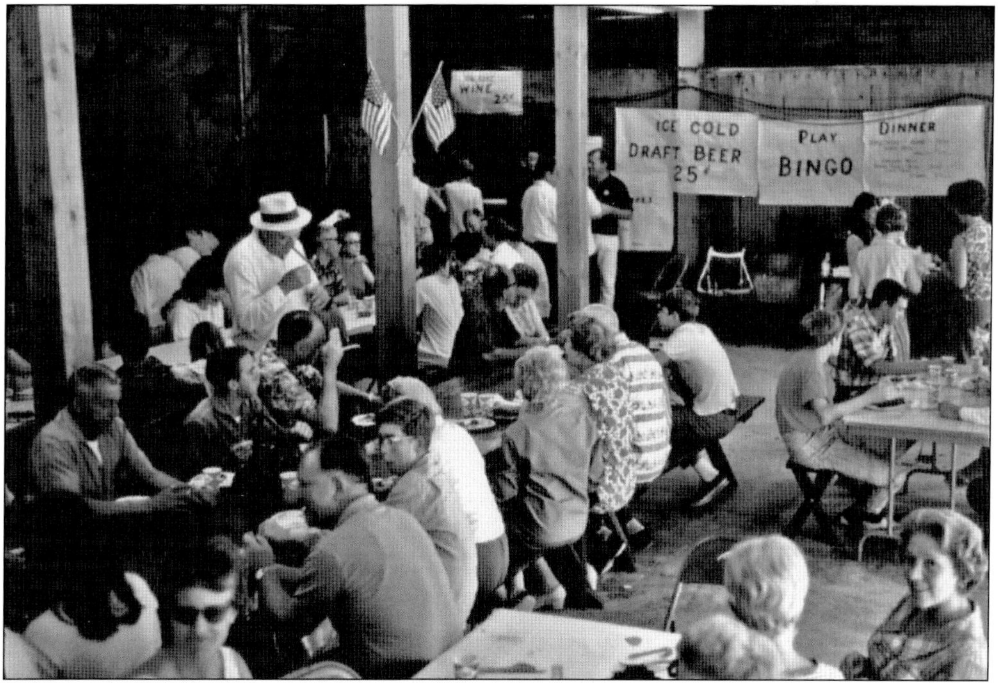

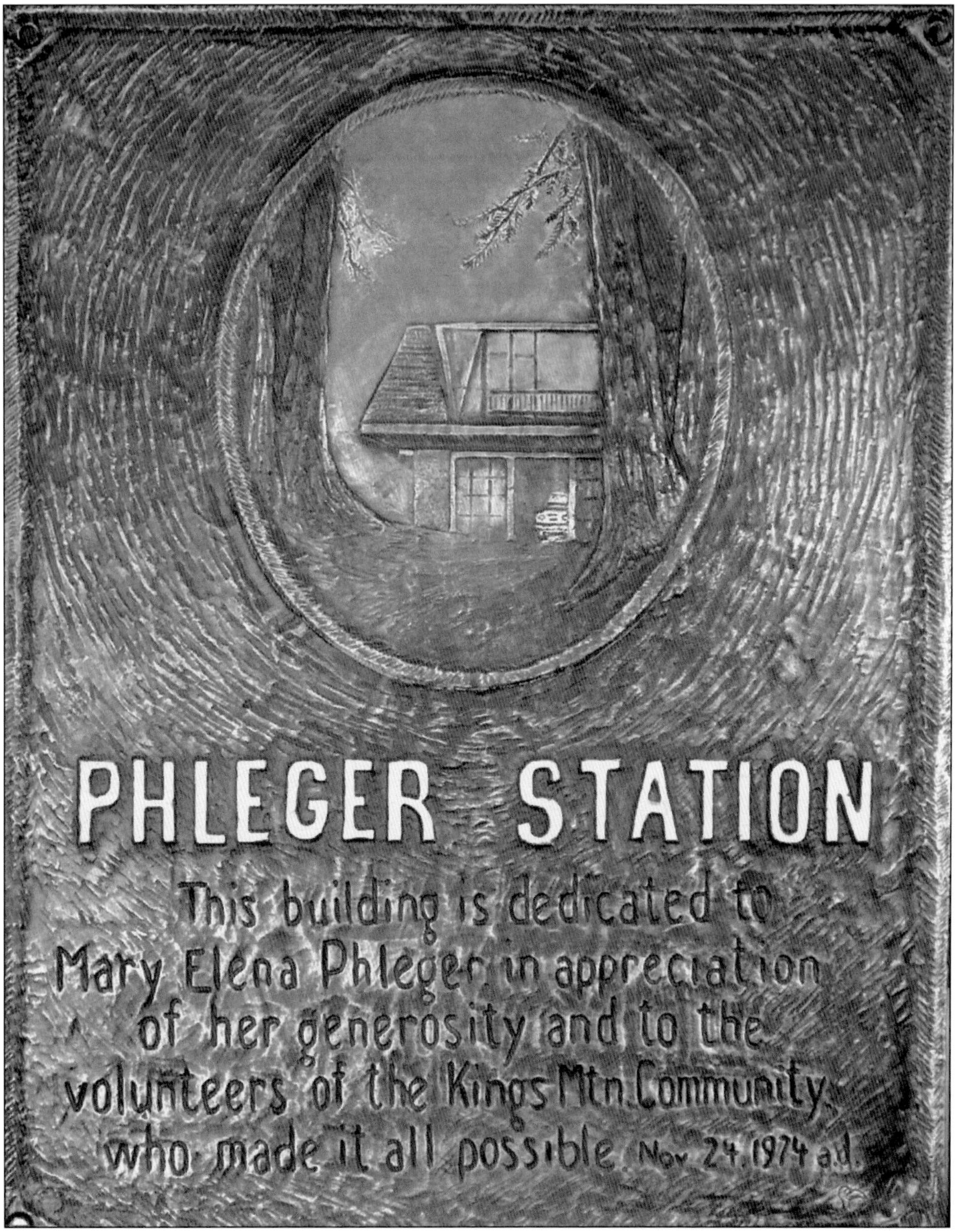

Beginning in the early 1960s, Herman and Mary Elena Phleger gave the fledgling volunteer fire brigade a $1-a-year lease on land. They continued supporting the fair as it outgrew the fire station and spread into the trees, eventually donating more than five acres to the brigade. When the new fire station was dedicated on November 11, 1974, they were the guests of honor along with the Coles, Sen. Arlen Gregorio, and then-Supervisor-elect John Ward. Cofounding artist Rebecca Holland designed and gave the Phlegers this commemorative plaque for display at the building. By then, the center had been adapted to its intended uses: the ground floor housed the fire brigade's engines, equipment, and operations, and the second story was used for community gatherings, classes, meetings, and activities. (Courtesy Rebecca Holland.)

Either a throwback or in a wry tribute to the days of shingle mills, Jean Cole hands up a stack of shingles for the center's new roof to George Rust, third volunteer fire brigade chief, who reportedly always wore his fire chief's hat. It was 1968, and finishing touches were going onto the building. (Courtesy Ardyth Woodruff.)

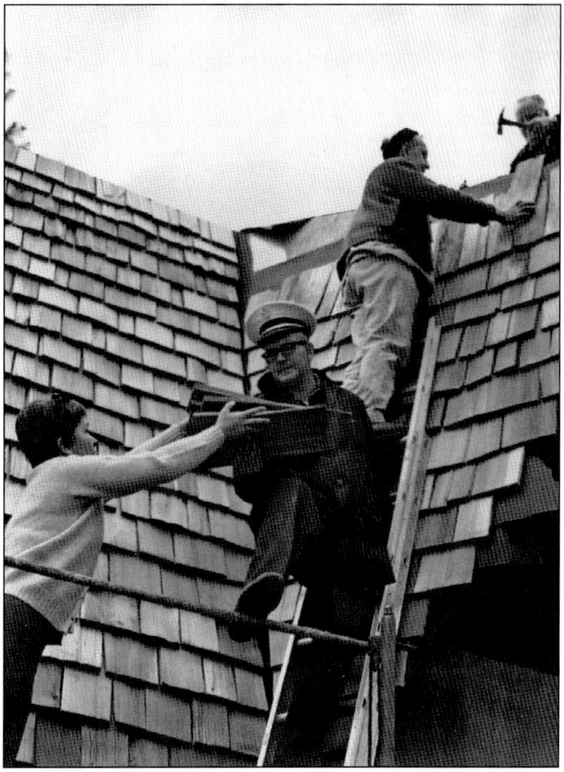

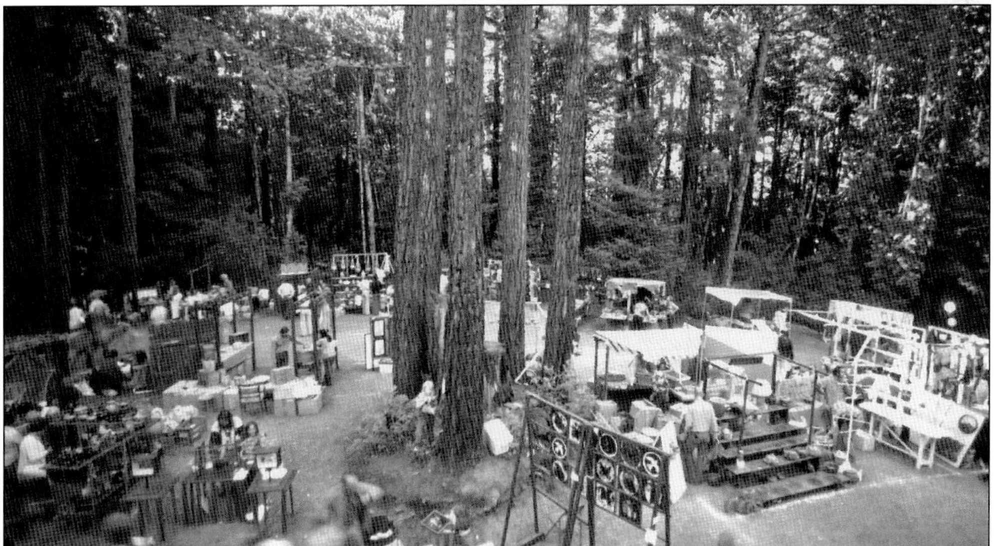

The gleaming new Kings Mountain Community Center was ready for the 1972 fair. The next year, it moved to Labor Day weekend with 90-plus artists. The 1974 fair, shown here, stretched into the trees. By 1976, artists were chosen by jury and the net income was an encouraging $19,000, including $386 from the new Mountain Folk Art section. The 1978 fair netted $24,500, and the building was finally done by 1979. By the early 1980s, organizers were dividing $30,000 proceeds among the fire brigade, elementary school, 4-H club, and ongoing building improvement. (Courtesy Bill Goebner.)

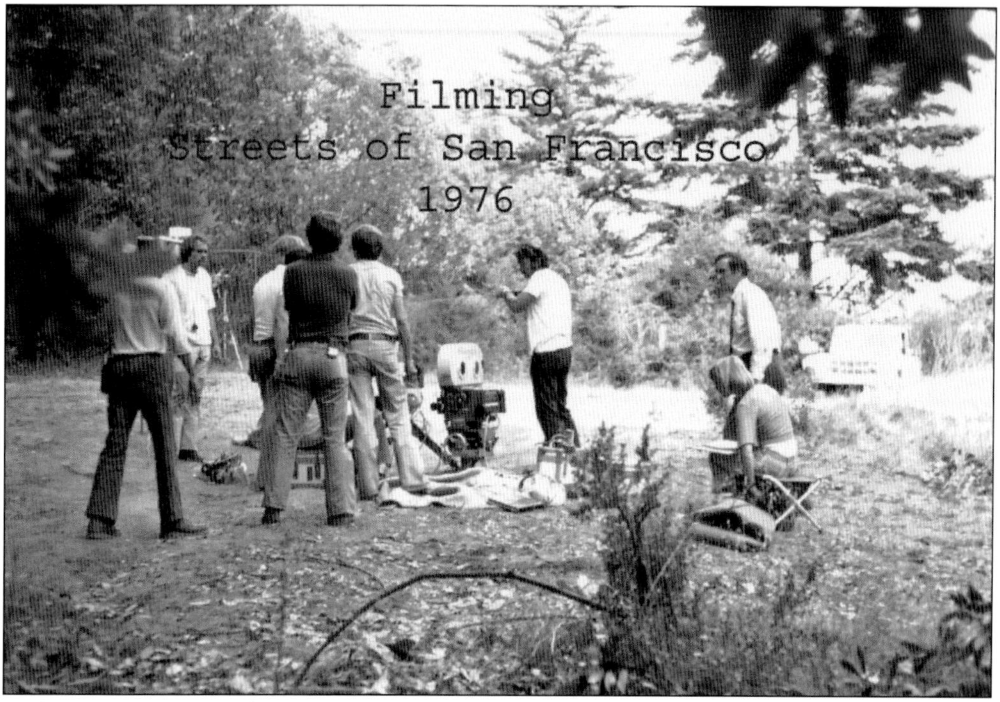

In August 1976, art took a temporary backseat to Hollywood when segments of an episode of *Streets of San Francisco* were filmed on the mountain. (Courtesy Bill Goebner.)

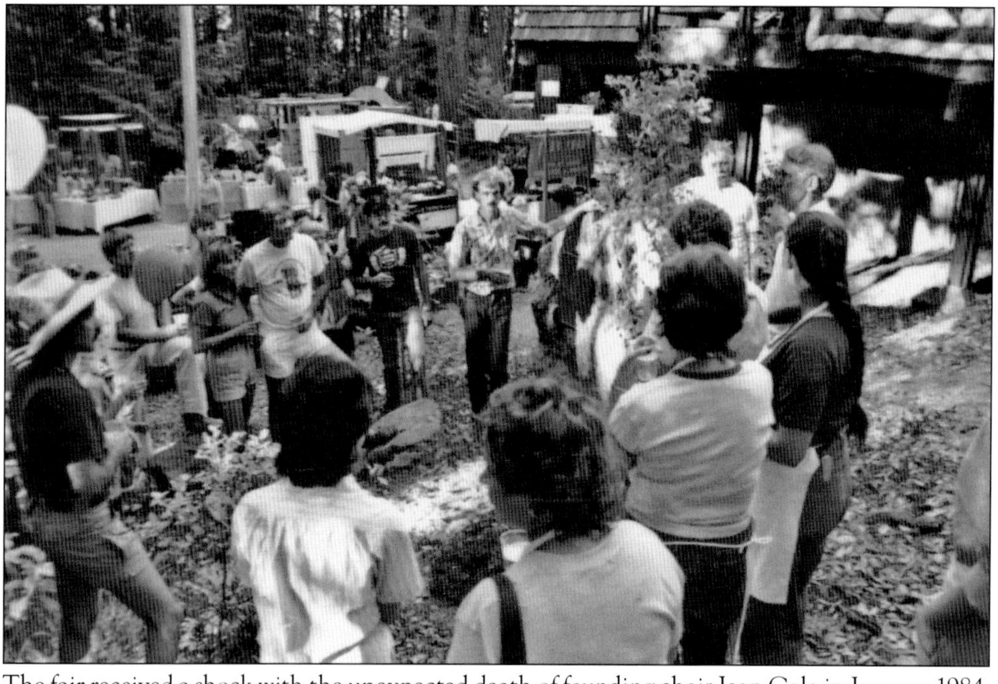

The fair received a shock with the unexpected death of founding chair Jean Cole in January 1984. Fears that the fair might die with her were quelled when mountain residents Dick and Carol Funk stepped in with a message of "Don't worry, keep on." Here trees are planted in memory of Jean during the fair of 1984. (Courtesy Ardyth Woodruff.)

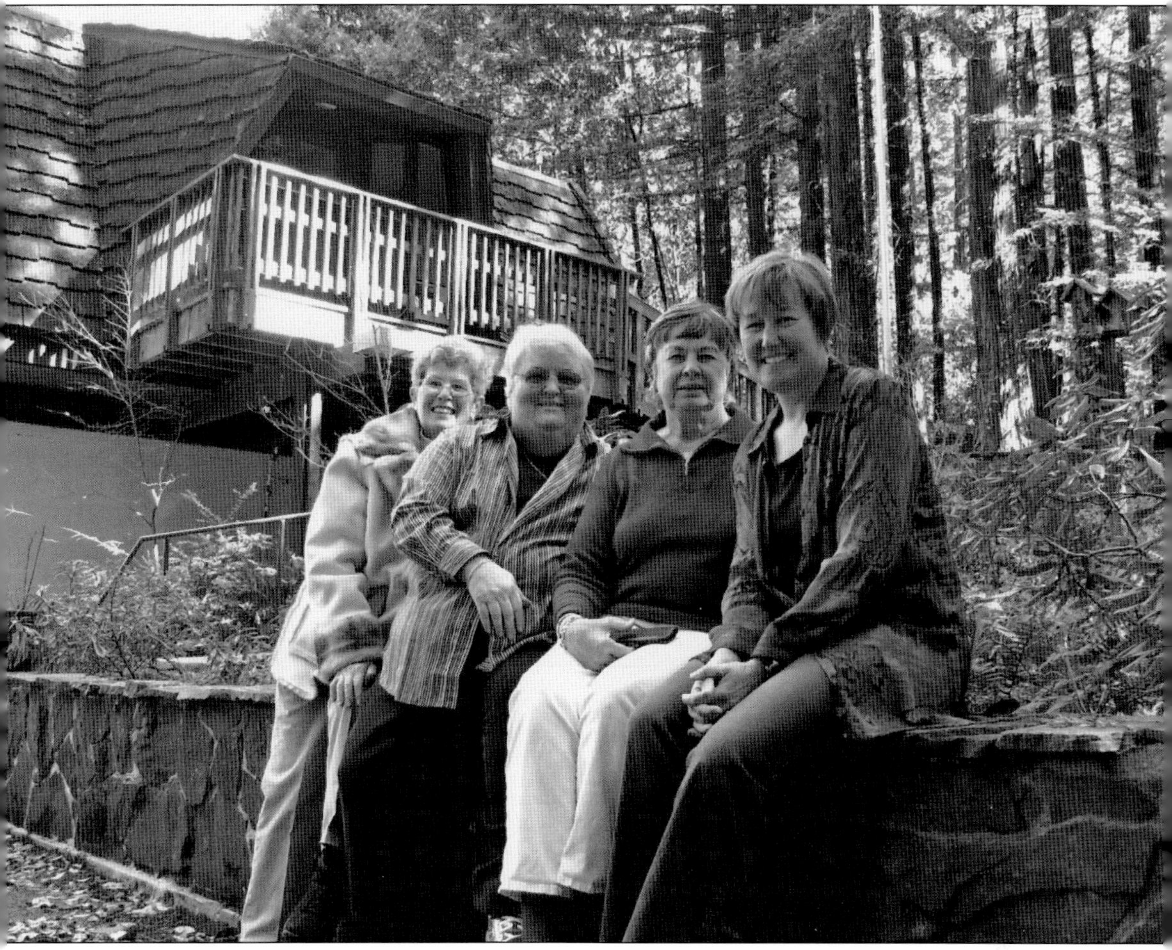

Succeeding Jean Cole as fair chairs were the following people, shown from left to right. Carol Funk (1984–1991) helped Jean as liaison with the artists while her husband, Dick, handled finances. "That relationship with the artists makes it a whole show; complete, cohesive, special," Carol says. Vi Croop (1992–1997), granddaughter of Pine Needle Ruth Harder, volunteered as treasurer and at the "cook shack" (food area) before seeking out new artists as chair. Vi commented, "It amazes me, over these many years, it continues to bring the community, all types of people, together with the goal of improving this community." Sybil Plank (1998–2004) helped artists sell work and at the "cook shack" before bringing her business background into her chair duties: "The art fair, and its connection to the fire brigade, is absolutely the heart and soul of the Kings Mountain community. . . . If the roads close, we depend on each other so it's in our best interest to care about each other, something I think is rare in a quasi-metropolitan area." Dawn Neisser (2005–present) helped in publicity and managed the "cook shack" before overseeing the many operations that dovetail into the fair. "There's always a way to get ingrained into the community, because you meet everybody," Dawn says. (Courtesy the author.)

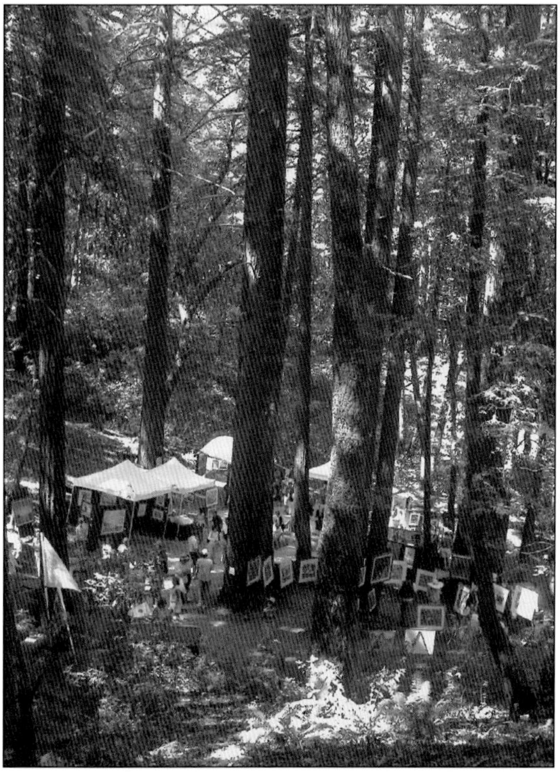

The Kings Mountain Art Fair is a living art gallery every Labor Day weekend. Display racks and tables are set up along winding trails and in idyllic groves. All is run by tireless volunteers, who refuse corporate sponsorship and other forms of commercialism. "Founders' values and beliefs made this fair what it is," says former chair Vi Croop. (Courtesy the author.)

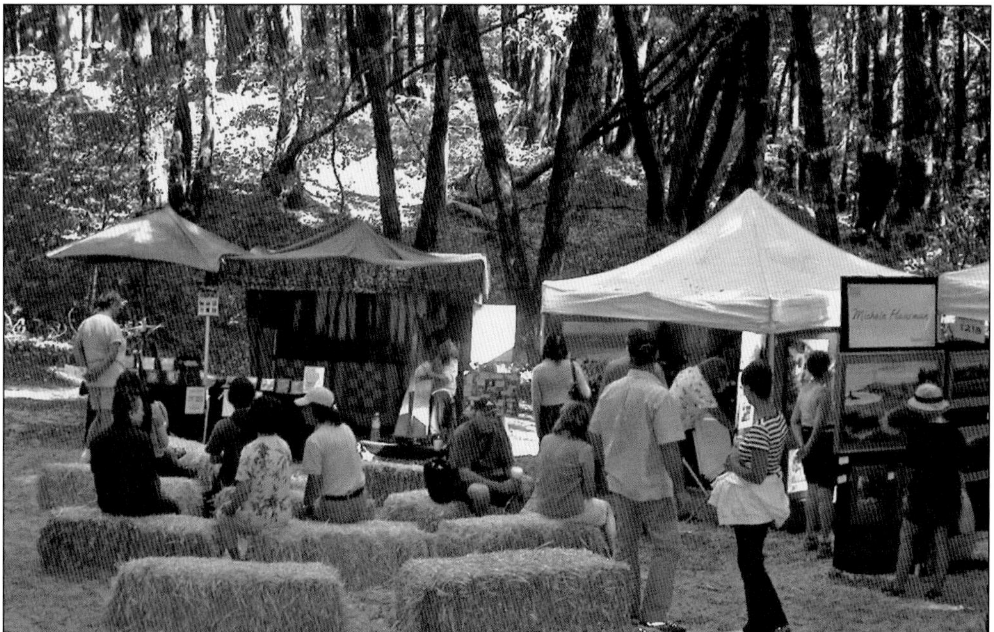

The only live music at the fair are softly wafting strains of harpist Aryeh Frankfurter, who plays on a tiny platform in one corner of a grove usually dedicated to fine art paintings. A few hay bales provide casual seating. The presence of the musician is low-key so as to not interfere with visitors' experience of the art. (Courtesy the author.)

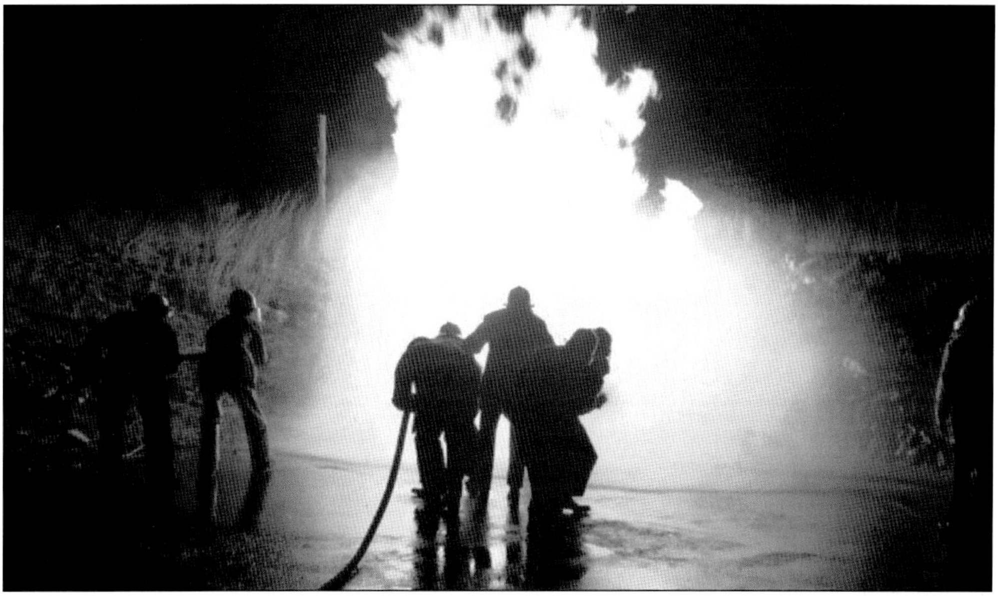

Fund-raisers, donations, and mostly the fair support the nonprofit Kings Mountain Volunteer Fire Brigade, Inc. Having incorporated in the early 1980s, it manages the Kings Mountain Fire Department and owns the community center and fire equipment. The roughly 15 firefighter/EMTs respond to 150–200 calls per year. Its booth at the fair offers free blood-pressure screenings as part of what chief Jim Sullivan calls the "pretty special, pretty unique hard work it does for people in the community," as shown in this training exercise with a propane tank. (Courtesy Bill Goebner.)

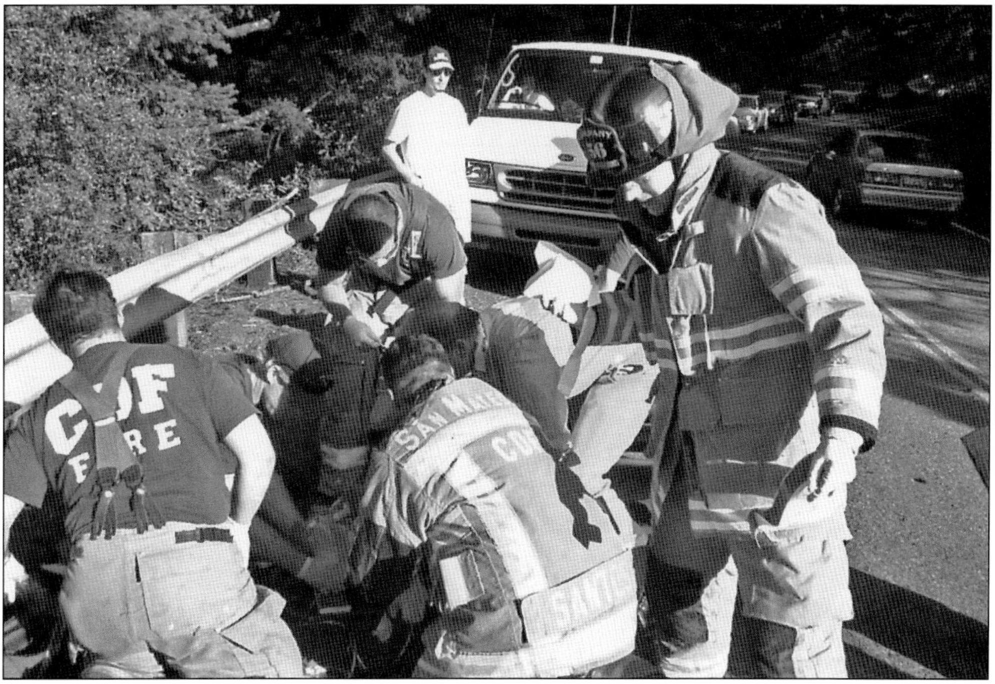

Eighty percent of the calls for the fire brigade are for medical aid; 20 percent are for fires. Most accidents, such as this one in 2002, involve motorcycles speeding down the twisty mountain roads. This rider survived without major injury. (Courtesy Bill Goebner.)

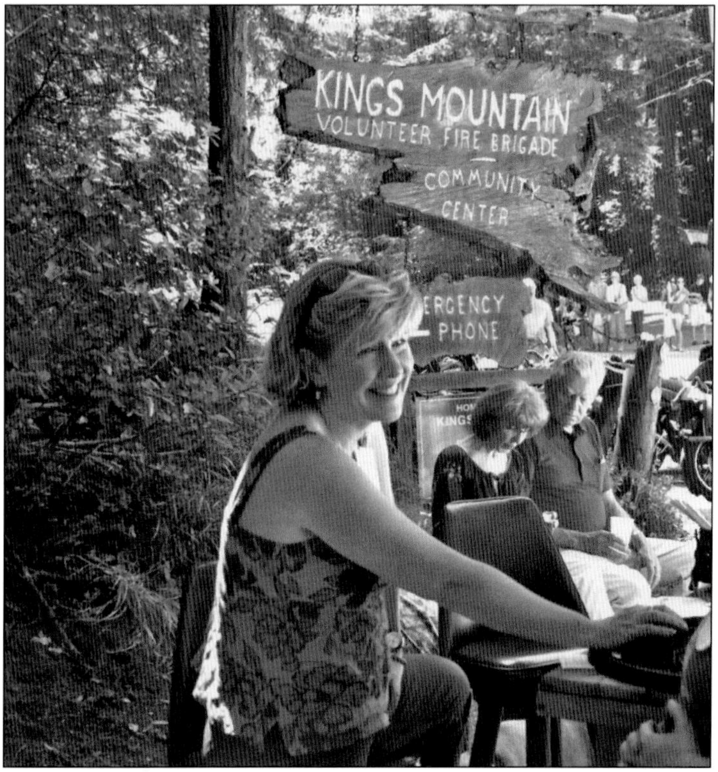

Inspired by early volunteers Walt and Dot McClary, Bill and Shirley Windle, Ollie and Marie Shane, and Wally and Luette Schmidt, around 300 mountain residents of all ages, more than a third of the community, fill the many slots it takes to make the fair run every year. Months earlier, current volunteer coordinator Patty O'Connell (left) lists what is needed in the mountain's Yahoo! network and *Echo* newsletter and fits volunteers into the right jobs. (Courtesy Bill Goebner.)

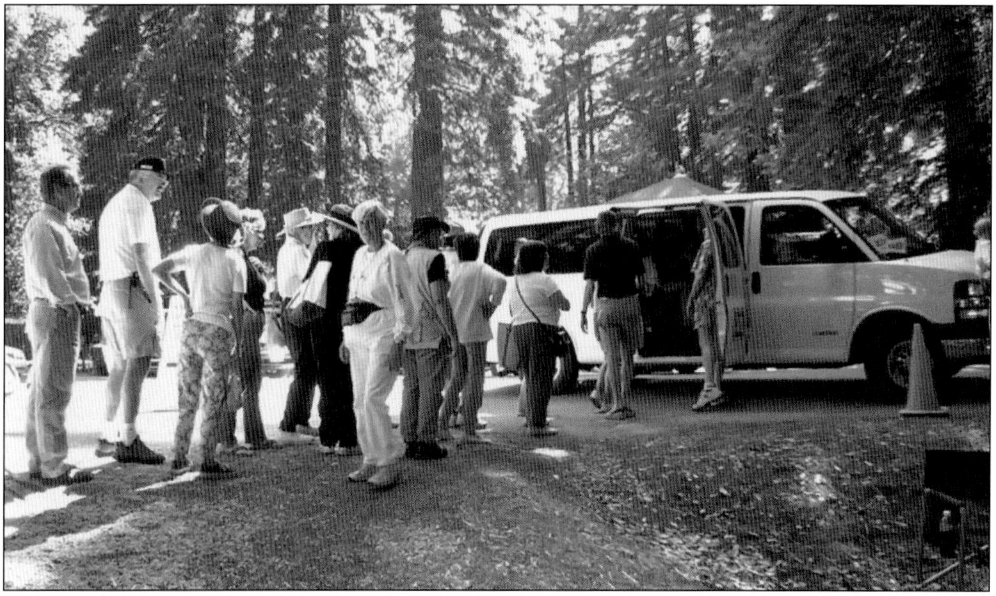

First, artists parked on land donated by the neighboring open space preserve. Then volunteers parked artists' cars after they unloaded their art. Then organizers rented 15-passenger vans. Now transportation chairs Chris Norling and Joe "Rocky" Rockmore hire motorized cable cars from San Francisco to shuttle artists and visitors between the fair and their cars from early morning to late afternoon. Riding the cars are volunteer hosts who welcome the public, hand out directories, and answer questions. (Courtesy Bill Goebner.)

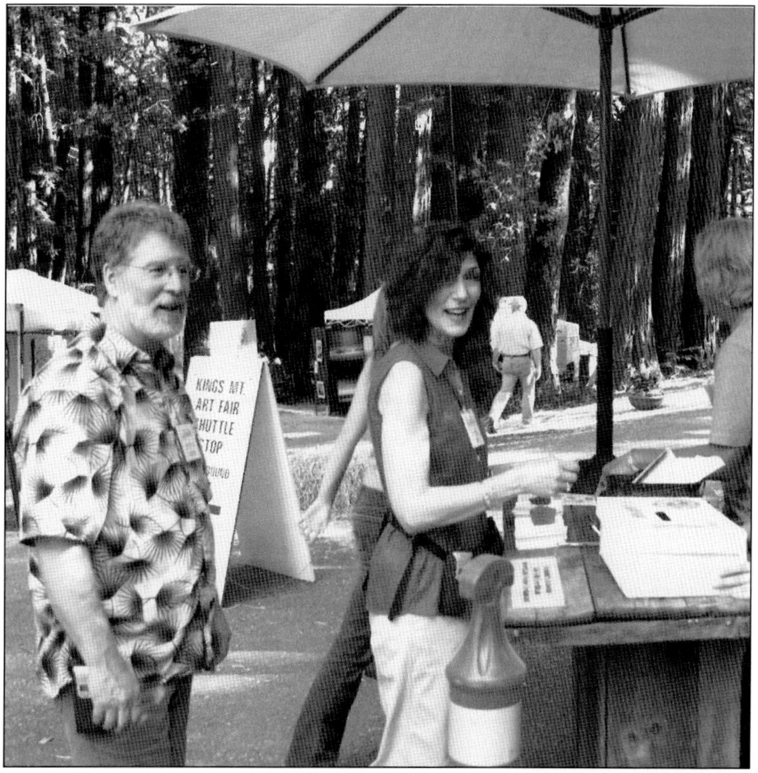

Working with her husband, Keith, information booth committee chair Bev Anderson structures the information booth to "make people feel as they would feel if they were guests in your home—they're guests in our forest," she says. It is a nerve center: 30-plus volunteers with walkie-talkies help find lost children, greet visitors, keep directories stocked, make sure the ATM is running, and maintain a lost-and-found. (Courtesy Bill Goebner.)

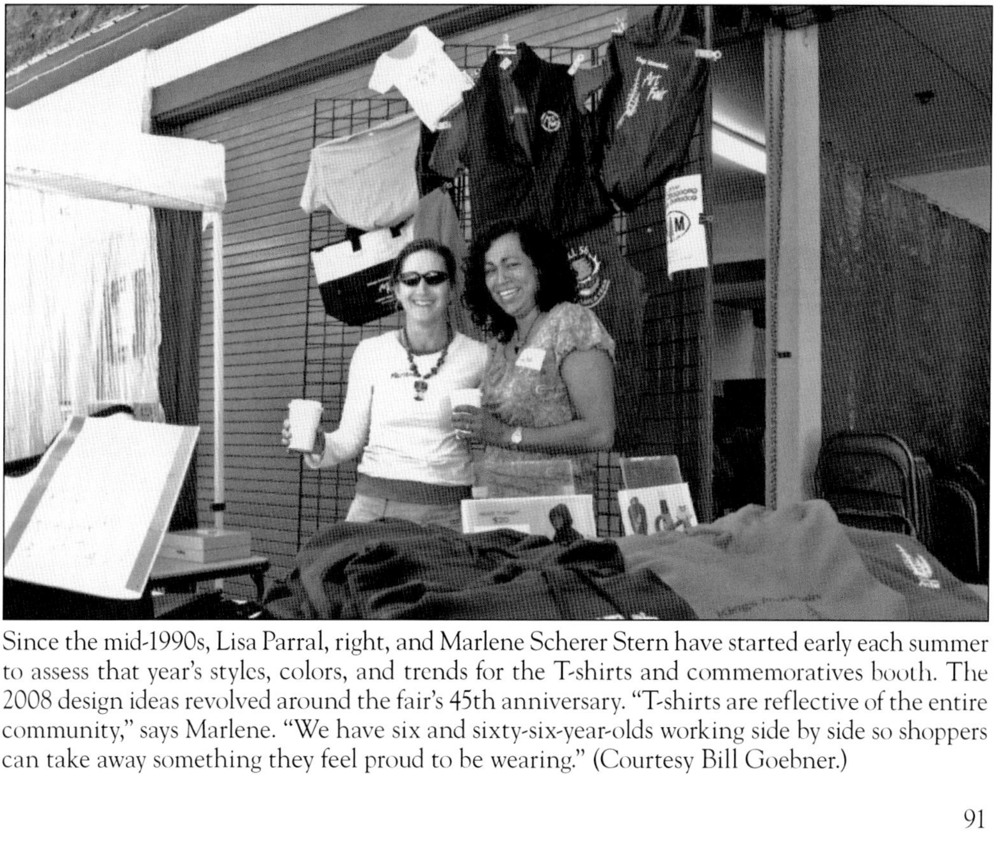

Since the mid-1990s, Lisa Parral, right, and Marlene Scherer Stern have started early each summer to assess that year's styles, colors, and trends for the T-shirts and commemoratives booth. The 2008 design ideas revolved around the fair's 45th anniversary. "T-shirts are reflective of the entire community," says Marlene. "We have six and sixty-six-year-olds working side by side so shoppers can take away something they feel proud to be wearing." (Courtesy Bill Goebner.)

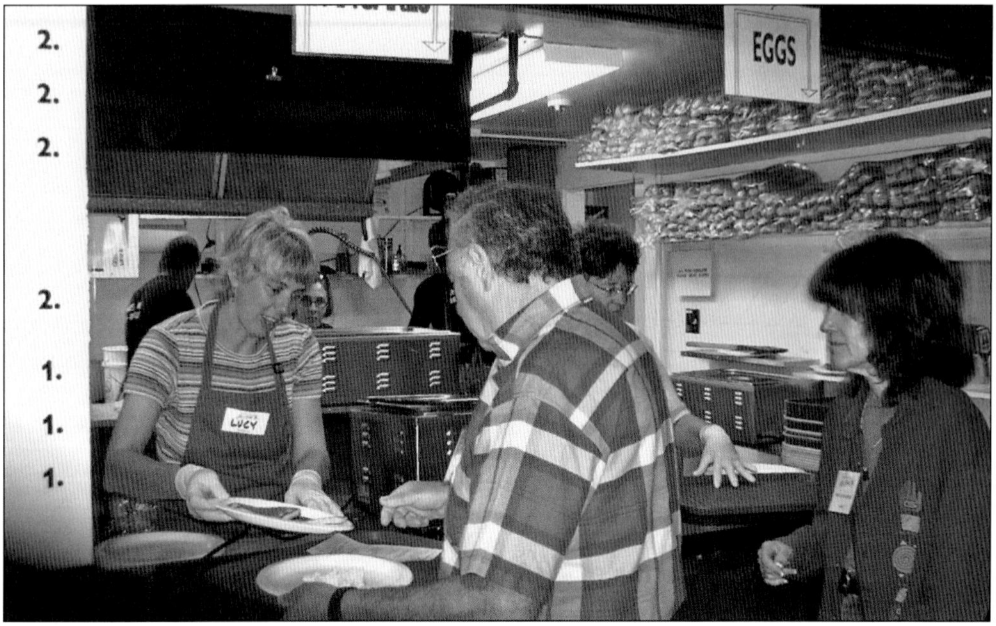

Colloquially called the "cook shack," now Grill 56 after the brigade's Engine 56, the food court calls for the largest pool of volunteers at the fair. More than 100 each day cover breakfast and lunch, processing orders and preparing food with friendly precision. For some, this is a chance to catch up with neighbors. "It's a huge social thing," says committee chair Cindy Phelps. (Courtesy Bill Goebner.)

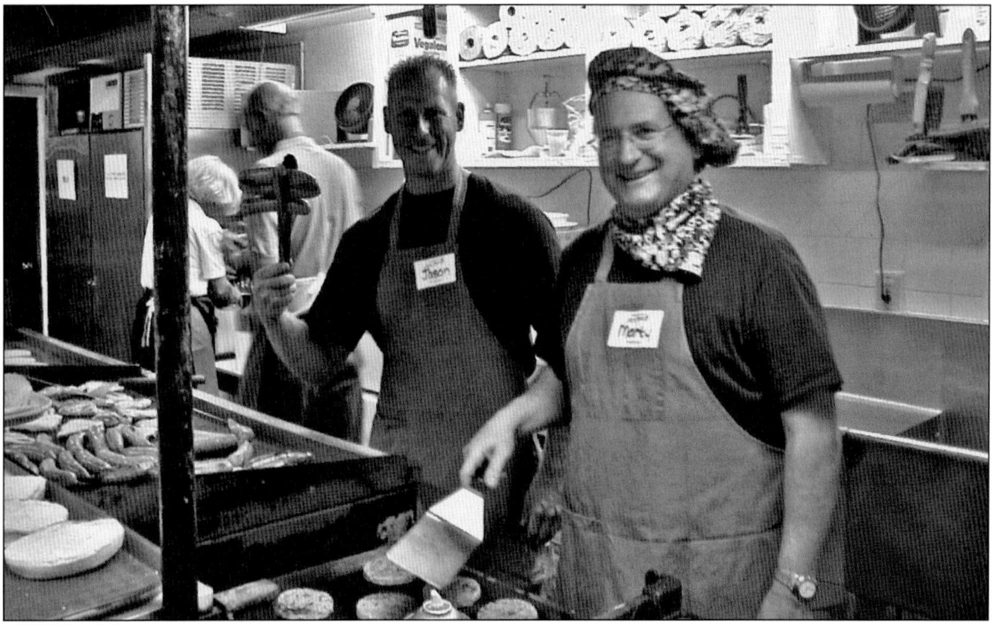

Civil litigation attorney and "cook shack" manager Martin Eisenberg, right, flips burgers like anyone else at Grill 56. He calls it a "sort of equalizer": its volunteers are everyday folks to a consultant with the Washington defense department. He also orders its food from the U.S. Food Service. "This is a community that supports itself," he says. "Volunteers built the building. Volunteers are on the fire brigade. You want to be a part of that." (Courtesy Bill Goebner.)

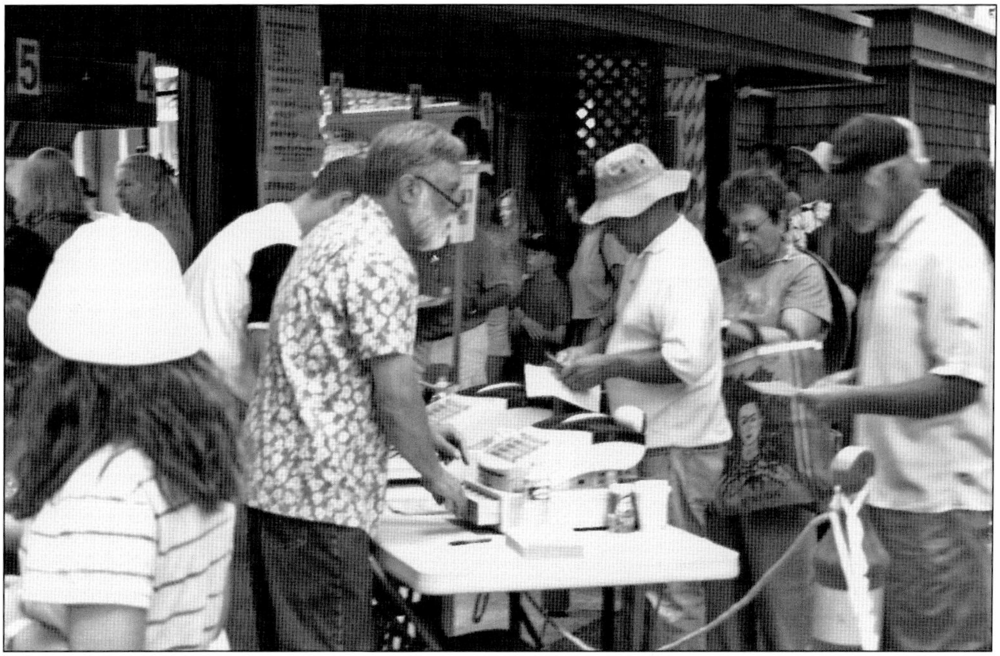

Volunteer jobs at Grill 56 start with order-takers who go down the lines to keep them moving to line monitors to cashiers to cooks—pancakes at breakfast, which is well-attended by the artists, burgers and chili for some 7,500 lunches each day—to those assembling sandwiches, busing tables, and washing trays. (Courtesy Bill Goebner.)

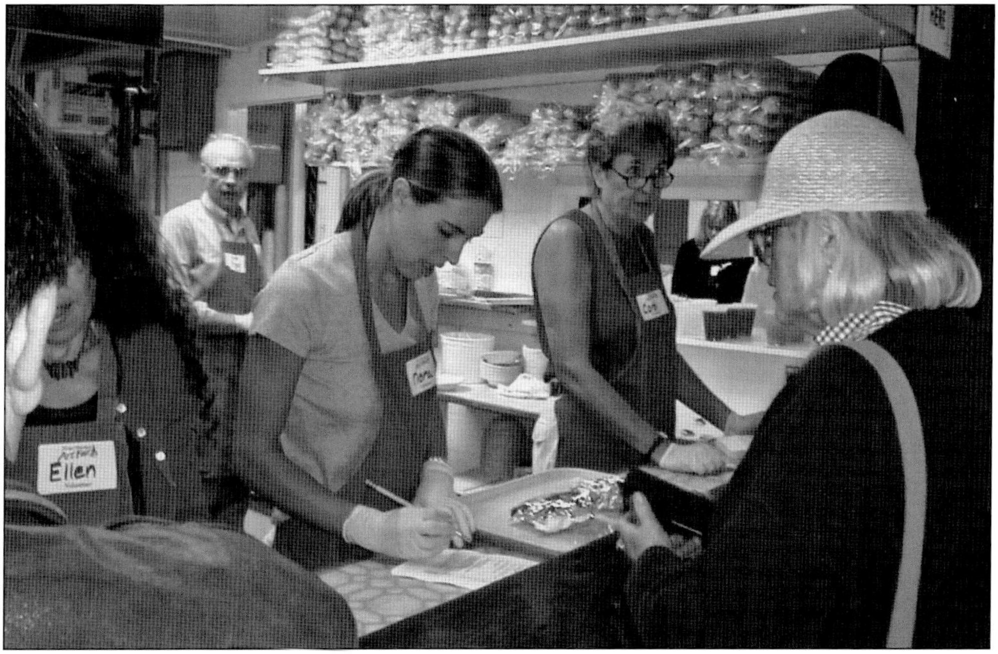

It is not unusual for volunteers to include residents' relatives and friends, former residents who visit to help onetime neighbors, and entire mountain families, such as the Culver family at the "cook shack": novelist Carol Culver (right), her husband, Craig, and daughter, Nora. (Courtesy Bill Goebner.)

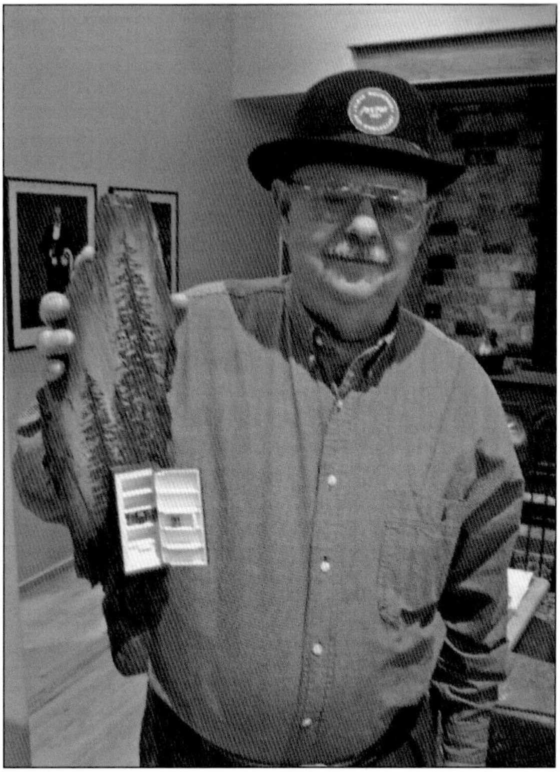

A member of the fair's board of directors since 1979, attorney Don Roesch lent his legal savvy to help the fair become a nonprofit in the early 1980s and channel proceeds to the school, community, and sustainability. In 1986, the board awarded him "Don's Golden Freezer" for his active role in getting freezer equipment donated and a freezer installed. (Courtesy the author.)

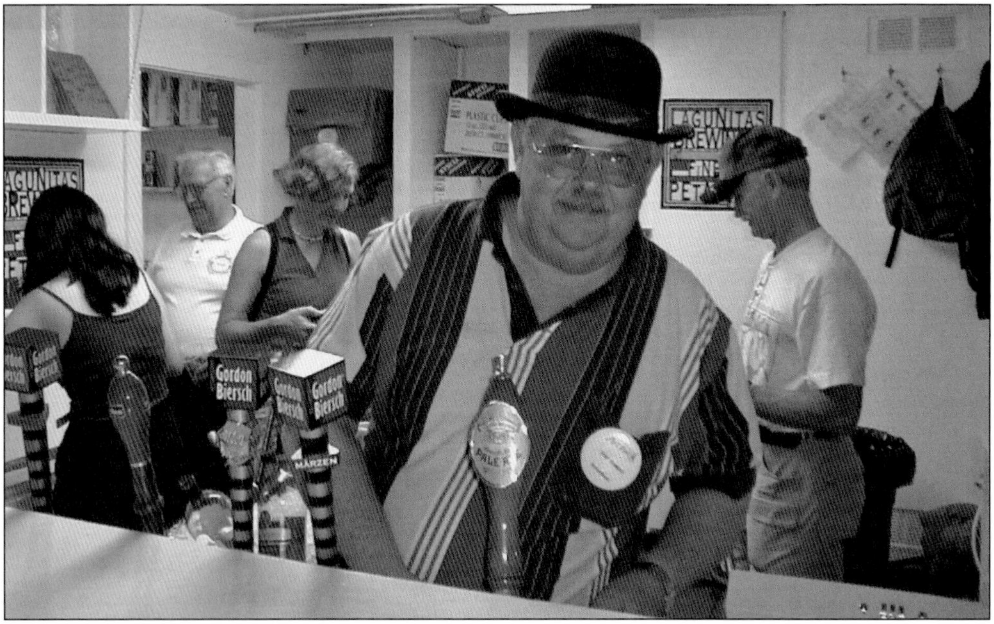

Aided by Dennis Ruby, who orders the wine, Don Roesch orders the beer, waters, and soft drinks for the two beverage booths, which require nearly 80 volunteers per weekend, and also oversees the 3,000-pound pallets of ice to keep beverages and food cool through the fair. He works in tandem with Grill 56 to have beverages waiting for food orders in what he calls "one of the most efficient food operations you'll ever see." (Courtesy Bill Goebner.)

Even the youngest mountain residents volunteer at the fair. Children as young as seven, like Rebecca (left) and Lauren, with helpful parents nearby, take seriously the task of busing the picnic tables outside the "cook shack." Teens socialize over washing trays behind the kitchen. "There's just a certain spirit," said one teen. (Courtesy Bill Goebner.)

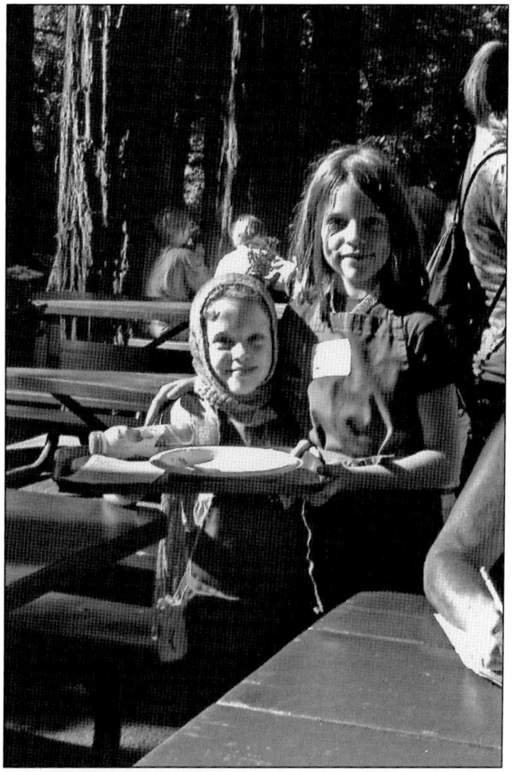

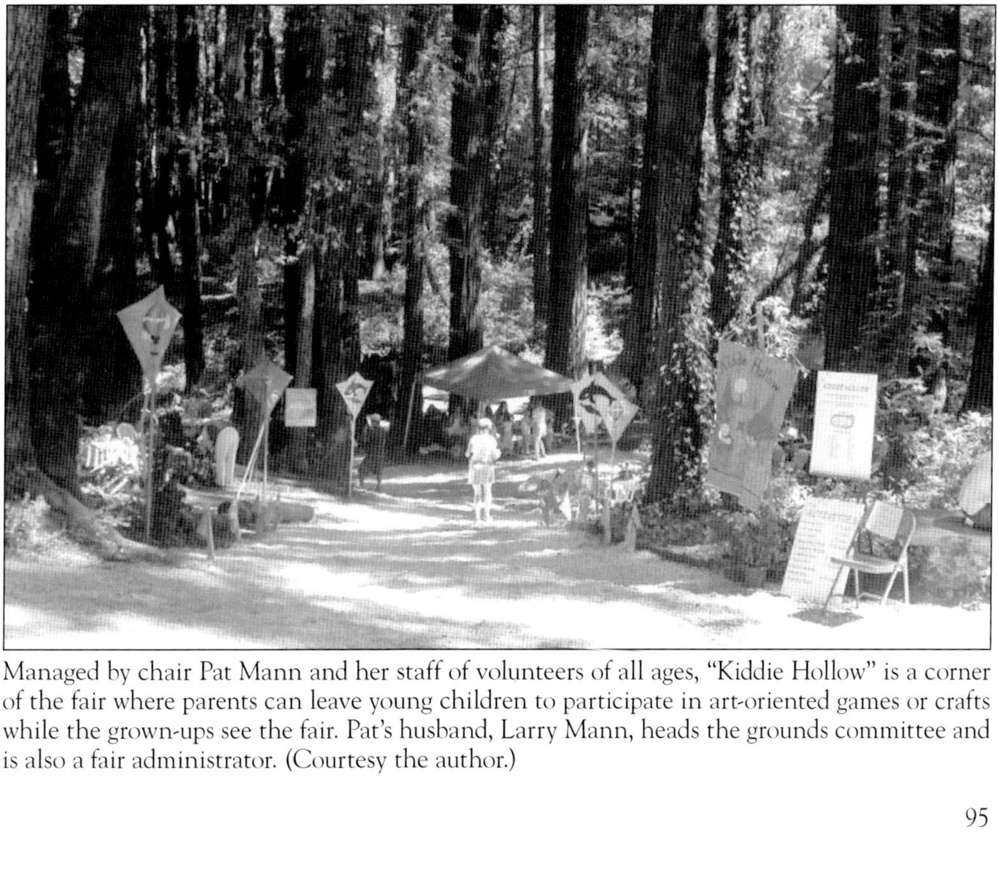

Managed by chair Pat Mann and her staff of volunteers of all ages, "Kiddie Hollow" is a corner of the fair where parents can leave young children to participate in art-oriented games or crafts while the grown-ups see the fair. Pat's husband, Larry Mann, heads the grounds committee and is also a fair administrator. (Courtesy the author.)

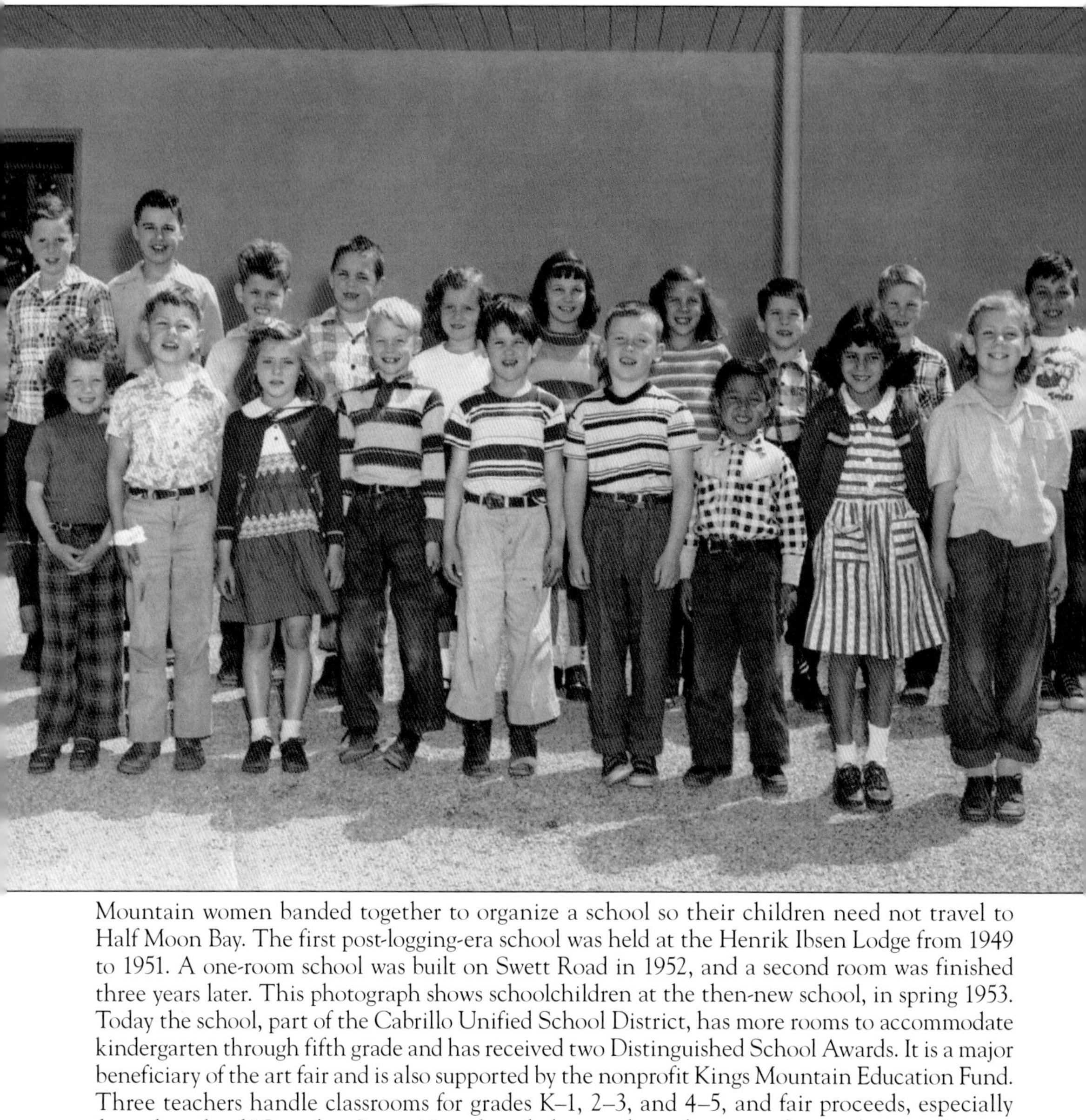

Mountain women banded together to organize a school so their children need not travel to Half Moon Bay. The first post-logging-era school was held at the Henrik Ibsen Lodge from 1949 to 1951. A one-room school was built on Swett Road in 1952, and a second room was finished three years later. This photograph shows schoolchildren at the then-new school, in spring 1953. Today the school, part of the Cabrillo Unified School District, has more rooms to accommodate kindergarten through fifth grade and has received two Distinguished School Awards. It is a major beneficiary of the art fair and is also supported by the nonprofit Kings Mountain Education Fund. Three teachers handle classrooms for grades K–1, 2–3, and 4–5, and fair proceeds, especially from the sale of "Grandma Jennie's" cookies, help round out the curriculum with art and music. (Courtesy Sue Bolton.)

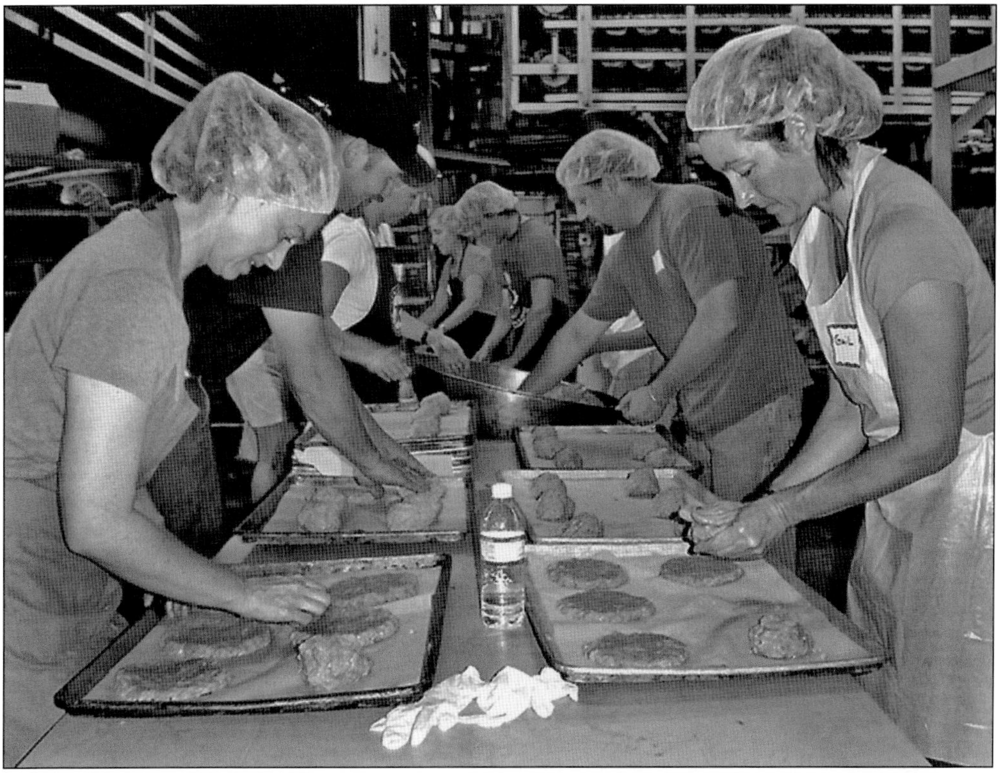

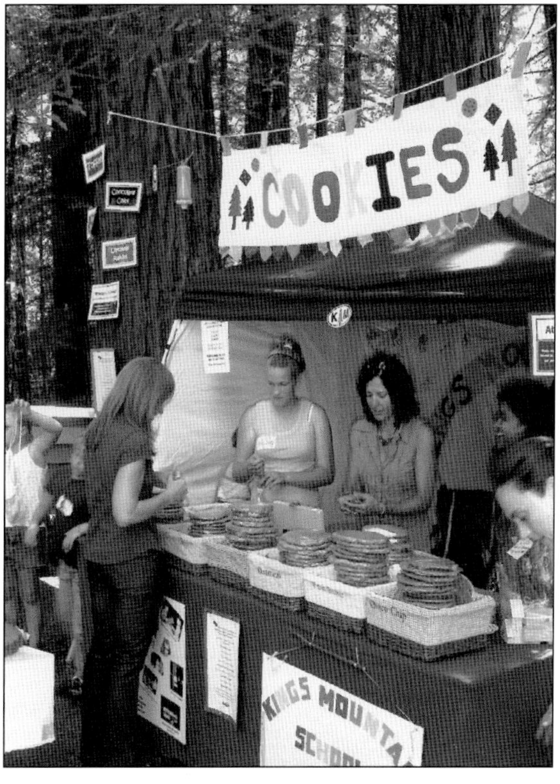

Above from left to right, mountain residents Teffaney Ebert, Shawn Moore, Gail Hanna, and Tom McLarty shape dough into "Grandma Jennie's" cookies to raise funds for the Kings Mountain Elementary School. There was a real Jennie, who had a knack for cookies. Each year, parents, relatives, and friends gather a week before the fair at Wedemeyer's Bakery in South San Francisco to use its industrial-size kitchens to turn hundreds of pounds of ingredients into more than 3,500 eight-inch chocolate chip, peanut butter, oatmeal, toffee crunch, and annual "mystery flavor" cookies. At right, volunteers run the fair's cookie booth. Children with parents travel through the fair all weekend, selling cookies from wagons to peckish browsers. Ninety percent of cookie proceeds fund the school's site director, special programs, and supplies. By midday Labor Day, the cookies are usually gone. (Above, courtesy the author/*Half Moon Bay Review*; right, courtesy the author.)

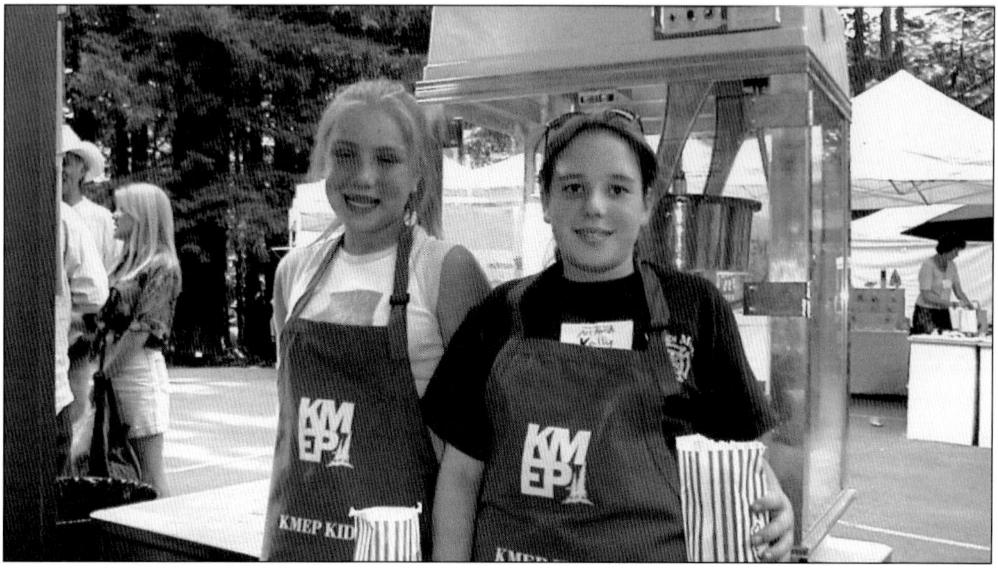

Children sell popcorn to raise money for Kings Mountain Emergency Preparedness, started in 1992 by Pat Wurster. It holds two community drills a year: in April, anniversary of the 1906 San Francisco earthquake, and October, anniversary of the 1989 Loma Prieta temblor. KMEP tends the community after fierce winter storms: the mountain is mapped into a grid covered by "area captains," who patrol after disasters or serious storms looking for colored placards residents hang on their doors. A green placard signals that everyone within is all right, a red one calls for help. (Courtesy Bill Goebner.)

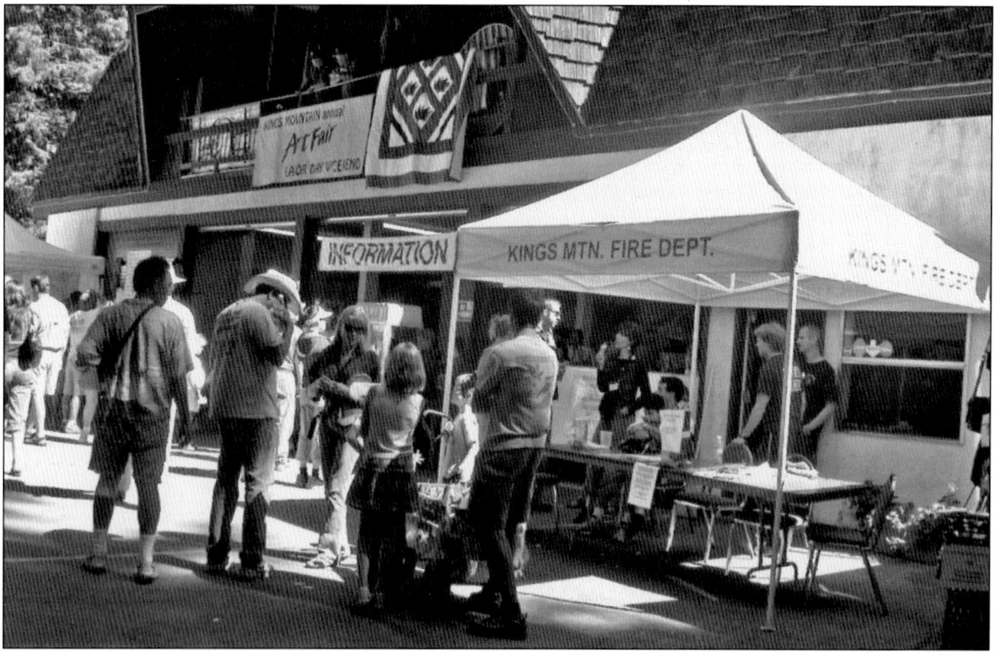

The 15 members of the Kings Mountain Volunteer Fire Brigade put in 250 hours of initial training, regular drills, and advanced training. The next-closest help is not close: "If there's a life-threatening emergency, or a fire, (help is) 15 minutes away," says fire chief Jim Sullivan. "When you call 911, it's comforting to know someone you know can help you." (Courtesy the author.)

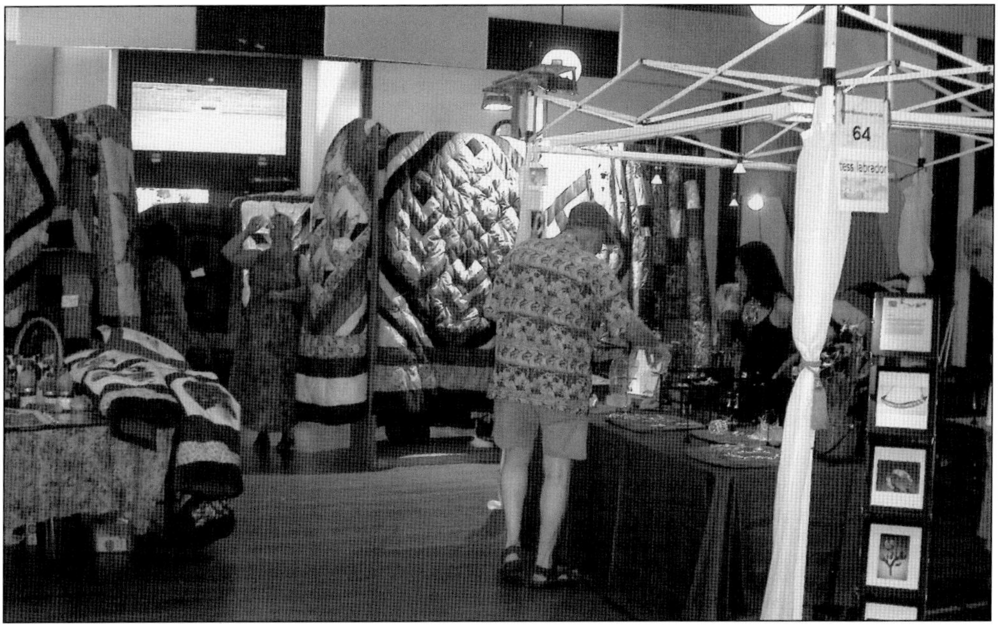

The interior of the community center, second floor, is used all year for meetings of the many special-interest groups like the book or gardening club, the Kings Mountain Association, Pilates or yoga classes, or holiday or social activities. At the fair, it is used to display professional art: high-quality, colorful quilts and thick comforters, fine jewelry, or exquisite clothing. Even the balcony is used to display fine jewelry or ceramic art. (Courtesy the author.)

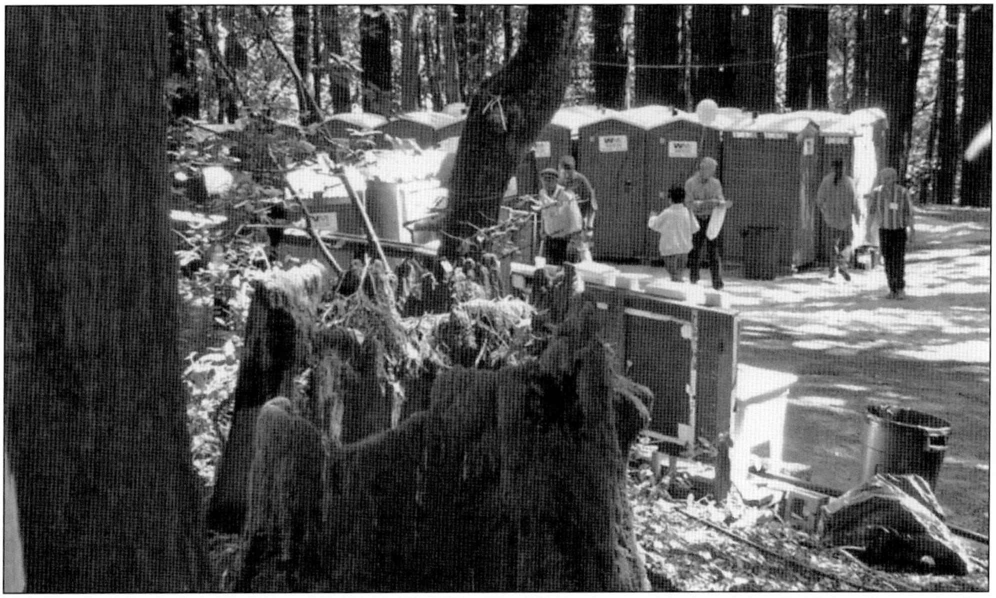

Even portable toilets—whimsically dubbed "biffies" by some participants—look aesthetic at the fair. Volunteers monitor the grounds, spreading sawdust and posting signs, and longtime volunteers Sherri Fisher, Carrie German, and Michele Wilson map out professional artists' booths according to their needs. "Everyone in the community and their friends come together to do something to raise money for our fire department which doesn't get federal money," says Wilson. "People love the fair and what it's doing." (Courtesy Bill Goebner.)

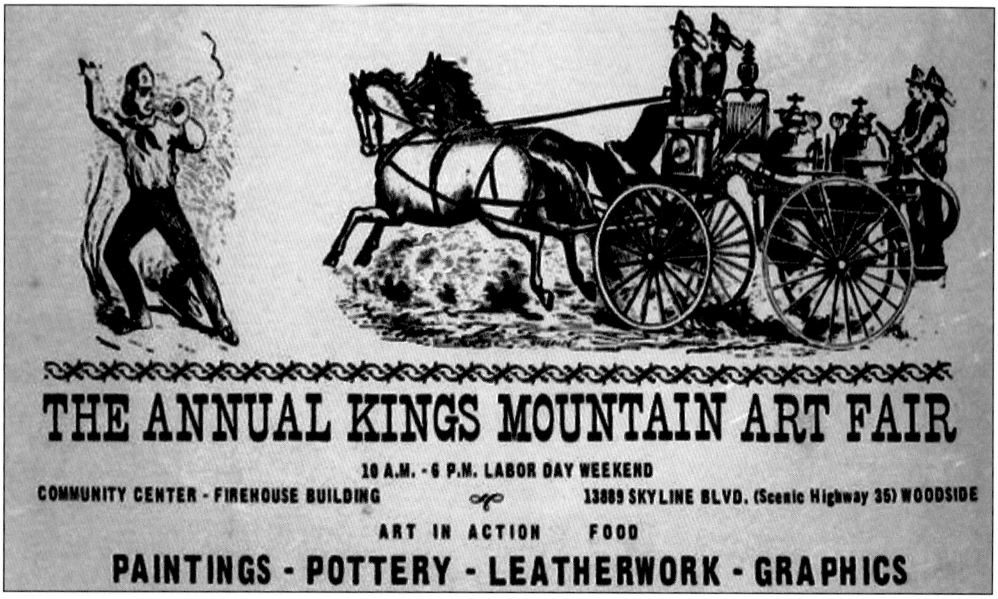

Well before the fair, a publicity committee gets word out to community and regional newspapers, television, radio, the Internet, and the AAA magazine. Volunteers post signs and posters, like this one *c.* mid-1970s, on major roadways like Skyline Boulevard, Highway 92, and arteries into Woodside and Portola Valley. The committee has four organizers and about 20 others working under them. (Courtesy Bill Goebner.)

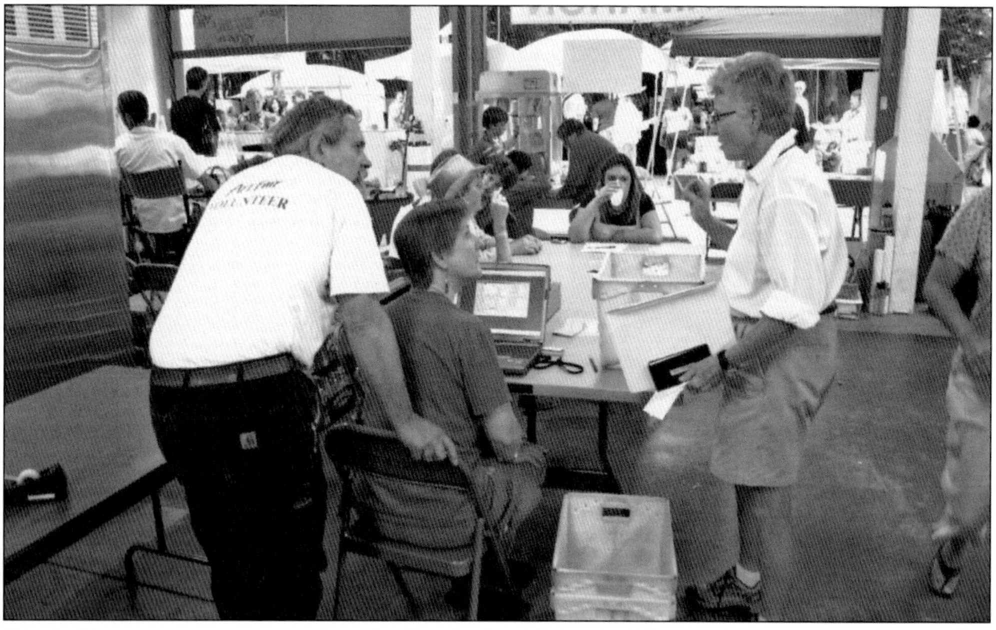

Carrie German, center, started at the "cook shack" but in 20 years became an indispensable administrator, handling paperwork for an artist. Her husband, Tim, left, is also active in multiple volunteer tasks. She brushes aside accolades, preferring to focus on the community. "It amazes me how every year it comes together and goes so smoothly, like oiled clockwork," she says. "This community is what makes Kings Mountain, Kings Mountain. It's what holds us together." (Courtesy Bill Goebner.)

Eight

Treetop Talent
Mountain Folk Artists

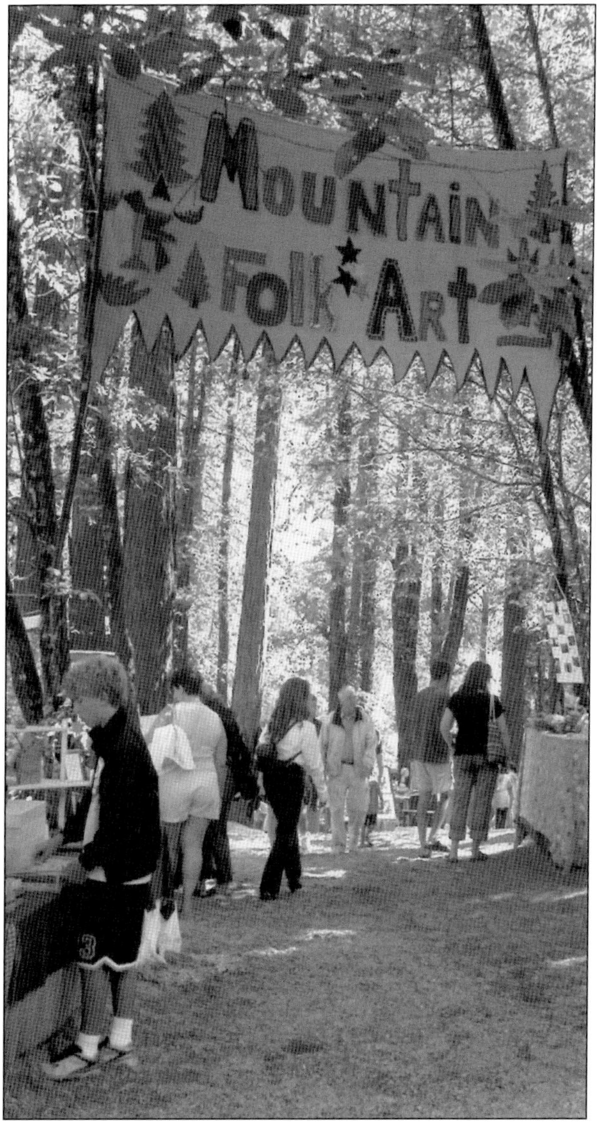

High-end fine art and highest-quality crafts define and drive the Kings Mountain Art Fair. One hundred and thirty-five professional artists from the Western states and beyond make up the professional complement, and each returns 15 percent of his/her profits to the board of Kings Mountain Art Fair, Inc. The artists apply by late January and are juried in February by a strictly anonymous panel of arts professionals who do not live on the mountain. One corner of the fair houses the local Mountain Folk artists, some of whom are professional artists and who display high-quality paintings, sculpture, and fine crafts. Mountain Folk artists must live within the volunteer brigade's call area (Highway 92 to Bear Gulch West and one-and-a-half miles off Skyline Boulevard in both directions), register, pay a nominal fee, and hand over 10 percent of profits to the fair. Some longtime Mountain Folk artists who have moved off the mountain are grandfathered in, and their artistic grown children who live elsewhere have a four-year grace period to participate. Mountain Folk organizer Deb Rockmore, with her natural-stone and freshwater-pearl Design 23 jewelry, says, "I like the feeling of local artists having a place to show their stuff. Community's gotta be our middle name." (Courtesy the author.)

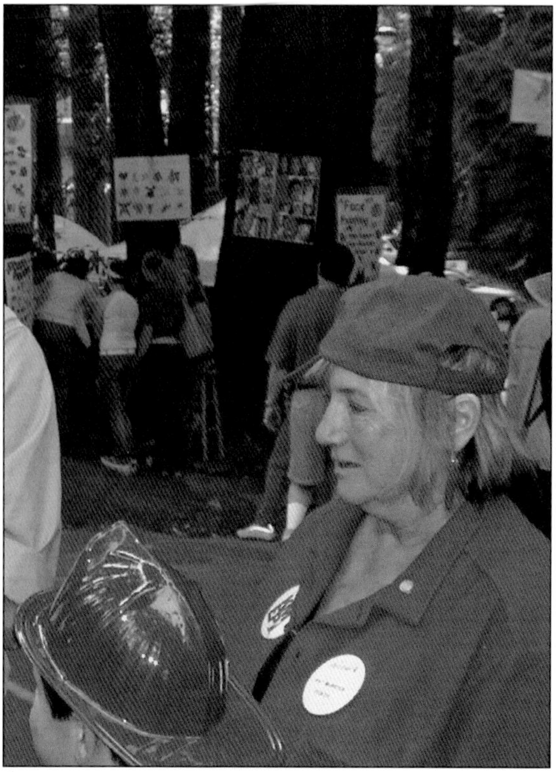

Artists' registration chair Pat Wurster prepares information packets and tally sheets for the artists, a task she enjoys because "I get to meet every single artist." She is not the only one who benefits from the mountain community's awareness of the value of the artists: "I hear over and over how (the artists) love the redwoods and the support they get from the community. They say they don't see that anywhere else." (Courtesy Bill Goebner.)

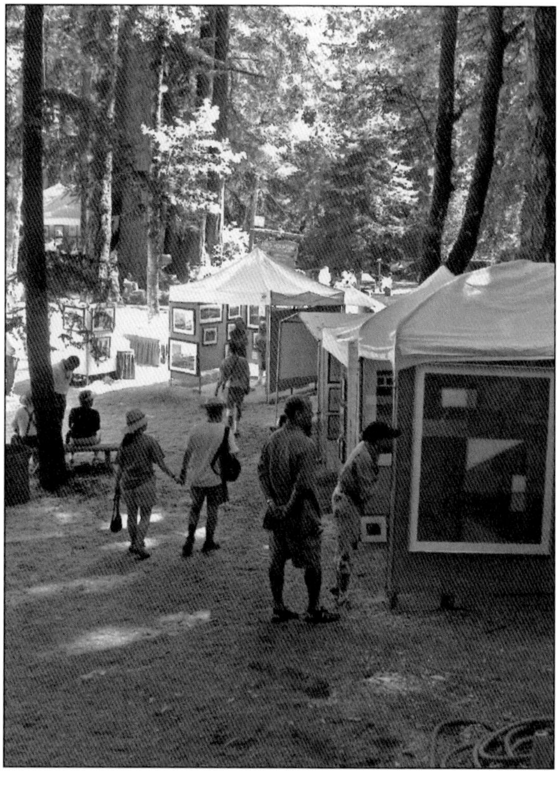

Roaming the fair are volunteers wearing distinctive aprons, easily recognizable as "booth sitters," who tend booths like these when artists need to step out or who get lunch for them. Chair Linda Schweitzer, who organizes the 35 to 40 volunteers—five to six per two-hour shifts—with Tish Strother, says the consideration makes the artists feel special. "This fair is so different in the way we treat them," she said. "They say it's such a community feeling." (Courtesy the author.)

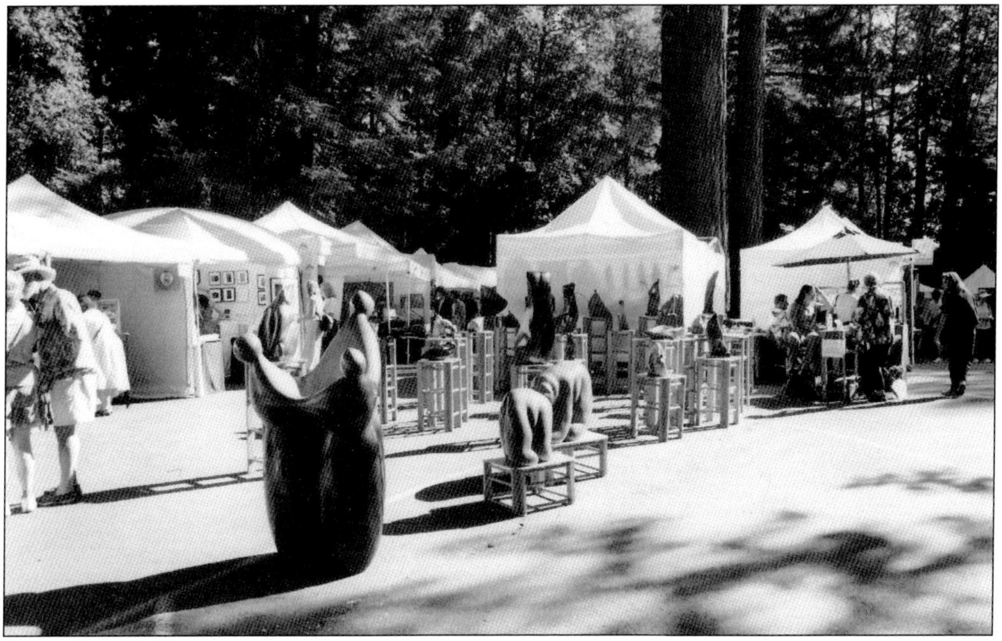

Sharon Spencer of Washington State left a career as a high school physical education and science teacher to follow her heart into art. She has shown her bronze and marble sculptures, which command prices of $450 to $30,000, at the fair since 1975. She says, "The whole reason I do this show is the wonderful philosophy behind it."

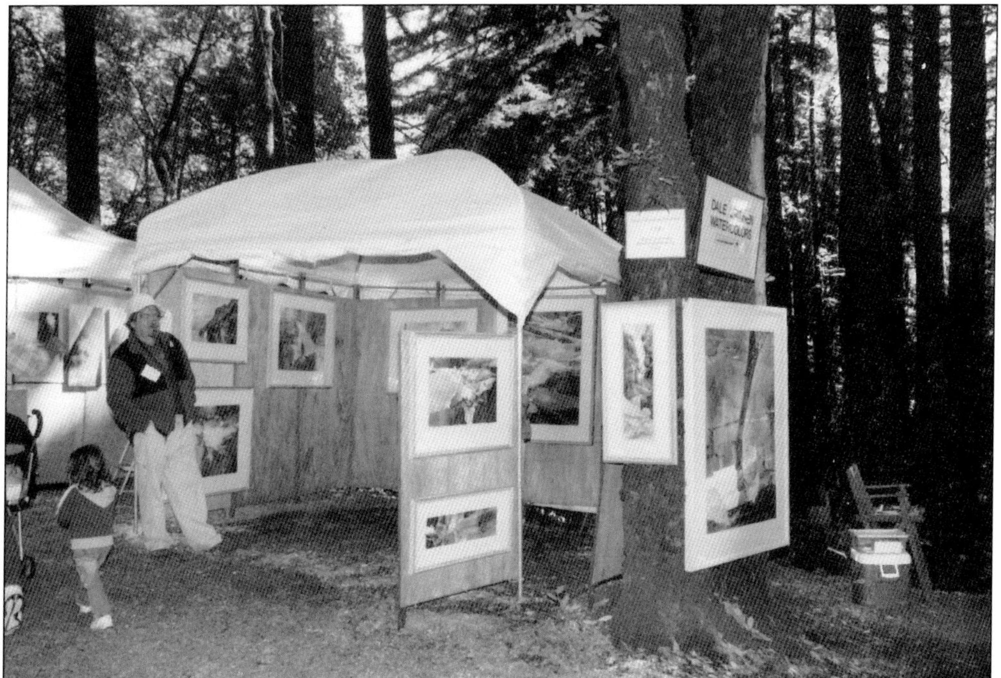

Fine artist Dale Laitinen of California's gold country says the fair is "the one show I am always excited to come to every year. There's such nice people, atmosphere, sense of community." His landscapes and abstract watercolor paintings draw from $575 to $4,500.

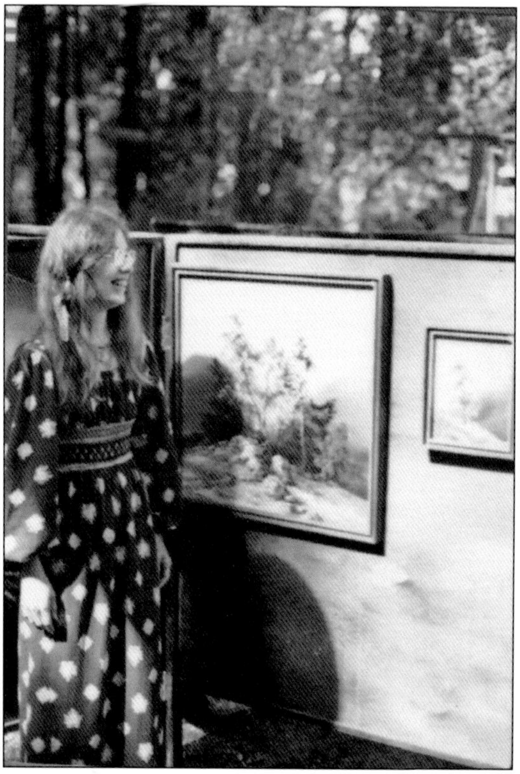

Mountain Folk matriarch Rebecca Holland has shown her oil paintings of stately redwoods, idyllic landscapes, tossing seascapes, or rustic buildings in every art fair except one. When she moved halfway down the mountain after 35 years there, she was "grandmothered" into the Mountain Folk Art. She has painted since age nine, preferring thin brushes to thick ones because "I was seeing in detail." Her work has gone into Western galleries, offices, and private collections, and her early "rock art" went into posters, publicity art, or T-shirts for rock musicians. Mountain Folk, she said, "maintains the personality of the community. It's the best reflection of why we were there." (Left, courtesy Ardyth Woodruff; below, courtesy the author.)

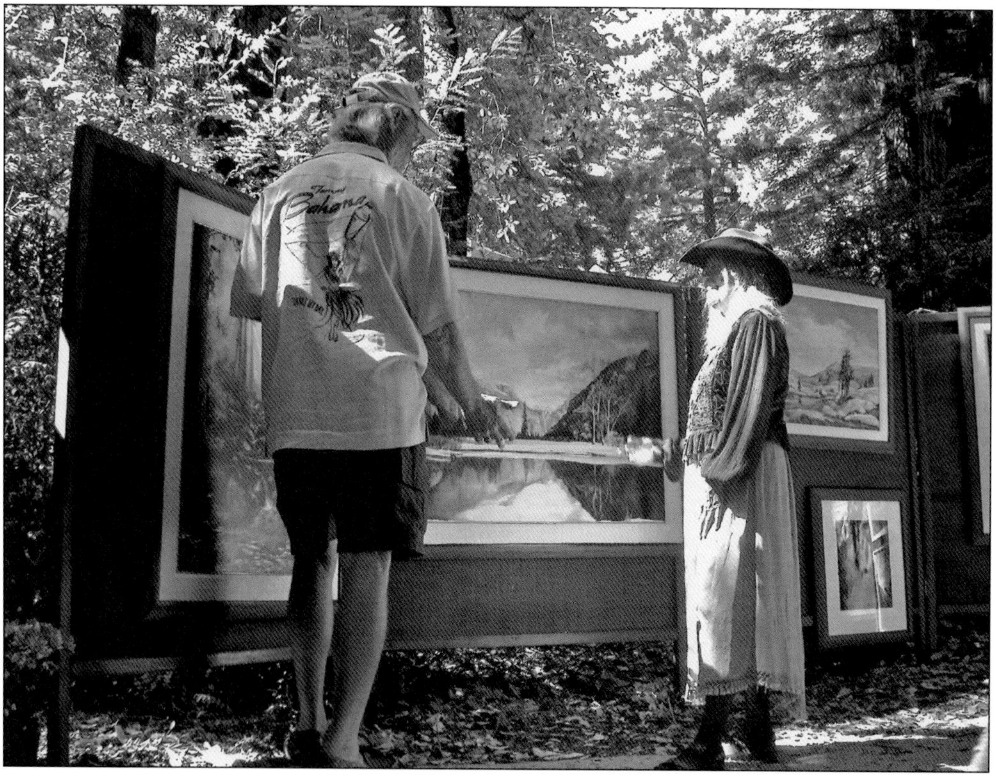

Renate Hettrich envisioned a family business around her colorful, intertwined candles, but her children wanted nothing to do with chain stores. "Everything looked alike. They said it was too boring—not as creative," says Renate. So for more than 10 years, she stuck with small stores and the fair to sell her candles. The children help her shape, tint, and arrange them. "It's much more creative." (Courtesy the author.)

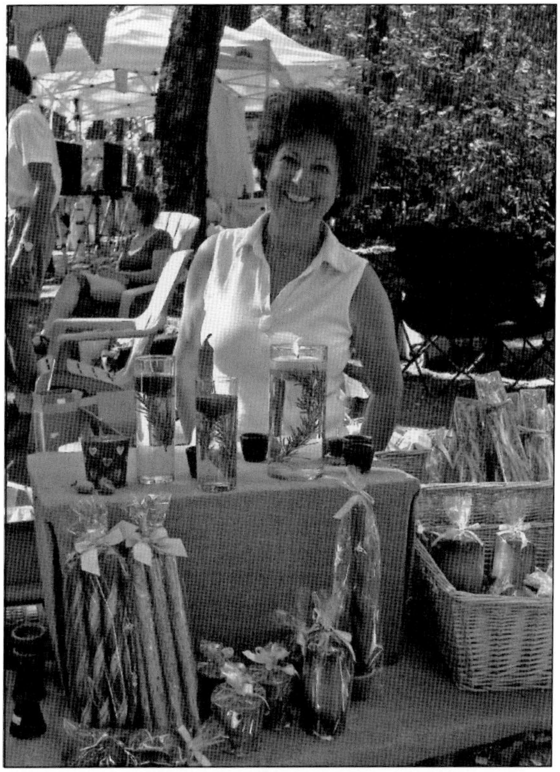

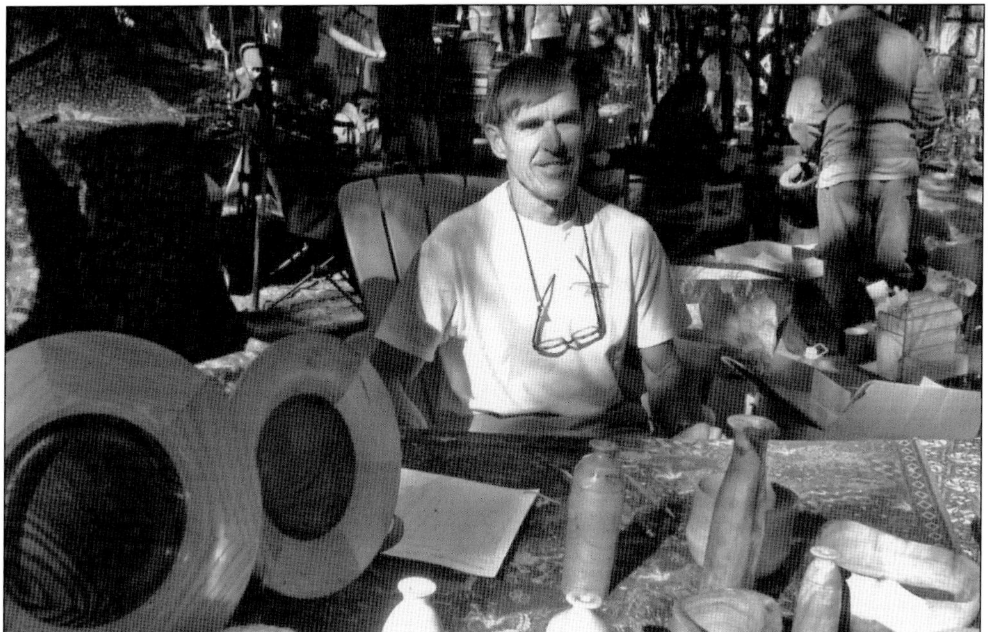

Woodworking was just a hobby for 35-year mountain resident Gene Frantz, but after retiring from representing clothing lines, he found a downed madrone tree and made his first turned-wood creation. Now, using only found birch, alder, or walnut, he creates bowls, candleholders, or vases. For him, he says, the fun part is turning the wood. (Courtesy the author.)

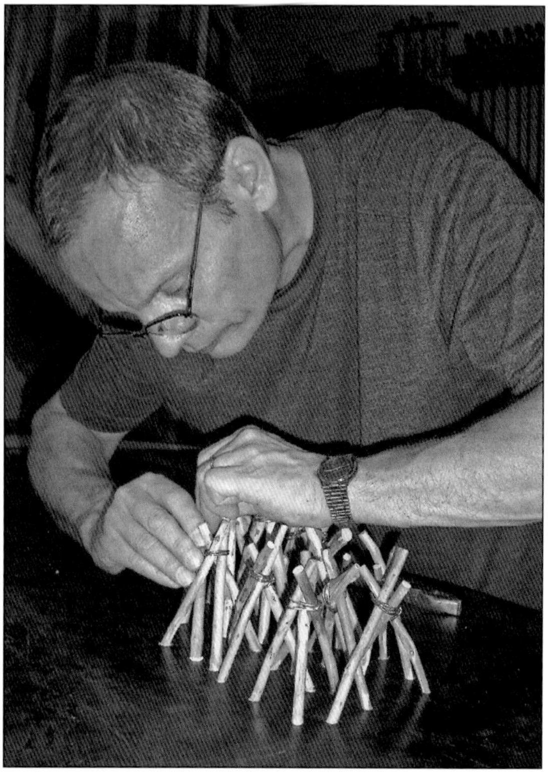

A Kings Mountain resident since 1997 and a native of Gelsenkichen, Germany, Werner Glinka creates "urban totems": contemporary, upscale, three-dimensional wall sculptures using found natural or man-made objects "where I can explore three-dimensionality. Texture is something that I use everywhere." He says, "The real thing about the mountain is the community. That's the whole idea of the art fair." Here he fits redwood twigs into one-third of a triptych. (Courtesy the author.)

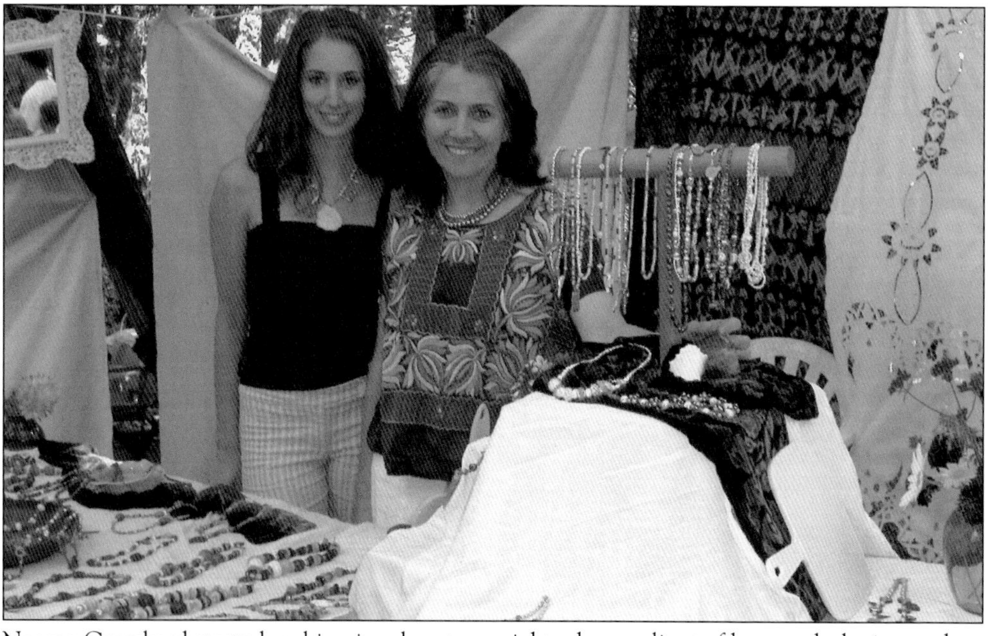

Naama Grossbard started making jewelry at age eight when a client of her psychologist mother, Francoise Bourzat, traded a session for beads for little Naama to play with. "I started stringing them randomly," she says, "and my parents got me a booth at the fair." After selling $300 worth of jewelry, "I realized this was a good gig." Now mother and daughter share a booth. (Courtesy the author.)

Since 1990, Clovis professional artist William Livingston refuses to sell his fine, salvaged-wood handmade furniture, commanding four figures per piece, anywhere but the Kings Mountain fair. His customers are just as loyal: one saved pocket change for 10 years to buy a rocking chair. When Livingston later asked the customer if he had regrets about the purchase, Livingston said, he "only had one: that he didn't do it ten years ago. I sell happiness. It changes people's lives." (Courtesy the author.)

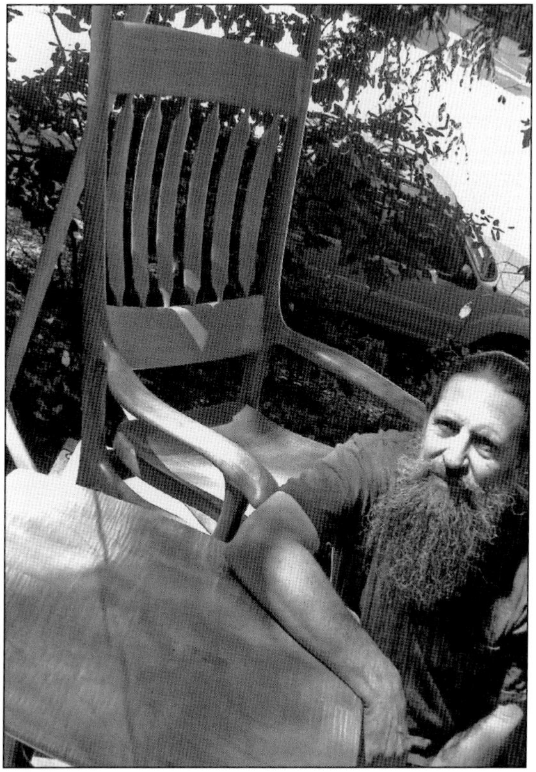

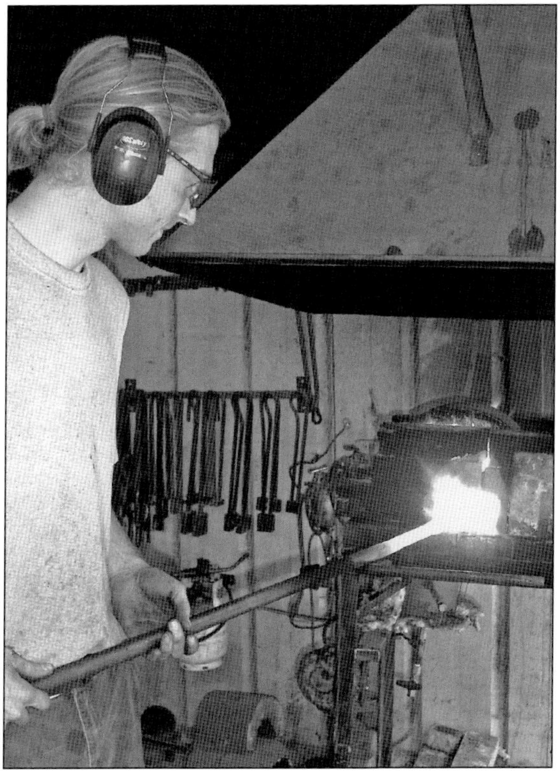

"On a hot summer day, I go and light a fire. I think I'm crazy sometimes," says 20-something blacksmith Erik Newquist, who made his own tools and forge, which runs on vegetable oil. "Hooked" at 16 by his blacksmith uncle, he studied at the Penland School of Crafts in North Carolina. He fires up his forge to 2,200 degrees to craft candlesticks, hooks, garden gates, stair rails, patio furniture, or curtain rods for home or business. "It wasn't like I made the choice. It chose me," he said. (Courtesy the author.)

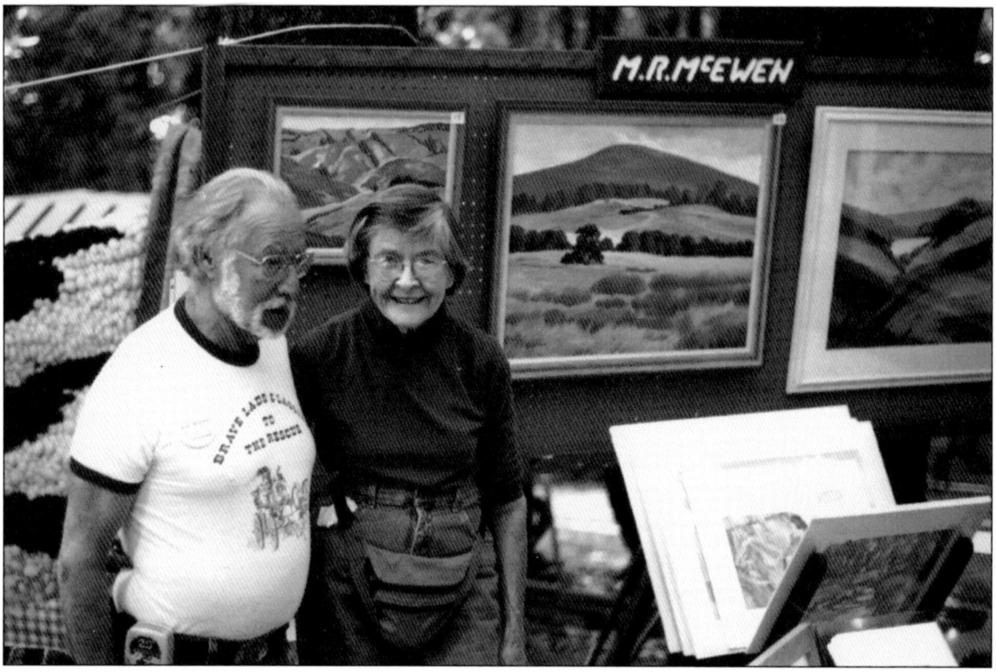

Marjorie "Midge" McEwen showed her pastels, watercolors, and original silk screens at the art fair from 1963 until 2004. Her husband, Bob, made the display boards that formed her booth. Their son Robert (below), who calls Kings Mountain "a wonderful place to grow up," swept out the barn for the first fair. Now a Belmont resident, he is grandfathered into Mountain Folk with handmade wood games like checkers, penny hockey, or jump-the-pegs. "I come back every year to see who's here," he said. "That's what makes it unique." (Above, courtesy Midge McEwen; below, courtesy the author.)

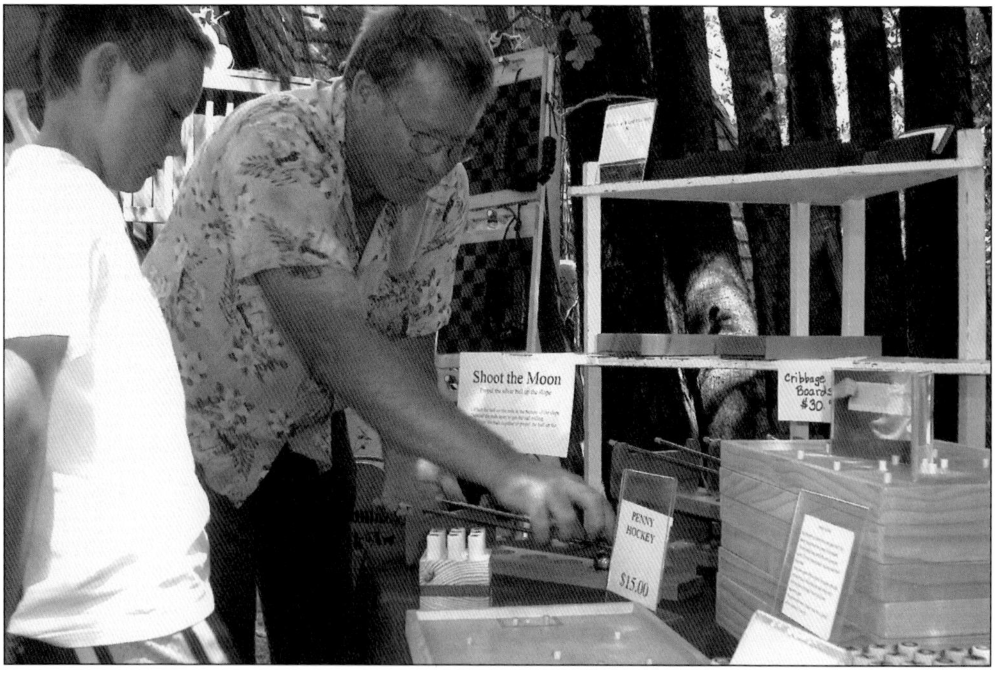

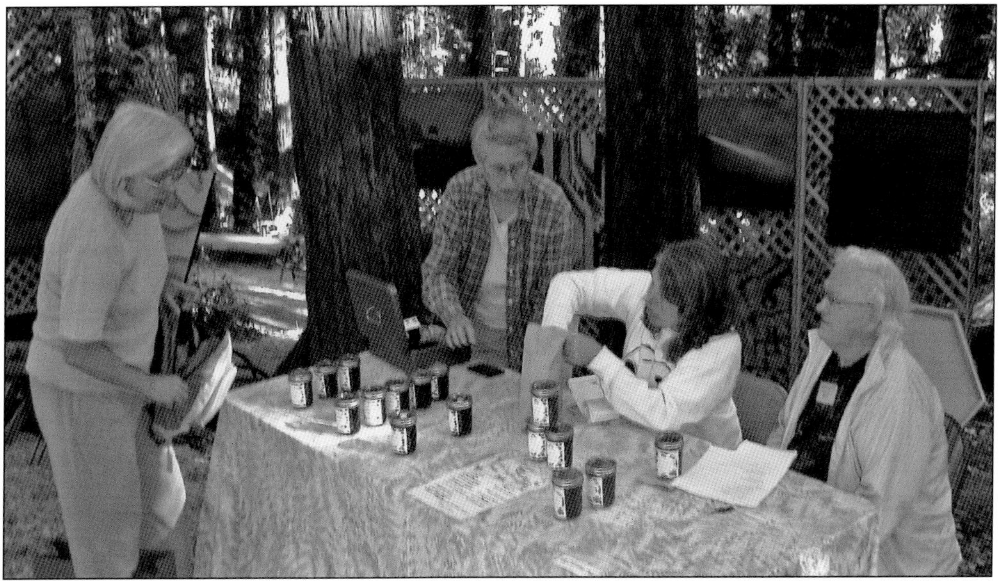

In the early 1970s, Beverly Oaks's 4-H group wanted to show homemade jams and jellies at the fair, and soon her daughters Virginia, Patricia, and Marilyn and husband, Norman, joined her. The family grows the fruit on their mountain farm and spends the winter making Bewitching Blackberry, Magic Mint, Perky Plum, and Laudable Loganberry only for the fair. (Courtesy the author.)

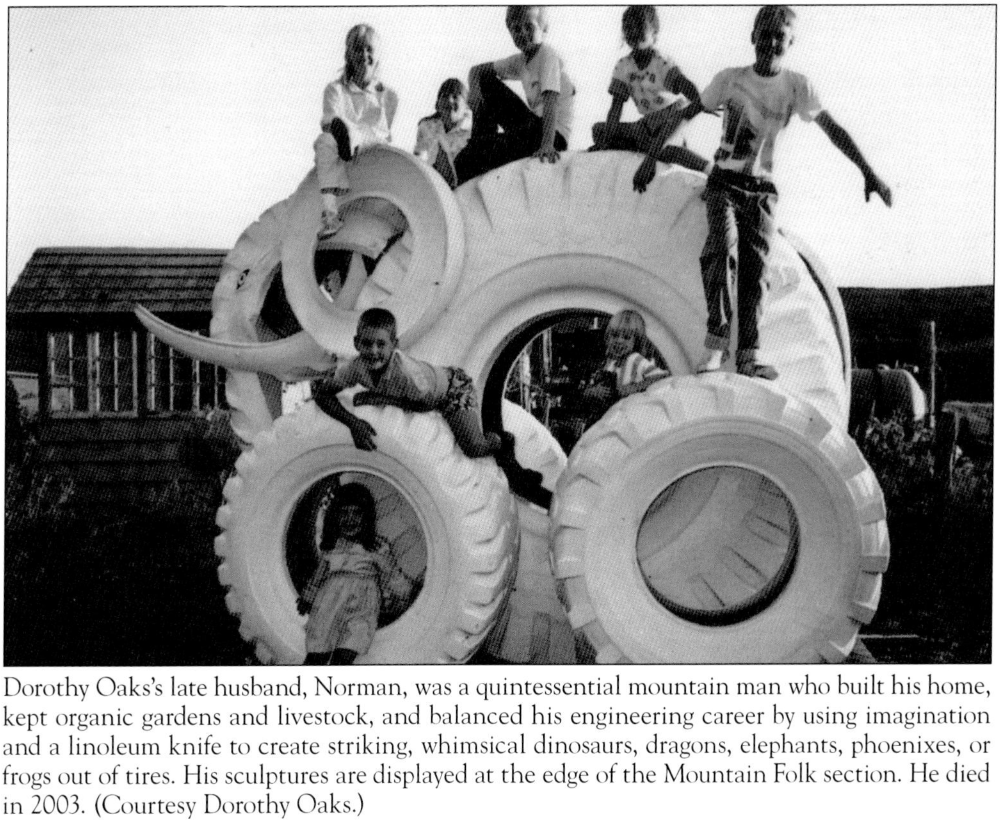

Dorothy Oaks's late husband, Norman, was a quintessential mountain man who built his home, kept organic gardens and livestock, and balanced his engineering career by using imagination and a linoleum knife to create striking, whimsical dinosaurs, dragons, elephants, phoenixes, or frogs out of tires. His sculptures are displayed at the edge of the Mountain Folk section. He died in 2003. (Courtesy Dorothy Oaks.)

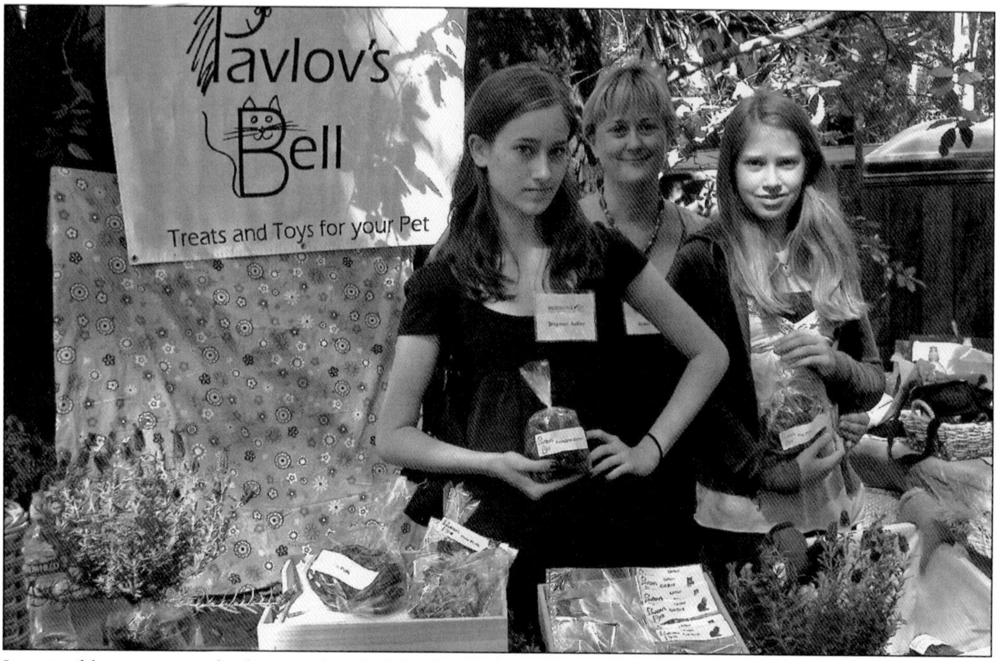

Inspired by an aunt, the homeschooled Anker kids make seafood treats for dogs, molasses or alfalfa treats for horses, and colorful cat or dog toys and sell them with help from their dad, Andrew, and brother Zachary. "We even get along," says Dagmar, left. Everything possible is organic, says mom Renee, and the family sews the toys to last. (Courtesy the author.)

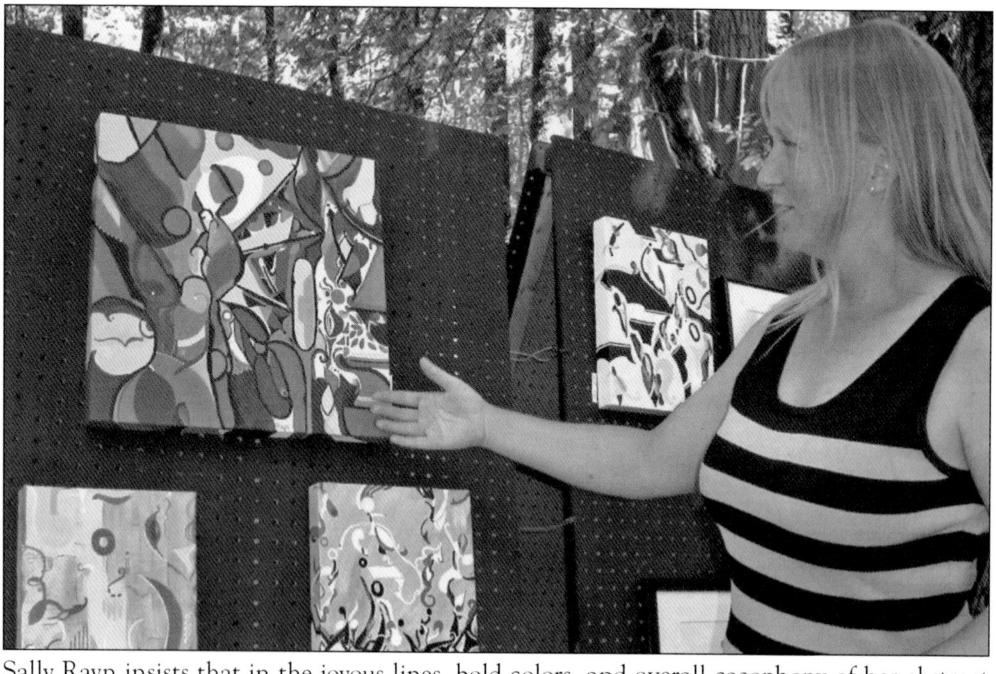

Sally Rayn insists that in the joyous lines, bold colors, and overall cacophony of her abstract paintings, she strives for balance. People see in her art what they will. "Different people from different cultures see different pictures," says the fifth-grade teacher, who also puts wild color and free-flowing lines into her decorative candles. (Courtesy the author.)

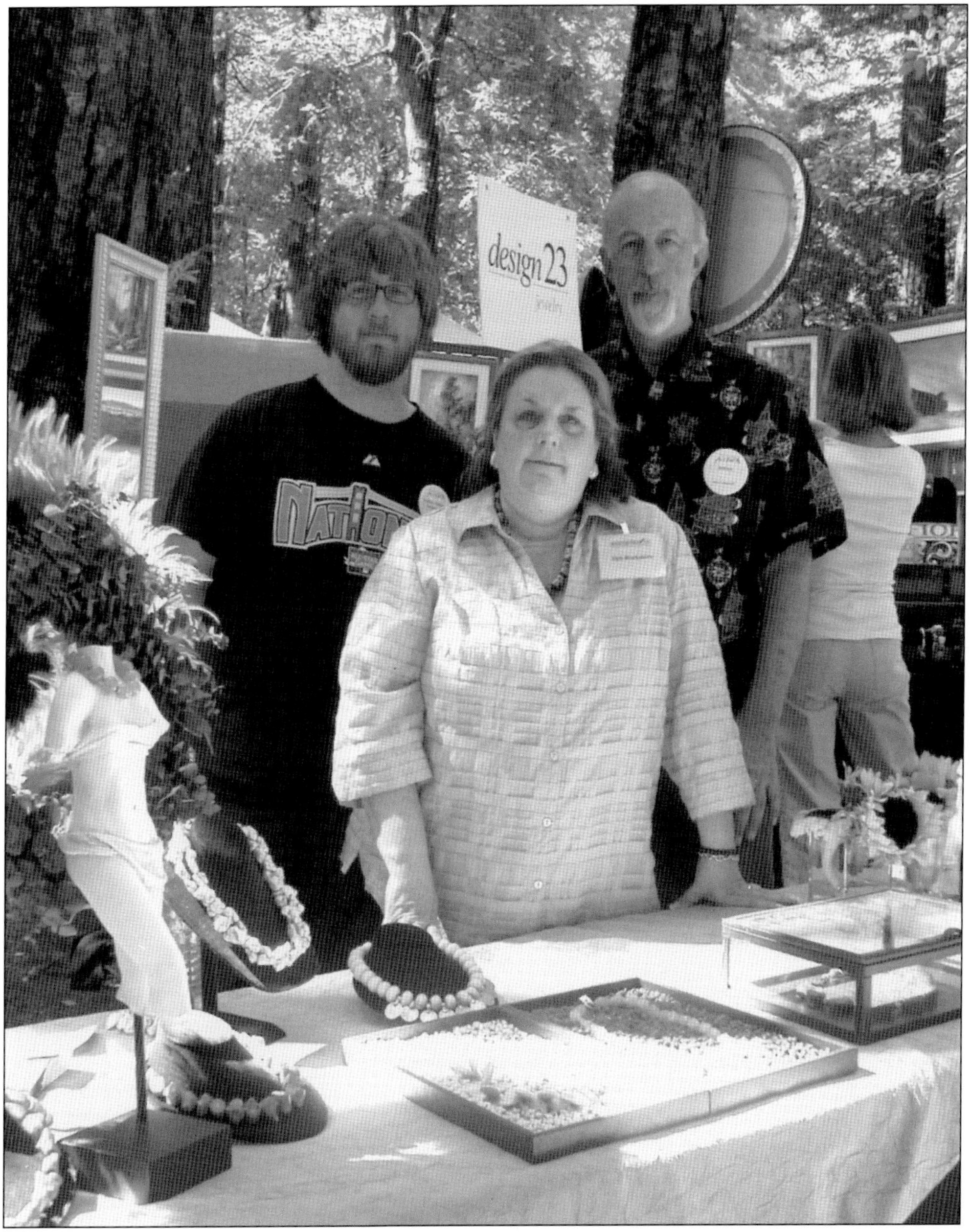

Joe "Rocky" Rockmore told his wife, Deb, about the art fair when they were dating, and since their 1985 wedding, the whole family has been involved. Joe, retired after 29 years with the volunteer Kings Mountain Fire Brigade, is half-owner of an information technology consulting company working largely for the federal government, and is a hands-off leader as he books, organizes, and runs the fair's shuttles. Son Logan has updated information as the fair's Webmaster since he was 10, and daughter Casey is a tireless helper. Deb has run the fair's Mountain Folk Art section since 1991. "Kings Mountain has plenty of artists tucked away off Skyline Boulevard," says Deb, who also sells her own Design 23 beaded and natural-stones jewelry with Mountain Folk. "I've been here 30 years," Joe says of the fair. "What higher recommendation can you give a community?" (Courtesy the author.)

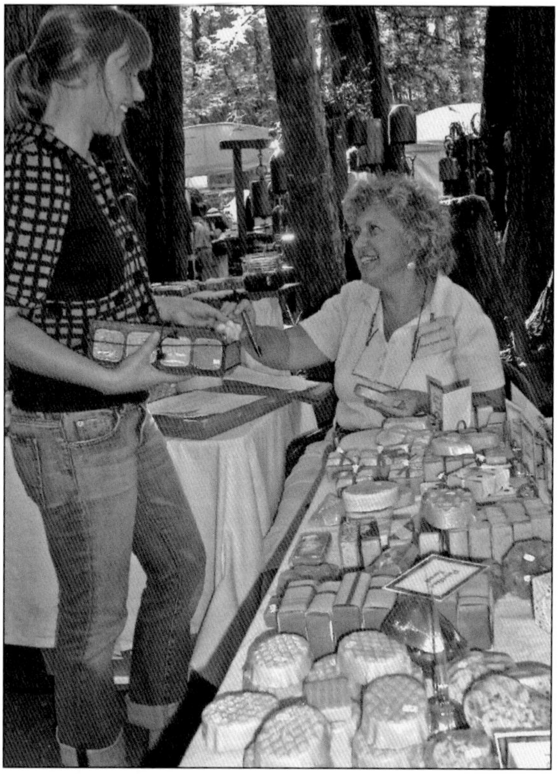

Mary Lynn Seaby, right, not only loves bath and body products, she "was fascinated by the idea I could make them myself. There's a sense of mixology, because I love to cook." She and daughter Lauren create and package soaps of varied scents, shapes, and images, from flowers to mythological figures, to sell at fairs and their holiday "driveway boutique." (Courtesy the author.)

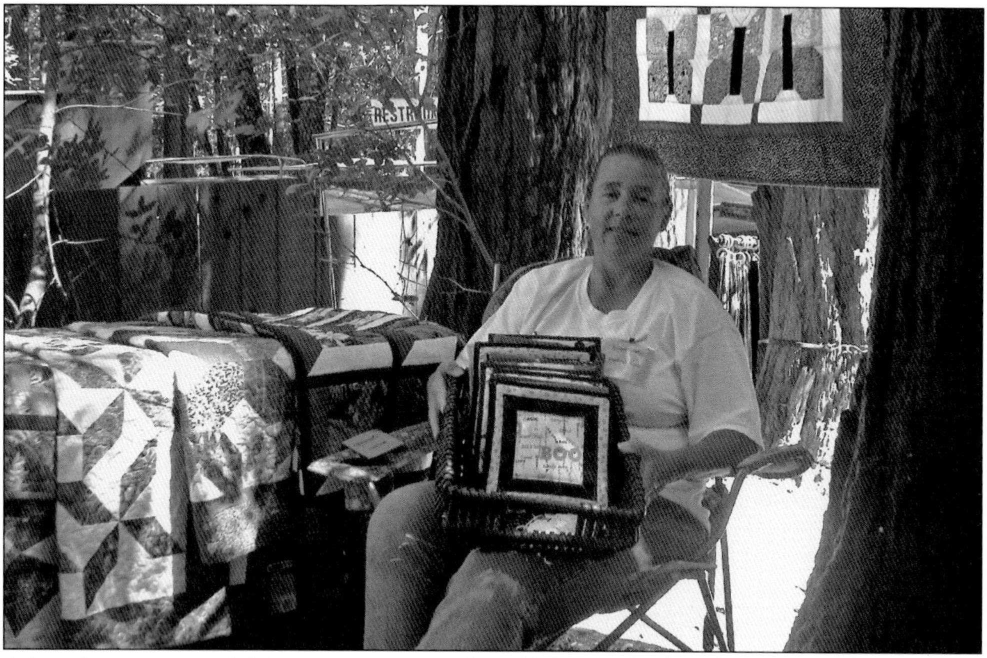

A fourth-generation, lifelong mountain resident, Deborah Soult makes her booth, where she sells handmade baby- and twin-size quilts and whimsical pot holders, a family affair: friends and her teenage daughter also quilt. Soult has lived half her life in the same house in Henrik Ibsen Park. (Courtesy the author.)

The fair is a family affair for the Stergers: parents Eric and Bev put up road signs, daughter Ocean makes jewelry, and son Reef does trash duty. Bev, a preschool/elementary teacher at Kings Mountain School, also presents her Mystic Moon jewelry made with crystals, semiprecious stones, shells, glass, or found objects. "It feels good to be part of the community," she says. (Courtesy the author.)

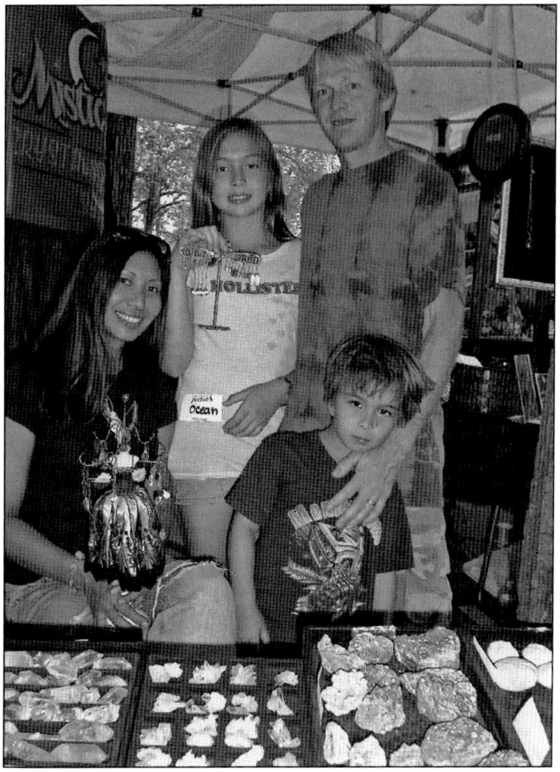

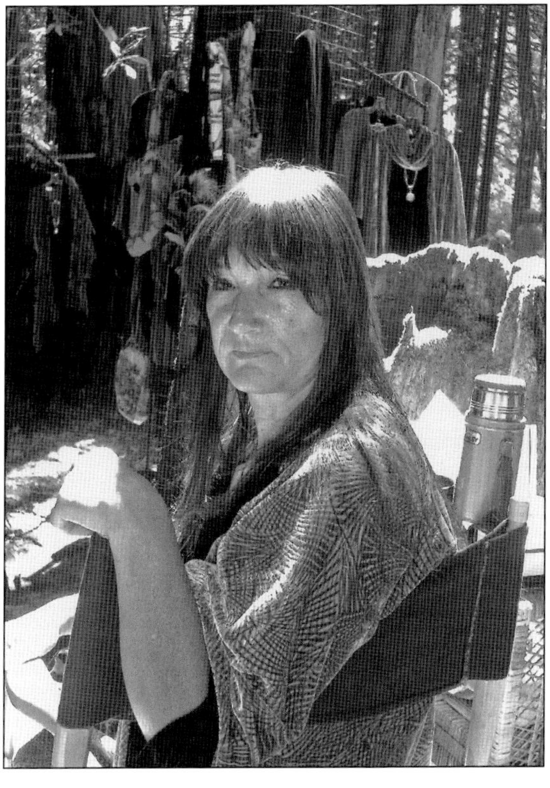

A Mountain Folk artist since 1976, Kim Ward began with hand-woven chenille jackets and crocheted vests and scarves, and she now creates silk velvet, high-end casual contemporary pieces for adults. Since her kids finished college, she tried search-and-rescue work and now teaches Pilates, but Ward will always return to Mountain Folk. "My kids went to school here. This supports the fire house, supports the community," she said. "I'll always keep doing this one." (Courtesy the author.)

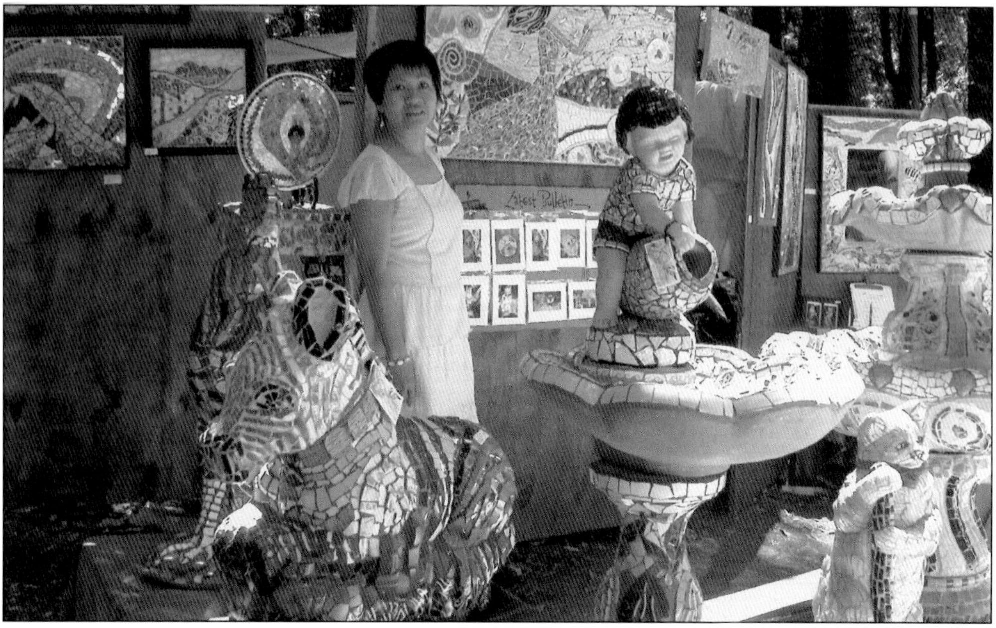

Seeing the work of Spanish artist Antonin Gaudi introduced mosaic to Xuan My Ho. "I found my passion," she said. She shows colorful two- and three-dimensional wall hangings, vessels, and sculptures on the mountain and in galleries. "My pieces always flow in curves," she explains. Her art balances her day as a software engineer: Both are analytical, but she finds it "therapeutic" to follow technology with color. (Courtesy the author.)

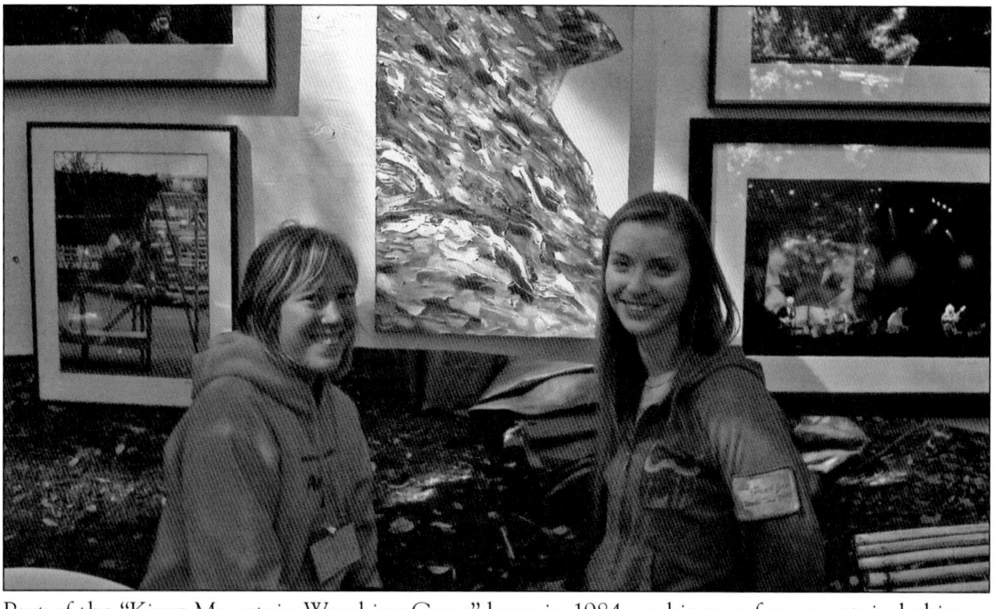

Part of the "Kings Mountain Wrecking Crew," born in 1984—a big year for mountain babies—Amber Young, left, with paintings and Erika Carrillo with photographs of Bridge School concerts, do the fair together. "It's a very important part of all of us to get together and stay together," said lifelong artist Amber. Her father, rocker Neil Young, "a mellow dude who happens to rock really well," with mom, Pegi, always "encouraged what he saw already developing." (Courtesy the author.)

Nine

FULL CIRCLE
KINGS MOUNTAIN TODAY

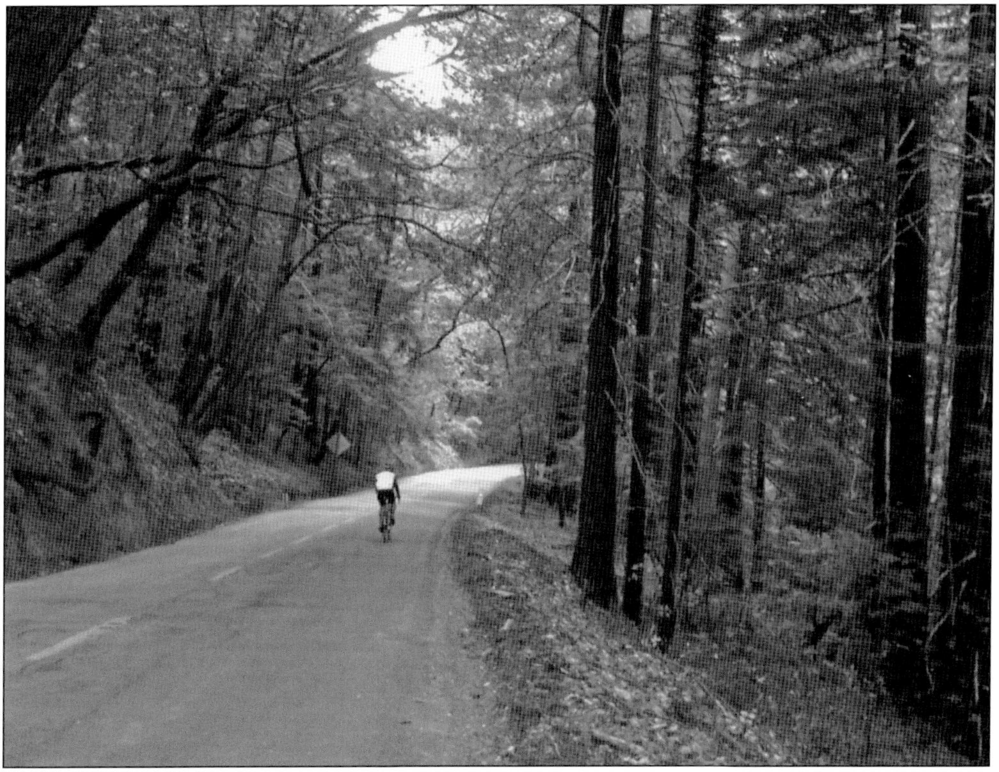

The motto of the Kings Mountain *Echo*, the community's monthly paper that has been in publication for decades, says it best: "The strength of the hills is in the people." Where teamsters and oxen once plodded, bicyclists and hikers now explore, sometimes coming across ghosts of the past: the remains of the mills. More than a century has passed since pioneers faced grizzlies, but today's residents still have that can-do resourcefulness and color. Mills have been replaced by a tightly knit community with common interests such as writing, books, hiking, yoga, and more. The independent Kings Mountain Association provides a forum for residents to debate and plan action on larger issues. Social ties through holiday or recreational activities counterbalance the mountain's geographical isolation. Homes range from modest to multimillion-dollar. Residents succeed in literature, the arts, and the international financial world—until wintertime storms rouse them from their fireplaces to brave wind and rain to tend to one another. (Courtesy the author.)

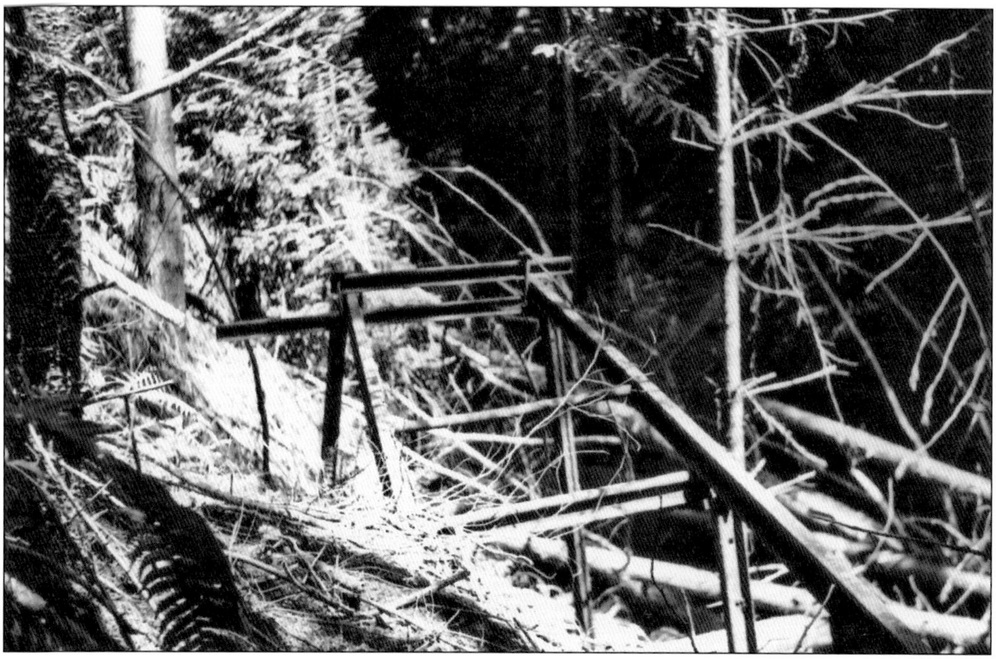

There is an eerily skeletal aspect to the remains of the tramway of the Virginia Mill on the west bank of Corte Madera Creek. Once this tramway angled down a steep (700 feet) incline to the creek. At least into the 1960s, other remnants of the mill included a fallen smokestack and rusting cables. In time, second-growth redwoods obscured the ghosts. (Courtesy Phil Kreiss.)

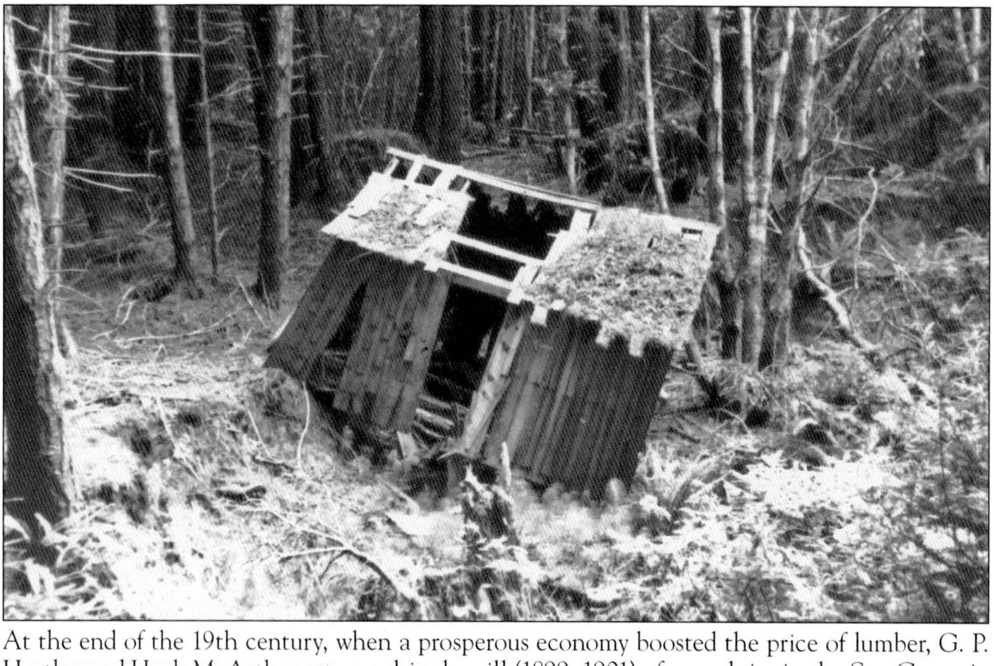

At the end of the 19th century, when a prosperous economy boosted the price of lumber, G. P. Hartley and Hugh McArthur set up a shingle mill (1899–1901) of record size in the San Gregorio basin. After Hartley's death, McArthur bought 552 acres of timber land to the south and moved the mill, which lasted until 1906. This cabin, sliding downhill, is a *c.* 1950s remnant of those mills. (Courtesy Phil Kreiss.)

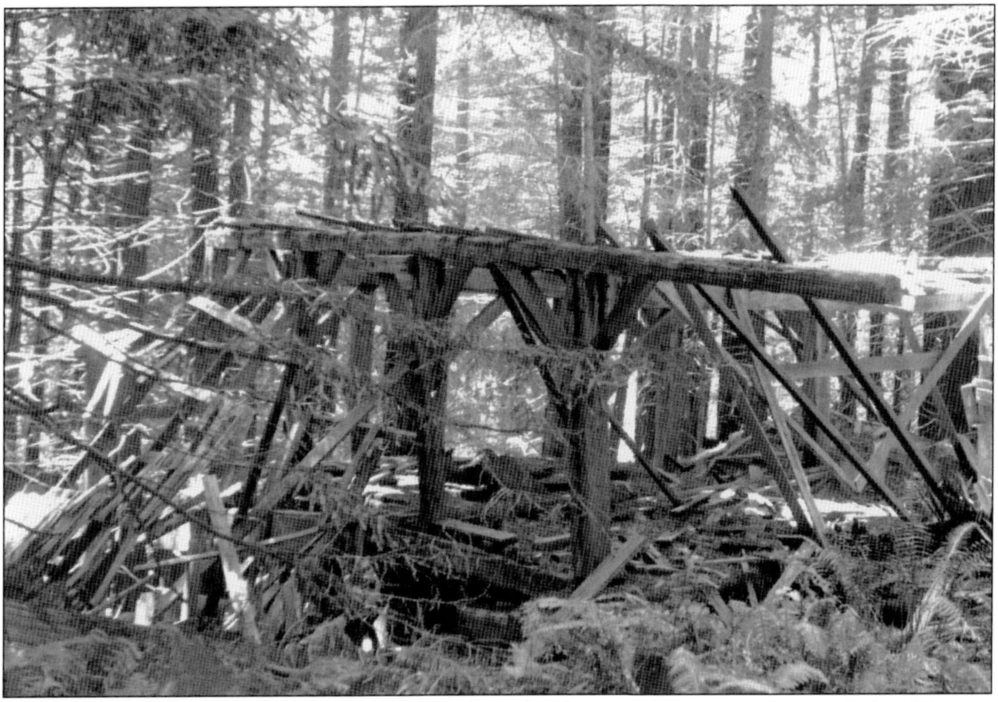

B. D. Hayward and son had a small shingle mill in the Tunitas Canyon, on the east fork of Tunitas Creek, in the 1880s. The photograph above, taken in the 1950s, shows the ruins that were left 70 years later. Below is the Hayward mill outhouse in a photograph taken at about the same time. (Both courtesy Phil Kreiss.)

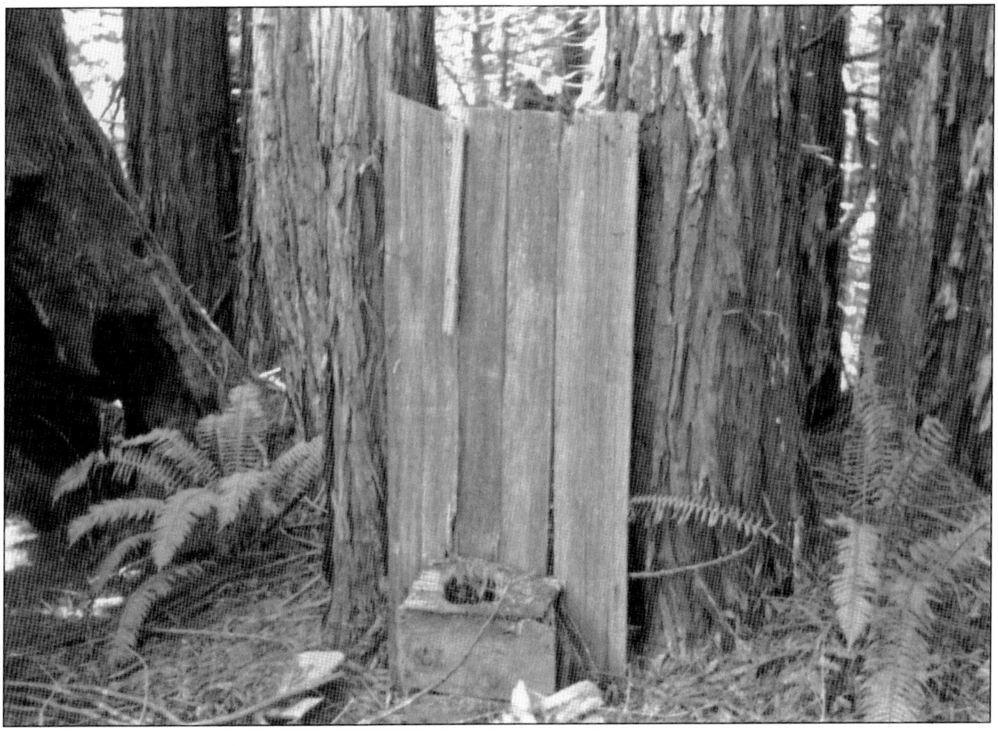

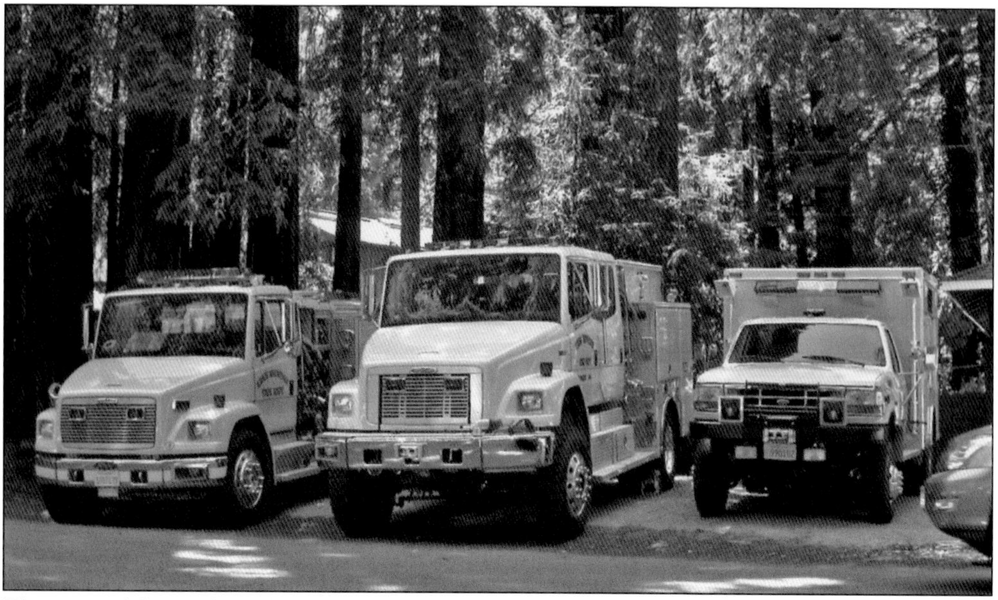

The state-of-the-art fire vehicles obtained through art fair funds are proudly displayed right across Skyline Boulevard from the fair's entrance every Labor Day weekend. The vehicles include a Type I vehicle designed for fighting structure fires, purchased in 1998; a Type III vehicle for fighting fires inside wildlands, purchased in 2004; a LIWD rescue and medical vehicle purchased in 1997 (all owned by Kings Mountain Volunteer Fire Brigade, Inc.); and a water tank truck, the only piece owned by San Mateo County but stored on Kings Mountain. (Courtesy the author.)

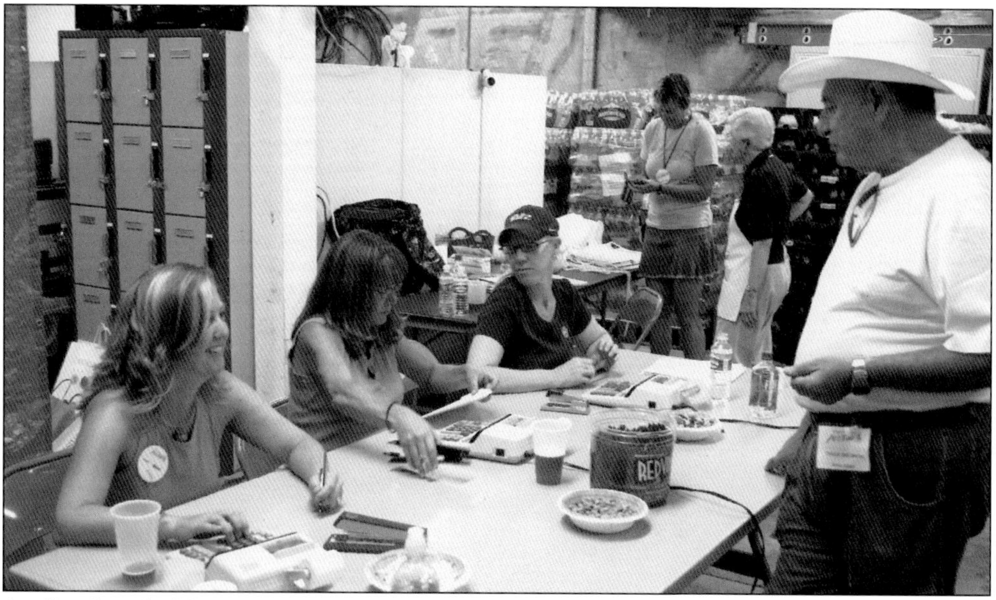

Art Fair board of directors treasurer Marty Phelps balances the books for the $75,000 to $80,000 the fair averages each year. Funds are tallied, by volunteers shown here, at the end of each fair day. Major beneficiaries are the volunteer fire brigade and the Kings Mountain Education Fund, which funds enrichment programs like art and music, and there are minor grants as well. "This is an event that involves a least one-third of the population," Marty said. "That really unites the community." (Courtesy Bill Goebner.)

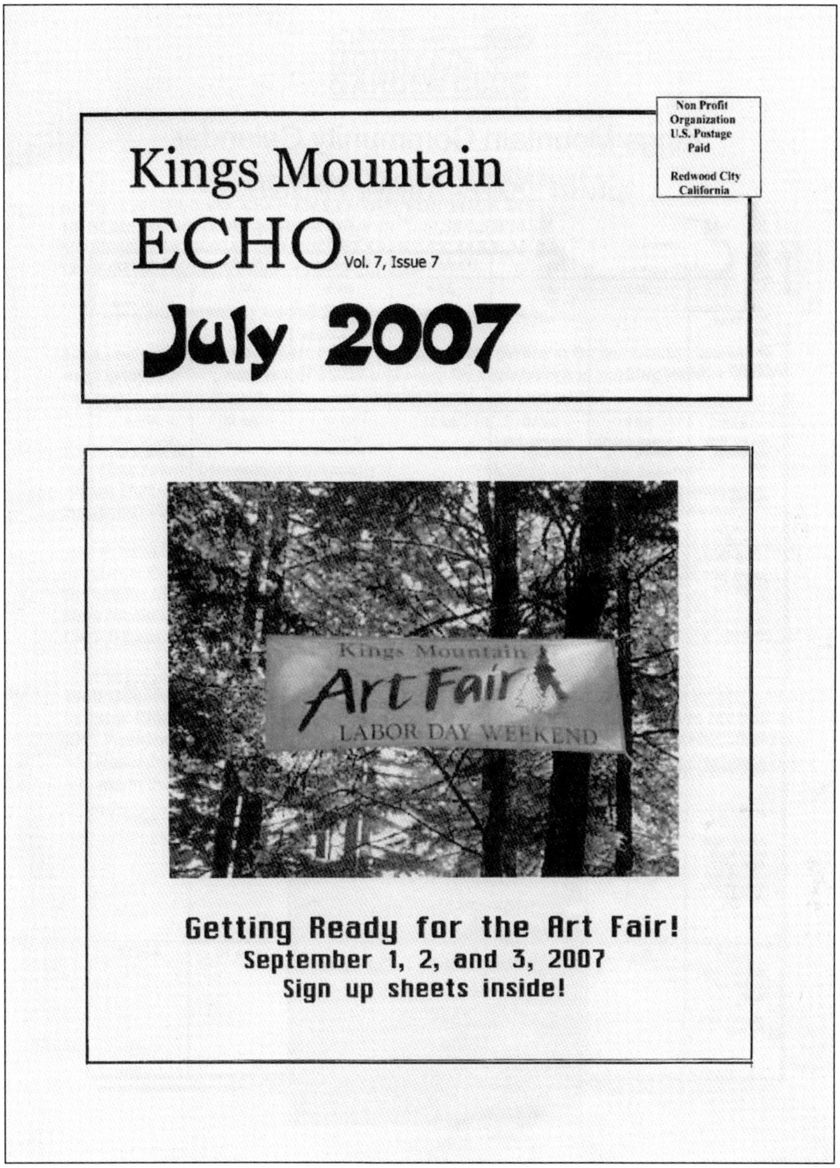
Non Profit
Organization
U.S. Postage
Paid

Redwood City
California

Kings Mountain
ECHO Vol. 7, Issue 7
July 2007

Getting Ready for the Art Fair!
September 1, 2, and 3, 2007
Sign up sheets inside!

Communication on the mountain comes from a network of local volunteers drawing on the technologies of today and yesteryear. Four hundred and fifty copies of the monthly *Echo* mountain newsletter have been assembled for the past decade by mountain resident Jack Rix on his dining-room table, with help from his wife, Betsy. (Prior editors include Jim Warren, Bob Seaby, Leigh Norling, and Pat Wurster.) From a few sheets of paper mimeographed and stapled in the early 1970s to today's computer technology, it contains community announcements, information on the special-interest groups, a calendar of community center events, regular "who's who" features, an "animal hotline," features by local historian Ken Fisher, emergency information, and entertaining "Mountain Musings." Articles are submitted by mountain neighbors; Rix puts it all together and mails it, with a little financial help from art fair grants and private donations. About half of the community is part of an online mountain Yahoo! group, maintained as a community service by Mary Lynn and Robert Seaby and including only mountain residents. It also provides an informational network. (Courtesy Bill Goebner.)

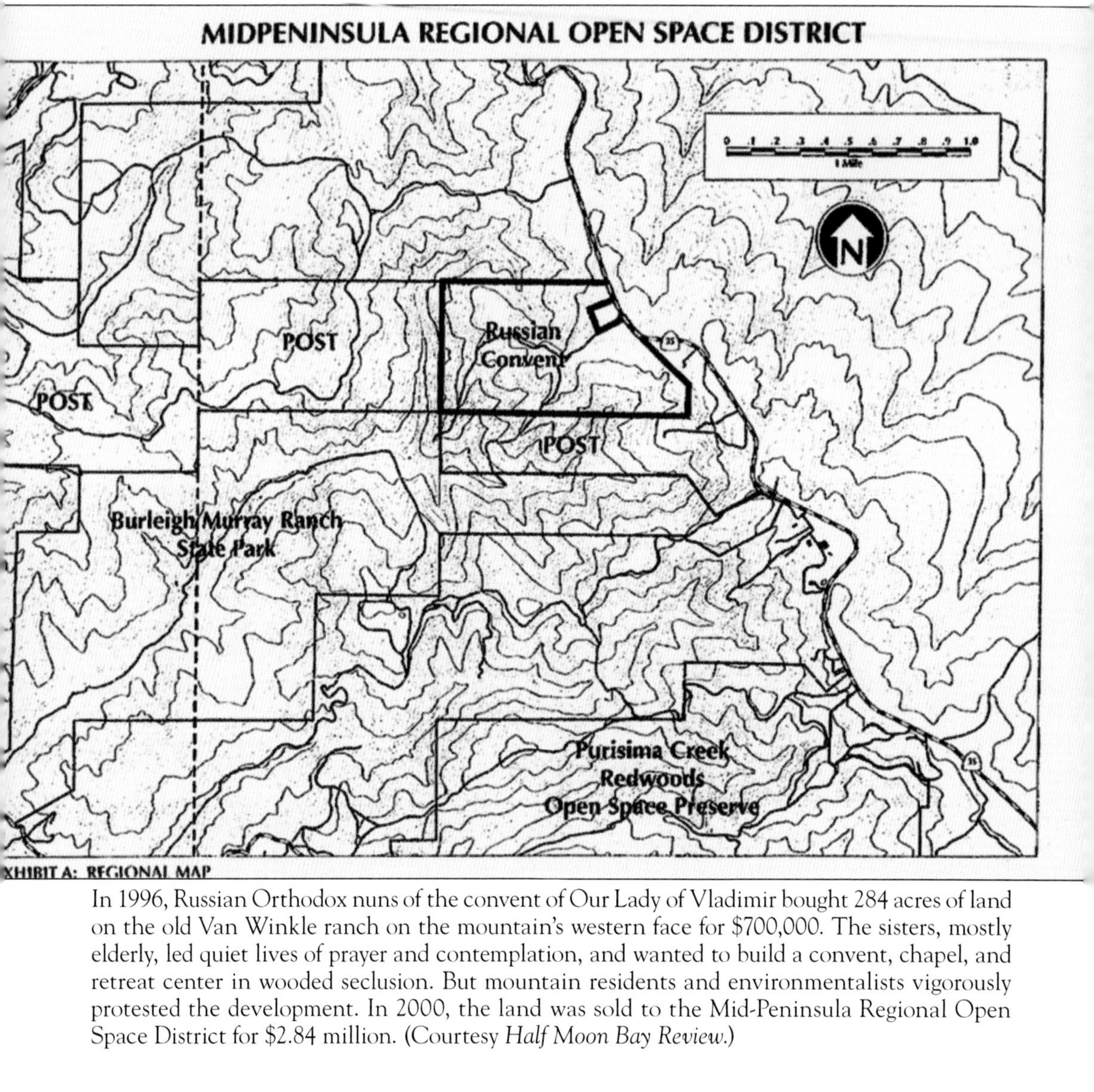

In 1996, Russian Orthodox nuns of the convent of Our Lady of Vladimir bought 284 acres of land on the old Van Winkle ranch on the mountain's western face for $700,000. The sisters, mostly elderly, led quiet lives of prayer and contemplation, and wanted to build a convent, chapel, and retreat center in wooded seclusion. But mountain residents and environmentalists vigorously protested the development. In 2000, the land was sold to the Mid-Peninsula Regional Open Space District for $2.84 million. (Courtesy *Half Moon Bay Review*.)

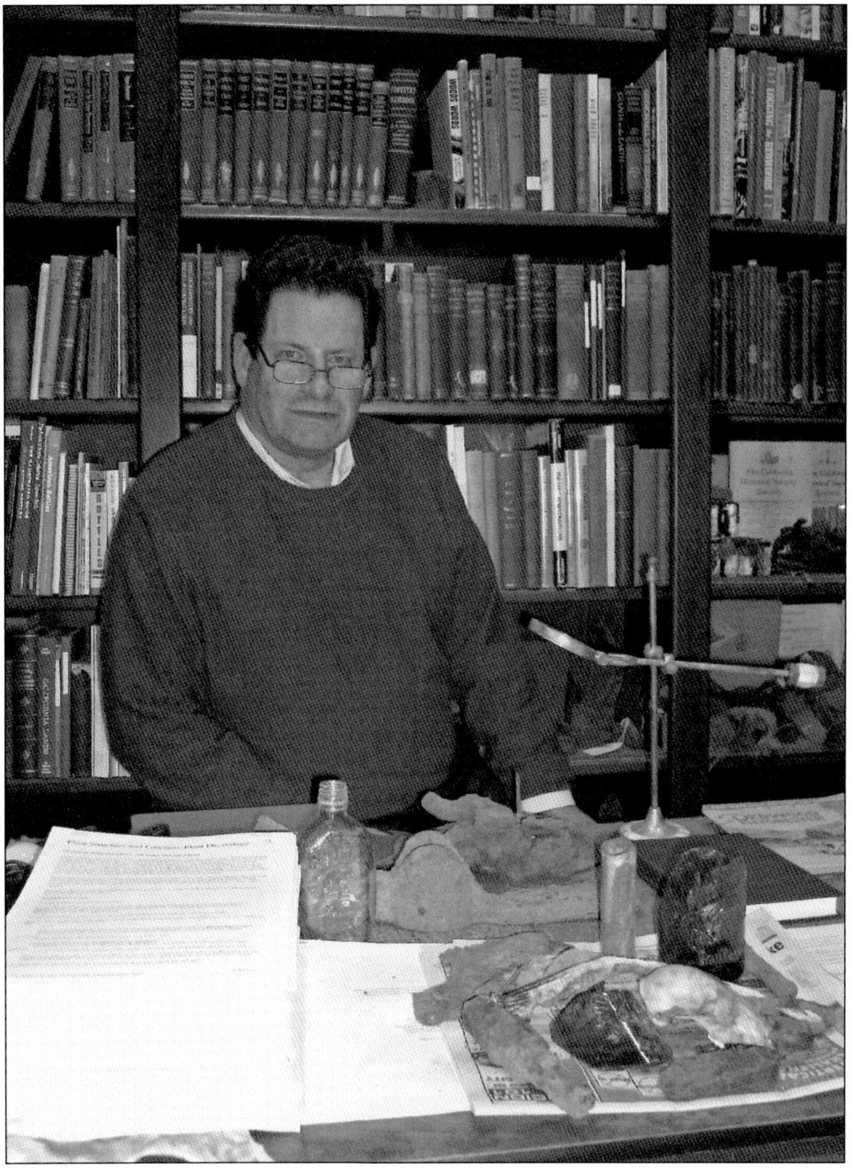

Growing up in San Mateo, Ken Fisher stumbled on a deserted, *c.* 1930s Kings Mountain trapper's cabin, fixed it up, and camped there; in 1973, he made Kings Mountain his permanent home. Ken is the founder, chairman, and CEO of Fisher Investments, a $45-billion independent global money management firm. He is the fourth-longest-running columnist in *Forbes Magazine*'s history with his monthly "Portfolio Strategy" column and author of four bestselling investment-related books, multiple articles, and scholarly research papers. He was ranked No. 271 on the 2007 Forbes 400 list of richest Americans. He has endowed the world's only academic chair devoted to any single tree species, the Kenneth L. Fisher Chair in redwood forest ecology at Humboldt State University, currently held by leading redwood scientist Dr. Stephen Sillett. While he and his wife, Sherrilyn, raised their three sons, Ken sought clues to the mountain's past by hiking its trails and ravines, exploring, analyzing, documenting, and collecting thousands of photographs, histories, artifacts, maps, letters, and more into his extensive library. He is the mountain community's undisputed historian, as well as a quiet benefactor. (Courtesy the author.)

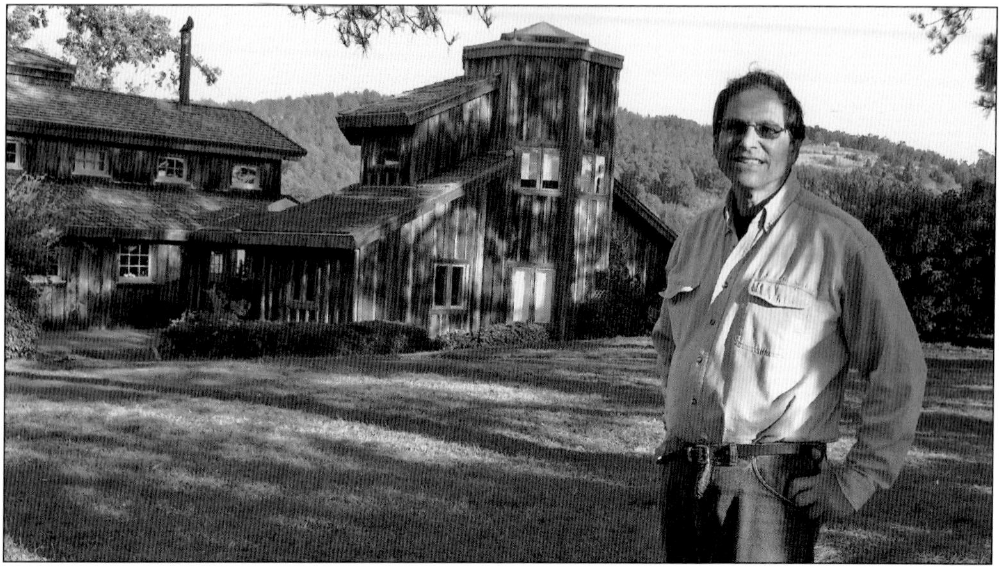

Rebecca Holland's domestic partner since the mid-1990s, filmmaker Steve Michelson started Gilbert Award–winning, major Bay Area film and video post-production studio One Pass in 1975. He is now the executive producer for Lobitos Creek Ranch and Specialty Studios, which specializes in documentary and special-interest programs for international clients—and taught Kings Mountain Elementary School children to make videos that raised funds for the school, which his three and Holland's two children attended. Rebecca works with him on the ranch, where they raise horses. (Courtesy the author.)

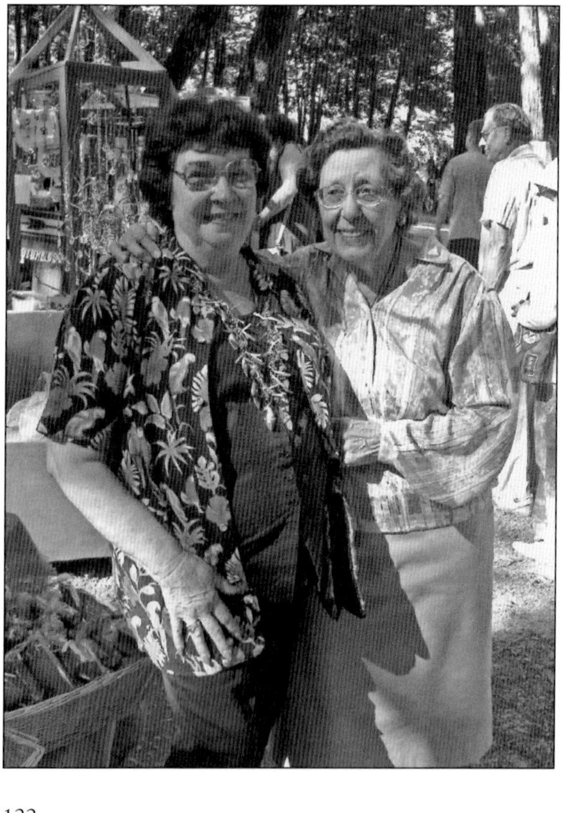

Visiting the fair in 2007 to look over the art and see how it has evolved in 45 years are 40-year volunteer Ardyth Woodruff (left) and 20-year "poster chair" and 2003 Volunteer of the Year Zanette Cornman. (Courtesy the author.)

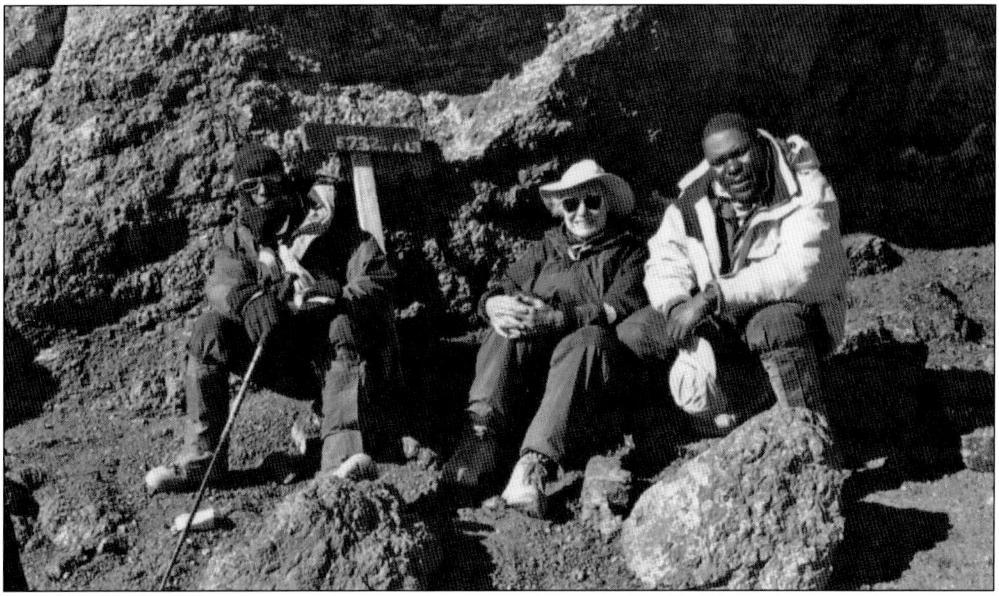

A mountain dweller since 1962, Alma Fletcher (center) has vigorously fought proposed development and promoted open space. A former reporter, an English teacher who inspired students during civil rights unrest in Mississippi, and an avid outdoorswoman, she and her husband, Jim, raised children Mark and Austri on the mountain. She and Austri have backpacked hundreds of miles on the Appalachian Trail and internationally. In 2006, spry septuagenarian Alma joined Austri in successfully climbing another mountain—Kilimanjaro. (Courtesy Alma Fletcher.)

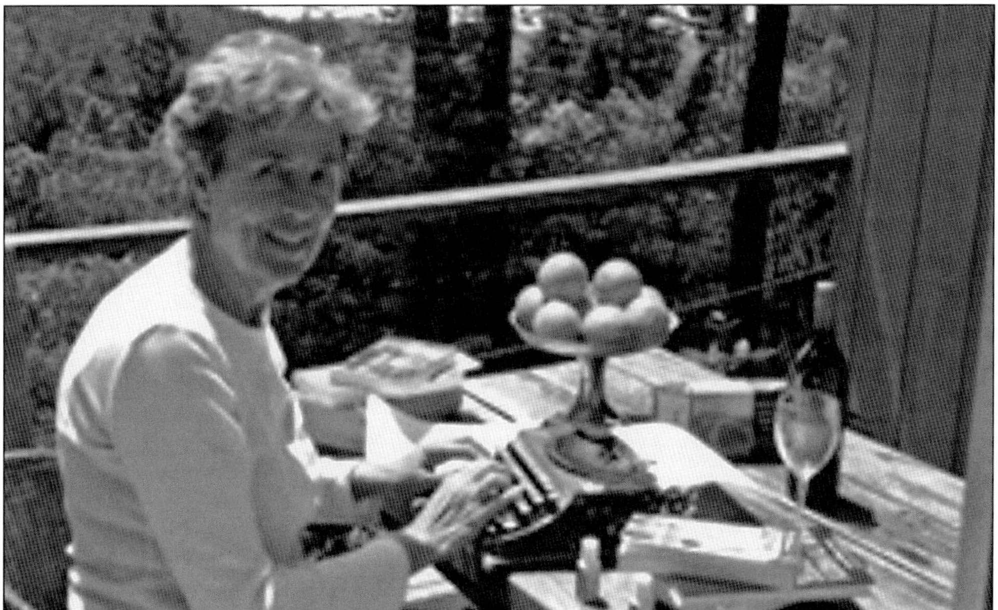

Morning walks along redwood trails have energized mountain resident Carol Culver into producing 30 books since her debut novel in 1989. Most are romances, written under her pen name Carol Grace, with a recent foray into young-adult fiction. Working at the art fair's "cook shack" and her local writers' group have kept her on the mountain since the 1970s. (Courtesy Carol Culver.)

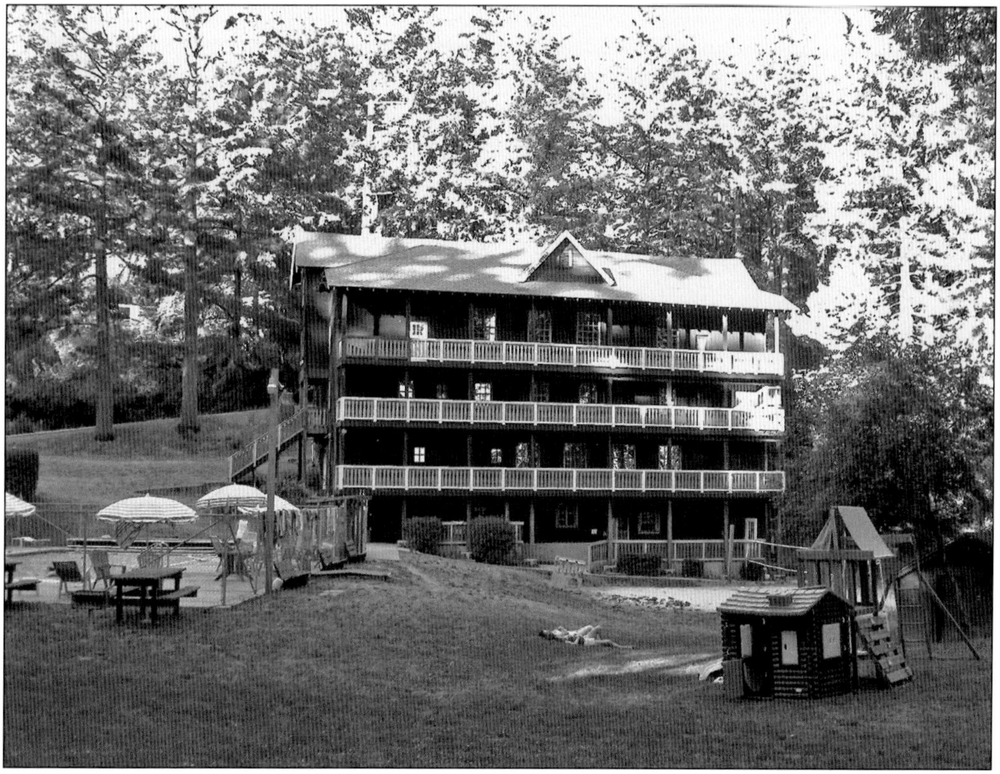

The Sons of Norway clubhouse, built in 1923, towers today over the Olympic-sized pool and sprawling lawns encircled by redwoods that offer privacy from the road. In the vicinity are some 31 cabins scattered over roughly 33 acres. The cabins are owned by members; the land is owned by and leased from the lodge. (Courtesy the author.)

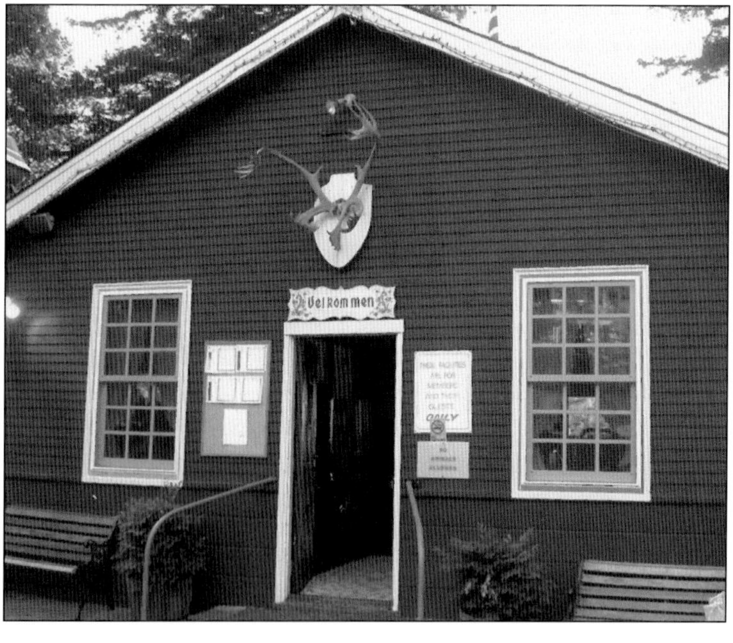

Festive social life flourished at Henrik Ibsen Lodge with the dance hall, built by hand in 1927–1930. Octagonal, with an overhead star-shaped beam pattern and one open wall, the hall is the scene of festivities that hailed the 1,000th anniversary of the voyage of Leif Eriksen. The Norwegian club is "one big happy family," said member, lifelong mountain resident, and artist Deborah Soult. (Courtesy the author.)

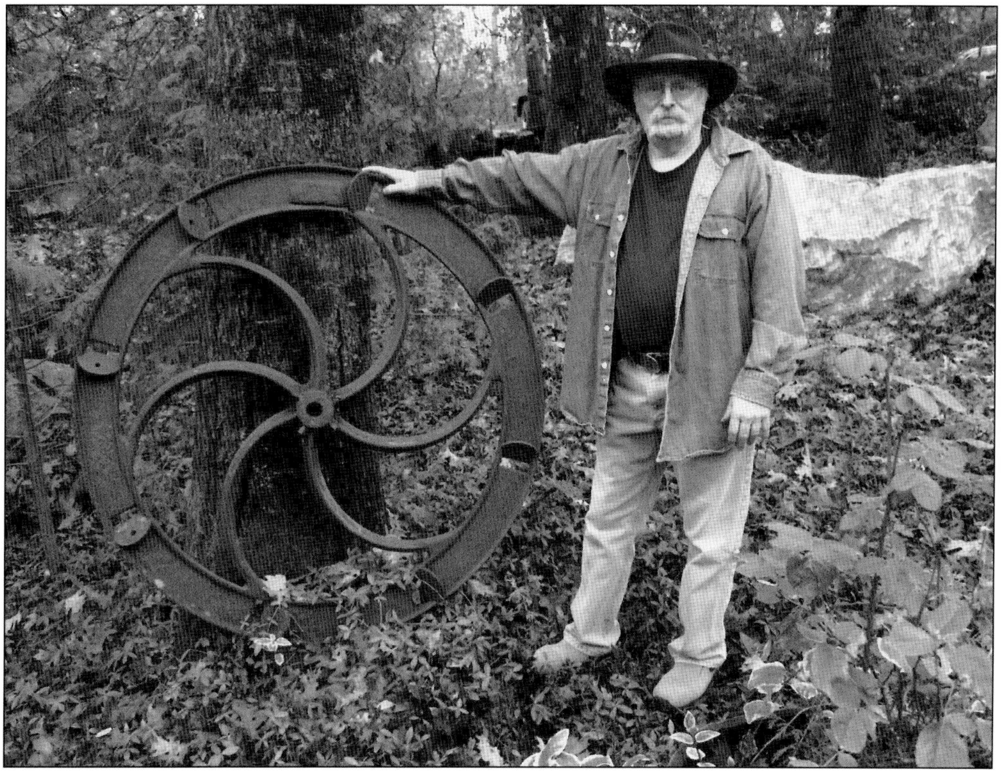

Phil Kreiss combed Kings Mountain and environs in the 1950s and 1960s as a boy with his father, Don Kreiss, in search of whiskey bottles abandoned by millmen. Today at home in Amador County, he stands by his own pride and joy—a large planing wheel he salvaged from the abandoned *c.* 1862 Taylor mill site. Logs were run through it to square the sides before cutting shingles. (Courtesy the author.)

Among Phil Kreiss's own bottle collection inherited from his father are, from left to right, a *c.* 1880 whiskey flask, a bottle for spices or pepper sauce, a bottle for Hoods sarsaparilla, and a bottle that probably contained medicine from an early drugstore. Hundreds were found by Don Kreiss, discarded by lumbermen and embedded in dirt and history on the mountain. (Courtesy the author, from Phil Kreiss's collection.)

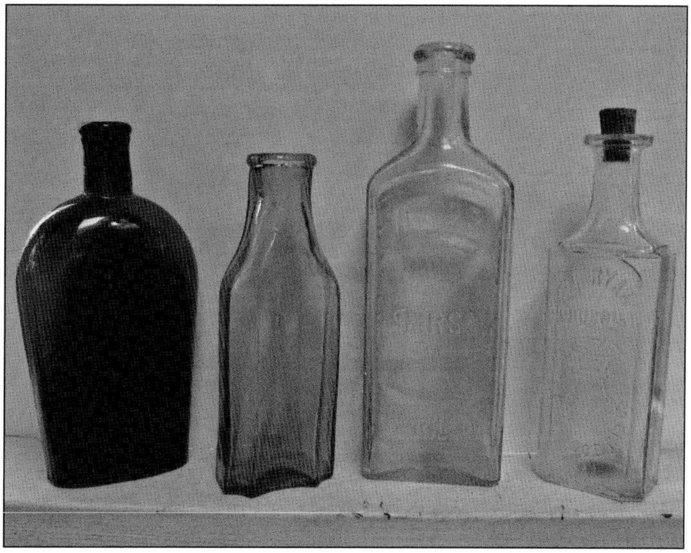

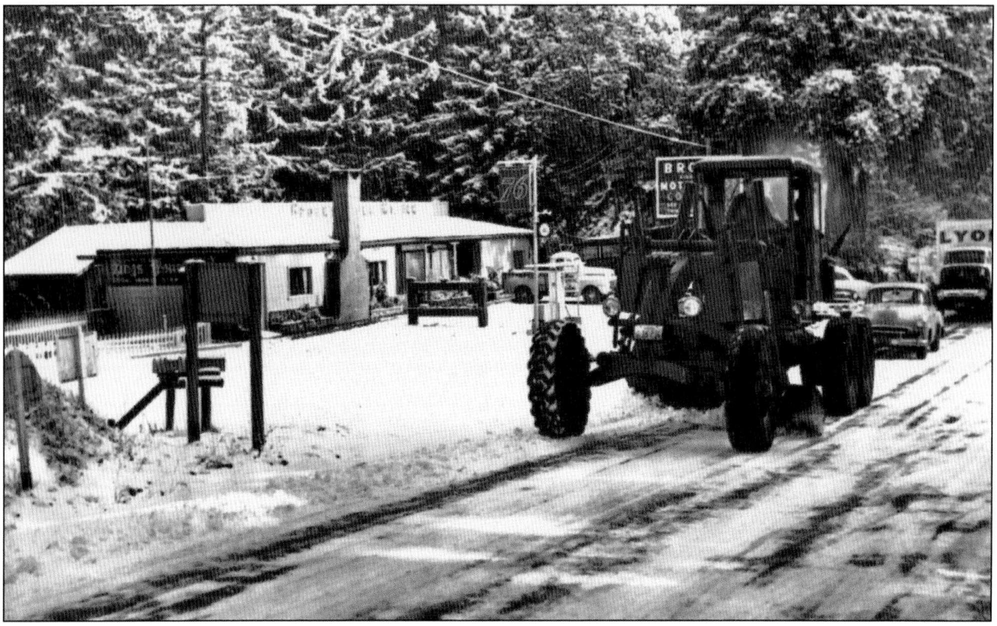

Even on the temperate California coast, climate extremes can make for interesting local color. Sunny weather warms the Labor Day art fair. Winter storms clog narrow roads with toppled branches and send some mountain residents to the protection of bayside hotels. Cold weather brings occasional snow, generally a cause for recreation but rarely heavy, as in this case in 1974. (Courtesy Bill Goebner.)

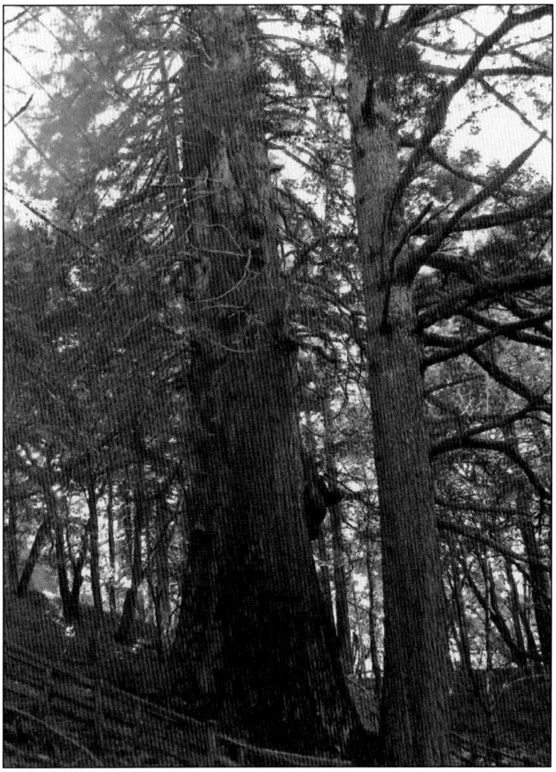

The gentle slopes around the remaining stump of old-growth redwood Methuselah were, like most slopes and gulches on the mountain, cleared by 19th-century loggers and up to the 1930s, when the upper portion of the tree fell away. Today second-growth trees like these, growing relatively rapidly, have restored the forest so that, once more, green redwood sails open to the wind. (Courtesy the author.)

BIBLIOGRAPHY

Becher, Sherri D. "Evolution of the Dairy Industry in San Mateo County 1776–1977." San Mateo, CA: College of San Mateo student monograph, 1970.

Bromfield, D. Gordon. "The San Mateo We Knew." Santa Barbara, CA: privately published, 1957.

Bromfield, J. D. "History of San Mateo County,"

Cook, Dorothy. "Some People and Events on Kings Mountain." San Mateo, CA: College of San Mateo student monograph, 1941–1942.

Fisher, Kenneth L. "The Crash of '53: Our County's Worst Aviation Tragedy." San Mateo, CA: *La Peninsula: A Journal of the San Mateo County Historical Association*, 1991–1992.

———"Kings Mountain's Colorful History." San Mateo, CA: *La Peninsula: A Journal of the San Mateo County History Association*, November 1990.

Gilman, J. N. "The Story of Willowmoor Vesta IV," Woodside, CA: They Ayrshire Advocate, 1923.

Johnston, Hank. *They Felled The Redwoods*. Los Angeles, CA: Transangelo Books, 1966.

Kalenborn, Mrs. A. S. "Early Lumbering Industry of San Mateo County." San Mateo, CA: San Mateo County Historical Archives manuscript, 1944.

Maskell, Theadate. "The History of Kings Mountain." San Mateo, CA: College of San Mateo student monograph, 1942.

Moore and DePue. *The Illustrated History of San Mateo County*, Woodside, CA: Gilbert Richards Publications, 1974.

Nicoli, A. H. "The Lumbering Industry of San Mateo County." San Mateo, CA: College of San Mateo student monograph, 1940.

Richards, Gilbert. *Crossroads: People and Events of the Redwoods of San Mateo County*. Woodside, CA: Gilbert Richards Publications, 1973.

Stanger, Frank M. "History of San Mateo County," San Mateo, CA: *San Mateo Times*, 1938.

——— *Sawmillls in the Redwoods: Logging on the San Francisco Peninsula 1849-1967*. San Mateo, CA: San Mateo County Historical Association, 1967.

Springer Texts in Statistics

Springer Texts in Statistics (STS) includes advanced textbooks from 3rd- to 4th-year undergraduate levels to 1st- to 2nd-year graduate levels. Exercise sets should be included. The series editors are currently Genevera I. Allen, Richard D. De Veaux, and Rebecca Nugent. Stephen Fienberg, George Casella, and Ingram Olkin were editors of the series for many years.

Frederic Schoenberg

Space-Time Point Processes

An Applied Statistics Course

Springer

Frederic Schoenberg
Department of Statistics
and Data Science
UCLA
Los Angeles, CA, USA

ISSN 1431-875X ISSN 2197-4136 (electronic)
Springer Texts in Statistics
ISBN 978-3-032-20789-0 ISBN 978-3-032-20790-6 (eBook)
https://doi.org/10.1007/978-3-032-20790-6

This Springer imprint is published by the registered company Springer Nature Switzerland AG
The registered company address is: Gewerbestrasse 11, 6330 Cham, Switzerland

Foreword

If we were really honest, every book would be called "stuff I've done", and this one is no exception. What I mean is, when writing a book on some subject, there is a pretense that the book is a thorough treatment of what everyone in the world has discovered about the topic, but in reality, such an undertaking would be too difficult, and due to laziness and ego, we end up mostly writing about our own contributions. Although I know this is common practice, I am nevertheless embarrassed of the extent to which I have emphasized my own work, and sincerely apologize to the reader and my colleagues for this.

One pet peeve of mine is when people make something seem easy, and then I try to do it and it doesn't work. It is especially bad when books or papers contain code that does not actually work. Although I certainly have neglected many topics within the realm of point processes, for those topics I discuss here, I have made a concerted effort not to avoid the annoying little issues and decisions that arise when implementing them in practice. This comes at a cost of some elegance and brevity, but I hope the reader finds this useful, including the R code to implement the methods discussed here, for instance. I promise that, other than a few of the plots of the introductory examples in Chap. 1, all of the figures in this book were actually made with the code contained in this book.

Thanks so much to my family: my wife Victoria, my kids Max and Gemma, my step-daughters, parents, siblings, and their families. Huge thanks also to all my students, especially Conor Kresin, and to my wonderful Ph.D. advisor, David Brillinger.

This might be the last statistics book ever written without absolutely any use of AI.

Los Angeles, USA Frederic Schoenberg

Contents

1 Introduction 1
1.1 Basics 2
1.2 Examples of Point Processes 2
1.3 Characterizations of Point Processes 6
1.3.1 Stochastic Processes 7
1.3.2 Lists of Points 8
1.3.3 Random Measures 9
1.4 Integration 10
1.5 Stationarity, Simplicity, and Orderliness 12
1.6 Conditional Intensity 14
1.7 Simple Hypothetical Examples 16
1.8 Martingale Theorem 18
1.9 Purely Spatial Processes, Papangelou Intensity, and the Georgii-Zessin-Nguyen Formula 18
1.10 Exercises 19
References 20

2 Models 21
2.1 Poisson Processes and Their Variants 21
2.2 Mixed Poisson Processes 24
2.3 Compound Poisson Processes 25
2.4 Poisson Cluster Processes 27
2.5 Cox Processes 28
2.6 Gibbs Processes 30
2.7 Matern Processes 31
2.8 Hawkes Processes and Their Variants 32
2.9 Totally Independent Non-simple Point Processes 39
2.10 Exercises 44
References 46

3 Estimation 49
3.1 Maximum Likelihood 49
3.2 Likelihood 49
3.3 Maximum Likelihood Estimates 50
3.4 Integral Approximation for Hawkes, ETAS, and Recursive Models 52
3.5 Separable Estimation 57
3.6 Least Squares for Aggregated Data 61

3.7 Estimation via Functional Summaries and Score Functions ... 62
3.8 Non-parametric Estimation for Hawkes Processes ... 66
3.9 Method of Moments Estimation ... 70
3.10 Cross-Excitation Estimation ... 71
3.11 Exercises ... 71
References ... 72

4 Adjectives ... 75
4.1 Descriptions of Clustering and Inhibition ... 75
4.2 Nearest Neighbor-Type Functions ... 75
4.3 R/S Statistic ... 82
4.4 Causality ... 83
4.5 Prototypes ... 86
4.6 Exercises ... 93
References ... 93

5 Model Evaluation ... 97
5.1 Pixel-Based Residuals ... 98
5.1.1 Raw Residuals ... 98
5.1.2 Pearson Residuals ... 98
5.1.3 Pixel Size ... 99
5.1.4 Examples ... 100
5.1.5 Numerical Summaries of Residuals ... 105
5.1.6 Deviance Residuals ... 106
5.2 Rescaling ... 109
5.3 Super-Thinning ... 111
5.4 Voronoi Residuals ... 116
5.5 Numerical Tests ... 121
5.5.1 L-Test and N-Test ... 121
5.5.2 Magnitude-Weighted Scores ... 123
5.6 Weighted Second-Order Statistics ... 126
5.7 Exercises ... 129
References ... 131

1 Introduction

This book is meant to accompany a one-semester course in point processes, either at the graduate or undergraduate level, for students focused primarily on applied statistics and data science. The goal is to educate and train students in the practical aspects of the summary, description, and forecasting of spatial-temporal point process data. While very thorough treatments of the theoretical aspects of point processes already exist, this book's aim is to summarize the main issues in the practical applications associated with space-time point processes. In particular, some of the questions addressed in this book are:

- How can one summarize space-time point process data?
- How are space-time point processes modeled?
- How can one use a space-time point process model to forecast the probability of future events?
- What are the different ways of estimating parameters in space-time point process models, and how do they compare?
- How can space-time point process models be estimated non-parametrically?
- What techniques exist for assessing how well a space-time point process model fits to data, or for comparing the fit of multiple models?

The focus is on applied methodology, and only theory that is essentially and directly linked to these applied questions is included. Applied examples are used throughout the book, and the text includes *R* code for implementing all the techniques discussed in the book. The reader unfamiliar with *R* should start by downloading *R* which is freely available from www.r-project.org.

The style of the book is meant to emulate the excellent textbooks on other statistical subjects by Julian Faraway, Chris Chatfield, Rafael Irizarry, William Venables, and Brian Ripley. Important and difficult concepts and methods are not shied away from, but the book aims to explain these topics in as direct, simple, and straightforward a way as possible, with simple language and minimal notation. The book is meant to be used for teaching at the graduate or undergraduate levels. Sample exercises are given at the end of each chapter, and these problems are straightforward and thus suitable for undergraduate or graduate students in applied statistics and data science.

The book covers standard, classical methods for point processes, such as Poisson processes, Cox processes, Hawkes models, conditional intensities, kernel smoothing, and Ripley's K-function, and also describes important recent advances for space-time point processes, such as Model-Independent Stochastic Declustering (MISD), Stoyan-Grabarnik parameter estimation, Voronoi deviance residual analysis, and super-thinned residual analysis.

F. Schoenberg, *Space-Time Point Processes*, Springer Texts in Statistics,
https://doi.org/10.1007/978-3-032-20790-6_1

When I taught this course in the past, a common question some students had at the outset was "How much calculus do I need to know for this class?" Although in many ways this course assumes very little prior information, and while I have tried to emphasize practical, statistical topics as much as possible, placing less emphasis on mathematical topics of primarily theoretical interest, nevertheless some background mathematical knowledge is expected, particularly integral calculus. My answer is the very basics of integrals, like the fact that $\int[f(x)+g(x)]dx = \int f(x)dx + \int g(x)dx$, and the ability to compute basic integrals such as $\int c\,dx$, $\int \log(x)dx$, $\int x^a dx$, or $\int e^{ax}dx$, where a is a real number. For instance, the reader, or student taking this course, should be expected to know how to compute $\int_1^3 \int_1^3 (4+3/x)dxdy$. I will assume a similar understanding of derivatives, and a basic understanding of limits, such as L'Hôpital's rule. I also assume a solid understanding of basic statistical concepts such as distributions, expected value, variance, and covariance. In a few cases, the proofs of certain results refer to specific theorems or concepts from previous books or papers; the unfamiliar and uninterested reader may skip these parts if desired, as their understanding is not really vital to the understanding of this book.

1.1 Basics

This chapter defines most of the terms we will use in discussing space-time point processes, and the next chapters describe some of the models and methods used to describe point processes. As a result, these first chapters contain many definitions and theoretical constructs. Do not worry, applied statisticians: examples involving inference and data analysis are coming soon!

1.2 Examples of Point Processes

A point process is a random collection of points falling in some metric space. For a spatial-temporal point process, the metric space is a portion of space-time, $S = \mathbf{R}^d \times \mathbf{R}$. That is, for each point, one observes the coordinates of its spatial location in $\mathbf{R}^d$, and its time coordinate in $\mathbf{R}$. Often $d = 2$, but sometimes $d = 3$ when three-dimensional locations of events are available. We will typically assume $d = 2$ in what follows, and the extension to $d = 3$ will usually be evident.

Examples of spatial-temporal point processes include incidence of disease, sightings or births of a species, and occurrences of wildfires, earthquakes, lightning strikes, tsunamis, volcanic eruptions, terrorist strikes, crimes, UFO sightings, and rare financial events. For some reason, the points typically represent unfortunate or scary events in most applications, though there are exceptions, such as the analysis of lottery winners.

The origin times and epicenters of microearthquakes in Parkfield, California, between 1988 and 1995, recorded by the US High-Resolution Seismographic Station Network, are shown in Fig. 1.1. These are earthquakes detected by a very highly sensitive array of local seismometers, and some of the earthquakes have magnitudes as low as –1 (magnitude is the logarithm of energy released in an earthquake, so earthquakes can have negative magnitude). One sees immediately that the microearthquakes are highly clustered, particularly in time, with several bursts of seismicity featuring dozens of events occurring close together geographically and at practically the same time.

Figure 1.2 shows the locations of wildfires between 1876 and 1996 in Los Angeles County, CA, recorded by the Los Angeles County Department of Public Works. The points are far from uniformly distributed. There clearly are some areas, such as the Southern part of the County as well as the main metropolitan portion of Los Angeles, with no wildfires at all, while other areas have very high incidence of wildfires. As with the example of earthquakes, one goal of the statistical analysis of the data is to

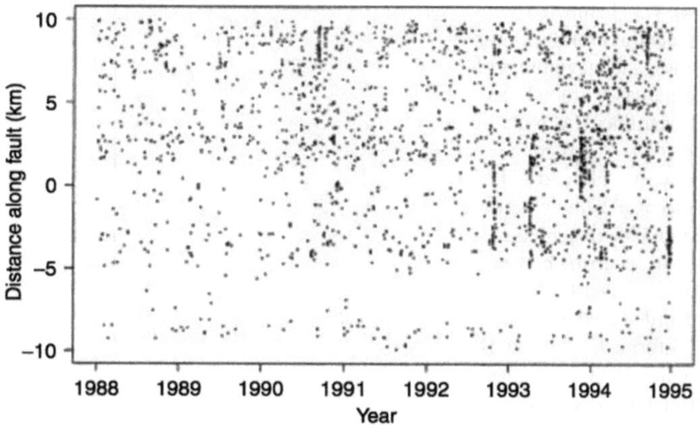

Fig. 1.1 Microearthquakes in Parkfield, CA, recorded by the US High-Resolution Seismographic Station Network, occurring from 1988 to 1995

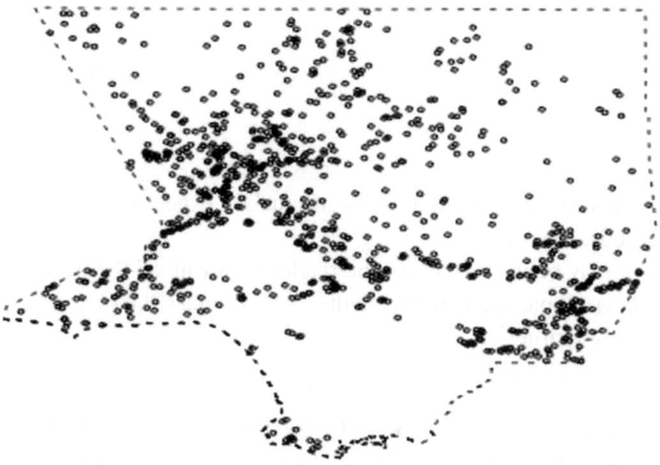

Fig. 1.2 Centroids of wildfires in Los Angeles County, CA, occurring from 1876 to 1996, recorded by the Los Angeles County Department of Public Works

use information from the past to estimate the probability of a point occurring in the future within some spatial or spatial-temporal region.

I have tried throughout this book to distinguish carefully between the terms *point* and *location*. By a *location* in space-time, I simply mean any possible value of (t, x, y). In other courses and contexts, such locations are sometimes called "points" in space-time. To avoid confusion, in this book, a *point* always refers exclusively to one of the events being studied, such as an earthquake or wildfire, or whatever the case may be.

For a *marked* point process, each point has some mark or random variable associated with it. For example, consider Fig. 1.3, which shows the locations, times, and magnitudes of earthquakes of magnitude at least 3.0 around San Bernardino, California, between 1970 and 2025. Specifically, the earthquake epicenters depicted all fall within longitude –118 to –117, and within latitude 34–35. In a sense, four dimensions are shown on the plot: for each point, one may discern not only its epicentral longitude and latitude but also its corresponding origin time and magnitude. It is natural to consider times and locations to be coordinates where the points occur, and magnitude to be a mark associated with each point. In some rare situations, one may be able to treat the marks just as one treats the coordinates, but typically they are most naturally kept distinct and treated very differently. For example, one would not typically be interested in characterizing the degree of clustering in the magnitudes, and while most models for earthquake occurrences have the feature that bigger earthquakes have more aftershocks,

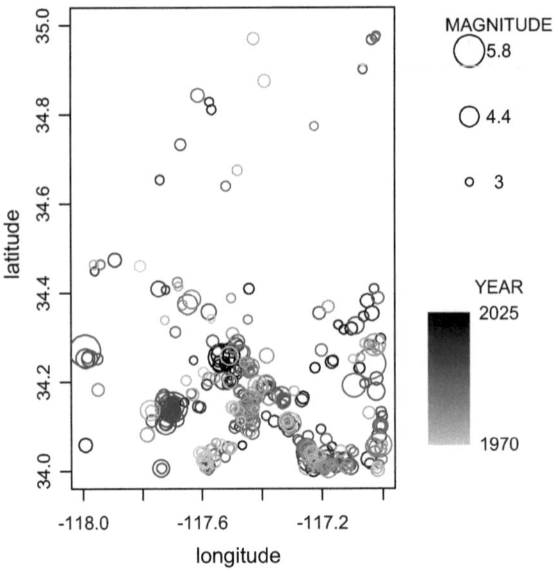

Fig. 1.3 Estimated epicentral locations, origin times, and magnitudes of earthquakes around San Bernardino, CA, with epicentral longitude between –118 and –117, epicentral latitude between 34 and 35, magnitude ≥3.0, occurring between 1/1/1970 and 12/31/2024, recorded by the Southern California Earthquake Data Center. Data are available from https://service.scedc.caltech.edu/eq-catalogs

the models do not posit that an earthquake's expected number of aftershocks depends on its longitude, latitude, or year.

It may be instructive for the reader to download the data for Fig. 1.3, which we will be revisiting in later chapters, and re-create this plot. To make the plot in Fig. 1.3, first download the data from the web by visiting

{https://service.scedc.caltech.edu/eq-catalogs/date_mag_loc.php}

(use minimum magnitude = 3.0, maximum magnitude = 9.0, min depth = 0, max depth = 100km, Southern latitude 34, Northern latitude 35, West longitude –118, East longitude –117, event type = earthquake, geographic type = local), and save the data to a file, which by default will be called "SearchResults.txt". Set your *R* directory so that this file is in your local *R* directory. Then using any text editor, delete the last 2 lines of the file "SearchResults.txt", and change all colons to spaces using the "find and change" feature your text editor. Next, implement the following *R* code:

```
x = read.table("SearchResults.txt",skip=2,fill=TRUE)
t = julian(as.Date(x$V1),origin = as.Date("1970-01-01")) + x$V2/24 +
    x$V3/24/60 + x$V4/24/60/60
maxt = julian(as.Date("2025-01-01"),origin = as.Date("1970-01-01"))
par(mfrow=c(1,2)) ## this just makes a 1x2 matrix of plots.
## the main image plot will be on the left,
## and the legends will be on the right.
plot(c(-118,-117),c(34,35),xlab="longitude",ylab="latitude",type="n")
points(x$V10,x$V9,cex=x$V7-2,col=grey(.8*t/maxt))
   ## The rest below is just to add the legends:
   plot(c(0,10),c(.8,4.2),type="n",axes=F,xlab="",ylab="")
   image(c(-1:1),seq(1,2,length=100),matrix(rep(seq(0,0.8,length=100),
     2),ncol=100,byrow=T), add=T,col=grey((80:0)/100))
   text(c(2,2),c(1,2),c("1970","2025"))
   text(2,2.2,"YEAR")
   points(c(1,1,1),c(3,3.5,4),cex=c(min(x$V7)-2,.5*(min(x$V7)+
     max(x$V7))-2,max(x$V7)-2))
   text(c(2,2,2),c(3,3.5,4),as.character(signif(c(min(x$V7),
     (max(x$V7)+min(x$V7))/2,max(x$V7)),2)))
```

```
text(2,4.2,"MAGNITUDE")
```

After running the code above, if you are done with a 1×2 matrix of plots and want to go back to a plotting device with simply one plot on it, do

```
par(mfrow=c(1,1))
```

Figure 1.4 shows the locations of red banana plants, *Musa Velutina*, detected in Costa Rica between December 2006 and January 2008. The marks, in this case heights, are indicated by the circle sizes. Despite the nice sounding name, the red bananas are a poisonous, invasive species that can be dangerous. Questions of interest are how clustered the plant locations are, and how quickly they might be spreading.

Figure 1.5 shows the locations of reported gang-related violent crimes in Los Angeles County, California, from 2014 to 2017, as collected by the Los Angeles Police Department (LAPD), with responses made by the City of Los Angeles Mayor's Office of Gang Reduction Youth Development (GRYD). GRYD operated in 23 zones throughout Los Angeles; reported crimes in 10 of these 23 zones are shown in Fig. 1.5. Questions of primary interest are whether the clustering in these reported gang-related violent crimes appears to be attributable to crimes triggering other crimes, perhaps due to retaliation, whether GRYD is effective at reducing the rate of these retaliations, and to what degree covariates such as income and education can explain the spatial-temporal patterns in reported crimes.

It is important to distinguish point process data from conventional geostatistical data, for which quite different models and methods are used. Geostatistical data are those where the locations are fixed in advance, and at each location, one observes some variable or collection of variables. Plots of geostatistical data also look like points with differing values and thus closely resemble plots of marked point process data. However, with geostatistical data, the locations and times of the points are not random, but are fixed and typically known in advance, and forecasting these spatial-temporal locations in the future is not of primary interest.

For instance, an example of a geostatistical dataset would be records of daily 1pm temperatures at a collection of weather stations in Los Angeles County, whose locations are depicted in Fig. 1.6. The locations of these weather stations are known, and although occasional slight changes in the locations

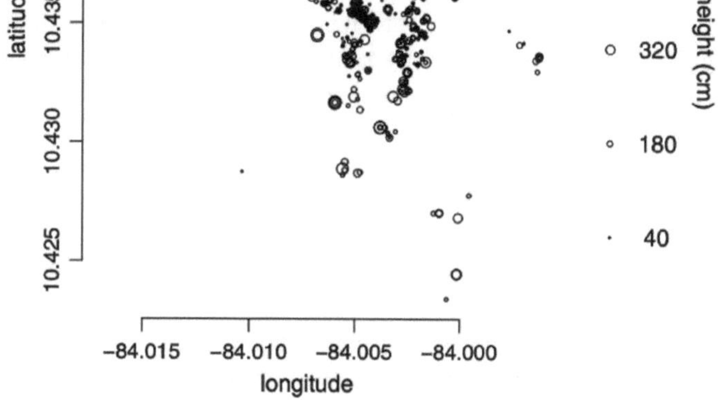

Fig. 1.4 Locations and heights of *Musa Velutina* (red banana) records in Costa Rica, December 2006–January 2008

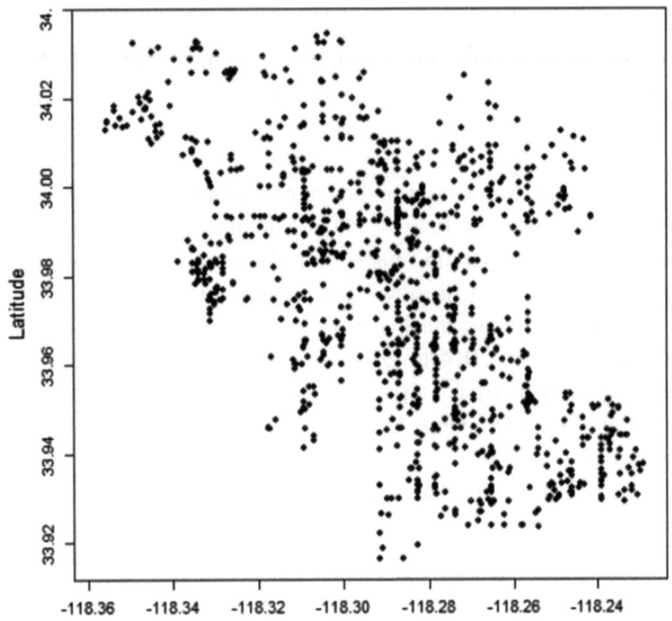

Fig. 1.5 Reports of gang-related violent crimes to which GRYD responded, in Los Angeles County, CA, from 2014 to 2017. Locations of crimes are reported at the level of street addresses or intersections by LAPD officials, and for privacy reasons, latitudes and longitudes are randomized uniformly over 15 m intervals

might occur, forecasting these locations is not a main problem of interest. Instead, one is interested in forecasting the values of temperature recorded at these locations, and/or interpolating the values at other spatial-temporal locations. With geostatistical data, the values (or marks) are unknown and of primary interest for forecasting, and may be considered random, whereas with point process data, the spatial-temporal locations themselves are unknown and the primary goal is to forecast future point locations. Thus, with geostatistical data, methods like variograms, covariograms, kriging, and fitting spatial autoregressive and conditional autoregressive models can be very useful, as ways to describe how the recorded values (e.g. temperatures) are related to one another, and for forecasting future values. With point process data, by contrast, such as the times, locations, and magnitudes of earthquakes in a given region, the methods used are primarily designed to characterize how clustered the observations are, and to forecast where and when future events are likely to occur.

In some situations, the line between geostatistical data and point process data can be a bit blurry, especially when the events observed are recorded with low spatial-temporal resolution. For instance, suppose one considers records of daily totals of the number of cases of COVID-19 in each of various cities in the United States, where within each city, only the daily totals are observed, rather than more precise spatial or temporal information. This may be considered a spatial-temporal point process, where each case is a point, but where the resolution is low, or alternatively, one may consider this data geostatistical, where for each spatial-temporal location (a city on a particular day), one observes a case count. For such cases, both point process and geostatistical methods might be useful.

1.3 Characterizations of Point Processes

Point processes have been characterized in a variety of ways. Daley and Vere-Jones (2003) detail the history originating from life tables, dating back to the 1700s. It is desirable to view point processes as particular examples of some general kind of mathematical construct, rather than as unique constructs that are fundamentally different from any others, so that one may apply results, theorems, and techniques

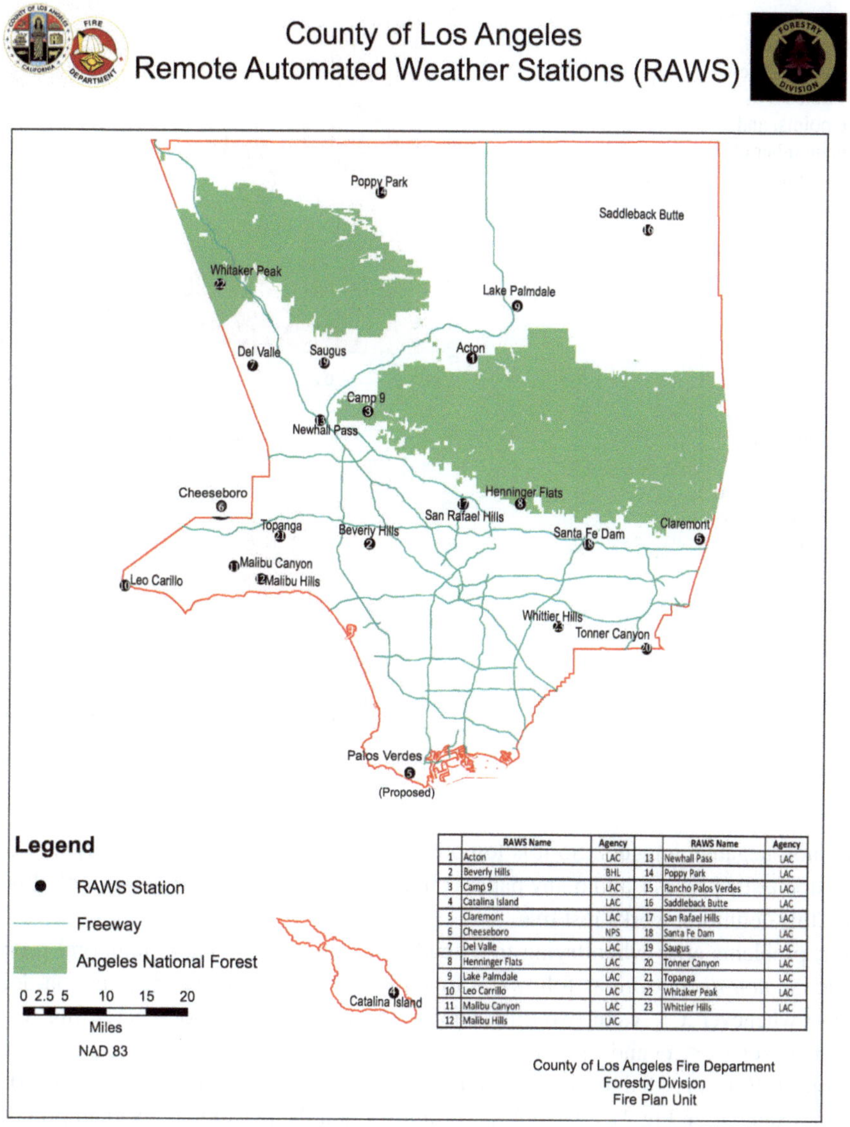

Fig. 1.6 Locations of Remote Automatic Weather Stations (RAWS) in Los Angeles County, California, in August 2019, according to fire.lacounty.gov

from the more general and well-studied mathematical domain to the particular field of point processes. But what is the most natural general construct, of which point processes are a special case? This question is not so easy to answer, and attempts have varied over the years from stochastic processes, to random sets, to random measures.

1.3.1 Stochastic Processes

Point processes on the line were originally characterized as examples of stochastic processes on the line, but special cases because point processes must be non-decreasing and Z^+-valued, where Z^+

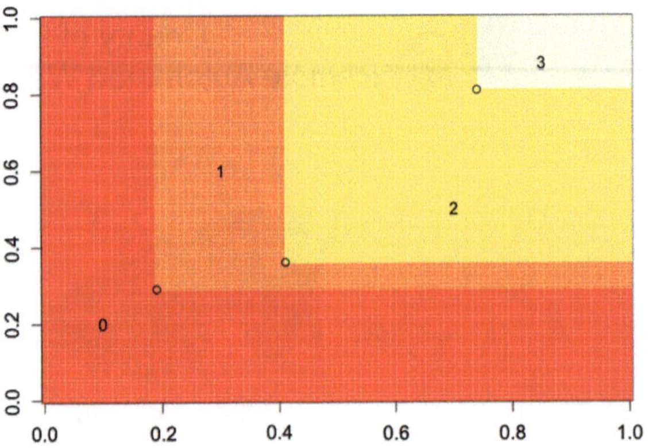

Fig. 1.7 Illustration where N is a non-decreasing Z^+-valued process. The small black circles represent the points, and $N(x, y)$ is the number of points (x_i, y_i) with $x_i \leq x$ and $y_i \leq y$

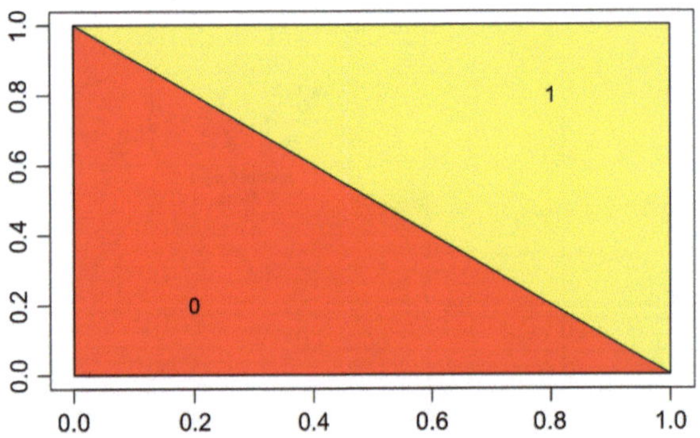

Fig. 1.8 Example of a troublesome non-decreasing Z^+-valued process. What collection of points does this function correspond to?

denotes the non-negative integers. So it is tempting to define a point process as any non-decreasing, Z^+-valued stochastic process, and many papers published in the 1970s and 1980s took this approach. On the line, this definition works just fine.

However, problems arise when trying to extend this definition to spatial-temporal processes. We generally define *non-decreasing* as follows: a function or random process $f(x)$ is non-decreasing if $f(x) \leq f(y)$ whenever $x \leq y$. In two dimensions, we say $f(x, y)$ is non-decreasing if $f(x_1, y_1) \leq f(x_2, y_2)$ whenever $x_1 \leq x_2$ and $y_1 \leq y_2$.

Now, suppose $N(x, y)$ is defined to be the number of points (x_i, y_i) with $0 \leq x_i \leq x$ and $0 \leq y_i \leq y$, as shown, for example, in Fig. 1.7. Then N is certainly a non-decreasing, Z^+-valued process.

However, there are other non-decreasing, Z^+-valued processes that are not point processes. For instance, if $N(x, y) = 0$ for $y \leq 1 - x$ and $N(x, y) = 1$ for $y > 1 - x$, as in Fig. 1.8, then N is technically a non-decreasing Z^+-valued stochastic process, but it clearly does not correspond to any collection of points. As a result, few authors currently define a point process as a non-decreasing, Z^+-valued stochastic process.

1.3.2 Lists of Points

If N is a finite collection of points, one could represent it simply as a finite list, $N = \{x_1, x_2, ...\}$, where each x_i represents one of the points. This is the approach taken, for example, by Møller and Waagepetersen (2003). In this framework, what kind of object is N?

If $S = \mathbf{R}^d \times \mathbf{R}$ is the spatial-temporal domain where each point occurs, then N is a vector in $\emptyset \cup S \cup S^2 \cup S^3 \cup ....$ This sort of definition may be suitable for finite point processes, and point

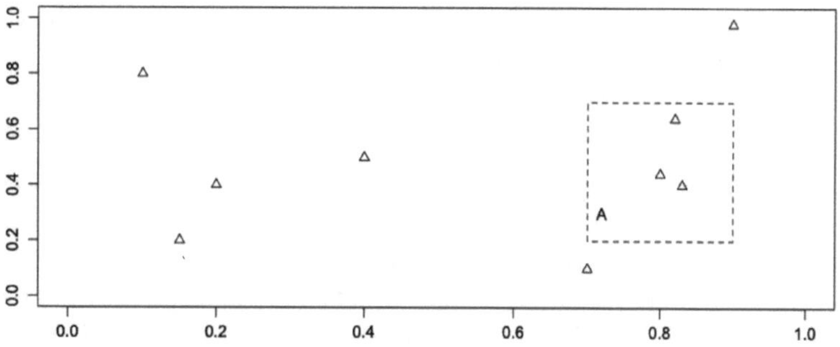

Fig. 1.9 N viewed as a random measure. The triangles represent points, and A represents a portion of the observation region, where $N(A) = 3$

processes with a countable number of points. However, one can imagine wanting to consider the point process with points at all irrational times, or some other uncountable collection of points. It is possible to restrict the definition to include only point processes with points on a set of measure zero, but then what if, for instance, N has points at all times in the Cantor set? Such a process would not even meet the basic definition of a list of points. These kinds of concerns can actually befuddle the stochastic process and random measure formulations as well, so typically we require a point process to have only finitely many points in any bounded region of space-time, regardless of whether we view point processes as stochastic processes, random lists of points, or random measures.

A more serious drawback of the random list formulation is it does not embed point processes within some well-established branch of mathematics with a wide variety of useful tools and results to apply to point processes. Unlike the stochastic process and random measure formulations, defining a point process as a random collection of points does not allow us to borrow mathematical properties, define integrals, use the martingale property, etc., so typically the random measure definition is used instead.

1.3.3 Random Measures

A Z^+-valued random measure is now widely regarded as the preferred mathematical definition of a point process. In this context, for a region A in the observed space-time domain S, the measure $N(A)$ represents the number of points falling in the region A. For the square A in Fig. 1.9, for example, the value of $N(A)$ is 3. As mentioned previously, attention is typically restricted to processes with only a finite number of points in any bounded subset of S.

In the 1950s–1970s, considerable attention was paid to the idea that there are non-measurable sets, such as the Vitali set, for instance. In light of this, we should mention that $N(A)$ technically needs only be defined for *measurable* A.

The random measure definition may initially seem quite strange. After all, in Fig. 1.9, while the set A contains three points, it may seem odd to consider its *size*, or *measure*, to be three. The notion that we are essentially *measuring* a set based on how many points it contains seems peculiar to most readers at first. On the other hand, the random measure formulation is practically ideal, for several reasons. First, every Z^+-valued random measure corresponds to a random collection of points, and vice versa. Second, the definition applies to temporal point processes, where the domain S is the line or a portion thereof, and extends immediately to space-time or more abstract domains. Brillinger (1997, 2000) analyzed point processes on the surface of a sphere or on an ellipse, for instance. Third, the definition embeds point processes within the context of an extremely rich and well-studied area of mathematics, allowing one to borrow results from random measure theory and apply those results to point processes. In particular, martingale theory, a main result of which is described in Chap. 1.6, has been especially relevant for the study of point processes, as we will see in later chapters. We will therefore use this random measure definition throughout.

Note that not every Z^+-valued function on subsets of space-time corresponds to a point process. In order for N to be a measure, it must satisfy the property that if $\{A_i\}$ are disjoint sets then $N(\bigcup_i A_i) = \sum_i N(A_i)$. To see why this matters, consider the case of two point processes, N_1 and N_2, with points at different locations and times, and suppose $M = N_1 \times N_2$. That is, for any measurable set B, $M(B) =$ the product $N_1(B) \times N_2(B)$. Is M a point process?

It is easy to see that M is Z^+-valued, but is not a point process. For instance, suppose N_1 has a point only at (0.25, 0.5), and N_2 also only has one point and it is at (0.75, 0.5). Let $A_1 = [0, 0.5] \times [0, 1]$ and $A_2 = [0.5, 1] \times [0, 1]$. Then since $N_2(A_1) = 0$ and $N_1(A_2) = 0$, we have $M(A_1) = M(A_2) = 0$, but $M(A_1 \cup A_2) = 1 \times 1 = 1$, so M is not a well-defined measure. Thus, M is an example of a $\mathbf{Z}^+$-valued function on subsets of S that is not a measure, and does not correspond to a collection of points.

A key feature of point processes is their assumed *randomness*. We use the term *point pattern* or *realization* to mean a particular collection of points, such as a particular dataset or simulation, and a *point process* to mean a random collection of points that could in principle be observed repeatedly, with points possibly occurring in very different spatial-temporal locations in different realizations. Thus, a point process is a random point pattern, or, to use the random measure formulation, a point pattern on S is a Z^+-valued measure on S, and a point process on S is a *random* Z^+-valued measure on S.

In what follows, we will sometimes use the notation τ_i to represent point i, whose spatial-temporal coordinates are (t_i, x_i, y_i).

1.4 Integration

One fundamental concept that simply must be discussed when learning about point processes is what is meant by integrating with respect to a point process. That is, if N is a spatial-temporal point process, then what is $\int_t \int_x \int_y f(t, x, y)dN$? Or a bit more simply, if N is a temporal point process on the line, what is $\int_t f(t)dN$?

The answers to these questions may simply be explained in analogy with ordinary integrals on the line. Think of $\int f(t)dt$ as the limiting sum of the areas of a sequence of rectangles, whose widths dt get smaller and smaller, and whose heights are given by $f(t)$. One such rectangle is shown in Fig. 1.10.

When considering $\int f(t)dN$, we imagine now measuring the width of any such rectangle using the random measure N. So, for example, the width of a rectangle whose base is [1.0, 1.001] is no longer measured as 0.001, but rather as the number of points that happen to occur in the interval [1.0, 1.001].

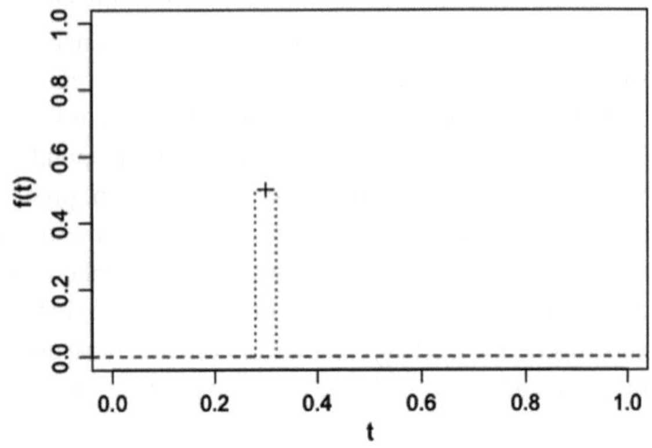

Fig. 1.10 In $\int f(t)dN$, the width of each rectangle is measured by how many points it contains

When the intervals are small, this number of points in an interval may be zero for most intervals, but when an interval contains a single point, that interval will have a measure of 1. If the interval contains two points, it will have a measure of 2, etc. Thus, the sum of the *areas* of these rectangles, where by *area* we mean the height, $f(t)$, multiplied by the *measure* of the base, will simply be the sum

$$\sum_{i=1}^{n} f(t_i), \tag{1.1}$$

where the sum in (1.1) is over all n *points* t_i that happen to occur.

Similarly, for a space-time point process,

$$\int_t \int_x \int_y f(t, x, y) dN = \sum_{i=1}^{n} f(t_i, x_i, y_i). \tag{1.2}$$

As a special example, consider the case where $f(t, x, y) = 1$ for all t, x, y. Then for any region B in space-time, $\int_B f(t, x, y) dN = \int_B dN = \sum_{i=1}^{n} 1 = N(B)$, which is the number of points in B.

In some cases, notation such as $\int_B f(t) dN(t)$ or $\int_B f(t, x, y) dN(t, x, y)$ is used, where the very last parts, "(t)" or "(t, x, y)", signify that the points are represented by t or by (t, x, y). For instance, for a space-time point process, suppose one were interested in the sum of the squares of the x-coordinates of all the observed points. This could be represented as $\int x^2 dN(t, x, y)$.

A basic example involves *kernel smoothing* a point process (Diggle 1983). Suppose N is a purely spatial point process, with points at locations $\{(x_1, y_1), (x_2, y_2), ..., (x_n, y_n)$. It may in some cases be desirable to obtain a smoothing of the points, via kernel smoothing using some spatial density function f, resulting in the quantity

$$\begin{aligned} K(x, y) &= \int_x \int_y f(x - x', y - y') dN(x', y') \\ &= \sum_{i=1}^{n} f(x - x_i, y - y_i), \end{aligned} \tag{1.3}$$

which can be computed for any location (x, y). For instance, Fig. 1.11 shows the epicentral locations of the San Bernardino earthquakes shown in Fig. 1.3, together with a kernel smoothing of these locations using a bivariate normal density for f. The code to produce Fig. 1.11 is below, using the function *kernel2d()* from the *splancs* library in *R*.

```
## After loading in the data using the code in Chapter 1.1
install.packages("splancs")
library(splancs)
plot(c(-118,-117),c(34,35),xlab="longitude",ylab="latitude",type="n")
bdry = matrix(c(-118+c(0,1,1,0,0),34+c(0,0,1,1,0)),ncol=2) ## boundary
image(kernel2d(as.points(x$V10,x$V9),bdry,h0=.15),add=T)
points(x$V10,x$V9,cex=.25)
```

Another example that arises in the study of Hawkes processes and their likelihoods involves integrals such as

$$\int_0^T \left[\int_0^t (t - u) dN(u) \right] dN(t), \tag{1.4}$$

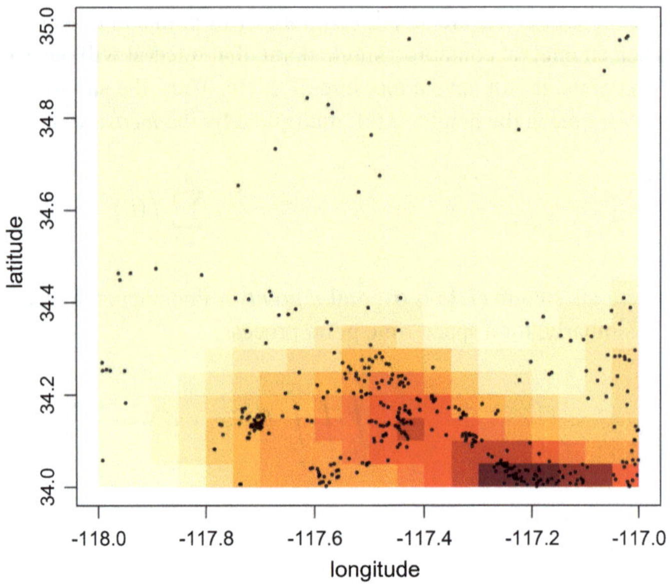

Fig. 1.11 Kernel smoothing, using a bivariate normal kernel with bandwidth 0.15^o, of the recorded epicentral locations of San Bernardino earthquakes between 1/1/1970 and 12/31/2024, recorded by the Southern California Earthquake Data Center. The epicentral locations are overlaid

where here we are imagining a purely temporal point process N.

What is meant by the double integral in (1.4)? Consider first the outer integral, $\int_0^T [...] dN(t)$, ignoring for the moment what is in the brackets. This notation means we are summing up whatever is in brackets, over all points, where each point is referred to as t. In other words, any time a t appears inside the brackets, this is referring to the times of the points, and we are summing whatever is in brackets over all of these points. Examining the portion inside the brackets now, $\int_0^t (t-u)dN(u)$ means the sum, over all points between time 0 and time t, of the function (t-u), where now the points we are summing over are labeled u. Thus, for each point t, we are summing the time $(t-u)$ elapsed between this point and a previous point, u. In other words, the integral in (1.4) is equal to $\sum_i \sum_{j=1}^i (t_i - t_j)$.

Perhaps a more specific example can help to illustrate this notation. Suppose the temporal point process is observed from time 0 to time 100, and only 4 points occur, and those points happen to occur at times 12.2, 35.4, 58.5, and 77.7. Then in this case

$$\begin{aligned}\int_0^T \left[\int_0^t (t-u)dN(u)\right] dN(t) &= \sum_{i=1}^{4}\sum_{j=1}^{i}(t_i - t_j) \\ &= (35.4 - 12.2) \\ &+ (58.5 - 12.2) + (58.5 - 35.4) \\ &+ (77.7 - 12.2) + (77.5 - 35.4) + (77.7 - 58.5) \\ &= 23.2 + 46.3 + 23.1 + 65.5 + 42.1 + 19.2 \\ &= 219.4.\end{aligned}$$

1.5 Stationarity, Simplicity, and Orderliness

Stationarity is a very basic but also quite difficult concept to discuss. It is basic because it is a feature of most of the simplest point process models, and the general idea, when expressed informally in words, is quite easy to understand. The essential idea is this: a point process is stationary if the statistical properties of the point process are the same in any one part of the observation region as they are anywhere else. However, this is a concept difficult to formalize mathematically without considerable notation.

Mathematically, we say a point process is *stationary* (or equivalently, *homogeneous*) if, for any positive integer k and any collection $B_1, B_2, \ldots, B_k$ of measurable sets, the joint distribution of the collection $\{N(B_1 + \Delta), N(B_2 + \Delta), \ldots, N(B_k + \Delta)\}$ does not depend on Δ. Here $B_i + \Delta$ refers to the set $\{(t, x, y) + \Delta : (t, x, y) \in B_i\}$. In particular, letting $k = 1$, stationarity implies that the distribution of the number of points on some day within some circular spatial region of radius r is the same as the distribution of the number of points occurring within any other circular spatial region of radius r on any other day.

Note that a stationary point process does not necessarily have points that are uniformly dispersed across the observation region, S. As we will see, a stationary point process can have clusters of points in certain regions of space-time, and few or even zero points in other regions of space-time. We will discuss many examples of such point processes, especially Poisson cluster processes and Hawkes processes, for instance. However, if there are certain times or locations that are a priori more likely to have a higher density of points in them than other times or locations, then the process is not stationary.

In order to really make sense of this, one must imagine being able to observe the process many times. If there are certain regions of S that are more likely to exhibit a high density of points in each realization, and other regions of S where points are less likely to occur in each realization, then the process is not stationary. Further, if there are certain regions of S where the degree of clustering is likely to be higher than in other regions, or where the clusters are more likely to be more diffuse than elsewhere in S, or where points are more likely to overlap, or to very nearly overlap, then again, the process is not stationary. If one is modeling the spread of a contagious disease, for instance, and the disease is likely to spread more quickly in places with hotter, more humid climates, then the process is not stationary. But if the distribution of points, and of collections of points, is the same everywhere, then the process is stationary.

If a point process is observed repeatedly, it may be possible to discern whether the assumption of stationarity is reasonable. For instance, one could examine whether there seem to be similar distributions of points in different spatial-temporal intervals of the same size. However, for a particular realization, the points are seldom distributed perfectly uniformly, and there is typically some non-uniformity, even if just by chance. This non-uniformity could be due to inhomogeneity, meaning certain locations and times are simply more likely to observe a higher density of points in each realization. In this case the process is not stationary. Alternatively, non-uniformity may be the result of triggering, or what is sometimes called *causal* clustering, meaning points that just happen to occur in a location of space-time tend to cause other points to be more likely to appear nearby. In this latter case, the process might be stationary. The difference boils down to whether one believes the clusters would likely occur in the same places and times if the point process were observed all over again. Distinguishing whether non-uniformity in the data should be attributed to causal clustering or to inhomogeneity with a single realization is very difficult. We will explore these issues further in Chap. 4.

A point process is called *simple* if all the points are distinct, i.e. P(there are distinct indices i and j where $\tau_i = \tau_j) = 0$.

A closely related concept is orderliness. A point process is *orderly* if for any time t and any spatial interval B, $\lim_{\Delta t \to 0} \frac{P(N([t, t+\Delta t) \times B) > 1)}{\Delta t |B|} = 0$. It turns out that if N is simple and stationary, then it is orderly (Daley and Vere-Jones, 2003, 3.3.V and 3.3.VI).

The times $\{t_1, t_2, \ldots, t_n\}$ at which the points occur are sometimes said to form the *ground process*. N has simple ground process if with probability 1, all the times are distinct. Figure 1.12 shows illustrations

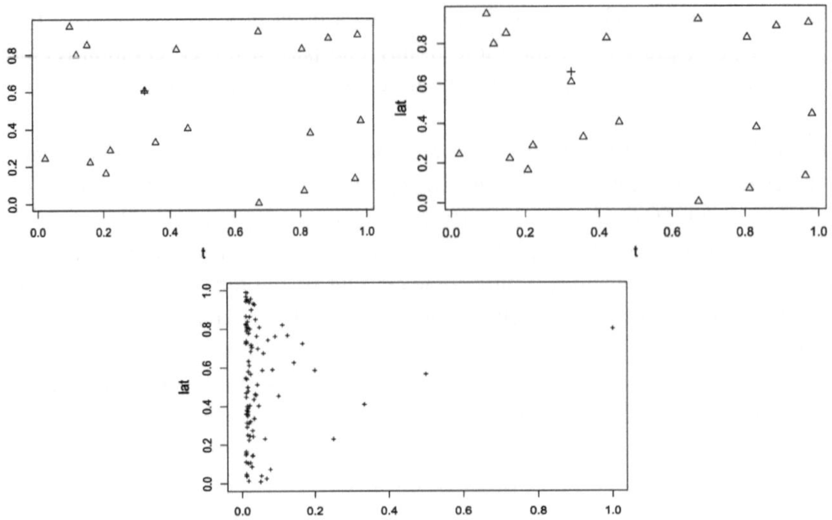

Fig. 1.12 Illustrations of **a** a non-simple process, N, with overlapping points at (0.34, 0.6), **b** a simple process N with non-simple ground process as two points occur at exactly time 0.34, and **c** a non-orderly point process with points at $\{(1/i, U(0,1)), i = 1, 2, ...\}$. The process is only shown for $i = 1$ to 100 here

of a non-simple process, N, a simple process N with non-simple ground process, and a non-orderly point process where the locations on the y-axis are uniformly distributed and the time of each point i occurs at exactly time $1/i$ for each i.

The *R* code used to produce Fig. 1.12 is as follows:

```
## nonsimple point process
n = 20
x = runif(n)
y = runif(n)
plot(x,y,xlab="t",ylab="lat",pch=2)
points(x[20],y[20],pch=3)

## nonsimple ground process
plot(x,y,xlab="t",ylab="lat",pch=2)
points(x[20],y[20]+.05,pch=3)

## nonorderly process
plot(c(0,1),c(0,1),type="n",xlab="t",ylab="lat")
n = 100
for(i in 1:n) points(1/i,runif(1),pch=3,cex=.5)
```

1.6 Conditional Intensity

The key to modeling most space-time point processes is to model the conditional intensity process, λ. We first define the overall rate, μ, and then the conditional intensity as a simple extension.

Fix any space-time location (t, x, y). The *overall rate* $\mu(t, x, y)$ is defined as the limiting rate, in points per unit of space-time, at which points are expected to occur around the location (t, x, y). Think of $\mu(t, x, y)$ as the expected number of points occurring in a small ball around the location (t, x, y), divided by the size of the ball, and let the size of the ball shrink to zero. That is,

$$\mu(t, x, y) = \lim_{\Delta t, r \to 0} \frac{E\{N([t, t + \Delta t) \times B(x, y, r))\}}{\Delta t \pi r^2}, \tag{1.5}$$

where $B(x, y, r)$ is a circle of radius r around (x, y).

The *conditional intensity* $\lambda(t, x, y)$ is the limiting expected rate of accumulation of points around (t, x, y), given all information prior to time t. Mathematically, we can write this as

$$\lambda(t, x, y) = \lim_{\Delta t, r \to 0} \frac{E\{N([t, t + \Delta t) \times B(x, y, r))|H_t\}}{\Delta t \pi r^2}, \tag{1.6}$$

where H_t is the history of the process up to but not including time t. The conditional intensity is also sometimes referred to as the *conditional rate.*

Technically, the conditional intensity depends on a particular *filtration*, $\mathcal{F}_t$, which indicates the information available at time t. For example, at any time t, one might have information only on what wildfires have occurred before time t. Alternatively, one might have information not only on what wildfires have occurred previously but also on other random variables such as the temperature, precipitation, and windspeed at various locations before time t, and in principle these might influence the probability of points occurring at or after time t. Thus, some authors sometimes refer to an $\mathcal{F}-$conditional intensity, for example. At a minimum, the filtration must at least contain all information on where and when all previous points have occurred, and the filtration containing only this information is called the *minimal* filtration to which the point process is adapted. In what follows, we will typically ignore this issue and just refer to λ as the *conditional intensity*, and the filtration will either be assumed to be the minimal filtration or, in the case of modeling using covariates such as temperature, precipitation, and windspeed, the filtration will be information on these covariates as well as the points that have occurred.

If N is orderly, then the conditional intensity can alternatively be written in terms of a conditional probability, instead of a conditional expectation. That is, if N is orderly, then

$$\lambda(t, x, y) = \lim_{\Delta t, r \to 0} \frac{P(N([t, t + \Delta t) \times B(x, y, r)) > 0|H_t)}{\Delta t \pi r^2}. \tag{1.7}$$

In fact, Eq. (1.7) seems to be the only reason for defining orderliness. The idea behind (1.7) is that, for any random variable X that must either take the value 0 or 1, $P(X > 0) = E(X)$. If N is orderly, then in a small space-time ball B around location (t, x, y), the probability that there are at least two points in B goes to zero as B gets sufficiently small. As a result, with probability going to 1, effectively $N(B)$ is either 0 or 1, and therefore the probability $P\{N(B) > 0\}$ is the same as $EN(B)$.

Note that the conditional intensity λ is random. It not only can vary across space and time, but may depend on what points have occurred previously, and these might be different with every realization. In later chapters, we will see many examples of point process models where λ depends very critically on what points have occurred previously. For instance, in modeling earthquakes, a fundamental observation is that after an earthquake occurs, it is likely to trigger aftershocks in its near vicinity. Therefore, the conditional intensity λ at any location (t, x, y) in space-time depends very much on whether there has recently been an earthquake nearby, and thus is a random variable. The overall rate, $\mu(t, x, y)$, is not random, and $\mu(t, x, y) = E[\lambda(t, x, y)]$.

It is important to point out that λ is *predictable*, a principle that becomes especially significant when using the martingale formula described in Chap. 1.6. Predictability has a very technical mathematical definition: predictable means adapted to the filtration generated by the left-continuous processes. For our practical purposes, though, we can think of *predictability* as just a slight generalization of left-continuity. Essentially, a process $Z(t, x, y)$ is *predictable* if knowing the value of Z at all previous times and locations allows you to know for certain what the value of $Z(t, x, y)$ will be. If Z is left-continuous, then Z is predictable, because at any location (x, y), no sudden jump would be permitted to occur at time 1.0 to separate Z from its values at times 0.999, 0.9999, 0.99999, etc. It makes intuitive sense that $\lambda(t)$ is predictable, since if you know all information leading up to time t, then you can determine what the *expected* rate of points around time t will be. However, $N(\{t\})$ is not predictable, because information prior to time t does not typically allow you to determine for sure whether or not a point will occur precisely at time t.

If for any (t, x, y), the limit in (1.6) does not exist or is ∞, we say $\lambda(t, x, y)$ does not exist. Assuming it exists everywhere, λ uniquely determines the distributions of any simple point process (Daley and Vere-Jones, 2003, Proposition 7.2.IV). This is an amazing fact. For many stochastic processes, one needs to know the conditional mean and variance and maybe more information in order to specify the distributions of the process. For Gaussian processes, for instance, one needs to specify the mean, variance, and covariance of the process in order to specify all its finite-dimensional distributions. For simple point processes, all you need is the conditional mean, λ. In modeling a point process, we typically assume it is simple and then just write down a model for λ.

1.7 Simple Hypothetical Examples

In this section, some very simple examples of point processes are discussed. These examples may not be realistic descriptions of datasets at all. The purpose is merely to ensure proper understanding of the definitions and concepts defined previously, especially conditional intensity.

Example 1. A single point, uniformly distributed. Perhaps one of the simplest examples of a point process one could imagine would be the case of a purely temporal point process where a single point is placed uniformly somewhere on the unit interval (0, 1), and there are no other points. One might suspect that such a process would have conditional intensity 1, since after all there will be one point in a time span of length 1, so the overall rate at which points are generated is one point per time unit. Note that for any small value of Δ, the probability of a point occurring in $(0, \Delta)$ is Δ, and the expected number of points in $(0, \Delta)$ is $0 \times P\{\text{no points in } (0, \Delta)\} + 1 \times P\{\text{one point in } (0, \Delta)\} = \Delta$, so $\lambda(0) = \lim_{\Delta \downarrow 0} \frac{EN(0,\Delta)}{\Delta} = \frac{\Delta}{\Delta} = 1$, i.e. the conditional intensity at time 0 is indeed 1.

Even this basic process has surprising complexity, however. What would you guess is the conditional intensity at time 0.9? The answer is: it depends! If a point has already occurred at or before time 0.9, then there is no chance for any point to occur after time 0.9, so the conditional intensity at time 0.9 would be 0. However, if a point has not occurred in the time span [0, 0.9), then for any small number Δ, the probability of a point occurring in $(0.9, 0.9 + \Delta)$ is $\Delta/0.1 = 10\Delta$, so $\lambda(0.9) = \lim_{\Delta \downarrow 0} 10\Delta/\Delta = 10$.

Thus, even for this very elementary example of a point process, there is considerable complexity. $\lambda(0.9)$ takes the value 0 if a point has occurred previously, and $\lambda(0.9) = 10$ if no point has occurred.

Note that the expected value $E\{\lambda(0.9)\} = 1$, since P(no point has occurred before time 0.9) $= 1/10$. For this single point process, $\mu(t) = E\{\lambda(t)\} = 1$ for all t, even though $\lambda(t)$ varies. An important idea highlighted by this example is that the conditional intensity λ is in general *random*, meaning its value at a given time depends on what points have occurred previously.

Example 2. A single point, exponentially distributed. Another example of a very basic, elementary temporal point process may be instructive. Consider again the case of a point process with only one point, but suppose now that this point is not uniformly distributed but instead exponentially distributed on $(0, \infty)$, with density $f(t) = exp(-t)$. Now what is the conditional intensity, $\lambda(t)$?

The answer again is: it depends. If a point has occurred prior to time t, then obviously $\lambda(t) = 0$. However, if no point has occurred yet, then $\lambda(t) = 1$, for any t. To see this, suppose first $t = 0$. Then since N cannot possibly have more than one point,

$$\begin{aligned}
\lambda(0) &= \lim_{\Delta \downarrow 0} EN(0, \Delta)/\Delta \\
&= \lim_{\Delta \downarrow 0} P\{N(0, \Delta) = 1\}/\Delta \\
&= \lim_{\Delta \downarrow 0} \int_0^{\Delta} e^{-t} dt/\Delta \\
&= \lim_{\Delta \downarrow 0} (1 - e^{-\Delta})/\Delta \\
&= \lim_{\Delta \downarrow 0} e^{-\Delta} \\
&= 1,
\end{aligned}$$

by L'Hôpital's rule.

Similarly, for any other value of t, if no point has occurred previously and this information is denoted H_t, then note that $P(H_t) = e^{-t}$, and, using the definition of conditional probability $[P(A|B) = P(A$ and $B)/P(B)]$,

$$\begin{aligned}
\lambda(t) &= \lim_{\Delta \downarrow 0} EN(t, t + \Delta | H_t)/\Delta \\
&= \lim_{\Delta \downarrow 0} P\{N(t, t + \Delta) = 1 | H_t\}/\Delta \\
&= \lim_{\Delta \downarrow 0} \frac{\int_t^{t+\Delta} e^{-t} dt}{\Delta P(H_t)} \\
&= \lim_{\Delta \downarrow 0} \frac{e^{-t} - e^{-(t+\Delta)}}{\Delta e^{-t}} \\
&= \lim_{\Delta \downarrow 0} \frac{e^{-(t+\Delta)}}{e^{-t}} \\
&= 1,
\end{aligned}$$

again using L'Hôpital's rule.

In the last two examples, we have seen a point process with $E\{\lambda(t)\} = 1$ for all t, and a point process where $\lambda(t) = 1$ for all t provided no point has occurred yet, but in both of these examples, $\lambda(t)$ depends critically on whether or not a point has occurred previously. In both examples, if a point *has* occurred previously, then $\lambda(t) = 0$. So is there a process where $\lambda(t) = 1$ for all t, regardless of what points have occurred previously? The answer is yes. In the special case of a simple point process where the conditional intensity happens to be independent of what happened previously, we call the process a Poisson process, and these types of processes are described in the next chapter.

1.8 Martingale Theorem

The rich theory of martingales supplies many results that are important for the study of point processes. A temporal process $X(t)$ is said to be a *martingale* if for any time t, any time horizon u, and any prior times $s_1, s_2, ..., \leq t$, $E\{X(t+u)|X(s_1), X(s_2), ..., X(t)\} = X(t)$. That is, given prior values of X, our expectation of the value X will take in the future is simply given by the last observed value, $X(t)$. If X represents the price of a stock, for instance, then to say X is a martingale means there is no momentum and no correction, and regardless of what price movements have occurred in the past, there is no reason to expect the stock price to be more likely to go up in the future or to go down in the future; our expectation of what value the stock will take in the future is always simply whatever value it is at currently. Martingales have been studied extensively by mathematicians, and some very useful results involving martingales can be applied to point processes.

The connection between point processes and martingales is this. Fix any spatial region, S. The integral of λ, $A(t, S) = \int_0^t \int_S \lambda(t, x, y)dxdydt$ is called the *compensator* of N. For any S, $N(t, S) - A(t, S)$ is a martingale.

Technical note: some authors (e.g. Jacod, 1975) actually define the compensator A as a predictable process such that $N - A$ is a martingale, and then define the conditional intensity λ as the Radon-Nikodym derivative of A, assuming this derivative exists.

Like the conditional intensity, the compensator A also uniquely defines any simple point process (Jacod, 1975). Thus, one way of proving that a point process has some particular distribution is to show that its compensator has the corresponding form.

A key formula for space-time point processes is called the martingale formula: for any predictable function $f(t, x, y)$,

$$\begin{aligned} E\int f(t,x,y)dN &:= E\sum_i f(t_i, x_i, y_i) \\ &= E\int f(t,x,y)\lambda(t,x,y)dtdxdy. \end{aligned} \tag{1.8}$$

The notation ":=" is meant purely to signify that the first equality is simply the *definition* of $E\int f(t, x, y)dN$. The fact that this sum can equivalently be computed as the integral in (1.8) is key to a lot of computation in later chapters. Note that when $f(t, x, y) = 1$, the martingale formula reduces to $EN(B) = E\int_B \lambda(t, x, y)dtdxdy$, which should make intuitive sense: the expected total number of points is equal to the total expected rate.

1.9 Purely Spatial Processes, Papangelou Intensity, and the Georgii-Zessin-Nguyen Formula

For point processes in $\mathbf{R}^2$, there is no natural ordering as there is in time. One could just use the x-coordinate in place of time and define a conditional intensity, but most models for spatial processes would be very awkward to define this way.

Instead, a more natural and useful tool is the Papangelou intensity, $\lambda_P(x, y)$, which is the conditional rate of points around location (x, y), given information on everywhere else. Letting $L_P(\theta) = \sum \log\{\lambda_P(\tau_i)\} - \int \lambda_P(x, y)dxdy$, where $\lambda_P(x, y)$ is the Papangelou intensity, $L_P(\theta)$ is called the pseudo-log-likelihood.

For spatial point processes there is a formula corresponding to (1.8), namely, $E\int f(x, y)dN = E\int f(x, y)\lambda_P(x, y)dxdy$ which also holds, for any deterministic function f, and this is called the

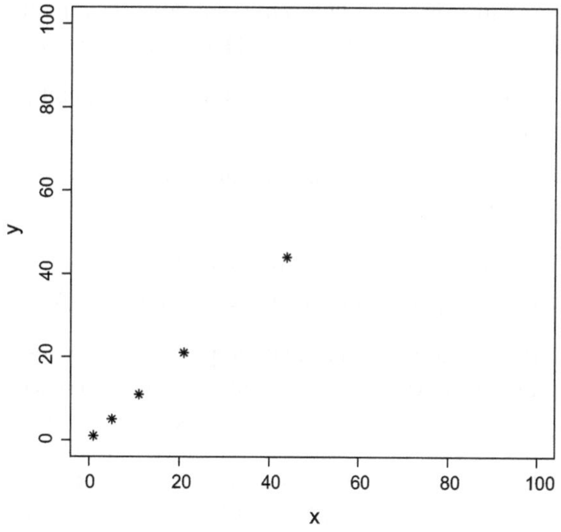

Fig. 1.13 A point process with points at (i, i, i) with probability $1/i$. Only the first two coordinates (x, y) are shown, and the process is only shown for $i = 1$ to 100 here

Georgii-Zessin-Nguyen formula (Nguyen & Zessin, 1979; Georgii, 1988). When $f = 1$ this means $EN(B) = E \int_B \lambda_P(x, y)dxdy$, and when both $f = 1$ and $\lambda_P = 1$, this means $EN(B) = |B|$, the size of the spatial observation region.

1.10 Exercises

1.1. Suppose the spatial-temporal point process N has points at the three space-time locations ($t = 1.2$, $x = 2$, $y = 3$), ($t = 2.4, x = 3, y = 0.5$), and ($t = 8.7, x = 2, y = 1$). Let $B = [0, 10]$ (time) $\times[1.5, 2.5] \times [0, 5]$. What is $\int\limits_B dN$?

1.2. Suppose the spatial-temporal point process N has points at the three space-time locations ($t = 1.2, x = 2, y = 3$), ($t = 2.4, x = 3, y = 0.5$), and ($t = 8.7, x = 2, y = 1$). Let $B = [0, 10] \times [0, 5] \times [0, 5]$. What is $\int_B (t + x^2 y) dN$?

1.3. Suppose N is generated as follows. For each integer $i = 1, 2, ...,$ N has a point at (i, i, i) with probability $1/i$, independently of the other points, and N has no other points. An example is shown in Fig. 1.13. What is $\lambda(2, 2, 2)$?
(a) 2. (b) 1. (c) 0. (d) does not exist.

The *R* code for producing Fig. 1.13 is as follows:

```
## points at (i,i) with prob. 1/i.
plot(c(0,100),c(0,100),type="n",xlab="x",ylab="y")
for(i in 1:100) if(runif(1) < 1/i) points(i,i,pch=8)
```

1.4. Suppose N is generated as follows. For each integer $i = 1, 2, ...,$ N has a point at (i, i, i) with probability $1/i$, independently of the other points, and N has no other points. N is
(a) simple but not orderly. (b) orderly but not simple. (c) simple and orderly. (d) neither simple nor orderly.

1.5. Suppose N always has one point distributed uniformly on the unit cube $B = [0, 1] \times [0, 1] \times [0, 1]$. What is $\lambda(0.5, 0.5, 0.5)$?

1.6. Suppose N is a *binomial* point process, with 100 points independently distributed uniformly on the unit cube $B = [0, 1] \times [0, 1] \times [0, 1]$. What is $\lambda(0.5, 0.5, 0.5)$?

1.7. Show that the distribution of any simple point process is uniquely determined by the void probabilities.

1.8. Suppose N has a single point in time somewhere on $[0, 1]$, and that the point must be at a rational time. What is λ?

1.9. Suppose N is a temporal point process where only 3 points occur between time 0 and time 100, and they happen at times 10.0, 25.0, and 82.0. What is $\int_0^{100} \left[\int_0^t (t-u)^2\, dN(u)\right] dN(t)$?

1.10. Suppose N is a spatial-temporal point process where only 3 points occur on the unit square S between time 0 and time 100, and they happen at space-time locations $(t, x, y) = (10.0, 0.4, 0.7)$, (25.0, 0.2, 0.9) and (82.0, 0.5, 0.4). What is $\int_0^{100} \int_S \left[\int_0^t (t-u)^2 xy\, dN(u)\right] dN(t, x, y)$?

1.11. Suppose N is a simple point process with conditional intensity $\lambda(t, x, y) = 1 + 2t + 3x + 4y$ on the unit cube $B = [0, 1] \times [0, 1] \times [0, 1]$. Let the statistic R denote the total rate at the observed points, $R = \sum_{i=1}^{N(B)} \lambda(t, x, y)$, where $R = 0$ if $N(B) = 0$. Find $E(R)$.

1.12. Suppose N is a simple purely spatial point process on the unit square $S = [0, 1] \times [0, 1]$ with Papangelou intensity $\lambda(x, y) = e^x$. Let L_P be the pseudo-log-likelihood. What is $E(L_P)$? Hint: you will need to use the integration by parts formula: $\int u dv = uv - \int v du$.

References

Brillinger, D. R. (1997). A particle migrating randomly on a sphere. *Journal of Theoretical Probability, 10*, 429–433.

Brillinger, D. R. (2000). Some examples of random process environmental data analysis. In C. R. Rao & P. K. Sen (Eds.), *Handbook of Statistics* (Vol. 18, pp. 33–56). NorthHolland.

Daley, D. J., & Jones, D. V. (2003). *An introduction to the theory of point processes: Elementary theory of point processes*. New York: Springer.

Diggle, P. J. (1983). *Statistical analysis of spatial point patterns*. Academic.

Georgii, H.-O. (1988). *Gibbs measures and phase transitions*. Walter de Gruyter.

Jacod, J. (1975). Multivariate point processes: predictable projections, Radon-Nikodym derivatives, representation of martingales. *Zeitschrift für Wahrscheinlichkeitstheorie und verwandte Gebiete, 31*, 235–253.

Nguyen, X. X., & Zessin, H. (1979). Integral and differential characterizations of the Gibbs point process. *Mathematische Nachrichten, 88*, 105–115.

2 Models

In some cases, point patterns can be analyzed without models. If one's goal is merely to summarize the overall rate of points per unit of space-time, to smooth out the points in order to detect potential hotspots of activity, or perhaps even to detect clustering or trends, all of these tasks can sometimes be performed without considering point process models. Chapter 4 is devoted to ways of describing point patterns, many of which do not involve modeling at all. However, if one's goal is to forecast future behavior, to characterize and understand complex behavior, to distinguish inhomogeneity from triggering, to estimate the probability of an event occurring in some spatial-temporal region, or to determine whether a particular characteristic of the data is statistically significant, then some sort of point process model will typically be necessary. Further, the main way to understand the behavior of descriptors of point processes is by studying their properties for particular point process models.

2.1 Poisson Processes and Their Variants

The most basic model for point processes is the Poisson process. If N is a simple point process with conditional intensity λ, where λ does not depend on what points have occurred previously, then N is a *Poisson process*. The name comes from the fact that for such a process, for any spatial-temporal interval B, $N(B)$ has a Poisson distribution (the proof of this fact will be shown momentarily).

The Poisson distribution has a very particular form. $P\{N(B) = k\} = e^{-A}A^k/k!$, for $k = 0, 1, 2, \ldots$, where $A = \int_B \lambda(t, x, y)dtdxdy$, and with the convention $0! = 1$. The mean of $N(B)$ is A and the variance of $N(B)$ is also A.

Note that a Poisson process does not have to be stationary. A simple point process with $\lambda(t, x, y) = 10.5 + 2t + 4x + e^{-y}$, for example, is a Poisson process. If λ is constant for all t, x, and y, and N is simple, then N is a *stationary* (or equivalently, homogeneous) Poisson process, and is sometimes called *completely random*. Figure 2.1 shows a realization of a stationary Poisson process with $\lambda(t, x) = 2.5$ on $[0, 1] \times [0, 10]$, a realization of a non-stationary (inhomogeneous) Poisson process where the rate of points increases as t or x increase, and a realization of a non-stationary Poisson process where the rate is higher inside the circle of radius 0.2 centered at (0.4, 0.7) than outside it.

Simulating a stationary Poisson process is very easy. To generate the left panel in Fig. 2.1, for instance, the following *R* code can be used.

F. Schoenberg, *Space-Time Point Processes*, Springer Texts in Statistics,
https://doi.org/10.1007/978-3-032-20790-6_2

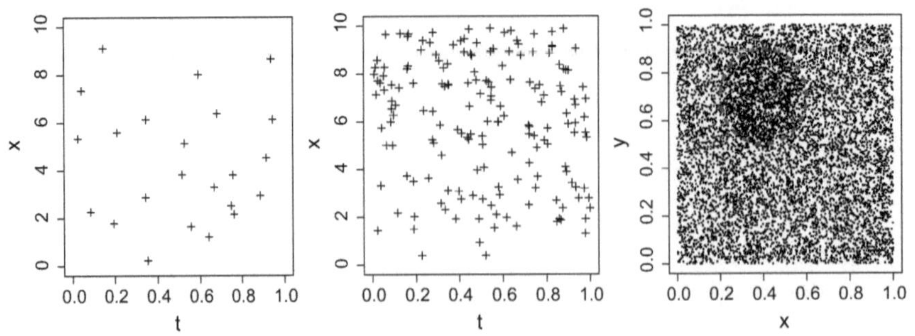

Fig. 2.1 Left: stationary Poisson process with $\lambda(t, x) = 2.5$, for $t \in [0, 1]$, $x \in [0, 10]$. Middle: inhomogeneous Poisson process with $\lambda(t, x) = 1.5 + 10t + 2x$, for $t \in [0, 1]$, $x \in [0, 10]$. Right: inhomogeneous Poisson process with $\lambda(t, x, y) = 1 + \mathbf{1}_{\{||(x,y)-(0.4,0.7)||<0.2\}}$ for $t \in [0, 8000]$, $x, y \in [0, 1]$

```
n = rpois(1,2.5*10)
t = runif(n)
x = runif(n)*10
plot(c(0,1),c(0,10),xlab="t",ylab="x",type="n")
points(t,x,pch=3)
```

One way to simulate an inhomogeneous Poisson process with rate $\lambda(t, x, y)$ is by *thinning*. One first generates candidate points according to a homogeneous Poisson process with rate b, where $b \geq \lambda(t, x, y)$ for all t, x, y in the space-time domain. For instance, to generate the inhomogeneous Poisson process with rate $\lambda(t, x) = 1.5 + 10t + 2x$ on $[0, 1] \times [0, 10]$ as shown in the middle in Fig. 2.1, one may do:

```
n = rpois(1, 31.5*10)  ## on the domain [0,1]x[0,10],
## lambda <= 1.5 + 10(1) + 2(20) = 31.5, and domain has area 10.
candt = runif(n); candx = runif(n)*10
accept = (runif(n) < (1.5 + 10*candt + 2*candx)/31.5) ## logical
## vector of TRUE/FALSEs, indicating if we accept the point or not.
t = candt[accept]
x = candx[accept]
plot(c(0,1),c(0,10),xlab="t",ylab="x",type="n")
points(t,x,pch=3)
```

The following code simulates the inhomogeneous Poisson process with rate $\lambda(t, x, y) = 1 + \mathbf{1}_{\{||(x,y)-(0.4,0.7)||<0.2\}}$ for $t \in [0, 8000]$ and $x, y \in [0, 1]$, shown in the right in Fig. 2.1. Here the maximum possible value of λ is simply 2.

```
n = rpois(1, 2*8000*1*1)  ## on the domain [0,8000] x [0,1] x [0,1],
candx = runif(n); candy = runif(n)
accept = (runif(n) < (1 + ((candx-.4)^2 + (candy-.7)^2 < .2^2))/2)
x = candx[accept]; y = candy[accept]
plot(c(0,1),c(0,1),xlab="x",ylab="y",type="n")
points(x,y,pch=1,cex=.2)
a = seq(.201,.599,length=100); b = sqrt(.04-(a-.4)^2) ## red circle
lines(a[c(1:100,100:1)],c(b+.7,.7-b),lty=3,col="red",lwd=3)
```

The key thing about Poisson processes is their *complete independence*. For a Poisson process N, $N(B_1)$, $N(B_2)$, ..., $N(B_j)$ are independent for any disjoint sets B_1, B_2, ..., B_j. This complete independence property follows immediately from the property that, for a Poisson process, the conditional intensity $\lambda(t, x, y)$ at a particular location (t, x, y) does not depend on the number of points occurring previously, and the fact that the distribution of N is completely determined by λ.

In fact, if a simple, orderly point process with conditional rate λ obeys the complete independence property, then it is a Poisson process. To see why, fix any region B, and suppose for any n, we divide the region B into little disjoint intervals $B_1^{(n)}$, ..., $B_n^{(n)}$, each containing an equal expected number of points, such that $EN(B_i^{(n)}) = E(N(B))/n$. Now let each interval get smaller and smaller as $n \to \infty$. If N is simple and orderly, then this can be done so that ultimately each of the intervals is so small that no interval contains more than one point, i.e. for sufficiently large n, $P(N(B_i^{(n)}) > 1) \to 0$ and thus $EN(B_i^{(n)}) = P(N(B_i^{(n)}) > 0)$. For any n, the number of intervals with at least one point is a binomial random variable, because of the complete independence property. And as $n \to \infty$, it is well known that the binomial converges to the Poisson distribution. Specifically, if $np \to \lambda$ as $n \to \infty$, then $P\{N(B) = k\} = \lim_{n\to\infty} C_{n,k} p^k (1-p)^{n-k} = \lim_{n\to\infty} e^{-np}(np)^k/k! = e^{-\lambda}\lambda^k/k!$. To complete the proof, note that the total number of points, $N(B)$, has the same limiting distribution as the number of intervals with at least one point, since as n gets large the probability of an interval having two or more points converges to zero.

Counterexample. Note that it is technically possible for a simple point process with the complete independence property not to be Poisson. Consider a process N that is destined to have, with certainty, exactly one point at the origin, (0, 0, 0), and no other points. For any region B containing the origin, $N(B) = 1$ with probability 100%, which is different from a Poisson random variable with mean 1. In this counterexample, the expected number of points around the origin per unit of space-time diverges to infinity, so the conditional intensity does not exist, at least at the origin. The reader who goes back to check the definition of a Poisson process will note that we subtly assumed that the conditional intensity exists by assuming that "N is a simple point process with conditional intensity λ".

Since a Poisson process obeys the complete independence property, the conditional rate λ never depends on what occurred previously, so in discussing Poisson processes, we often omit the term *conditional* because it is superfluous. Instead, one models the *rate* of the Poisson process, which in general might vary as t, x, and y vary. To put it another way, for a Poisson process, the conditional rate $\lambda(t, x, y)$ is identical to the overall rate $\mu(t, x, y)$.

What types of datasets may be modeled using Poisson processes? In order for the Poisson model to be appropriate, the complete independence property must be reasonable. The best examples are ones where there is a very small probability of some event occurring in any particular location, but there are many opportunities for it to occur, and any single instance of the event occurring neither triggers nor inhibits future events. The Poisson distribution's original formulation by Siméon Denis Poisson was motivated by considering the number of defendants wrongly convicted of crimes each year in a given country. Another early example studied by Ladislaus Bortkiewicz was instances of soldiers in the Prussian army dying by being kicked by horses. With both of these examples, though the probability of an instance occurring for any particular defendant or soldier may be very small, the total number of occurrences, aggregated over all individuals, may be well approximated by the Poisson distribution.

While it is inappropriate to use a Poisson process model to describe earthquake occurrences in general due to the obvious triggering of aftershocks especially by large earthquakes, Poisson processes have nevertheless been used to describe *declustered* sequences of earthquakes consisting of only the largest events. Poisson processes have also been used in some situations as null hypothesis models in order to assess whether a certain degree of clustering or other behavior is real: if the data exhibit some property more than one would observe 95% of the time from a Poisson process, then we might say the behavior is *statistically significant*. Poisson processes have thus been used in all sorts of applications, including environmental sciences, cellular biology, neurology, forestry, and astronomy.

2.2 Mixed Poisson Processes

Suppose $\lambda(t, x, y) = c$, where c is a random variable. For example, c might be Poisson or exponential, or half normal, or something constrained to be positive. Conditional on c, let N be a stationary Poisson process with rate c. Then N is called a *mixed* Poisson process.

For a mixed Poisson process N, $E(N(B)|c) = V(N(B)|c) = c|B|$, but unconditionally, $N(B)$ is not Poisson distributed. If we imagine simulating the process repeatedly, each time with a different draw of c, then the distribution of $N(B)$ will not be Poisson. $N(B)$ will typically be *overdispersed* relative to the Poisson process, meaning it will have higher variance.

To see this, note that for any random variable X with finite mean and variance, $V(X) = E(X^2) - [E(X)]^2$, and if X is a Poisson random variable, then $V(X) = E(X)$, so $E(X^2) = [E(X)]^2 + E(X)$. Now observe that, for a mixed Poisson process, conditioning on c,

$E(N(B)) = \int E(N(B)|c)f(c)dc = \int c|B|f(c)dc = |B|E(c)$.
$E(N(B)^2) = \int E(N(B)^2|c)f(c)dc = \int[c^2|B|^2 + c|B|]f(c)dc = |B|^2E(c^2) + |B|E(c)$,
so $V(N(B)) = |B|^2E(c^2) + |B|E(c) - |B|^2[E(c)]^2 = E(N(B)) + |B|^2V(c)$. Thus, $V(N(B)) \geq E(N(B))$.

Figure 2.2 illustrates three realizations of a mixed Poisson process. One sees that the rate is sometimes low, sometimes medium, and sometimes high, but whatever the rate happens to be, the points will be uniformly distributed throughout the space-time region.

Simulations of mixed Poisson processes, like those in Fig. 2.2, can be generated by repeatedly running the *R* code below.

```
m = rexp(1,rate=.5)
n1 = rpois(1,m*10*10)
x1 = runif(n1)*10; y1 = runif(n1)*10
plot(c(0,10),c(0,10),xlab="lon",ylab="lat",type="n")
points(x1,y1)
```

An example of a mixed Poisson process might be the locations of people seen on a portion of a University campus at some randomly chosen time during the week. If one happens to choose a time

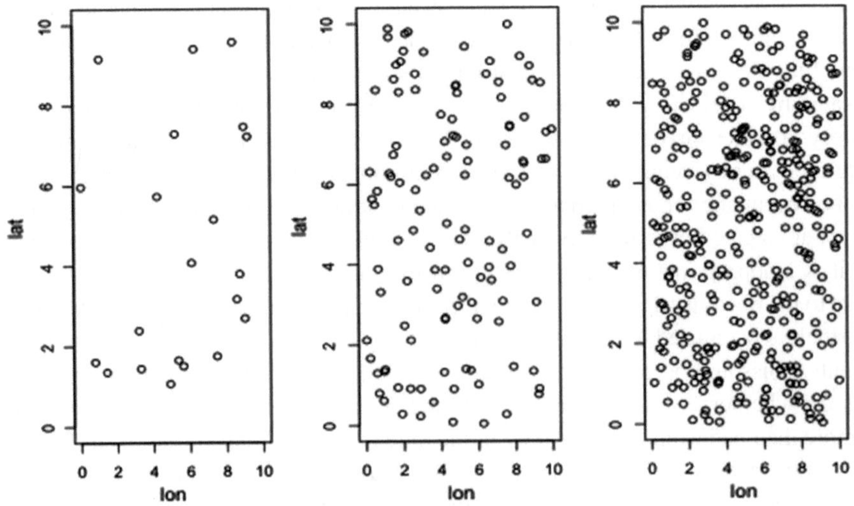

Fig. 2.2 Mixed Poisson process where c is an exponential (0.5) random variable

when the campus is more crowded, then there will tend to be more people observed, but one might choose a time during the night or the weekend when the campus is more sparse. The mixed Poisson process has been used in engineering to model repairs required for certain products; some products are more faulty and need many repairs, while some need fewer, and the failure rate for a given product may be unknown ahead of time and thus considered random (Cha & Finkelstein, 2018). Another example application involves warranty pricing, for modeling the times of failures of products, some of which were purchased new and some purchased used (Nguyen & Murthy, 1984).

2.3 Compound Poisson Processes

Recall that a point process is *simple* if with probability 1, no two of the points coincide exactly. The requirement of simplicity does not appear to be met for some applications to data. For example, seismological research on faulting suggests that earthquakes may begin with multiple ruptures at the same or infinitesimally different times (Kagan, 1994); in such cases even if the underlying earthquake process is simple, the recorded observations of such events may not be.

Some interesting examples of non-simple point processes are worth discussing. For example, suppose M is a stationary Poisson process with rate 1, N_1 is a non-simple process with 2 points wherever M has a point, and N_2 is a stationary Poisson process with rate 2. Then both N_1 and N_2 have a rate of 2 everywhere, but they are obviously not the same process. Indeed, if we calculate, for example, the probability that each of them has at least 2 points in some region B of volume 0.1, then we see quite a substantial difference.

$$P\{N_1(B) \geq 2\} = 1 - P\{M(B) = 0\} = 1 - \exp(-0.1) \approx 9.52\%.$$

However,

$$P\{N_2(B) \geq 2\} = 1 - P\{N_1(B) = 0\} - P\{N_1(B) = 1\} = 1 - \exp(-0.2) - 0.2\exp(-0.2) \approx 1.75\%.$$

More generally, suppose N is not simple, and is generated as follows. First generate a stationary Poisson process M with intensity c, and then for each point τ_i of M, let N have some non-negative number Z_i of points right at τ_i, where Z_i are all independent and identically distributed (iid) and independent of M. Then N is a *compound Poisson process.*

For a compound Poisson process, like the mixed Poisson process, the variance is greater than or equal to the mean.

$$\begin{aligned}
\mathbb{E}[N(B)] &= \sum_m \mathbb{E}[N(B)|M(B) = m]f(m) \\
&= \sum_m \mathbb{E}[Z_1 + Z_2 + \cdots + Z_m]f(m) \\
&= \sum_m m\mathbb{E}[Z]f(m) \\
&= \mathbb{E}[Z]\sum_m mf(m) \\
&= \mathbb{E}[Z]\,\mathbb{E}[M].
\end{aligned}$$

Similarly, one can condition on $M(B) = m$ in computing $\mathbb{E}(N^2)$ and $Var(N)$.

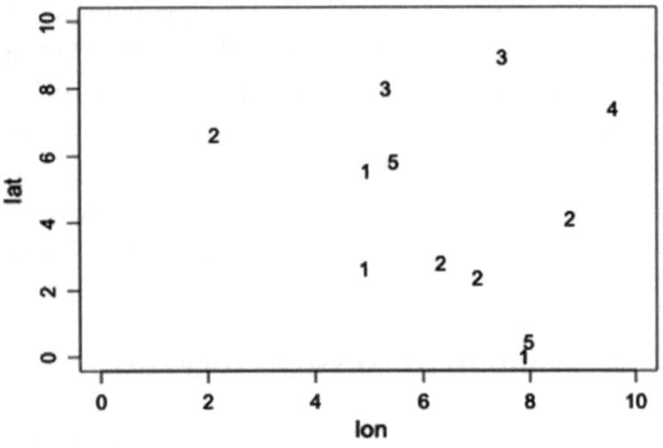

Fig. 2.3 Compound Poisson process where each Z_i is a Poisson (3) random variable. The integrers represent the number of points at each location

$$
\begin{aligned}
\mathbb{E}[N(B)^2] &= \sum_m \mathbb{E}[N(B)^2 | M(B) = m] f(m) \\
&= \sum_m \mathbb{E}[(Z_1 + Z_2 + \cdots + Z_m)^2] f(m) \\
&= \sum_m \left(m\mathbb{E}[Z^2] + (m^2 - m)\mathbb{E}[Z]^2 \right) f(m) \qquad (*) \\
&= \mathbb{E}[Z^2] \sum_m m f(m) + \mathbb{E}[Z]^2 \sum_m m^2 f(m) - \mathbb{E}[Z]^2 \sum_m m f(m) \\
&= \mathbb{E}[Z^2]\mathbb{E}[M] + \mathbb{E}[Z]^2\mathbb{E}[M^2] - \mathbb{E}[Z]^2\mathbb{E}[M] \\
&= \mathbb{E}[M]\mathbb{V}(Z) + \mathbb{E}[Z]^2\mathbb{E}[M^2].
\end{aligned}
$$

Therefore,

$$
\begin{aligned}
\mathbb{V}(N(B)) &= \mathbb{E}[M]\mathbb{V}(Z) + \mathbb{E}[Z]^2\mathbb{E}[M^2] - (\mathbb{E}[Z]\mathbb{E}[M])^2 \\
&= \mathbb{E}[M]\mathbb{V}(Z) + \mathbb{E}[Z]^2\mathbb{V}(M) \\
&= c|B|(\mathbb{V}(Z) + \mathbb{E}[Z]^2) \\
&= c|B| \ \mathbb{E}[Z^2].
\end{aligned}
$$

Thus, $\mathbb{V}(N(B)) = c|B|\mathbb{V}(Z) + c|B|(\mathbb{E}(Z))^2 = c|B|\mathbb{E}(Z^2) \geq \mathbb{E}(N(B))$, because, for any non-negative integer-valued random variable Z, $\mathbb{E}(Z^2) \geq \mathbb{E}(Z)$ with equality if and only if Z can only be 0 or 1.

A realization of a compound Poisson process is in Fig. 2.3, and the code used to generate it is below.

```
n1 = rpois(1,.12*10*10)
x1 = runif(n1)*10; y1 = runif(n1)*10
a = as.character(rpois(n1,3))
plot(c(0,10),c(0,10),xlab="lon",ylab="lat",type="n")
text(x1,y1,a)
```

A hypothetical example of a compound Poisson process might be the number of different loaves of bread in markets throughout Los Angeles during the beginning of the COVID-19 pandemic. Many markets have zero loaves, and some might have 1, or 2, or 5, occurring essentially at the exact same location. Another example is the locations of baby birds, where nests occur randomly within the space,

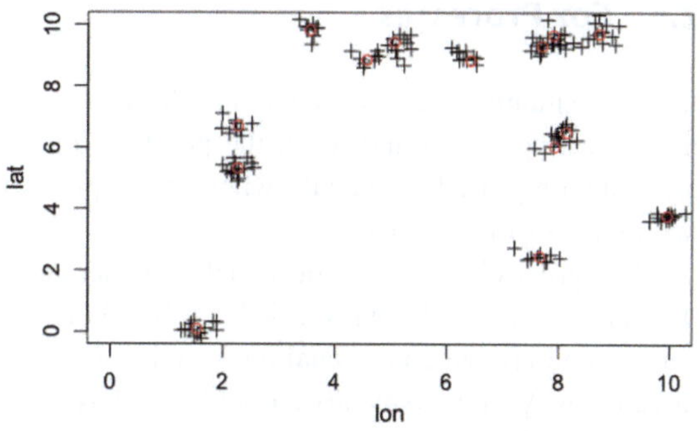

Fig. 2.4 Simulated Neyman-Scott process. The points of the Neyman-Scott process are in black, and the underlying parent points used to generate them are shown in red

and within each nest one might find multiple birds. Compound Poisson processes have been used to model deaths from violent crimes, for example, (Kegler, 2007), where many times there is only one victim but for some crimes there is more than one victim.

Other models for non-simple point processes will be discussed in Sect. 2.9.

2.4 Poisson Cluster Processes

Another extension of the Poisson process is the Poisson cluster process. Imagine first generating parent points M according to a Poisson process. Then for each parent point s_i, generate some random number Z_i of offspring points, where these offspring points are scattered spatially and temporally, independently of each other, with some distribution centered at s_i. Let N be the collection of just the offspring, not the parents. N is called a *Poisson cluster process*. Usually M is assumed stationary Poisson, and in the particular case where the Z_i are iid Poisson random variables independent of M, the process is called a Neyman-Scott cluster process.

Figure 2.4 shows a realization of a Neyman-Scott cluster process. The code used to make Fig. 2.4 is below.

```
n1 = rpois(1,.12*10*10)
x1 = runif(n1)*10; y1 = runif(n1)*10
x2 = c(); y2 = c() ## parents are (x1,y1).
for(i in 1:n1){
c = rpois(1,8) ## number of offspring
if(c>0) for(j in 1:c){
x2 = c(x2,rnorm(1,sd=.2)+x1[i])
y2 = c(y2,rnorm(1,sd=.2)+y1[i])
}}
plot(c(0,10),c(0,10),xlab="lon",ylab="lat",type="n")
points(x2,y2,pch=3)
points(x1,y1,col="red")
```

Neyman-Scott models have been used to describe rainfall patterns, for example (Wheater et al., 2005). The idea is that storms arrive randomly according to a Poisson process, and then each storm spreads some random amount of precipitation to the areas around it.

2.5 Cox Processes

In some situations, a researcher may have access to some *covariate*, i.e. a variable that can help in forecasting where and when the points are more likely to occur. In these cases, Cox processes are commonly used, especially when one is primarily interested in how the covariate influences the occurrences of the points.

More precisely, suppose you somehow generate a stochastic process $\lambda(t, x, y)$ such that $\lambda(t, x, y) \geq 0$ for all t, x, and y. Then given λ, let N be a Poisson process with intensity $\lambda(t, x, y)$. Thus, $\lambda(t, x, y)$ can be random, but conditional on λ, N is a Poisson process. In this case we say N is a *Cox process* directed by λ, or equivalently a doubly stochastic Poisson process (Stoyan et al., 1995).

A realization of a Cox process is shown in Fig. 2.5. Cox processes arise in practice when modeling events depending on some covariate that may reasonably be considered random, or unpredictable. Even if the covariate in question may be forecast to some degree of precision, typically that precision is not perfect and it may make sense to consider the covariate random.

For instance, the points of N might be the times and locations where subjects were identified with a particular disease. The incidence of this disease might depend on the temperature, and these temperatures might in turn be modeled as evolving randomly. Another example of Cox processes applied to real data is in the analysis of automobile accidents, where the idea is that an individual's chance of getting in an accident on a given day seems to vary throughout the year (Bartlett, 1986), with some dates and times experiencing more traffic or more hazardous conditions, thus increasing the risk of traffic accidents at these times.

With a Cox process model, one is assuming that, although the points might tend to aggregate in certain areas of space-time because the covariate takes especially high or especially low values in those areas, the process is not clustered in the sense that the occurrence of a point is not directly causing other points to occur. In the automobile accident application, for instance, one may expect the accidents to occur predominately where there is more traffic. However, the Cox model posits that the random occurrence of an accident somewhere does not trigger other accidents, but rather that, given the traffic conditions, the accident occurrences occur randomly and independently of one another.

An example is given in Fig. 2.5, where the covariate (e.g. traffic) is simulated according to a discretized Brownian Sheet (which just means you start with one value in the lower left corner and then add in normal noise as you move up and to the right; that is, the value in pixel $[i, j]$ is the average of the values in pixels $[i-1, j]$ and $[i, j-1]$, plus the sum of two independent normals).

A particularly important and commonly used model is the Log-Gaussian Cox Process (LGCP) model, where $\log \lambda(t, x, y)$ is a Gaussian random field with mean μ and covariance $c(r)$, for spatial-temporal radius r. The function rLGCP() in the *R* package *spatstat* can automatically generate λ for you according to this model, and then generate points according to a Cox process directed by λ. The function $rLGCP()$ can alternatively be used just to generate the points of the Cox process, when you supply it with λ.

Code to simulate both the Brownian sheet covariate and the resulting points of the LGCP is below, and relies on the function *rLGCP* in the *R* package *spatstat*.

```
## First, generate a discretized 100x100 Brownian Sheet.
d = 100
z = matrix(rep(-3,m*m),ncol=m)
for(i in c(2:d)) z[1,i] = z[1,(i-1)] + rnorm(1,sd=.1)/2
for(i in c(2:d)) z[i,1] = z[(i-1),1] + rnorm(1,sd=.1)/2
for(i in c(2:d)){ for(j in c(2:d)){
z[i,j] = (z[(i-1),j] + rnorm(1,sd=.1))/2 + (z[i,(j-1)] + rnorm(1,sd=.1))/2}}
## Now generate the points, x, using LGCP, and plot.
install.packages("spatstat")
```

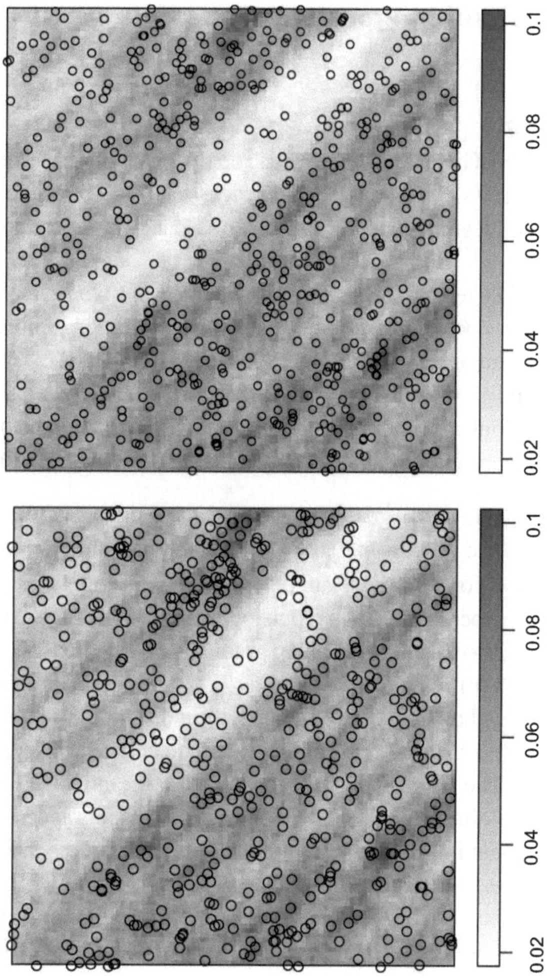

Fig. 2.5 Log-Gaussian Cox processes driven by a Brownian Sheet. Left: points generated using rLGCP(). Right: points generated using rpois() and runif()

```
library(spatstat)
m = as.im(z)
x = rLGCP(model="gauss", mu = m,var=0,scale=1)
image(exp(m),col=gray((64:20)/64),main="")
points(x)
```

Instead of using *spatstat*, one could alternatively generate the points in each pixel individually according to a Poisson process with mean μ, using the *R* function rpois(), where μ is some function of the covariate (traffic), as in the code below.

```
image(exp(m),col=gray((64:20)/64),main="")
for(i in 1:d){for(j in 1:d){
n = rpois(1,exp(z[j,i])); if(n>0){x = runif(n)+i-1;y=runif(n)+j-1
points(x,y)}}}
```

2.6 Gibbs Processes

For any finite collection $(\tau_1, \tau_2, ..., \tau_n)$ of points in space-time, if the joint density is $C(q)exp\left[-q\{\sum_i \nu_1(\tau_i) + \sum_{i \neq j} \nu_2(\tau_i, \tau_j)\}\right]$, then N is a *Gibbs process* (Goulard et al., 1996; Stoyan & Stoyan, 1998). Given a distance metric on the given observation region, such as Euclidean distance, for instance, in the case of purely spatial processes, or perhaps the sum of some multiple of temporal distance plus Euclidean distance in the case of space-time processes, $\nu_2(\tau_i, \tau_j)$ can often be written $\nu(r)$, where $r = |\tau_i - \tau_j|$.

The term $\nu(r)$ is called the *interaction potential.* Note that for a Gibbs process in general, provided $\nu(r) \neq 0$, the process has *causal* clustering or inhibition, in the sense that the random occurrence of a point at τ_i actually makes it more likely (if $\nu(r) < 0$) or less likely (if $\nu(r) > 0$) that a subsequent point τ_j would occur a distance r away from τ_i.

Some special cases are important. For examples, (b)–(e) below, suppose $\sigma > 0$ is some constant, perhaps chosen or known by the user or perhaps estimated using the data.

(a) When $\nu(r) = 0$, there are no interactions, and the process is a Poisson process with intensity $\nu_1(s)$. The process may be homogeneous or inhomogeneous; examples are shown in Fig. 2.1.

(b) If for some constant $\sigma > 0$, $\nu(r) = -\log[1 - e^{-(r/\sigma)^2}]$, then N is called a *soft-core* process. The process has weak repulsion because $\nu(r)$ is always non-negative, taking values approaching ∞ as $r \to 0$, and decreasing gradually as r increases.

(c) $\nu(r) = \infty$ for $r \leq \sigma$, and $\nu(r) = 0$ for $r > \sigma$ defines a *hard-core* process, as the likelihood is zero of having any two points within distance σ of each other.

(d) $\nu(r) = (\sigma/r)^k$ is an intermediate choice between the soft-core and hard-core models.

(e) The *Strauss process* has $\nu_1(s) = \alpha$, and $\nu(r) = \gamma$ for $r \leq \sigma$, while $\nu(r) = 0$ for $r > \sigma$. Thus, points within σ of each other are discouraged by the Strauss model by some amount γ but are not impossible as with the hard-core process, and for distances greater than σ the Strauss process is effectively ambivalent, as such pairs are neither more likely nor less likely than for a Poisson process. To the reader wondering why some of the same terms are used for these models as for pornography, perhaps it is because of how titilating the subject of point processes can be.

Figure 2.6 shows examples of simulated purely spatial Gibbs processes on the square $[0, 100] \times [0, 100]$. One can see that, for the hard-core process there are no pairs of points very close together, whereas for the Strauss process, such pairs of points are rare but occasionally occur. Code for the simulations in Fig. 2.6.

```
par(mfrow=c(1,2))
plot(rHardcore(0.1,2,square(100)),main="",pch=".",cex=2)
plot(rStrauss(0.1,.3,2,square(100)),main="",pch=".",cex=2)
```

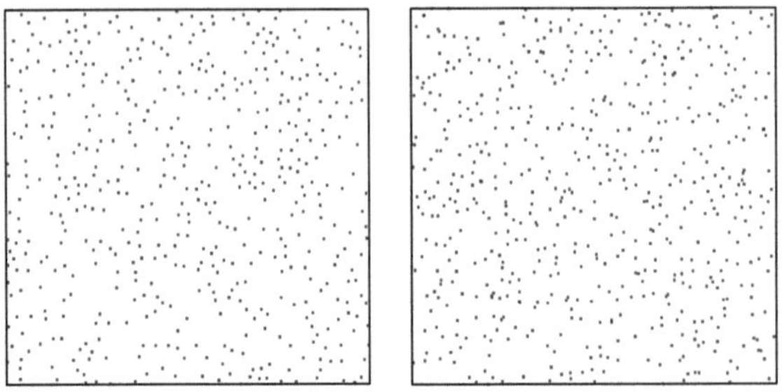

Fig. 2.6 Simulated spatial Gibbs point processes on $[0, 100] \times [0, 100]$. Left: hard-core process with $\nu_1 = 0.1$ and $\sigma = 2$. Right: Strauss process with $\alpha = 0.1$, $\sigma = 2$, and $\gamma = 0.3$

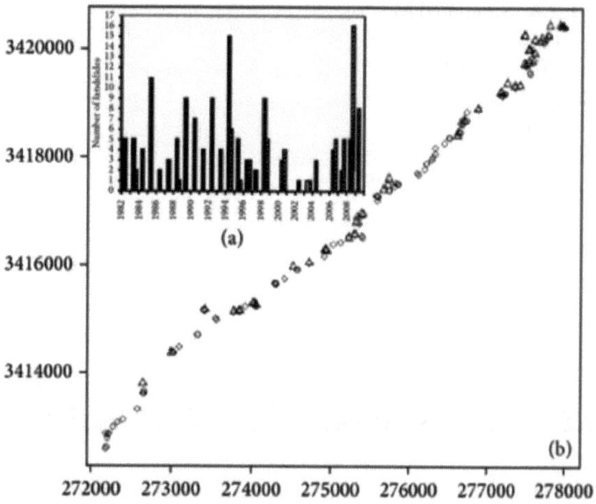

Fig. 2.7 From Das and Stein (2016): **a** Temporal distribution of small (solid bar) and large (dashed bar) landslides along the 12 km road corridor in the Indian Himalayas between 1982 and 2009 and **b** the spatial distribution of small (represented by circles) and large (represented by triangles) landslides along the road corridor with UTM coordinates

The Strauss process model has been used to model the spatial locations of landslides along a 12 km road corridor in the Indian Himalayas, for example (Das & Stein, 2016). As seen in Fig. 2.7, for example, the locations are rather regularly scattered, with very few pairs of landslides within a distances of 30 m or so.

2.7 Matern Processes

The Matern I and Matern II processes are very simple processes to simulate, and thus nice elementary examples of processes exhibiting repulsion. As with the Gibbs processes, we will assume there is some distance metric on the observation region, such as a linear combination of temporal difference and Euclidean distance in space, and suppose the constant $\sigma > 0$ described below is some value chosen or known by the user or estimated using data.

The *Matern(I)* process is generated as follows. First, generate M according to a stationary Poisson process with rate μ. Then let N be all points of M that are not within distance σ of any other point of M. Thus, the process by construction cannot possibly have any pairs of points within distance σ of each other.

The *Matern(II)* process is similar, in that it too cannot possibly have any pairs of points separated by a distance less than σ. For the Matern(II) process, one first generates points $\tau_1, \tau_2, \ldots$ according to a stationary Poisson process of rate μ. Then for $i = 1, 2, \ldots$, keep point i if there is no previous kept point τ_j with $|t_i - t_j| \leq \sigma$.

Sample simulations of Matern(I) and Matern(II) processes on the square $[0, 100] \times [0, 100]$ are shown in Fig. 2.8. The two processes are generated using identical values of μ and σ, but the Matern(II) process results in more points, because if two candidate points are within σ of each other, Matern(I) throws both of them out whereas Matern(II) discards only the second one.

Code for generating the simulations in Fig. 2.8.

```
library(spatstat)
par(mfrow=c(1,2))
plot(rMaternI(.01,5,square(100)),main="",pch=".",cex=2)
plot(rMaternII(0.01,5,square(100)),main="",pch=".",cex=2)
```

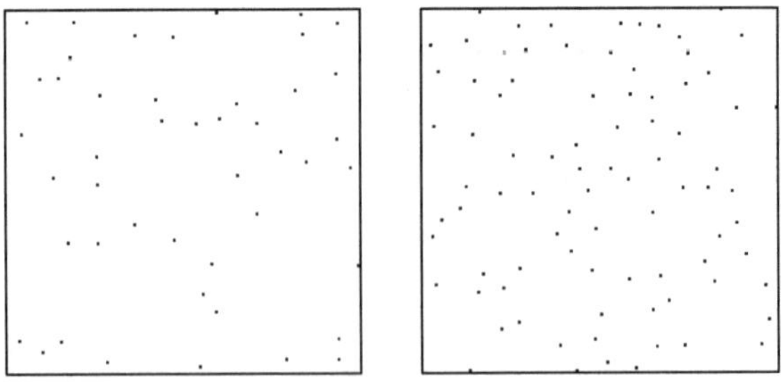

Fig. 2.8 Simulated Matern point processes on $[0, 100] \times [0, 100]$. Left: Matern(I) process with $\mu = 0.01$ and $\sigma = 5.0$. Right: Matern(II) process with $\mu = 0.01$ and $\sigma = 5.0$

2.8 Hawkes Processes and Their Variants

A *Hawkes process* or *self-exciting point process* has conditional intensity

$$\lambda(t, x, y) = \mu(x, y) + K \int_{t'<t} g(t - t', x - x', y - y') dN(t', x', y') \tag{2.9}$$

$$= \mu(x, y) + K \sum_{(t',x',y'):t'<t} g(t - t', x - x', y - y'). \tag{2.10}$$

The function g is typically assumed to be a density, i.e. to be non-negative and to integrate to 1 over all time and space, and is called the *triggering function* or *triggering density*. The constant K is called the *productivity*. If g is a density function, then K is the expected number of points triggered directly by each point. The idea is that background points (parents) are appearing with rate $\mu(x, y)$, and then each parent point generates some offspring points, and those offspring generate further offspring, and so on. Each point, whether a parent or offspring, generates an expected number K of further offspring, and those descendants are distributed spatially and temporally around their parents according to the density g. If $K \geq 1$, then the process is *explosive* and the overall density of points will quickly diverge to infinity. If $K = 1$, the process is said to be *critical*, and if $K < 1$, then each parent point is expected to generate $K + K^2 + K^3 + \cdots = 1/(1 - K) - 1 = K/(1 - K)$ descendants in total. As a result, in a Hawkes process with $K < 1$, if we expect m parent points then we expect $m\frac{K}{1-K}$ children, so the expected fraction of points that are parents is $\frac{m}{m+m\frac{K}{1-K}} = \frac{1}{1+\frac{K}{1-K}} = \frac{1}{\frac{1-K+K}{1-K}} = 1 - K$, and therefore the expected fraction of offspring points is simply K.

A simulated Hawkes process is shown in Fig. 2.9. The Hawkes model is useful for describing clustered phenomena, including the spread of invasive species or contagious diseases, especially when an underlying branching structure of the spread is implicit. The model has also been used for modeling behaviors where retaliations are possible, such as violent crimes or terrorist attacks.

The simulation in Fig. 2.9 was generated using the following code. It uses a general function called simhawk() for simulating many types of Hawkes process, by loading it in from my website.

```
source(url("http://www.stat.ucla.edu/~frederic/book/simhawk.r"))
mu = 1; theta_K = 0.7; unif_t_length = 2;
unif_xy_rad = .04; theta_b = 2; theta_m0 = 4.5
z = simhawk(T=200,gmi=pointprod, gt=unifgt, gxy = unifxy)
par(mfrow=c(1,2))
plot(c(0,1),c(0,1),xlab="longitude",ylab="latitude",type="n")
points(z$lon,z$lat,col=grey(.8*z$t/200),cex=.5)
```

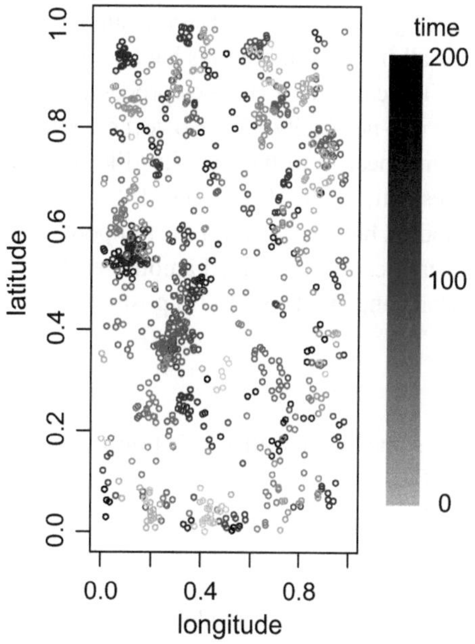

Fig. 2.9 Simulated Hawkes point process on $[0, 1] \times [0, 1]$ from time 0 to 200, with $\mu = 1$, $K = 0.7$, and where $g(t)$ is uniform(0, 2) and $g(x, y)$ is uniform on the circle with radius 0.04 centered at $(0, 0)$

```
## to add the legend:
plot(c(0,10),c(.8,4.2),type="n",axes=F,xlab="",ylab="")
image(c(-1:1),seq(1,4,length=100),matrix(rep(seq(0,0.8,length=100),
  2),ncol=100,byrow=T), add=T,col=grey((80:0)/100))
text(c(2,2,2,1),c(1,2.5,4,4.2),c("0","100","200","time"))
text(1.5,4.2,"time")
```

For a stationary Hawkes process with homogeneous background rate $\mu(x, y) = \mu$, productivity K satisfying $0 \le K < 1$, and triggering density g with finite support, the mean number of points per unit space-time is particularly easy to calculate, using the martingale property. Suppose the observed spatial-temporal domain is $B \times [0, T]$ at time T, for some fixed measurable spatial region B. Letting $a = \lim_{T\to\infty} \frac{1}{T|B|} EN(B \times [0, T])$,

$$
\begin{aligned}
a &= \frac{1}{T|B|} E \int_{B\times[0,T]} dN \\
&= \lim_{T\to\infty} \frac{1}{T|B|} E \int_B \int \int_0^T \lambda(t)dtdxdy \\
&= \lim_{T\to\infty} \frac{1}{T|B|} E \int_B \int \int_0^T \left\{ \mu + K \int_B \int \int_0^t g(t-t', x-x', y-y')dN(t', x', y') \right\} dtdxdy \\
&= \mu + K \lim_{T\to\infty} \frac{1}{T|B|} E \int_B \int \int_0^T \left\{ \int_B \int \int_0^{T-t'} g(t-t', x-x', y-y')dt \right\} dN(t', x', y') \\
&= \mu + K \lim_{T\to\infty} \frac{1}{T|B|} EN(B \times [0, T]),
\end{aligned}
\tag{2.11}
$$

since g is a density with finite support and thus $\lim_{T\to\infty}\int_B\int\int_0^{T-t'} g(t-t', x-x', y-y')dt = 1$, for all (t', x', y'). We thus have $a = \mu + Ka$, so $a = \frac{\mu}{1-K}$.

Typically for a Hawkes process, the productivity K is restricted to non-negative values to ensure the non-negativity of λ. However, a related model where the occurrence of each point τ_i causes future points nearby to become *less* likely is the self-correcting model or stress-release model (Isham & Westcott, 1979; Vere-Jones, 1988; Vere-Jones & Ogata, 1984). There are several versions of these models, but basically, for the temporal case, the conditional intensity gradually increases over time but decreases by some fixed amount each time a point occurs. For instance, the self-correcting model of Isham and Westcott (1979) posits

$$\lambda(t) = \alpha\phi(N(t) - \alpha t), \tag{2.12}$$

for some non-negative function ϕ. Similarly, for the stress-release model of Vere-Jones and Ogata (1984),

$$\lambda(t) = \exp\{\alpha + \beta t - \gamma N(t)\}. \tag{2.13}$$

The idea behind the model as applied to seismology by Vere-Jones and Ogata (1984), and Vere-Jones (1988), is that the stress along earthquake faults is constantly increasing with time, causing the rate of earthquakes to increase, but when an earthquake occurs, some of this stress is released, reducing the rate in the future until the stress builds back up again. This has been extended to collections of faults connected together in linked stress-release models (e.g. Bebbington & Harte, 2001).

A seemingly natural application of Hawkes processes is earthquakes and their aftershocks. However, it has long been observed that earthquakes of larger magnitudes tend to have far more aftershocks than smaller earthquakes. As a result, a variant of the Hawkes model called the Epidemic-Type Aftershock Sequence (ETAS) process was developed.

ETAS is a marked version of the Hawkes process introduced by Ogata (1988, 1998), where points have different productivities depending on their magnitudes. The model is specified as

$$\lambda(t, x, y) = \mu(x, y) + \sum_{t', x', y' : t' < t} g(t-t', x-x', y-y')h(m'), \tag{2.14}$$

where $\mu(x, y)$ is usually estimated by smoothing observed large earthquakes, $h(m) = ke^{a(m-m_0)}$, where m_0 is the catalog cutoff magnitude, and $g(t, x, y) = g_1(t)g_2(r^2)$, where $r^2 = ||(x, y)||^2$. Typically g_1 and g_2 are power-law (also called Pareto) densities, i.e. $g_1(t) = (p-1)c^{p-1}(t+c)^{-p}$. An alternative is where g_1 and/or g_2 are exponential or the sum of exponentials.

A simulation of the ETAS model is shown in Fig. 2.10. Although the ETAS model in (2.10) might look somewhat complicated, it really is quite simple. The model forecasts earthquake rates using only past seismicity, and ignoring all sorts of potential covariates such as observed tectonic deformation and strain rates, radon levels, water levels, animal behaviors, electro-magnetic signals, and paleoseismic information, all of which have been posited to aid in earthquake forecasting. Nevertheless, the ETAS model has so far outperformed alternative models in earthquake forecasting experiments such as the Collaboratory for the Study of Earthquake Predictability (CSEP).

The code used to generate the simulation in Fig. 2.10, and like the simulated Hawkes process, it again uses the function simhawk(), which we assume the user has already loaded.

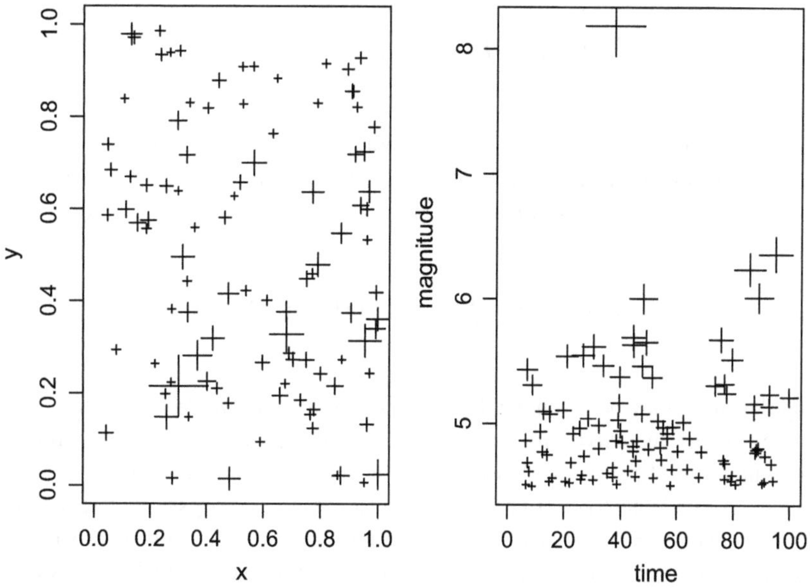

Fig. 2.10 Simulation of ETAS on [0, 1] × [0, 1] from time 0 to 100, with $\mu(x, y) = 1, k = 0.5, a = 0.8$, and where $g(t)$ and $g(x, y)$ are Pareto with parameters $(c, p) = (3, 2.5)$ and $(d, q) = (4, 3.5)$, respectively. The earthquake magnitudes are assumed to come from an exponential distribution with $\beta = 2$ and lower magnitude cutoff $m_0 = 4.5$

```
mu = 1; theta_K = 0.5; theta_a = .8; theta_b = 2; theta_m0 = 4.5
theta_c = 3; theta_p = 2.5; theta_d = 4; theta_q = 3.5
z = simhawk()
par(mfrow=c(1,2))
plot(c(0,1),c(0,1),xlab="x",ylab="y",type="n")
points(z$lon,z$lat,pch=3,cex=z$m-4)
plot(c(0,100),c(4.5,max(z$m)),xlab="time",ylab="magnitude",type="n")
points(z$t,z$m,pch=3,cex=z$m-4)
```

Another variant of the Hawkes process is the *recursive* process. Just as the ETAS model assigns different productivities for different earthquakes based on their magnitudes, similarly, one may question the assumption of constant productivity for epidemic diseases based on what we know from both specific disease epidemics (Cauchemez et al., 2016; Wallinga & Teunis, 2004) and general modeling of outbreaks (Lloyd-Smith et al., 2015). For instance, when the prevalence of the disease is low or zero in a region, as is the case when the epidemic has never struck before or has not struck in considerable time, then the conditional intensity λ is small and one would expect the rate of transmission for each infected person to be quite high, as a majority of hosts are likely immunologically naive, and a carrier of the disease may be expected to infect many others. When the epidemic is at its peak and many subjects have contracted the disease, on the other hand, λ is large and one might expect the rate of transmission to be lower due to human efforts at containment and intervention of the disease, and because many subjects may have already been exposed and thus might be recovered and immune to further infection, or deceased (in either case no longer part of a susceptible pool). These considerations suggest a point process model where the productivity for a subject infected at time t is inversely related to the conditional intensity at time t. Since the conditional intensity in turn depends critically on this productivity, we call the model recursive. For the purely temporal case, we may write this model

$$\lambda(t) = \mu + \int_0^t H[\lambda(u)]g(t-u)dN(u), \tag{2.15}$$

where $\mu > 0$, and $g > 0$ is a density function. The productivity function H should typically be decreasing in light of the considerations above regarding the transmission of disease, and particular focus is on the case where $H(x) = \kappa x^{-\alpha}$, with $\kappa > 0$, so that

$$\lambda(t) = \mu + \kappa \int_0^t [\lambda(u)]^{-\alpha} g(t-u)dN(u). \tag{2.16}$$

The triggering density g may be given e.g. by an exponential density, $g(u) = \beta exp(\beta u)$.

The existence of the recursive process (2.16) as a valid point process (i.e. with almost surely no infinite accumulation of points in a bounded region) for any positive values of α and κ is given in Schoenberg et al. (2019). When $\alpha = 0$, (2.16) reduces to a Hawkes process. We refer to the special case where $\alpha = 1$, i.e. where $\lambda(t) = \mu + \kappa \int_0^t \frac{g(t-u)}{\lambda(u)} dN(u)$ as the *standard* recursive process. The standard version of the model has especially simple and attractive features, some of which are described below.

The mean of the recursive process (2.16) can be obtained simply by using the martingale property for point processes. For $B = [0, T]$,

$$\begin{aligned}
\frac{1}{T} EN(B) &= \frac{1}{T} E \int_B dN \\
&= \frac{1}{T} E \int_0^T \lambda(t)dt \\
&= \frac{1}{T} E \int_0^T \left\{ \mu + \kappa \int_0^t [\lambda(u)]^{-\alpha} g(t-u)dN(u) \right\} dt \\
&= \mu + \frac{\kappa}{T} E \int_0^T \int_0^t [\lambda(u)]^{1-\alpha} g(t-u)dtdu \\
&= \mu + \frac{\kappa}{T} E \int_0^T [\lambda(u)]^{1-\alpha} \left\{ \int_0^{T-u} g(t-u)dt \right\} du \\
&\to \mu + \frac{\kappa}{T} E \int_0^T [\lambda(u)]^{1-\alpha} du,
\end{aligned} \tag{2.17}$$

as $T \to \infty$, provided $\lim_{T\to\infty} \int_0^{T-u} g(t-u)dt = 1$, for all $u > 0$. If this assumption is violated, then Eq. (2.17) is merely an approximation. Impacts of violations to this assumption were investigated in Schoenberg (2016).

For the standard recursive model, $\alpha = 1$, and (2.17) reduces simply to $\mu + \kappa$. This highlights a major distinction between Hawkes models and recursive models. For a Hawkes process, doubling the background rate amounts to doubling the total expected number of points, but this is far from true for the recursive process. As an example, if $\mu = 0.1$ and $\kappa = 2$, then doubling μ would only increase the total expected number of points by less than 5%. In the situation where $\mu = 0.01$ and $\kappa = 2$, doubling μ would increase the total expected number of points by less than 0.5%.

A version of the law of large numbers for the recursive process can be proven to show that for the standard recursive process, $\frac{N(0,T)}{T}$ converges to $\mu + \kappa$ as $T \to \infty$ with rate of convergence $\sqrt{T}$ in L^2. To be specific, if $\lim\sup_{T\to\infty} \sqrt{T} \int_T^\infty g(t)dt < \infty$, then

$$\sup_T T E \left\{ \left(\frac{N(0,T)}{T} - (\mu + \kappa) \right) \right\} < \infty. \tag{2.18}$$

The proof of (2.18) is given in Schoenberg et al. (2019).

The productivity of a point τ_i is typically defined in the context of Hawkes or ETAS processes as the expected number of first generation offspring of the point τ_i. For a Hawkes process, the productivity of each point is simply κ. In the case of the recursive model (2.16), the productivity of any point τ_i is given by $H\{\lambda(\tau_i)\}$. Thus, the total productivity, for n points $\tau_1, \tau_2, ..., \tau_n$, is $\sum_{i=1}^n H\{\lambda(\tau_i)\}$, and for the special case of the standard recursive model, the expected value of the total productivity is

$$\kappa E \int_0^T \frac{1}{\lambda(t)} dN = \kappa E \int_0^T \frac{1}{\lambda(t)} \lambda(t)dt = \kappa T.$$

Thus, provided again that $\lim_{T\to\infty} \int_0^{T-u} g(t-u)dt = 1$ for all $u > 0$, the average productivity for the standard recursive model is $\kappa T/N(B) \to \kappa/(\mu + \kappa)$ a.s., since $N(B)/T \to \mu + \kappa$ a.s. This highlights another difference between the recursive and Hawkes models. For a Hawkes process, the points $\tau_1, \tau_2, ...$ all have constant productivity, κ. For a standard recursive process, the productivity for the first point τ_1 is κ/μ, which is larger than the productivity for any subsequent point. The productivity of the second point is $\frac{\kappa}{\mu + \frac{\kappa g(\tau_2-\tau_1)}{\mu}}$, the productivity of the third point is $\frac{\kappa}{\mu + \frac{\kappa g(\tau_3-\tau_1)}{\mu} + \frac{\kappa g(\tau_3-\tau_2)}{(\mu+\kappa g(\tau_2-\tau_1)/\mu)}}$, etc., and the productivity of the points ultimately averages $\frac{\kappa}{\mu+\kappa}$.

Figure 2.11 shows simulations of a recursive process and a Hawkes process over the same domain, with the same exponential triggering density, and the same background rate μ. In the top panels, $\mu = 0.05$ and $\beta = 0.8$, and in the bottom panels, $\mu = 0.1$ and $\beta = 1$. In each case, the parameter K of the Hawkes process was selected as $K = \kappa/(\mu + \kappa)$ so that the Hawkes and recursive processes would have the same expected numbers of points. One sees also how the parameter β influences the degree of clustering in the processes. One main difference between the Hawkes and recursive models is that the former exhibits occasional small clusters with just a few or even just one isolated point, whereas the latter produces almost exclusively large clusters. The form for $H(\lambda)$ implies that events occurring following a period of no events or relatively few events will trigger more offspring. In models for earthquakes such as ETAS, rare events trigger more offspring only in the sense that larger magnitude events are rare. However, in ETAS and other Hawkes-type models for earthquakes, two events of the same magnitude have the same productivity regardless of when they occur. In the epidemic disease context, this may be violated since diseases may spread more rapidly when the disease has been dormant for a while and human attempts to curb contagion are not in place. In the earthquake context, it has been noted by some authors, including notably (Ogata, 1988), that large earthquakes have frequently followed periods of relative quiescence, but this effect has not typically been incorporated into models such as ETAS for forecasting earthquakes.

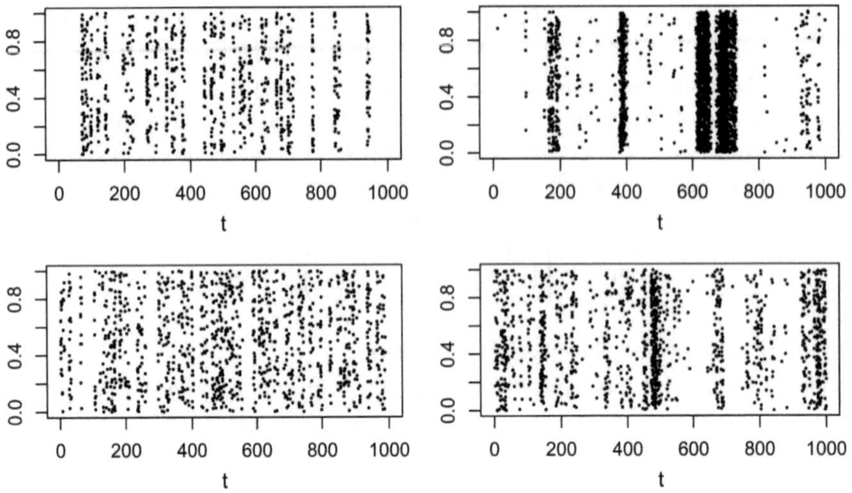

Fig. 2.11 Simulated recursive and Hawkes processes, from time 0 to 1000. The panels on the left are recursive processes, those on the right are Hawkes processes, and all four have exponential triggering function, $g(u) = \beta \exp(\beta u)$. For the top panels, $(\mu, \kappa, \beta) = (0.05, 2, 0.8)$. For the bottom panels, $(\mu, \kappa, \beta) = (0.1, 2, 1)$. For the Hawkes processes, $K = \kappa/(\mu + \kappa)$ so that the Hawkes and recursive processes in each row have the same expected numbers of points The y-coordinates of the points are drawn uniformly for ease of visualization

One way to simulate the recursive model is by thinning, the same technique that was used to simulate inhomogeneous Poisson processes. Code to generate the simulated standard recursive processes in Fig. 2.11 is below.

```
par(mfrow=c(2,2))
## First recursive
mu = .05; k = 2; beta=.8; T = 1000; b = 10*(mu+k)
n = rpois(1,b*T); candt = sort(runif(n))*T ## candidate pts
t = c(); lams = c(); m = 0; lambda = mu
for(i in 1:n){
if(m > 0) lambda = mu + sum(beta/lams * exp(-beta*(candt[i]-t)))
if(runif(1) < lambda/b){m = m+1; t[m] = candt[i]; lams[m] = lambda}
}
plot(c(0,1000),c(0,1),xlab="t",ylab="",type="n")
points(t,runif(m),cex=.2)
## Now Hawkes
mu = .05; theta_K = k/(mu+k); theta_b = 2; theta_m0 = 4.5
theta_beta = .8;
z = simhawk(T=1000,gt=expgt, gxy = pointxy, gmi = pointprod)
plot(c(0,1000),c(0,1),xlab="t",ylab="",type="n")
points(z$t,runif(z$n),cex=.2)
## Now recursive again
mu = .1; k = 2; beta=1; T = 1000; b = 10*(mu+k)
n = rpois(1,b*T); candt = sort(runif(n))*T ## candidate pts
t = c(); lams = c(); m = 0; lambda = mu
for(i in 1:n){
if(m > 0) lambda = mu + sum(beta/lams * exp(-beta*(candt[i]-t)))
if(runif(1) < lambda/b){m = m+1; t[m] = candt[i]; lams[m] = lambda}
}
plot(c(0,1000),c(0,1),xlab="t",ylab="",type="n")
```

```
points(t,runif(m),cex=.2)
## Now Hawkes again
mu = .1; theta_K = k/(mu+k); theta_b = 2; theta_m0 = 4.5
theta_beta = 1;
z = simhawk(T=1000,gt=expgt, gxy = pointxy, gmi = pointprod)
plot(c(0,1000),c(0,1),xlab="t",ylab="",type="n")
points(z$t,runif(z$n),cex=.2)
```

2.9 Totally Independent Non-simple Point Processes

Recall that the compound Poisson process is an example of a point process that is non-simple, i.e. can have overlapping points. This section deals with models for non-simple multivariate point processes.

For a *multivariate* point process, each point is associated with a mark in some countable mark space, such as the positive integers, and sometimes the mark indicates the number of overlapping points. An elementary example might be the times and locations where ladybugs are observed, and the marks could be the number of spots on each ladybug. I use the word *elementary* rather than *simple*, because we typically say such a process is *simple* if no two points can occur simultaneously, and the idea of this section is to explore models for non-simple processes, where not only can multiple points happen simultaneously, but there can even be simultaneous points with the same mark. In particular, is it possible for such a process to have the complete independence property, so that the occurrence of one point has no influence at all on the distribution of other points? That is, is it possible for a model to have the feature that the occurrence of one ladybug with some number of spots to have no influence on the occurrences of ladybugs of any number of spots, whether at the same time or in the future?

We might say a non-simple point process is *totally independent* if it obeys the complete independence property and in addition, if the information that at least one point of a certain mark (or a collection of points of certain marks) occurs at time t does not influence the distribution of other points occurring at time t. The question, then, is what type of point process has this total independence property.

To simplify the discussion, suppose first that there is only one type of mark (or equivalently, that there are no marks at all). Suppose further that at least one point occurs at some space-time location t, and let the random variable m denote the number of points occurring at time t. Let $\alpha = P(m > 2|m > 1)$. In this case, total independence implies that

$$\alpha = P(m > 3|m > 2) = P(m > 4|m > 3) = \cdots,$$

$$P(m > 3|m > 1) = P(m > 3|m > 2)P(m > 2|m > 1) = \alpha^2,$$

and in general, for any non-negative integers i and j with $j > i$,

$$P(m > j|m > i) = \alpha^{j-i}. \tag{2.19}$$

The relation (2.19) is satisfied if and only if m is geometrically distributed, i.e.

$$P(m = i) = (1 - \alpha)\alpha^i,$$

where $0 < \alpha < 1$.

Thus, in the unmarked case, a compound Poisson process with geometric mark distribution is the only totally independent process. For the case of a multivariate point process with multiple marks, the same logic as above can be used to show that if the process is totally independent, then it must be a compound Poisson process with mark distribution of the form $P(\underline{x}) \propto \prod_{i=1}^{k} \alpha_i^{a_i}$, for $\underline{x} = \{x_1^{a_1}, ..., x_k^{a_k}\}$.

Non-simple marked point processes can be tricky to model. While the conditional intensity uniquely specifies simple point processes, as noted in Chap. 1.6, it does not uniquely specify non-simple processes. One way to characterize uniquely a non-simple marked point process is via a change in the mark space M. The method involves identifying with the point process its associated point process on a different space with an expanded mark space. The resulting associated process is simple by construction, and hence may be characterized uniquely by its conditional intensity on the expanded space. The construction is as follows; see also Exercise 7.1.6 of Daley and Vere-Jones (1988) or p. 195 of Daley and Vere-Jones (2003).

Let M^* denote the collection of all subsets of M, i.e. $M^* = \cup_{k=1}^{\infty} M^k$, where $M^k = M \times \cdots \times M$, the collection of all possible combinations of k marks.

Let the function $\phi_i(\underline{x})$ denote the multiplicity of the mark x_i in the vector $\underline{x}$, for $x_i \in M$ and $x \in M^*$, and let $\phi(\underline{x}) = \sum_i \phi_i(\underline{x})$. In other words, if $\underline{x} = \{x_1^{a_1}, x_2^{a_2}, ...\}$, then $\phi_1(\underline{x}) = a_1, \phi_2(\underline{x}) = a_2$, etc., and $\phi(\underline{x}) = \sum_i a_1$.

Define the function $\psi(\underline{x})$ as the number of distinct marks in $\underline{x}$. That is, $\psi(\underline{x}) := \sum_i \mathbf{I}_{\phi_i(\underline{x})>0}$, where $\mathbf{I}$ is the indicator function.

Given a non-simple marked point process N with mark space M, one may define the *simplified* marked point process N^* on the expanded mark space M^* as the collection of processes $\{N_{\underline{x}}^*\}$, for $\underline{x} \in M^*$, each defined via

$$N_{\underline{x}}^*(\{t\}) := \prod_i \mathbf{I}_{\{N_i(\{t\})=\phi_i(\underline{x})\}}, \tag{2.20}$$

for each space-time location, t.

Thus, $N_{\underline{x}}^*$ has a single point at space-time location t iff. N has a_i points at time t and mark x_i for each i, where $\underline{x} = \{x_1^{a_1}, x_2^{a_2}, ...\}$. N^* is then a simple point process by construction, and therefore its conditional intensity (assuming it exists) uniquely characterizes the finite-dimensional distributions of N^* and hence those of N as well. Let λ^* denote the conditional intensity of N^*, which we might also call the *simplified* conditional intensity of N. Thus, for any space-time location t and any collection $\underline{x}$ of marks, $\lambda^*(t, \underline{x})$ is the conditional rate at which points of marks $\underline{x}$ are occurring per unit of space-time, given the past, and let $\lambda^*(t) := \sum_{\underline{x} \in M^*} \lambda^*(t, \underline{x})$ represent the total ground rate of N^* over all possible collections of marks.

One may ask how λ, the conditional intensity of N, is related to λ^*, the conditional intensity of λ^*. Assuming both exist, the two intensities are related via the following result.

Theorem 2.9.1 *Suppose the multivariate marked point process N has conditional intensity λ and that its simplified version N^* has conditional intensity λ^*. Then for each i, for almost all t,*

$$\lambda_i(t) = \sum_{\underline{x} \in M^*} \phi_i(\underline{x}) \lambda_{\underline{x}}^*(t). \tag{2.21}$$

Proof Fix i. Observe from (2.20) that $N_i(t) = \sum_{\underline{x} \in M^*} \phi_i(\underline{x}) N_{\underline{x}}^*(t)$. So

$$N_i(t) - \int_0^t \sum_{\underline{x} \in M^*} \phi_i(\underline{x}) \lambda^*_{\underline{x}}(u) du = \sum_{\underline{x} \in M^*} \phi_i(\underline{x}) \left[N^*_{\underline{x}}(t) - \int_0^t \lambda^*_{\underline{x}}(u) du \right],$$

which is a linear combination of $\mathcal{F}$-martingales and is therefore itself an $\mathcal{F}$-martingale. Hence, the sum in (2.21) is an $\mathcal{F}$-conditional intensity of N_i, and thus coincides almost everywhere with λ_i by the uniqueness theorem for point process compensators (Jacod, 1975). □

Theorem 2.9.1 shows that a non-simple temporal marked point process N may be characterized via its simplified conditional intensity λ^*, assuming it exists. The relation between the simple point process N^* on the expanded mark space and the non-simple point process N on the original mark space is analogous to the relation between a (possibly infinite-dimensional) multivariate distribution and its marginal distributions, where attention is restricted exclusively to non-negative integer-valued distributions and where the sum of the values must be at least one.

Certain special cases of non-simple point processes are worthy of closer attention. One natural case to consider is where the process N is totally independent. More generally, N may be a non-Poisson point process lacking complete independence, but may nevertheless have independence of the marks at any space-time location t, given that at least one point occurs at t. In this case the simplified conditional intensity $\lambda^*(t, \underline{x})$ has the form

$$\lambda^*(t, \underline{x}) = [\lambda^*(t)]^{1-a} \prod_{i=1}^{k} [\lambda^*(t, \{x_i\})]^{a_i}, \tag{2.22}$$

where $\underline{x} = \{x_1^{a_1}, ..., x_k^{a_k}\}$ and $a := \sum a_k$.

Under this assumption, the ordinary conditional intensity λ can be written directly in terms of the simplified conditional intensity λ^* as in the following result.

Theorem 2.9.2 *Suppose N is a totally independent non-simple marked point process with conditional intensity λ and simplified conditional intensity λ^*. Then for all i and almost all t,*

$$\lambda_i(t) = \frac{2\, \lambda^*_{\{x_i\}}(t)\, \lambda^*(t)}{\lambda^*(t) - \lambda^*_{\{x_i\}}(t)}. \tag{2.23}$$

Proof The following proof makes repeated use of the idea that for any i, the set M^* corresponds one-to-one with the collection $\{\underline{x} : \phi_i(\underline{x}) > 0; \phi(\underline{x}) > 1\}$, where the correspondence is simply the augmentation by one of the multiplicity $\phi_i(\underline{x})$.

Fix i. In what follows, I will suppress t for brevity, as what follows is true for almost all t.

Consider the collection of all $\underline{x}$ such that the multiplicity $\phi_i(\underline{x})$ of the mark x_i is positive. Complete separability implies that the sum of $\lambda^*_{\underline{x}}$ over all such $\underline{x}$ is given by

$$
\begin{aligned}
\bar{\lambda}_i^* &:= \sum_{\underline{x}:\phi_i(\underline{x})>0} \lambda_{\underline{x}}^* \\
&= \lambda_{\{x_i\}}^* + \sum_{\underline{x}:\phi_i(\underline{x})>0;\phi(\underline{x})>1} \lambda_{\underline{x}}^* \\
&= \lambda_{\{x_i\}}^* + \sum_{\underline{x}:\phi(\underline{x})>0} \left(\lambda_{\{x_i\}}^*/\lambda^*\right) \lambda_{\underline{x}}^* \\
&= \lambda_{\{x_i\}}^* + \left(\lambda_{\{x_i\}}^*/\lambda^*\right) \lambda^* \\
&= 2\lambda_{\{x_i\}}^*. \qquad (2.24)
\end{aligned}
$$

One may now write λ_i in terms of λ^*, summing over all possible $\underline{x} \in \mathcal{X}^*$, as follows:

$$
\begin{aligned}
\lambda_i &= \sum_{j=1}^{\infty} \sum_{\underline{x}:\phi_i(\underline{x})=j} j\lambda_{\underline{x}}^* \\
&= \sum_{j=1}^{\infty} j\lambda_{\{x_i^j\}}^* + \sum_{j=1}^{\infty} \sum_{\underline{x}:j=\phi_i(\underline{x})<\phi(\underline{x})} j\lambda_{\underline{x}}^* \\
&= \sum_{j=1}^{\infty} j(\lambda^*)^{1-j}(\lambda_{\{x_i\}}^*)^j + \sum_{j=1}^{\infty} \sum_{\underline{x}':\phi_i(\underline{x}')=0} j(\lambda^*)^{-j}(\lambda_{\{x_i\}}^*)^j \lambda_{\underline{x}'}^* \qquad (2.25) \\
&= \left[\sum_{j=1}^{\infty} j \left(\frac{\lambda_{\{x_i\}}^*}{\lambda^*}\right)^j\right] [\lambda^* + (\lambda^* - \bar{\lambda}_i^*)] \qquad (2.26) \\
&= \frac{(\lambda_{\{x_i\}}^*/\lambda^*)}{[1-\lambda_{\{x_i\}}^*/\lambda^*]^2} \left[2\lambda^* - 2\lambda_{\{x_i\}}^*\right] \qquad (2.27) \\
&= \frac{2\lambda_{\{x_i\}}^*\lambda^*}{\lambda^* - \lambda_{\{x_i\}}^*},
\end{aligned}
$$

where the observation that $\sum_{\underline{x}':\phi_i(\underline{x}')=0} \lambda_{\underline{x}'}^* = \lambda^* - \bar{\lambda}_i^*$ is used to go from (2.25) to (2.26), and the relation $\bar{\lambda}_i^* = 2\lambda_{\{x_i\}}^*$ of (2.24) is used to go from (2.26) to (2.27). □

Now consider the case where N may have multiple points simultaneously, but where no two such points may occur at the same mark. Such a process was previously called simple, but to distinguish it from a simple process on the expanded mark space, in what follows we will use the term singular instead. Specifically, λ^* is *singular* if for all $\underline{x}$ such that $\phi_i(\underline{x}) > 1$ for any i, $\lambda_{\underline{x}}^*(t) = 0$ for almost all t.

It is obvious that, given the same values of the simplified conditional intensity $\lambda^*(t, \{x_i\})$, the ordinary conditional intensity $\lambda(t, x_i)$ will generally be smaller for a singular point process than in the non-singular case, since singularity prohibits the existence of multiple points at mark x_i.

We will say the simplified conditional intensity λ^* is *separable* if, for all $\underline{x} \in M^*$ and almost all $t \in (0, \infty)$,

$$
\lambda_{\underline{x}}^*(t) = \left(\lambda^*(t)\right)^{(1-\psi(\underline{x}))} \prod_{\underline{x}'=\{x_i^a\};a=\phi_i(\underline{x})>0} \lambda_{\underline{x}'}^*(t), \qquad (2.28)
$$

where $\lambda^*(t) := \sum_{\underline{x} \in M^*} \lambda^*_{\underline{x}}(t)$, and $\psi(\underline{x}) := \sum_i \mathbf{1}_{\phi_i(\underline{x})>0}$ is the number of distinct marks in $\underline{x}$.

Note that relation (2.28) implies that for all $\underline{x} = \{x_1^{a_1}, x_2^{a_2}, \ldots, x_k^{a_k}\}$, for almost all t,

$$\lambda^*_{\{x_1^{a_1}, x_2^{a_2}, \ldots, x_k^{a_k}\}}(t) = \lambda^*_{\{x_1^{a_1}, \ldots, x_{k-1}^{a_{k-1}}\}}(t)\ \lambda^*_{\{x_k^{a_k}\}}(t) \ / \ \lambda^*(t).$$

Heuristically, separability means that the likelihood of N simultaneously having a_1 overlapping points at mark x_1, and a_2 overlapping points at mark x_2, etc., is proportional to the products of the likelihoods of each of these phenomena occurring individually. Note also that if λ^* is separable then the finite-dimensional distributions of N are completely determined by the collection of processes $\{\lambda^*_{\{x^a\}}(t)\}$ alone.

Interestingly, if N is separable and singular, then the form of its ordinary conditional rate of points of mark x_i is very similar to that of processes with conditional intensity obeying (2.22), except that the difference between the two terms in the denominator of (2.23) is replaced by their sum.

Theorem 2.9.3 *Suppose N is a singular and separable non-simple point process with conditional intensity λ and simplified conditional intensity λ^*. Then for all i, for almost all t,*

$$\lambda_i(t) = \frac{2\lambda^*_{\{x_i\}}(t)\lambda^*(t)}{\lambda^*(t) + \lambda^*_{\{x_i\}}(t)}. \tag{2.29}$$

Proof Again, t will be suppressed; the following is true for almost all t.

$$\begin{aligned}
\lambda_i &= \lambda^*_{\{x_i\}} + \sum_{\underline{x}:\phi_i(\underline{x})=1;\phi(\underline{x})>1} \lambda^*(\underline{x}) \\
&= \lambda^*_{\{x_i\}} + \frac{\lambda^*_{\{x_i\}}}{\lambda^*} \sum_{\underline{x}:\phi_i(\underline{x})=0} \lambda^*_{\underline{x}} \\
&= \lambda^*_{\{x_i\}} + \frac{\lambda^*_{\{x_i\}}}{\lambda^*}\left(\lambda^* - \lambda_i\right).
\end{aligned}$$

So $\lambda_i\left(1 + \frac{\lambda^*_{\{x_i\}}}{\lambda^*}\right) = 2\lambda^*_{\{x_i\}}$, which establishes (2.29). □

We now consider the antithesis of singularity, i.e. the case where N may have multiple points at a given time, but such multiple points must all occur at the same mark.

Theorem 2.9.4 *Suppose N is a non-simple marked point process with conditional intensity λ and that $\lambda^*_{\underline{x}}(t) = 0$ a.e. for all $\underline{x}$ such that $\phi(\underline{x}) > \phi_i(\underline{x})$ for all i. Suppose also that for almost all t, $\lambda^*_{\{x_i^{a_i}\}} = (\lambda^*)^{1-a_i}\left(\lambda^*_{\{x_i\}}\right)^{a_i}$. Then for each i, for almost all t,*

$$\lambda_i(t) = \frac{\lambda^*_{\{x_i\}}(t)\,(\lambda^*(t))^2}{\left(\lambda^*(t) - \lambda^*_{\{x_i\}}(t)\right)^2}.$$

Proof Again let t be suppressed in the notation that follows, and the following is true for almost all t. Under the stated conditions, one need only consider elements of M^* of the form $\underline{x} = \{x_i^k\}$. Hence,

$$\begin{aligned}\lambda_i &= \lambda^*_{\{x_i\}} + 2\lambda^*_{\{x_i^2\}} + 3\lambda^*_{\{x_i^3\}} + \cdots \\ &= \lambda^* \sum_{k=1}^{\infty} k \left(\frac{\lambda^*_{\{x_i\}}}{\lambda^*} \right)^k \\ &= \frac{\lambda^* \left(\lambda^*_{\{x_i\}} / \lambda^* \right)}{\left(1 - (\lambda^*_{\{x_i\}} / \lambda^*) \right)^2} \\ &= \frac{\lambda^*_{\{x_i\}} (\lambda^*)^2}{(\lambda^* - \lambda^*_{\{x_i\}})^2}.\end{aligned}$$

□

2.10 Exercises

2.1. Suppose N is a Poisson process with $\lambda(t, x, y) = 1.5 + 10t + 2x$ on $B = [0, 1]x[0, 10]x[0, 1]$. What is $EN(B)$?

2.2. Why is the process N in the counterexample in Sect. 2.1, with one point at the origin and no other points, not a Poisson process? What assumption is violated? Is N simple? orderly? completely independent? Does λ exist?

2.3. Suppose N is a Poisson process on $S = [0, T] \times [0, 1] \times [0, 1]$ with rate 3, and M has the same points N has, plus one extra point somewhere distributed uniformly on S if $N(S)$ is odd. Write an expression for $\lambda_M(t, x, y)$, the conditional intensity of M at time t and location (x, y), given the points in M occurring before time t. For example, if $t = 0.6$ and M has had points at times 0.2, 0.4, and 0.5 before time t, then what is $\lambda(t, x, y)$?

2.4. Which of the following is correct? A mixed Poisson process is a Cox process where
a. $\lambda(t, x, y) = E(\lambda(t, x, y))$ for all t, x, y, in every realization.
b. $\lambda(t, x, y) = \lambda(t', x', y')$, for any locations (t, x, y) and (t', x', y').
c. The cluster sizes are Poisson distributed with mean λ.
d. $\lambda = 1$.

2.5. For each of the following processes, indicate (a) Is it a point process? (b) Is it simple? (c) Is it Poisson? (d) What is its conditional intensity?
(i) N is a process with 1 point placed uniformly in the unit square and with a time uniformly between 0 and 1.
(ii) N is a process with 2 points placed uniformly in the unit square and with times uniformly distributed between 0 and 1, and the two locations and times independent of each other.
(iii) N is a process with 2 points placed at exactly the same location and time as each other, and this location is uniformly distributed on the unit square and the time is uniform on (0, 1).
(iv) N is a simple point process with $\lambda(t, x, y) = 2 + t + 3x + 4y^2$, for $(x, y) \in$ the unit square $[0, 1]^2$, and for $tin(0, \infty)$.
(v) N is a temporal process on (0, 1) with only one point and that point is at time $1/2$.
(vi) N is a temporal process on (0, 1) with a point at every rational time between 0 and 1.
(vii) N is a temporal process on (0, 1) with points at every time between 0 and 1.
(viii) N is a temporal process on (0, 1) with one point placed at some time τ_1 uniformly distributed on $(0, 1/2)$, and another point τ_2 placed exactly at time $\tau_1 + 1/2$.

2.6. Suppose M is a stationary Poisson process with rate 1, and let $N = 2M$, i.e. N has two overlapping points wherever M has a point. Then (a) What is the conditional rate for N? (b) Does N obey the complete independence property? (c) Is N simple? (d) Is N a Poisson process? Prove either that N is a Poisson process or that it is not.

2.7. For each of the following datasets, indicate what type of model you might suggest using. In some cases, there might be more than one correct answer.
(a) Data on polar bear sightings, where one is especially interested in seeing if there are more or fewer as you go North.
(b) Data on the number of winning lottery tickets purchased at various merchants in a certain city, where one is interested in whether they seem to be uniformly distributed or whether certain stores seem to have been especially lucky.
(c) Data on lightning strikes, where one is interested in whether they are more likely on hot, rainy days than on cold, rainy days.
(d) Data on mosquitos carrying a certain virus, where one is interested in whether they are significantly clustered or not.
(e) Data on suicides, where one is interested in whether there is social contagion or not.
(f) Data on the number of failing test grades for students in each classroom at a certain school, where one is interested in whether certain classes have more failing students than others.
(g) Data on sightings of poison oak, where one is interested in characterizing its rate of spread.
(h) Data on the locations of children playing in a particular park, where one is interested in whether they are clustered or unifornly scattered.
(i) Data on locations of employees' desks in a certain company, where conceivably the desks are not overly close together so that each employee can carve out a bit of their own space.

2.8. Simulate and plot two realizations of each of the following models: homogeneous Poisson process, inhomogeneous Poisson process, mixed Poisson process, compound Poisson process, Neyman-Scott process, Cox process, Gibbs process, Matern process, Hawkes process, ETAS process, recursive process. For each plot, label it accordingly, specifying which type of model is being simulated and indicate the parameters as well. Choose parameters that are slightly different from the examples in this book.

2.9. Which of the following is a Poisson process?
(a.) a Hawkes process with productivity $K = 1$.
(b.) a Poisson cluster process with mean cluster size of 4.5.
(c.) a simple point process with conditional intensity $\lambda(t, x, y) = 1 + N\{(0, t)xS\}$.
(d.) a soft-core Gibbs process with $s = 1$.
(e.) a simple point process with conditional intensity $\lambda(t, x, y) = 1 + log(3 + x + yt)$.
(f.) None of the above.

2.10. Let B mean the spatial-temporal region $[0, 10] \times [0, 1] \times [0, 1]$, i.e. the unit square S observed from time 0 to time 10 days. Suppose N is a Poisson process on B with rate 3 everywhere. What is the expected value of the sum of the *times* of the events in B? That is, what is $E \sum_{i=1}^{t} t_i$?

For the next two problems, suppose the point process N is generated as follows. A uniform random variable U is drawn between 0 and 1. If $U < 0.5$, then {
– A single point is placed uniformly in the unit square, with a time uniformly distributed between time 0 and time 5.
– And, an independent uniform random variable is drawn between 0 and 1, and if it is less then 0.4, then another point is placed uniformly in the unit square, but with a time uniformly distributed between time 5 and time 10.}

If $U \geq 0.5$, then a single point is placed uniformly in the unit square with a time uniformly distributed between 5 and 10.

2.11. What is $E \int dN$?

2.12. Suppose there is a point at $(4, 0.5, 0.8)$, i.e. at time $t = 4$, $x = 0.5$, and $y = 0.8$. What is $\lambda(5, 0.5, 0.8)$?

For the next three problems, suppose N is the single point process, where N has one point for sure, i.e. $P\{N(B) = 1\} = 1$. The one point of N is distributed uniformly in B, where B is the spatial-temporal region $[0, 10] \times [0, 1] \times [0, 1]$, i.e. the unit square S observed from time 0 to time 10 days.

2.13. What is $E \int_B \lambda(t, x, y)dtdxdy$?

2.14. Suppose N happens to have a point at $(7.5, 0.5, 0.8)$. What is $\lambda(8, 0.5, 0.8)$?

2.15. Suppose again that N happens to have a point at $(7.5, 0.5, 0.8)$. What is $\lambda(7.5, 0.5, 0.8)$?

For the next two problems, suppose N is a rate decreasing point process with points distributed spatially in the unit square S and with times from time 0 to ∞, and suppose $\lambda(t, x, y) = 5 - N\{[0, t)xS\}$.

2.16. What is $E \int_0^\infty \int_S \lambda(t, x, y)dtdxdy$?

2.17. What is $E \int_0^\infty \int_S \lambda^2(t, x, y)dtdxdy$?

References

Bartlett, M. (1986). Mixed Cox processes, with an application to accident statistics. *Journal of Applied Probability, 23*, 321–333.

Bebbington, M., & Harte, D. S. (2001). On the statistics of the linked stress release model. *Journal of Applied Probability, 38*, 176–187.

Cauchemez, S., Nouvellet, P., Cori, A., Jombart, T., Garske, T., Clapham, H., Moore, S., Mills, H. L., Salje, H., Collins, C., Rodriguez-Barraquer, I., Riley, S., Truelove, S., Algarni, H., Alhakeem, R., AlHarbi, K., Turkistani, A., Aguas, R. J., Cummings, D. A. T., et al. (2016). Unraveling the drivers of MERS-CoV transmission. *Proceedings of the National Academy of Sciences, 113*(32), 9081–9086.

Cha, J. H., & Finkelstein, M. (2018). Applications of the mixed Poisson process. In Springer series in reliability engineering, *Point processes for reliability analysis*. Springer. https://doi.org/10.1007/978-3-319-73540-5_11

Daley, D. J., & Jones, D. V. (2003). *An introduction to the theory of point processes: Elementary theory of point processes*. Springer.

Daley, D., & Vere-Jones, D. (1988). *An introduction to the theory of point processes*. Springer.

Das, I., & Stein, A. (2016). Application of the multitype Strauss point model for characterizing the spatial distribution of landslides. *Mathematical Problems in Engineering, 1612901*, 1–12.

Goulard, M., Grabarnik, P., & Sarkka, A. (1996). Parameter estimation for marked Gibbs point processes through the maximum pseudo-likelihood method. *Scandinavian Journal of Statistics, 23*, 365–379.

Isham, V., & Westcott, M. (1979). A self-correcting point process. *Stochastic Processes and Their Applications, 8*(3), 335–347.

Jacod, J. (1975). Multivariate point processes: predictable projections, Radon-Nikodym derivatives, representation of martingales. *Zeitschrift für Wahrscheinlichkeitstheorie und verwandte Gebiete, 31*, 235–253.

Kagan, Y. Y. (1994). Observational evidence for earthquakes as a nonlinear dynamic process. *Physica D, 77*, 160–192.

Kegler, S. R. (2007). Applying the compound Poisson process model to the reporting of injury-related mortality rates. *Epidemiologic Perspectives and Innovations, 16*(4), 1–9.

Lloyd-Smith, J. O., Funk, S., McLean, A. R., Riley, S., & Wood, J. L. N. (2015). Nine challenges in modelling the emergence of novel pathogens. *Epidemics, 10*, 35–39.

Nguyen, D. G., & Murthy, D. N. P. (1984). Cost analysis of warranty policies. *Naval Research Logistics Quarterly, 31*(4), 525–541.

Ogata, Y. (1988). Statistical models for earthquake occurrences and residual analysis for point processes. *Journal of the American Statistical Association, 83*, 9–27.

Ogata, Y. (1998). Space-time point-process models for earthquake occurrences. *Annals of the Institute of Statistical Mathematics, 50*(2), 379–402.

Schoenberg, F. (2016). A note on the consistent estimation of spatial-temporal point process parameters. *Statistica Sinica, 26*, 861–879.

Schoenberg, F., Hoffmann, M., & Harrigan, R. (2019). A recursive point process model for infectious diseases. *AISM, 71*(5), 1271–1287.

Stoyan, D., & Stoyan, H. (1998). Non-homogeneous Gibbs process models for forestry—a case study. *Biometrical Journal, 40*, 521–531.

Stoyan, D., Kendall, W. S., & Mecke, J. (1995). *Stochastic geometry and its applications* (2nd ed.). Wiley.

Vere-Jones, D. (1988). On the variance properties of stress release models. *Australian and New Zealand Journal of Statistics, 30A*(1), 123–135.

Vere-Jones, D., & Ogata, Y. (1984). On the moments of a self-correcting point process. *The Journal of Applied Probability, 21*, 315–342.

Wallinga, J., & Teunis, P. (2004). Different epidemic curves for severe acute respiratory syndrome reveal similar impacts of control measures. *American Journal of Epidemiology, 160*(6), 509–516.

Wheater, H. S., Chandler, R. E., Onof, C., Isham, V. S., Bellone, E., Yang, C., Lekkas, D., Lourmas, G., & Segond, M. L. (2005). Spatial-temporal rainfall modelling for flood risk estimation. *Stochastic Environmental Research and Risk Assessment, 19*(6), 403–416.

3 Estimation

Throughout this chapter, we suppose that a model for a point process has been specified but there are some parameters in the model whose values are unknown, and one seeks to use the observations to find values of the parameters so that the model best fits the data. In the case of non-parametric estimation, the setup is similar, but we might suppose that there are certain *functions* that must be estimated, rather than parameters. In geophysics and some other fields, they often use the term *inversion* where we use the term *estimation*. I wish someone had told me this back when I was a graduate student; I spent so much time wondering what they were talking about inverting!

3.1 Maximum Likelihood

Point process models are usually estimated via maximum likelihood. Before we describe the maximum likelihood estimate (MLE) and its properties, we first motivate the definition of the likelihood for a point process.

3.2 Likelihood

Recall that for a temporal Poisson process N, the probability of observing exactly k points in the interval (τ_1, τ_2) is

$$P\{N(\tau_1, \tau_2) = k\} = \frac{e^{-B} B^k}{k!},$$

with $B = A(\tau_2) - A(\tau_1)$, where $A(t) = \int_0^t \lambda(u)du$, and with the convention that $0! = 1$. So for $k = 0$, $P\{N$ has 0 points in $(\tau_1, \tau_2)\} = exp(-B) = e^{-A(\tau_2)+A(\tau_1)}$. That is, for a simple non-stationary temporal Poisson process with intensity $\lambda(t)$ on $[0, T]$, the likelihood of observing zero points in the interior of the interval (τ_1, τ_2) is $e^{-A(\tau_2)+A(\tau_1)}$, and the probability of observing zero points in $(\tau_2, \tau_3)\}$ is $e^{-A(\tau_3)+A(\tau_2)}$, etc. Meanwhile, the probability density of observing a point at τ_i is given by $\lambda(\tau_i)$. Therefore, the likelihood of observing the particular collection of points $\{\tau_1, \tau_2, \ldots, \tau_n\}$ on $[0, T]$ is simply the product of the densities at the points times the probability of observing zero points in $(0, \tau_1)$ times the probability of observing zero points in (τ_1, τ_2), ..., times the probability of observing zero

F. Schoenberg, *Space-Time Point Processes*, Springer Texts in Statistics,
https://doi.org/10.1007/978-3-032-20790-6_3

points in (τ_n, T). In other words, the likelihood for such a process is $\lambda(\tau_1) \times \lambda(\tau_2) \times \cdots \times \lambda(\tau_n) \times e^{-A(\tau_1)} \times e^{-A(\tau_2)+A(\tau_1)} \times \cdots \times e^{-A(T)+A(\tau_n)} = \prod_{i=1}^{n} \lambda(\tau_i) e^{-A(T)}$.

In general, even for general point processes that are not Poisson, we define the likelihood as $\prod_{i=1}^{n} \lambda(\tau_i) e^{-A(T)}$, and thus the log-likelihood is $\sum_{i=1}^{n} \log \lambda(\tau_i) - A(T)$, and in the spatial-temporal case this is simply

$$l = \sum_{i=1}^{n} \log \lambda(\tau_i) - \int \lambda(t, x, y) dt dx dy.$$

The log-likelihood can be positive or negative, depends on the spatial-temporal units of analysis (e.g. km versus meters versus degrees), and is not usually interpreted directly. Instead, the log-likelihood of one model is interpreted relative to another model, or the log-likelihoods can be compared for the same model but two different parameter vectors.

3.3 Maximum Likelihood Estimates

One way to estimate the vector θ of parameters governing the conditional intensity λ is to find the vector θ maximizing the log-likelihood

$$l(\theta) = \sum \log \lambda(t_i, x_i, y_i; \theta) - \int \lambda(t, x, y; \theta) dt dx dy. \tag{3.1}$$

The result is called the maximum likelihood estimate (MLE) of θ.

Ogata (1978) showed that the resulting estimate, $\hat{\theta}$, is, under standard conditions, asymptotically unbiased [meaning $E(\hat{\theta}) \to \theta$ as $T \to \infty$], consistent [$P(|\hat{\theta} - \theta| > \epsilon) \to 0$ as $T \to \infty$, for any $\epsilon > 0$], asymptotically normal [$\hat{\theta} \to$ Normal in distribution as $T \to \infty$], and asymptotically efficient [possessing minimal variance among asymptotically unbiased estimators]. Further, he showed standard errors for $\hat{\theta}$ can be constructed using the diagonal elements of the inverse of the Hessian of l evaluated at $\hat{\theta}$.

The conditions of Ogata (1978) can be relaxed a bit for Poisson processes (Rathbun & Cressie, 1994), and for certain spatial-temporal process in general (Rathbun, 1996). Even if the process is not Poisson, under some circumstances (Schoenberg, 2004) the parameters governing the unconditional intensity, $E\lambda$, can be consistently estimated by maximizing the Poisson likelihood $L_P(\theta) = \sum_{i=1}^{n} \log(E\lambda(t_i)) - \int E\lambda(t, x, y) dt dx dy$. Another way to think of this is as the likelihood if we were to pretend the process was Poisson, even though it is not.

Another convenient property of the MLE is this: Suppose you are missing some covariate that might affect λ. Under general conditions, the MLE will nevertheless be consistent, provided the effect of the missing covariate is small (Schoenberg, 2016).

Maximum likelihood estimation seems like it should be easy. Most statistical software packages, like *R*, have excellent functions (like *optim*) that can find the parameters that maximize a function, using Newton-Raphson or other techniques. So, given a dataset and a model for λ, to find the parameters maximizing (3.1), all you have to do is write a function that takes the parameters as inputs, and outputs the log-likelihood in (3.1), and pass that function into *optim()*. It seems easy, right?

Before getting into what makes maximum likelihood difficult in actual practice, let us study some instances where it is easy and straightforward. A first example has nothing to do with point processes, but is simply to show how *optim()* works in *R*. Imagine one wants to find the values of the parameters a and b minimizing the function

$$f(a, b) = (a - 87.1)^2 + (b - 59.2)^2. \tag{3.2}$$

The following code can be used to find the optimal values of a and b to minimize the function f in (3.2).

```
pstart = c(10,20) ## starting guesses for (a,b)
f = function(p) (p[1]-87.1)^2 + (p[2]-59.2)^2
optim(pstart,f)$par
```

Running the code above produces the estimates (87.09549, 59.20400). Even after starting with the poor guesses of $a = 10$ and $b = 20$, optim() achieves estimates that are quite close to the true optimal values of $a = 87.1$ and $b = 59.2$.

Returning to point process estimation, suppose one aims to fit the inhomogeneous Poisson process model described near the beginning of Chap. 2, where $\lambda(t, x, y) = 2$ for (x, y) in a circle of radius 0.2 centered at (a, b), and $\lambda = 1$ everywhere else. In the example in Chap. 2, $(a, b) = (0.4, 0.7)$, and is simulated using the function *simcirc* below.

```
simcirc = function(T=8000,X1=1,Y1=1,a=.4,b=.7,lam1=1,lam2=1,r=.2){
## simulate a Poisson process with intensity lam_1 + lam_2 1_{||(x-a,y-b)|| < r}
## on [0,T] x [0,X1] x [0,Y1]
tot = lam1+lam2; n = rpois(1, tot*T*X1*Y1)
candx = runif(n); candy = runif(n)
accept = (runif(n) < (lam1+((candx-a)^2 + (candy-b)^2 < r^2))/tot)
x <<- candx[accept]; y <<- candy[accept];
t <<- runif(length(x))*T; n <<- length(x)
}
simcirc()
```

Suppose the values a and b are unknown and to be estimated. The following code estimates them by maximum likelihood, using the starting guesses $a = 0.8$ and $b = 0.3$. In this code, the function f outputs the negative log-likelihood, which is then minimized by *optim()*. Here the integral $\int_S \lambda(t, x, y)dtdxdy = 8000(1 + \pi 0.2^2)$.

```
pstart = c(.5,.5) ## starting guesses for (a,b)
f = function(p){
lam = 1 + 1*((x-p[1])^2 + (y-p[2])^2 < .04)
int = 8000*(1+pi*.04)
int-sum(log(lam))
}
optim(pstart,f)$par
```

Again, the maximum likelihood estimates are quite close to the true parameters $a = 0.4$ and $b = 0.7$. Every run will be a bit different as it depends on the simulation of the process which is different each time, but one example on my computer yields $(a, b) = (0.3986697, 0.7005818)$.

Unfortunately, although Eq. (3.1) might look simple, and although in the example above everything was straightforward and worked well, in most applications, writing a function to compute (3.1) is very problematic. Actually, the first term in (3.1), $\sum \log \lambda(t_i, x_i, y_i; \theta)$, is usually very easy to compute. Given a model and estimates of the parameters θ, it is typically very straightforward to compute the conditional intensity λ at any point (t_i, x_i, y_i), and then taking the logarithm of those values and summing them up is quick and easy.

The problem is the integral term, $\int \lambda(t, x, y; \theta)dtdxdy$. This means the integral, over *all* spatial and temporal locations in your observation region, of the conditional intensity λ. Even if λ is easy to compute at any single given location and time, it is usually not so easy to compute or even approximate the integral of λ over all locations and times.

In the example above where $\lambda = 2$ in the circle of radius 0.2 and $\lambda = 1$ everywhere else in the unit square, and where t ranged from 0 to 8000, the integral of λ just happened to be very simple to compute as $8000(1 + \pi 0.2^2)$. Furthermore, this integral did not even depend on the parameters being estimated, although technically, if the parameters (a, b) were near the border of the unit square, then the integral over the unit square would decrease.

In general, with most models, the integral $\int_S \lambda(t, x, y; \theta)dtdxdy$ depends on the parameters θ, and can be difficult to compute, especially if λ is complex and highly volatile. One option is to approximate the integral numerically, e.g. by computing λ at thousands or even millions of space-time locations, and averaging the results. However, if λ is highly variable and the spatial-temporal domain is large, then even millions of locations might not be enough for the approximation to be accurate. Moreover, if the integral of λ depends on the parameters, θ, then when using *optim()* to search over the parameter space for the best fitting parameters, this integral of λ would have to be approximated repeatedly, for every candidate value of θ in the search. Furthermore, if the approximation is good for some values of θ but is poor for others, as is often the case, for instance, if λ is extremely volatile for certain possible values of θ, then *optim()* may falsely select or falsely reject those poorly approximated values of θ in its optimization. For some models, there may be analytic ways to approximate the integral of λ over the spatial-temporal domain, but again, it generally is not enough for these approximations to be good for some or even most choices of θ; unless the approximation is close for *all* values of θ, *optim()* may converge to a value of θ that is not actually the maximum likelihood estimate.

3.4 Integral Approximation for Hawkes, ETAS, and Recursive Models

As mentioned in the previous section, in maximizing $l(\theta) = \sum \log \lambda(t_i, x_i, y_i; \theta) - \int\int\int_0^T \lambda(t, x, y)dtdxdy$, it is typically straightforward to compute the sum, but the integral can be problematic especially when the conditional intensity is very volatile. There is a trick, however, for Hawkes processes (Schoenberg, 2013). Suppose $\lambda(t, x, y) = \alpha\mu(x, y) + \kappa \sum_{t',x',y':t'<t} g(t - t', x - x', y - y')$, where g and μ are density functions, so $\int\int \mu(x, y)dxdy = 1$ and $\int\int\int g(t, x, y)dtdxdy = 1$. In this case $\int\int\int_0^T \lambda(t, x, y)dtdxdy$

$$
\begin{aligned}
&= \int\int\int_0^T \alpha\mu(x, y) + \kappa \sum_{t',x',y':t'<t} g(t - t', x - x', y - y')dtdxdy \\
&= \alpha T + \kappa \int\int\int \sum g(t - t', x - x', y - y')dtdxdy \\
&= \alpha T + \kappa \sum \int\int\int g(t - t', x - x', y - y')dtdxdy \\
&\approx \alpha T + \kappa N, \qquad (3.3)
\end{aligned}
$$

where $N = N([0, T] \times S)$ is the total number of observed points.

The reason why the approximation is not an equality is that, while the integral $\int\int\int g = 1$ when g is integrated over all of time and space, technically here we are integrating $g(t - t', x - x', y - y')$ only over the remainder of the observation region $[t', T] \times S$, for each observed point (t', x', y'). If the process is such that the points triggered by a point (t_i, x_i, y_i) are sure to fall within the observation region $[0, T] \times S$, then the approximation would be perfect, but otherwise $\int\int\int_0^T \lambda(t, x, y)dtdxdy <$

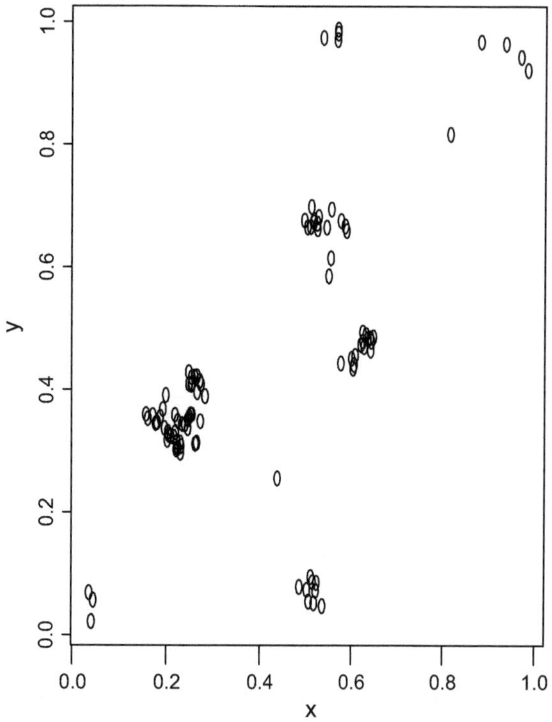

Fig. 3.1 Hawkes process on $[0, 1] \times [0, 1] \times [0, 1]$ with $\mu = 10$ and $\kappa = 0.9$, and with exponential spatial triggering function with parameter $\alpha = 2000$ and exponential temporal triggering function with parameter $\beta = 3000$

$\alpha T + \kappa N$. In the case where triggered points fall outside the observation region, we may refer to this as *leakage*. Importantly, if for some values of θ, there is significant leakage, so that the approximation is poor, then since in maximum likelihood estimation one seeks a value of θ maximizing $l(\theta)$, a search for values of θ maximizing $\sum \log(\lambda(t_i, x_i, y_i; \theta)) - (\alpha T + \kappa N)$ will tend to avoid such values of θ. As a result, the use of the approximation above tends to result in reasonable estimates of θ, and leakage in this integral approximation tends to be a negligible problem for Hawkes processes.

To illustrate, suppose we use the code below to simulate and plot a Hawkes process with exponential triggering function in both time and space, on the space-time domain $[0, 1] \times [0, 1] \times [0, 1]$. The simulation is depicted in Fig. 3.1.

```
source(url("http://www.stat.ucla.edu/~frederic/book/simhawk.r"))
T = 1; X1=1; Y1=1; mu = 10; theta_K = 0.9; theta_alpha = 2000
theta_beta = 3000; theta_b = 2; theta_m0 = 3.5
z = simhawk(T=T,gmi=pointprod, gt=expgt, gxy = expxy)
plot(z$lon,z$lat,xlab="x",ylab="y")
```

The code below is then used to fit the parameters of the model, $\theta = \{\mu, \kappa, \alpha, \beta\}$. Approximate standard errors (SEs) of $\hat{\theta} = \{\hat{\mu}, \hat{\kappa}, \hat{\alpha}, \hat{\beta}\}$ are also computed, using the square roots of the diagonal elements of the inverse of the Hessian of the log-likelihood at $\hat{\theta}$.

```
source(url("http://www.stat.ucla.edu/~frederic/book/fithawk.r"))
theta1 = c(15,.5,1000,1000)
b1 = optim(theta1,loglhawk,hessian=T)
b1$par
sqrt(diag(solve(b1$hess)))
```

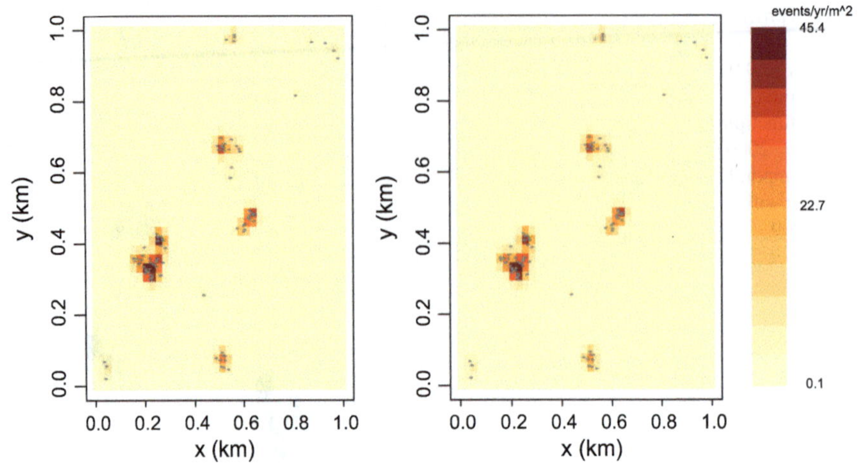

Fig. 3.2 (left) True conditional intensity of Hawkes process on $[0, 1] \times [0, 1] \times [0, 1]$ with $\mu = 10$ and $\kappa = 0.9$, and with exponential spatial triggering function with parameter $\alpha = 2000$ and exponential temporal triggering function with parameter $\beta = 3000$. (right) Estimated conditional intensity of the same process, with parameters α, β, μ, and κ estimated by MLE using *optim()*. For both plots, conditional intensities are evaluated at the centers of a 40×40 grid of x and y values, and summed over 10, 000 equally spaced times. The points are overlaid in gray

The code above uses the function *loglhawk()*, which assumes the triggering function is exponential in space and time, and returns the negative log-likelihood. If a different triggering function is used, then *loglhawk()* needs to be altered. In particular, the lines

```
const = K*alpha/pi*beta
```

and

```
    r2 = (z$lon[j]-z$lon[i])^2+(z$lat[j]-z$lat[i])^2
    gij = gij + exp(-beta*(z$t[j]-z$t[i])-alpha*r2)
```

would need to be changed.

The estimates obtained for this simulation, with SEs in parentheses are $\{\hat{\mu}, \hat{\kappa}, \hat{\alpha}, \hat{\beta}\} = \{11.96(3.45), 0.8835(0.0953), 1890(246), 3119(405)\}$, which are reasonably close to the true values of $\{\mu, \kappa, \alpha, \beta\} = 10, 0.9, 2000, 3000\}$ used in the simulation. Figure 3.2 shows the true conditional intensity $\lambda(t, x, y)$ as well as the estimate $\hat{\lambda}(t, x, y)$ where λ is estimated by MLE, both summed at 10,000 times between time 0 and time 1. The left-most image, showing the sum of the *true* conditional intensity λ, was made using the following code.

```
a = seq(0,1,length=40); b = a; m = matrix(0,nrow=40,ncol=40)
mu = 10; k = 0.9; alpha = 2000; beta = 3000; const = k*alpha/pi*beta
for(t in seq(0,1,length=10000)){
for(i in c(1:40)){ for(j in c(1:40)){
    r2 = (a[i]-z$lon[z$t<t])^2+(b[j]-z$lat[z$t<t])^2
    m[i,j] = m[i,j] + mu + const*sum(exp(-beta*(t-z$t[z$t<t])-alpha*r2))
    }}}
plot(c(0,1),c(0,1),xlab="x (km)",ylab="y (km)",type="n")
image(a,b,m,add=T)
points(z$lon,z$lat,pch=3,cex=.2,col=grey(.5))
```

The code above constructs a 40×40 grid, and for each gridpoint, calculates $\lambda(t, x, y)$ at the center of the grid, for 10, 000 times equally spaced between 0 and 1, and adds them up. The results are then plotted using *image()*, and the points overlaid using the *R* function *points()*.

Similarly, the following code adds up the *estimated* conditional intensity $\hat{\lambda}$, using the parameters estimated by MLE with the integral approximation described above, and plots the result shown in the middle of Fig. 3.2. The estimated and true intensity appear to be nearly indistinguishable in this example.

```
m2 = matrix(0,nrow=40,ncol=40)
mu = 11.96; k = 0.8835; alpha = 1890; beta = 3119
const = k*alpha/pi*beta
for(t in seq(0,1,length=10000)){
for(i in c(1:40)){ for(j in c(1:40)){
    r2 = (a[i]-z$lon[z$t<t])^2+(b[j]-z$lat[z$t<t])^2
    m2[i,j] = m2[i,j] + mu + const*sum(exp(-beta*(t-z$t[z$t<t])-alpha*r2))
    }}}
plot(c(0,1),c(0,1),xlab="x (km)",ylab="y (km)",type="n")
image(a,b,m2,add=T,zlim=range(m))
points(z$lon,z$lat,pch=3,cex=.2,col=grey(.5))
```

To plot the legend on the right of Fig. 3.2, one can implement the code below.

```
w = c(m,m2)/10^6
plot(c(0,10),range(w),type="n",axes=F,xlab="",ylab="")
  image(c(-1:1),seq(min(w),max(w),length=100),matrix(rep(seq(0,0.8,
    length=100),2),ncol=100,byrow=T), add=T)
  text(c(2.7,2.7,2.7),c(min(w),.5*(min(w)+max(w)),max(w)),c(m3(
    min(w)),m3(.5*(min(w)+max(w))),m3(max(w))))
  text(2.8,1.02*max(w),"events/yr/m^2")
```

In finding the MLE using *optim()*, an initial guess at θ is required. Unfortunately, the final result often depends on the starting guess, which is typically determined rather arbitrarily. The problem is essentially multi-modality, as *optim()* is prone to finding a local optimum when in theory one desires the global optimum. However, this problem can usually be readily remedied with a bit of effort; one can try a bunch of starting guesses, and in the end simply choose the result where *optim()* found the value of highest log-likelihood. Furthermore, in many cases, even when *optim()* finds an estimate where the individual parameter estimates are far from the maximum likelihood estimates, often the resulting estimates of the conditional intensity λ are quite similar. In such cases, the apparently large differences in particular parameter estimates can be of small importance.

In the case where the productivity κ varies from event to event, such as in the ETAS model, the simplification above can still be used. If, for instance, $\lambda(t,x,y) = \alpha\mu(x,y) + \sum_{t',x',y',m':t'<t} h(m')g(t-t',x-x',y-y')$, where g and μ are density functions, then $\int\int\int_0^T \lambda(t,x,y)dtdxdy$

$$
\begin{aligned}
&= \int\int\int_0^T \alpha\mu(x,y) + \sum_{t',x',y',m':t'<t} h(m')g(t-t',x-x',y-y')dtdxdy \\
&= \alpha T + \int\int\int \sum h(m')g(t-t',x-x',y-y')dtdxdy \\
&= \alpha T + \sum h(m') \int\int\int g(t-t',x-x',y-y')dtdxdy \\
&\approx \alpha T + \sum_{i=1}^{N} h(m_i).
\end{aligned}
$$

To fit the ETAS model with power-law triggering in space and time to the San Bernardino earthquake data from Fig. 1.3 of Chap. 1, for instance, one could use the following code, after downloading the data and editing it to form the file SearchResults.txt, as described around Fig. 1.3 in Chap. 1.

```
x = read.table("SearchResults.txt",skip=2,fill=TRUE)
t = julian(as.Date(x$V1),origin = as.Date("1970-01-01")) + x$V2/24 +
    x$V3/24/60 + x$V4/24/60/60
maxt = julian(as.Date("2025-01-01"),origin = as.Date("1970-01-01"))
z = list(); z$t = t; z$lon = x$V10+118; z$lat = x$V9-34;
z$m = x$V7; z$n = length(z$t)
X1 = 1; Y1 = 1; T = maxt; M0 = 3.5
source(url("http://www.stat.ucla.edu/~frederic/book/fitetas.r"))
theta1 = c(z$n/maxt*.1,.1,2,2,2,2,3)
b1 = optim(theta1,logletas,hessian=T)
theta2 = b1$par
b1 = optim(theta2,logletas,hessian=T)
theta2 = b1$par
sqrt(diag(solve(b1$hess))) ## for SEs
```

This results in the parameter estimates (with approximate SEs) $\{\hat{\mu}, \hat{K}, \hat{c}, \hat{p}, \hat{a}, \hat{d}, \hat{q}\} = \{0.0138(.00106), 0.390(0.0351), 0.00480(0.00205), 1.14(0.0126), 1.08(0.145), 0.00346(.00000635), 3.86(0.302)\}$. For a dataset like this with only 405 points and 7 parameters to estimate, the variances of the estimates are rather large.

With only 405 events observed, computation is very fast, but with many points, computation of the log-likelihood can be prohibitively slow. One way to speed up maximum likelihood estimation is to do the computation of the log-likelihood in C, and then have optim() find the minimum of some simple *R* function that basically just calls this C function.

In some situations, when computing the approximate standard errors using the square root of the inverse Hessian of the log-likelihood, the output is *NaN*. Usually this occurs when *optim()* has stopped running without finding a local minimum. The default in *optim()* is to run 500 iterations for the Nelder-Mead algorithm, which is the default algorithm implemented by *optim()*. It is for this reason that, in the code above, *optim()* is run twice, where for the second run, the initial guess is the final parameter estimate from the first run. Another way to address this problem is to try various different starting values and choose the final value for $\hat{\theta}$ that achieves the highest log-likelihood.

In the case of the recursive model, one must first note that, despite the recursive nature of the model, the log-likelihood can be computed quite directly. For any given realization of points $\{\tau_1, \tau_2, \ldots, \tau_n\}$, given a particular value of the parameter vector θ, $\lambda(\tau_1) = \mu$, so one can immediately compute $H\{\lambda(\tau_1)\} = H(\mu)$, and thus $\lambda(\tau_2) = \mu + H(\mu)g(\tau_2 - \tau_1)$. One therefore has $H\{\lambda(\tau_2)\} = H\{\mu + H(\mu)g(\tau_2 - \tau_1)\}$, and one can continue in this fashion to compute $\lambda(\tau_i)$ for $i = 1, 2, \ldots, n$. Further, the integral term in the log-likelihood may be approximated in a fashion similar to that for Hawkes and ETAS models, namely, assuming $g(t)$ has negligible mass for $t > T - \tau_i$,

$$\int_0^T \lambda(t)dt = \int_0^T \{\mu + \int_0^t H\{\lambda(s)\}g(t-s)dN(s)\}dt$$
$$= \mu T + \int_0^T H\{\lambda(s)\} \int_0^{T-s} g(u)dN(s)du$$
$$\approx \mu T + \int_0^T H\{\lambda(s)\}dN(s)$$
$$= \mu T + \sum_{i=1}^{n} H\{\lambda(\tau_i)\},$$

which is very easy to compute.

For example, suppose one wishes to fit the recursive model to just the times of the San Bernardino earthquakes considered above. The code below can be used to fit the model

$$\lambda(t) = \mu + \kappa \int_0^t [\lambda(u)]^{-\alpha} g(t-u)dN(u),$$

by MLE, where $g(u) = \beta e^{-\beta u}$, to find estimates of the parameters $\{\mu, \kappa, \alpha, \beta\}$.

```
x = read.table("SearchResults.txt",skip=2,fill=TRUE)
t = julian(as.Date(x$V1),origin = as.Date("1970-01-01")) + x$V2/24 +
    x$V3/24/60 + x$V4/24/60/60; n = length(t)
T= julian(as.Date("2025-01-01"),origin = as.Date("1970-01-01"))
source(url("http://www.stat.ucla.edu/~frederic/book/fitrecursive.r"))
theta1 = c(.01,.2,1,2)
b1 = optim(theta1,loglrecursive,hessian=T)
theta2 = b1$par
sqrt(diag(solve(b1$hess))) ## for SEs
```

The resulting parameter estimates for the recursive model (with SEs) are $\{\hat{\mu}, \hat{K}, \hat{\alpha}, \hat{\beta}\} = \{0.0163(.000924), 0.183(0.0231), 0.0000000443(0.00000638), 2.60(0.631)\}$.

3.5 Separable Estimation

One topic that always comes up in practice yet has been discussed far too rarely in publications is how to formulate your own model. Given data, it can be very tricky to decide what type of model to fit, and even within one class of models, deciding on the particular functional form for components of the model can be difficult and very consequential.

In order to try to avoid gross mis-specification, an approach I generally recommend is to start simple and gradually add complexity to the model. In particular, a very useful approach that can be effective for some types of point process data is to start out by assuming the process is *separable*, i.e. that different components of the process can be estimated individually, essentially ignoring the other components. For example, given the times and locations of wildfires, one may first estimate the temporal distribution by smoothing the number of wildfires observed as a function of the calendar date, since more wildfires are generally observed in the hotter summer months than in the colder winter months. Then one could separately estimate how wildfire incidence varies according to location within the observation region, since certain areas may be much more prone to wildfires than others. Multiplying these two components together, one can construct a simple Poisson process model for wildfires. Since each of these components can readily be inspected individually, there is hope that at least the functional forms chosen may fit the data well. As one adds further complexity into the model, e.g. by incorporating spatial-temporal interactions as well as relevant covariates such as windspeed and relative humidity, one can gradually build a model that may remain faithfully close to the data. In my experience, the opposite approach, working from the top down by combining lots of covariates and components at once, typically results in a grossly mis-specified and over-parameterized model with high variance and large predictive errors.

Recent increases in spatial-temporal marked point process data with multiple covariates have led to the development of point process models with relatively large numbers of parameters. The high dimensionality of the models can pose problems when it comes to the improvement, evaluation, and estimation of these models. In such situations, one may initially choose to focus on an individual portion of the process, e.g. by modeling first the purely temporal aspects of the process, and then adding spatial, mark, and covariate components. In seismology, for instance, a decade elapsed between the introduction of temporal marked Epidemic-Type Aftershock Sequence (ETAS) models (Ogata, 1988) and the development of spatial-temporal marked versions (Ogata, 1988) that are now commonly used. When examining just a portion of the process, however, one may inquire whether the modeled process may be accurately estimated in the absence of the components being ignored. In modeling the times and marks of a spatial-temporal marked point process, for instance, it is important to determine under what conditions the spatial components of the process may be ancillary to the parameters governing the temporal and mark components, or when ignoring the spatial coordinates of the observations would substantially bias estimates of temporal and mark parameters.

In this section, we discuss conditions under which different components of a point process model can be well estimated separably. Again, the purpose here is really to avoid mis-specification. If one desires to describe how wildfire incidence changes as a function of temperature, for instance, a very convenient place to start is by plotting wildfire incidence versus temperature. However, since the distribution of temperatures is not homogeneous, and since temperatures surely interact in complex ways with month and latitude as well as other weather related covariates, such a simple plot of incidence versus temperature can potentially be misleading, so it is important to understand under what conditions the relationship between temperature and incidence can be well estimated individually.

In addition, there is a sense among point process practitioners that, when certain possibly confounding variables have been omitted from the analysis, the resulting estimates of parameters should not be too substantially biased provided the omitted variables have a small influence on the conditional rate. Theoretical justification for this idea is hard to find, however. Below, I provide some results showing that omitted variables with small effects on the conditional rate should have small effects on parameter estimates, and conditions are described under which conventional maximum likelihood estimates are consistent despite the omission of certain variables.

The overall purpose here is to find conditions under which such partial models may be consistently estimated despite missing information. Certain special cases are well known. In point process models for earthquake occurrences, for instance, the distribution of earthquake magnitudes is typically modeled as constant over time. Thus, while earthquake magnitudes can affect the times and locations of future earthquakes, the magnitude distribution of an event at a particular location and time, given that an event occurs, is typically thought to be constant. Under this assumption, the estimation of the earthquake size distribution is especially straightforward. When one or more dimensions of a point process have coordinates whose entries are iid draws from a fixed distribution, the process is called separable; see e.g.

Rathbun (1996) or Schoenberg (2004) for examples. Under far more general conditions, components of a point process, when estimated separably using maximum likelihood methods, still yield consistent parameter estimates.

Suppose that N is a marked spatial-temporal point process, with k marks observed at each point, and with conditional intensity λ that is governed by a parameter vector θ from some compact parameter space Θ. We say the conditional intensity is *completely separable* if

$$\lambda(t, x, y, m_1, \ldots, m_k; \theta) = \theta_{k+1}\lambda_0(t, x, y; \theta_0)\lambda_1(t, x, y, m_1; \theta_1) \cdots \lambda_k(t, x, y, m_k; \theta_k), \quad (3.4)$$

where $\theta_i \in \Theta_i$, and each λ_i is predictable. In some applications, it may be unreasonable to suppose that the process is completely separable. However, more generally one might suppose that a given component is separable, as in the following definition.

We say λ (or equivalently, the point process N) is *separable in mark* m_i if the conditional intensity may be written as

$$\lambda(t, x, y, m_1, \ldots, m_k; \theta) = \theta_{k+1}\lambda_i(t, x, y, m_i; \theta_i)\lambda_{-i}(t, x, y, m_{-i}; \theta_{-i}), \quad (3.5)$$

where $m_{-i} = \{m_1, m_2, \ldots, m_{i-1}, m_{j+1}, m_{j+2}, \ldots, m_k\}$, and θ_{-i} denotes the parameter vector $\{\theta_0, \theta_1, \ldots, \theta_{i-1}, \theta_{i+1}, \theta_{i+2}, \ldots, \theta_k\}$. Mark m_i may be multiplicative and yet may influence the conditional rates λ_i and λ_{-i} at future times and the distribution of mark mi may vary with t, x, y and may depend on any facets of the history of the process. The key feature for separability of a mark is that the parameter θ_i only influences the process λ_i. The idea is that the rate λ may vary in time and space and might depend on mark m_i in potentially complicated ways, but the component related to mark m_i and the components related to other marks m_{-i} influence the rate in multiplicative fashion.

The separability of a component in a point process model is very important in that if a parameter or collection of parameters may be estimated individually, this greatly facilitates model building, fitting, and assessment. For multidimensional models, the rate at which points occur versus each separable coordinate may be plotted individually to suggest functional forms for the model, and also the fit of the model is much more readily inspected from such a plot due to the reduction in the number of dimensions. Further, while maximum likelihood estimates have such well-understood properties as consistency and asymptotic efficiency under rather general conditions, in practice maximum likelihood typically requires an iterative optimization procedure which, when many parameters are being estimated, can fail to converge to a global maximum and which often relies heavily on starting values, the choice of which can be very problematic. Estimation is greatly facilitated when only a few parameters are estimated at a time. Hence, it is worth exploring situations in which point process models can be decomposed so that certain parameters can be consistently estimated separably, without optimizing over all values of the other parameters.

Tests for separability of point process models have been proposed by Schoenberg (2004) and Chang and Schoenberg (2011). Rathbun (1996) noted that models that are multiplicative in all dimensions may be estimated separably, and methods for estimating such models are detailed by Baddeley and Turner (2000). In Schoenberg (2016), a much wider class of models is treated, and while we gloss over the mathematical details here, the main results may roughly be summarized as follows: **for models that are multiplicative in the coordinates of the point process (i.e. locations and times of the points), and either multiplicative or additive in the covariates, the individual components of the model may, under general conditions, be consistently estimated separately.** The resulting estimates will be equivalent, or, in the case of Theorem 2 of Schoenberg (2016), will converge in probability to the ordinary maximum likelihood estimates.

The conditions in Theorems 1 and 2 of Schoenberg (2016) essentially mandate that the impacts of the missing covariates on the conditional intensity are not too large. Thus, these results are not surprising, and the general conclusion that parameters may be well estimated in the absence of data on covariates that do not greatly affect the conditional intensity of the process seems to be widely acknowledged among practitioners.

As mentioned above, these results may have implications for point process estimation. It is typically far easier (and faster) to obtain a partial maximum likelihood estimate for a parameter governing one aspect of the point process (e.g. the magnitude distribution of earthquakes) than to search over values of all parameters simultaneously in order to find the value maximizing the full likelihood. It is important to note, however, that I do not advocate ignoring relevant covariates. Indeed, if such information can lead to more accurate forecasts then of course it should be included. The argument here is that a model's omission of variables with little influence on the conditional intensity need not cause one to doubt the accuracy of all parameter estimates and inferences based on the model. The idea of separable estimation may have implications for model building as well. It is typically extremely difficult to construct realistic models for multidimensional point processes with many covariates. Ideally such models should be based on well-understood physical principles and subject matter expertise. However, in some situations empirically based models may be sought, and one method for constructing such a model would be to individually investigate the distribution of the coordinates, and the individual contribution to the conditional intensity of each (or perhaps small collections of) covariates. These marginal distributions of the process could then be estimated separately, and the parametric forms for each could readily be inspected for goodness-of-fit.

Considering the San Bernardino earthquake data with $M \geq 3.5$, for example, if one were constructing a model from scratch to try to describe these observations, one might start by inspecting the frequency of points versus time, and the density of points versus location, and the density of points as a function of magnitude. For instance, one may estimate the intensity of earthquakes as a function of time simple using kernel smoothing, obtaining estimates $\hat{f}_1(t) = \sum_{i=1}^{n} w(t - t_i)$ for some *weight* or *kernel* density w. Typically w is chosen to be a density that peaks at 0, so that points near time t are given the most weight, and points far from time t are given little weight. In Fig. 3.3, the Gaussian density with mean 0 and standard deviation σ is selected for w, and the parameter σ, which is called the *bandwidth*, is computed using the simple default rule of thumb proposed by Silverman (1986). These intensity estimates as separate functions of time, location, and magnitude could then be combined to form a simple Poisson model via $\lambda(t, x, y, m) = \alpha f_1(t) f_2(x, y) f_3(m)$, and such a model might successively be refined using covariates and/or clustering features (such as ETAS).

Code to produce Fig. 3.3 is below.

```
y=density(t/365+1970)
plot(y$x,y$y*z$n,xlab="yr",ylab="events/yr", type="l",xlim=c(1970,2025))
rug(t/365+1970)
library(splancs)
mypoly = matrix(c(-118,-117,-117,-118,-118,34,34,35,35,34),ncol=2,byrow=F)
filled.contour(kernel2d(as.points(z$lon-118,z$lat+34),mypoly,.1))
points(z$lon*.7-118,z$lat+34,cex=.2)
a=density(z$m,cut=-2)
plot(a$x,a$y*z$n,xlab="magnitude",ylab="events / unit M", type="l")
rug(z$m)
```

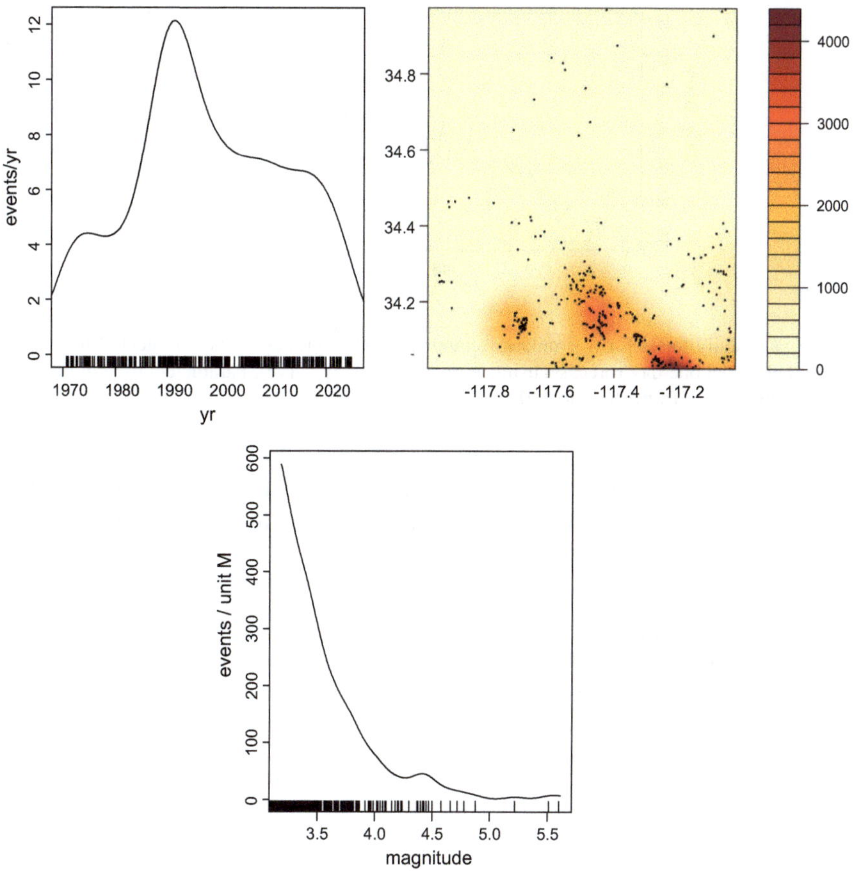

Fig. 3.3 Separate components of the San Bernardino earthquake data. (left) Smooth estimated density of earthquakes versus time, with earthquake times denoted by line segments at bottom. (middle) Smooth density estimate of earthquakes as a function of location, with earthquake epicenters overlaid in black. (right) Smooth density estimate of earthquakes versus magnitude

3.6 Least Squares for Aggregated Data

Point process data are sometimes aggregated over time and/or space, and one observes only the aggregated totals. For instance, in epidemiology, it is common only to report the daily (or weekly) total number of cases of a disease, rather than the precise time each individual case was discovered. In such situations, it is often convenient to estimate the parameters in point process models by least squares, simply minimizing the sum of squared differences between the number of cases expected each day, according to the fitted model, and the number of daily cases observed.

In particular, for the problem of fitting a Hawkes model using daily aggregated counts, the use of least squares estimation is particularly justified in light of the correspondence between Hawkes processes and autoregressive time series derived in Kirchner (2016, 2017).

For example, Fig. 3.4 shows the times of points in a simulated temporal Hawkes process, aggregated daily. A Hawkes model is fit to the aggregated daily totals via least squares, and the fitted model is also shown in Fig. 3.4. The true parameters for the simulated Hawkes model are selected to be $\mu =$

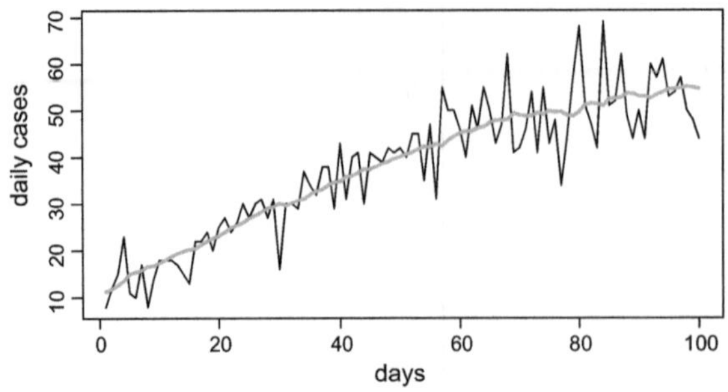

Fig. 3.4 Aggregated daily totals for a simulated temporal Hawkes process with exponential triggering (black line segments) and fitted model one-day forecasts using least squares (gray curve). Parameters used in the simulation were $\mu = 10$, $K = 0.8$, and $\beta = 3$, from day 0 to 100

10, $K = 0.8$, $\beta = 0.1$, and the triggering function is exponential, $g(u) = \beta \exp(\beta u)$. After running *optim()*, with starting values of $\{20, 0.5, 0.5\}$, the least squares estimates (with SEs) are $\{\hat{mu}, \hat{K}, \hat{\beta}\} = \{11.2(0.235), 0.875(0.00507), 0.0896(0.00301).\}$

The *R* code used for the simulation and estimation in Fig. 3.4 is as follows.

```
source(url("http://www.stat.ucla.edu/~frederic/book/simhawk.r"))
T = 100; mu = 10; theta_K = 0.85; theta_beta = .1; theta_b=0; theta_m0=0
z = simhawk(T=T,gmi=pointprod, gt=expgt, gxy = pointxy)
count = rep(0,T)
for(i in 1:z$n) count[ceiling(z$t[i])] = count[ceiling(z$t[i])]+1
plot(1:T,count,xlab="days",ylab="daily cases",type="l")
ssq = function(theta){
est = rep(theta[1],T)
for(i in 2:T){
  est[i] = theta[1] + sum(count[(i-1):1]*theta[2]*
    theta[3]*exp(-theta[3]*(1:(i-1))))
  }
sum((count-est)^2)
}
theta = c(20,.5,.5)
b1 = optim(theta,ssq,hessian=T)
b1$par
sqrt(diag(solve(b1$hess))) ## for SEs
theta = b1$par
est = rep(theta[1],T)
for(i in 2:T){
  est[i] = theta[1] + sum(count[(i-1):1]*theta[2]*
    theta[3]*exp(-theta[3]*(1:(i-1))))
  }
lines(1:T,est,col="grey",lwd=3)
```

3.7 Estimation via Functional Summaries and Score Functions

An alternative way to estimate parameters is by choosing some other property of interest and finding the values of the parameters that optimize this property. Ideally the property chosen should summarize the quality of fit in a way that is practically important, a topic we will revisit in Sect. 5.5.2 when discussing magnitude-weighted likelihood scores. One could view maximum likelihood as an example of this approach where the summary chosen is the likelihood, which is typically a very useful measure of overall fit. However, when one is primarily interested in describing the degree of clustering, a summary of this clustering can be used instead.

Diggle (2014), Gneiting and Raftery (2007), and others consider various situations where particular score functions can be shown to be optimal. When clustering is the primary focus, for example, the parameters in the model are chosen so that the amount of clustering in the model best matches the amount of clustering in the data. Specifically, one may find the parameters that minimize the sum of squared differences between $K(r)$ and $\hat{K}(r)$ at various distances r, where $K(r)$ is the K-function of the fitted model, and $\hat{K}(r)$ is the estimated K-function for the data. See Chap. 4 for a definition of the K-function and other functions summarizing the degree of clustering. Such estimation is considered in Diggle (2014). Diggle et al. (2010) and Diggle (2014) also consider maximizing the partial log-likelihood, $\sum_{i=1}^{n} \log P_i$, where $P_i = \frac{\lambda(t_i, x_i)}{\sum_{R_i} \lambda(t_i, x_j)}$, and where R_i is a *risk set* which is normally the collection of points (t_j, x_j) for $j = i, i+1, \ldots, n$. The maximum partial likelihood estimates can be problematic in some situations and lack the theoretical optimality characteristic of maximum likelihood estimates, but can be computed much more simply, without requiring the computation or approximation of an integral.

If one is particularly interested in finding a model whose mean and variance match closely with that of the data, then it might make sense to estimate the model parameters by minimizing the sum of squared differences between the theoretical mean and variance of the fitted model and the estimated mean and variance for the data, perhaps estimated by dividing the observation region S up into a regular grid and computing the sample mean and sample variance of the number of points per grid cell. This is essentially the logic behind method of moments estimation, which is considered further in Sect. 3.9 in the context of estimating the background and productivity parameters in Hawkes models.

One promising way to estimate parameters in a point process model is by minimizing the sum of squares of the Stoyan-Grabarnik statistic. For any interval B of the spatial-temporal domain, let $T(B)$ denote the sum

$$T(B) = \sum_{j:(t_j, x_j, y_j) \in B} 1/\lambda(t_j, x_j, y_j). \tag{3.6}$$

That is, $T(B)$ is the sum of the reciprocals of the conditional intensities of the points in B. As mentioned in Stoyan and Grabarnik (1991), the martingale formula (see Sect. 1.6) implies that

$$ET(B) = E \sum_{j:(t_j, x_j, y_j) \in B} 1/\lambda(t_j, x_j, y_j) = E \int_B 1/\lambda(t, x, y) dN = E \int_B d\mu = |B|, \tag{3.7}$$

where $|B|$ denotes the size of the region B.

Formula (3.7) suggests searching for parameters that make $T(B)$ as close as possible to $|B|$. More specifically, one may divide the observation region into subregions, B_1, B_2, ..., B_k, and search for parameters minimizing the sum of squared differences

$$\sum_{i=1}^{k} (T(B_i) - |B_i|)^2. \tag{3.8}$$

Such a procedure was proposed by Cronie and van Lieshout (2018) in order to choose an optimal bandwidth parameter for kernel smoothing the points of a point process in order to estimate the overall intensity, $E[\lambda(t, x, y)]$. However, more generally one can also estimate the parameters governing the conditional intensity of a spatial-temporal point process by finding the parameters minimizing (3.8).

The resulting estimator, which we might call the *Stoyan-Grabarnik (SG)* estimator, has some very compelling properties. First, under quite general conditions, the SG estimator is consistent, as shown in Kresin and Schoenberg (2023). Second, unlike maximum likelihood estimates, the SG estimator can be computed without having to approximate an integral. As mentioned previously in Sect. 3.3 and as pointed out by Harte (2013) and others, the integral term in the log-likelihood is by far the largest source of computational problems in attempts to maximize the log-likelihood. For some models, sometimes the integral can be well approximated numerically or using calculus, as in Ogata (1998), or for the case of a Hawkes process as described in Sect. 3.4, but even in these special cases, one must ensure that the approximation is close for all possible values of the parameters, or else the optimization routine might converge to those parameter values where the approximation breaks down.

A third, rather mysterious advantage of the SG estimator is that because it only involves the computation of the conditional intensity at the points that occur, the model allows one to fit parameters to models where the conditional intensity at certain locations in space-time might be unspecified or might perhaps not even exist. This can have important practical applications, especially in cases where data on important covariates are unavailable at some (or all) locations where points do not occur. For example, suppose you are modeling wildfire occurrences, in an area where many of the fires are ignited due to campfires. An important covariate you might want to have in your model is the proximity of the closest fire personnel to the scene, as this may influence whether an ignition is extinguished before it can cover enough area to be officially recognized as a wildfire. However, it may be that data on proximity to fire personnel are available for each wildfire, but not for other space-time locations in your observation region. With SG estimation, the missing data do not prevent you from fitting a model with proximity to wildfire personnel as a covariate! I say this is mysterious because, one might suspect that it would be impossible to estimate the effect of proximity to wildfire personnel without observing this variable everywhere: if, for instance, most wildfires occur at a distance of roughly 10km from fire personnel, and few occur at 5km from fire personnel, it seems impossible to conclude anything about the effect of this covariate without knowing how many locations and times that did *not* experience wildfires were 5km or 10km from fire personnel. But nevertheless, SG estimation allows parameters governing the relationship between distance to fire personnel and wildfire occurrence to be consistently estimated. One way to think about it is, for any values of these parameters, the sum of squares in (3.8) is evaluating how well the fitted model agrees with the data at the locations where fires occurred, and for some values it will fit better than others.

As an illustration, consider again the inhomogeneous Poisson process model described near the beginning of Chap. 2, with intensity $\lambda_1 = 1$ except inside a circle of radius $r = 0.2$ centered at $(a = 0.4, b = 0.7)$, in which the intensity is raised by an amount $\lambda_2 = 1$. Previously, in the beginning of this chapter, we considered estimating a and b via MLE. We now consider the more difficult task of estimating the five parameters $\theta = (a, b, r, \lambda_1, \lambda_2)$ simultaneously, via the SG estimator. For the SG estimation below, x, y, and t are each divided into 10 equally sized slices, so the space is divided into $10 \times 10 \times 10 = 1000$ regular bins.

Figure 3.5 shows a simulation of this inhomogeneous Poisson process, simulated using the *R* function *simcirc* defined earlier in this chapter. The code for simulating and plotting the resulting points and true intensity is below.

```
simcirc()
par(mfrow=c(1,3)) ## PLOT SIMULATED PTS AND TRUE INTENSITY
plot(x,y,cex=0.3,xlim=c(0,1),ylim=c(0,1))
plot(c(0,1),c(0,1),type="n",xlab="x",ylab="y")
polygon(c(0,1,1,0,0),c(0,0,1,1,0), col=grey(.9))
i1 = seq(.2,.6,length=1000); i2 = i1[1000:1]
j1 =.7+sqrt(.2^2 - (.4-i1)^2); j2 = .7-sqrt(.2^2 - (.4-i2)^2)
polygon(c(i1,i2),c(j1,j2),col=grey(.8))
```

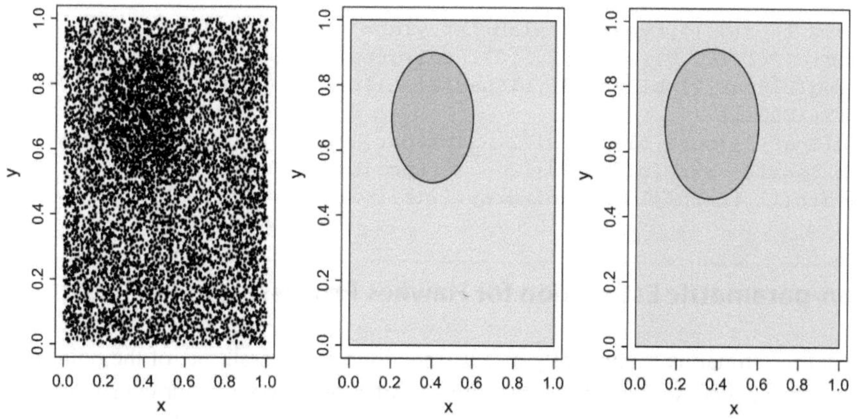

Fig. 3.5 Simulation and estimation via SG estimation of an inhomogeneous Poisson process with intensity $\lambda(t, x, y) = \lambda_1 + \lambda_2 \mathbf{1}_{\{||(x-a, y-b)||<r\}}$. (left) Simulated process with parameters $(a, b, r, \lambda_1, \lambda_2) = (0.4, 0.7, 0.2, 1, 1)$, from $t = 0$ to 8000. (middle) True intensity used in the simulation. (right) Intensity fit via SG estimation

The simulated data were then used to estimate θ by SG estimation. The resulting estimates were $\hat{\theta} = (0.367, 0.685, 0.230, 1.11, 0.774)$, and one can see from the resulting estimate in Fig. 3.5 that the intensity is estimated rather accurately in this case. Because no integrals are involved, the code for SG estimation is incredibly simple. The only slightly complicated part is figuring out and keeping track of which point is in which bin, which is accomplished in the code below.

```
## Construct a list, wbin, where wbin[[17]] = c() if bin 17 is empty, and
## if wbin[[17]] = c(1,2,10), then points 1,2,and 10 are in bin 17.
wbin = list()
for(i in 1:1000) wbin[[i]] = c(0)
for(m in 1:n) {
    gridindex = 10*10*floor(t[m]*10/T)+
    10*floor(x[m]*10/X1)+ceiling(y[m]*10/Y1)
    wbin[[gridindex]] = c(wbin[[gridindex]],m)
}
for(i in 1:1000) wbin[[i]] = wbin[[i]][-1]
```

The code used for SG estimation is below. Because no calculation of an integral is required, all that is needed is to compute the very simple sum $T(B)$ in (3.6), for each bin B, compare with the bin size $|B|$, and add up the squared differences.

```
sumsg = function(theta){
  cat(theta)
  if(min(c(theta[4],theta[4]+theta[5]))<0) return(1e10)
  b = T*X1*Y1/10/10/10 ## the area of each bin
  lam = theta[4]+theta[5]*((x-theta[1])^2+(y-theta[2])^2<theta[3]^2)
  mysum = rep(b,1000)
  for(i in 1:1000) if(length(wbin[[i]]) > 0) mysum[i] = sum(1/lam[wbin[[i]]])
  sum((mysum-b)^2)
}
theta = c(.5,.5,.5,.8,.8)
b1 = optim(theta,sumsg)
```

The following is the code to draw the fitted intensity after SG estimation, as shown in the rightmost panel of Fig. 3.5.

```
plot(c(0,1),c(0,1),type="n",xlab="x",ylab="y")
polygon(c(0,1,1,0,0),c(0,0,1,1,0), col=grey(1-b1$par[4]/10))
i1 = seq(b1$par[1]-b1$par[3],b1$par[1]+b1$par[3]-.00001,length=1000)
i2 = i1[1000:1]
j1 = b1$par[2]+sqrt(b1$par[3]^2 - (b1$par[1]-i1)^2)
j2 = b1$par[2]-sqrt(b1$par[3]^2 - (b1$par[1]-i2)^2)
polygon(c(i1,i2),c(j1,j2),col=grey(1-(b1$par[4]+b1$par[5])/10))
```

3.8 Non-parametric Estimation for Hawkes Processes

Non-parametric estimation traditionally meant smoothing the overall rate of the point process using some smoothing method, such as kernel smoothing, splines, wavelets, or Fourier methods. For example, earlier in this chapter, we explored the use of kernel smoothers for separable estimates of the intensity in Fig. 3.3. Such smoothings can be useful especially for modeling Poisson processes.

For Hawkes processes, non-parametric estimates can also be used, and these methods are fundamentally different from these overall rate smoothers. An ingenious idea of Marsan and Lengliné (2008) was to estimate the triggering function of a Hawkes process non-parametrically. Their idea was to assume the triggering function, g, could be written as $g(t, x, y) = g_1(t)g_2(x, y)$, to assume g_1 and g_2 were step functions, and then to estimate the step heights in each of these functions by maximum likelihood. (Technically, Marsan and Lengliné (2008) used a variant of the E-M algorithm suggested by Veen and Schoenberg (2008), but the idea is extremely similar.) The procedure thus does not rely on a parametric form for the triggering function, and is extremely useful as a tool for a variety of purposes including suggesting the functional form of a triggering function, assessing the goodness-of-fit of a particular proposed functional form, and simulating or forecasting the process without relying on a particular and possibly mis-specified functional form for the triggering function.

As an illustration, the *R* code below simulates a Hawkes process with g_1 and g_2 estimated non-parametrically. The model is $\lambda(t, x, y) = \mu + \kappa \sum_{t',x',y':t'<t} g_1(t - t')g_2(||(x, y) - (x', y')||)$, where g_1 and g_2 are power-law densities: $g_1t(t) = (p - 1)c^{p-1}(t + c)^{-p}$, and $g_2(r) = \frac{q-1}{\pi} d^{q-1}(r^2 + d)^{-q}$.

```
source(url("http://www.stat.ucla.edu/~frederic/book/simhawk.r"))
T = 1000; mu = .1; theta_K = 0.85; theta_beta = .1; theta_b=0
theta_m0=0; theta_c = 0.4; theta_p = 2; theta_d = 0.2
theta_q = 5; x1=1; y1=1; K = .85
z = simhawk(T=T,gmi=pointprod, gt=powergt, gxy = powerxy)
```

Before running *optim* to try to find the best fitting parameters, it is a good idea to make the function optimized by *optim* as fast as possible, and one way to do this is to do some of the computations just once, outside of this function, and store the results. That is what is done in the code immediately below when it comes to constructing and storing the adjacency matrix, A, so that $A[i, j]$ is the number of pairs of points (t, x, y), (t', x', y') such that $t - t' \in [i - 1, i)$ and $||(x, y) - (x', y')|| \in 0.01[j - 1, j)$.

```
t = z$t; x = z$lon; y = z$lat; n = z$n; A = list()
for(i in 1:n) A[[i]] = matrix(0,ncol=10,nrow=10)
for(i in 2:n) { for(j in 1:(i-1)){
 dt = ceiling(t[i] - t[j])
 dx = ceiling(10*sqrt((x[i]-x[j])^2 + (y[i]-y[j])^2))
 if((dt<=10)&&(dx<=10)) A[[i]][dt,dx] = A[[i]][dt,dx]+1
}}
```

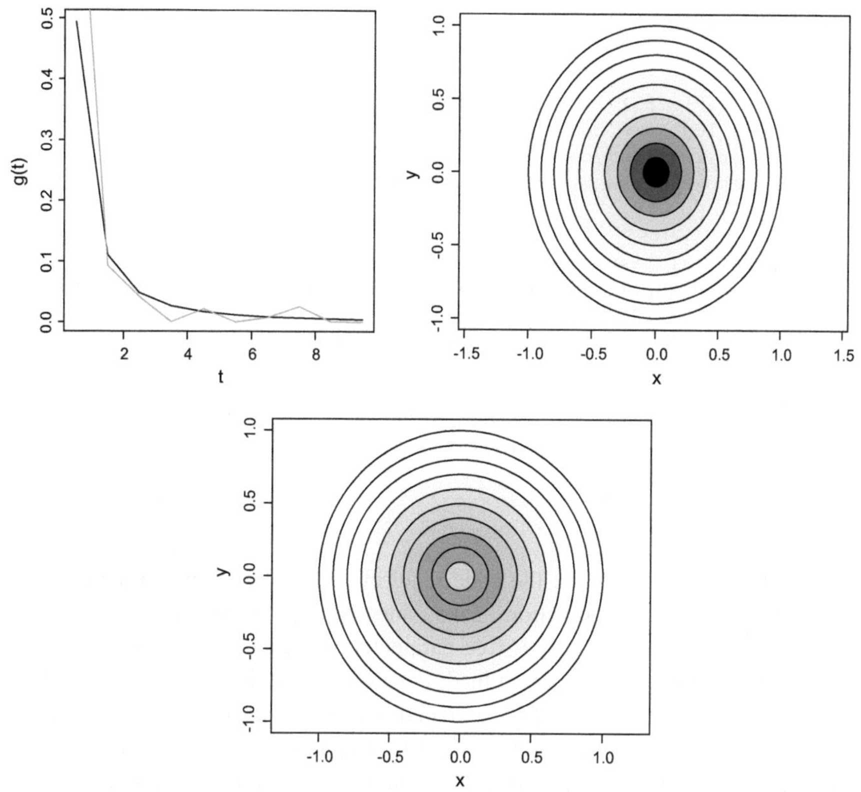

Fig. 3.6 True and non-parametrically estimated triggering functions for a simulated Hawkes process with power-law triggering in space and time, and with parameters $\mu = 0.1$, $\kappa = 0.85$, $c = 0.4$, $p = 2$, $d = 0.2$, $q = 5$, on the unit square and from $T = 0$ to 1000. (left) true (black) and estimated temporal triggering function $g_1(t)$. (middle) true spatial triggering function $g_2(r)$. (right) estimated spatial triggering function $\hat{g}_2(r)$

Next, in the *R* code that follows, the process simulated above is then fit by MLE, where in the estimation, g_1 and g_2 are assumed to be step functions with 10 steps each, with $g_1(u) = \beta_i$ if $i - 1 \leq u < i$, for $i = 1, 2, \ldots, 10$, and $g_1(u) = 0$ otherwise, and $g_2(r) = \gamma_i$ if $0.1(i-1) \leq r < (0.1)i$, for $i = 1, 2, \ldots, 10$, and $g_2(r) = 0$ otherwise. The code below uses *optim()* to find the maximum likelihood estimates of the parameters $\Theta = \{\mu, \kappa, \beta_1, \ldots, \beta_9, \gamma_1, \ldots, \gamma_9\}$, and then constructs Fig. 3.6 which shows the non-parametrically estimated temporal and spatial triggering functions, $\hat{g}_1$ and $\hat{g}_2$, as well as the true power-law triggering functions g_1 and g_2 used in the simulations.

```
loglnonp = function(theta){
  thetat = c(theta[1:9],1-sum(theta[1:9]))
  thetax = c(theta[10:18],(1-sum(pi*((1:9)*0.02-0.01)*theta[10:18]))/(0.19*pi))
  mu = theta[19]; K = theta[20]
  if(min(c(thetat,thetax,mu,K))<0) return(99999)
  lam = rep(mu,n)
  intlam = mu*T + K*n
  for(i in 2:(z$n)){
       lam[i] = mu + K * thetat %*% A[[i]]  %*% thetax
       }
   if(min(lam) > 0) sumlog = sum(log(lam)) else return(99999)
   loglik = sumlog - intlam
   cat("loglike is ", loglik, ". sumlog = ",
    sumlog,". integral = ", intlam,".\n")
```

```
    return(-1.0*loglik)
}

theta = c(rep(.1,19),.85)
b1 = optim(theta,loglnonp,control=list(maxit = 500000))
b1 = optim(b1$par,loglnonp,control=list(maxit = 500000))
## repeat line above a few times until it converges
b1$par
theta = b1$par
thetat = c(theta[1:9],1-sum(theta[1:9]))
thetax = c(theta[10:18],(1-sum(pi*((1:9)*0.02-0.01)*theta[10:18]))/(0.19*pi))
b = seq(.5,9.5,length=10)
plot(b,(2-1)*0.4^(2-1)*(b+.4)^(-2),xlab="t",ylab="g(t)",type="l")
lines(b,thetat,col="grey")
theta_d = 0.2; theta_q = 5
plot(1,type="n",xlim=c(-.7,.7),ylim=c(-1,1),xlab="x",ylab="y",asp=1)
cl1 = grey(1-(5-1)*.2^(5-1)/pi*((b[10:1]/10)^2+.2)^(-5)/6)
cl2 = grey(1-thetax[10:1]/6)
symbols(rep(0,10),rep(0,10),circles=seq(1,.1,-.1),inches=F,add=T,bg=cl1)
symbols(rep(0,10),rep(0,10),circles=seq(1,.1,-.1),inches=F,add=T,bg=cl2)
```

There are two little tricky things in the code requiring a bit of explanation here, both related to the fact that g_1 and g_2 are *density* functions. First, since both g_1 and g_2 must integrate to 1, if each has 10 steps, then there are really only 9 free parameters for each, since given the heights of the first 9 steps, the height of the 10th is determined. For instance, in the case of g_1, $1 = \int_0^{10} g_1(t)dt = \sum_{i=1}^{10} \alpha_i$, so $\alpha_{10} = 1 - \sum_{i=1}^{9} \alpha_i$. Second, the spatial density g_2 must integrate to 1 over the whole plane, i.e. $\int g_2(x, y)dxdy = 1$. This can be solved by changing to polar coordinates, or simply by requiring that the disk-shaped areas multiplied by their corresponding values of g_2 in Fig. 3.6 sum to 1. These 10 disks have areas $0.01\pi, 0.03\pi, 0.05\pi, \ldots, 0.19\pi$, so the value in the 10th disk must equal $\frac{1}{0.19\pi}(1 - 0.01\pi\alpha_1 - 0.03\pi\alpha_2 - \cdots - 0.17\pi\alpha_9) = \frac{1}{0.19\pi}\left[1 - \sum_{i=1}^{9}(0.02i - 0.01)\alpha_i\right]$.

Although the non-parametric estimates of the temporal triggering function are quite accurate, the relatively poor fit for the spatial triggering may possibly be due to the fact that the step function assumption is so badly violated for the case of a power-law spatial triggering density, or perhaps more likely due to problems *optim()* seems to encounter when estimating many parameters simultaneously. The problem is most likely not due to the small sample size, since in my experience even for larger T the inaccuracy seems to persist.

As mentioned previously, the tactic used by Marsan and Lengliné (2008) is to assume the estimated triggering function is a step function with q steps of fixed widths and unknown heights, and then to estimate the q step heights via maximum likelihood. However, Instead of using *optim()* to obtain maximum likelihood estimates of the step heights, one might consider other methods. When $g(u)$ is a step function with value β_k for u in the range U_k, setting the partial derivatives of the log-likelihood with respect to each β_k to zero, for $k = 1, \ldots, q$, reduces to Schoenberg et al. (2018)

$$0 = \partial l(\theta)/\partial \beta_k = \sum_{(i,j):\tau_j - \tau_i \in U_k} K/\lambda(\tau_i) - Kn|U_k|, \tag{3.9}$$

where i and j are indices ranging from 1 to n, and the sum is over all pairs of points τ_i and τ_j with $i < j$ such that the distance between τ_i and τ_j is in the interval U_k.

Relation (3.9), for $k = 1, 2, \ldots, q$, amounts to q equations with q unknowns. However, the equations are nonlinear, depending in particular on $1/\lambda(\tau_i)$, which in turn depends on the q unknowns. One may attempt to resort to gradient descent or other optimization routines to find approximate solutions, but these are typically prohibitively slow, since they rely on computing or approximating the log-likelihood l and its derivatives many times, and each computation of l requires $O(n^2)$ computations. Thus, Marsan and Lengliné (2008) and Marsan and Lengliné (2010) find approximate maximum likelihood estimates using the E-M-based algorithm of Veen and Schoenberg (2008), which is an iterative procedure requiring substantial computation time. A relatively simple mathematical curiosity enables us to reduce the computation time dramatically, however, for the special case when $q = n$.

For a simple Hawkes process, at the n points $\tau_1, \ldots, \tau_n$, we have the n equations,

$$\lambda(\tau_j) = \mu + K \sum_{i<j} g(\tau_j - \tau_i), \tag{3.10}$$

for $j = 1, 2, \ldots, n$. For simplicity, assume for the moment that μ and K are known. The case where μ and K are unknown, and other issues arising in practical implementation, are discussed in Schoenberg et al. (2018).

As with Marsan and Lengliné (2008), we assume our estimate $\hat{g}(u)$ will be a step function, so that for u in a given interval U_k, we have $\hat{g}(u) = \beta_k$. Again, for simplicity, let us assume that the process is observed over a spatial region S and time interval [0, T], and that the intervals U_k are time intervals of equal size Δ, so that the size $|U_k|$ of each interval is simply $\Delta|S|$. Setting the derivative of the log-likelihood l with respect to β_k to zero yields the q equations in (3.9), for $k = 1, 2, \ldots, q$.

Unfortunately the terms on the right hand side of (3.9) are highly nonlinear functions of the desired parameters, $\beta = \{\beta_1, \beta_2, \ldots, \beta_q\}$. However, (3.9) consists of q linear equations in terms of the n constants $1/\lambda(\tau_j)$. Thus, if $q = n$, we may readily use Eq. (3.9) to solve for $1/\lambda(\tau_j)$, which therefore yields $\lambda(\tau_j)$, and subsequently use the n linear Eq. (3.10) to solve for β.

Indeed, with some additional notation we may write the resulting estimator in a very simple and condensed form as follows. First, let us use the following notation: for any vector $z = \{z_1, z_2, \ldots, z_k\}$, let $1/z$ represent the vector $\{1/z_1, 1/z_2, \ldots, 1/z_k\}$. Next, consider the $q \times q$ adjacency matrix A defined so that, for $j, k \in \{1, 2, \ldots, q\}$, $A[k, j]$ is the number of points τ_i such that $\tau_j - \tau_i \in U_k$. Let λ represent the n-vector $\{\lambda(\tau_1), \lambda(\tau_2), \ldots, \lambda(\tau_n)\}$, and let $\mathbf{1}$ denote the n-vector $\{1, 1, \ldots, 1\}$.

With this notation, (3.9) can be rewritten as

$$0 = KA(1/\lambda) - Kb, \tag{3.11}$$

where $b = n|S|\Delta\mathbf{1}$. The estimate of $1/\lambda$ satisfying Eq. (3.11) is thus $A^{-1}b$, assuming A is invertible. Similarly, Eq. (3.10) may be rewritten

$$\lambda = \mu + KA^T\beta, \tag{3.12}$$

whose solution is $\beta = (KA^T)^{-1}(\lambda - \mu)$. Combining these two formulas, the resulting vector $\hat{\beta}$ of estimates may be written

$$\hat{\beta} = (KA^T)^{-1}[1/(A^{-1}b) - \mu]. \tag{3.13}$$

Equation (3.13) is remarkably simple and extremely rapid to compute. The speed with which these non-parametric estimates can be obtained facilitates certain computations that might otherwise be prohibitively time consuming. For instance, one may obtain approximate standard errors for these estimates by repeated simulation and estimation of the triggering function. While the estimates in (3.13) tend to have extremely high variance, when it is reasonable to assume that g is smooth, these estimates may be smoothed to provide more stable estimates of g, as described in Phillips and Schoenberg (2024).

Also, one must be careful in constructing the estimates (3.13) to ensure that the system of equations is not underdetermined, which would occur if, for instance, one fits an inhomogeneous background rate with more than one parameter and also fits $n-1$ parameters for the triggering density. Marsan and Lengliné (2008) avoid this issue because in their case $q << n$.

3.9 Method of Moments Estimation

Another way to estimate point process parameters is via method of moments. Often one can write the first few (usually 2) moments of $N(S)/|S|$ in terms of the same number of parameters of the process, and then given data, substitute the sample moments in for the moments and solve for the parameter values.

For example, given a Hawkes process, one may write the mean of $N(S)/|S|$ as $\frac{\mu}{1-K}$ as seen in Eq. 2.17, and similarly one may obtain an expression for the variance of $N(S)/|S|$ in terms of μ and K, namely $var\{N(S)/|S|\} = \frac{\mu}{K^2(1-K)}$. Then, substituting the sample mean of $N(S)/|S|$ and sample variance of $N(S)/|S|$ for the true mean and variance, one can obtain estimates of μ and K. These estimates do not require iteration using *optim()*, and therefore can often be more stable and accurate than maximum likelihood estimates, especially when many other parameters must be estimated as well.

For the Hawkes process, this results in an estimate of κ via

$$\hat{\kappa} = \sqrt{\frac{\bar{N}}{\hat{v}(N)}}, \tag{3.14}$$

where $\bar{N}$ and $\hat{v}(N)$ are the sample mean and sample variance, respectively, of $N(S)/|S|$, as shown in Eq. (7) of Hardiman and Bouchard (2014), and

$$\hat{\mu} = \frac{(1-\hat{\kappa})N(S)}{|S|}. \tag{3.15}$$

In computing $\bar{N}$ and $\hat{v}(N)$ to obtain $\hat{\kappa}$ via Eq. (3.14), one may divide the observed space-time region into W bins, and use the sample mean and sample variance of the number of points in each bin per unit of space-time. For estimating μ via Eq. (3.15), however, one may simply use the entire observation region, S. A similar type of estimation using cumulants is discussed by Bacry et al. (2016).

The code below implements these estimates for the Hawkes process simulation of Fig. 3.6. The true values of (μ, κ) used in the simulation were $(0.1, 0.85)$. The maximum likelihood estimates, obtained when simultaneously estimating the temporal and spatial triggering functions g_1 and g_2 non-parametrically, were $(0.133, 0.707)$, and the method of moment estimates for this simulation were $(0.100, 0.78)$.

```
W = 10 ## number of bins.
intervalsize = T/W
mycount = rep(0,W)
for(i in 1:W)
    mycount[i] = sum((t< i*intervalsize) & (t >= (i-1)*intervalsize))
mymean = mean(mycount)
myvar = var(mycount)
khat = 1 - sqrt(mymean/myvar)
muhat = mymean*(1-khat)/intervalsize
```

3.10 Cross-Excitation Estimation

Consider the case where one observes a temporal Hawkes process in each of several locations, e.g. incidence of some disease in various different cities. Together, this can be viewed as a multivariate Hawkes process, $\{N_i; i = 1, 2, \ldots, M\}$, where, for instance, N_1 is a temporal point process representing cases in Los Angeles, N_2 represents cases in New York City, etc. Suppose further that individuals in one location may infect individuals in another location. In this situation, both MLE and least squares perform poorly. Indeed, both methods appear to grossly overestimate the cross-productivity, i.e. the rate at which those from one location infect others at a different location. A major problem is multi-collinearity: if, for instance, cases are rising in Los Angeles and New York City at similar rates, then the model tends vastly to overestimate the rate at which those in Los Angeles are infecting those in New York City and vice versa, since the model, a priori, has no reason to suspect that those in New York City are any less likely to be infected by Los Angelenos than by other New Yorkers.

A major goal in current research is to mitigate this problem, i.e. false cross-excitations in multivariate Hawkes processes for epidemic diseases using data involving spatial components (different locations). Seven different estimation methods are proposed in Diouane et al. (2024), for instance, including ridge regression, elastic net, and multi-stage estimation techniques, with varying results. Of these, the one I consider most interesting and worth discussing briefly here is multi-stage estimation. The idea is to first fit Hawkes process parameters to each city individually, e.g. by maximum likelihood or least squares. In this first stage of estimation, essentially the cross-productivities, i.e. the rates at which people from Los Angeles are infecting those in New York City, are fixed at zero. In the second stage of estimation, all the parameters estimated in the first stage of estimation are held fixed, and only the cross-productivities are estimated, again by MLE or least squares. The idea is that, in the first stage, the model is fit as well as possible without cross-productivities and essentially finds parameters that best account for the transmission of the disease locally. Then, in stage two, essentially only *excess* transmission, not already accounted for in stage one, is accounted for via cross-productivities, and this forces them to assume smaller and much more reasonable values.

3.11 Exercises

3.1. Suppose N is a Poisson process with intensity $\lambda(t, x, y) = exp(-3t)$ over t in [0,10], x in [0,1], y in [0,1]. N happens to have points at $(t, x, y) = (1.5, .4, .2)$, $(2, .52, .31)$, $(4, .1, .33)$, and $(5, .71, .29)$. What is the log-likelihood of this realization?

3.2. Which of the following is not typically true of the MLE of a spatial-temporal point process?

a. It is unbiased.
b. It is consistent.
c. It is asymptotically normal.
d. It is asymptotically efficient.

3.3. Suppose N is a Hawkes process on $[0, T] \times S$ with conditional rate $\lambda(t, x, y) = 1 + 0.7 \sum_{t_i<t} g(t - t_i)h(x - x_i, y - y_i)$, where $T = 100$, S is the unit square, and $g(u)$ is uniform on $[0, 1]$, and $h(x', y')$ is uniform on the square centered at $(0, 0)$ with each side having length 0.4. Suppose that in one realization, N happens to have points at $(37, 0.3, 0.5)$ and $(58, 0.9, 0.9)$. If one uses the approximation (3.3), compute the amount of *leakage*.

3.4. (a) Simulate a Hawkes process with conditional rate $\lambda(t, x, y) = \mu + \kappa \sum_{t_i<t} \alpha \exp\{\alpha(t - t_i)\}g(x - x_i, y - y_i)$, where $g(x, y)$ is uniform on the circle with radius β centered at $(0, 0)$, and

where $\mu = 1$, $\kappa = 0.6$, $\alpha = 3$, and $\beta = 0.1$. Plot the x- and y-coordinates of the realization. (b) Estimate the parameters μ, κ, α, and β by MLE. Provide your estimates and standard errors.

3.5. Using the San Bernardino earthquake data shown in Fig. 1.3 of Chap. 1, fit a Hawkes model to the locations and times of the earthquakes, and compute approximate standard errors. Comment on your results. Show a plot of the fitted conditional intensity as a function of longitude and latitude, summed over 10, 000 times spanning the observation window.

3.6. Using the San Bernardino earthquake data shown in Fig. 1.3 of Chap. 1, fit an ETAS model to the locations and times of the earthquakes, and compute approximate standard errors. Comment on your results. Show a plot of the fitted conditional intensity as a function of longitude and latitude, summed over 10, 000 times spanning the observation window.

3.7. Using the San Bernardino earthquake data shown in Fig. 1.3 of Chap. 1, restrict your dataset to only those 58 earthquakes of magnitude 3.8 or more, and fit a Recursive model to the times of these earthquakes of magnitude at least 3.8. Compute approximate standard errors.

3.8. Using the San Bernardino earthquake data shown in Fig. 1.3 of Chap. 1, aggregate the total number of earthquakes per month, for each month, and fit a purely temporal Hawkes model with exponential triggering function by least squares using just the aggregated monthly totals.

3.9. Simulate an inhomogeneous Poisson process with intensity $\lambda(t, x, y) = \theta_1 + \theta_2 x + \theta_3 y$, using values of $\theta = (\theta_1, \theta_2, \theta_3)$ of your choice, and then estimate θ by SG estimation. Plot the simulated points, plot the true λ used in the simulations versus x and y, and plot $\hat{\lambda}$ fit by SG estimation.

3.10. Let B mean the spatial-temporal region $[0, 10] \times [0, 1] \times [0, 1]$, i.e. the unit square S observed from time 0 to time 10 days. Suppose N is a Poisson process on B with rate 3 everywhere, and N happens to have 25 points occur on B. What is the log-likelihood, L?

3.11. Suppose N is a rate decreasing point process with points distributed spatially in the unit square S and with times from time 0 to ∞, and suppose $\lambda(t, x, y) = 5 - N\{[0, t)xS\}$. Let L be the log-likelihood. What is $E(L)$?

References

Bacry, E., Gaiffas, S., Mastromatteo, I., & Muzy, J.-F. (2016). Mean-field inference of Hawkes point processes. *Journal of Physics A: Mathematical and Theoretical, 49*, Article 174006.

Baddeley, A. J., & Turner, R. (2000). Practical maximum pseudolikelihood for spatial point patterns. *Australian and New Zealand Journal of Statistics, 42*(3), 283–322.

Chang, C., & Schoenberg, F. (2011). Testing separability in multi-dimensional point processes with covariates. *Annals of the Institute of Statistical Mathematics, 63*(6), 1103–1122.

Cronie, O., & Van Lieshout, M. N. M. (2018). A non-model-based approach to bandwidth selection for kernel estimators of spatial intensity functions. *Biometrika, 105*(2), 455–462.

Diggle, P. J. (2014). Statistical analysis of spatial and spatio-temporal point patterns, 3rd ed. Monographs on statistics and applied probability, vol. 128. Boca Raton, FL: CRC Press.

Diggle, P. J., Kaimi, I., & Abellana, R. (2010). Partial-likelihood analysis of spatio- temporal point-process data. *Biometrics, 66*(2), 347–354.

Diouane, Y., Schoenberg, F., & Mohler, G. (2024). Accurate estimation of cross-excitation in multivariate Hawkes process models of infectious diseases. In *11th IEEE International Conference on Data Science and Advanced Analytics (DSAA 2024)* (pp. 1–8).

Gneiting, T., & Raftery, A. E. (2007). Strictly proper scoring rules, prediction, and estimation. *Journal of the American Statistical Association, 102*, 359–378.

Hardiman, S. J., & Bouchaud, J. P. (2014). Branching-ratio approximation for the self-exciting Hawkes process. *Physical Review. E, Statistical, Nonlinear, and Soft Matter Physics, 90*(6), 062807.

Harte, D. (2013). Bias in fitting the ETAS model: A case study based on New Zealand seismicity. *Geophysical Journal International, 192*(1), 390–412.

Kirchner, M. (2016). Hawkes and INAR(∞) processes. *Stochastic Processes and their Applications, 26*(8), 2494–2525.

Kirchner, M. (2017). An estimation procedure for the Hawkes process. *Quantitative Finance, 17*(4), 571–595.

Kresin, C., & Schoenberg, F. (2023). Parametric estimation of spatial-temporal point processes using the Stoyan-Grabarnik statistic. *Annals of the Institute of Statistical Mathematics, 75*, 887–909.
Marsan, D., & Lengliné, O. (2008). Extending earthquakes' reach through cascading. *Science, 319*(5866), 1076–1079.
Marsan, D., & Lengliné, O. (2010). A new estimation of the decay of aftershock density with distance to the mainshock. *Journal of Geophysical Research, 115*, B09302.
Ogata, Y. (1978). The asymptotic behaviour of maximum likelihood estimators for stationary point processes. *Annals of the Institute of Statistical Mathematics, 30*, 243–261.
Ogata, Y. (1988). Statistical models for earthquake occurrences and residual analysis for point processes. *Journal of the American Statistical Association, 83*, 9–27.
Ogata, Y. (1998). Space-time point-process models for earthquake occurrences. *Annals of the Institute of Statistical Mathematics, 50*(2), 379–402.
Phillips, S., & Schoenberg, F. (2024). Efficient non-parametric estimation of variable productivity Hawkes processes. *Journal of Applied Statistics*, 1–18.
Rathbun, S. L. (1996). Asymptotic properties of the maximum likelihood estimator for spatio-temporal point processes. *Journal of Statistical Planning and Inference, 51*, 55–74.
Rathbun, S. L., & Cressie, N. (1994). Asymptotic properties of estimators for the parameters of spatial inhomogeneous Poisson point processes. *Advances in Applied Probability, 26*, 122–154.
Schoenberg, F. (2004). Consistent parametric estimation of the intensity of a spatial-temporal point process. *Journal of Statistical Planning and Inference, 128*(1), 79–93.
Schoenberg, F. (2013). Facilitated estimation of ETAS. *Bulletin of the Seismological Society of America, 103*(1), 1–7.
Schoenberg, F. (2016). A note on the consistent estimation of spatial-temporal point process parameters. *Statistica Sinica, 26*, 861–879.
Schoenberg, F., Gordon, J. S., & Harrigan, R. (2018). Analytic computation of nonparametric Marsan-Lengliné estimates for Hawkes point processes. *Journal of Nonparametric Statistics, 30*(3), 742–757.
Silverman, B. W. (1986). *Density estimation for statistics and data analysis*. Boca Raton: Chapman and Hall.
Stoyan, D., & Grabarnik, P. (1991). Second-order characteristics for stochastic structures connected with Gibbs point processes. *Mathematische Nachrichten, 151*(1), 95–100.
Veen, A., & Schoenberg, F. (2008). Estimation of space-time branching process models in seismology using an EM-type algorithm. *JASA, 103*(482), 614–624.

Adjectives

4

One of the purposes of modeling is to summarize the main characteristics of the data in a useful way. However, models are typically mis-specified and reliant on questionable assumptions, so it is desirable to describe the data in other ways that might not require the assumption of a particular model. This chapter details some of these ways.

While the title of this chapter is meant to be tongue-in-cheek, and perhaps a more apt title would be "descriptors" since most of the topics here are actually nouns, the main point of the title is to emphasize that the purpose here is simply to describe some properties of the data. Since most of the methods in this chapter do not require models, one might think it would make more sense for this chapter to precede Chaps. 2 and 3. On the other hand, I thought it would be better to place it after the discussion of models, so that we can discuss what properties these descriptors have for various different models.

4.1 Descriptions of Clustering and Inhibition

Clustering and inhibition are sometimes referred to as *second-order* properties of a point process. We say a simple temporal point process N on the line $\mathbb{R}$ is *inhibitory* or *self-correcting* if, for $0 < a \leq b < c$, $cov\{N(a, b), N(b, c)\} < 0$. N is *clustered* if this covariance is positive. These definitions extend readily to space-time processes as well: N is self-exciting, for instance, if for any spatial region B and for $0 < a \leq b < c, cov\{N[(a, b) \times B], N[(b, c) \times B]\} > 0$. Well-known examples of self-correcting and clustered point processes, respectively, are the stress-release process (Isham & Westcott, 1979) and the Hawkes process (Hawkes, 1971). The term *self-exciting* is sometimes used as a synonym for *clustered*, but some authors distinguish the two terms by referring only to causal clustering as self-excitation, such as that in the Hawkes process, whereas clustering in general may be attributable to inhomogeneity.

4.2 Nearest Neighbor-Type Functions

There are several methods that have been proposed for describing the degree of clustering in spatial or spatial-temporal point process data.

One such function that can be used to summarize the degree of clustering in a spatial or spatial-temporal point process is the F-function, which is also sometimes called the *empty space function*. $F(r)$ is typically defined for purely spatial processes, as the probability that the distance from a randomly chosen location in the spatial domain to the nearest point of the process N is less than or equal to r. That

F. Schoenberg, *Space-Time Point Processes*, Springer Texts in Statistics,
https://doi.org/10.1007/978-3-032-20790-6_4

is, F is the cumulative distribution function (cdf) of the distance between a randomly selected location to its nearest observed point. As with all of the descriptors in this section, the F-function is typically used to describe the purely spatial behavior of the process, and can be extended to the spatial-temporal case provided one has some meaningful way of measuring spatial-temporal distance. For instance, one may define spatial-temporal distance by combining spatial distance and difference in time, such as

$$d\{(x_1, y_1, t_1), (x_2, y_2, t_2)\} = \alpha||(x_1, y_1) - (x_2, y_2)|| + \beta|t_1 - t_2|, \tag{4.1}$$

for some non-negative real numbers α and β.

The F-function can readily be interpreted. If $F(0.2) = 0.4$, for instance, then 40% of locations in the domain will be within distance 0.2 of a point of the point process. Lower values of the F-function indicate clustering and higher values indicate inhibition.

A closely related descriptor is the *nearest neighbor distribution function*, $G(r)$, which is the cdf of the distance between a randomly selected *point* of the process to its nearest observed point. In other words, $G(r)$ is the probability that the distance from a randomly chosen *point* of the point process N to its nearest other point in N is less than or equal to r.

In defining F and G, it is crucial to differentiate a *location* from a *point*. Here and throughout this text, I will use the word *location* to mean a position in the spatial-temporal domain. A *point*, by contrast, is a place where one of the observed events happens to occur. For instance, when considering the origin times and locations of earthquakes in California between 2010 and 2020, any spot in California between 2010 and 2020 is a *location*, whereas only a place and time when an earthquake occurred would be a *point*. Every point occurs at a location, but not every location is a point.

For a Poisson process, $F(r) = G(r)$, as the occurrence of a point at a particular location has no effect on the distance from the location to the nearest other point, because of the complete independence property. For a homogeneous Poisson process in the plane,

$$F(r) = G(r) = 1 - \exp(-\lambda\pi r^2).$$

There are actually two F-functions and two G-functions. As with most other statistical constructs, there is the theoretical value, and this is distinct from our best estimate of its value given the data. Thus, we should differentiate the theoretical F-function from the estimated F-function, and similarly for the G-function, J-function, and other summaries in this section.

The F- and G-functions can be estimated simply using the empirical distribution of distances from locations in the spatial domain to points of the point process, or the empirical distribution of distances from points to other points in the point process, respectively. That is, one can estimate $F(r)$ via

$$\hat{F}(r) = \frac{1}{m}\sum_{j=1}^{m} \mathbb{1}\{\exists i : |\tau_i - \nu_j| \le r\} = \frac{1}{m}\sum_{j=1}^{m} \mathbb{1}\{\min_i |\tau_i - \nu_j| \le r\},$$

where $n = N(S)$ is the number of observed points, $\{\tau_i, i = 1, \ldots, n\}$ are the points of the point process and $\{\nu_j, j = 1, \ldots, m\}$ are m locations in the spatial domain S distributed uniformly at random. Similarly, one can estimate $G(r)$ with

$$\hat{G}(r) = \frac{1}{n}\sum_{i=1}^{n} \mathbb{1}\{\exists j : |\tau_i - \tau_j| \le r\} = \frac{1}{n}\sum_{i=1}^{n} \mathbb{1}\{\min_{i \ne j} |\tau_i - \tau_j| \le r\}.$$

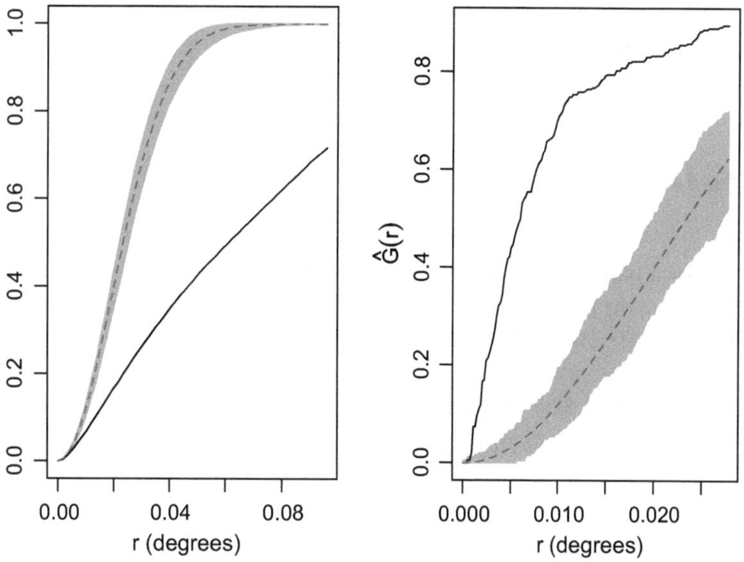

Fig. 4.1 (solid black curves) Estimated F-function and G-function for San Bernardino earthquake data shown in Fig. 1.3 of Chap. 1, along with theoretical F-function and G-function for a stationary Poisson process (red dashed curves). Grey 95% confidence bounds are based on 200 simulations of stationary Poisson processes on the same domain, each with rate equal to the mean rate for the earthquake data

If the point process N is stationary with points throughout the plane $\mathbf{R}^2$, but observed only in some portion of the plane S, then these estimates $\hat{F}$ and $\hat{G}$ will be biased because of edge effects, so various corrections are typically used in practice to correct for the fact that a typical location near the boundary may actually have more points within r of it that are outside of the observation window (Stoyan & Stoyan, 1994, Stoyan et al., 1995).

Estimates of F and G applied to the San Bernardino earthquake data described in Chap. 1 are shown in Fig. 4.1, along with the theoretical F- and G-functions for the stationary Poisson process and 95% confidence bounds based on simulated stationary Poisson processes. The code for producing these estimates and making Fig. 4.1 (after downloading the data and editing it to form the file SearchResults.txt, as described around Fig. 1.3 in Chap. 1) is shown below. The estimates of the F-function and G-function for the earthquake data are showing that the earthquakes are statistically significantly more clustered than a stationary Poisson, at scales of 0 to 0.04 degrees.

```
install.packages("spatstat")
library(spatstat)
par(mfrow=c(1,2))
a = read.table("SearchResults.txt",skip=2,fill=TRUE)
x = a$V10; y = a$V9; z = cbind(x,y); n = length(x)
b = as.ppp(z, W = c(-118,-117,34,35))
env = envelope(b,Fest,nsim=200)
plot(env,legend=F,main="",xlab="r (degrees)",ylab="")
mtext(s=2,l=2,expression(hat(F)(r)))
env2 = envelope(b,Gest,nsim=200)
plot(env2,legend=F,main="",xlab="r (degrees)",ylab="")
mtext(s=2,l=2,expression(hat(G)(r)))
```

The F- and G-functions can easily be interpreted. If $F(0.02) = 0.18$, for instance, then 18% of locations in the domain have a point within distance 0.02 of them. If $G(0.02) = 0.80$, then 80% of *points* have another point within distance 0.02.

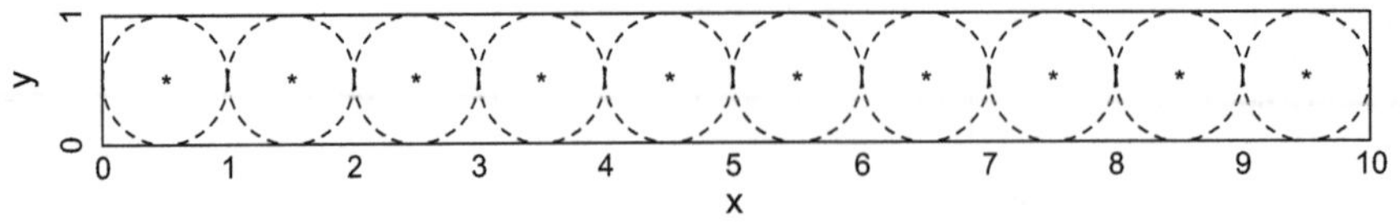

Fig. 4.2 Point pattern with 10 optimally separated points in $S = (0, 10) \times (0, 1)$

For a particular value of r and a fixed total number of points, the larger $F(r)$ is, the more well-dispersed the points are. For instance, if there are 10 points and they are perfectly evenly spaced across the space $(0, 10) \times (0, 1)$, as in Fig. 4.2, then

$$\begin{aligned} F(0.5) &= P(\text{a randomly selected location in S is within distance 0.5 of a point}) \\ &= P(\text{a randomly selected location in S falls within one of the 10 circles} \\ &\qquad \text{shown in Fig. 32}) \\ &= 10(\pi/4)/10 \\ &= \pi/4. \end{aligned}$$

However, if instead all 10 points occurred at (0.5, 0.5), then

$$\begin{aligned} F(0.5) &= P\{\text{a randomly selected location in S is within distance 0.5 of (0.5, 0.5)}\} \\ &= \text{the area of the first circle / the area of S} \\ &= (\pi/4)/10 \\ &= \pi/40. \end{aligned}$$

By contrast, for a particular value of r and a fixed total number of points, the smaller $G(r)$ is, the more well-dispersed the points are. For instance, if there are 10 points and they are perfectly evenly spaced across the space $(0, 10) \times (0, 1)$, as in Fig. 4.2, then

$$\begin{aligned} G(0.5) &= P(\text{a randomly selected point of } N \text{ is within distance 0.5 of another} \\ &\qquad \text{point of } N) \\ &= 0. \end{aligned}$$

If, instead, all the points happen to occur at the location (0.5, 0.5), then $G(0.5) = 1$.
Below is *R* code to construct Fig. 4.2.

```
plot(c(0,10),c(0,1),xlab="x",ylab="y",type="n",axes=F)
lines(c(0,0,10,10,0),c(0,1,1,0,0) )
mtext(s=1,at=0:10,as.character(0:10))
mtext(s=2,at=c(0,1),as.character(c(0,1)))
for(i in 1:10){
points(i-.5,.5,pch="*")
j = seq(-.5,.5,length=100)
lines(i - .5 + j, .5 + sqrt(.5^2 - j^2),lty=2)
lines(i - .5 + j, .5 - sqrt(.5^2 - j^2),lty=2)
}
```

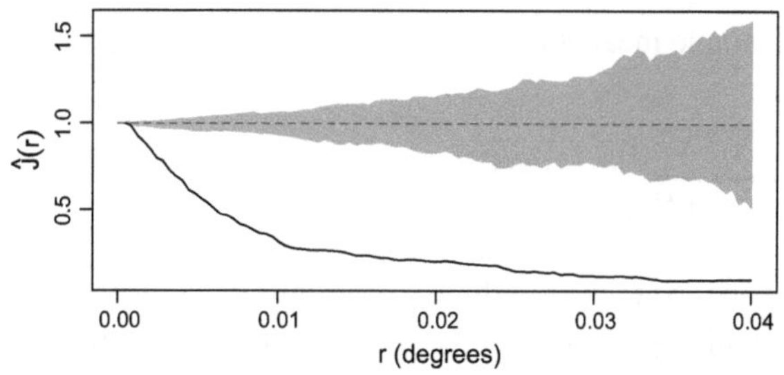

Fig. 4.3 (solid black curves) Estimated J-function for San Bernardino earthquake data shown in Fig. 1.3 of Chap. 1 (solid black curve), along with theoretical J-function for a stationary Poisson process (red dashed curve), and 95% confidence bounds (gray shaded areas) based on 200 simulations of stationary Poisson processes on the same domain, each with rate equal to the mean rate for the earthquake data

Since the G-function describes how clustered points are around other points, and the F-function describes how clustered they are around a randomly selected location, it makes sense to consider them in combination. For instance, it is common to consider their ratio, the J-function, defined as

$$J(r) = \frac{1 - G(r)}{1 - F(r)},$$

for r such that $F(r) < 1$. Note that $J(r) > 1$ indicates inhibition at distance scale r, and $J(r) < 1$ indicates clustering at scale r, because processes with more intense clustering have larger values of $G(r)$ and smaller values of $F(r)$. For a homogeneous Poisson process, $J(r) = 1$ for all r.

The code below produces the estimates of the J-function for the San Bernardino earthquake data, as shown in Fig. 4.3. The estimated J-function for the data is less than 1 because the earthquake locations are so tightly clustered.

```
env = envelope(b,Jest,nsim=200,r=seq(0,.04,length=100))
plot(env,legend=F,main="",xlab="r (degrees)",ylab="")
mtext(s=2,l=2,expression(hat(J)(r)))
```

Another functional summary more frequently used than the F-, G-, and J-functions is Ripley's K-function (Ripley, 1976). For a stationary process with mean rate $E[\lambda(t, x, y)] = \mu$, let

$$K(r) = \frac{1}{\mu}\mathbb{E}[\# \text{ of points within distance } r \text{ of a randomly chosen point}].$$

Distance here usually means ordinary Euclidean distance between spatial locations, but can be extended to spatial-temporal distance as well, just as with the F, G, and J-functions. Since the expected number of points within distance r of any given point of a purely spatial stationary Poisson process is simply $\mu\pi r^2$, for such a process, $K(r) = \frac{1}{\mu}(\mu\pi r^2) = \pi r^2$. In practice, one typically obtains an estimate of $K(r)$ for the spatial locations of points using data, and compares the estimate to πr^2 to investigate clustering. If the estimate of $K(r)$ is significantly higher than πr^2, then there is significant clustering within distances up to r, whereas if the estimate $\hat{K}(r)$ is significantly less than πr^2, then there is significant inhibition within distances up to r.

An obvious way to estimate the overall rate μ is simply using $\hat{\mu} = N(S)/|S|$, i.e. the overall observed rate at which points occurred in the dataset, and therefore, letting $n = N(S)$, a simple way to estimate $K(r)$ is via

$$\check{K}(r) = \frac{1}{\hat{\mu}}[\text{sample mean \# of points within distance } r \text{ of points in the data}]$$
$$= \frac{1}{\hat{\mu}n}\sum_{i=1}^{n}\sum_{j\neq i}\mathbf{1}_{\{|\tau_i-\tau_j|\leq r\}}.$$

As the area of observation $|S|$ tends to infinity, $\check{K}(r)$ is asymptotically normal with mean πr^2 and variance $\frac{2\pi r^2}{\lambda^2|S|}$, under the null hypothesis that the point process is a spatial stationary Poisson process with intensity λ. (see Cressie 1993, p. 642; Ripley 1988 pp. 28–48; Heinrich 1988).

However, as with naive estimates of the F- and G-functions, the estimate $\check{K}(r)$ will typically be biased because of boundary effects. Specifically, if N is a stationary spatial point process on the plane but only observed on a rectangular region S, then $\check{K}(r)$ will typically underestimate $K(r)$ because the observation region is missing points occurring outside of S but near its boundary of S, and such points may have increased the estimate of $K(r)$ had they been included. Such boundary effect considerations have led $K(r)$ instead to be conventionally estimated via

$$\hat{K}(r) = \frac{1}{\hat{\mu}n}\sum_{i=1}^{n}\sum_{j\neq i}\mathbf{1}_{\{|\tau_i-\tau_j|\leq r\}}w(\tau_i,\tau_j), \tag{4.2}$$

where $w(\tau_i, \tau_j)$ is the inverse of the proportion of the circle centered at τ_i passing through τ_j that is inside the observation region S. The idea is that this weight $w(\tau_i, \tau_j)$ is chosen so that a pair of points lying near the boundary of S is given a weight greater than 1 in order to compensate for unobserved points that may be lying just outside of the observation window, and the resulting estimator $\hat{K}$ can easily be shown to be unbiased if N is a stationary Poisson process observed on a portion of $\mathbb{R}^2$.

Some authors prefer to estimate the (scaled) derivative of the K-function, also called the *pair correlation function*. Specifically, for a spatial point process with overall rate $\mu(\tau) = E[\lambda(\tau)]$, suppose one defines the *second-order intensity*

$$\lambda_2(\tau_1,\tau_2) = \lim_{\Delta\downarrow 0}\frac{EN(B_{\tau_1,\Delta}B_{\tau_2,\Delta})}{\Delta^2},$$

assuming it exists, for locations $\tau_1 \neq \tau_2$, where $B_{x,\Delta}$ means a circle with radius Δ centered at τ. Then the pair correlation function $g_2(\tau_1, \tau_2)$ is defined for $\tau_1 \neq \tau_2$ as

$$g2(\tau_1,\tau_2) = \frac{\lambda_2(\tau_1,\tau_2)}{\mu(\tau_1)\mu(\tau_2)}.$$

Often it is convenient to assume that the pair correlation g_2 is *isotropic*, i.e. it depends only on the distance between the locations τ_1 and τ_2, so that $g_2(\tau_1, \tau_2) = \phi(r)$, where $r = ||\tau_1 - \tau_2||$. For a stationary spatial Poisson process, $\phi(r) = 1$. If N exhibits spatial clustering at scale r then $\phi(r) > 1$, and if N exhibits inhibition at distance r then $\phi(r) < 1$ (Illian et al., 2008; Baddeley et al., 2015). For a spatial point process with isotropic pair correlation ϕ, the pair correlation obeys (Baddeley et al., 2025)

$$\phi(r) = \frac{\partial K(r)/\partial r}{2\pi r}),$$

and can be estimated using kernel smoothing techniques (Guan, 2007a, b; Jalilian & Waagepetersen, 2018; Jalilian et al., 2019).

The scaled and centered version of Ripley's K-function is called the L-function (Besag, 1977). Scaling and centering can be important here because the human eye is not very good at detecting departures from πr^2, whereas we can very easily see if values of a function are positive or negative. Thus, one typically inspects estimates of $L(r) - r$ versus r, where

$$L(r) = \sqrt{\frac{K(r)}{\pi}}.$$

For the stationary Poisson process on $\mathbb{R}^2$, $K(r) = \pi r^2$, so $L(r) = r$, and $L(r) - r = 0$. The L-function is typically estimated simply via

$$\hat{L}(r) = \sqrt{\frac{\hat{K}(r)}{\pi}},$$

and positive values of $\hat{L}(r) - r$ indicate clustering of the process up to distance r, and negative values indicate inhibition. Simulations of stationary Poisson processes can readily be used to generate 95%-confidence bands, so that values of $\hat{L}(r) - r$ outside these bands indicate statistically significant clustering or inhibition.

Figure 4.4 shows the estimated K-function and L-function for the San Bernardino earthquake data. Because the earthquakes are so tightly spatially clustered, the estimated K and L-functions greatly exceed the 95%-bounds based on simulations of stationary Poisson processes. The code below generates the estimates $\hat{K}(r)$ and $\hat{L}(r) - r$ shown in Fig. 4.4.

```
par(mfrow=c(1,2))
env = envelope(b,Kest,nsim=200,r=seq(0,.15,length=100))
plot(env,legend=F,main="",xlab="r (degrees)",ylab="")
mtext(s=2,l=2,expression(hat(K)(r)))
L = Lest(b,r=seq(0,.15,length=100))
env = envelope(b,Lest,nsim=200,r=seq(0,.15,length=100))
plot(L$r,L$bord-L$r,type="l",xlab="r (degrees)",ylab="",
ylim=c(min(env$lo-L$r),max(L$bord-L$r)))
mtext(s=2,l=2,expression(hat(L)(r)-r))
lines(L$r,env$lo-L$r, lty=2)
lines(L$r,env$hi-L$r,lty=2)
```

The F, G, J, K, and L-functions can all be extended to describe marked or multivariate point processes. For example, one can define the marked G-function, $G_m(r)$ as the probability that a randomly chosen point with mark m has another point with mark m within distance r of it. Similarly, the marked K-function, $K_m(r)$, is defined as $\frac{1}{\mu_m}\mathbb{E}$ [# of points of mark m within distance r of a randomly chosen point of mark m], where μ_m is the rate of points of mark m. If one is interested in the relationships between points of different marks, the *cross* K-function, $K_{ab}(r)$, is defined as $\frac{1}{\mu_b}\mathbb{E}$ [# of points of mark b within distance r of a randomly chosen point of mark a].

Summaries like the K-function are useful for examining whether the points of a point process are significantly more or less clustered than those of a stationary Poisson process. However, in some situations it may be of interest to discern whether the points are significantly more or less clustered than those of some other point process. In the case of earthquakes, for example, it is obvious that the

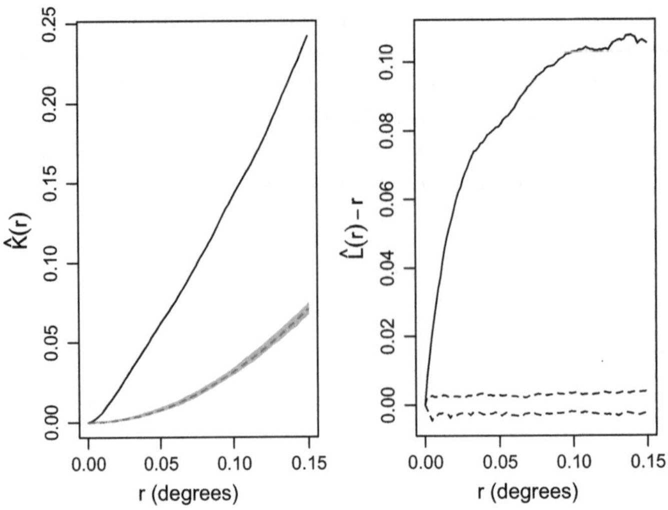

Fig. 4.4 Estimated border-corrected K-function (left) and L-function (right) for San Bernardino earthquake data shown in Fig. 1.3 of Chap. 1. Estimates based on the data are represented by solid black curves. On left, theoretical K-function for a stationary Poisson process is shown in red, along with 95% confidence bounds (gray shaded areas) based on 200 simulations of stationary Poisson processes on the same domain, each with rate equal to the mean rate for the earthquake data. On right, dashed curves define 95% confidence bounds for $\hat{L}(r) - r$ based on 200 simulated stationary Poisson processes on the same domain, again with rates equal to that of the earthquake data

data are far more clustered than a stationary Poisson process, and a more interesting question may be whether the observations are significantly more or less clustered than an ETAS process. For this purpose, the inhomogeneous K-function, or other weighted versions of second-order summaries, may be useful. Such an analysis is really an assessment of how well the model captures the clustering in the data rather than a description of the data, so topics such as the *inhomogeneous* or *weighted* K-function are discussed in Chap. 5 in the context of model evaluation.

4.3 R/S Statistic

The rescaled range statistic, R/S, was introduced by Hurst (1951), who monitored the Nile river flow and attempted to describe the distribution of the time until the river overflowed or ran dry. The R/S statistic was later used as a graphical technique for the study of long-range dependence properties of temporal processes (Mandelbrot & Wallis, 1969). Ogata and Abe (1991) used the R/S statistic to investigate the long-range dependence of Japanese earthquakes, and Daley (1999) studied the properties of R/S for long-range renewal processes.

Suppose N is a purely temporal simple point process observed on $[0, T]$ and let $Z(t) = N[0, t)$ denote the cumulative number of points up to time t. Consider an arbitrary interval $(t_0, t_0 + \delta)$ of length δ, where $t_0 + \delta \leq T$, and define the deviation function $D(u, t_0, \delta) = [Z(u + t_0) - Z(t)] - \frac{u}{\delta}[Z(t_0 + \delta) - Z(t_0)]$. Further, define the range $R(t_0; \delta) = \max_{0 \leq u \leq \delta} D(u, t_0, \delta) - \min_{0 \leq u \leq \delta} D(u, t_0, \delta)$, and the sample variance $S^2(t_0; \delta) = \frac{Z(t_0+\delta)-Z(t_0)}{\delta} - \left[\frac{Z(t_0+\delta)-Z(t_0)}{\delta}\right]^2$. Then the R/S statistic is the ratio $\frac{R(t_0;\delta)}{S(t_0;\delta)}$. The log-log plot of R/S versus δ should have a constant slope H as δ becomes large and this slope is called the H-constant or Hurst's number (Harte, 2001; Clegg, 2006). For a random walk, this

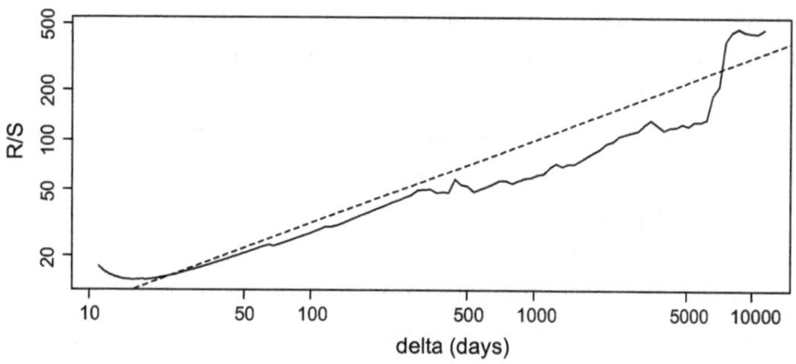

Fig. 4.5 Rescaled range (R/S) plot for San Bernardino earthquake event times, for $t_0 = 250$. Dashed line has slope 0.5 and intercept 0.5

slope H is $1/2$, and for processes with long-range dependence, H is greater than $1/2$, so estimates of H are often used to characterize the degree of long-range dependence in the data.

There are several methods for estimating H; the most commonly used among these is the R/S plot, or Pox diagram, which is a plot of the rescaled range statistic R/S against δ on log-log scale; for large δ, R/S is scattered around a straight line with slope H. To obtain a parametric estimate of H, an approximate MLE is typically used. The large sample theory for the maximum spectral likelihood has been developed by Whittle (1962). Under the hypothesis of independent and identically distributed increments, the R/S statistic is asymptotically distributed as the range of a Brownian bridge (Mandelbrot, 1975). Using the extended continuous mapping theorem, Herrnordf's theorem (Billingsley, 1968; Lo, 1991) showed that $\frac{1}{\sqrt{n}}R/S$, for short-range dependent point processes, converges to the range of a Brownian bridge.

The code below, applied to the San Bernardino earthquake data, yields the plot in Fig. 4.5. Although the earthquakes are clearly clustered over short time scales, their long-term temporal dependence appears to be minimal.

```
t = z$t ## times of earthquakes from 0 to maxt = 20089.
t0 = 250; Zt = sum(t<t0); m = rep(0,140)
for(j in 1:140){
delta = 10+exp(j/15)
Zd = sum(t < t0+delta)
u = seq(0,delta,length=1000)
d = rep(0,1000)
for(i in 1:1000){
    d[i] = (sum(t<t0+u[i]) - Zt) - u[i]/delta*(Zd-Zt)
    }
R = max(d) - min(d)
s1 = (Zd-Zt)/delta
S = sqrt(s1 - s1^2)
m[j] = R/S
}
plot(10+exp((1:140)/15),m,log="xy",type="l",xlab="delta (days)",ylab="R/S")
abline(lty=2,a=.5,b=.5)
```

4.4 Causality

A very important problem in the analysis of clustered point processes is discriminating between triggering and inhomogeneity. Indeed, Diggle (2014) describes this problem as one of the most important challenges currently facing point process analysts. Both causal clustering and inhomogeneity can lead to aggregation of points in certain locations, though the mechanisms for this aggregation have very different implications. Causal clustering, or triggering, refers to the situation where the random occurrence of a point causes other points to be more likely to occur in the near vicinity of space-time. Inhomogeneity refers to the case where, because of differences in the background environment, points are simply more likely to occur at certain locations of space-time than others. Discriminating between these two phenomena can be very difficult in practice.

For example, suppose one is analyzing catalogs of reported gang-related violent crimes, and many occurrences are present in one spatial-temporal area. Is this aggregation of points due to the socio-economic and geographical circumstances in the particular location, in which case the explanation is inhomogeneity? Or is the aggregation due at least partly to retaliation, where one such crime that just happens to occur in the region may spark several retaliations, each of which might yield further retaliations, and so on, in which case the explanation is triggering?

One approach suggested by Diggle (2014) is to observe the point process repeatedly and inspect whether the clustering of points appears to occur predominantly in the same spatial-temporal locations, which would suggest the aggregation of points may be attributable to inhomogeneity. If the clusters of points occur in different locations, then they are more likely the result of triggering. However, very often in practice, obtaining repeatedly observed point process data is not feasible. Furthermore, it is possible for a process, such as a Neyman-Scott process, to exhibit aggregation of points at certain random hot-spots, which may be different in each realization, yet the aggregation of points is still not causal in the sense of individual points triggering others as in a Hawkes process.

An approach taken in several papers including Park et al. (2021) is to attempt to fit a Hawkes model with both inhomogeneity and triggering, and where the spatially and temporally varying background rate is modeled as accurately as possible, for instance using kernel smoothing of previously occurring points as well as covariate information that may influence the background rate, such as demographic information on each census tract. The idea is that if the inhomogeneity is accurately modeled via the background rate, then any triggering estimated in the resulting Hawkes model may be attributed to causal clustering. While this idea is sensible, it can be difficult to assess whether the background rate indeed accurately models all the inhomogeneity in the spatial-temporal environment, and any inhomogeneity not adequately captured by the model will leak into the triggering function and be incorrectly characterized as causal clustering.

Another idea explored in Cordi et al. (2017) is to fit a Hawkes model to the data and another to the data with the times reversed. If the model fits significantly better to the forward-time data, then this suggests the aggregation of points may indeed be causal, whereas if the model fits equally well with the times reversed, then the aggregation is most likely due to inhomogeneity. The idea is that typically in applications it would make no sense for points to trigger the occurrence of prior points, so the observation that a Hawkes model fits as well to the time-reversed data as it does to the forward-time data is incompatible with actual causal clustering but is consistent with the notion that the Hawkes model's background rate term is not accurately describing the inhomogeneity in the process and thus incorrectly classifying some of the inhomogeneity as triggering. While the idea of Cordi et al. (2017) is very clever, its extension to the case where the inhomogeneity may vary over space instead of (or in addition to) time is unclear. Also, there is no guarantee that a process with causal triggering would not have the property that a Hawkes model fits equally well with the times reversed.

Figure 4.6 shows the fitted conditional intensity for the ETAS model with power-law triggering in both space and time, as fit in Chap. 3, but now fit to the data both forward and backward in time. The log-likelihood for the model fit to the data is –924.6, and the log-likelihood for the model fit with times reversed is –943.8. In general, when comparing nested models with the same dataset, a difference in log-likelihoods of 2 or more can be considered statistically significant. Here, where the dataset itself is changed, the situation is a bit different, but 2 is still a good rule of thumb benchmark to use when comparing the fit of the model forward and in reversed. In this example, the difference is 19.2, so the

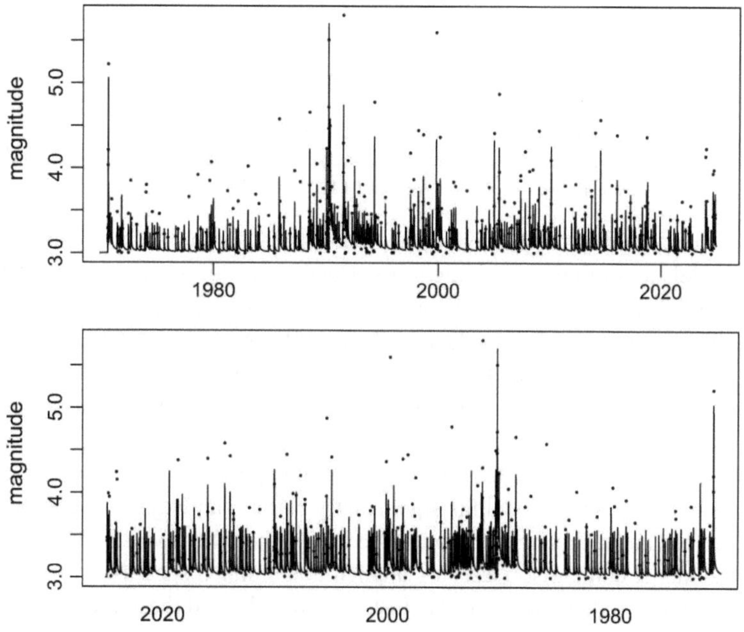

Fig. 4.6 (top) San Bernardino earthquake event times and magnitudes, with estimate of λ fit according to the ETAS model power-law triggering in space and time by MLE. (bottom) San Bernardino earthquake event times and magnitudes with time-reversed, along with estimate of λ fit according to the ETAS model power-law triggering in space and time by MLE to reversed times. Fitted intensities are calculated daily, and shown on logarithmic scale after smoothing and scaling

fit is significantly better with the data in their original order, suggesting that the clustering in the data is due to triggering rather than inhomogeneity.

The code below was used to produce Fig. 4.6, after running the code in Chap. 3 to fit the ETAS model to this dataset.

```
mu = theta2[1]; K = theta2[2]; c = theta2[3]; p = theta2[4]
a = theta2[5]; d = theta2[6]; q = theta2[7]; n = z$n
lam = rep(mu,T)
const = K*(p-1)*c^(p-1)
for(j in ceiling(t[1]):T){
  v = max(c(1:n)[t[1:n]<j]) ## index of last pt before time j
  lam[j] = mu + const*sum(exp(a*(z$m[1:v]-M0))*(j-t[1:v]+c)^(-p))
  }
plot(as.Date(x$V1),z$m,xlab="",ylab="magnitude",cex=.2)
lam2 = smooth(log(lam),twiceit=T)
lam3 = (lam2 - min(lam2))/(max(lam2)-min(lam2))*2.7+3
lines(as.Date(x$V1[1])-t[1]+1:T,lam3)
t2 = T-t[n:1]
z = list(); z$t = t2; z$lon = x$V10[n:1]+118; z$lat = x$V9[n:1]-34;
z$m = x$V7[n:1]; z$n = length(z$t)
theta1 = c(z$n/maxt*.1,.1,2,2,2,2,3)
b1 = optim(theta1,logletas,hessian=T)
theta2 = b1$par
b1 = optim(theta2,logletas,hessian=T)
theta2 = b1$par
mu = theta2[1]; K = theta2[2]; c = theta2[3]; p = theta2[4]
a = theta2[5]; d = theta2[6]; q = theta2[7]; n = z$n
lam = rep(mu,T)
const = K*(p-1)*c^(p-1)
for(j in ceiling(t2[1]):T){
  v = max(c(1:n)[t2[1:n]<j]) ## index of last pt before time j
  lam[j] = mu + const*sum(exp(a*(z$m[1:v]-M0))*(j-t2[1:v]+c)^(-p))
```

```
  }
plot(t2,z$m,xaxt="n",
xlab="",ylab="magnitude",cex=.2)
mtext(s=1,l=1,c("1980","2000","2020"),at=T-c(10*365,30*365,50*365))
lam2 = smooth(log(lam),twiceit=T)
lam3 = (lam2 - min(lam2))/(max(lam2)-min(lam2))*2.7+3
lines(as.Date(x$V1[1])-t[1]+1:T,lam3)
```

Yet another alternative idea is to fit both a Hawkes model with causal clustering as well as non-causal models as similar as possible to the Hawkes model but without causal clustering, such as Neyman-Scott, Poisson cluster, or inhomogeneous Poisson models, and compare how these models fit. This allows one to quantify the degree of causal clustering in the data, and, provided the models are sensible and fit well, if the Hawkes model fits significantly better than the alternative models without causal clustering, then this is potentially strong evidence that the causal triggering identified by the Hawkes model is real.

McGovern et al. (2025) consider formal hypothesis tests using the log-likelihood statistic to determine if a Hawkes model fits significantly better than Neyman-Scott or inhomogeneous Poisson alternatives, and a similar test is performed using the time-reversal method. Both the time-reversal test and the model comparison tests are applied to simulated spatial-temporal point processes to quantify the accuracy in identifying causal clustering models, and these methods are applied to reported shooting data from Boston. The analysis for the simulated data show that accuracy in correctly identifying causal structures is generally very high under most conditions. The application to the reported Boston shootings data suggest that there is indeed causal triggering in certain locations, perhaps due to retaliatory crime activity. Similar likelihood ratio tests are applied in McGovern and Schoenberg (2024) to data on measles, Chlamydia, Lyme disease, and suicide, showing that the Hawkes model fits significantly better than a Poisson cluster model for the cases of measles, Chlamydia, and suicide, but not significantly better for Lyme disease, which makes sense since Lyme disease is thought to be spread by ticks and other pests rather than by direct contagion from human to human. For suicide, which has been posited to have an element of social contagion (Bearman & Moody, 2004; Ali et al., 2011; Cheng et al., 2014), the data were fit statistically significantly better by a Hawkes model than by a corresponding Poisson cluster process, although the estimated degree of triggering (productivity) was very low, at just 0.128, and not statistically significant.

4.5 Prototypes

Given a collection $\{X_i; i = 1, 2, \ldots, m\}$ of point patterns, one may define its prototype as a point pattern Y minimizing the sum $\sum_{i=1}^{m} d(X_i, Y)$, where d is some distance function, i.e. $d(X, Y)$ is the distance between the two-point patterns X and Y. Some constraints on the function d are required in order for d to be a well-defined distance function; see, for example, p. 370 of Appendix 1 of Daley and Vere-Jones (2003).

Many choices of d are possible. The spike-time distance, used successfully in the description of neuron firings by Victor and Purpura (1997), defines $d(X, Y)$ as the minimal cost needed to transform point pattern X into the pattern Y using a series of elementary operations. These elementary operations include adding a point to X, which is given some cost p_a, deleting a point from X, which is given cost p_d, and moving a point of X by some amount in time and/or space, which is given a cost of p_t and/or p_s. The cost parameters p_a, p_d, p_t, and p_s must be non-negative and p_a must equal p_d in order for d to be a well-defined symmetric distance function (Victor and Purpura, 1997).

This spike-time distance metric is somewhat similar to the Earth Movers Distance (EMD) described by Rubner et al. (2000) in that it measures the amount of movement necessary to transform one random collection into another. EMD measures the minimum amount of work required to match the histogram of shades of pixels in one image with those of another image. As with spike-time distance, this work is measured as the sum of costs associated with certain basic operations, such as increasing or decreasing the shading of one pixel or set of pixels by a certain amount. Computation of EMD is closely related to the solution of Hitchcock (1941) to the classic transportation problem first discussed by Monge (1781) where of interest was the best way to ship goods from suppliers to consumers while satisfying varying levels of consumer demand. The key distinctions between spike-time distance and EMD are that the latter is typically used to determine the distance between histograms of observations rather than the observations themselves, which are typically pixellated values recorded in discrete time rather than points in continuous time, and that the spike-time distance allows the addition and deletion of new points whereas EMD merely involves changing the values associated with existing pixels. Indeed, if addition and deletion are not allowed (or equivalently, if the addition and deletion penalties are prohibitively large), then the spike time distance is essentially the same as the integrated difference between the cumulative functions associated with the two temporal point patterns.

Some problems of how to determine the spike-time distance between two-point patterns and how to find the prototype for a collection of point patterns are discussed in Tranbarger and Schoenberg (2004). I list here two key facts facilitating the solution to these problems. The first is that the spike time distance between two temporal point patterns X and Y is simply given by the sum of the penalties associated with adding or deleting points, plus the sum $\sum_{j=1}^{J} p_t|x(j) - y(j)|$, where $x(1), \ldots, x(J)$ and $y(1), \ldots, y(J)$ are the sorted remaining points of X and Y, respectively. Hence, for purely temporal point patterns, the problem of determining which point of X gets moved to which point of Y is not an issue, and finding the distance between X and Y simply amounts to deciding which points are added or deleted and which are moved. For multidimensional point patterns, no such obvious shortcut exists, however, but an algorithm that attempts all possible additions, deletions, and pairings of the points in X and Y might not be prohibitively slow for point patterns each of which contains a relatively small number of points (see Sect. 3.2 of Tranbarger and Schoenberg (2004) for a discussion of computational approaches and their run times).

A second fact worth mentioning is that, for a given collection of multidimensional point patterns, using the spike-time distance, there exists a prototype for which each coordinate of each point in the prototype is equal to a coordinate of a point in one of the point patterns in the collection. Therefore one way of finding a collection's prototype is by searching over all combinations of coordinates of points in the collection, or by using the step-wise approach suggested in Tranbarger and Schoenberg (2010).

As noted in Victor and Purpura (1997), one of the main difficulties inherent in metric analyses of point patterns is that of determining the penalties for adding, deleting, and moving points. Only the relative values of these parameters are relevant for the determination of the prototype. The ratio of the adding/deleting penalty p_a to the moving penalties p_t, p_s can have a large impact on the resulting prototypes.

For a purely temporal point pattern, the prototype contains a point τ if an aftershock is present near the space-time location τ in a fraction of at least $p_a/(p_a + p_d)$ of the mainshocks in the dataset. This fraction can be seen as a lower bound on the proportion of point patterns with a point near time τ in order for a point τ to be considered a typical occurrence and thus be included in the prototype. Indeed, if a given point pattern has no aftershock in the interval $(\tau - p_a/p_t, \tau + p_a/p_t)$ after the mainshock, then the occurrence of a point in the prototype at time τ results in an increase by an amount p_a in the distance from this point pattern to the prototype. On the other hand, for each sequence with an aftershock near time τ after the mainshock, the lack of a point near time τ in the prototype causes the distance from the point pattern to the prototype to increase by the amount p_d. The prototype will contain a point at t if it is more economical to do so; ignoring moving penalties for the moment this means if $(m - m_\tau)p_a \leq m_\tau p_d$, where m_τ is the number of point patterns with an aftershock near time τ after the mainshock. It follows that the prototype will contain only those points where the fraction (m_τ/m) of point patterns in the dataset that contain nearby points is at least $p_a/(p_a + p_d)$.

The fact above can be helpful in determining appropriate values of p_a and p_d. If $p_a = p_d$, then the above ratio is 1/2, but it may be of interest to include points in the prototype even though nearby points may occur in less than half the point patterns in the dataset. If one desires that the prototype Y should represent all aftershocks occurring in at least some proportion p of the aftershock sequences in the dataset, then one may set the ratio of p_a to p_d to $p/(1-p)$. The prototype may still be defined as before, that is, as the point pattern Y minimizing the sum $\sum_i d(Xi, Y)$; the fact that the function d is no longer symmetric and thus not a proper distance function is immaterial. Provided d is any function such that a minimizer Y of $\sum_i d(X_i, Y)$ exists, the point pattern Y can be interpreted as a prototype and may represent a useful summary of the collection of point patterns.

If a symmetric distance function is desired, then the prototype can contain no more points than the median number of points in the collection. If one seeks a prototype that is typical in terms of its length, then with a symmetric distance, the moving penalties must be chosen to be minuscule in order to ensure that the prototype's length is close or equal to the median length of the point patterns. It may often be desirable to ensure that the prototype contains the median number of points $\tilde{n}$ of all point-process realizations in the dataset, however, and one way to ensure this is by allowing the addition and deletion penalties to differ. Diez (2010) and Diez et al. (2012), for example, suggest choosing p_a and p_d by maximizing $p_a p_d$ subject to the constraints that p_a and p_d must be non-negative with $p_a + p_d = 2$ and that the prototype must have $\tilde{n}$ points.

In addition to the determination of prototypes, the (possibly non-symmetric) distance function d can also be used for identification of outliers or clusters. One may classify certain individual wildfire seasons as outliers, for example, if their distance from the prototype is unusually large. Further, subgroups of wildfire seasons can be classified into clusters based on the principle of minimizing the total distance from the sequences of occurrences in the wildfire seasons to their respective cluster prototypes. For determining clusters and distances to the prototype, tiny moving penalties are no longer required and in fact comparably sized adding and moving penalties are preferable; these issues are discussed further in Tranbarger and Schoenberg (2010).

The top-left panel of Fig. 4.7 shows the locations of the 4 earthquakes with magnitude at least 5.0 in the San Bernardino earthquake dataset, along with all other recorded earthquakes of magnitude at least 3.5 occurring within 10 km and within 1 year afterward. The earthquake at longitude –117.04 and latitude 34.24, which had a magnitude of 5.6, had no recorded aftershocks in this range. This happens sometimes. The code to produce Fig. 4.7a is below.

```
dist = function(x1,y1,x2,y2) sqrt((x1-x2)^2+(y1-y2)^2)
indices = c(1:n)[m>=5]
v = list(); w = v
m1 = length(indices)
for(i in 1:m1){
ind = indices[i]
v[[i]] = c(1:n)[(dist(x,y,x[ind],y[ind])<1/11.1) &
  (t-t[ind] < 365) & (t>=t[ind])]
}
for(i in 1:m1) w[[i]] = as.ppp(cbind(x[v[[i]]],y[v[[i]]]),
  W = c(-118,-117,34,35))
plot(c(-118,-117),c(34,35),type="n",xlab="longitude (degrees)",
```

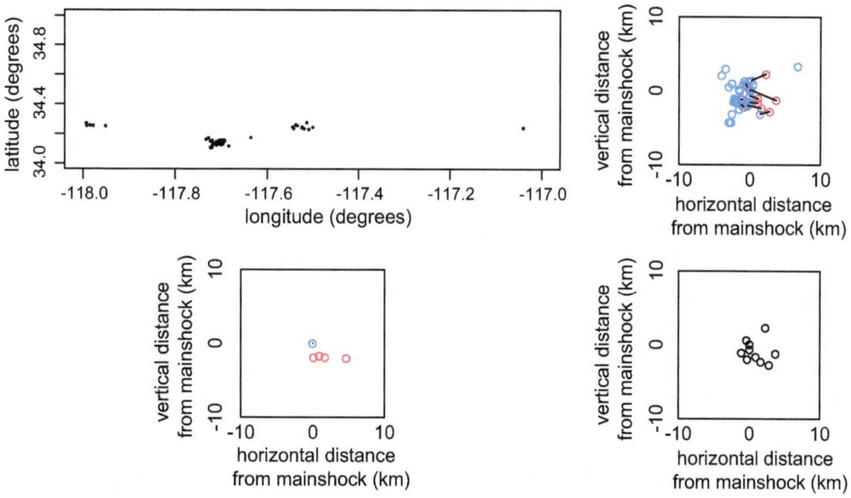

Fig. 4.7 (top-left) Locations of four San Bernardino mainshocks (earthquakes with magnitude ≥ 5.0) and their aftershocks within 10 km and within 1 year after mainshock. (top-right) Diagram showing how spike-time distance is computed from the pattern of the mainshock at longitude –117.5343 and its aftershocks, to the mainshock at longitude –117.697 and its aftershocks. (bottom-left) Diagram showing how spike-time distance is computed from the pattern of the mainshock at longitude –117.993 and its aftershocks, to the mainshock at longitude –117.04, which has no recorded aftershocks. Spike-time distances are computed here using penalties $p_a = p_d = p_m = 1$. (bottom-right) Estimated spatial prototype for the four mainshock-aftershock sequences

```
ylab="latitude (degrees)")
for(i in 1:m1) points(w[[i]],cex=.25)
```

Suppose these four earthquakes and their respective aftershocks are viewed as four distinct point patterns, each centered at the origin, with each point translated so that the original earthquake with magnitude at least 5.0 is placed exactly at the origin. The top-right panel of Fig. 4.7 diagrams the spike-time distance from the earthquake at longitude –117.5343 and its aftershocks, to the earthquake at longitude –117.697 and its aftershocks, using penalties of 1 for both the adding/deleting penalties p_a and p_d and moving penalty p_m. Figure 4.7's bottom-left panel diagrams the spike-time distance from the earthquake at longitude –117.993 and its aftershocks, to the earthquake at longitude –117.04, which has no recorded aftershocks. In this latter case, the spike-time distance simply involves adding/deleting points, as no points other than the original earthquakes of magnitude at least 5.0, which I am calling *mainshocks*, can be moved to align with points in the other pattern. The spike-time distance here is 4.0.

The code to produce the top-right and bottom-left panels of Fig. 4.7, and makes use of the function *ppdist()* in the *ttbary* library.

```
install.packages(c("ttbary","spatstat"))
library(ttbary); library(spatstat)
r = list() ## will be centered point patterns.
win = 1/11.1 * c(-1,1,-1,1) ## window
for(i in 1:m1) r[[i]] = as.ppp(cbind(x[v[[i]]]-x[v[[i]][1]],
  y[v[[i]]]-y[v[[i]][1]]),W = win)
dmat = crossdist(r[[1]],r[[2]])
res = ppdist(dmat, type="tt", ret_matching=TRUE)
plotmatch(r[[1]],r[[2]], dmat, res, penalty=1)
```

```
mtext(s=1,l=2,"horizontal distance \n from mainshock (km)")
mtext(s=1,l=0,c("-10","0","10"),at=c(-1/11.1,0,1/11.1))
mtext(s=2,l=-6,"vertical distance \n from mainshock (km)")
mtext(s=2,l=-8,c("-10","0","10"),at=c(-1/11.1,0,1/11.1))
res$dist ## 27.11279
dmat = crossdist(r[[3]],r[[4]])
res = ppdist(dmat, type="tt", ret_matching=TRUE)
plotmatch(r[[3]],r[[4]], dmat, res, penalty=1)
mtext(s=1,l=2,"horizontal distance \n from mainshock (km)")
mtext(s=1,l=0,c("-10","0","10"),at=c(-1/11.1,0,1/11.1))
mtext(s=2,l=-6,"vertical distance \n from mainshock (km)")
mtext(s=2,l=-8,c("-10","0","10"),at=c(-1/11.1,0,1/11.1))
```

The bottom-right panel of Fig. 4.7 shows the spatial prototype for these four point patterns shown in the top-left panel of Fig. 4.7. This prototype can be viewed as a median or typical mainshock-aftershock sequence for an earthquake of magnitude 5.0 or greater in this region, and its aftershocks within a distance of 10 km and a time interval of 1 year after the mainshock. The code to estimate the prototype is below, and uses the sequential algorithm suggested in Tranbarger and Schoenberg (2010). The algorithm works by searching over all potential locations, and adding to the prototype the location that minimizes the sum of spike-time distances. Then the algorithm proceeds by adding points one at a time, until no further additions would decrease the sum of spike-time distances. For each potential prototype point, the search is over all candidate locations whose x-coordinate is the same as one of the observed points in one of the point patterns, and similarly for the potential y-coordinates. Because the *ppdist()* function seems to have problems when there are duplicate points at exactly the same location, in the code below I remove the mainshocks from each sequence in computing the prototype, and the origin is then added to the prototype at the end.

```
candidatesx = c(); candidatesy = c()
for(i in 1:m1) {
candidatesx = c(candidatesx,r[[i]]$x)
candidatesy = c(candidatesy,r[[i]]$y)
}
candidatesx = unique(candidatesx)
candidatesy = unique(candidatesy)
ncanx = length(candidatesx)
ncany = length(candidatesy)
sumd = function(proto,r){
  ## calculates sum of dists from proto to r = list of ppps.
  m1 = length(r)
  if(length(proto$x)==0){
    sum0 = 0
    for(i in 1:m1) sum0 = sum0 + length(r[[i]]$x)
    return(sum0)
  }
  ans = 0
  for(i in 1:m1){
    dmat = crossdist(proto,r[[i]])
    if(sum(dmat)>0) ans = ans + ppdist(dmat, type="tt")
```

```
    }
    ans
  }
  proto = list(); canproto = proto
  dnow = sumd(proto,r)
  for(k in 1:100){
  dlast = dnow
  nextx = 0; nexty = 0
  for(i in 1:ncanx){ for(j in 1:ncany){
      canproto = as.ppp(cbind(c(proto$x,candidatesx[i]),
          c(proto$y,candidatesy[j])),W=win)
      a = sumd(canproto,r)
      if(a < dnow){
          nextx = candidatesx[i]; nexty = candidatesy[j]
          dnow = a
          }
  }}
  if(dnow == dlast) break
  cat(k,dnow,nextx,nexty,"\n")
  proto = as.ppp(cbind(c(proto$x,nextx),
          c(proto$y,nexty)),W=win)
  }
  plot(proto,main="")
  points(0,0)
  mtext(s=1,l=2,"horizontal distance \n from mainshock (km)")
    mtext(s=1,l=0,c("-10","0","10"),at=c(-1/11.1,0,1/11.1))
    mtext(s=2,l=-6,"vertical distance \n from mainshock (km)")
    mtext(s=2,l=-8,c("-10","0","10"),at=c(-1/11.1,0,1/11.1))
```

Given a collection of realizations of a marked point process, one approach to assigning marks to the prototype of the collection is to consider the mark to be an additional dimension of the point process. There are three main problems, however, with treating the marks similarly to how one treats spatial or temporal coordinates. The first is a computational problem and is especially important with large spatial-temporal datasets. Since each coordinate of every point in the prototype of a collection of point process realizations is equal to a coordinate in one of the points in the collection (Tranbarger and Schoenberg, 2010), prototypes are typically determined by searching over large subsets of combinations of observed coordinates (Diez, 2010). Sometimes after adding in another dimension, this exceeds reasonable computing capacity.

A second problem is that in computation of spike-time distance, when considering moving a point of one-point pattern to a point of another point pattern, treating differences in marks comparably to differences in spatial-temporal coordinates is problematic. One may choose movement penalties for the temporal and spatial domains objectively, using the criteria suggested by Tranbarger and Schoenberg (2010) or Diez et al. (2012). These suggested penalties are set so that in determining $d(X, Y)$, given two homogeneous Poisson processes X and Y with rate equal to the observed average rate of the realizations in the dataset, deleting any point in X or moving it the expected distance to its nearest neighbor in Y are equivalent. For a purely spatial point process, if $p_a = p_d = 1$, then the spatial movement cost $p_m(z)$ would simply be $\sqrt{\frac{\pi \bar{n}}{|S|}}$, where $\bar{n}$ is the mean number of points in each spatial-point process realization and $|S|$ represents the total area of the spatial support. Similarly, for a purely temporal point process, the temporal movement cost $p_m(t)$ would simply be $\frac{\bar{n}}{\Delta t}$, where Δt is the length of the temporal support for the data. Typically, distance for multiple-dimensional spike-time metrics are considered in the L1 norm, which conveniently allows for separate consideration of the spatial and temporal movement penalties for a spatial-temporal prototype. If $p_a \neq p_d$, then one may add the constraint that the prototype should have its number of points equal to the median number over the realizations in the dataset (Diez et al., 2012). The above criteria are shown in Schoenberg and Tranbarger (2008) and Diez et al. (2012) to yield useful summaries of central tendency for spatial-temporal point processes. In the case of marked point processes, distances in marks can be treated in a similar manner.

For applications to events such as earthquakes or wildfires, a third complication with treating the mark space in an analogous manner to the spatial and temporal coordinates lies in the fact that most of the events are small in size, but the largest earthquakes and wildfires are of critical importance in forecasting and in summarizing previous activity. In the computation of spike-time distance, assigning a sizable penalty for moving points in the mark dimension results in many of the points with large marks being deleted rather than moved to points in the prototype. Thus, the prototype is constructed essentially by ignoring many of the largest earthquakes or wildfires in the dataset. On the other hand, if a very small penalty is used for moving the marks of the points, then events with very different sizes will be given comparable weight in determining the prototype and, since most earthquakes and wildfires are small, the smallest ones will tend to have undue impact in determining the representation of the typical realization in the dataset.

In the *marked* case, given a collection of space-time (or purely spatial, or purely temporal) marked point patterns, one can first construct an initial prototype P of the realizations ignoring the marks. That is, find P by minimizing $\sum D(N_i, P)$ using spike-time distance in time and space only (or equivalently, setting the moving penalty for changes in mark to zero). If the spatial support may reasonably be approximated by a rectangle, then appropriate values for the moving penalty parameters p_m governing the spike-time distance metric may be set using the relations

$$p_m(t) = \frac{\bar{n}}{\Delta t}, \quad p_m(x) = \sqrt{\frac{\pi \bar{n}}{|S_x|}}, \quad \text{and} \quad p_m(y) = \sqrt{\frac{\pi \bar{n}}{|S_y|}},$$

where $p_m(t)$, $p_m(x)$, and $p_m(t)$ denote the moving penalties along the temporal axis, the x-axis, and the y-axis, respectively, and Δ_t, $|S_x|$, and $|S_y|$ represent the total duration, longitudinal range, and latitudinal range, respectively, of the spatial-temporal domain. To create a prototype of a purely spatial marked point process, one can either ignore the times associated with the points or simply set the movement penalty in the temporal direction to zero. Similarly, setting the spatial moving penalties to zero results in a prototype of the marginal temporal marked point process.

For a spatial-temporal *marked* point process, one approach can be to temporarily ignore the marks in constructing the spatial-temporal prototype, and then add in the marks later as follows. For each point P_j in the prototype, consider the collection of points x_{ij} across all observed point patterns such that the point x_{ij} is moved to P_j in the computation of the spike-time distance $D(N_i, P)$. These points $\{x_{ij} : i = 1, \ldots, m\}$ may be thought of as the points in the data most closely associated with the point P_j. The mark associated with the point P_j is defined as the mean of the marks associated with the points $\{x_{ij} : i = 1, \ldots, m\}$. The end result is a prototype P where each point P_j has an assigned value for its mark determined entirely by the observation points that contribute, in terms of spike-time distance, to that point of the prototype. This method was used for instance in Nichols et al. (2011) to delineate the wildfire seasons in Southern California.

4.6 Exercises

4.1. Suppose N is the one-point process on the unit circle, guaranteed to have a point at the origin and no other points. What is the F-function for this process? What is the G-function?

4.2. Suppose N is the non-simple process on $S =$ the unit circle, with two points occurring right at the origin. What is the F-function for this process? What is the G-function?

4.3. Suppose N is the two-point process on $S =$ the unit circle, with two points uniformly distributed independently on S. What is the F-function for this process? What is the G-function?

4.4. Simulate a stationary temporal Poisson process with rate 3 from time 0 to time 100, and construct the rescaled range (R/S) plot for the simulation.

4.5. Suppose N is a spatial point process on the unit square $[0, 1] \times [0, 1]$. Suppose in a given realization, N happens to have just 4 points and the points occur at (0.4, 0.7), (0.5, 0.6), (0.6, 0.5), and (0.8, 0.2). What is the naive estimate of the K-function, $\check{K}(r)$, at $r = 0.2$? Is this higher or lower than πr^2?

4.6. Simulate 10 stationary spatial Poisson processes on the unit square, and compute their prototype. Plot the 10 simulated processes and plot their prototype.

4.7. Compute the prototype for all 11 San Bernardino mainshock earthquakes with magnitude $\geq$4.5 and their aftershocks within 10 km and within 1 year after the corresponding mainshock.

4.8. Consider the times (in days) of aftershocks from the 4 San Bernardino mainshock earthquakes with magnitude ≥ 5.0 and their aftershocks within $10km$ and within 1 year after the corresponding mainshock. Ignoring spatial locations of the aftershocks, treat time since mainshock as the only coordinate, and compute the temporal prototype of the aftershocks.

4.9. Consider the time (in years) and magnitudes of aftershocks from the 4 San Bernardino mainshock earthquakes with magnitude ≥ 5.0 and their aftershocks within $10km$ and within 1 year after the corresponding mainshock. Ignoring spatial locations of the aftershocks, treat magnitude and time since mainshock in years as if they were spatial coordinates, and compute the time-magnitude prototype of the aftershocks.

4.10. Suppose $\{N_1, \ldots, N_k\}$ is a collection of m spatial stationary Poisson patterns on the unit circle, where k is very large. Suppose $p_a = p_d = 1$. Describe what the prototype of this collection would converge to as $p_m \to \infty$.

4.11. Continuing the previous problem, how would the prototype change as $p_m \to 0$?

4.12. Thought exercise: can point processes be described using group theory? Consider the collection of stationary purely temporal point processes each defined over the entire real line $\mathbf{R}$, and measured according to their K-function or some other measure of clustering. Let the stationary Poisson processes be zero, and let $+$ denote superposition. Then if N is clustered and M is inhibitory an equivalent degree, so that the superposition $N + M$ is neither clustered nor inhibitory, then $N + M = 0$. Thus, these point processes may form a group under superposition. Can you think of a useful homomorphism and apply the fundamental theorem of group theory?

References

Ali, M., Dwyer, D., & Rizzo, J. (2011). The social contagion effect of suicidal behavior in adolescents: Does it really exist? *Journal of Mental Health Policy and Economics, 14*(1), 3–12.

Baddeley A, Rubak E, & Turner R. (2015). *Spatial point patterns: methodology and applications with R.* London: CRC Press.

Baddeley, A., Davies, T. M., & Hazelton, M. L. (2025). An improved estimator of the pair correlation function of a spatial point process. *Biometrika, 112*(2), asaf021.

Bearman, P. S., & Moody, J. (2004). Suicide and friendships among American adolescents. *American Journal of Public Health, 94*(1), 89–95.
Besag, J. E. (1977). Discussion contribution to Ripley (1977). *Journal of the Royal Statistical Society, 39*, 193–195.
Billingsley, P. (1968). *Convergence of probability measures*. New York: Wiley.
Cheng, Q., Li, H., Silenzio, V., & Caine, E. (2014). Suicide contagion: A systematic review of definitions and research utility. *PLOS One, 9*(9), 1–9.
Clegg, R. (2006). A practical guide to measuring the hurst parameter. *International Journal of Simulation: Systems, Science and Technology, 7*(2), 3–14.
Cordi, M., Challet, D., & Toke, I.-M. (2017). Testing the causality of Hawkes processes with time reversal. *Journal of Statistical Mechanics: Theory and Experiment,2018*, Article 033408.
Cressie, N. A. C. (1993). *Statistics for spatial data (revised)*. New York: Wiley.
Daley, D. J. (1999). The Hurst index of long-range dependent renewal processes. *Annals of Probability, 27*(4), 2035–2041.
Daley, D. J., & Jones, D. V. (2003). *An introduction to the theory of point processes: Elementary theory of point processes*. New York: Springer.
Diez, D. (2010). Extensions of distance and prototype methods for point patterns. Los Angeles. Ph.D. Thesis.
Diez, D., Schoenberg, F., & Woody, C. D. (2012). Algorithms for computing spike time distance and point process prototypes with application to feline neuronal responses to acoustic stimuli. *Journal of Neuroscience Methods, 203*(1), 186–192.
Diggle, P. J. (2014). Statistical analysis of spatial and spatio-temporal point patterns. Monographs on statistics and applied probability 128. Boca Raton, FL: CRC Press. 3rd ed.
Guan, Y. (2007). A least-squares cross-validation bandwidth selection approach in pair correlation function estimation. *Statistics and Probability Letters, 77*, 1722–9.
Guan, Y. (2007). A composite likelihood cross-validation approach in selecting bandwidth for the estimation of the pair correlation function. *Scandinavian Journal of Statistics, 34*, 336–46.
Harte, D. (2001). *Multifractals: Theory and applications*. New York: Chapman and Hall/CRC.
Hawkes, A. G. (1971). Point spectra of some mutually exciting point processes. *Journal of the Royal Statistical Society Series B, 33*, 438–443.
Heinrich, L. (1988). Asymptotic Gaussianity of some estimators for reduced factorial moment measures and product densities of stationary Poisson cluster processes. *Statistics, 19*, 87–106.
Hitchcock, F. L. (1941). The distribution of a product from several sources to numerous localities. *Journal of Mathematical Physics, 20*, 224–230.
Hurst, H. E. (1951). Long term storage capacity of reservoirs. *Transactions of the American Society of Civil Engineers, 116*, 770–808.
Illian J, Penttinen A, Stoyan H, & Stoyan D. (2008). *Statistical analysis and modelling of spatial point patterns*. Chichester: John Wiley and Sons.
Isham V, & Westcott M. (1979). A self-correcting point process. *Stochastic Processes and their Applications, 8*(3), 335–347.
Jalilian, A., Guan, Y., & Waagepetersen, R. (2019). Orthogonal series estimation of the pair correlation function of a spatial point process. *Statistica Sinica, 29*, 769–87.
Jalilian, A., & Waagepetersen, R. (2018). Fast bandwidth selection for estimation of the pair correlation function. *Journal of Statistical Computation and Simulation, 88*, 2001–11.
Lo, A. W. (1991). Long-term memory in stock market prices. *Econometrica, 59*, 1279–1313.
Mandelbrot, B. B. (1975). Limit theorems on the self-normalized range for weakly and strongly dependent processes. *Zeitschrift fur Wahrscheinlichkeitstheorie und Verwandte Gebiete, 31*, 271–285.
Mandelbrot, B. B., & Wallis, J. R. (1969). Robustness of the rescaled range r/s in the measurement in non-cyclic long run statistical dependence. *Water Resources Research, 5*, 967–988.
McGovern, I., Brantingham, P. J., & Schoenberg, F. (2025). Testing for causal clustering in point processes. *Journal of Applied Science and Innovation Studies, 2*(1), 1–10.
McGovern, I., & Schoenberg, F. (2024). Application of tests for contagion in point processes to measles, Chlamydia, Lyme disease, and suicide. *Journal of Epidemiology and Community Health, Medical Research Archives, 12*(9), 1–12.
Monge, G. (1781). Mémoire sur la Théorie des Déblais et des Remblais. Histoire de l'Academie Royale des Sciences. Paris
Nichols, K., Schoenberg, F., Keeley, J., Bray, A., & Diez, D. (2011). The application of prototype point processes for the summary and description of California wildfires. *Journal of Time Series Analysis, 32*(4), 420–429.
Ogata, Y., & Abe, K. (1991). Some statistical features of the long-term variation of the global and regional seismic activity. *International Statistical Review, 59*(2), 139–161.
Park, J., Schoenberg, F., Brantingham, P. J., & Bertozzi, A. L. (2021). Investigating clustering and violence interruption in gang-related violent crime data using spatial-temporal point processes with covariates. *JASA, 116*(536), 1674–1687.
Ripley, B. D. (1976). The second-order analysis of stationary point processes. *Journal of Applied Probability, 13*(2), 255–266.

Ripley, B. D. (1988). *Statistical inference for spatial processes*. Cambridge: Cambridge University Press.
Rubner, Y., Tomasi, C., & Guias, L. (2000). The earth mover's distance as a metric for image retrieval. *International Journal of Computer Vision, 40*(2), 99–121.
Schoenberg, F., & Tranbarger, K. E. (2008). Description of earthquake aftershock sequences using prototype point processes. *Environmetrics, 19*, 271–286.
Stoyan, D., Kendall, W. S., & Mecke, J. (1995). *Stochastic geometry and its applications* (2nd ed.). New York: Wiley.
Stoyan, D., & Stoyan, H. (1994). *Fractals, random shapes and point fields*. Chichester: Wiley.
Tranbarger, K. E., & Schoenberg, F. (2010). On the computation and application of point process prototypes. *Open Applied Informatics Journal, 4*, 1–9.
Victor, J. D., & Purpura, K. P. (1997). Metric-space analysis of spike trains: Theory, algorithms and application. *Network Computation in Neural Systems, 8*, 127–164.
Whittle, P. (1962). Gaussian estimation in stationary time series. *Bulletin of the International Statistical Institute, 39*, 105–129.

5 Model Evaluation

Assessing the goodness-of-fit for point processes is much more difficult than for other types of data. With regression data or time series data, for every observation, there is a corresponding residual, indicating the amount the forecasted response would have been off by if the fitted model had been used to predict it, and a very natural first step in evaluating a model is simply to examine the residuals. Similarly, with many types of spatial or spatial-temporal data, such as geostatistical or lattice data, one similarly can define a residual corresponding to each observation as the observed response minus the fitted response according to the model. With point processes, however, where the observations are points but the fitted model is typically a fitted process λ, residuals are not quite as easy to define.

Fortunately, recent statistical developments in the assessment of space-time point process models have resulted in new, powerful model evaluation tools. These tools include residual point process methods such as rescaling, super-thinning, pixel-based methods such as Pearson residuals and deviance residuals, Voronoi residuals, and weighted second-order statistics for assessing particular features of a model such as its background rate or the degree of spatial clustering. Residual analysis methods for spatial point process models, such as rescaling and super-thinning, involve transforming the point process using a model for the conditional intensity λ and then inspecting the uniformity of the result. The difficult problem of evaluating the agreement between a possibly complex spatial-temporal point process model and data thus boils down to the apparently simpler problem of assessing the homogeneity of the residual point process, a task for which many standard tests are available.

A note of caution should be made concerning the use of the model assessment tools in this chapter. It is common to estimate the conditional intensity function non-parametrically, for example, using a kernel smoother. If the selection of the tuning parameter is done while simultaneously assessing the fit of the resulting model, this will likely lead to a model that is overfit. A simple way to avoid this danger is to have a clear separation between the model fitting stage and the model assessment stage, as occurs commonly in machine learning or when models are developed for prospective experiments, such as the Regional Earthquake Likelihood Models (RELM) project (Field et al., 2007) and its successor, the Collaboratory for the Study of Earthquake Predictability, or *CSEP* (Schorlemmer & Gerstenberger, 2007), which is discussed later in this chapter.

CSEP, which is run by the Southern California Earthquake Center, has since 2007 hosted a variety of models in prospective experiments that forecast the expected number of earthquakes to occur in particular magnitude ranges occurring in predetermined spatial-temporal grid cells. The forecasts in CSEP must be made on a purely prospective basis: the computer code for calculating forecasts must be submitted completely in advance, and no changes or retrospective adjustments may be made by humans

F. Schoenberg, *Space-Time Point Processes*, Springer Texts in Statistics,
https://doi.org/10.1007/978-3-032-20790-6_5

after the fact. As a result, the analyses in CSEP are not fraught with problems such as overfitting, publication bias, and other problems common in retrospective analyses of earthquake forecasts. In particular, the problem of overfitting is not a major concern for forecasts in CSEP. However, when models are fit retrospectively and then their goodness-of-fit is assessed, overfitting can be a serious problem, especially when elements of the model are fit non-parametrically.

5.1 Pixel-Based Residuals

Perhaps the most obvious way to obtain a kind of analogue of regression residuals in the context of space-time point processes is to divide the observation region up into spatial-temporal grid cells or *pixels*, $B_1, \ldots, B_m$, and compare the observed and expected number of points in each pixel. That is, for each pixel (or *cell*), one computes either the difference between the observed and expected numbers of points, or some other measure of goodness-of-fit.

5.1.1 Raw Residuals

Given a model for the conditional intensity $\hat{\lambda}$, the most natural way to define a residual for pixel B_i would be

$$R(B_i) = N(B_i) - \int_{B_i} \hat{\lambda}(t, x, y) dt dx dy. \tag{5.1}$$

Such residuals $R(B_i)$ are sometimes called *raw* residuals. Baddeley et al. (2005) introduced methods for residual analysis of purely spatial point processes, based on comparing the total number of points to the number forecast by the model as in (5.1). Baddeley et al. (2005) considered a residual *field* which then could be smoothed or aggregated over an arbitrary portion of the space; in practice, these residuals are typically evaluated over predetermined pixels. For instance, in evaluating forecasts of CSEP models for earthquake occurrences, the models are essentially constrained to have a constant conditional intensity within pre-specified pixels established by CSEP, so these same pixels are very natural units for assessment. In other cases, it is up to the evaluator to determine these spatial or spatial-temporal grid cells.

5.1.2 Pearson Residuals

Baddeley et al. (2005) proposed various ways to standardize the raw residuals, and although they considered purely spatial point processes characterized by their Papangelou intensities, their methods extend readily to the spatial-temporal case as well, with the Papangelou intensity replaced by the conditional intensity, λ. Some of these standardized residuals are described below.

One may wish to rescale the raw residuals in such a way that they have mean 0 and variance approximately equal to 1. *Pearson residuals* are defined as

$$R_P(B_i) = \sum_{(t_j, x_j, y_j) \in B_i} \frac{1}{\sqrt{\hat{\lambda}(t_j x_j, y_j)}} - \int_{B_i} \sqrt{\hat{\lambda}(t, x, y)} dt dx dy,$$

for all points (t_j, x_j, y_j) with $\hat{\lambda}(t_j, x_j, y_j) > 0$. These residuals are analogous to Pearson residuals in Poisson regression.

Standardization is important for both residual plots and goodness-of-fit tests, since otherwise plots of the residuals will tend to overemphasize deviations in pixels where the rate is high. Behind the term Pearson residuals lies the implication that these standardized residuals should be approximately standard normally distributed, so that the squared residuals, or their sum, are distributed approximately according to Pearson's χ^2-distribution.

5.1.3 Pixel Size

The excellent treatment of Pearson residuals and other scaled residuals by Baddeley et al. (2005), the thorough discussion of their properties in Baddeley et al. (2008), their use for formal inference using score and pseudo-score statistics as described in Baddeley et al. (2011), and the fact that such residuals extend so readily to the case of spatial-temporal point processes may suggest that the problem of residual analysis for such point processes is generally solved. In practice, however, such residuals, when examined over a fixed rectangular grid, tend to be problematic.

As noted in Bray et al. (2014), if the pixels are too large, then their power to detect local inconsistencies between the model and data is low, as locations in the interior of a pixel where the modeled conditional rate is too high may cancel out with places where the model underestimates the conditional rate. There is essentially a loss of information in such situations.

On the other hand, when spatial-temporal pixels are small and/or the estimated conditional intensity in some pixels is very low, the raw and standardized residuals tend to be highly skewed. In these situations where the residuals have a highly skewed distribution, the skew is typically intensified by the standardization to Pearson residuals.

Since Pearson residuals are standardized to have mean zero and unit (or approximately unit) variance under the null hypothesis that the modeled conditional intensity is correct (see Baddeley et al., 2007), one may inquire whether the skew of these residuals is indeed problematic. Consider, for instance, the case of a spatial-temporal Poisson process where the estimate of the intensity $\lambda(t, x, y)$ is exactly correct, that is, $\hat{\lambda}(t, x, y) = \lambda(t, x, y)$ at all space-time locations, and where one elects to use Pearson residuals on pixels. Suppose that there are several pixels where the integral of λ over the pixel is roughly 0.01. Given many of these pixels, it is not unlikely that at least one of them will contain a point of the process. In such pixels, the raw residual will be 0.99, and the standard deviation of the number of points in the pixel is $\sqrt{0.01} = 0.1$, so the Pearson residual is 9.90.

In such cases, the skew may severely complicate the analysis. Often the majority of the raw residuals are close to zero while those that contain an event are close to one, and thus graphical displays of the raw or Pearson residuals usually highlight little more than the locations of the points themselves. As a result, in these situations plots of both the raw and the Pearson residuals are not informative, and merely highlight the pixels where events occur regardless of the fit of the model. A few highly skewed Pearson residuals may overwhelm the others in a visual inspection, rendering a plot of the Pearson residuals largely useless in terms of evaluating the quality of the fit of the model. Further, conventional tests based on the normal approximation may have grossly incorrect p-values, and will commonly reject the null model even when it is correct. In the hypothetical example described above where the Pearson residual is 9.90, even if one adjusts for the non-normality of the residual and instead uses exact p-values based on the Poisson distribution, such a test applied to any such pixel containing a point will still reject the model at the significance level of 0.01.

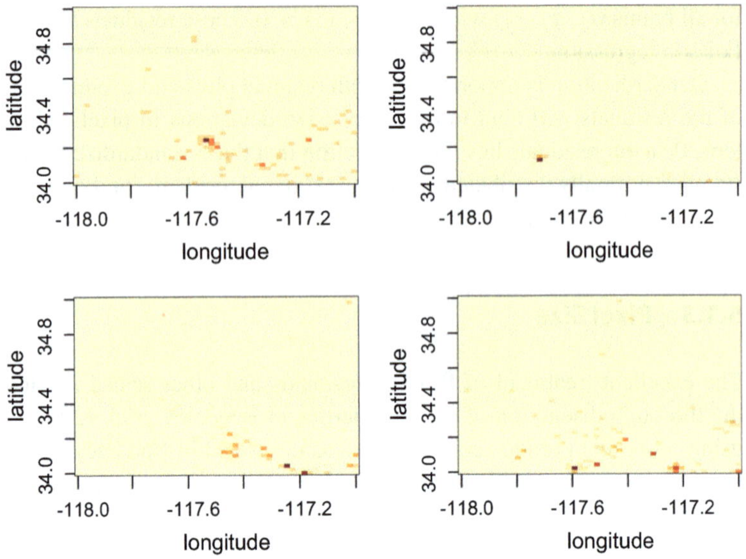

Fig. 5.1 Counts of number of San Bernardino earthquakes recorded in each pixel, for a regular 4 × 50 × 50 grid of pixels. (top-left) Counts of San Bernardino earthquakes from 1/1/1970 through 12/31/1983. (top-right) San Bernardino earthquake counts from 1/1/1984 to 12/31/1997. (bottom-left) Counts of San Bernardino earthquakes from 1/1/1998 through 12/31/2011. (bottom-right) Counts of San Bernardino earthquakes from 1/1/2012 to 12/31/2025

5.1.4 Examples

Figure 5.1 shows the number of San Bernardino earthquakes is each pixel, for a regular grid of $4 \times 50 \times 50$ pixels, with each pixel representing a 14 years $\times 0.02^\circ \times 0.02^\circ$ grid. Below is the code to construct Fig. 5.1, after downloading and editing the file "SearchResults.txt" as described in Chap. 1.

```
x = read.table("SearchResults.txt",skip=2,fill=TRUE)
t = julian(as.Date(x$V1),origin = as.Date("1970-01-01")) + x$V2/24 +
    x$V3/24/60 + x$V4/24/60/60
maxt = julian(as.Date("2025-01-01"),origin = as.Date("1970-01-01"))
z = list(); z$t = t; z$lon = x$V10+118; z$lat = x$V9-34;
z$m = x$V7; z$n = length(z$t); n = z$n; M0 = 3.5
dat = array(0,dim=c(4,50,50))
for(i in 1:n){
  j1 = ceiling(z$t[i]/maxt*4)
  j2 =  ceiling(z$lon[i]*50)
  j3 = ceiling(z$lat[i]*50)
  dat[j1,j2,j3] = dat[j1,j2,j3] + 1
  }
par(mfrow=c(2,2))
xs = seq(-118,-117,length=50); ys = seq(34,35,length=50)
image(xs,ys,dat[1,,],xlab="longitude",ylab="latitude")
image(xs,ys,dat[2,,],xlab="longitude",ylab="latitude")
image(xs,ys,dat[3,,],xlab="longitude",ylab="latitude")
image(xs,ys,dat[4,,],xlab="longitude",ylab="latitude")
```

Figures 5.2 and 5.3 show the raw and Pearson residuals, respectively, for the $4 \times 50 \times 50$ pixel grid for the fitted ETAS model fit to the San Bernardino earthquakes times and locations. Standardization via Pearson residuals does taper down the very large residuals near longitude –117.5 and latitude 34.1. However, in the other pixels, because of the problem of skew, the raw residuals simply mirror the pixels that happen to have earthquakes, rather than highlighting where the model fits well or poorly, and the standardization to Pearson residuals actually makes the problem worse.

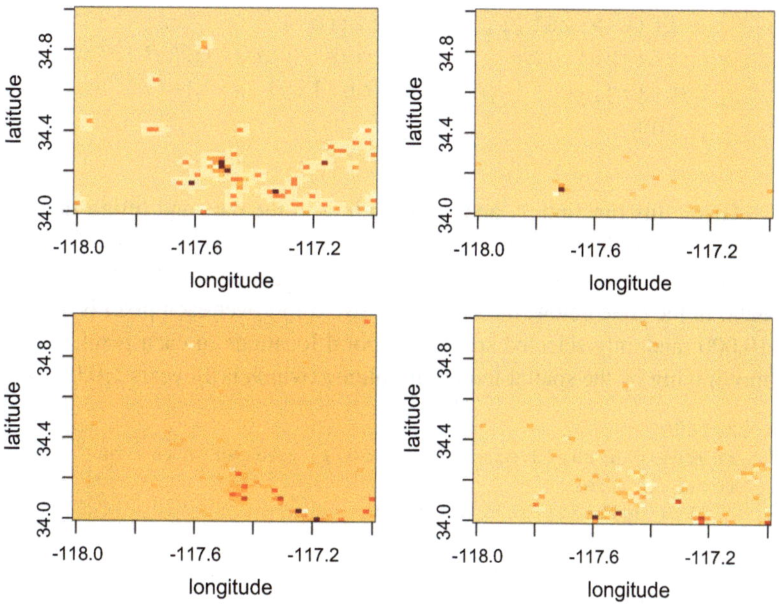

Fig. 5.2 (left) Raw residuals for ETAS model fit to San Bernardino earthquakes, for a regular 4 × 50 × 50 grid of pixels. (top-left) Raw residuals from 1/1/1970 through 12/31/1983. (top-right) Raw residuals from 1/1/1984 to 12/31/1997. (bottom-left) Raw residuals from 1/1/1998 through 12/31/2011. (bottom-right) Raw residuals from 1/1/2012 to 12/31/2025

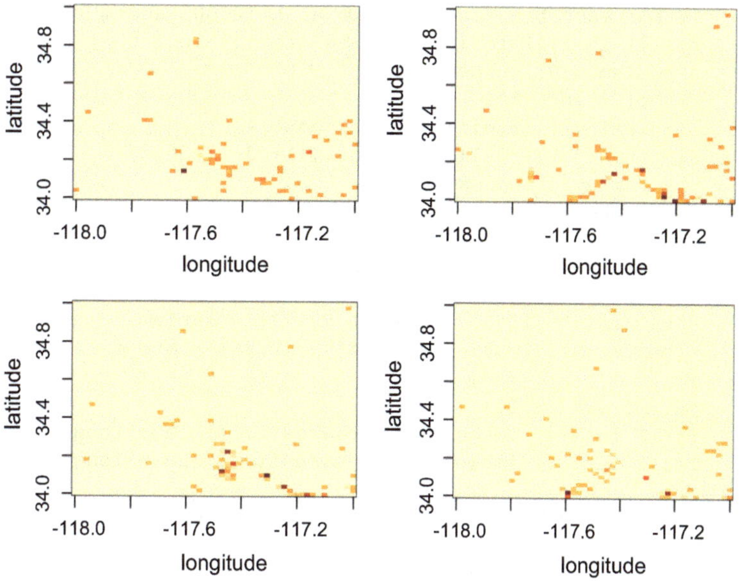

Fig. 5.3 (left) Pearson residuals for ETAS model fit to San Bernardino earthquakes, for the same regular 4 × 50 × 50 grid of pixels. (top-left) Peason residuals from 1/1/1970 through 12/31/1983. (top-right) Pearson residuals from 1/1/1984 to 12/31/1997. (bottom-left) Pearson residuals from 1/1/1998 through 12/31/2011. (bottom-right) Pearson residuals from 1/1/2012 to 12/31/2025

Before providing the code to construct Figs. 5.2 and 5.3, it will be useful, here and in what follows later in this chapter, to have a function, *f*, that computes the conditional intensity, $\lambda(t, x, y)$, for the ETAS model fit by MLE, at any spatial-temporal location (t, x, y) in the observation region.

```
mu = theta2[1]; K = theta2[2]; c = theta2[3]; p = theta2[4]
a = theta2[5]; d = theta2[6]; q = theta2[7]; n = z$n;
f = function(t,x,y,z){ ## compute lambda(t,x,y) given data z
    j = 0
    gij = 0
    lam = mu
```

```
    if(t > z$t[1]) j = max(c(1:z$n)[z$t<t])
    if(j>0) lam = mu + const*sum(exp(a*(z$m[1:j]-M0))*(t -
  z$t[1:j]+c)^(-p)*((z$lon[1:j]-x)^2+(z$lat[1:j]-y)^2+d)^(-q))
    lam
}
```

Given this function f, and after reading in the data and fitting the model as described in Chaps. 1 and 3, the following code can be used to construct Figs. 5.2 and 5.3, which show the raw residuals and Pearson residuals, respectively, for the ETAS model, fit by MLE to the San Bernardino earthquake data. In the code below, the integral of $\lambda(t, x, y)$ over each pixel is approximated by calculating λ at 10,000 randomly selected spatial-temporal locations in each pixel, averaging these values of λ and multiplying by the spatial-temporal volume (which is 14 years $\times 0.02° \times 0.02°$).

```
k=10000
rawres = array(0,dim=c(4,50,50)); peares = rawres
for(i in 1:n){
  j1 = ceiling(z$t[i]/maxt*4)
  j2 =  ceiling(z$lon[i]*50)
  j3 = ceiling(z$lat[i]*50)
  peares[j1,j2,j3] = peares[j1,j2,j3] + 1/sqrt(f(z$t[i],z$lon[i],z$lat[i],z))
  }
## For each bin, average lam at k=10000 random locations.
for(j1 in 1:4) for(j2 in 1:50) for(j3 in 1:50){
  sumlam = 0; sumpea = 0
  for(j4 in 1:k){
    lam1 = f((runif(1)+j1-1)*maxt/4,
    (runif(1)+j2-1)/50,(runif(1)+j3-1)/50,z)
    sumlam = sumlam + lam1
    sumpea = sumpea + sqrt(lam1)
    }
  intlam = sumlam/k*maxt/4/50/50
  intpea = sumpea/k*maxt/4/50/50
  rawres[j1,j2,j3] = dat[j1,j2,j3] - intlam
  peares[j1,j2,j3] = peares[j1,j2,j3] -intpea
}
par(mfrow=c(2,2))
for(i in 1:4) image(xs,ys,rawres[i,,],xlab="longitude",ylab="latitude")
for(i in 1:4) image(xs,ys,peares[i,,],xlab="longitude",ylab="latitude")
```

Consider a poorly fitting model for comparison. For instance, suppose we fit a Poisson model with rate

$$\lambda(t, x, y) = \beta_1 + \beta_2 t + \beta_3 t^2 + \beta_4 x + \beta_5 x^2 + \beta_6 y + \beta_7 y^2. \tag{5.2}$$

The model (5.2) has no clustering at all and is therefore incapable of fitting the highly clustered San Bernardino earthquake data well.

The code below can be used to fit the model (5.2) to the San Bernardino earthquake data by MLE (again, after having loaded in the data). One thing to watch out for with a model such as (5.2) is that the conditional intensity λ could be negative for some spatial-temporal locations, or zero at one of the points, for some values of the parameters. In order to try to avoid this scenario, in the code below, if the conditional intensity is less than 10^{-20} at any of the points or at any of the corners of the spatial-temporal observation region, then a very large positive value is returned for the negative log-likelihood, which is then minimized, so such values for the parameters will be averted. The model

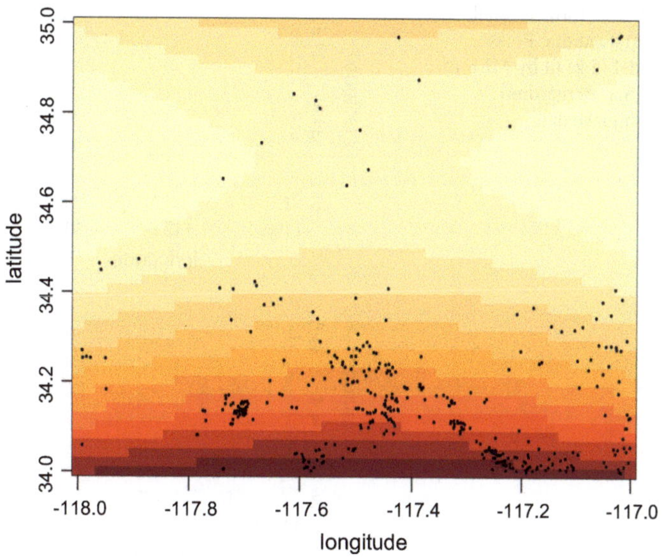

Fig. 5.4 Quadratic Poisson model (5.2) fit by MLE to the San Bernardino earthquake data. Rates λ are aggregated over all days. Earthquakes are shown in black

(5.2) has the advantages of simplicity and ease of interpretation, but an alternative would be to model $\log(\lambda)$ as a quadratic in t, x, and y, in order to ensure that λ is positive at all locations for any values of the parameters.

```
loglpois = function(beta){
cat("\n",beta,"\n")
## I am assuming here that t goes from 0 to maxt and x and y from 0 to 1.
intlam = maxt*(beta[1]+beta[2]*maxt/2 + beta[3]*maxt^2/3 + beta[4]/2 +
        beta[5]/3 + beta[6]/2 + beta[7]/3)
if(intlam < 0) return(1e+20)
lam = beta[1] + beta[2]*z$t + beta[3]*z$t^2 + beta[4]*z$lon +
        beta[5]*z$lon^2 + beta[6]*z$lat + beta[7]*z$lat^2
## make sure lambda is positive at the pts
if(min(lam)<1e-20) return(1e+20)
## make sure lambda is positive at the corners of the space
cornert = c(rep(0,4),rep(maxt,4))
cornerx = rep(c(0,1),4); cornery = rep(c(0,0,1,1),2)
lamcorn = beta[1] + beta[2]*cornert + beta[3]*cornert^2 + beta[4]*cornerx +
             beta[5]*cornerx^2 + beta[6]*cornery + beta[7]*cornery^2
if(min(lamcorn)<1e-20) return(1e+20)
sumlog = sum(log(lam))
loglik = sumlog - intlam
cat("loglike is ", loglik, ". sumlog = ", sumlog,". integral = ", intlam,".\n")
return(-1.0*loglik)
}
theta1 = c(z$n/maxt,rep(0,6))
b1 = optim(theta1,loglpois)
b2 = optim(b1$par,loglpois)
```

The fit of the model is shown in Fig. 5.4. The model fits especially poorly to the cluster of events around longitude –117.75 and latitude 34.15.

The code below was used to make Fig. 5.4. It also creates a function, g, that computes the estimated rate $\hat{\lambda}(t, x, y)$ according to model (5.2), for any spatial-temporal location (t, x, y).

```
beta = b2$par
```

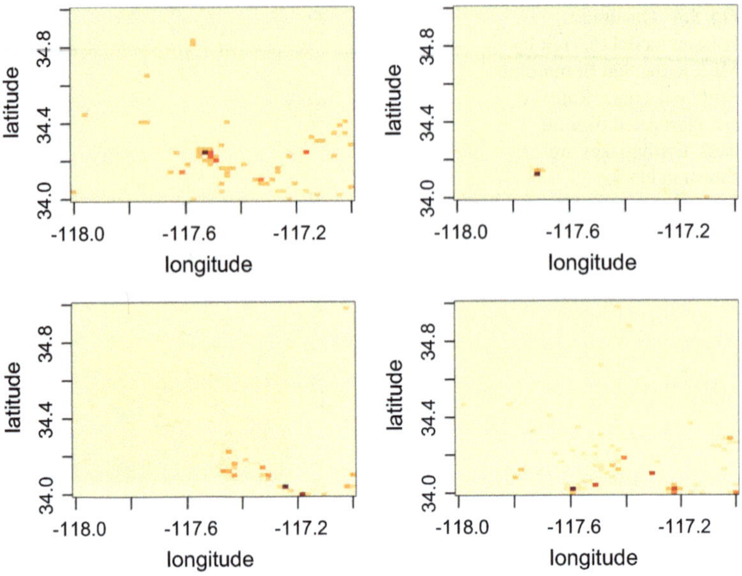

Fig. 5.5 Raw residuals from quadratic Poisson model (5.2) fit by MLE to the San Bernardino earthquake data

```
fit = matrix(0,ncol=50,nrow=50)
for(i in 1:50) for(j in 1:50)
    fit[i,j] = maxt*(beta[1] + beta[2]*maxt/2 + beta[3]*maxt^2/3 +
    beta[4]*i/50 + beta[5]*(i/50)^2 + beta[6]*j/50 + beta[7]*(j/50)^2)
image(xs,ys,fit,xlab="longitude",ylab="latitude")
points(-118+z$lon,34+z$lat,cex=.2)
g = function(t,x,y) beta[1] + beta[2]*t + beta[3]*t^2 + beta[4]*x +
    beta[5]*x^2 + beta[6]*y + beta[7]*y^2
```

Using this function g, we can now easily create raw and Pearson residuals for the fitted Poisson model fit to the San Bernardino earthquakes. The results are shown in Figs. 5.5 and 5.6. For datasets such as these, whether the model fits very poorly, like the Poisson model, or relatively well, like the ETAS model, the resulting plots look roughly similar either way, and seem to merely highlight where most of the events happened to occur. Code for producing these plots is below.

```
k=10000
rawrespois = array(0,dim=c(4,50,50)); pearespois = rawrespois
for(i in 1:n){
  j1 = ceiling(z$t[i]/maxt*4)
  j2 =  ceiling(z$lon[i]*50)
  j3 = ceiling(z$lat[i]*50)
  pearespois[j1,j2,j3] = pearespois[j1,j2,j3] +
    1/sqrt(g(z$t[i],z$lon[i],z$lat[i]))
  }
## For each bin, average lam at k=10000 random locations.
for(j1 in 1:4) for(j2 in 1:50) for(j3 in 1:50){
  sumlam = 0; sumpea = 0
  for(j4 in 1:k){
    lam1 = g((runif(1)+j1-1)*maxt/4,
    (runif(1)+j2-1)/50,(runif(1)+j3-1)/50)
    sumlam = sumlam + lam1
    sumpea = sumpea + sqrt(lam1)
    }
  intlam = sumlam/k*maxt/4/50/50
```

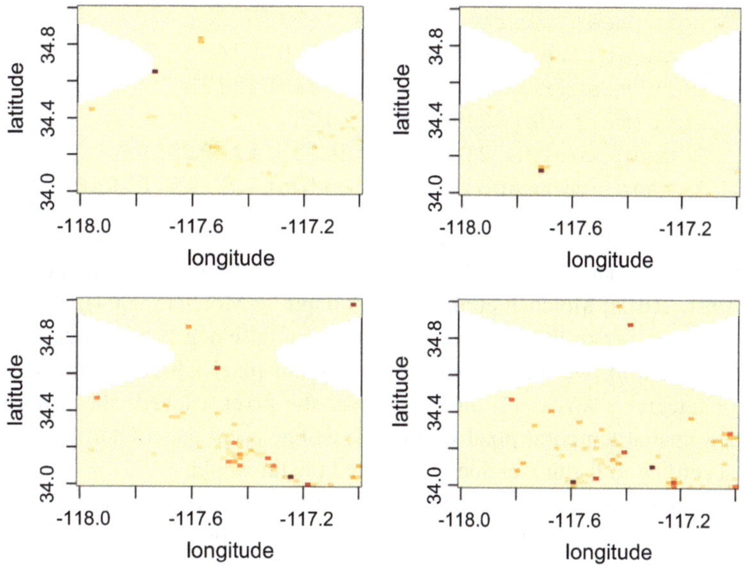

Fig. 5.6 Pearson residuals from quadratic Poisson model (5.2) fit by MLE to the San Bernardino earthquake data

```
    intpea = sumpea/k*maxt/4/50/50
    rawrespois[j1,j2,j3] = dat[j1,j2,j3] - intlam
    pearespois[j1,j2,j3] = pearespois[j1,j2,j3] -intpea
  }
  par(mfrow=c(2,2))
  for(i in 1:4) image(xs,ys,rawrespois[i,,],xlab="longitude",ylab="latitude")
  for(i in 1:4) image(xs,ys,pearespois[i,,],xlab="longitude",ylab="latitude")
```

5.1.5 Numerical Summaries of Residuals

Although graphical displays of the raw and Pearson residuals are not very useful in cases such as the San Bernardino earthquake data, a very useful statistic is the mean of the absolute values of the residuals, sometimes called the MAE (for Mean Absolute Error). The MAE can be interpreted as the typical amount the model would have been "off" by if used to estimate the number of points in each pixel. The root-mean-square (RMS) residual is an alternative that can be interpreted similarly.

For the ETAS model applied to the San Bernardino earthquake data, for instance, the MAE is 0.06373 and the RMS residual is 0.2776. For the quadratic Poisson model (5.2) applied to the San Bernardino earthquake data, by contrast, the MAE is 0.07674 and the RMS residual is 0.3375. Thus, the MAE and RMS residual for the Poisson model are 20.4 and 21.6% higher, respectively, than their counterparts for the ETAS model.

1 minus the ratio of the mean of the squared residuals to the mean of the mean of the squares of the total number of events in each pixel can be interpreted similarly to the R^2 in regression, as the proportion of variation explained by the model. In this case these proportions are 35% for the ETAS model, and just over 4% for the quadratic Poisson model. The code to produce these summaries is below. If standard errors are desired for any of these statistics, they can typically be obtained either by simulating the model and re-estimating it, or by drawing bootstrap samples from the distribution of residuals.

```
mean(abs(rawres)) ## 0.06373
```

```
sqrt(mean(rawres^2)) ## 0.2776
mean(abs(rawrespois)) ## 0.07674
sqrt(mean(rawrespois^2)) ## 0.3375
sqrt(mean(dat^2)) ## 0.3445
1-mean(rawres^2)/mean(dat^2) ## 0.3509
1-mean(rawrespois^2)/mean(dat^2) ## 0.04019
```

Another way to summarize residuals is via error diagrams, which are also sometimes called receiver operating characteristic (ROC) curves (Swets, 1973) or Molchan diagrams (Kagan, 2009; Molchan, 1991, 2010a; Molchan et al., 1997; Zaliapin & Molchan 2004), which plot the (normalized) number of alarms versus the (normalized) number of false negatives, for each possible alarm threshold, where by an *alarm*, we mean any spatial-temporal pixel where the modeled expected number of points, or integral $\int \hat{\lambda}(t, x, y)$, integrated over the pixel, exceeds the given threshold. A *false negative* is any spatial-temporal pixel where at least one point occurs but where the expected number of points according to the model does not exceed the threshold.

Plotting error diagrams with multiple models on the same plot can be a useful way to compare the models' overall forecasting efficacy. For the purpose of comparing models, one may normalize the error diagram so that the false negative rates are considered relative to one of the given models in consideration as in Kagan (2007b). This tends to alleviate a common problem with error diagrams as applied to earthquake forecasts, which is that most of the relevant focus is typically very near the axes and thus it can be difficult to inspect differences between the models graphically. While error diagrams can be useful overall summaries of goodness-of-fit, they unfortunately provide little information regarding where models are fitting poorly or how they may be improved.

5.1.6 Deviance Residuals

A useful method for comparing models is the deviance residual plot proposed in Wong and Schoenberg (2009), in analogy with deviances defined for generalized linear models in the regression framework. As with raw and Pearson residuals, the spatial-temporal domain S is divided into (usually evenly spaced) pixels. Then, the differences between the log-likelihoods within each pixel for the two competing models are examined. That is, given two models for the conditional intensity, $\hat{\lambda}_1$ and $\hat{\lambda}_2$, the deviance residual in any bin, B, of $\hat{\lambda}_1$ against $\hat{\lambda}_2$ is given by $R_{\mathrm{D}}(B) =$

$$\sum_{i:\tau_i \in B} \log(\hat{\lambda}_1(\tau_i)) - \int_B \hat{\lambda}_1(t, x, y)dtdxdy - \left(\sum_{i:\tau_i \in B} \log(\hat{\lambda}_2(\tau_i)) - \int_B \hat{\lambda}_2(t, x, y)dtdxdy \right).$$

Positive residuals imply that the model $\hat{\lambda}_1$ fits better in the given pixel and negative residuals imply that $\hat{\lambda}_2$ provides better fit. By taking the sum of the deviance residuals, $\sum_j R_{\mathrm{D}}(B_j)$, one obtains the overall log-likelihood ratio score, providing an overall measure of relative goodness-of-fit of the two models.

Figures 5.7 and 5.8 show the deviance residuals for the ETAS model versus the quadratic Poisson model, applied to the San Bernardino earthquake data. In Fig. 5.7 the color scale is linear and in Fig. 5.8 the color scale is made to highlight deviances closer to zero. In both plots, the ETAS model fits better than the Poisson model in locations colored red, and the Poisson model fits better in locations colored blue. From Fig. 5.7 one sees that the main difference is that the ETAS model fits much better to the main earthquake clusters, especially that around longitude –117.7 and latitude 34.15. As seen in Fig. 5.8, the Poisson model tends to fit slightly better in the areas in the Northern portion of the observation region where no events occurred, and around many of the events in the Southern portion of the observation

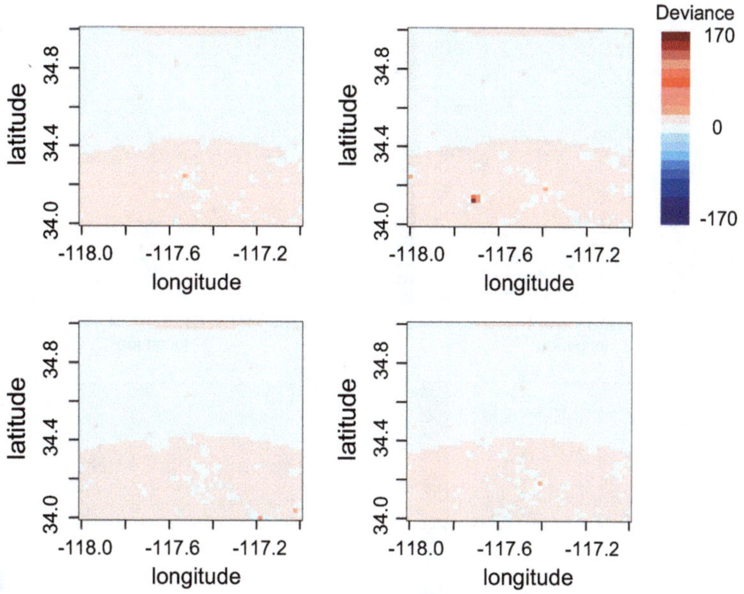

Fig. 5.7 Deviance residuals, for ETAS model relative to quadratic Poisson model (5.2), fit by MLE to the San Bernardino earthquake data, with linear color scale extending to the maximum observed deviance. Positive deviances indicate locations where the log-likelihood for ETAS is higher. Negative deviances indicate locations where the log-likelihood for the Poisson model is higher

region, but in the other areas the ETAS model fits a bit better. Overall, the log-likelihood ratio score is over 700, favoring the ETAS model very substantially, and again, most of this deviance results from the improved fit of ETAS to the earthquake cluster around longitude –117.7 and latitude 34.15. For nested models, the log-likelihood ratio is generally approximately Chi-square distributed, but here the models are non-nested and have differing numbers of estimated parameters. In such cases, the Akaike Information Criterion (AIC) or Bayes Information Criterion (BIC) are often used. The AIC is defined as 2 times the log-likelihood minus 2 times the number of fitted parameters. For competing models, even if non-nested, differences in the AIC of more than the critical value of the Chi-square distribution, with degrees of freedom equal to the difference in the number of parameters estimated for the two models, are generally deemed to indicate statistically significantly better fit (Akaike 1974, 1983; Ogata 1988). In the case considered here, both the ETAS model and the quadratic Poisson model have 7 parameters estimated by MLE; in such cases, differences in AIC greater than 2 are generally considered statistically significant, though more precise estimates can be obtained via simulation and re-estimation.

The code below can be used to generate Figs. 5.7 and 5.8.

```
devr = array(0,dim=c(4,50,50))
for(i in 1:n){
  j1 = ceiling(z$t[i]/maxt*4)
  j2 =  ceiling(z$lon[i]*50)
  j3 = ceiling(z$lat[i]*50)
  devr[j1,j2,j3] = devr[j1,j2,j3] + log(f(z$t[i],z$lon[i],z$lat[i],z)) -
           log(g(z$t[i],z$lon[i],z$lat[i]))
  }
devr = devr + rawres - rawrespois
## we want the sum log(lambda_E) - int_E - sum log(lambda_P) - int_P
## the integral of lambda for each cell is (dat - rawres) for ETAS
## and (dat - rawrespois) for Poisson.
```

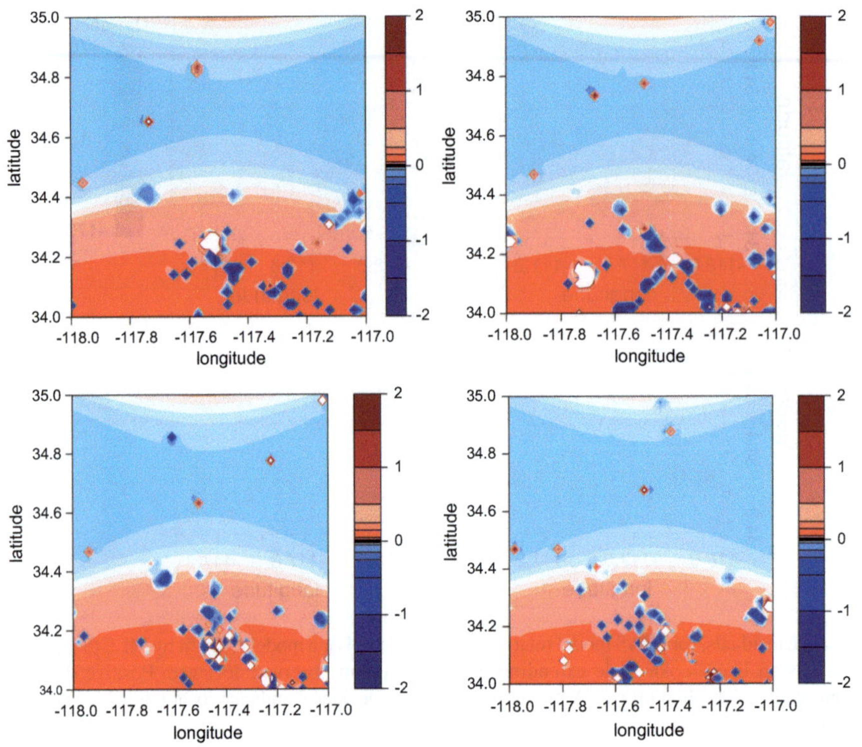

Fig. 5.8 Smoothed deviance residuals less than 2 in absolute value, for ETAS model relative to quadratic Poisson model (5.2), fit by MLE to the San Bernardino earthquake data, with color scale made to highlight the small deviances. Positive deviances indicate locations where the log-likelihood for ETAS is higher. Negative deviances indicate locations where the log-likelihood for the Poisson model is higher

```
mycol = c("Midnight Blue","Navy","Medium Blue","Blue","Royal Blue",
"Dodger Blue", "Deep Sky Blue", "Light Sky Blue", "Light Blue", "Light Cyan",
"Misty Rose", "Light Salmon", "Salmon", "Light Coral", "Orange Red",
"Tomato", "Dark Salmon", "Indian Red", "Firebrick","Dark Red")
mymax = max(abs(devr))
bre = seq(-mymax,mymax,length=21)
par(mfrow=c(2,3))
image(xs,ys,devr[1,,],xlab="longitude",ylab="latitude",breaks=bre,col=mycol)
image(xs,ys,devr[2,,],xlab="longitude",ylab="latitude",breaks=bre,col=mycol)
plot(c(0,10),c(min(bre),max(bre)),type="n",axes=F,xlab="",ylab="")
image(c(-1:1),bre,matrix(rep(bre,2),ncol=21,byrow=T),add=T,col=mycol)
text(2.5,min(bre),as.character(signif(min(bre),2)),cex=1)
text(2.5,0,"0",cex=1)
text(2.5,max(bre),as.character(signif(max(bre),2)),cex=1)
mtext(s=3,l=0,at=1,"Deviance",cex=.75)
image(xs,ys,devr[3,,],xlab="longitude",ylab="latitude",breaks=bre,col=mycol)
image(xs,ys,devr[4,,],xlab="longitude",ylab="latitude",breaks=bre,col=mycol)
sum(devr) ## 744.6
lev = c(-2,-1.5,-1,-.5,-.25,-.15,-.05,-.02,-.01,-.005,0,.005,.01,.02,.05,.15,.25,.5,1,1.5,2)
par(mfrow=c(1,1))
filled.contour(xs,ys,devr[1,,],xlab="longitude",ylab="latitude",levels=lev,col=mycol)
filled.contour(xs,ys,devr[2,,],xlab="longitude",ylab="latitude",levels=lev,col=mycol)
filled.contour(xs,ys,devr[3,,],xlab="longitude",ylab="latitude",levels=lev,col=mycol)
filled.contour(xs,ys,devr[4,,],xlab="longitude",ylab="latitude",levels=lev,col=mycol)
```

The raw, Pearson, or deviance residuals may be smoothed, as in Baddeley et al. (2005). In fact, the deviance residuals in Fig. 5.8 are slightly smoothed in the *R* function *filled.contour()*. This results in very minimal smoothing by default, and if the smoothing is substantial, the resulting plot typically only reveals gross, large-scale inconsistencies between the model and data. It is usually preferable to consider alternative types of residuals, such as those described below.

5.2 Rescaling

Meyer (1971a) investigated rescaling a point process according to its compensator, the integrated conditional intensity. The method involves moving each point to a new time (or location), creating a transformed space in which the rescaled points are homogeneous Poisson of rate one if the model used in the rescaling is correct. This method was used in Ogata (1988) to assess models for earthquake times and magnitudes and extended in Merzbach and Nualart (1986), Nair (1990), Schoenberg (1999), and Vere-Jones and Schoenberg (2004) to the spatial and spatial-temporal cases.

The procedure amounts to stretching or compressing a simple point process according to its compensator, which is the integral of the conditional intensity, λ, in such a way that the times (or any one dimension, really) of the point process N are rescaled in order to obtain a Poisson process with intensity one as long as the model for λ used in the rescaling is correct. More precisely, for each point (t_i, x_i, y_i) of the original point process N on $\mathbb{R}^+ \times \mathbb{R}^2$, the rescaled point process M has a point at $(\int_0^{t_i} \lambda(s, x_i, y_i)ds, x_i, y_i)$. For a purely temporal point process N, each point t_i of N corresponds to a point of the rescaled process M at time $\int_0^{t_i} \lambda(s)ds$. For instance, if N is a stationary Poisson process on $(0, \infty)$ with intensity $\lambda(t)$, the rescaled process M satisfies $M(\int_0^a \lambda(t)dt, \int_0^b \lambda(t)dt) = N(a, b)$. Whether in the spatial-temporal case or the purely temporal case, the resulting process M is a stationary Poisson process with rate one. Heuristically, the space is compressed when λ is small and stretched when λ is large, so that the points are ultimately uniformly distributed in the resulting transformed space, if the model for λ is correct. The interpretation given by Papangelou (1972) for the temporal case was "Roughly, moving in $[0, \infty)$ so as to meet expected future points at a rate of one per time unit (given at each instant complete knowledge of the past), we meet them at the times of a Poisson process".

Meyer (1971a) also observed that for a simple multivariate point process, the temporal coordinates can be rescaled according to the compensator in this way in order to form a sequence of stationary Poisson processes. For a simple space-time point process, one may choose any one axis and rescale it. For instance, one may choose to rescale the x-axis, and move each observation (t_i, x_i, y_i), to the new rescaled position $(t_i, \int_0^{x_i} \hat{\lambda}(t_i, x, y_i)dx, y_i)$, and assess the space-time homogeneity of the resulting process. This sort of method was used for model evaluation by Berman (1986) and by Ogata (1988) to assess an ETAS model fit to earthquake data, and by Schoenberg (2003) for the spatial-temporal case. The spatial homogeneity of these residual points may be assessed, for instance, using Ripley's K-function.

If λ is spatially and temporally volatile, the transformed space bounding the rescaled residuals can be highly irregular, which makes it difficult to detect uniformity using the K-function. In this case, one can rescale the points along a different axis as in Schoenberg (1999) and see if there is any improvement. Unfortunately, most models for earthquake occurrences, such as those in CSEP, have volatile conditional intensities resulting in a highly irregular boundary regardless of which axis is chosen for rescaling. In such cases, the K-function is dominated by boundary effects and has little power to detect excessive clustering or inhibition in the residuals.

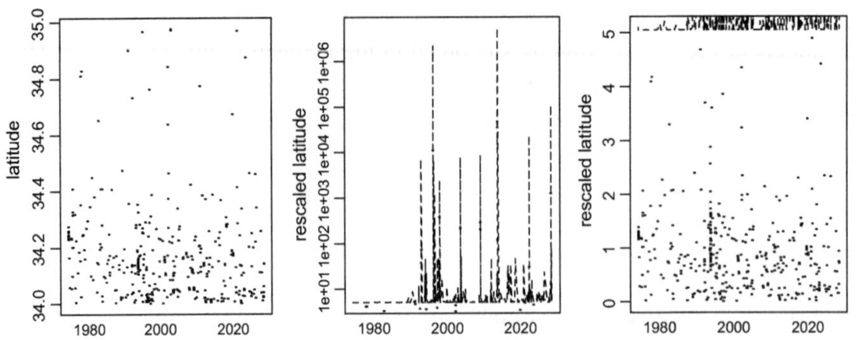

Fig. 5.9 (left) Recorded origin times and latitudes of San Bernardino earthquakes shown in Fig. 3 of Chap. 1. (middle) Rescaled residuals, for San Bernardino earthquakes rescaled using the ETAS model fit by MLE, with latitudes rescaled. Rescaled latitudes are shown on logarithmic scale. (right) Rescaled residuals for San Bernardino earthquakes rescaled using the ETAS model fit by MLE, with latitudes rescaled. Only the rescaled residuals with rescaled latitudes less than the median value 0.014 of the upper boundary are shown, and rescaled latitudes are shown on linear scale

Figure 5.9 shows the rescaled residuals for the ETAS model fit to the San Bernardino earthquake data. The fitted model was shown in Fig. 36 in Chap. 4. In Fig. 5.9, the latitudes of the points are rescaled using the fitted model $\hat{\lambda}(t, x, y)$. As seen in the middle panel of Fig. 5.9, $\hat{\lambda}$ is so highly volatile that even on logarithmic scale, it is impossible to discern if the points beneath the boundary are clustered or not. Comparing the leftmost and rightmost panels of Fig. 5.9, the clustering in the data is substantially decreased after rescaling, though some clustering clearly remains after rescaling. This indicates some clustering in the observations not adequately accounted for by the fitted ETAS model, and implies some lack of fit, particularly for the 19 events occurring on March 1, 1990. One must be somewhat cautious, however, in interpreting rescaled residuals, because sometimes patterns observed in the points in the rescaled coordinates may be difficult to interpret due to the rescaling.

The code to produce Fig. 5.9 (again, after reading in the data and fitting the model as described in Chaps. 1 and 3) is below. For each point (t_i, x_i, y_i), the integral $\int_0^{y_i} \lambda(t_i, x_i, y)dy$ is approximated by computing λ at 100,000 locations (t_i, x_i, y) with y equally spaced between 34.0 and y_i. Similarly, the height of the boundary is also computed via approximation using 100,000 equally spaced latitude coordinates.

```
mu = theta2[1]; K = theta2[2]; c = theta2[3]; p = theta2[4]
a = theta2[5]; d = theta2[6]; q = theta2[7]; n = z$n; k=100000
par(mfrow=c(1,3))
plot(t,34+z$lat,xaxt="n",xlab="",ylab="latitude",cex=0.2)
mtext(s=1,l=1,c("1980","2000","2020"),at=c(10*365,30*365,50*365))
newy = rep(365*mu*z$lat[1],n); newtop = rep(365*mu,n)
for(i in 2:n){
  y = seq(0,z$lat[i],l=k); y2 = seq(0,1,l=k)
  lam = rep(mu,k); lam2 = lam
  const = K*(p-1)*c^(p-1)*(q-1)*d^(q-1)/pi
  for(j in 1:k){
    lam[j] = mu + const*sum(exp(a*(z$m[1:(i-1)]-M0))*(t[i] - t[1:(i-1)]+c)^(-p)*
        ((z$lon[1:(i-1)]-z$lon[i])^2+(z$lat[1:(i-1)]-y[i])^2+d)^(-q))
    lam2[j] = mu + const*sum(exp(a*(z$m[1:(i-1)]-M0))*(t[i] - t[1:(i-1)]+c)^(-p)*
        ((z$lon[1:(i-1)]-z$lon[i])^2+(z$lat[1:(i-1)]-y2[i])^2+d)^(-q))
  }
  newy[i] = 365*mean(lam)*z$lat[i]
  newtop[i] = 365*mean(lam2)
}
plot(range(t),range(newtop),xaxt="n",xlab="",ylab="rescaled latitude",
```

```
    type="n",log="y")
lines(t,newtop,lty=2)
points(t,newy,cex=0.2)
mtext(s=1,l=1,c("1980","2000","2020"),at=c(10*365,30*365,50*365))
plot(range(t),c(0,median(newtop)),xaxt="n",xlab="",
    ylab="rescaled latitude",type="n")
lines(t,newtop,lty=2)
points(t,newy,cex=0.2)
mtext(s=1,l=1,c("1980","2000","2020"),at=c(10*365,30*365,50*365))
```

The result of Meyer (1971a) requires that the conditional intensity λ of the point process N be known. Thus, one may question whether the rescaled process is similar to a Poisson process when λ is estimated rather than known. Even in the simplest case when N is a stationary Poisson process with unknown rate λ, when λ is estimated by maximum likelihood and the process N is rescaled according to this estimate $\hat{\lambda}$ to form the rescaled process $\hat{M}$, the fact that $\hat{M}$ is not a Poisson process, or equivalently that $N(0,t) - \hat{\lambda}t$ is not a martingale, has been observed by several authors including Aalen and Hoem (1978), Brown and Nair (1988), Heinrich (1991), and Solow (1993).

It has been argued that the difference between $\hat{M}$ and a Poisson process with rate one is negligible, since $\hat{\lambda}$ converges a.s. to λ, or because certain statistics, such as the Kolmogorov-Smirnov statistic, when applied to $\hat{M}$, have asymptotically the same distribution as the statistics corresponding to the Poisson process (Arsham, 1987; Davies, 1977; Heinrich, 1991; Karr, 1991; Kutoyants, 1984; Lisek & Lisek, 1985; Lee, 1986; Ogata & Vere-Jones, 1984; Saw, 1975; Yokoyama et al., 1993). However, when T is small, the asymptotic arguments above are less relevant, and the exact properties of $\hat{M}$ may be important. It turns out that $\hat{M}$ is self-correcting, with a highly fluctuating conditional intensity process. This suggests that caution should be used in assuming that $\hat{M}$ is similar to a stationary Poisson process, particularly when the original point process N is observed over a short time scale. Further, although certain functionals of $\hat{M}$ may asymptotically approach those of a Poisson process, the asymptotic behavior of $\hat{M}$ may more accurately be characterized in relation to the Brownian Bridge (Schoenberg, 2002).

5.3 Super-Thinning

Let $\hat{\lambda}(t,x,y)$ be an estimate (either parametric or non-parametric) of the conditional intensity $\lambda(t,x,y)$. The method of randomly thinning a point process is based on the works of Lewis and Shedler (1979) and Ogata (1981), who used random thinning as a means of simulating spatial-temporal point processes. For residual analysis, one can similarly thin, or randomly remove points from, a point process so that the points that remain after thinning form a homogeneous Poisson process if and only if the model $\hat{\lambda}$ used to perform the thinning is correct. These remaining points are called the thinned residuals.

In residual thinning, each observed point is retained independently with probability $b/\hat{\lambda}(t_i, x_i, y_i)$, where $b = \inf_{(t,x,y)\in S}\{\hat{\lambda}(t,x,y)\}$. The points that remain are called *thinned residual points*, and if the estimate $\hat{\lambda}(t,x,y) = \lambda(t,x,y)$ almost everywhere, then the residual process, Z, will be homogeneous Poisson with rate b. To detect clustering or inhibition in the residual point pattern, one may use some summary statistic such as the K-function or L-function, for example. In practice, one may generate several realizations of thinned residuals and analyze each of them to get an overall assessment of the goodness-of-fit.

The power of thinned residuals may suffer in part due to the variability and lack of independence in the thinned residual points and especially due to the loss of information when removing observed points. Indeed, if b is small, as is often the case when modeling spatially inhomogeneous phenomena such as earthquakes or wildfires, then thinning may result in very few residual points, so that tests, both formal and informal, will have little power to detect inhomogeneity.

An opposite approach was proposed by Brémaud (1981), who suggested superposing a simulated point process onto an observed point process realization so as to yield a homogeneous Poisson process. Residual superposition involves transforming the point process N into a homogeneous Poisson process by simulating points rather than removing points. A residual point process is created by simulating a Cox process directed by $d - \hat{\lambda}(t, x, y)$, where $d = \sup_{(t,x,y)\in\mathcal{S}}\{\hat{\lambda}(t, x, y)\}$. That is, one first determines $d - \hat{\lambda}(t, x, y)$ for all spatial-temporal locations (t, x, y), and then simulates a Poisson process with that intensity.

The simulated process is then superposed onto N, creating a homogeneous Poisson point process of rate d if and only if $\hat{\lambda} = \lambda$ almost everywhere. Any significant clustering, inhibition, or inhomogeneity in the superposed residuals indicates a lack of fit of the model $\hat{\lambda}$, and as with thinning, several realizations of superposed residuals may be generated and assessed for uniformity.

Residual analysis using superposition has limited power when the supremum of $\hat{\lambda}$ is much larger than the mean of $\hat{\lambda}$ over the observation region $\mathcal{S}$, as is often the case with models of highly inhomogeneous or clustered phenomena. In such cases, the simulated points are by construction approximately homogeneous in regions where $d >> \hat{\lambda}$, and since the number of such simulated points is large, their inclusion in the residuals tends to overwhelm any information provided by N in standard tests of homogeneity, resulting in little power to detect inhomogeneity in the residuals as a whole.

A more powerful approach is super-thinning, which is a combination of thinning observed points and superimposing simulated points, leading to a homogeneous residual point process if and only if the estimate $\hat{\lambda}$ of the original point process is correct. With super-thinning, the relative amount of thinning and superposition can be controlled through the choice of a tuning parameter, k. With a prudent choice of k, the method can be substantially more powerful than either thinning or superposition alone.

Suppose that one desires to transform the point process N into a residual Poisson process with rate k, where $\inf\{\hat{\lambda}(t_i, x_i, y_i)\} \leq k \leq \sup\{\hat{\lambda}(t_i, x_i, y_i)\}$. One may first thin N, keeping each point (t_i, x_i, y_i) independently with probability $\min\{k/\hat{\lambda}(t_i, x_i, y_i), 1\}$ to obtain a thinned residual process Z_1. Next, one simulates a Cox process Z_2 directed by $\max\{k - \hat{\lambda}(t, x, y), 0\}$. That is, conditional on k and $\hat{\lambda}$, Z_2 is a Poisson process whose rate at location (t, x, y) is $\max\{k - \hat{\lambda}(t, x, y), 0\}$. Note that this second step can easily be performed by simulating a homogeneous Poisson process with rate k and independently keeping each simulated point $(\tilde{t}_i, \tilde{x}_i, \tilde{y}_i)$ with probability $\max\{\frac{k-\hat{\lambda}(\tilde{t}_i,\tilde{x}_i,\tilde{y}_i)}{k}, 0\}$. The points of the residual point process $Z = Z_1 + Z_2$, obtained by superposing the thinned residuals and the simulated Poisson process, are called *super-thinned residual points*. Because Z is homogeneous Poisson with rate k if and only if $\hat{\lambda} = \lambda$ almost everywhere, as shown below, one may inspect the points in Z for uniformity as a way of assessing the goodness-of-fit of the estimate $\hat{\lambda}$.

The super-thinned residual process, Z, may be formally defined as follows. Suppose N is a point process adapted to the filtration $\mathcal{F}$. Let W_t be a Uniform(0, 1) white noise process adapted to $\mathcal{F}$ and independent of N. Let Q be a Poisson process with rate k adapted to $\mathcal{F}$ and independent of N and W.

Given an estimate $\hat{\lambda} > 0$ of λ, let $Z_1(t, x, y) = N(t, x, y)\mathbf{1}_{(W_t<k/\hat{\lambda}(t,x,y))}$ and $Z_2(t, x, y) = Q(t, x, y)\mathbf{1}_{(W_t<(k-\hat{\lambda}(t,x,y))/k)}$. The superposition $Z = Z_1 + Z_2$ defines the super-thinned residual process, and Z is a Poisson process with rate k if and only if $\hat{\lambda} = \lambda$ almost everywhere.

To prove the preceding sentence, note that if Z has simple ground process and has compensator $k\mu$, then Z is a Poisson process with rate k (see e.g., Nair, 1990, Proposition 4.2). Since N has simple ground process, and since Q is a Poisson process independent of N, it is trivially true that the superposition $N + Q$ has simple ground process, and therefore the same is true of Z.

To show that if $\hat{\lambda} = \lambda$ almost everywhere, then Z has compensator $k\mu$, fix any spatial-temporal location (t, x, y) and let F be any event in $\mathcal{F}_{t,x,y}$. Let C denote a set of the form $(t, u) \times X$, where X is a measurable subset of the spatial domain. Since $0 \leq W(y) \leq 1$,

$$\begin{aligned}
E[Z(C)|F] = \; & E\left[\int_C \mathbf{1}_{(\hat{\lambda}(y)\geq k)}\mathbf{1}_{(W(y)<\frac{k}{\hat{\lambda}(y)})} dN(y)|F\right] \\
& + E\left[\int_C \mathbf{1}_{(\hat{\lambda}(y)<k)} dN(y)|F\right] \\
& + E\left[\int_C \mathbf{1}_{(\hat{\lambda}(y)<k)}\mathbf{1}_{(W(y)<\frac{k-\hat{\lambda}(y)}{k})} dQ(y)|F\right] \\
= \; & E\left[\int_C E\left[\mathbf{1}_{(\hat{\lambda}(y)\geq k)}\mathbf{1}_{(W(y)<\frac{k}{\hat{\lambda}(y)})}|F_y\right] dN(y)|F\right] \\
& + E\left[\int_C \mathbf{1}_{(\hat{\lambda}(y)<k)} dN(y)|F\right] \\
& + E\left[\int_C E\left[\mathbf{1}_{(\hat{\lambda}(y)<k)}\mathbf{1}_{(W(y)<\frac{k-\hat{\lambda}(y)}{k})}|F_y\right] dQ(y)|F\right] \\
= \; & E\left[\int_C \mathbf{1}_{(\hat{\lambda}(y)\geq k)}\frac{k}{\hat{\lambda}(y)} dN(y)|F\right] \\
& + E\left[\int_C \mathbf{1}_{(\hat{\lambda}(y)<k)} dN(y)|F\right] \\
& + E\left[\int_C \mathbf{1}_{(\hat{\lambda}(y)<k)}\frac{k-\hat{\lambda}(y)}{k} dQ(y)|F\right]
\end{aligned}$$

Thus, by the martingale property,

$$\begin{aligned}
E[Z(C)|F] = \; & E\left[\int_C \mathbf{1}_{(\hat{\lambda}(y)\geq k)}\frac{k}{\hat{\lambda}(y)}\lambda(y) d\mu|F\right] \\
& + E\left[\int_C \mathbf{1}_{(\hat{\lambda}(y)<k)}\lambda(y) d\mu|F\right] \\
& + E\left[\int_C \mathbf{1}_{(\hat{\lambda}(y)<k)}\frac{(k-\hat{\lambda}(y))}{k}(k) d\mu|F\right].
\end{aligned} \tag{5.3}$$

If $\hat{\lambda} = \lambda$ almost everywhere, then the sum of the three terms in (5.3) reduces immediately to

$$E[Z(C)|F] = (k)E\left[\int_C \mathbf{1}_{(\lambda(y)\geq k)} + \int_C \mathbf{1}_{(\lambda(y)<k)} d\mu | F\right] = k\mu(C),$$

so that $k\mu$ is the compensator of Z and thus Z is a Poisson process with rate k.

The converse is quite easy to show. If $\hat{\lambda}$ is not equal to λ almost everywhere, then at least one of the four sets $B_1 = \{\hat{\lambda} > \lambda\} \cup \{\hat{\lambda} \geq k\}$, $B_2 = \{\hat{\lambda} < \lambda\} \cup \{\hat{\lambda} \geq k\}$, $B_3 = \{\hat{\lambda} > \lambda\} \cup \{\hat{\lambda} < k\}$, or $B_4 = \{\hat{\lambda} < \lambda\} \cup \{\hat{\lambda} < k\}$ must have measure greater than zero. Without loss of generality, suppose that B_1 has positive measure. The indicator 1_{B_1} is predictable, since $\hat{\lambda}$ and λ are predictable, so as in (5.3),

$$E\int 1_{B_1} dZ = E\int 1_{B_1} \frac{k}{\hat{\lambda}(y)} \lambda(y) d\mu < kE\int 1_{B_1} d\mu,$$

so Z is not a Poisson process with rate k, since for a Poisson process with rate k, one would have equality in the above relation by the martingale property, and the proof is complete.

In super-thinning, the tuning parameter k allows the user to control the rate of thinning and superposition. As a result, super-thinning is potentially much more powerful than either thinning or superposition alone. In application to earthquake forecasts, a natural choice for k is the total number of expected earthquakes according to the model being investigated. The parameter k can also be chosen in a way that optimizes the power of formal tests of homogeneity of the residuals.

One suggested approach is to super-thin a point process by thinning out and superposing as few points as possible in order to retain as much of the original data as possible. This suggests choosing the value of k minimizing the sum of the absolute deviations of the estimated conditional intensity from k, i.e., solving

$$\operatorname*{argmin}_k \int\int_S\int_t |\hat{\lambda}(t, x, y) - k| dt dx dy,$$

i.e., letting k equal the median of $\hat{\lambda}$. In some cases a unique median might not exist, however.

Alternatively, one may choose the value of k minimizing the sum of the squared deviations of the estimated conditional intensity from k, letting k equal the mean of $\hat{\lambda}$,

$$k = \frac{1}{|S|}\int\int_S\int_t \hat{\lambda}(t, x, y) dt dx dy,$$

where $|S|$ is the volume of the observation region. In this case, the expected number of points in the resulting residual process is equal to the number of points in N. Depending on one's choice of test statistic performed on the residual process, it may be possible to choose k so that the resulting residual test has optimal power.

Below is the code to produce Fig. 5.10, after reading in the data and fitting the model as described in Chaps. 1 and 3, and after running the rescaling code above.

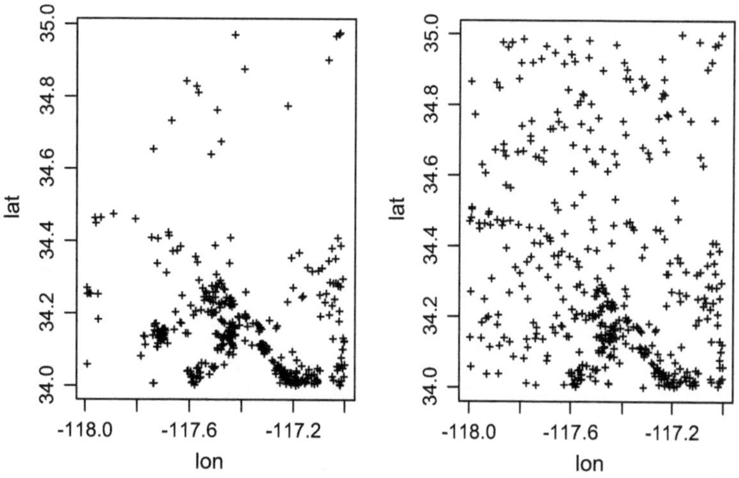

Fig. 5.10 (left) Recorded epicentral latitudes and longitudes of San Bernardino earthquakes. (right) super-thinned residuals, for San Bernardino earthquakes using the ETAS model fit by MLE. The parameter k used in super-thinning is the mean of $\hat{\lambda}$ at the observed events

```
source(url("http://www.stat.ucla.edu/~frederic/book/super-thin.r"))
lam = rep(mu,n); X1 = 1; Y1 = 1
const = K*(p-1)*c^(p-1)*(q-1)*d^(q-1)/pi
for(i in 2:n) lam[i] = mu + const*sum(exp(a*(z$m[1:(i-1)]-M0))*(t[i] -
  t[1:(i-1)]+c)^(-p)*((z$lon[1:(i-1)]-z$lon[i])^2+(z$lat[1:(i-1)]-
  z$lat[i])^2+d)^(-q))
s = supthin(z,lam,f,median(lam))
par(mfrow=c(1,2))
plot(-118+z$lon,34+z$lat,pch=3,cex=.5,xlab="lon",ylab="lat")
plot(-118+s$lon,34+s$lat,pch=3,cex=.5,xlab="lon",ylab="lat")
```

Figure 5.10 shows an example of super-thinning the San Bernardino earthquake data, using the ETAS model. Again, the clustering in the data is substantially decreased after super-thinning, but the remaining clustering in the super-thinned residuals indicates that the fitted ETAS model is not quite sufficiently accounting for the high degree of clustering in the data, especially for the events around longitude −117.2 and latitude just above 34.0.

The left-over clustering in the super-thinned residuals is confirmed from the estimated K-function of the spatial locations of the residuals, as shown in Fig. 5.11. The estimated K-function of the super-thinned residuals is much lower than that of the raw data, since much of the clustering has been removed, but is still above the 95% confidence bounds based on 200 simulations of homogeneous Poisson processes with the same rate as the super-thinned process. The code to produce Fig. 5.11 is below.

```
b = as.ppp(cbind(s$lon,s$lat), W = c(0,1,0,1))
b2 = as.ppp(cbind(z$lon,z$lat), W = c(0,1,0,1))
env = envelope(b,Kest,nsim=200,r=seq(0,.05,length=100))
z = Kest(b2,r=seq(0,.05,length=100))
plot(z$r,z$bord,lty=2,col="green",type="l",xlab="r (degrees)",ylab="")
plot(env,legend=F,main="",add=T)
mtext(s=2,l=2,expression(hat(K)(r)))
```

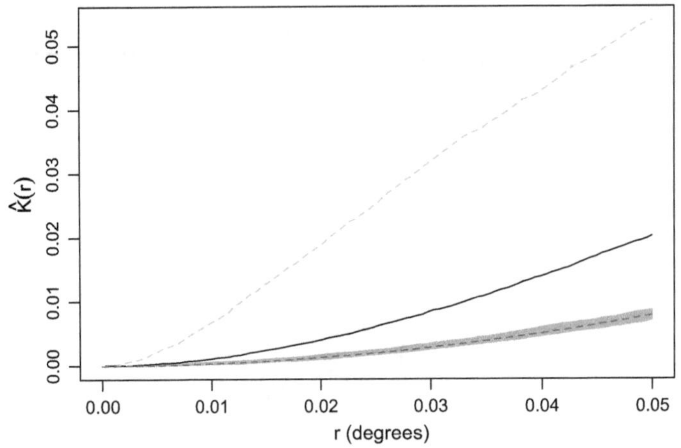

Fig. 5.11 Estimated K-function for super-thinned residuals of San Bernardino earthquakes (solid black curve), super-thinned using the ETAS model fit by MLE; 95% bounds (gray) based on simulated stationary Poisson processes of the same rate; K-function of stationary Poisson process (red dashed curve); and estimated K-function for the raw data, i.e., the epicentral latitudes and longitudes of San Bernardino earthquakes (green dashed curve)

5.4 Voronoi Residuals

When discussing pixel sizes in Sect. 5.1.3, it was mentioned that with raw and Pearson residuals, the choice of pixel size can be problematic. One method of addressing this problem of pixel size specification is to use a data-driven, spatially adaptive partition such as the Voronoi tessellation, as suggested in Bray et al. (2014).

Given a simple space-time point process N, one may obtain a collection of n Voronoi cells, $C_1, \ldots, C_n$, where cell C_i is defined as the collection of spatial-temporal locations closer to the partic-

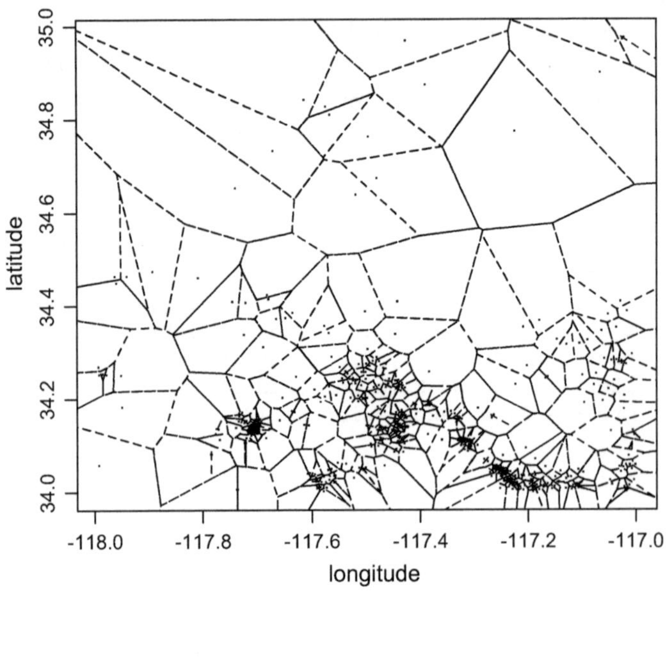

Fig. 5.12 Voronoi tessellation of San Bernardino earthquake locations

ular point τ_i than to any of the other observed points τ_j, $j \neq i$. The collection of cells C_i is called the Voronoi tessellation of N. For a simple point process, each cell C_i must contain the point τ_i and not other points, so by construction, $N(C_i) = 1$ for each cell C_i.

Figure 5.12 shows the Voronoi tessellation of the San Bernardino earthquakes. The code to produce Fig. 5.12 (again, after having loaded in the data as *z*) is below, and uses the *R* function *deldir()* from the package also called *deldir*. Since in what follows we will also use some functions in the *splints* library, the code below loads in that library as well.

```
install.packages(c("deldir","splancs"))
library(deldir,splancs)
dd <- deldir(-118+z$lon, 34+z$lat)
plot(-118+z$lon,34+z$lat,pch=".",xlab="longitude",ylab="latitude")
tl = tile.list(dd)
for(i in 1:z$n) polygon(tl[[i]],lty=2)
```

Many fascinating geometric properties of planar Voronoi tessellations have been discovered. For instance, for a planar process, for any two adjacent Voronoi cells containing points τ_i and τ_j, the segment common to the boundaries of both cells is a perpendicular bisector of the segment $\overline{\tau_i \tau_j}$; each Voronoi cell boundary is a convex polygon; each vertex is the circumcenter of the points whose cells share the vertex; the average number of segments per cell may not exceed 6; and the Voronoi tessellation generated by a stationary Poisson process in the plane has cells averaging exactly 6 sides per cell (see e.g., Okabe et al., 2000).

Given a model for the conditional intensity of a spatial or spaceâŁ"time point process, one may construct residuals simply by evaluating the residual process over Voronoi cells rather than over rectangular pixels. Such residuals are referred to as *Voronoi residuals.*

For the purpose of considering the distribution of Voronoi residuals, a few more properties of Voronoi cells are relevant. When N is a homogeneous Poisson process, the sizes $|C_i|$ of the Voronoi cells are approximately gamma distributed. More specifically, for a planar homogeneous Poisson process with rate λ, the expected area of a Voronoi cell is equal to the $1/\lambda$ (Meijering, 1953), and simulation studies have shown that the area of a typical Voronoi cell is approximately gamma distributed (Hinde & Miles, 1980; Tanemura, 2003; Ferenc & Néda, 2007).

For each Voronoi cell C_i, given a model $\hat{\lambda}(t, x, y)$, one may compute the raw residual, $r_i = 1 - \int_{C_i} \hat{\lambda}(t, x, y)$, where the 1 appears because each Voronoi cell has exactly one point inside it by construction. Alternatively, one may compute the standardized residual $s_i = \frac{1-\int \hat{\lambda}(s,t)\, dt\, ds}{\sqrt{\int \hat{\lambda}(s,t)\, dt\, ds}}$ over the Voronoi cells C_i. When comparing two models, it can be useful to compare the log-likelihoods of the two models, aggregated over each Voronoi cell, and the results are called *Voronoi deviance residuals.*

One advantage of Voronoi residuals compared to conventional pixel-based methods is that the partition is entirely automatic and spatially adaptive. In addition, as shown in Bray et al. (2014), Voronoi residuals have a distribution that tends to be far less skewed than pixel-based residuals, and are approximately Gamma distributed under quite general regularity conditions. More specifically, for the case of a stationary Poisson process in the plane, the distribution of the term $\int_{C_i} \lambda(t, x, y)$ is well approximated by a Gamma distribution with parameters $a = 2.2975$, $b = 3.01116$, $c = 1.0825$ (Ferenc & Néda, 2007), and this approximation for $\int_{C_i} \hat{\lambda}(t, x, y)$ is also close more generally, provided that the conditional intensity is approximately constant near the location in question (Barr & Schoenberg, 2010). By contrast, for pixels over which the integrated conditional intensity is close to zero, the conventional raw residuals are approximately Bernoulli distributed.

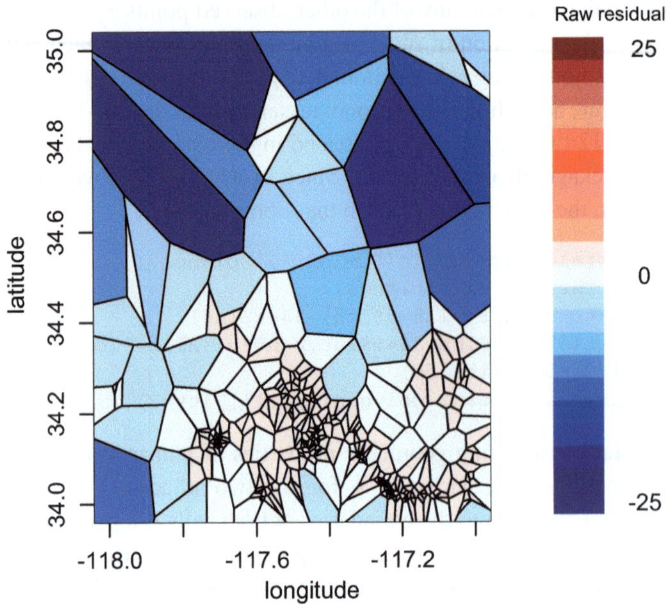

Fig. 5.13 Raw Voronoi residuals for ETAS model fit by MLE to San Bernardino earthquake data

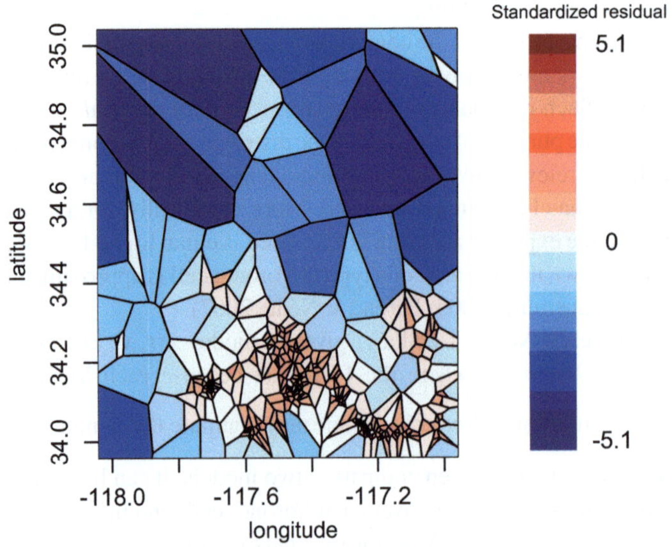

Fig. 5.14 Standardized Voronoi residuals for ETAS model fit by MLE to San Bernardino earthquake data

In practice, rather than construct Voronoi cells based on spatial-temporal distance, such as (4.1), it seems usually to be best to construct the Voronoi tessellation of all the spatial locations of the points, ignoring time in the calculations of distance. Alternatively, one may divide the temporal observation region up and consider the Voronoi tessellation of the spatial locations of the points within each temporal division.

Using the functions f and g and the list *mycol* of colors defined earlier in this chapter, the code to follow constructs the raw Voronoi, standardized Voronoi, and Voronoi deviance residuals plotted in Figs. 5.13, 5.14, and 5.15. For these plots, the integral of λ over each cell is approximated by averaging the values of λ calculated at 100,000 random spatial-temporal locations uniformly distributed within the cell.

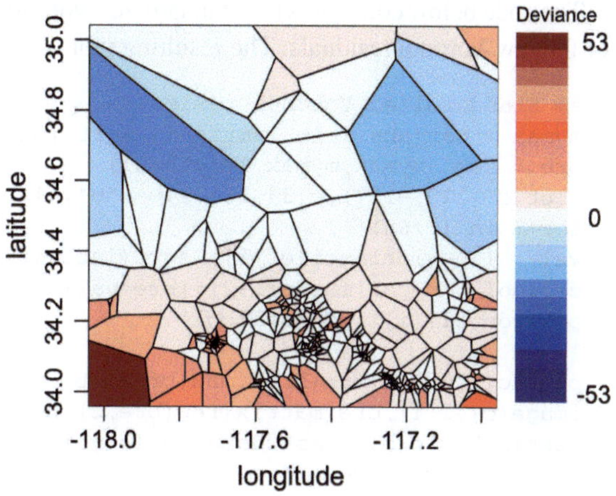

Fig. 5.15 Voronoi deviance residuals for ETAS relative to quadratic Poisson model (5.2) fit by MLE to San Bernardino earthquake data. Positive deviances indicate locations where the log-likelihood for ETAS is higher. Negative deviances indicate locations where the log-likelihood for the quadratic Poisson model is higher

We begin with code to approximate the integral of $\lambda(t, x, y)$ over each of the Voronoi cells.

```
## integrate lambda over each cell
m = 100000
intlamtilef = rep(0,n)
intlamtileg = rep(0,n)
lamf = rep(0,m)
lamg = rep(0,m)
for(i in 1:z$n){
bound = cbind(tl[[i]]$x+118, y = tl[[i]]$y-34)
randxy = csr(bound,m)
for(j in 1:m) lamf[j] = f(runif(1)*maxt,randxy[j,1],randxy[j,2],z)
for(j in 1:m) lamg[j] = g(runif(1)*maxt,randxy[j,1],randxy[j,2])
intlamtilef[i] = mean(lamf) * tl[[i]]$area * maxt
intlamtileg[i] = mean(lamg) * tl[[i]]$area * maxt
}
```

Given these integrals, constructing the raw Voronoi residuals is now a simple matter. The only slightly hard parts are figuring out which value corresponds to which color, and constructing the legend! The result is shown in Fig. 5.13.

```
## raw Voronoi residuals
mymax = max(abs(1-intlamtilef))+.01
bre = seq(-mymax,mymax,length=21)
par(mfrow=c(1,2))
plot(c(-118,-117),c(34,35),type="n",xlab="longitude",ylab="latitude")
for(i in 1:z$n){
val = 1 - intlamtilef[i]
cellcol = mycol[max(c(1:21)[bre<val])]
polygon(tl[[i]],col=cellcol)
}
plot(c(0,10),c(min(bre),max(bre)),type="n",axes=F,xlab="",ylab="")
image(c(-1:1),bre,matrix(rep(bre,2),ncol=21,byrow=T),add=T,col=mycol)
text(2.5,min(bre),as.character(signif(min(bre),2)),cex=1)
text(2.5,0,"0",cex=1)
text(2.5,max(bre),as.character(signif(max(bre),2)),cex=1)
mtext(s=3,l=0,at=1,"Raw residual",cex=.75)
```

The code below constructs the standardized Voronoi residuals, and is otherwise identical to the code for the raw Voronoi residuals. The resulting plot is shown in Fig. 5.14.

```
## Standardized Voronoi residuals.
mymax = max(abs(1-intlamtilef)/sqrt(intlamtilef))+.01
bre = seq(-mymax,mymax,length=21)
plot(c(-118,-117),c(34,35),type="n",xlab="longitude",ylab="latitude")
for(i in 1:z$n){
val = (1 - intlamtilef[i])/sqrt(intlamtilef[i])
cellcol = mycol[max(c(1:21)[bre<val])]
polygon(tl[[i]],col=cellcol)
}
plot(c(0,10),c(min(bre),max(bre)),type="n",axes=F,xlab="",ylab="")
image(c(-1:1),bre,matrix(rep(bre,2),ncol=21,byrow=T),add=T,col=mycol)
text(2.5,min(bre),as.character(signif(min(bre),2)),cex=1)
text(2.5,0,"0",cex=1)
text(2.5,max(bre),as.character(signif(max(bre),2)),cex=1)
mtext(s=3,l=0,at=1,"Standardized residual",cex=.75)
```

Finally, the code below constructs Voronoi deviance residuals for comparing the ETAS model (2.10), fit by MLE, to the quadratic Poisson model (5.2), also fit by MLE, again using the San Bernardino earthquake data. The result is shown in Fig. 5.15.

```
## Voronoi deviance residuals.
loglamf = rep(0,z$n); loglamg = loglamf
for(i in 1:z$n){
  loglamf[i] = log(f(z$t[i],z$lon[i],z$lat[i],z))
  loglamg[i] = log(g(z$t[i],z$lon[i],z$lat[i]))
  }
mymax = max(abs(loglamf-loglamg-intlamtilef+intlamtileg))+.01
bre = seq(-mymax,mymax,length=21)
plot(c(-118,-117),c(34,35),type="n",xlab="longitude",ylab="latitude")
val = loglamf - loglamg - intlamtilef + intlamtileg
for(i in 1:z$n){
cellcol = mycol[max(c(1:21)[bre<val[i]])]
polygon(tl[[i]],col=cellcol)
}
plot(c(0,10),c(min(bre),max(bre)),type="n",axes=F,xlab="",ylab="")
image(c(-1:1),bre,matrix(rep(bre,2),ncol=21,byrow=T),add=T,col=mycol)
text(2.5,min(bre),as.character(signif(min(bre),2)),cex=1)
text(2.5,0,"0",cex=1)
text(2.5,max(bre),as.character(signif(max(bre),2)),cex=1)
mtext(s=3,l=0,at=1,"Deviance",cex=.75)
```

One sees from Figs. 5.13 and 5.14 that this fitted ETAS model tended to overpredict seismicity in the Northern portion of the observation region, where fewer earthquakes occurred. The problem stems from the fact that we fit the ETAS model (2.10) with constant background rate, and this background rate fits the data poorly, as the clusters of points are far from uniformly distributed throughout the observation region. This also explains why the fitted ETAS model somewhat underpredicts the rate of events in the areas of high seismicity. Note that the raw Voronoi residuals cannot possibly be greater than 1; the asymmetry in the raw Voronoi residuals seen in Fig. 5.13 is not at all unusual. The standardization in Fig. 5.14 appears to solve the asymmetry issue, and Fig. 5.15 clearly shows that the ETAS model fits substantially better than the quadratic Poisson model especially in areas of high seismicity.

5.5 Numerical Tests

A host of numerical tests to assess the goodness-of-fit for spatial-temporal point process models have been proposed. The most often used numerical summary of fit for point processes is simply the log-likelihood, $l = \sum_{i=1}^{n} \log \lambda(\tau_i) - \int \lambda(t, x, y)dtdxdy$. When comparing two nested models, a likelihood ratio test can be performed, where the difference of log-likelihoods is approximately χ^2-distributed. A closely related summary is the Akaike Information Criterion (AIC), defined as 2 times the log-likelihood minus 2 times the number of fitted parameters, where again, for nested models, differences in the AIC should be approximately χ^2-distributed, with degrees of freedom equal to the difference in the number of parameters estimated for the two models (Akaike 1974, 1983; Ogata 1988).

Another very natural summary of overall goodness-of-fit is the Stoyan-Grabarnik statistic, T in (3.6), which should be close to the size $|B|$ of the spatial-temporal window if the model fits well, since $E(T) = |B|$ if the model is correct (Baddeley et al., 2005). Several other summaries have been specifically designed and tailored for use on models for earthquake occurrences, such as those used in RELM or CSEP. Such tests include the N-Test comparing the total expected and observed number of points, the L-Test comparing the likelihood with that expected according to the model, and the R-Test comparing the performance of two models.

5.5.1 L-Test and N-Test

The L-test, described in Schorlemmer et al. (2007), is similar to a likelihood ratio test, but is performed on one model at a time, and does not assume a particular distribution, relying instead on simulation. The L-test works by first simulating some fixed number of realizations from the forecast model. The log-likelihood (ℓ_j) for the given model is then computed for each simulation, j, as well as the log-likelihood ℓ_{obs} for the observed dataset, given the fitted model. One then determines the fraction of simulated log-likelihoods that are less than the log-likelihood for the observed dataset:

$$\gamma = \frac{\sum_{j=1}^{S} \mathbf{1}_{\{\ell_j < \ell_{\text{obs}}\}}}{S},$$

where $\mathbf{1}$ denotes the indicator function. The L-test is one-sided: if γ is close to zero, then the model is considered to be inconsistent with the data, and can be rejected. Otherwise, the model is not rejected and further tests may be desired.

The N-test is similar to the L-test, except that the quantile score examined is instead the fraction of simulations that contain fewer points than the actual observed number of points in the catalog, N_{obs}. That is,

$$\delta = \frac{\sum_{j=1}^{S} \mathbf{1}_{\{N_j < N_{\text{obs}}\}}}{S},$$

where N_j is the number of points in the jth simulation of the model. If the number of observed earthquakes is unusually large or small relative to this distribution, the data are considered inconsistent with the model. The N-test is two-sided, and the model is rejected if δ is close either to 0 or to 1. If a model is under-predicting or over-predicting the total number of earthquakes, then $\delta \sim 1$ or 0, respectively, and the model will likely be rejected with the N-test.

In practice, for many point process models, the log-likelihood for a given simulation depends critically on the total number of points in the simulation. Unfortunately, in such situations, both statistics γ and δ test essentially the same thing, namely the agreement between the observed and modeled *total* number of points. Even when the N and L tests do reject a model, they do not typically indicate *where* or *when* the model fit poorly, or how it could be improved.

Furthermore, the N-test and L-test have relatively low power and are typically unable to discern significant lack of fit unless the model fits extremely poorly. For instance, consider assessing the fit of a simple stationary Cox process model, i.e., a stationary mixed Poisson process where the rate is either 10, 20, or 40, each with probability $1/3$. Suppose that the alternative hypothesis, i.e., the true process generating the data, is a stationary Poisson process of rate 25, and that this process is observed on a spatial-temporal region of unit size. The L-test and N-test will virtually never reject the Cox model. Indeed, the code below performed 10,000 simulations of the above scenario, and also used 10,000 simulations of the Cox model to generate the null distribution, and the Cox model was rejected 0 times at the 5% significance level by either the L-test or N-test in these simulations. In other words, the power of these tests is minimal; the type II error probability is nearly 100% in this case.

```
m = 10000
rates = sample(c(10,20,40),m,rep=T)
n1 = rpois(m,rates)
cutoff1 = quantile(n1,.025)
cutoff2 = quantile(n1,.975)
n = rpois(m,25)
sum(n < cutoff1) ## 0
sum(n > cutoff2) ## 0
Ldata = 1/3*exp(-10)*10^n/factorial(n) + 1/3*exp(-20)*20^n/factorial(n) +
    1/3*exp(-40)*40^n/factorial(n)
Lsim = 1/3*exp(-10)*10^n1/factorial(n1) + 1/3*exp(-20)*20^n1/factorial(n1) +
    1/3*exp(-40)*40^n1/factorial(n1)
cutoff3 = quantile(Lsim,.05)
sum(Ldata < cutoff3)
```

This example is not entirely unrealistic for the case of evaluating earthquake forecasts. Several earthquake occurrence models, such as the ETAS models of Ogata (1988, 1998), are occasionally explosive, so that the number of points in a fixed spatial-temporal region may vary between realizations from just a few points to many, and this agrees with the intense heterogeneity and clustering observed in actual earthquake catalogs (see e.g., Kagan, 2004).

The L-test is considered more comprehensive in that it evaluates the forecast in terms of magnitude, spatial location, and number of events, while the N-test restricts its attention to the number of events. Numerical tests such as the L-test can be viewed as examples of scoring rules (see Gneiting & Raftery, 2007, or Heinrich-Mertsching et al., 2024), and developing research on scoring rules may result in numerical tests of improved power and efficiency.

In CSEP, two additional data consistency tests were proposed to assess the magnitude and spatial components of the forecasts, respectively: the M-test and the S-test (Zechar et al., 2010). The M-test isolates the forecasted magnitude distribution by counting the observed number of events in each magnitude bin without regard to their temporal or spatial locations, standardized so that the observed and expected total number of events under the model agree, and computing the joint (Poisson) likelihood of the observed numbers of events in the magnitude bins. As with the L-test, the null distribution of this statistic under the forecast model is approximated via simulations.

For the S-test, the spatial locations in the observation region are organized into small bins. The test focuses on the forecasted spatial distribution by summing the numbers of observed events over all times and over all magnitude ranges. The event counts within each of the spatial bins are again standardized so that the observed and expected total number of events under the model agree, and then one computes the joint (Poisson) likelihood of the observed numbers of events in the spatial bins. Again, the result is compared to the null distribution obtained using simulations of the model in question.

The above tests measure the degree to which the observations agree with a particular model, in terms of the likelihood of these observations under the given model. As noted in Zechar et al. (2013), tests such as the L-test and N-test are really tests of the consistency between the data and a particular model, and are not ideal for comparing two models. Schorlemmer et al. (2007) proposed an additional test to allow for the direct comparison of the performance of two models: the Ratio test, or *R-test*. The test statistic R is defined as the log-likelihood of the data according to model A minus the corresponding log-likelihood for model B. The null distribution of R is constructed under the null hypothesis that model A is correct, by simulating from model A and calculating R for each realization. The resulting test is one-sided, and can be supplemented with the corresponding test using model B as the null hypothesis. The T-test and W-test of Rhoades et al. (2011) are very similar to the R-test, except that instead of using simulations to find the null distribution of the difference between log-likelihoods, with the T-test and W-test, the differences between log-likelihoods within each space-time-magnitude bin for models A and B are treated as independent normal or symmetric random variables, respectively, and a t-test or Wilcoxon signed rank test, respectively, is performed.

Unfortunately, when used to compare various models, such likelihood-based tests suffer from the problem of variable null hypotheses and can lead to highly misleading and even seemingly contradictory results. For instance, suppose model A has a higher likelihood than model B. Thus, in a concrete sense, model A fits the data better than model B. It is nevertheless quite possible for model A to be rejected according to the L-test and model B not to be rejected using the L-test. Similarly, the R-test with model A as the null might indicate that model A performs statistically significantly better than model B, while the R-test with model B as the null hypothesis may indicate that the difference in likelihoods is not statistically significant. Seemingly paradoxical results like these occur frequently, and at a recent meeting of the Seismological Society of America, much confusion was expressed over such results; even some seismologists quite well versed in statistics referred to results in such circumstances as "somewhat mixed", even though model A clearly fit better according to the likelihood criterion than model B.

The explanation for such results is that the null hypotheses of the two tests are different: when model A is tested using the L-test, the null hypothesis is model A, and when model B is tested, the null hypothesis is model B. The test statistic may have very different distributions under these different hypotheses.

Unfortunately, these types of discrepancies seem to occur frequently, and hence the results of these numerical tests may not only be uninformative for model comparison, but in fact misleading. A striking example is given in Fig. 4 of Zechar et al. (2013), where the Shen et al. (2007) model produces the highest likelihood of the five models considered in this portion of the analysis, and yet under the L-test has the lowest corresponding p-value of the five models.

5.5.2 Magnitude-Weighted Scores

Most assessments of point process models use metrics that do not properly emphasize forecasting the largest events. The N-test, for example, quite literally counts each event equivalently, regardless of its size. Similarly, the log-likelihood

$$l = \sum_{i=1}^{N} \log \lambda(\tau_i) - \int \lambda(t, x, y, m) dt dx dy dm, \tag{5.4}$$

involves summing up the log conditional intensity at each point, over all events large and small, and subtracting the integral of the intensity over the entire spacc-time-magnitude observation range, without weighting the larger events any more heavily than the smaller ones. This can have a large impact on model selection: since earthquake forecasting experiments like CSEP have used evaluation methods that do not assign more weight to the largest events, such experiments and retrospective analyses have tended to favor models that accurately forecast the smallest events, which typically constitute the bulk of the data in seismic catalogs.

Instead, it may be desirable to assess the fit of models for forecasting using weighted measures that properly account for the fact that the largest events are typically of primary interest and importance. Such weighted measures, especially weighted likelihood, might allow models that successfully forecast the largest events to emerge, even if they might not forecast the smallest events as well, and may also be used in finding the best fitting parameters for a particular model or class of models, using data. The purpose is similar to that of LISA functions and other local point features for marked point processes (Ghorbani et al., 2021; Mateu et al., 2007), in that the goal is to focus specifically on the forecasting or understanding of a particular subset of points whose marks are in a certain class, namely, the largest magnitudes.

For fitting parameters to earthquake occurrence models such as ETAS, and especially for evaluating their goodness-of-fit, one might assign more weight to the largest events. Thus, instead of using the log-likelihood score in (5.4), one could instead use, as a goodness-of-fit statistic, the weighted log-likelihood

$$L_W = \sum_{i=1}^{N} w(m_i) \log \lambda(\tau_i) - \int w(m)\lambda(t, x, y, m)dtdxdydm, \tag{5.5}$$

where $w(m)$ is a weight corresponding to an event of magnitude m.

There are several different possible choices one might select for the weight function, W. One may choose to weight according to energy release, which for moment magnitude approximately follows the relation $logE = 11.8 + 1.5m$ (Gutenberg & Richter, 1954; Kanamori, 1977). A more physically justified choice would be to use the potency (Ben-Zion, 2001, 2003), or geometric moment, which quantifies an earthquake's observable size according to physical principles, and represents the volume of material associated with permanent inelastic deformation at the earthquake source. If an alternative is desired, weights could be determined according to some other measure such as the corresponding total energy released in the corresponding earthquake, the Modified Mercalli Intensity (MMI), or some function of the moment magnitude. The relationship between earthquake potency, P, in cm/km^2, and moment magnitude, m_w, in dyn×cm,

$$\log_{10} P = 1.5m_w - \log_{10} r + 5.1, \tag{5.6}$$

where r is the rigidity, has been extensively studied (Ben-Zion & Zhu, 2002, Ben-Zion, 2003, Trugman & Ben-Zion, 2024), and for earthquakes in the Western United States the rigidity is approximately 36 GPa (Ichinose et al., 2003; Trugman & Ben-Zion, 2024). Note that the ordinary log-likelihood corresponds to the weight function $w(m) = 1$, and the identity function, $w(m) = m$, seems similarly inappropriate, since, for instance, this would weight an earthquake of magnitude 6 only 20% more than an earthquake of magnitude 5, which is inadequate given the enormous disparity in energy released and damage potential between the two events.

Given a suitable weight function $w(m)$, such as the potency of an earthquake of magnitude m, one may readily form weighted versions of other traditional measures of goodness-of-fit as well. For instance, consider the case where the observation region is divided into J spatial-temporal-magnitude grid cells, as has been the case with CSEP, where the model in question outputs an expected number of events λ_j in cell j, and where n_j is the number of observed events in cell j, most of which are either 0 or 1. Then the traditional binary score (see e.g., Bayona et al., 2022), which is given by

$$\sum_j \mathbf{1}_{\{n_j \geq 1\}} \log(1 - e^{-\lambda_j}) + \lambda_j (\mathbf{1}_{\{n_j \geq 1\}} - 1), \tag{5.7}$$

may be replaced by the weighted binary score

$$\sum_j w_j \mathbf{1}_{\{n_j \geq 1\}} \log(1 - e^{-\lambda_j}) + w_j \lambda_j (\mathbf{1}_{\{n_j \geq 1\}} - 1), \tag{5.8}$$

where w_j is the potency (or other weight) that would correspond to an event in cell j.

Similarly, if for the model in question, one has estimates of the probability of observing exactly k events in cell j, then the often used Brier score (Brier, 1950),

$$\frac{1}{J} \sum_{j=1}^{J} \sum_{k=0}^{\infty} [\mathbf{1}_{\{n_j = k\}} - \hat{P}(n_j = k)]^2, \tag{5.9}$$

may be replaced by the weighted Brier score

$$\frac{1}{J} \sum_{j=1}^{J} \sum_{k=0}^{\infty} w_j [\mathbf{1}_{\{n_j = k\}} - \hat{P}(n_j = k)]^2. \tag{5.10}$$

Another useful magnitude-weighted summary statistic recently proposed in Schoenberg and Schorlemmer (2024) is the quotient

$$Q = \frac{\text{mean}\ \{\lambda_i : m_i > m^{[0.95]}\}}{\text{mean}\{\lambda(t, x, y)\}}, \tag{5.11}$$

where $m^{[0.95]}$ is the 95th percentile of the earthquake size distribution, with size measured either by potency or magnitude, and the denominator, $mean\{\lambda(t, x, y)\}$, may be estimated using either the conditional intensity at the observed earthquake locations, or using several thousand locations selected at random from the space-time-magnitude observation region. Note that the conditional intensity in both the numerator and denominator of (5.11) should be purely spatial-temporal, i.e., the integral of $\lambda(t, x, y, m)$ over all magnitudes. The higher the value of Q, the better the model appears to be forecasting the spatial-temporal locations of the largest 5% of events. For a homogeneous Poisson model with uniform magnitude density, Q will be close to 1. Any model that adequately accounts for the spatial inhomogeneity of seismicity will have $Q > 1$, as it should since such a model will tend to vastly outperform a homogeneous Poisson model at forecasting the largest events. Among competing models, the model that forecasts the larger events more accurately will tend to be the model with higher Q, especially if all the models are similarly calibrated overall [i.e., the mean of $\lambda(t, x, y)$ is close to the overall rate of events] which can readily be checked via other methods, such as the N-test.

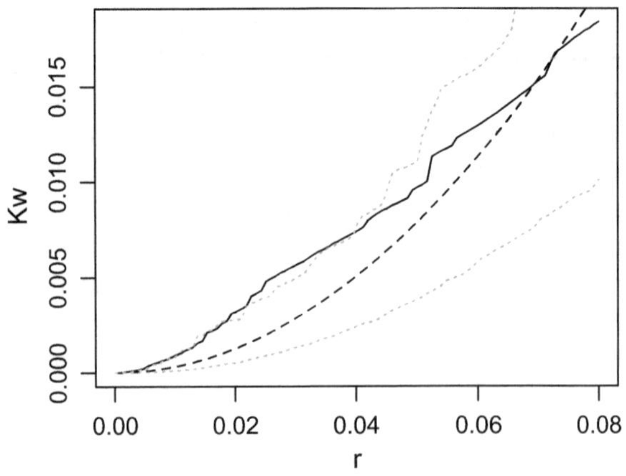

Fig. 5.16 Weighted K-function $K_W(r)$ (solid black curve) for quadratic Poisson model (5.2) fit by MLE to San Bernardino earthquake data. Dashed curve is πr^2, and dotted gray curves are upper and lower 95% bounds for $K_W(r)$ based on 200 simulations of model (5.2)

In the code below, the quadratic Poisson model is simulated via thinning, 200 times, and the 2.5th and 97.5th percentiles of the weighted K-functions of these simulations are used to construct the 95% confidence bands.

```
    ## Compute lam = lambda(x,y) at each point.
lam = maxt*(beta[1] + beta[2]*maxt/2 + beta[3]*maxt^2/3 + beta[4]*z$lon +
    beta[5]*z$lon^2 + beta[6]*z$lat + beta[7]*z$lat^2)
    ## Compute d = the interpoint distances.
d = matrix(0,ncol=z$n,nrow=z$n)
for(i in 1:(z$n-1)) for(j in (i+1):z$n) d[i,j] =
    sqrt((z$lon[j]-z$lon[i])^2+(z$lat[j]-z$lat[i])^2)
    ## Compute Kw.
m = 100
r = seq(0,.08,length=m)
Kw = rep(0,m)
for(k in 1:m){
for(i in 1:(z$n-1)){
for(j in (i+1):z$n){
if(d[i,j] < r[k]) Kw[k] = Kw[k] + 2/(lam[i]*lam[j])
}}}
plot(r,Kw,type="l")
lines(r,pi*r^2,lty=2)
    ## Simulate the quadratic Poisson model
Kw2 = matrix(0,nrow=200,ncol=m)
for(sim in 1:200){
  b = 2*max(lam)
  n1 = rpois(1,b); x1 = runif(n1); y1 = runif(n1)
  lamsim = maxt*(beta[1] + beta[2]*maxt/2 + beta[3]*maxt^2/3 + beta[4]*x1 +
      beta[5]*x1^2 + beta[6]*y1 + beta[7]*y1^2)
  keep = c(1:n1)[runif(n1) < lamsim/b]
  n2 = length(keep); x2 = x1[keep]; y2 = y1[keep]; lam2 = lamsim[keep]
      ## Compute d2 = the interpoint distances for the sim.
  d2 = matrix(0,ncol=n2,nrow=n2)
  for(i in 1:(n2-1)) for(j in (i+1):n2)
    d2[i,j] = sqrt((x2[j]-x2[i])^2+(y2[j]-y2[i])^2)
      ## Compute Kw2 = Kw for the sim.
  for(k in 1:m){for(i in 1:(n2-1)){for(j in (i+1):n2){
  if(d2[i,j] < r[k]) Kw2[sim,k] = Kw2[sim,k] + 2/(lam2[i]*lam2[j])}}}
}
```

```
mylow = function(t) quantile(t,.025)
myhigh = function(t) quantile(t,.975)
low = apply(Kw2,2,mylow)
high = apply(Kw2,2,myhigh)
lines(r,low,lty=3,col="grey")
lines(r,high,lty=3,col="grey")
```

In order to prove results regarding weighted second-order statistics such as the weighted K-function, a weighted point process N_w is a useful construct. Suppose there is some positive number $\lambda_{\min}$, such that $\lambda(s) \geq \lambda_{\min} > 0$ for all s. Then N_w is defined as the real-valued random measure such that for any set B, $N_w(B) = \int_B \frac{\lambda_{\min}}{\lambda(s)} dN$.

Since $\lambda(s)$ is F_s-measurable, $\lim_{\delta\to 0} E[N_w(s, s+\delta)|F_s]/\delta = \lambda_{\min} \lim_{\delta\to 0} \frac{1}{\lambda(s)} E[N(s, s+\delta) |F_s]/\delta = \lambda_{\min}$. Assuming that the original process N is orderly, the second moment of N_w may be derived similarly: $\lim_{\delta\to 0} E\left\{[N_w(s, s+\delta)|F_s]^2\right\}/\delta = \lambda_{\min}^2 \lim_{\delta\to 0} \frac{1}{\delta} E\left\{E\left[(\frac{N(s,s+\delta)}{\lambda(s)})^2|F_s\right]\right\} = \frac{\lambda_{\min}^2}{\lambda(s)}$.

Like the weighted K-function, the weighted R/S statistic can similarly be informative about the data's second-order properties relative to a given model. Let $D_w(u, t, \delta) = [N_w(u+t) - N_w(t)] - \frac{u}{\delta}[N_w(t+\delta) - N_w(t)]$, i.e., the weighted version of the deviation from the average in the interval $(t, t+\delta)$. The weighted rescaled range is $R_w(t;\delta) = \max_{0\leq u\leq\delta} D_w(u, t, \delta) - \min_{0\leq u\leq\delta} D_w(u, t, \delta)$. Assuming N is simple, the sample variance of the random variable $N_w(t, t+d) = Nw(t+d) - Nw(t)$ around the sample average is given by $S_w^2(t;\delta) = \frac{N_w(t+\delta)-N_w(t)}{\delta} - \left(\frac{N_w(t+\delta)-N_w(t)}{\delta}\right)^2$. Thus, as a diagnostic tool, the weighted R/S statistic is defined as $R/S_w = \frac{R_w(t;\delta)}{S_w(t;\delta)}$.

As shown in Adelfio and Schoenberg (2009), under general conditions involving the 2nd moment of N, i.e., provided N is not extremely explosive, the weighted R/S statistic R/S_w converges weakly to the range of the Brownian bridge.

Weighted versions of other second-order summaries of point processes, where the weighting is similarly performed by weighting each point by the inverse of its conditional intensity, can be obtained. Some of these are described and their properties derived in Adelfio and Schoenberg (2009).

5.7 Exercises

5.1. Suppose a purely spatial point process on S is observed, and the model considered is a stationary Poisson process with rate 2. Suppose the Voronoi cell for a given point has an area of 0.7. What is the Voronoi residual corresponding to this cell, for the stationary Poisson model with rate 2?

5.2. Why is it necessary that the point process be simple in order for rescaling to result in a Poisson process of rate 1? Can you think of an example of a non-simple point process for which rescaling by the compensator does not yield a rate 1 Poisson process?

5.3. Simulate a spatial-temporal Poisson process N on $[0, 1] \times [0, 1] \times [0, 1]$ with rate $\lambda(t, x, y) = 10 + t + 10x + 2y$. Rescale the y-values of N, but not using the true λ and instead using $\hat{\lambda} = 10 + t + 2x + 4y$. Plot the (x, y)-coordinates of the data, and then plot the (x, y)-coordinates of the rescaled residuals.

5.4. Suppose a spatial-temporal point process N on $[0, 1] \times [0, 1] \times [0, 1]$ has conditional intensity $\lambda(t, x, y) = 10 + t + 10x + 2y - 5\mathbf{I}_{N((t-0.1,t)\times(x-0.1,x)\times(y-0.1,y))>0}$. That is, the conditional intensity is $10 + t + 10x + 2y$ if there is no point within 0.1 days and within 0.1 to the West and within 0.1 South of the current location, and otherwise the conditional intensity is $5 + t + 10x + 2y$. Suppose the process N happens to have only two points, at (0.5, 0.5, 0.5) and at (0.7, 0.7, 0.7). If the times of the process are rescaled, what will be the coordinates of the rescaled points?

5.5. Simulate a spatial-temporal Poisson process N on $[0, 1] \times [0, 1] \times [0, 1]$ with rate $\lambda(t, x, y) = 10 + t + 10x + 2y$. Construct super-thinned residuals of N using $k = 20$, but not using the true λ and instead using $\hat{\lambda} = 10 + t + 2x + 4y$. Plot the (x, y)-coordinates of the simulated points, and then plot the (x, y)-coordinates of the super-thinned residuals.

5.6. Simulate a spatial-temporal Poisson process N on $[0, 1] \times [0, 1] \times [0, 1]$ with rate $\lambda(t, x, y) = 10 + t + 10x + 2y$. Construct raw, Pearson, and deviance residuals on a $1 \times 10 \times 10$ grid, so that all times are contained in the same pixel and spatially the unit square is divided into a 10×10 grid of pixels. For your residuals, do not use the true λ and instead use $\hat{\lambda} = 10 + t + 2x + 4y$. Plot the (x, y)-coordinates of the simulated points, and then plot the raw, Pearson, and deviance residuals, each as separate plots.

5.7. Suppose N is a spatial-temporal Poisson process N on $[0, 10] \times [0, 10] \times [0, 10]$ with rate $\lambda(t, x, y) = 10 + t + 10x + 2y$. Suppose one examines the raw residual for the pixel $[0, 1] \times [0, 1] \times [0, 1]$, for the true model. What is the distribution of this raw residual? Provide the name of the distribution as well as its mean and variance.

5.8. Suppose a spatial-temporal point process N on $[0, 1] \times [0, 1] \times [0, 1]$ has conditional intensity $\lambda(t, x, y) = 10 + t + 10x + 2y - 5\mathbf{I}_{N((t-0.1,t)\times(x-0.1,x)\times(y-0.1,y))>0}$. That is, the conditional intensity is $10 + t + 10x + 2y$ if there is no point within 0.1 days and within 0.1 to the West and within 0.1 South of the current location, and otherwise the conditional intensity is $5 + t + 10x + 2y$. Suppose the process N happens to have only two points, at (0.5, 0.5, 0.5) and at (0.7, 0.7, 0.7). If one constructs the super-thinned residuals of N, with $k = 20$ and using the true model for the super-thinning, what is the mean number of points that will be *superposed* in the super-thinning? What is the variance of the number of points that will be superposed in the super-thinning?

5.9. Simulate a spatial-temporal Poisson process N on $[0, 1] \times [0, 1] \times [0, 1]$ with rate $\lambda(t, x, y) = 2 + 3t + exp(x) + y^2$. Construct and plot the raw Voronoi residuals for the true model, assuming no parameter estimation is needed.

5.10. Simulate a spatial-temporal Poisson process N on $[0, 1] \times [0, 1] \times [0, 1]$ with rate $\lambda(t, x, y) = 2 + 3t + exp(x) + y^2$. Construct and plot the raw Voronoi residuals, but instead of using the true model, use the model $\lambda(t, x, y) = 2 + 3t + 2x + y$ in computing your residuals. Assume no parameter estimation is needed.

5.11. Suppose a spatial-temporal Poisson process N on $[0, 1] \times [0, 1] \times [0, 1]$ has rate $\lambda(t, x, y) = 2 + 3t + exp(x) + y^2$. What is the expected value of the mean area of the Voronoi cells?

5.12. Suppose a spatial-temporal Poisson process N on $[0, 1] \times [0, 1] \times [0, 1]$ has rate $\lambda(t, x, y) = 2 + 3t + 4x + 5y$, and happens to have 4 points, occurring at (0.2, 0.2, 0.2), (0.3, 0.4, 0.5), (0.4, 0.8, 0.9), and (0.8, 0.5, 0.8). Compute the statistic T in (3.6).

References

Aalen, O., & Hoem, J. (1978). Random time changes for multivariate counting processes. *Scandinavian Actuarial Journal, 17*, 81–101.

Adelfio, G., & Schoenberg, F. (2009). Point process diagnostics based on weighted second-order statistics and their asymptotic properties. *Annals of the Institute of Statistical Mathematics, 61*(4), 929–948.

Akaike H. (1974). A new look at the statistical model identification. *IEEE Transactions on Automatic Control, AC-19*, 716–723.

Akaike, H. (1983). Information measure and model selection. *Bulletin of the International Statistical Institute, 50*(1), 277–291.

Albrecht P. (1982). Testing the goodness-of-fit of a mixed Poisson process. *Insurance: Mathematics and Economics*, 1(1), 27–33.

Arsham, H. (1987). A modified one-sided K-S confidence region narrower in one tail. *Communications in Statistics-A: Theory and Methods, 16*, 17–28.

Baddeley, A., & Turner, R. (2005). Spatstat: An R package for analyzing spatial point patterns. *Journal of Statistical Software, 12*, 1–42.

Baddeley, A., Bárány, I., & Schneider, R. (2007). Spatial point processes and their applications. *Stochastic geometry: Lectures given at the CIME summer school held in Martina Franca, Italy, September 13–18, 2004* (pp. 1–75).

Baddeley, A., Møller, J., & Pakes, A. G. (2008). Properties of residuals for spatial point processes. *Annals of the Institute of Statistical Mathematics, 60*, 627–649.

Baddeley, A., Møller, J., & Waagepetersen, R. (2000). Non- and semi-parametric estimation of interaction in inhomogeneous point patterns. *Statistica Neerlandica, 54*(3), 329–350.

Baddeley, A., Rubak, E., & Møller, J. (2011). Score, pseudo-score and residual diagnostics for spatial point process models. *Statistical Science, 26*, 613–646.

Baddeley, A., Turner, R., Møller, J., & Hazelton, M. (2005). Residual analysis for spatial point processes (with discussion). *Journal of the Royal Statistical Society: Series B (Statistical Methodology), 67*(5), 617–666.

Barr, C. D., & Schoenberg, F. (2010). On the Voronoi estimator for the intensity of an inhomogeneous planar Poisson process. *Biometrika, 97*(4), 977–984.

Bayona, J. A., Savran, W. H., Rhoades, D. A., & Werner, M. J. (2022). Prospective evaluation of multiplicative hybrid earthquake forecasting models in California. *Geophysical Journal International, 229*(3), 1736–53.

Ben-Zion, Y. (2001). On quantification of the earthquake source. *Seismological Research Letters, 72*(2), 151–152.

Ben-Zion, Y. (2003). Appendix 2—Key formulas in earthquake seismology. International Geophysics, in W. H. K. Lee, H. Kanamori, P. C. Jennings, & C. Kisslinger (Eds.), *International Handbook of Earthquake and Engineering Seismology, Part B* (pp. 1857–1875). Academic. https://doi.org/10.1016/S0074-6142(03)80304-2

Ben–Zion, Y., & Zhu L. (2002). Potency–magnitude scaling relations for southern California earthquakes with 1.0<ML<7.0. *Geophysical Journal International, 148*(3), F1–F5.

Berman, M. (1986). Testing for spatial association between a point process and another stochastic process. *Journal of the Royal Statistical Society Series C: Applied Statistics, 35*(1), 54–62.

Besag, J. E. (1977). Discussion contribution to Ripley (1977). *Journal of the Royal Statistical Society, 39*, 193–195.

Bray, A., Wong, K., Barr, C. D., & Schoenberg, F. (2014). Voronoi cell based residual analysis of spatial point process models with applications to Southern California earthquake forecasts. *Annals of Applied Statistics, 8*(4), 2247–2267.

Brémaud, P. (1981). *Point Processes and Queues: Martingale Dynamics*. Springer.

Brier, G. W. (1950). Verification of forecasts expressed in terms of probability. *Monthly Weather Review, 78*(1), 1–3.

Brown, T., & Nair, M. (1988). Poisson approximations for time-changed point processes. *Stochastic Processes and Their Applications, 29*, 247–256.

Cressie, N. A. C. (1993). *Statistics for spatial data* (revised). Wiley.

Davies, R. (1977). Testing the hypothesis that a point process is Poisson. *Advances in Applied Probability, 9*, 724–746.

Diggle, P. J. (1983). *Statistical analysis of spatial point patterns*. Academic.

Ferenc, J.-S., & Néda, Z. (2007). On the size distribution of Poisson Voronoi cells. *Physica A: Statistical Mechanics and Its Applications, 385*(2), 518–526.

Field, E. H. (2007). Overview of the working group for the development of regional earthquake models (RELM). *Seismological Research Letters, 78*, 7–16.

Ghorbani, M., Cronie, O., Mateu, J., & Yu, J. (2021). Functional marked point processes: a natural structure to unify spatio-temporal frameworks and to analyse dependent functional data. *TEST, 30*, 529–568.

Gneiting, T., & Raftery, A. E. (2007). Strictly proper scoring rules, prediction, and estimation. *Journal of the American Statistical Association, 102*, 359–378.

Gutenberg, B., & Richter, C. F. (1954). *Seismicity of the Earth* (2nd ed.). Princeton University Press.

Heinrich, L. (1991). Goodness-of-fit tests for the second moment function of a stationary multidimensional Poisson process. *Statistics, 22*, 245–278.

Heinrich-Mertsching, C., Thorarinsdottir, T. L., Guttorp, P., & Schneider, M. (2024). Validation of point process predictions with proper scoring rules. *Scandinavian Journal of Statistics, 51*(4), 1533–1566.

Hinde, A. L., & Miles, R. E. (1980). Monte Carlo estimates of the distributions of the random polygons of the Voronoi tessellation with respect to a Poisson process. *Journal of Statistical Computation and Simulation, 10*, 205–223.

Ichinose, G. A., Anderson, J. G., Smith, K. D., & Zeng, Y. (2003). Source parameters of Eastern California and Western Nevada earthquakes from regional moment tensor inversion. *Bulletin of the Seismological Society of America, 93*(1), 61–84.

Kagan, Y. Y. (2004). Short-term properties of earthquake catalogs and models of earthquake source. *Bulletin of the Seismological Society of America, 94*(4), 1207–1228.

Kagan, Y. Y. (2007). On earthquake predictability measurement: Information score and error diagram. *Pure and Applied Geophysics, 164*(10), 1947–1962.

Kanamori H. (1977). The energy release in great earthquakes. *Journal of Geophysical Research (1896–1977), 82*(20), 2981–2987.

Karr, A. (1991). *Point processes and their statistical inference* (2nd ed.). Dekker.

Kutoyants, Y. (1984). On nonparametric estimation of intensity function of inhomogeneous Poisson process. *Problems of Control and Information Theory,13*, 253–258.

Lawson, A. B. (1988). On tests for spatial trend in a non-homogeneous Poisson process. *Journal of Applied Statistics, 15*(2), 225–234.

Lee, C. (1986). Estimation of the intensity of a Poisson process. *Communications in Statistics-B Simulation and Computation, 15*, 747–759.

Lewis, P., & Shedler, G. (1979). Simulation of nonhomogeneous Poisson processes by thinning. *Naval Research Logistics Quarterly,26*, 403–413.

Liebetrau, A. M. (1978). The weak convergence of a class of estimators of the variance function of a two-dimensional Poisson process. *Journal of Applied Probability, 15*(2), 433–439.

Lisek, B., & Lisek, M. (1985). A new method for testing whether a point process is Poisson. *Statistics, 16*, 445–450.

Mateu, J., Lorenzo, G., & Porcu, E. (2007). Detecting features in spatial point processes with clutter via local indicators of spatial association. *Journal of Computational and Graphical Statistics, 16*, 968–990.

Meijering, J. L. (1953). Interface area, edge length, and number of vertices in crystal aggregation with random nucleation. *Philips Research Reports, 8*, 270–290.

Merzbach, E., & Nualart, D. (1986). A characterization of the spatial Poisson process and changing time. *Annals of Probability, 14*, 1380–1390.

Meyer, P. (1971). Demonstration simplifiée d'un théorème de Knight. *Séminaire de Probabilités V,191*, 191–195.

Molchan, G. M. (1991). Structure of optimal strategies in earthquake prediction. *Tectonophysics, 193*, 267–276.

Molchan, G. (2010). Space-time earthquake prediction: the error diagrams. *Pure and Applied Geophysics, 167*, 907–917.

Molchan, G., Kronrod, T., & Panza, G. F. (1997). Multi-scale seismicity model for seismic risk. *Bulletin of the Seismological Society of America, 87*, 1220–1229.

Nair, M. (1990). Random space change for multiparameter point processes. *Annals of Probability, 18*, 1222–1231.

Ogata Y. (1981). On Lewis' simulation method for point processes. *IEEE Transactions on Information Theory, IT-27*, 23–31.

Ogata, Y. (1978). The asymptotic behaviour of maximum likelihood estimators for stationary point processes. *Annals of the Institute of Statistical Mathematics, 30*, 243–261.

Ogata, Y. (1998). Space-time point-process models for earthquake occurrences. *Annals of the Institute of Statistical Mathematics, 50*(2), 379–402.

Ogata, Y., & Vere-Jones, D. (1984). Inference for earthquake models: A self-correcting model. *Stochastic Processes and Their Applications, 17*, 337–347.

Ogata, Y. (1988). Statistical models for earthquake occurrences and residual analysis for point processes. *Journal of the American Statistical Association,83*, 9–27.

Okabe, A., Boots, B., Sugihara, K., & Chiu, S. (2000). *Spatial tessellations* (2nd ed.). Wiley.

Papangelou, F. (1972). Integrability of expected increments of point processes and a related random change of scale. *Transactions of the American Mathematical Society, 165*, 483–506.

Rhoades, D. A., Schorlemmer, D., Gerstenberger, M. C., Christophersen, A., Zechar, J. D., & Imoto, M. (2011). Efficient testing of earthquake forecasting models. *Acta Geophysica, 59*(4), 728–747.

Ripley, B. D. (1977). Modelling spatial patterns (with discussion). *Journal of the Royal Statistical Society, 39*, 172–212.

Ripley, B. (1981). *Spatial statistics*. Wiley.
Saw, J. (1975). Tests on the intensity of a Poisson process. *Communications in Statistics, 4*, 777–782.
Schoenberg, F. (1999). Transforming spatial point processes into Poisson processes. *Stochastic Processes and Their Applications,81*, 155–164.
Schoenberg, F. (2002). On rescaled Poisson processes and the Brownian bridge. *The Annals of the Institute of Statistical Mathematics, 54*(2), 445–457.
Schoenberg, F. (2003). Multi-dimensional residual analysis of point process models for earthquake occurrences. *Journal of the American Statistical Association, 98*(464), 789–795.
Schoenberg, F. (2004). Consistent parametric estimation of the intensity of a spatial-temporal point process. *Journal of Statistical Planning and Inference, 128*(1), 79–93.
Schoenberg, F. P. (2006). On non-simple marked point processes. *Annals of the Institute of Statistical Mathematics, 58*(2), 223–233.
Schoenberg, F., & Schorlemmer, D. (2024). Critical questions about CSEP, in the spirit of Yan, Dave, and Ilya. *SRL, 95*(6), 3617–3625.
Schorlemmer, D., & Gerstenberger, M. C. (2007). RELM testing center. *Seismological Research Letters, 78*(1), 30–35.
Schorlemmer, D., Gerstenberger, M. C., Wiemer, S., Jackson, D. D., & Rhoades, D. A. (2007). Earthquake likelihood model testing. *Seismological Research Letters, 78*, 17–27.
Shen, Z.-K., Jackson, D. D., & Kagan, Y. Y. (2007). Implications of geodetic strain rate for future earthquakes, with a five-year forecast of M5 earthquakes in southern California. *Seismological Research Letters, 78*, 116–120.
Solow, A. (1993). Model-checking in non-stationary Poisson processes. *Applied Stochastic Models and Data Analysis, 8*, 129–132.
Stark, P. B. (1997). Earthquake prediction: the null hypothesis. *Geophysical Journal International, 131*(3), 495–499.
Sundt, B. (1982). On the problem of testing whether a mixed Poisson process is homogeneous. *Insurance, Mathematics and Economics, 1*(4), 253–254.
Swets, J. A. (1973). The relative operating characteristic in psychology. *Science, 182*, 990–1000.
Tanemura, M. (2003). Statistical distributions of Poisson Voronoi cells in two and three dimensions. *Forma, 18*, 221–247.
Trugman, D. T., & Ben-Zion, Y. (2024). Potency-magnitude scaling relations and a unified earthquake catalog for the Western US. *The Seismic Record, 4*(3), 223–230.
Wong, K., & Schoenberg, F. (2009). On mainshock focal mechanisms and the spatial distribution of aftershocks. *The Bulletin of the Seismological Society of America, 99*(6), 3402–3412.
Yokoyama, S., Miyawaki, N., & Sakamoto, H. (1993). On the estimation problem in the analysis of the time-dependent Poisson process. *Communications in Statistics B: Simulation and Computation, 22*, 591–614.
Zaliapin, I., & Molchan, G. (2004). Tossing the earth: How to reliably test earthquake prediction methods. *Eos, Transaction AGU, 85*(47), S23A–0302.
Zechar, J. D., Gerstenberger, M. C., & Rhoades, D. A. (2010). Likelihood-based tests for evaluating space-rate-magnitude earthquake forecasts. *Bulletin of the Seismological Society of America, 100*(3), 1184–1195.
Zechar, J. D., Schorlemmer, D., Werner, M. J., Gerstenberger, M. C., Rhoades, D. A., & Jordan, T. H. (2013). Regional earthquake likelihood models I: First-order results. *Bulletin of the Seismological Society of America, 103*(2A), 787–798.
Zhuang, J. (2006). Second-order residual analysis of spatiotemporal point processes and applications in model evaluation. *The Journal of the Royal Statistical Society, Series B, 68*, 635–653.

MIX
Papier aus verantwortungsvollen Quellen
Paper from responsible sources
FSC® C105338
FSC
www.fsc.org

If you have any concerns about our products,
you can contact us on
ProductSafety@springernature.com

In case Publisher is established outside the EU,
the EU authorized representative is:
Springer Nature Customer Service Center GmbH
Europaplatz 3, 69115 Heidelberg, Germany

Printed by Libri Plureos GmbH
in Hamburg, Germany